THE
EASTERN
EUROPE
COLLECTION

HISTORY

OF THE

HOUSE OF AUSTRIA

Volume II

William Coxe

ARNO PRESS & THE NEW YORK TIMES

New York · 1971

Reprint Edition 1971 by Arno Press Inc.

Reprinted from a copy in
The Columbia University Library

LC# 72-135801

ISBN for Volumes I, II, III: 0-405-02743-5

ISBN for Vol. II: 0-405-02791-5

The Eastern Europe Collection
ISBN for complete set: 0-405-02730-3

Manufactured in the United States of America

HISTORY

OF THE

HOUSE OF AUSTRIA

VOL. II

Soutman   Hinchliff.

Rhodolph of Hapsburgh

HISTORY

OF THE

HOUSE OF AUSTRIA,

FROM THE

Foundation of the Monarchy

BY RHODOLPH OF HAPSBURGH,

TO THE DEATH OF

LEOPOLD THE SECOND:

1218 TO 1792.

BY WILLIAM COXE, F.R.S. F.A.S.

ARCHDEACON OF WILTS, AND RECTOR OF BEMERTON.

THIRD EDITION.

IN THREE VOLUMES.

VOL. II.

LONDON:

HENRY G. BOHN, YORK STREET, COVENT GARDEN.

1847.

LONDON:
SPOTTISWOODE and SHAW,
New-street Square.

CONTENTS

OF

THE SECOND VOLUME.

CHAP. XXXV. 1522–1564. — Ferdinand baffles the Views of Charles to procure the Reversion of the Imperial Crown for his Son Philip. Abdication of Charles, and Accession and Capitulation of Ferdinand. Emancipates the Imperial Crown from its Dependence on the See of Rome. Suspends the religious Disturbances in the hereditary Countries. His Conduct as Emperor, in regard to religious Affairs. Fruitless Attempts to obtain a Reformation of the Church, and to re-unite the Catholics and Protestants. Renewal and Dissolution of the Council of Trent. Ferdinand conciliates both Sects, and maintains the Peace of the Empire. Changes in the Constitution of Germany during his Reign. Election of his Son Maximilian as King of the Romans. Division of his Territories among his three Sons, and Establishment of the Branches of Austria, Tyrol, and Styria. His Death, Character, and Issue - - Page 1

CHAP. XXXVI. 1527–1566. — Situation of the House of Austria in consequence of the Separation of the two Branches, and the Introduction of the Lutheran Doctrines into Germany and the Hereditary Dominions. Birth and Education of Maximilian. His early Attachment to the Lutheran Doctrines. Motives which induced him not to quit the Catholic Church. The Effects of his tolerant and judicious Conduct. Diet of Augsburgh. Attempts of Maximilian to prevent the Dissensions in the Protestant Body. Progress of Calvinism, and Rise of the Disputes between the Lutherans and Calvinists - - - - - - - 19

CHAP. XXXVII. 1564–1574. — Troubles derived from the Introduction of the Reformation into the different Countries of Europe. Rise of the Huguenot Party, and Civil Wars in France. Massacre of St. Bartholomew. Maximilian endeavours to check these Persecutions. Introduces Regulations to prevent these Troubles from spreading into Germany. Commotions in the Netherlands. Character and Conduct of Philip II. Sanguinary Administration of the Duke of Alva. Rise and Progress of the Rebellion. Ineffectual Endeavours of Maximilian to mediate an Accommodation. Suppression of the Troubles in the Empire, occasioned by Grumbach and his Protector the Duke of Saxe Gotha. Maximilian eludes the demands of the Teutonic Knights, relative to the Recovery of Prussia and Livonia. His Connections with the Czar of Muscovy. Disputes with the Pope relative to Tuscany - Page 27

CHAP. XXXVIII. 1567–1576. — Affairs of Religion in the hereditary Countries. Toleration of Maximilian towards his Protestant Subjects of every Description. Affairs of Hungary. Renewal of the War with the Prince of Transylvania and the Turks. Siege of Zigeth, and Death of Solyman. Conclusion of Peace with Selim and the Prince of Transylvania - - - - 43

CHAP. XXXIX. 1572–1576. — Rhodolph, son of Maximilian, crowned King of Hungary and Bohemia. Elected King of the Romans. Maximilian's Attempts to procure the Crown of Poland for one of his Sons. Himself elected. Opposed by Stephen Bathori. Death, Character, and Issue - - - - - - 50

CHAP. XL. 1576–1603. — Accession of Rhodolph II. Right of Primogeniture established in the Succession to the Archduchy of Austria. Character, Principles, and Education of Rhodolph. His impolitic Endeavours to diminish the Ascendency of the Protestants and restore the Catholic Religion in his own Territories and the Empire. Schism, and mutual Persecutions among the Protestants. Systematic Plan for the Depression of the Protestants. Religious Troubles of Aix-la-Chapelle. Disputes Relative to the Ecclesiastical Reservation. Attempt of the Elector of Cologne to retain his ecclesiastical Dignity after his Renunciation of the Catholic Religion. Deposed and driven into Exile. Similar Contest for the Bishopric of Strasburgh. Rise and Progress of the Protestant Union under the Elector Palatine. Confederacies of Heidelberg and Frankfort - - - - - - - 62

CHAP. XLI. 1576–1609. — Persecution of the Protestants in the Austrian Dominions, and in the Empire. Execution of the Imperial Ban against Aix-la-Chapelle. Donawerth deprived of its civil and religious Rights. Diet of Ratisbon. Alarm of the Protestants. Increase of their Confederacy - - - - 79

CHAP. XLII. 1576–1606. — Rhodolph cedes the Frontier Garrisons of Hungary to his Uncle Charles, Duke of Styria. Construction of Carlstadt, and establishment of the Military Colonies against the Turks. Rise and Exploits of the Uscocks. Their Depredations occasion a War with the Turks. Contests in Hungary. Alliance of Sigismond Bathori, Prince of Transylvania, with the House of Austria. He cedes Transylvania to Rhodolph. Subsequent Contests for the Possession of that Principality. Exactions and Tyranny of the Austrian Governors and Generals. Rebellion of Botskai. Rise of the Civil Troubles in Hungary and Transylvania. State of Bohemia, Austria, and the Empire. Change in the Character, Manners, and Principles of Rhodolph - - - - 85

CHAP. XLIII. 1606–1609. — Education, Character, and early Life

of Matthias, Brother of Rhodolph. His Disputes with Rhodolph.
Becomes presumptive Heir to the Austrian Territories by the Death
of his Brother Ernest. Intrusted with the Government of Hungary
and Austria. Forms the Design of wresting the Sovereignty from
Rhodolph. Concludes a Peace with the Prince of Transylvania
and the Turks. Attempts of Rhodolph to entail the Succession on
Ferdinand, Duke of Styria. Matthias invades Bohemia, and extorts
from his Brother the Cession of Austria and Hungary. Involved in
Disputes with the Protestants of Austria. Conciliates the Hun-
garians, and is elected King. Grants Toleration to the Protestants
of Austria, and receives the Homage of the States - Page 95
CHAP. XLIV. 1609-1612. — Recommencement of the Troubles in
Bohemia. Disputes of Rhodolph with his Protestant Subjects.
Compelled to grant Religious Toleration. Rising Troubles in the
Empire. Union of the Protestants. Contested Succession of Juliers
and Berg. Plan of Henry IV. to humble the House of Austria.
Frustrated by his Assassination. Accommodation between the
Catholics and Protestants. Attempts of Rhodolph to transfer the
Succession of Bohemia to his Cousin the Archduke Leopold. Bohe-
mia invaded by the troops of Leopold. The States call in the Assistance of Matthias. Expulsion of Leopold, and Deposition of
Rhodolph. Matthias crowned King of Bohemia. Preparations of
the German Electors to choose a new Chief of the Empire. Death
of Rhodolph - - - - - - 108
CHAP. XLV. 1612-1618. — Disturbed Situation of Germany during
the Interregnum. Matthias elected Emperor, after much Opposition. His Capitulation. Difficulties attending the Commencement of his Administration, as well in the Empire as in his own
Dominions. Foiled in his Endeavours to obtain Succours for expelling the Turks from Transylvania. Makes a Peace with the
Sultan. Recommencement of the religious Disputes in Germany.
Divisions among the Protestants. Occupation of Juliers and Cleves
by the Dutch and Spaniards. Ineffectual Appeals made to the Emperor. Embarrassments of Matthias. Endeavours to entail the Succession to his Dominions on Ferdinand, Duke of Styria. Character
of Ferdinand. He is elected King of Hungary and Bohemia - 131
CHAP. XLVI. 1619. — Rise of the religious Troubles in Bohemia.
Persecution of the Protestants under the Auspices of Ferdinand.
Character and Principles of Count Thurn. He rouses the People
to Rebellion. Formation of an insurgent Government and Army.
Conciliating Conduct of Matthias. Offers Terms of Accommodation
to the Insurgents. Ferdinand seizes and imprisons Klesel, the
Minister of Matthias, and gains the Ascendency in the Cabinet.
Commencement of the Civil War in Bohemia. Military Operations.
Attempts to negotiate an Accommodation. Death of Matthias 144
CHAP. XLVII. 1619. — Accession of Ferdinand II. Dangers and
Difficulties of his Situation. State of his Dominions. Affairs of
Bohemia. Invasion of Moravia and Austria by the Insurgents.
Ferdinand besieged in Vienna. His Fortitude and extraordinary

Escape.   Elected Emperor.   The Elector Palatine chosen King of
Bohemia.   Irruption of Bethlehem Gabor and Count Thurn into
Austria.   Second Siege of Vienna   -   -   - Page 159
CHAP. XLVIII. 1619, 1620. — The Siege of Vienna raised.   Beth-
lehem Gabor proclaimed King of Hungary.   Attempts of the
Elector Palatine to engage the Protestant Union in his Cause.
Ferdinand baffles the Intrigues of his Rival.   Gains the Duke of
Bavaria, and the Catholic League.   Detaches the Elector of Saxony.
Obtains the Support of France.   Assisted by the King of Spain and
the Pope.   Concludes a Truce with Bethlehem Gabor.   The Pro-
testant Union refuses to interfere in the Affairs of Bohemia, and
enters into a Truce with the Catholics.   Invasion of the Palatinate
and Bohemia.   Battle of Prague.   Flight of the Elector Palatine
                                                             169
CHAP. XLIX. 1621–1623. — Re-establishment of the Austrian Government in Bohemia.   Rigorous Punishment of the Insurgents.
Plans of Ferdinand to divide the Palatine Territories.   Issues the
Ban of the Empire against the Elector Palatine and his Adherents.
Dissolution of the Protestant Union.   Conquest of the Palatinate.
Mansfeld, Christian of Brunswick, and the Margrave of Baden
support the Palatine Cause.   The Elector induced to disavow his
Partisans, and to make Offers of Submission to Ferdinand.   In-
vasion of Hungary by Bethlehem Gabor.   His Accommodation
with Ferdinand.   Transfer of the Palatine Electorate to the Duke
of Bavaria.   Alarm of the Protestants   -   -   - 180
CHAP. L. 1624–1629. — Hostile Views of England against the House
of Austria.   Character and Situation of the Kings of Denmark and
Sweden.   The King of Denmark heads the League formed by the
States of Lower Saxony against the Emperor.   Rise of Wallenstein,
and Formation of an Austrian Army, independent of the Catholic
League.   Military Operations.   Defeat of the King of Denmark
and Successes of Tilly and Wallenstein.   Irruption of Mansfeld into
Hungary.   Hostilities of Bethlehem Gabor.   Armistice.   Death
of Mansfeld.   Power and Arrogance of Ferdinand.   Completes the
Transfer of the Palatine Electorate to the House of Bavaria.
Wallenstein overruns Pomerania.   Attempts to form a naval Establish-
ment on the Baltic.   Siege of Stralsund.   Peace with Denmark 191
CHAP. LI. 1628–1630. — Ascendency and ambitious Designs of
Ferdinand.   Abolishes the Protestant Religion in Austria.   His
Civil and Religious Persecutions in Bohemia.   Nominates his
Son Ferdinand as his Successor in the Bohemian Throne.   His
Plan to suppress the Protestant Religion in Germany.   Edict of
Restitution.   Opposed by both Catholics and Protestants.   His
interference in the Affairs of Italy.   Diet of Ratisbon.   Intrigues
of Cardinal Richelieu with the German Princes.   Ferdinand per-
suaded to suspend the Edict of Restitution, to disband a Part of his
Army, dismiss Wallenstein, and agree to an Accommodation in regard▪
to the Affairs of Italy.   Disappointed in his Attempts to procure
the Election of his Son as King of the Romans   -   - 205

Chap. LII. 1630, 1631. — Situation of Sweden. Character and Exploits of Gustavus Adolphus. His Invasion of Germany. Obtains Possession of Pomerania. Concludes an Alliance with France. Meeting of the Protestants at Leipzic. Situation and Conduct of the Emperor and Empire. Tilly obtains the Command of the Imperial Forces. Repulsed in his Attempts to recover Pomerania. Siege and Sack of Magdeburgh. Invasion of the Territories of Hesse - - - - - Page 218

Chap. LIII. 1631, 1632.—Gustavus compels the Elector of Brandenburgh to enter into an Alliance, and deliver up his Fortresses. Restores the Dukes of Mecklenburgh. Concludes an Alliance with the Landgrave of Hesse. Supports the Elector of Saxony against Tilly. Gains the Battle of Leipzic. Narrow Escape and Retreat of Tilly. Rapid Progress of Gustavus along the Maine and the Rhine. Successes of his German Allies. Conquest of Bohemia by the Elector of Saxony. Conduct of Ferdinand. Ineffectual Attempt to detach France. Designs of Gustavus against the Catholic League. Repulses Tilly, and attacks Bavaria. Passage of the Leck, and Death of Tilly - - - - - 234

Chap. LIV. 1632. — Dangerous situation of Ferdinand. Restores Wallenstein to the Supreme Command. Character and Conduct of Wallenstein. Rapid Formation of a new Army. Military Operations. Wallenstein attempts to overpower or detach the Elector of Saxony. Battle of Lutzen. Death and Character of Gustavus 251

Chap. LV. 1632–1634. — Transactions after the Death of Gustavus. Oxenstiern intrusted with the Conduct of Affairs in Germany. Forms a League of the German Princes at Heilbron. Renews the Alliance with France. Military Operations of Wallenstein after the Battle of Lutzen. His Disgrace and Assassination - - 268

Chap. LVI. 1634–1637. — Arrangements after the Assassination of Wallenstein. Ferdinand, King of Hungary, the new Generalissimo, takes Ratisbon. Routs the Confederates at the Battle of Nordlingen. Consequences of the Victory. Consternation of the Protestant League. Firmness and Conduct of Oxenstiern. France takes the principal Share in the Contest. Declares War against Spain. Progress of the Imperialists. Defection of the Elector of Saxony. Peace of Prague. Dissolution of the Protestant Confederacy. Military Operations of 1635 and 1636. Electoral Diet of Ratisbon. The King of Hungary chosen King of the Romans. Death, Character, and Family of Ferdinand. Law of Primogeniture established in the Austrian Dominions - - 284

Chap. LVII. 1637–1641. — Accession of Ferdinand III. Partial Success of the Imperial Arms. Losses of the Emperor on the side of the Rhine. Splendid Victories and Death of the Duke of Weimar. France acquires Alsace. Declining Fortunes of Spain. Revolution of Portugal. Diet of Nuremberg. Commencement of Negotiations for Peace. Increasing Influence of the House of Brandenburgh - - - - . - 301

Chap. LVIII. 1640–1648. — Continuation of the War. Repeated

Distresses and Firmness of the Emperor.   Death of Richelieu, and
Louis XIII.   Administration and Views of Mazarin.   Election of
the Archduke Ferdinand as King of Hungary and Bohemia.
Memorable Siege of Prague.   Conclusion of Peace   -   Page 309
CHAP. LIX. 1637–1648. — Account of the Negotiations which terminated in the Peace of Westphalia.   Accommodation between Spain
and the United Provinces.   Contents of the Treaties of Osnaburgh
and Munster.   Remarks on the Peace   -   -   - 328
CHAP. LX. 1648–1657. — Delays and Difficulties in executing the
Peace of Westphalia.   The Archduke Ferdinand elected King of
the Romans. His Death.   Leopold crowned King of Hungary and
Bohemia.   The Emperor suppresses the rising Troubles in Ger-
many.   Terminates the Contest for the Succession of Juliers and
Berg.   Preserves the Independence of Bremen.   Successes of
Charles Gustavus, King of Sweden, in the War against Poland.
Death, Character, and Family of Ferdinand III.   -   - 342
CHAP. LXI. 1657–1660. — Accession of Leopold I.   After many
Difficulties and great Opposition from France, he obtains the
Imperial Crown.   Articles of his Capitulation.   League of the
Rhine.   Takes part in the War against Sweden.   Progress of Hosti-
lities.   Conquests, Reverses, and Death of Charles Gustavus.
Treaties of Roskild, Oliva, and Copenhagen.   Affairs of Spain.
Peace of the Pyrenees.   Marriage of Louis XIV. with the eldest
Infanta   -   -   -   -   -   -   - 350
CHAP. LXII. 1660–1664. — Affairs of Hungary and Transylvania.
State of the Ottoman Empire.   Renewal of the Turkish War.
Discontents in Hungary.   Contests of Leopold with the States.
Progress of the Turks.   Leopold obtains Succours from the Empire
and Christendom.   Establishment of a permanent Diet in Germany.
Defeat of the Turks at the Battle of St. Gothard.   Conclusion of a
Truce   -   -   -   -   -   -   - 362
CHAP. LXIII. 1664. — State of the European Powers.   Comparative
Estimate of the Strength and Influence possessed by the Houses of
Austria and Bourbon.   State of Germany.   Situation, Resources,
and Authority of Leopold   -   -   -   - 372
CHAP. LXIV. 1664–1679. — Death of Philip IV. of Spain, and
Accession of Charles II.   Distracted Situation of Spain under the
Regency of the Queen.   Marriage of Leopold with Margaret
Theresa, the second Infanta.   Louis XIV. invades the Spanish
Netherlands.   Temporising Conduct of Leopold and the German
States.   Peace of Aix-la-Chapelle dictated by the Triple Alliance.
Louis declares War against the United Provinces, in Conjunction
with England.   Successful Invasion of Holland.   Consternation of
the Dutch.   Overthrow of the Republican Party.   Heroic Exer-
tions of William Prince of Orange.   General Alarm among the
European States.   Leopold and the Elector of Brandenburgh assist
the United Provinces.   Peace of Breda between England and
Holland.   The Empire declares War against France.   Military
Operations.   Negotiations, which terminated in the Peace of
Nimeguen   -   -   -   -   -   - 393

CHAP. LXV. 1679–1697. — Usurpations and Incroachments of Louis XIV. on the Empire and Spain. Chambers of Re-union. Leopold makes fruitless Remonstrances. Improves the Military System of Germany. Forms defensive Associations. His Endeavours to consolidate a general League against France. Louis continues his Usurpations. Invades the Netherlands. Truce of Ratisbon. France attains her highest Elevation of Power and Influence. Louis irritates and alarms the States of Europe by repeated Aggressions. Counter Efforts of Leopold and William Prince of Orange. Disputes for the Palatine Succession. League of Augsburgh. French invasion of the Palatinate. Effects of the Revolution in England. Leopold and the Empire declare War against France. Grand Alliance. Rising Influence of Leopold in Germany. Leopold suspends his Design to create the Ninth Electorate, and restore the Electoral Privileges of Bohemia. Louis divides the Members of the Grand Alliance. Detaches the Duke of Savoy, and gains England and Holland. Peace of Ryswick. Remarks on the Treaty. Obnoxious Clause relative to the Restoration of the Catholic Religion in the Countries invaded by France   -   -   Page 409

CHAP. LXVI. 1667–1699. — Revival of the Discontents in Hungary. Conspiracies for throwing off the Austrian Yoke. Leopold abrogates the Privileges of the Nation, and establishes a Military Government. Rise and Progress of the Rebellion under Tekeli. The Turks invade Hungary, and lay Siege to Vienna. Formation of a Christian Army. John Sobieski, King of Poland, and the Duke of Loraine, raise the Siege. Interview of Leopold and Sobieski. The Turks expelled from Hungary. Progress of the Imperial Arms. Severities exercised against the Hungarians. Accommodation between the Court and the Malecontents. The Monarchy declared hereditary. The Venetians, Poles, and Russians concur in the War against the Porte. Defeat of the Turks at Zenta, by Prince Eugene. Peace of Carlovitz. Acquisitions of Leopold   -   -   -   -   -   -   -   437

CHAP. LXVII. 1697–1700. — Views of Leopold on the Spanish Succession. Different Pretenders. State of the Spanish Court. Successful Intrigues of Louis XIV. at Madrid. Partition Treaties. Nomination of Philip of Anjou, and Death of Charles. Accession of the new Monarch   -   -   -   -   -   459

CHAP. LXVIII. 1702, 1703. — Indignation excited at Vienna by the Transfer of the Spanish Monarchy to the House of Bourbon. Leopold prepares to assert his Claims by force of Arms. The French obtain Possession of the Netherlands. Acknowledgment of Philip by all the Powers in Europe except Leopold. Splendid Campaign of Eugene in Italy. Change in England and Holland in favour of the House of Austria. Renewal of the Grand Alliance, and general Declaration of War against France and Spain. Death of William, and Accession of Anne. Influence of Marlborough. Military Operations of 1702. Declaration of the Elector of Bavaria in favour of France. Ineffectual Descent at Cadiz, and Destruction of the Fleet at Vigo   -   -   -   -   -   -   478

Chap. LXIX. 1703, 1704. — Campaign of 1703, in the Netherlands, Germany, and Italy. The Duke of Savoy and the King of Portugal join the Grand Alliance. Disturbed Situation of Spain. The Archduke Charles proclaimed, and acknowledged King. Passes through Holland to England, and is escorted by an English Fleet to Lisbon - - . - - Page 490

Chap. LXX. 1704. — Critical Situation of the Emperor. Plans of the French and Bavarians to invade the Austrian Territories. Successful Rebellion of Ragotsky in Hungary. Leopold obtains the Assistance of Great Britain. Stupendous March of Marlborough from the Low Countries to the Danube. His interview with Eugene and the Margrave of Baden. Defeat of the Bavarians at Schellenberg. Siege of Ingoldstadt. Junction of Marlborough and Eugene. Victory of Blenheim. Successful Progress of the Allies. Reduction of Bavaria. Defeat of the Hungarian Rebels. Grateful Letter of Leopold to Marlborough - - - - 500

Chap. LXXI. 1705. — Death, Character, and Family of Leopold 513

HISTORY

OF

THE HOUSE OF AUSTRIA.

CHAP. XXXV. — FERDINAND I. — 1522–1564.

IN the midst of these events in Hungary and Bohemia,
Ferdinand became head of the empire, by the abdication of
his brother.

We have already related the attempts of Charles to procure the reversion of the imperial crown for Philip, a
project which both astonished and embarrassed Ferdinand,
who was accustomed to bend to the persevering inflexibility of his brother. After some difficulties he affected a
ready compliance, and even sent his ambassadors to solicit
the votes of the electors ; but at the same time he interposed an insuperable obstacle to the transfer of the imperial dignity, by demanding, as an indispensable condition,
that on the succession of Philip to the empire, his own son
Maximilian should be elected king of the Romans ; he also
secretly made overtures to Maurice of Saxony, and by his
means influenced the electors Palatine and Brandenburgh.
To avoid the appearance of public opposition, he next referred Charles to Maurice, as the head of the Protestant
body ; and on this occasion Maurice, acting with his characteristic address and duplicity, by affected ardour for the
accomplishment of the emperor's wishes, succeeded in persuading him to reserve the intended plan for a more
favourable opportunity.

VOL. II.   B

Charles, however, till the very moment of his retreat, did not relinquish his favourite object ; and retained the imperial crown some months after the renunciation of his other dignities, with the vain hope of prevailing on his brother, or at least of securing the imperial dignity for his posterity ; but Ferdinand, who had been little inclined to comply with the solicitations of the emperor in the pride of power and victory, received with indifference the last overture of an abdicated sovereign. Another attempt made by Charles to procure for Philip the perpetual vicariate of Italy, was equally fruitless ; for Ferdinand, aware that this office would enable the Spanish branch to appropriate the Italian fiefs, gave a peremptory refusal, replying that as he intended to leave the empire entire to his successors, he expected his brother would act in the same manner towards him. At length, Charles, disappointed in all his endeavours, by a formal deed, dated August 7th, 1556, resigned his claims of allegiance from the Germanic body to his brother, the king of the Romans.

The voluntary abdication of an emperor being a new event in the political history of Germany, some difficulties arose on the manner of accepting the resignation, which produced a delay of nearly two years before Ferdinand was formally acknowledged and proclaimed. Although he had signed, on the 15th of February, 1558, a capitulation when chosen king of the Romans ; and although it was unusual to exact new conditions from a king of the Romans, when he succeeded to the imperial dignity ; yet the electors, on this occasion, presented another capitulation for the purpose of including the religious peace, which had been arranged since the election of Ferdinand.

The accession of Ferdinand was also distinguished by an event which exalted the dignity of the imperial crown, by rescuing it from servile dependence on the see of Rome. Hitherto, a personal coronation by the pope had been considered as necessary to confer the title of emperor, and to enable him to secure the reversion of the imperial crown for another person, by the nomination of a king of the Romans. Maximilian had, indeed, with the consent of Julius II., assumed the title of emperor elect ; but the title was of no advantage, for he could not prevail on the electors to nominate his grandson Charles as his successor, because he had never been crowned at Rome. Charles himself had respected the privileges or prejudices of the German nation; and, however urgent the circumstances of the times, had not attempted to obtain the appointment of Ferdinand before his own coronation.

The impolitic and overbearing conduct of the aged pontiff, Paul IV., deprived the Roman see of this honour, which had frequently enabled his predecessors to interfere with effect in the affairs of Germany. The first step of Ferdinand, after his inauguration, was to send an embassy to Rome, respectfully announcing his accession and expressing his wishes to receive the imperial crown from the hands of the pontiff; but this submissive application was contemptuously received by Paul, whose romantic imagination was filled with the most extravagant ideas of spiritual power and pre-eminence, and who was personally offended with Ferdinand for the concessions he had granted to the Protestants in the religious peace. He treated the abdication of Charles as the act of a madman; declared that he ought to have resigned the imperial dignity to the head of the church, from whom he had received it; and annulled the nomination of Ferdinand, because it was made with the concurrence of electors who were tainted with heresy. He therefore refused to receive his ambassador, and required him to relinquish the imperial crown, and submit to a new election.

On receiving the haughty message, Ferdinand acted with a firmness and dignity becoming his high rank, and ordered his ambassador to quit Rome within three days, if the pope still refused to grant him an audience. Paul was embarrassed with this unexpected firmness, and, as the means of avoiding an immediate rupture, granted the ambassador a private interview, without retracting his arrogant pretensions, and promised an explanation of his conduct through the intervention of a legate. This discussion, however, was highly prejudicial to the arrogated supremacy of the pope; for it irritated both Catholics and Protestants, and led to an examination, in consequence of which the personal coronation by the pope was declared unnecessary. Paul dying the same year, his successor, Pius IV., made overtures of reconciliation to the emperor, and these overtures produced a new embassy, by which Ferdinand expressed the accustomed devotion and reverence, but omitted the usual profession of obedience to the head of the church. This omission was far from being grateful to the court of Rome, which never willingly relinquished its slightest pretensions, and succeeded by artifice and cajolery in persuading the imperial ambassador to introduce the word *obedience* in his public compliment. In consequence of this addition, the pope acknowledged the title of the emperor; and Ferdinand, who was too prudent to cavil at words, when he had in reality gained his object, did not disavow, though he did not formally approve, the concession made in his name.

Soon afterwards Maximilian, eldest son of Ferdinand, was elected, without the smallest difficulty, king of the Romans, notwithstanding the opposition of the pope; and, in his public compliment to the head of the church, substituted the word *obsequium* for *obedientiam*. Thus terminated the long dependence of the emperors on the see of Rome, which had been established in ages of darkness and ignorance, had been continued from respect and habit, and which in all periods had involved the empire in innumerable embarrassments and calamities, without producing a single real advantage.

The example of Ferdinand, in neglecting to receive the crown from the pope, has been followed by his successors; from this period, the chiefs of the empire have avoided an expensive and difficult journey, and are totally emancipated from the most distant dependence on the see of Rome.

As emperor, Ferdinand pursued the same system of policy as when king of the Romans, particularly in regard to religious affairs; and he had occasion for all his foresight, caution, and forbearance, to prevent the religious feuds from again breaking out into civil wars. Though like his brother, sincerely attached to the church of Rome, and anxious to prevent the diffusion of doctrines which he considered as heretical, he was of a more flexible and forbearing disposition, and felt himself interested to conciliate the Protestants as well as the Catholics, for the sake of procuring their support against the Turks. Hence he acted with the most impartial justice towards both parties, maintained the letter and spirit of the terms concluded by his interference at Passau; and equally resisted all the encroachments, both of Catholics and Protestants. As the only means of maintaining the balance which existed between the two parties, he persevered in resisting all the attempts of the Protestants to obtain the repeal of the ecclesiastical reservation, and equally discountenanced the efforts of the Catholics to prevent the toleration of the Protestant doctrines in the territories of Catholic prelates.

Sensible of the mutual jealousy which reigned between the Catholics and Protestants, dreading the renewal of the religious warfare, and appreciating the political advantages which might arise to the empire and Christianity from the re-union of all parties under one system of doctrine and worship, he never relaxed in his endeavours to heal the schism of the church, or to obtain from the court of Rome such concessions as might receive the approbation of all. With this view, he procured the renewal of the conferences on points of religion, and when these failed of success, he pressed the Protestants, at the diet of Augsburgh, to acknowledge the council of Trent. But they refused, unless the pope should agree to act as a party only, instead of presiding; unless the Protestant divines were treated on the same footing as the Catholic bishops, and the council held at some other town, either in or near Germany. These demands, being incompatible with the Catholic principles, were necessarily rejected; and, in order to avoid any discussion which might offend either party, the recess was framed without any mention of the proposed council, postponing the affairs of religion to a favourable occasion, and confirming the treaty of Passau, and the religious peace.

From these circumstances, Ferdinand seems for a time to have abandoned his design of procuring the convocation of a general council, till the alarming progress of the Protestant doctrines, and the interference of Spain and France, compelled him again to interfere in religious disputes.

The Protestant was now become the dominant religion in Sweden and Denmark, and by the accession of Elizabeth was established in England. In France, no longer confined to the great body of the people, it found partisans among the higher orders of the state, and became a bond of union for all the parties in opposition to the government. Its progress was favoured by the weak state of the administration under Francis II., who was wholly swayed by his wife, Mary queen of Scots, and by her uncles, the duke of Guise, and the cardinal of Loraine ; and was still more promoted under the unpopular and sanguinary administration of Catherine de' Medici, who at this time held the reins of government, during the minority of her son, Charles IX. From France and Germany it spread into the Low Countries ; and all the vigilance of the inquisition, and the severity of the government, scarcely sufficed to prevent its introduction into Spain and Portugal.

The courts of France and Spain were more particularly interested to prevent the progress of the schism ; and, with that view, Philip and Henry II. had concluded the treaty of Chateau Cambresis, in the same manner as Francis I. and Charles suspended their own disputes, for the purpose of crushing the Lutherans. A favourable opportunity presenting itself on the election of pope Pius IV., who was of a far less obstinate and overbearing temper than his predecessor Paul, the courts of France and Spain joined in requiring the convocation of a council, and finally extorted his acquiescence.

The meeting of a council being now not far distant, Ferdinand endeavoured to render it subservient to his views for securing the peace of Germany. For this purpose he joined with France and Spain, and exerted all his influence with the pope, to obtain the convocation of a *new* council in some town of Germany, and not the resumption of the former council at Trent, which, as it would occasion the confirmation of the former decisions, would only tend still farther to irritate the Protestants. He represented, also, the necessity of directing its first attention to the essential point of general reformation, rather than to articles of faith ; he enforced the expediency of commencing the cure with the source of the evil, by bringing back the ecclesiastical state to its ancient constitutions, and tendered his zealous co-operation as the first protector of the church. He also imparted to the pope the resolutions passed by the Protestants at the diet of Augsburgh ; and, after expatiating on their strength and union, urged the imprudence of attempting to compel so powerful a body to adopt principles which they had so long rejected, and the danger of again involving Christendom in a perilous warfare. Finally, he concluded with the most earnest solicitations, that the pope would at least condescend to gratify the Protestants, by permitting the marriage of the clergy, and the administration of the communion under both kinds ; and he enforced the demand with arguments founded no less on moral principles than political expediency, which must have convinced all who were not blinded by prejudice, or interested to maintain their errors.

This memorial was far from being grateful to the court of Rome ; but its indiscreet publication by the pope rendered Ferdinand still more popular in Germany, and removed those suspicions, which the Protestants began to entertain of his sincerity. All his endeavours, however, failed in obtaining a new council ; and, after much difficulty, he consented to the resumption of the former council of Trent. This important point being arranged, the pope issued the requisite bulls, and sent two cardinals, Commendon and Delfino, as his legates, to invite the Protestants to the assembly.

As the proposals and language of the pope were far more mild and plausible than on preceding occasions, Ferdinand hoped to overcome their repugnance to take part in the deliberations of this council, and submit to its decisions ; and, for this purpose, he sent his own ambassadors with the papal legates, to a meeting of the whole body, which, with his permission, had assembled in 1560 at Naumburgh, a city in Upper Saxony. But the renewal of the council at Trent, which had formerly taken such a decided part against the Protestants, was too disagreeable a measure to be rendered palatable by any address of the court of Rome. The assembly, therefore, far from being inclined to submit to the council, and unite with the Catholics, gave proofs of the most inveterate hostility to the Roman see, for they contemptuously sent back to the legates, unopened, the papal briefs, which were addressed to them by the usual title of " Sons," with the reply, that as they did not acknowledge the bishop of Rome as their father, they could neither receive his letters nor accept the title. This was but the prelude to a formal answer, which, amidst the bitterest invectives, contained the declaration, that they would receive no invitation from the pope to repair to a council which he had no power to convoke, that being the prerogative of the emperor, to whom as their sovereign, they were alone amenable.*

At this meeting, the Protestants, for the purpose of strengthening their union, declared their resolution to adhere to the confession of Augsburgh, whatever were the decrees of the council of Trent. But this very resolution was a proof of that diversity of opinions which afterwards occasioned as great a schism among themselves as that by which they had separated from the church of Rome. Some proposed to retain that confession in the original and primitive sense, and adhere strictly to the doctrines of Luther ; others, of whom the chief was the elector Palatine, to explain and modify those articles in such a manner as to accommodate them to the doctrines of that reformed church, first established by Zuingle, and afterwards systematised by Calvin. So violent were the dissensions on this subject, that, for some time, the elector Palatine refused to affix his signature to this confession ; and, on the other side, John Frederic, son of the deposed elector of Saxony, publicly stigmatised the elector Palatine, although his father-in-law, with the reproachful epithet of Sacramentarian, and indignantly quitted the assembly.

Ferdinand saw, with secret satisfaction, these tokens of rising disunion ; and, leaving this cause to operate, hastened the meeting of the council at Trent, which, after many delays and difficulties, resumed its sittings on the 15th of January, 1562. It is unnecessary to dwell on the proceedings of this memorable council; it will be sufficient to observe, that the papal party was so powerful as to prevent the decision of any point contrary to the wishes and interests of the see of Rome ; and therefore, that, after long

---

* An interesting account of this transaction is given in the life of the celebrated cardinal Commendon, one of the legates, written by Gratiana, and translated by Flechier, lib. ii. ch. iii.

cavils and disputes, cabals, and intrigues, no essential reformation was suffered to take place.

Ferdinand himself stood in a delicate situation; and, by his attempts to mediate between the two parties, was exposed to the suspicions and obloquy of both. By the Protestants, he was accused of persecution and intolerance, and even by the Catholics, whose party he saved from total annihilation in Germany, he was charged with lukewarmness to his religion, and with dishonouring the church, by requiring concessions hostile to its authority, doctrines, and usages. But neither obloquy nor persuasion could induce him to swerve from that line of conduct which he had adopted from motives of duty and interest.

At length, perceiving that the principal changes made by the council were trifling, or in matters of no import, and that the most essential questions were referred to the decision of the pope, he himself brought forward several grievances, of which he required the redress. He urged the council particularly to exhort the pope to examine if any amendment was necessary in his own person, state, and court; "because," he observed, "the only true method to obtain authority for the reformation of others, is to begin by amending oneself." He required the reduction of the number of cardinals to twenty-six; the discontinuance of scandalous dispensations and exemptions from common law; the abolition of pluralities and simony, and of the farming of ecclesiastical offices. He proposed, that bishops should be compelled to reside in their dioceses; that no fees should be demanded for the administration of the sacrament; that excommunication should be used only for mortal sins and manifest irregularities; that the prayers and divine offices should be performed in the vulgar tongue; breviaries and missals corrected, and a new ritual made for the use of the church; that the clergy and monks should be reformed according to ancient institutions; the rigour of fasts abated; the communion administered under both kinds; and marriage allowed to the clergy. These articles were supported by the king of Spain; and some others, of still stronger import, were added by the French monarch.

It is easy to conceive the indignation and surprise of the court of Rome at these demands, made by the protector and advocate of the church ; but it is unnecessary to dwell on the cavils, chicanery, and disputes, employed to defeat every effort for real reformation, and which induced the emperor himself to permit the dissolution of an assembly, from which, according to his own expression, "nothing good could be expected, even if it continued its sittings for a hundred years."

Thus terminated this celebrated council, which had been so long expected, and called with the hope of uniting all Christendom under one system of worship and doctrine ; but which, by its decrees, declared the principal errors and abuses of the church of Rome articles of faith, even on points hitherto problematical ; and thus set an insuperable barrier between the Catholic Church and the Protestants of every sect and denomination. But although these decisions were in almost every respect contrary to the wishes and expectations of Ferdinand, yet with a view to prevent a new schism in the church, he did not withhold his assent to its decrees, and continued his negotiations, with the hope of obtaining for the subjects of his hereditary countries, at least the permission to administer the communion under both kinds, and the marriage of priests. Notwithstanding the refusal of the Protestants to accept the decrees of the council, and the incessant bickerings between the two parties, Ferdinand, by a strict adherence to the articles of his capitulation, and by a mixture of moderation and firmness, succeeded in maintaining the public peace ; and, though he could not annihilate, he repressed those religious feuds, which, under a less prudent sovereign, would have again involved the empire in a civil war.

While all Germany had been the theatre of religious discussion, the hereditary dominions of the house of Austria could not escape the general contagion. In the earliest period of the Lutheran dispute, the reformed doctrines spread into Austria, and found numerous adherents in the capital, and even in the university ; but more particularly among the territorial lords, who maintained domestic priests of the reformed opinions, and held a regular correspondence with Luther. These innovations had not escaped the attention of Ferdinand, and he omitted no endeavours to check their progress. He rigorously enforced the execution of the edict of the Worms, and strictly forbade the distribution of Luther's translation of the Bible.   But, notwithstanding all his vigilance, the Lutheran doctrines prospered no less in Austria than in Germany; and, in the space of a few years, the majority of the states were either openly or secretly attached to the Reformation.

The invasion of the Turks, and the other embarrassments of Ferdinand, encouraged the Lutherans to demand a public toleration; and although their petition was not formally granted, he was so desirous to obtain the support of the states that he connived at their private conventicles. This tacit toleration, however, occasioned a rapid increase of the Protestant party; Ferdinand, to counteract its effects, prohibited the preaching of the new opinions, and introduced the community of Jesuits into every part of his hereditary dominions, as the most able defenders of the Catholic faith.   After concluding the peace of Passau, he took more decided steps; he issued a general edict, ordering all his subjects to continue in the ancient religion, and pay due obedience to the Catholic church; and in particular to discontinue the administration of the sacrament under two kinds.

The states, encouraged by the example and success of the Protestants in Germany, made repeated attempts to procure the revocation of this edict, and even at one period threatened to withhold their subsidy for the support of the war against the Turks.   At length, Ferdinand perceiving that his opposition did not retard the diffusion of the Protestant doctrines, and aware that persecution would only increase their adherents, endeavoured to prevent the formal separation of his subjects from the church, by obtaining an indulgence for the marriage of priests, and the reception of the communion under both kinds, the two articles on which the Protestants most earnestly insisted.   He laboured with uncommon ardour to gain these points, first from the council of Trent, and afterwards from the pope himself, by employing every argument which could be deduced from considerations of morality and expedience.   " In Bohemia," he said, " from the days of Jacobel and Huss, no persuasion, no argument, no violence, not even arms and war, have succeeded in abolishing the use of the cup in the sa-

crament. In fact, the church itself permitted it, although
the popes revoked it by a breach of the conditions on
which it was granted; and if ever there was an opportunity
of re-uniting the Calixtins to the church, it is in the present moment, when, after an interval of one hundred and
forty years, the archiepiscopal see is re-established in
Prague, and the Calixtins have agreed to the consecration
of their priests, by the new prelate, and when this re-union
can be effected by the simple restoration of the cup."

"In the other states, Hungary, Austria, Silesia, Styria,
Carinthia, Carniola, Bavaria, and other parts of Germany,
many desire, with ardour, the same indulgence; if this
concession is granted, they may be re-united to the church,
but if refused, they will be driven into the party of
the Protestants. In Hungary, things are carried to such
an unfortunate extremity, that the priests have been compelled by violence to administer the sacrament under both
kinds. Those who have given way to this irregularity,
have been punished and degraded by their diocesans; and,
in consequence of this persecution, the country is almost
deprived of priests. Hence children die, or grow up to maturity, without baptism; and men and women, of all ages
and of all ranks, live like the brutes, in the grossest ignorance of God and of religion."

For the marriage of priests, it was urged, "There is
such a want of ministers of the altar, that it becomes necessary to examine, whether divine or positive law will not
allow to priests the liberty of marrying. If such a permission cannot be granted, may not married men of learning
and probity be ordained, according to the custom of the
eastern church, or married priests be tolerated for a time,
provided they act according to the Catholic and Christian
faith? And it may justly be asked, whether such concessions would not be far more preferable than to tolerate, as
has unfortunately been done, fornication and concubinage."

On another occasion, after observing that in Germany,
and particularly in his hereditary countries, there was
scarcely a single person capable of executing the office of
priest, unmarried, he continues in still stronger expressions,
"I cannot avoid adding, what is a common observation,
that priests, who live in concubinage, are guilty of greater

sin than those who are married; for the last only transgress a law which is capable of being changed, whereas the first sin against a divine law, which is neither capable of change nor dispensation."

These arguments made perhaps some impression on the council; but, by papal influence, the two questions were left undecided, and, with the concurrence of Ferdinand, referred to the decision of the pope. But although the legate had obtained his acquiescence in the dissolution of the council, by the most solemn assurances that these concessions would be granted, the pope with difficulty consented that the cup should be administered to the laity in the communion, and refused to approve the marriage of priests. Ferdinand instantly promulgated this concession, and persevered in his solicitations for the other article, during the short interval which elapsed before his death, on the 25th of July, 1564.

As the constitution of Germany had now begun to assume consistency, the reign of Ferdinand is necessarily less distinguished for a variety of new regulations than those of the preceding emperors. The religious regulations have already been detailed; and those which he introduced, as emperor were, a change in the system of the Aulic council, a complete reformation of the coinage, and an improvement in the institutions for the maintenance of the public peace, which was greatly disturbed by the licentiousness of military levies, raised without the countenance of any regular government, and under the pretence of foreign service.

The first of these regulations, for the maintenance of peace was, by substituting for the general diets, of which the proceedings were uncertain and dilatory, diets of deputation, which consisting only of the electors and of deputies from the other members of the empire, were easily convoked, and speedy in their decisions. The other was, by increasing the power of the military chief in each circle, which rendered the conduct of military affairs more prompt and effectual; a measure which was proposed under Ferdinand, but received its completion during the reign of his successor. The Aulic council, instituted by Maximilian, was retained and improved by Charles; but as he submitted to its decisions the affairs of Italy and the Low

Countries, as well as those of Germany, it was gradually
filled with foreign members, who introduced some changes in
the form of its proceedings. The states of the empire, both
at the conclusion of the peace of Passau and of the peace of
religion, had remonstrated against these innovations, and
Ferdinand, in the name of his brother, promised redress ;
and as no amelioration took place during the reign of
Charles, the first object of the new emperor was, to fulfil
his promise. With this view he purged the council of
foreign members, and published an ordinance relative to its
jurisdiction, forms of proceeding and ceremonial, which
still continues in force ; and from this amelioration, he has
often been considered as the original institutor.

In regard to the public coinage, at his accession extremely debased and defective, Germany owes to him an
edict, which has likewise formed the foundation of all
subsequent regulations. By this edict, the alloy, the value,
the title, form, and assay of the coins are regulated ; and
all the states are forbidden to issue money which does not
bear the bust, or at least the designation of the reigning
sovereign.

So greatly was Ferdinand beloved, and so much was the
jealousy entertained by the Germans of the power of his
illustrious house diminished by the separation of the two
branches, that he found no difficulty in obtaining the election of his son as king of the Romans ; and, as a short time
before, he had been crowned at Prague as hereditary sovereign of Bohemia, and the following year at Presburgh, as
successor to the throne of Hungary, Ferdinand was
enabled to secure to his successor the three dignities,
which it had always been the ambition of his ancestor to
obtain. To prevent also those family contests which had
hitherto weakened his illustrious house, Ferdinand settled
by his testament, dated August 10th, 1555, the succession
to the archduchy of Austria on his eldest son alone, and
his posterity ; to his second son, Ferdinand, he devised the
Tyrol, and the exterior provinces ; to Charles, his third
son, Carinthia, Styria, and Carniola : he secured the fulfilment of these bequests, by obtaining the signature of his
three sons to this testament.

Ferdinand died on the 25th of July, 1564, in the sixty-second year of his age, of a fever which was occasioned by the chagrin arising from the religious troubles in his own dominions, and the failure of all his attempts to heal the schism of the church.

Though as Protestants it is impossible not to consider Ferdinand as the great oppugner of religious truth, and the principal supporter of Catholic errors, yet we cannot deny him the praise of an ardent and sincere attachment to the religion of his ancestors, free from bigotry and intolerance, to a degree unusual in his age and family. He saw and lamented the abuses of the church, and by his attempts to procure a real reformation, exposed himself to the odium of the Catholics; but he left an unequivocal proof of his religious sentiments in a paper annexed to his will, with the hope that this last memorial of a deceased parent would make a deep impression on the minds of his children. In this paper, he exhorted them with paternal tenderness to maintain an inflexible attachment to their religion; and corroborated his arguments by detailing the troubles and calamities which he considered as derived from the introduction of the Lutheran doctrines, and by holding forth to them the prospect both of celestial and terrestrial blessings as the reward of their obedience.

Ferdinand in his youth possessed uncommon beauty of countenance, and, in his more advanced age, united with a graceful deportment the dignity and gravity of a sovereign. To the completion of his education according to the plan of Erasmus, he probably owed a greater degree of taste and erudition than usually falls to the lot of a monarch. Besides the Spanish, Italian, German, and French languages, he was well acquainted with classical literature, and possessed a general knowledge of the arts and sciences. He evinced his taste and disposition by the great delight which he found in perusing the Greek writers, and the predilection he showed for Cæsar and Cicero. He was attached to the society of the learned, whom he treated with freedom and familiarity, patronised men of letters, and maintained an intimate correspondence with Erasmus, on whom he conferred marks of distinction and liberality expressive of his gratitude and respect. Among others, he also employed and favoured the learned Busbequius, who is distin guished for his embassy to Constantinople, and his excellent account of the Turks.

In domestic life he was a model of temperance, decorum, and sobriety ; and was remarkable for a placid and forgiving disposition. He was faithful to the marriage bed ; and even after the death of a beloved wife, preserved an inviolable continence.

Bred up by Spanish priests, and led astray by the example of his brother, Ferdinand gave, in the fervour of youth, and the career of victory, proofs of intolerance and despotism ; but, unlike Charles, he became more wise and moderate as he advanced in years, varied and adapted his conduct to contingencies, and gradually corrected those arbitrary and persecuting principles which he had imbibed in the school of Ferdinand the Catholic. The characteristic qualities of Ferdinand, when matured by experience, were application, vigilance, mildness, and impartiality ; policy without deceit, courage without ostentation. He did not possess the brilliant talents of his brother, yet neither did he inherit that restless and despotic genius, which led Charles to sacrifice to his own ambitious views the tranquillity and happiness of his people. Though he did not attract the wonder of his age, he deserved and obtained what was far more desirable, the esteem of his contemporaries and the love of his subjects. He may justly be called the pacificator of Germany ; and to him may be attributed the lustre of that branch of the house of Austria of which he was the head.

A blind attachment to his ministers, and a facility of temper easily wrought upon by ambitious or interested men, were his principal foibles, and to them may be imputed that indelible stain on his memory, with which history reproaches him, the assassination of Martinuzzi. In a sovereign so just and moderate, so remarkable for strict adherence to truth, his conduct towards the Bohemians is another defect. But although this breach of his solemn engagements, and his extreme severity towards the malecontents cannot be excused, they may at least be palliated by the peculiar difficulties of his situation, and the turbulent character of the people.

His wife Anne, daughter of Ladislaus, king of Hungary

and Bohemia, was born in 1503, and espoused him in 1521. She seems to have borne, at least by courtesy, the title of queen, even before her husband became sovereign of Hungary and Bohemia, and this privilege was derived from an incident which occurred during her childhood. On the coronation of her infant brother, in the cathedral of Prague, Anne, who was only six years old, burst into tears, because she was not crowned ; and, to appease her, Ladislaus took the diadem and placed it on her head. This circumstance being considered as auspicious, a sudden acclamation burst forth from the nobles and deputies ; they instantly declared her successor to her brother, should he die without issue, and the king, on his part, promised not to give her in marriage without the approbation of the states. This trivial incident greatly contributed to secure the election of her husband Ferdinand.

Anne was a princess equally beautiful, sensible, humble, and pious, of a compassionate and forgiving temper, modest and decent in her attire. She paid a peculiar attention to the education of her children, and, instead of indulging them in the luxuries of a court, had the good sense to train them in habits of humility, temperance, and self-control, that they might be prepared for every change of fortune, and be enabled to bear want, hunger, and thirst. She died in 1547, in the midst of the Bohemian rebellion ; and her death was a real loss to the people, who in her had frequently found a powerful mediator with Ferdinand. She bore fifteen children, of whom three sons and nine daughters arrived at years of maturity.

The three sons formed the lines of Austria, Tyrol, and Styria.

1. Maximilian, who succeeded his father in the archduchy of Austria, and in the empire.

2. Ferdinand, who inherited the Tyrol, and the exterior provinces. His first wife was Phillippa Welseren, a woman of great beauty and accomplishments, but being only of a patrician family, the alliance was considered as degrading, and the emperor, complacent and forgiving as he was in temper, was too jealous of the honour of his family to ratify or approve the marriage. After some years, his daughter-in-law found means to gain admittance into his

presence, and, throwing herself at his feet, her beauty and
attractive manners won his forgiveness. He acknowledged
her as his daughter-in-law; but he was unable to oblite-
rate the stigma which German prejudice has affixed to dis-
proportionate matches; and her children, though deemed
legitimate, were declared incapable of inheriting. She died
in 1580, leaving two sons, Andrew and Charles. Andrew
obtained the margraviate of Burgau, entered into holy
orders, became bishop of Brixen and Constance, and was
raised to the dignity of cardinal. He was likewise sub-
governor of the Netherlands. On his death, in 1600, the
margraviate of Burgau descended to his brother Charles,
who afterwards was raised to the dignity of a prince of the
empire, and, dying without issue, in 1619, the lands which
had been conferred on him reverted to the Styrian line. The
second wife of Ferdinand was his cousin, Anne Catherine,
daughter of William, duke of Mantua. When she became
a widow, she refused the hand of the emperor Matthias;
and died in a nunnery, in 1621.

Charles, the third and youngest son of Ferdinand, founder
of the Styrian line, was born in 1540. A marriage was
proposed between him and the unfortunate Mary queen of
Scots, by her confidant Melville, who came to Innspruck
in 1562. He was also a candidate for the hand of Elizabeth of England, and, like other princes, was disappointed
by her maiden coyness, or independent spirit. He was
anxious to urge his suit in person, and received the
strongest encouragement from the royal coquette, but the
prudence or pride of his brother prevented him from going,
like the duke of Anjou, to swell the train of his mistress,
by requiring the previous adjustment and ratification of
the articles of marriage.* He died in 1590, leaving by his
wife Maria, the daughter of Albert of Bavaria, several
daughters. His sons were : — 1. Ferdinand, who, on the
death of Matthias, became emperor, and head of the house
of Austria, and king of Hungary and Bohemia. 2. Maximilian Ernest, grand-master of the Teutonic order. 3. Leopold, first bishop of Passau and Strasburgh, in 1519, and
afterwards, on quitting the ecclesiastical profession, sovereign of Tyrol and the exterior provinces, in virtue of the

* Rapin, vol. vii. 8vo., p. 222. 244. 299.

family compact with his brother Ferdinand. His territories devolved successively on his two sons, Ferdinand Charles and Sigismond Francis, both of whom dying without male issue, all the collateral branches of the house of Austria became extinct, in 1665, and the whole inheritance reverted to the elder branch, in the person of Leopold. 4. Charles, bishop of Breslau and Brixen ; after the death of his brother Maximilian Ernest, he became grand-master of the Teutonic order. He was nominated governor of the Low Countries, but died in Spain before he could assume the government, in 1624.*

The daughters of Ferdinand were : — 1. Elizabeth, married to Sigismond Augustus, duke of Lithuania, and afterwards king of Poland. 2. Maria, to William, duke of Cleves. 3. Magdalen, abbess of the nunnery of Hall, in the Tyrol, which her father built at her request. 4. Catherine, wife, first of Francis, duke of Mantua ; and, secondly, of Sigismond Augustus, after the death of her sister Elizabeth, but divorced for barrenness. 5. Eleonora, who married William, duke of Mantua. 6. Barbara, wife of Alphonso, duke of Ferrara. 7. Joanna, who espoused Francis Maria de' Medici, great duke of Florence. 8. and 9. Margaret and Helena, who took the veil.

Chap. XXXVI. — MAXIMILIAN II.—1527-1566.

BEFORE we commence the reign of Maximilian II., it is necessary to review the situation of the house of Austria, in consequence of the separation of the two branches, and the acquisition of Hungary and Bohemia, and to consider

* We do not deem it necessary to enter into any further account of the collateral branches of Styria and Tyrol, because those branches were comparatively insignificant, and because every fact of importance will find its proper place in the reigns of the succeeding sovereigns. Those who have taste and curiosity for these genealogical inquiries, will find ample information in Gebheardi Gen. Gesch. vol. ii. p. 448—484., and Pinacotheca Austriaca, p. 301—328.

the effects of the Reformation on the head of that house, as well in regard to his own territories as to the empire.

By the division of the two branches, the head of the German line for some time derived as little support from the sovereign of Spain and the Netherlands, as if those territories had been held by another family, although a domestic connection was still maintained, and two of the Austrian princes were educated in Spain, with the expectation of being called to the succession of the monarchy, should Philip die without issue. The ties of relationship were outweighed by political considerations, and the separation was widened by the disappointment of Philip in his attempt to obtain the imperial crown, and the discordance of religious sentiments between him and Maximilian. Even the result of their political conduct was different; for while Ferdinand and Maximilian, by toleration, mildness, and prudence, were preserving their dominions, and laying the foundation of future grandeur, Philip was rashly exhausting his vast resources, immense treasures, and numerous population, in pursuing the gigantic projects of his father.

The ill-judged division of the territories made by Ferdinand among his three sons contributed to weaken the German line; but while its influence was diminished on one side by the dismemberment of these dependent provinces, it obtained a more than equivalent aggrandisement by the acquisition of Bohemia; and had Maximilian secured tranquil possession of Hungary, of which he was nominal sovereign, he would have ranked among the greatest monarchs of Europe. But, in fact, the Turks possessed one half of the kingdom; the remainder was contested by the house of Zapoli; and even that portion which he held was preserved with difficulty, and agitated with endless feuds; while the perpetual wars, in which he and his father were engaged for the disputed territory, exhausted their resources, and fettered their exertions on the side of Europe.

It is a difficult question to solve, what would have been the condition of the church and of the empire, if the house of Austria had not taken part against the Reformation; at the same time it cannot be denied that the wars in which that house was engaged against the reformers, proved the greatest obstacle to its own aggrandisement. In no other cause, except that of religion, could the people have been induced to make such astonishing efforts in defence of their sovereigns ; and by no other bond of union would so many different states have been united against so formidable an adversary. Never was the house of Austria more powerful than after the victory of Muhlberg, when by the destruction of the league of Smalkalde, the liberties of the Germanic body appeared to be annihilated ; but these liberties revived under the auspices of Maurice of Saxony, and by the religious peace of Augsburgh, all the plans of Charles for the oppression of civil and religious liberty were overturned, and the Protestant religion established on a permanent basis.

In the diet of Augsburgh, Germany was first divided into different parties of religion and policy; and the schism was consolidated because it was then first legalised. From that period the members of the confession of Augsburgh were placed on an equality with the Catholics ; but after a contest attended with such violence and acrimony, it was impossible for the two parties to coalesce : and even the stipulations of the peace itself contained the seeds of future animosity, by furnishing each with a pretext for explaining the articles according to its interests or prejudices. The Protestants had infringed the ecclesiastical reservation, by procuring the election of Protestants into Catholic chapters ; and many of the Catholic prelates contravened the declaration of Ferdinand annexed to the religious peace, by withholding liberty of conscience from their Protestant subjects. But these very dissensions were, in the present instance, by no means disadvantageous to the head of the house of Austria as chief of the empire, nor detrimental to the empire itself. For the fermentation arising from the collision of the two parties, occasioned the establishment of regulations, which secured the liberty of the states, and affixed due bounds to the imperial prerogative ; while the emulation excited between the two sects enabled a moderate and prudent emperor to draw forth unusual support from the Protestants, by occasional acts of toleration, at the same time that he derived due assistance from the Catholics, from principles of religious attachment. From these causes Ferdinand and Maximilian obtained greater succours from the Protestants alone, than the whole empire had ever before furnished, even when not divided by religious feuds.

The same causes, however, did not operate with equal effect in the hereditary dominions of the house of Austria. The Protestants had gained such a preponderance in the states, both of Bohemia and Austria, and such influence in the country, that they were rather inclined to extort than to accept toleration ; and nothing but the extreme mildness and liberality of Maximilian, joined with equal firmness and decision, could have prevented the total extermination of the Catholic faith. From these circumstances his authority and views were perpetually shackled ; and the concessions which necessity or inclination induced him to make, gave rise to the troubles which involved all Europe in war, under his weaker and more bigoted successors.

Maximilian II. was born on the 1st of August, 1527, and educated in Spain with his cousin Philip, who was of the same age, under the auspices of the emperor, Charles V. But though brought up in so bigoted a court, and the associate of the morose and intolerant Philip, he imbibed, in his early years, and preserved through life, the most winning affability of manners, and the most liberal spirit of toleration. He principally owed these virtues and principles to the instructions of his early preceptor, Wolfgang Severus, a Silesian, who was secretly attached to the Lutheran doctrines. This impression was too deep to be ever obliterated, and resisted all the instructions of subsequent preceptors, and all the exhortations and advice of his family. As he advanced to manhood, he took a Lutheran priest into his service, under the title of secretary, from whom he was accustomed to receive the communion under both kinds ; and, by his intervention, entered into an intimate correspondence with the chiefs of the Protestant party, particularly with Frederic III., elector Palatine, and Augustus, elector of Saxony. When he had retired from Spain, he publicly evinced the most decided attachment to the Lutheran principles, often, assisted at their divine service, and replied to those who endeavoured to alarm him with the apprehension of losing the imperial crown, and with the anger of his family, "I will sacrifice all worldly interests for the sake of salvation." He for a long time resisted all the menaces of his father, who threatened to disinherit him for his attachment to the Protestant doctrines ; and, in a letter to the elector Palatine, he observes, "I have so deeply offended my father, by maintaining a Lutheran preacher in my service, that I am apprehensive of being expelled as a fugitive, and hope to find an asylum in your court."*

Such being the religious sentiments of Maximilian, his accession was dreaded by the Catholics, and hailed by the Protestants. Nor were the alarms of one party and the exultation of the other without foundation, for the abolition of the ecclesiastical reservation, and the admission of Protestant nobles into the Catholic chapters, would have broken down the barrier, which was the last defence of the Catholic church in Germany. But the interests of the sovereign soon outweighed the inclinations of the individual; Maximilian saw the Protestants weakened by schisms, and actuated by discordant views, while the Catholics were firmly united by a common principle, and alone capable of affording him a permanent and efficient support. He was aware that they would be assisted by all the power of Philip II., and all the intrigues and influence of the pope, and that their cause would find the most strenuous adherents, even in his own family. He hoped by moderate and timely concessions, to conciliate the Protestant body ; but he was sensible, that by quitting the pale of the church, he should render the Catholics his implacable enemies. It was likewise not the least powerful motive to a prince who was so anxiously attached to peace, to consider that his profession of the Protestant doctrines would not only revive the religious troubles, but induce the Catholics to raise Philip II., or some powerful rival, to the imperial throne. As a father who consulted the interests of his children, it is no discredit to the feelings of Maximilian to suppose, that he was

* Vie de Commendon, p. 286.; Haberlin's Reichs Geschichte, vol. vi. p. 91.

influenced by the dread of losing the Spanish succession, which, as Philip was at this time without issue male, was likely to devolve on his family; as a son, he was probably biassed by the injunctions of his dying father; as a husband and brother, he must have felt an unconquerable reluctance to shock the prejudices of his wife and brothers, who were zealously devoted to the Catholic faith.

Influenced by these motives, Maximilian determined to remain within the pale of the church; and adopted a line of conduct which reflects honour on his memory. He took his father's confessor, made a public profession of the Catholic faith, and maintained the establishment of the church; but he never swerved from the most liberal toleration, and in Germany, made the religious peace, which he had so great a share in promoting, the grand rule of his conduct.

The transactions of the first diet, which Maximilian summoned at Augsburgh, in March, 1566, sufficiently evinced his prudence and policy, as by no other means could he have baffled the intrigues of the pope, suspended the religious feuds, and, in the midst of interminable discussions, persuaded the princes of the empire to furnish such succours as were sufficient to preserve his dominions in Hungary from being overwhelmed by the Turks.

The diet was crowded beyond all former examples, and both parties met with the most decided hostility against each other. The Protestants presented a bitter remonstrance against the oppression of their brethren in the states of the Catholic prelates; and the Catholics equally complained of the breaches of the ecclesiastical reservation, and were stimulated and directed by the legate, cardinal Commendon, who had been deputed by the new pope, Pius V., to preserve unanimity in the Catholic body, and to deter the emperor from encroaching on the prerogatives of the church. Maximilian, who saw the danger of commencing a religious discussion, prevailed on both parties to open the business of the diet by voting succours against the Turks, as a matter which did not admit of delay. This proposal, if made by a sovereign of a different character, would have only provoked the discussion; yet such was the confidence of all parties in their new chief, that they agreed to it without a dissenting voice, and vying in their efforts to conciliate his favour, they voted succours in men and money far surpassing their contingents, both for the present exigency, and for the three succeeding years. To this grant, the indiscreet zeal of some of the states endeavoured to annex the condition that Hungary, which had absorbed so much of their blood and treasure, should be subject to the same taxes as the empire; but Maximilian contrived to elude this demand, without damping the ardour of the diet, by promising the full co-operation of all the forces of Hungary, whenever the empire was exposed to danger.

Having gained this point, he suffered the states to resume the discussion of religious affairs; though with his characteristic prudence, he did not irritate the minds of the two sects by taking a part in the dispute. Acting as a mere mediator, he transmitted their respective complaints and replies to each other; and thus showing that both had equal causes of complaint, brought them to a more reasonable temper, while he restrained both parties by evincing his firm resolution to maintain the peace of religion. This prudent impartiality was at the same time attended with another advantage; for the pope, who, from the character and principles of Maximilian, dreaded great innovations in religion, was conciliated by his conduct, and, at the conclusion of the diet, remitted to him the sum of 50,000 ducats as a subsidy against the Turks.*

At the same time that Maximilian laboured to preserve tranquillity between the Catholics and Protestants, he endeavoured to maintain the union of the Protestant body, as well from inclination as from a desire of securing the peace of Germany.

Frederic III., surnamed the Pious, the first elector Palatine of the branch of Simmern, has been already mentioned as a convert to Calvinism, and as having evinced opinions contrary to the Lutheran tenets at the meeting of Naumburgh. Since that period, he abolished Lutheranism, expelled its priests, persecuted its adherents, and established in his states that system of doctrine and worship which is followed by the reformed churches of Holland

* Vie de Commendon, p. 289.

and Switzerland. He had recently published the celebrated catechism of Heidelberg, which contained the Calvinistic system of worship and doctrine, and, like the confession of Augsburgh, became the symbolical book and creed of the Calvinists in Germany. In consequence of these innovations, the rigid Lutherans regarded Frederic with no less antipathy than they did the Catholics; and some of the most rash and zealous, among whom were the elector of Brandenburgh, and even his cousin Wolfgang, chief of the line of Deux Ponts, urged the emperor to exert his imperial authority in re-establishing the Lutheran worship. The Catholics adroitly availed themselves of this division, and Commendon captiously proposed to require from the Lutherans, in the public diet, an acknowledgment whether they considered the elector as a member of their confession. This question greatly embarrassed the Protestants; for they could not disavow the elector without losing the support of the reformed churches in France and Switzerland, and of the Calvinists in Germany, and, if they acknowledged him, they gave their public approbation to doctrines which they had constantly stigmatised as anti-christian. The elector Palatine endeavoured to justify his principles by public discussion, and appealed to the Bible and the confession of Augsburgh, while the Catholics and rigid Lutherans clamoured for his punishment or deposition.

Fortunately an open schism among the Protestants, and a civil war in the empire, were prevented by the intervention of the emperor. Though connected by long friendship with the elector Palatine, and though averse to every species of persecution, he could not approve the Calvinistic doctrines; and he considered himself bound to maintain the religious peace, and to exclude all new sects who dissented from the confession of Augsburgh. He therefore yielded, in appearance at least, to the instances of the Catholics and rigid Lutherans; but he contrived to prevent the Catholics from interfering in the discussion. The Protestants being thus left to settle the question themselves, were too prudent to weaken their party by mutual persecution; and while they disapproved the catechism of Heidelberg, they refused to exclude the elector or the Calvinists from the benefits of the religious peace. To satisfy, however, the Catholics and rigid Lutherans, a decree was passed by the diet, declaring, that no toleration should be allowed, except to the Catholics and the members of the confession of Augsburgh ; and although the elector Palatine refused to renounce his creed, the emperor suffered him to shelter himself under that system of doctrine, and thus allowed the Calvinists a tacit, though not a formal toleration.*

CHAP. XXXVII.—1564–1574.

THIS was a specimen of the conduct which Maximilian pursued during his whole reign, and of the means by which he prevented Germany from being disturbed by religious feuds, and obtained from the states repeated and unusual grants of succours against the Turks. Anxious to preserve the tranquillity of the empire, while the surrounding kingdoms were agitated by intestine dissensions or civil wars, he did not confine his attention to internal policy, but endeavoured to prevent the religious contests, which had arisen in France and the Netherlands, from extending into Germany.

In France, the Huguenots, or Protestants, had gradually increased, till they became equal in numbers, influence, and strength to the Catholics. The regent, Catherine de' Medici, aggravated the troubles of the state by imprudently opposing one party to the other, and alternately favouring the Catholics and Protestants, in order to establish her own dominion by their alternate support. This conduct rousing their mutual animosities into a civil war, the whole kingdom, from one extremity to the other, bore the marks of desolation and carnage, which equally attended the triumphs of the two parties. They were headed by chiefs, many of whom cloked their ambitious designs or personal enmities under the pretence of religion ; the prince of Condé, with the admiral Coligny, were the directors of the Huguenots, and the constable Montmorency, with the

* Vie de Commendon, passim ; Schmidt, b. x. ch. 21.

duke of Guise, were at the head of the Catholics. Under such able chiefs the kingdom was as much divided as if it consisted of different nations; an internal system of policy was established, and armies organised on each side, and the Protestants in particular, besides being in possession of the principal part of the northern provinces, and the chief ports on the channel, were masters of Orleans and Lyons. The king of Spain assisted the Catholics, Elizabeth of England the Huguenots, and the German states furnished mercenaries, who seem to have acted on both sides; but the great ornament and most promising chief of the Huguenots was Henry, the youthful king of Navarre, whose court and kingdom had long afforded a refuge to the persecuted Protestants, and whose dominions enabled him to interfere with such effect in the contests of France.

The Catholics, perceiving that they could not conquer their opponents by arms, had recourse to the most horrible and perfidious expedients. After lulling them into security by favourable terms of peace, they endeavoured to cut off the chiefs, and exterminate the whole party by a general massacre, which commenced in the capital on the day of St. Bartholomew, August 24th, 1572, and was to extend at the same moment to every part of the kingdom. This execrable deed, which surpasses every example of the most atrocious perfidy and savage barbarity, was not attended with the effects expected by its sanguinary projectors. Admiral Coligny, and some of the principal chiefs, were indeed assassinated; but the great bulwarks of the party, the king of Navarre and the prince of Condé, saved themselves by a pretended abjuration; others escaped, and in the more distant parts of the kingdom the Protestants were spared, and the cruel designs of the Catholic party disappointed, by the refusal of the royal officers and governors to execute their orders. The Protestants, sensible that they had far less to dread from the open enmity than from the secret perfidy of their opponents, renewed the contest with an unanimity and resolution proportionate to their danger; and the civil war was again prosecuted with all the fury which on one side arose from disappointed vengeance, and on the other from just resentment, and a desire of retaliating unmerited cruelties.

Although Maximilian was father-in-law to Charles IX., at whose command this massacre was perpetrated, he publicly expressed his abhorrence of such sanguinary proceedings. On the death of Charles, when Henry of Valois, in returning from Poland to take possession of the crown, passed through Vienna, he laboured to dissuade him from similar acts of persecution, and made that memorable observation, which has been recorded so much to his honour, " That no crime was greater in princes than to tyrannise over the consciences of their subjects ; that, far from honouring the common Father of all, by shedding the blood of heretics, they incurred the divine vengeance, and, while they aspired by such means to crowns in heaven, they justly exposed themselves to the loss of their earthly kingdoms."

While he was anxious to extend the principles of toleration, his sagacious mind was not insensible to the mischiefs arising from the interference of the German troops in these religious contests. He had often been a witness to the disorders committed by these tumultuary levies in the empire, and he was apprehensive lest, on their return, with the licentiousness contracted in camps, they might continue the predatory warfare to which they had been accustomed, and occasion the revival of the civil and religious troubles in Germany. He therefore proposed to the diet of Spire, which assembled in 1570, to forbid the enrolment of German troops in foreign service ; but he could not prevail on the states to accede to a proposition which they considered as an infringement of their liberties, and as tending to damp that military ardour which was the great characteristic of the Germans. Though unable to carry this point, Maximilian endeavoured at least to prevent the evils attending this privilege, and obtained the consent of the diet to the establishment of certain regulations, which prohibited any prince from making such enrolments without specifying to the emperor the numbers and quality of the levies ; engaging not to employ them against the head or members of the empire ; promising indemnification for the disorders which they might commit in their passage ; and agreeing not to disband them within the German territories.

But he was still more interested, no less as emperor than

as a prince of the house of Austria, in the civil and religious disturbances which broke out in the Netherlands, and finally produced that revolution which separated the United Provinces from the Spanish dominions.

The seventeen provinces of the Low Countries which Charles had inherited from the house of Burgundy, or obtained by purchase, comprised the country formed by the republic of the seven United Provinces, the nine provinces of the Spanish or Austrian Netherlands, and the county of Artois. Maximilian I. had formed these provinces, Franche Comté and their dependencies, into a circle of the empire, under the name of Burgundy; and this arrangement was ratified in 1548, by Charles, who endowed it with all the privileges and rights of the other circles, and imposed, as its contribution, a double electoral contingent; but confirmed the exemption which it had before enjoyed from the jurisdiction of the empire. Besides this general bond of union, which connected the Netherlands with the empire, each province was governed by peculiar statutes and usages, and the sovereign had no right to impose taxes or make laws without the consent of the respective states.

The reformed opinions, at an early period, had penetrated into the Low Countries, and found a ready reception among a people of an active and turbulent spirit, living under a free government, and, in consequence of their local position and commercial relations, intimately connected with those countries which were the scene of religious innovation. Charles had used the same efforts as in Spain and Germany to suppress the Reformation; he had even attempted to introduce the inquisition, and exercised such severity against the Protestants, that, if we may credit an historian of great caution and prudence, not less than 50,000 persons, during his reign, sealed their belief with their blood.* But these severe measures serving only to augment the numbers as well as zeal of the converts, and driving many of the most industrious and opulent merchants and manufacturers into exile, Charles at length ceased to enforce the execution of his sanguinary edicts; and, by the connivance of the magistrates, the Protestants enjoyed a tacit toleration.

* Father Paul's History of the council of Trent. According to Grotius, the number of sufferers amounted to 100,000.

Such was the situation of the country when Philip assumed the reins of government; and the striking difference between his manners, character, and principles and those of his father, inspired the natives with the most alarming apprehensions as well for their civil as for their religious liberties.

Charles, born and educated in the Netherlands, and accustomed to the manners and language of the country, was attached to his subjects from habit, and from that local partiality which renders early impressions almost indelible. He employed and favoured the Flemings even in his other dominions, and though cold and reserved in Spain, he was affable and familiar in his residence at Brussels and Ghent. He was intimately acquainted with the genius and temper of the people, as well as with the interests of the country, and benefited them by ameliorating their constitutions, and establishing laws for promoting and regulating their commerce. Although he had punished the refractory citizens of Ghent, and issued the most rigorous laws against the Protestants, yet he had generally respected the prejudices and privileges of the people, and, in return, possessed their esteem and confidence.

Philip, on the contrary, spoke scarcely any other language except Spanish, and reserved all his partiality for the country to which he owed his birth and education. His temper was severe, gloomy, and unrelenting; his deportment reserved and supercilious. Bred up in a kingdom where the sovereign authority was almost without restraint, and where the slightest deviation from the established worship was regarded with the utmost horror, he fostered an antipathy against the people of the Netherlands, who claimed such numerous immunities and privileges, and amongst whom the new opinions had made a most alarming progress. During his residence in the Netherlands, he had made no effort to conceal this disposition; and alienated his subjects as well by giving his whole confidence to foreigners as by drawing a considerable Spanish force into the country.

The first object of Philip, after the abdication of his father, was the extirpation of doctrines which he regarded with horror, and the annihilation of privileges which he

considered as injurious to his authority. The opposition
which he experienced from the prince of Orange *, count
Egmont †, and other considerable nobles, no less than from

* William, prince of Orange, the great founder of Belgic liberty,
was the representative of the ancient and illustrious family of Nassau,
in Germany, and son of William, count of Nassau Dillemburgh, who
at an early period had introduced the Reformation into his dominions.
William was born in 1533, and had received, in the house of his father,
a tincture of the Protestant doctrines; but in his youth he had been
removed to the court of the emperor Charles V., who himself superintended his education, and endeavoured to bring him up in the Catholic faith.   He inherited from his father great possessions in the
Netherlands and in Germany; and his inheritance was considerably
increased by the bequest of his uncle, René de Nassau, prince of
Orange, who, dying without issue male, left him the principality of
Orange, and the other possessions of the house of Chalons in France.
He was honoured with the favour of Charles V., who, notwithstanding his youth, intrusted him with various important military
commands, and continued to distinguish him with marks of friendship
and affection till the very last day of his reign.   These peculiar marks
of favour, and the influence which he possessed in the Netherlands,
were sufficient to draw on him the jealousy of Philip; this jealousy
was increased by his supposed attachment to the Protestant religion,
and by the part which he took in the removal of cardinal Granvella,
and in opposing the introduction of foreign troops and the establishment of the inquisition.   In consequence of this dislike, Philip never
admitted him into his confidence; and though he could not avoid
intrusting him with the government of Holland, Zealand, and Utrecht,
which was due to his great possessions and influence in the country,
yet he watched all his movements with jealousy and suspicion, and
reduced him to a mere cipher in the council of state.
William was admirably calculated to become the chief of a party,
and the head of a revolution.   He was remarkable for military skill,
and, as a general, distinguished in a high degree for those qualities
which are most requisite, and yet most seldom found, in civil contests:
an unshaken firmness in adverse circumstances, and a patient perseverance in watching for the return of favourable moments of action.
Though circumspect, prudent, and sagacious, he was active and enterprising ; and he possessed the rare talent of conciliating the minds of
men, and of infusing unanimity and spirit into a heterogeneous mass of
discordant parties.   Aubery, Mémoires pour servir à l'Histoire de la
Hollande; La Pise Histoire des Princes d'Orange.
† Count Egmont, who was descended from the dukes of Guelderland, possessed scarcely less influence than the prince of Orange.
Though a zealous Catholic, he was a friend to toleration, and warmly
attached to the constitution and privileges of his country.   He was
distinguished for his military talents, and had signalised himself at the
battles of St. Quintin and Gravelines; but his connections with the

the people of all ranks and sects who valued their rights and privileges, only stimulated his ardent and relentless temper, and impelled him to prosecute his designs with still greater severity and perseverance.

After various civil as well as religious innovations, calculated to further his projects, Philip despatched a considerable army of Spanish and Italian veterans into the Netherlands, and chose a fit instrument for his cruelty and vengeance in the duke of Alva, a Spanish nobleman of a ferocious and implacable temper, ardently attached to the Catholic religion, habituated to the severe discipline of camps, accustomed to enforce implicit obedience, and highly distinguished for military skill. Invested with almost absolute powers, the new general acted without control; for the regent Margaret being disgusted with bearing nothing but the name of a governess, and with witnessing a tyranny which she could not prevent, resigned her office, and left him in full possession of the sovereign authority.

Scarcely any period in the annals of modern history presents a more dreadful scene of horror than the administration of Alva. All the civil privileges of the natives were abolished, and arbitrary tribunals, composed of foreigners, were established, which, in contempt of all law and custom, disposed, without appeal, of life, property, and liberty. Neither long services nor exalted rank found protection or safety. The prince of Orange, who had prudently retired into Germany from the gathering storm, was deprived of his property, and declared, with all his adherents, guilty of high treason; the counts of Egmont and Horn, notwithstanding their known attachment to the Catholic religion, were brought to the scaffold; all who were distinguished for humanity or toleration, all who had evinced the slightest

Protestants, and his defence of the constitution and liberties of the country, were sufficient to eradicate all remains of gratitude from the bosom of Philip, and though intrusted with the government of Artois and Flanders, he was, like the prince of Orange, marked out as a destined victim.

He possessed neither the firmness nor decision of the prince of Orange, was deficient in sagacity and foresight, and, from the incumbrance of a numerous family, was influenced rather by the hope of personal advantage than by a consideration of the public good.

opposition to the establishment of civil and ecclesiastical tyranny, were marked as objects of vengeance. Philip, released from the solemn engagements which he had contracted as sovereign, by the dispensation of the pope, gave full scope to his gloomy, malignant, and vengeful temper; and, throughout the Netherlands, nothing was heard but lamentations and cries of despair; nothing seen but confiscation, imprisonment, exile, torture, and death.* By these measures Philip seemed to have succeeded in his plan of establishing an arbitrary authority on the ruins of civil and religious liberty. But his success was of short duration, he was made sensible that usurped power, though supported by a veteran army, and assisted by military skill and vast resources, was insufficient to resist the desperate efforts of a whole people, when directed by able leaders, and inspired by the ardour of liberty and religious zeal.

The prince of Orange having retired into Germany, was supported by the landgrave of Hesse, the electors of Saxony and Palatine, the duke of Wirtemberg, seventeen imperial cities, and by the king of Denmark; and, with their assistance and support, was enabled to levy a considerable force. A part of these troops, which had been assembled under his brother Louis, penetrated as far as Groningen; but, after some trifling success, were defeated by the duke of Alva, and Louis himself with difficulty escaped. This defeat hastening the march of the prince, whose troops had not been sufficiently ready to second the operations of his brother, he made an irruption into Brabant, as far as Tillemont. But Alva maintaining himself on the defensive, and declining an engagement, the prince was compelled to retreat and disband his troops for want of pay and provisions.

Meanwhile the prince of Orange and the persecuted inhabitants of the Netherlands claimed the protection of the emperor, as members of the circle of Burgundy; and their appeal was opposed by the duke of Alva, who demanded that the prince should be given up as a rebellious subject, and required the suspension of his levies in the empire. Maximilian, who joined with all Europe in expressing his abhorrence of the cruelties which Philip

* Hume, vol. v. p. 67. 199.

exercised towards the people of the Netherlands, boldly espoused the part of persecuted subjects against their tyrannical sovereign. In 1565, he sent his brother Charles into Spain, to exhort Philip, in his own name and that of the empire, to terminate the sanguinary persecutions of the duke of Alva, to recall the foreign troops, and adopt more moderate and lenient measures, as the only means of preventing the total loss of the Low Countries. But his benevolent application only drew from Philip an arrogant and disdainful reply, accompanied with the keenest personal reproaches to the archduke, who was contemptuously asked, "Why the emperor, instead of making these useless representations, did not prevent the prince of Orange and his brothers from levying troops in the empire?"

At the same time the emperor made attempts in favour of his intended son-in-law, Don Carlos, who had been imprisoned by his father, in consequence of his supposed connections with the rebels of the Low Countries, and his secret inclination to the reformed doctrines. But he was unable to awaken feelings of paternal affection in the morose, suspicious, and bigoted bosom of Philip, who coldly replied, that the imprisonment of the prince was indispensable, and conformable to the advice of the greatest theologians and jurists; and the subsequent fate of Don Carlos proved the sincerity of his horried declaration, " That he would cut off even his own hand if it contained a drop of blood which savoured of heresy!"

This conduct annihilating all hopes of reconciliation between Philip and his subjects, Maximilian directed his attention to lessen the evils attending those enrolments which he could not suppress, and to prevent the diffusion of the religious troubles into the empire. The tyranny of Philip, and the arbitrary measures enforced by the duke of Alva, convinced the unfortunate people of the Netherlands that they had no alternative but resistance or ruin, and a trifling instance of success roused them into open rebellion. A body of freebooters, who had fitted out small armaments by sea against the Spanish commerce, having succeeded in surprising Brill, the key of Holland, thus secured a place of arms for the disaffected. This event was followed by a general insurrection in the neighbour-

ing provinces; the Spanish garrisons were instantly expelled from Flushing and Vere, and, under the direction of
the prince of Orange, the rebellion spread in a few months,
through the provinces of Holland, Zealand, Overyssel,
Guelderland, and Friesland. It gradually assumed strength
and consistency, and was first formed into a regular system
on the 15th of September, 1572, in a meeting of the deputies from the revolted towns, at Dort, in which contributions were fixed for the maintenance of the public force,
the command and the principal administration intrusted to
the prince of Orange, and the free excercise of the reformed
religion established. All the attempts of Alva to crush the
rebellion, or conciliate the people, failing of success, Philip
was at length reduced to the humiliating necessity of recalling a governor who had so faithfully fulfilled his cruel
and impolitic orders, and of requesting the mediation of
the emperor, which he had before so arrogantly rejected.

Notwithstanding the repulsive manner in which the
former interference of Maximilian had been received, he
did not refuse his intercession; and sending count Schwart-
zenburgh, a relation of the prince of Orange, into Holland,
obtained his consent to assemble a congress at Breda. But
his efforts were defeated by the incurable jealousy of the
insurgents, and still more by the inflexibility of Philip,
who refused to dismiss his foreign troops, or to permit a
general assembly of the states for the purpose of arranging
the civil and religious points of controversy; nor could
any arguments induce him to grant even a partial and temporary toleration of the Protestant worship. In consequence of this obstinacy, Maximilian withdrew his mediation, and the insurgents renewed the contest with all the
resolution of despair. The sanguinary excesses committed
by the Spaniards drove the whole country, except Luxemburgh, to join in the insurrection; and before the close of
Maximilian's reign, the pacification or confederacy of
Ghent was, on the 8th of November, 1576, arranged under
the auspices of the prince of Orange, by which all the provinces, both Catholic and Protestant, except Luxemburgh,
united to form a common cause for the expulsion of foreign
troops; the re-establishment of the ancient constitution;
the suspension of the edicts against the Protestants, and

the restoration of all things to their pristine state before the tyrannical government of the duke of Alva.*

To the vigour and firmness of Maximilian, no less than to his moderation and personal address, must be attributed the tranquillity in which the empire was maintained during his pacific reign, notwithstanding the troubles without and the dissensions within. One event, alone of sufficient importance to deserve notice, disturbed the public peace, and that event derived its origin from the reign of Charles.

William, lord of Grumbach, a free noble of the circle of Franconia, and a feudatory of the see of Wurtzburgh, was one of those brave, turbulent, and enterprising adventurers with whom the empire had teemed before the abolition of the right of diffidation. He had acted a considerable part in the predatory wars of Albert of Brandenburgh, and had extorted from Melchior Zobel, bishop of Wurtzburgh, considerable sums of money and a valuable territory, together with the independence of his fiefs, as a reward for saving the domains of the see from devastation. This iniquitous agreement being cancelled by Charles V., Grumbach, in 1553, invaded the episcopal territories, and was in consequence declared guilty of high treason, and all his estates and property confiscated. Having in vain appealed to the emperor, the diet, and the imperial chamber, he procured the assassination of the bishop. After wandering as a fugitive from place to place, he suddenly assembled a corps of predatory troops, by an enterprise no less bold than successful, obtained possession of Wurtzburgh, and extorted from the new bishop and chapter an indemnification for the loss of his property, with a promise that they would not only suspend the process against the murderers of the late bishop, but would even assist him if attacked on that account.

This was too glaring a violation of the public peace to pass unpunished. In 1566, Ferdinand not only annulled

* Strada de Bello Belgico; Desormeaux, Histoire d'Espagne, tom. iv. passim; Ferreras, tom. ix. p. 404-533.; Schmidt, b. xi. ch. 2. 3.; Watson's History of Philip II. vol. ii. p. 150-159.; Kerroux, Histoire de la Hollande, tom. i. p. 245-305.; La Pise Histoire des Princes d'Orange, art. Guillaume IX.; Aubery, Mémoires pour servir à l'Histoire de la Hollande, p. 1-62.

the agreement, but issued the ban of the empire against the
offenders, and Grumbach took refuge under the protection
of John Frederic, duke of Saxe Gotha, who refused to
deliver him to justice. Such was the state of the affair
when Maximilian ascended the throne. The artful Grumbach soon obtained unbounded influence over the mind of
a credulous, ardent, and capricious prince, who was affected
by the loss of the electoral dignity and his paternal inheritance, and easily excited his resentment against the Albertine branch and the house of Austria. He urged him to
assert his rights; represented the princes, nobles, and
equestrian order of the empire as ripe for revolt against
the tyrannical administration of the Austrian family; and
promised the support of Elizabeth, queen of England, in
defence of the Protestant religion against the abettors of
popish despotism. To further his purposes he even employed magical incantations and secret rites. He introduced into the palace the son of a peasant who was called
the seer of angels, whom he described as capable of raising
spirits, and drawing from their responses the knowledge of
future events. By his agency he deluded the infatuated
prince into a confidence of success; induced him to expect
the death of the emperor and the elector of Saxony, with
the discovery of hidden treasures; and consummated this
series of deceptions by an optical illusion, which exhibited
to his astonished eyes his own figure, habited in the
electoral cap and robes.

Fascinated by these arts, the duke of Saxe Gotha consented to the assassination of Augustus, elector of Saxony,
as the means of recovering his paternal dominions, and
even raised his hopes to the imperial crown; Grumbach at
length deeming his projects complete, confidently appealed
to the equestrian order of the empire, over whom he flattered himself that he possessed unbounded influence.

The machinations and intrigues of this artful marauder
becoming daily more dangerous, Maximilian had recourse
to the most rigorous measures. At the diet of Augsburgh,
in 1566, the ban of the empire was fulminated against
Grumbach and all his protectors and adherents, and the
execution of the decree intrusted to the elector of Saxony.
The credulous duke, when exhorted to deliver up Grum-

bach, resisted all the instances of the emperor, of the
elector Augustus, of his brother John Frederic, and of his
father-in-law the elector Palatine, and made preparations
for resistance. All arguments being fruitless, Augustus,
at the head of a considerable army, laid siege to Gotha,
and obtained possession of the place and person of the
duke by the voluntary surrender of the garrison, who refused to sacrifice their lives in defence of such a traitor as
Grumbach. Maximilian, convinced that such disturbers
of the public peace ought to receive the punishment due to
their crimes, rejected all intercession in favour of the prisoners: Grumbach and his most guilty associates were
executed, the unfortunate Frederic was condemned to perpetual imprisonment, and his dominions transferred to his
two sons, Joseph Casimir and John Ernest. His wife
Elizabeth devoted herself to prison with her unfortunate
husband, where he died after a confinement of twenty-eight
years.*

Nothing had more tended to disturb the peace of Germany, and to embarrass Maximilian, than the promise extorted from him, as well as from every new emperor at his
election, to recover the dismembered fiefs, and to restore
the imperial authority. This promise had for some time
been deemed a matter of form, and the fulfilment merely
optional, because it solely regarded the foreign dependencies; but it could not be considered in the same light
when it related to territories within the empire itself, and
to a powerful body who held a high rank in the diet.
Such was the situation of the Teutonic knights who, during
the reign of Maximilian, came forward to claim the execution of this promise in the recovery of Prussia and Livonia,
which had been wrested from their order.

We have already alluded to the defection of Albert of
Brandenburgh, grand-master of the Teutonic order, from
the church of Rome ; his appropriation of eastern Prussia
as an hereditary duchy relevant from the crown of Poland;
and his cession of western Prussia to Sigismond I. In con-

* Barre, tom. ix. p. 82.; Struvius, p. 1143-1147 ; Schmidt,
vli. 10. passim ; and Heinrich, who has given the best and clearest
account of this singular transaction from authentic documents, vol. v.
p. 818-825.

sequence of this defection the Teutonic knights had elected a new grand-master, transferred his residence to Mariendahl, in Franconia, and obtained from the emperor, Charles V., a sentence of the imperial chamber for the restitution of their dismembered territories, and the ban of the empire against the new duke. Succours were frequently voted by the diet for their support; but all their attempts were rendered fruitless by the religious troubles in Germany; for Albert, assisted by the Lutheran princes, whose doctrines he had embraced, continued in quiet possession of the appropriated territories, and even obtained from the crown of Poland the extension of the investiture to the electoral branch of his family. This measure still further irritated the Teutonic knights, who had never intermitted their appeals to the empire; and at the diet of Spire, in 1570, the grand-master brought forward a demand requiring the states to enforce the execution of the sentence pronounced by their own tribunal. With a view to induce them to comply with this demand, he asserted that the natives were anxious to return under the dominion of their ancient masters; and offered to sequestrate the contested territories till the expenses of the war were repaid. He concluded with declaring that if the diet would not interfere, the order would risk their own blood and treasures to procure themselves justice; and demanded permission for the passage of foreign troops through the territories of the empire.

Maximilian was greatly embarrassed by this appeal; he was unwilling by a public refusal to implicate the honour and dignity of the empire; but he was still more unwilling either to offend the house of Brandenburgh or the Polish nation, whose good will he was desirous to conciliate, from the hope of securing the crown for one of his sons, on the death of Sigismond Augustus, who was without issue. He foresaw, likewise, that the contest would involve the empire both in a foreign and a civil war, as he was aware that the house of Brandenburgh would be supported by all the Protestant princes. He therefore pressed the grand-master to suspend his intended hostilities; and, being seconded by the majority of the states, his persuasions were successful. At the same time he did not attempt to annul the imperial ban, and saved the honour of the order, as well as his own dignity, by inserting in the recess a general declaration that he would zealously co-operate with the states, not only for the recovery of the dismembered provinces, but for increasing and protecting the territories of the empire.

The affairs of Livonia, which was another dismembered province of the Teutonic order, would likewise have embarrassed an emperor of less prudence and dexterity than Maximilian.

Livonia, with Esthonia Courland, and Semigallia, was conquered in the fourteenth century by the Teutonic knights, and governed by a provincial master, subordinate to the grand-master, resident at Marienburgh, in Prussia. In 1521, the independence of Livonia, and its annexed states, was purchased from Albert of Brandenburgh, by the celebrated Walter of Plettenberg*, the hero of the Teutonic order, who, after delivering his territories from the inroads of the neighbouring nations, introduced the Reformation, and was acknowledged as a prince of the empire by Charles V. Notwithstanding the change of religion, the knights of Livonia maintained their union, and were governed by an elective master; but as the successors of Plettenberg did not inherit his talents, the country became a prey to civil divisions, and was exposed to the perpetual inroads of the Poles, Russians, Swedes, and Danes, who were at different times called in by the contending parties.

In this situation, Ivan Vasilievitch II., czar of Muscovy, having consolidated the power established by his grandfather, turned his attention to the conquest of Livonia, and in a short time made himself master of a considerable part of the province. The knights in vain appealed to the empire, to Sweden, and to Denmark; but deriving no effectual assistance from either, Gothard Kettler, the provincial master, imitated the example of Albert of Brandenburgh, purchased the protection of Sigismond Augustus, king of Poland, by the cession of Livonia and its dependencies, and reserved to himself Courland and Semigallia, as an hereditary sovereignty. Meanwhile the city of Revel,

* The duke of Rohan observes, in his Parfait Capitaine, that the three great heroes of the world were Alexander, Julius Cæsar, and Plettenberg.

with the district of Esthonia, threw itself under the protection of Eric XIV., king of Sweden; and Magnus, bishop of Pilten, brother of the king of Denmark, obtained from the czar of Muscovy, Wenden, and the neighbouring district, with the title of king of Livonia. But this short-lived sovereignty was soon annihilated, and the czar appropriated the greater part of the province. In consequence of these different claims, the country became for more than a century a prey to the Russians, Danes, Swedes, and Poles, and was successively possessed and ravaged by each party.

At the present period Maximilian was appealed to by the order, as head of the empire; and the diet, alarmed at the progress of the Russians, proposed to send an embassy for the purpose of demanding from the czar the restitution of his conquests in a province which formed part of the empire. But Maximilian, who had now a near prospect of obtaining the crown of Poland, vacant by the abdication of Henry of Valois, was unwilling to irritate Ivan, from whose assistance he expected to derive the greatest advantage. He therefore despatched a private deputation, not to demand Livonia, but to prepare the mind of the czar for the reception of the German embassy, to obtain the promise of his support in the affairs of Poland, and to contract with him an alliance against the Turks. The effects of this mission surpassed his most sanguine expectations, for the czar promised his support, sent emissaries to Poland to promote the election of an Austrian prince, and offered to unite with the European states in an alliance against the Turks, their common enemy.

Though from prudence and policy Maximilian declined urging the pretensions of the empire, in regard to the dismembered fiefs, no emperor was more strenuous in preserving his rights and prerogatives against the encroachments of the Roman see.

A dispute for precedence arising between the duke of Ferrara and Cosmo de' Medici, who had recently assumed the title of duke of Florence, Cosmo proposed to refer the contest to the pope; but the duke of Ferrara, knowing the pope's partiality to the house of Medici, refused to abide by his arbitration, and contended that the decision ought to be submitted to the head of the empire. Cosmo could not object to the appeal ; and the pope acquiesced in the reference, provided Maximilian would act as a mere arbitrator, and not as emperor.

Maximilian rejected this attempt to restrict his prerogative with disdain ; and while the affair was pending, the pope endeavoured to terminate the dispute to his own advantage, by conferring on Cosmo the title of *great* duke. This expedient aggravated instead of terminating the contest, for Maximilian, considering Florence as a fief of the empire, sent ambassadors to Rome to make a solemn protest against the conduct of the pope, in arrogating a right which belonged to the emperor. These ambassadors were not admitted to an audience ; and the contest seemed likely to become serious, as neither party would relinquish his claims ; while Cosmo himself declared his territory independent, and not a fief of the empire. The pope sent Commendon into Germany, in order to pacify the emperor ; but all his efforts proved ineffectual, till Cosmo, dying in 1574, his son and heir, Francis Maria, purchased from the emperor, whose sister he had married, the confirmation of the title of Great Duke, which had been borne by his father.*

Chap. XXXVIII.— 1567–1576.

During the reign of Maximilian II., the hereditary countries were not the scene of great revolutions, or, as in former times, agitated by internal feuds ; and the principal object of his attention in Bohemia and Austria was the arrangement of religious affairs, in which he followed the same line of conduct, and the same prudent impartiality as in Germany.

No doubt can be entertained that he was always secretly and sincerely attached to the Lutheran doctrines ; and although, from prudence and policy, he continued to profess the Catholic religion, yet he endeavoured to make amends

* Muratori· Vie de Commendon, ch. viii.; Barre, tom. ix. p. 135.

for his apparent desertion of principles which he had adopted from conviction, by procuring concessions from the pope, or by granting the most enlarged toleration to the Protestants. He first attempted to obtain permission for the marriage of priests, and, failing in that endeavour, he resumed the well-meant, though impracticable plan of his father, to re-unite the two churches by mutual agreement. Finding, however, this plan equally disagreeable to both Catholics and Protestants, he finally resolved to tolerate those whom he could not bring back to the church. In the prosecution of this delicate design, he did not forget the dignity of his station, nor lessen the value of his toleration, by suffering it to appear as if extorted by interest or fear, but as the result of his unbiassed sentiments and good-will; for, when the states of Austria endeavoured to obtain toleration for the Protestants as the price of their assistance against the Turks, and demanded the expulsion of the Jesuits, he replied, that "he had convened them to receive contributions, not remonstrances; to expel the Turks, not the Jesuits." So great, however, was their confidence in his probity, and their love of his person, that this answer, which from another sovereign would have produced dangerous consequences, neither checked the promptitude nor lessened the amount of their contributions.

He maintained the same regard to his dignity in Bohemia and the dependent provinces, where he first essayed his meditated plan of toleration. Soon after his accession, he had granted a verbal protection to the ministers of the Lutheran church established at Breslau; but warned them against the new sects and heresies which had recently sprung up among the Protestants. In the first diet, which he held in person, at Prague, in March, 1567, for obtaining succours against the Turks, he annulled the compacts which had hitherto been the great barrier of the Catholic church. In consequence of this repeal, the majority of the Calixtins, who were mostly burghers, or of the lower orders of the people, and who enjoyed a tacit toleration under the compacts, openly professed Lutheranism; and other sects, when no longer compelled to conceal their tenets, publicly dissented from the hitherto established religion. Notwithstanding the Catholic church enjoyed, in their full extent, all its possessions and privileges, and was still professed by the principal nobility, yet the utmost concord and brotherhood prevailed throughout the country, and the different sects imitated the example of their sovereign, by vying in mutual forbearance and good-will. This innovation is remarkable, as the first proof of unlimited toleration, in a sovereign of any persuasion ; and is singular, as having been granted in an age of intolerance, persecution, and bigotry.

In the following year he prepared to introduce a similar innovation into his Austrian dominions, and commenced his reform by granting to the nobles, and equestrian order of the district below the Ems, liberty of worship, according to the confession of Augsburgh, in their own residences and domains. He would, probably, have extended this indulgence to the inhabitants of towns, had he not been prevented by the interference of the pope.

Pius V., who was a pontiff of an inflexible and overbearing temper, and who entertained a high opinion of the papal prerogatives, was equally alarmed and offended by these innovations, which threatened the total ruin of the Catholic church in the Austrian territories, and deputed cardinal Commendon, as his legate, to remonstrate with the emperor. Maximilian, desirous to evade the interference of the pope, and unwilling to relinquish his plan, endeavoured to prevent the legate from fulfilling his embassy ; but the peremptory orders of the pope inducing Commendon to persist, he was unable, as a Catholic prince, to refuse an embassy from the head of the church. He therefore received him with outward respect and cordiality; but continued firm to his purpose, in spite of all the remonstrances and arguments of the cardinal, or the menaces of the pope. The legate was supported by all the influence of the Spanish court; and his arguments were at length strengthened by the death of Elizabeth, queen of Spain. Maximilian, on one side lured by the prospect of seeing his eldest daughter become the wife of Philip, and, on the other, alarmed at the troubles which he had reason to apprehend from the enmity of the pope, and the opposition of the king of Spain, yielded at length to necessity and interest, not conviction. He promised to live in obedience to the see of Rome, and not to extend his meditated toleration in Austria; though he still either refused or avoided revoking the concessions which he had already granted.*

In addition to this compliance he soon afterwards filled the archbishoprics of Vienna and Gran, and several bishoprics in Hungary, which he had probably kept open with the view of promoting the progress of the Lutheran doctrines, and he permitted the legate to visit and reform the churches of his hereditary dominions. But the same year, and even before the cardinal had quitted his territories, he extended to the nobility and equestrian order of Austria above the Ems, the same toleration which he had before granted to those of Austria below the Ems. To prevent, however, the progress of those numerous sects which had already sprung up, Maximilian called upon the Protestants of his dominions for a formulary of their worship and doctrine, which, differing little from the confession of Augsburgh, received his approbation. At the same time he strictly fulfilled his promise to the pope, by maintaining the Catholic, as the dominant religion, in all its rights, possessions, and privileges; and by requiring, from the two tolerated Protestant orders a solemn engagement that they would strictly adhere to their formulary of faith, neither trench on the revenues, nor inveigh against the doctrines of the church, and not introduce their worship and tenets in the states and towns immediately dependent on his own domination. Notwithstanding the repeated instances of the states, he could not be persuaded to swerve from this principle, but persisted in refusing to grant toleration to the towns, and in repressing, to the utmost of his power, all the attempts of the burghers to introduce the illicit celebration of the Protestant worship.

During his pacific reign, Hungary alone, of all his dominions, was visited by the scourge of war.

We have already described the uncertain situation in which Hungary was left on the death of Ferdinand. Maxi-

* In the account of this transaction we have wholly relied on the authority of the Vie de Commendon, ch. iv. It is, however, not difficult to perceive, that the author has adopted the prejudices of the legate in exhibiting the conduct and motives of Maximilian in a more unfavourable light than they deserve.

milian had scarcely ascended the throne before the continued aggressions of John Sigismond provoked him to commence offensive operations. In the depth of winter, Swendy, a general distinguished for his military talents, marched, with a considerable Austrian force, against John Sigismond, and, after recovering the captured places, conquered Tokay. Kovar, Erdad, and Bathor. While Maximilian was thus engaged against the prince of Transylvania, he sent ambassadors to the sultan, offering to pay the arrears of the tribute, and demanding the continuance of the armistice concluded by his father : but Solyman sought a pretext for renewing hostilities, by demanding terms too dishonourable to be accepted, and made active preparations to invade Hungary. Maximilian exerted all his vigour and activity to resist the threatened aggression by obtaining considerable succours from the German diet, and raising levies in his own hereditary countries. Advancing into Hungary, he divided his forces into three bodies: one under the command of Swendy, on the Teiss, kept the Transylvanians in check ; a second, under the archduke Charles, secured Illyria ; and the main army, amounting to 80,000 men, under the emperor himself, encamped in the vicinity of Raab, to watch the motions of the Turks.

At the commencement of the spring, in 1566, Solyman again advanced at the head of his numerous multitudes. On arriving at Belgrade, he received John Sigismond with regal honours ; and declared that, notwithstanding his declining age, he had again taken arms in his cause, and would chastise the house of Austria, or perish under the walls of Vienna. He was preparing to ascend the course of the Danube, when the aggressions of the garrison of Zigeth, who, in a sally, killed one of his favourite bashas, induced him to direct his attention to that fortress. Fortunately, this little town was strongly fortified and situated in the midst of a marsh, was defended by count Zrini with a small but brave garrison of 1500 men, who distinguished themselves with the same intrepidity as the garrison of Guntz, in resisting, for thirty-four days, all the efforts of the Ottoman army. After enormous labour in forming roads across the marsh, and raising lofty mounds of earth for batteries ; and after twenty assaults, the Turks became masters of a part of the fortress, called the Old Town; but the brave governor continued to hold out till the garrison was reduced to 600 men, and the inner fort set on fire. Perceiving all further resistance to be vain, he determined to die with the same bravery as he had lived, and inspired his troops with a similar spirit. Taking the keys of the place, he armed himself with the sabre of his forefathers, and, sallying out with the remnant of his troops, found an honourable death in the midst of the enemy. His followers were driven back into the fortress, and, being pursued by the Turks, shared the fate of their gallant leader, except a few whose bravery won the protection even of the ferocious Janissaries. The Turks thus became masters of the place, after the loss of 20,000 men; but the sultan did not survive to witness this success, for he died on the 4th of September, 1566, in consequence of fatigue and the unwholesome air of the marshes.

The grand vizier concealed the death of Solyman until the arrival of the new sultan Selim, who, unwilling to continue hostilities in a distant country at the commencement of his reign, withdrew his army from Hungary, and returned to Constantinople.

Meanwhile Maximilian had continued on the defensive in his camp near Raab, and was unwilling for so inconsiderable a fortress to risk a battle with an army far superior in numbers, the loss of which would have established John Sigismond on the throne of Hungary, and opened the hereditary countries to the Turkish inroads. Apprised of the death of Solyman, and conscious that he had nothing further to apprehend, during that season, from the Turks, he disbanded part of his army, threw garrisons into the principal fortresses, and retired to Vienna. General Swendy, whom he left with a considerable corps to carry on offensive operations against the prince of Transylvania, engaged in a winter campaign, and not only compelled Sigismond to raise the siege of Tokay, but retook Zatmar, and captured the important and hitherto impregnable fortress of Mongatz.

In the midst of these successes Maximilian sent an embassy to Constantinople to offer terms of peace; but, to give weight to his negotiations, made the most active preparations for the renewal of hostilities, by procuring large contributions and levies from Bohemìa and Austria, and far more considerable succours from the empire. Backed by these preparations, his overtures found a ready reception ; for Selim, who was anxious to consolidate his authority, and to turn his arms against Cyprus, readily concluded an armistice in May, 1567, on the condition that both parties, as well as the prince of Transylvania, should retain the territories which they then held. This peace was both honourable and advantageous to Maximilian, as he lost only Zigeth and Giula, and extended his territory in Hungary from the borders of Transylvania to beyond the Teiss, a district important from its local situation, and comprising not less than two hundred miles in extent.* John Sigismond, refusing to be included in this peace, continued the war, and endeavoured to excite an insurrection among the proud magnates of Hungary, who were dissatisfied with Maximilian for his pacific inclinations, and for employing foreign troops. His intrigues being discovered, and two of the most considerable conspirators arrested, he had no resource but to accept the terms of peace offered by Maximilian, which were advantageous to both parties. He engaged not to assume the title of king of Hungary, except in his correspondence with the Turks, and to acknowledge the emperor as king, his superior and master ; in addition to Transylvania, as an hereditary principality, he was to retain for life the counties of Bihar and Marmarosch, with Crasna and Zolnok, and whatever territories he could recover from the Turks. In return, the emperor promised to confer on him one of his nieces in marriage, and to cede to him Oppelen in Silesia, if expelled from Transylvania. On the death of John Sigismond without issue male, Transylvania was to be considered as an elective principality, dependent on the crown of Hungary.

The intended marriage did not take place, for John Sigismond dying on the 16th of March, 1571, soon after the peace, all his possessions in Hungary reverted to Maximilian. The diet of Transylvania chose Stephen Bathori,

* Forty-five and a half German miles.

who had acted with great reputation as the general and minister of John Sigismond ; and Maximilian, although he had recommended another person, prudently confirmed the choice, from the apprehension of again exciting a Turkish war. The new waivode was accordingly confirmed, both by Maximilian and the Turks, took the oath of fidelity to the crown of Hungary, and continued to live on terms of friendship and concord with the emperor.

Maximilian was a prince of too much probity to break the armistice with Selim, notwithstanding the urgent exhortations of the pope, the king of Spain, and the Venetians ; when cardinal Commendon pressed him with all the specious arguments by which the church of Rome attempted to justify the breach of the most solemn engagements with infidels, he replied, " The faith of treaties ought to be considered as inviolable, and a christian can never be justified in breaking an oath." Such was his moderation, that, when the Turkish fleet was defeated by the allies at Lepanto, he would not permit any public mark of rejoicing, lest he should appear to insult the Turks in their distress, although he would not act against them when victorious.* In consequence of this conduct he maintained even Hungary in a state of tranquillity, and almost the last act of his reign was a renewal of the armistice with Amurath, the successor of Selim, in 1576.

Chap. XXXIX.—1572–1576.

MAXIMILIAN being of a delicate constitution, and declining in health, employed the last years of his reign in taking precautions to secure his dignities and possessions for his descendants. Having first obtained the consent of the Hungarian states, his eldest son Rhodolph was, in 1572, crowned king of Hungary, in a diet at Presburgh, and this example was not lost on those of Bohemia ; but as the elective right was still not considered as abrogated, Maximilian acted with his characteristic prudence, and adopted

* Vie de Commendon, p. 25-27.

a line of conduct which neither wounded the prejudices of
his subjects, nor contravened the right of hereditary succession established by Ferdinand. In a diet, convoked
with great solemnity at Prague, he himself introduced his
son to the states, and recommended him as their future
sovereign ; the states, satisfied with this appeal to their
choice, signified their unanimous consent, and Rhodolph,
was crowned on the 22nd of September, 1575, king of
Bohemia.

Having thus rendered his son successor to the crowns
of Hungary and Bohemia, he laboured to procure for him
the dignity of king of the Romans. He found a ready
assent from the states of the empire, who had sufficiently experienced the mischiefs of contested elections,
and who were apprehensive that, in case of an interregnum,
the kings of Spain and France would aspire to the imperial crown. The electors themselves were also inclined to
favour Maximilian from motives of personal friendship or
religious interest, and all appeared at the diet of Ratisbon,
except the elector Palatine, who, on account of age and
infirmities, deputed his son. No difficulties occurred in
the election of Rhodolph, but, in regard to the capitulation,
the zealous Protestants, at the instigation of the elector
Palatine, endeavoured to introduce articles which tended
to annihilate the Catholic religion. Of these, the principal
were, that the emperor should be styled the advocate of
the Christian church, instead of the see of Rome ; that the
declaration of Ferdinand should be inserted in, instead of
being annexed to, the religious peace ; the ecclesiastical
reservation abolished ; the annates and other revenues
taken from the pope, and applied to furnish succours
against the Turks. Finally, the emperor was not to assist
at any future election, that his presence might not influence the electoral suffrages.

These demands being indignantly rejected by the Catholics, the Protestants, by the interference of Augustus of
Saxony, were induced to withdraw all the articles, except
that relative to the declaration of Ferdinand, which they
considered as peculiarly necessary, because the Catholic
prelates had rejected it as not binding, and even disputed
its authenticity. This contest excited the warmest dis-

putes, and nearly occasioned the prorogation of the diet. Maximilian, who was sensible of the justice of this demand, endeavoured in vain to prevail on the Catholics; but failing in all his efforts, he candidly appealed to the Protestants, and induced them to recede, by promising to consider the declaration as a legal act of the emperor, and to endeavour to procure its authentication at a future diet, or at all events to exert his authority in protecting those who suffered by its infringement. This point being arranged, the election took place without contest or delay, and Rhodolph was unanimously chosen and crowned at Ratisbon by the elector of Mentz, on the 1st of November, 1575.

Besides these dignities, which from right or prescription belonged to his family, he endeavoured to procure the crown of Poland, with the duchy of Lithuania*, either for himself or one of his sons. On the decease of Sigismond Augustus, in July, 1572, Maximilian, as a descendant from a princess of the Jaghellon family†, offered his son Ernest as a candidate; he endeavoured to gain the Protestant party in Poland, which being tolerated under the name of dissidents‡, had become predominant, and pro-

* The duchy of Lithuania had at length been permanently united to Poland, by Sigismond Augustus, who renounced his right of inheritance, on the condition that the two countries should always choose the same sovereign. On the death of Sigismond Augustus, the last male of the Jaghellon line (July 7, 1572), Poland was converted into a real elective monarchy, by the establishment of a law restraining the sovereign from procuring the appointment of a successor during his lifetime.

† His mother, Anne, daughter of Ladislaus, king of Hungary and Bohemia, was grand-daughter of Cassimir, king of Poland.

‡ The Reformation was introduced into Poland under Sigismond I., and gained ground, notwithstanding the persecution of its adherents. They increased so much under Sigismond Augustus, who was himself secretly attached to the new doctrines, that they not only obtained liberty of worship, but were admitted, without distinction of sects, to a share in the diet, and to the privileges hitherto confined to the Catholics. These maxims of unlimited toleration gaining ground, the members of the diet, which assembled on the decease of Sigismond Augustus, entered into engagements for the reciprocal indulgence of their respective tenets. To avoid invidious distinctions, all who were not Catholics were designated by the name of dissidents in religion. This difference of religious sentiments was to occasion no difference of

posed that Ernest should espouse Anne, the only unmarried
sister of the deceased monarch, although she had attained
her fiftieth year.   Ernest was opposed, among other candidates, by John, king of Sweden, who had espoused Catherine, another sister of the deceased monarch; but the
prize was wrested from all by Henry, duke of Anjou,
brother of Charles IX., king of France, whose military
fame and romantic character rendered him popular in
Poland, and who secured his election by liberal promises
and bribes.

Maximilian, though thus disappointed, renewed his
pretensions, when Henry abandoned Poland to succeed to
the crown of France, vacant by the death of his brother.
He again proposed his son, but, contrary to his wishes and
expectations, was himself chosen king by a large party of
the principal nobles, and proclaimed by the primate : the
decree of election bears a just and honourable testimony to
his virtues and abilities, representing him as having consolidated the tranquillity of the Christian world, which was
broken by seditions and divisions, and as having acquired
more glory, by his pacific conduct, than other princes by
their military exploits.

However flattered by this eulogium, the satisfaction of
Maximilian was not of long continuance ; for a party,
instigated by the Turks and by the powers hostile to the
aggrandisement of the house of Austria, chose Stephen
Bathori, waivode of Transylvania, and gave him the princess Anne in marriage.   Maximilian was pressed by the
papal legate, and by his own adherents to receive the
crown ; but he delayed complying with their instances
from various motives, of which the principal were, a desire
to transfer the crown to his son Ernest, a dread of exciting
a war with the Turks, or a wish to obtain a modification of
the articles of the Pacta Conventa.*   Meanwhile his more

civil rights; and a clause was inserted in the Pacta Conventa, or capitulation of the new sovereign, by which he engaged to keep peace
among the dissidents.   Lengnich, Jus. Pub. Polon. tom. ii. p. 555. ;
Historia Poloniæ, ch. i.; Travels in Poland, b. i. ch. 2.

* These were extremely onerous, and such as Maximilian could not
sign without the consent of the empire.   Among other stipulations, he
was to engage to reside two years in the kingdom, and then not to

active rival hastened into Poland, espoused the princess Anne, and was crowned after signing the capitulation offered to Maximilian, on the 1st of May, 1575. His promptitude secured the possession of the throne, and his great talents and shining qualities increased his adherents even among those who had embraced the Austrian party. Maximilian, however, having concluded the truce with Amurath, at length endeavoured to compensate for his tardiness and indecision. He signed the Pacta Conventa, warmly appealed to the empire, and being secure of support from the czar, endeavoured to excite the kings of Sweden and Denmark against his rival, whom he stigmatised as a vassal of the Turks; but he was prevented, by death, from involving himself in a war at the close of his reign, which could not fail of being long and doubtful, and which it had ever been his principal object to avoid.

He had long felt his health declining, and his end was hastened by the anxiety and fatigue derived from mental and bodily exertions. Like his great ancestor Maximilian, he was fond of meditating and discoursing on the immortality of the soul: and he met his death with the calmness and resignation of a christian. He expired at Ratisbon, where he had been holding a diet, on the 12th of October, 1576, on the very day and hour in which the recess was published, in the fiftieth year of his age, and the twelfth of his reign.

Contemporary writers have left no specific description of the person and features of this amiable monarch; but all agree in extolling the grace and elegance of his manners, and the fascination of his conversation and deportment. His life and reign exhibit the fairest and most pleasing picture of the qualities of his mind.

Maximilian, by his vigour, activity, and address, gained,

quit it, except with the consent of the states. He was also required to construct, at his own expense, four fortresses, to discharge the debts of the late monarch, and the arrears of the troops, and to deposit a sum of money for the pay of 10,000 Polish horse. Considering the feeble health of Maximilian, and the nature of these onerous conditions, and, above all, that he could not obtain the nomination of a successor, we ought not to join the biographer of Commendon, in blaming him for delaying to purchase a temporary dignity at so high a price. It is rather a wonder that he at last deemed it worthy of his acceptance.

when young, the esteem and favour of Charles V., who used to call him his right hand, gave him his eldest daughter Mary in marriage, and, before he had attained the twenty-first year of his age, appointed him viceroy of Spain, during his absence with Philip in Germany and the Low Countries. But though instructed in the arts of government by Charles, Maximilian was not swayed by his example, or allured by the splendour of his achievements; for, instead of adopting those principles of dissimulation and duplicity, and that unbounded ambition which disgraced the head of the empire, he distinguished himself by frankness, candour, mildness, moderation, benevolence, and liberality of sentiment.

He loved, cultivated, and encouraged the arts and sciences, and held men of learning in the highest confidence and esteem. He was remarkable for his knowledge of languages, and was not unaptly compared to Mithridates, for the facility with which he spoke the different tongues of the various people over whom he reigned. He was, besides, well read in the Latin, and conversed in it with great ease, purity, and elegance. Though of a convivial disposition and fond of society, his course of life was sober and regular; lively and facetious in conversation, he tempered, without debasing, the dignity of his station, by the most affable and condescending behaviour, and Henry of Valois, himself a pattern of courtesy, declared, that in all his travels, he had never met a more accomplished gentleman. Nor were these pleasing qualities assumed merely for public occasions, and to dazzle the eyes of his courtiers; for in private he was equally good and amiable; a faithful and affectionate husband, a tender parent, and a kind and benevolent master.

Like our great Alfred, he was regular and systematical in the distribution of his time; and his hours were distinctly appropriated for prayer, business, diversion, and repose. In his consultations he listened with patience and complacency to the opinions of all; and it was justly observed by the vice-chancellor of the empire, that had he been a chancellor or secretary, he would have surpassed all his chancellors and secretaries, and rendered his ministers his scholars. He was accessible to persons of all distinctions;

after his dinner, he gave a general audience to his subjects, sitting or standing by the table; addressed himself with singular courtesy to the meanest persons, and possessed the rare talent of never dismissing his petitioners dissatisfied. He was economical without parsimony, fond of plainness and simplicity no less in his apparel than in his diet, and he carried his contempt of finery so far, that he never purchased a single jewel for his personal attire.

We recite with pleasure the testimony of the Bohemian ambassadors who were deputed to promote his interests with the Poles, no less as a true picture of his general conduct, than as a heartfelt testimony of gratitude from subjects to their sovereign. "We Bohemians are as happy under his government as if he were our father: our privileges, our laws, our rights, liberties, and usages are protected, maintained, defended, and confirmed. No less just than wise, he confers the offices and dignities of the kingdom only on natives of rank, and is not influenced by favour or artifice. He introduces no innovations contrary to our immunities; and, when the great expenses which he incurs for the good of Christendom render contributions necessary, he levies them without violence, and with the approbation of the states. But what may be almost considered as a miracle, is, the prudence and impartiality of his conduct towards persons of a different faith, always recommending union, concord, peace, toleration, and mutual regard. He listens even to the meanest of his subjects, readily receives their petitions, and renders impartial justice to all."

Historians, not distinguishing between a sovereign pacific from principle and reflection, or from indolence and pusillanimity, have censured Maximilian for dilatory and inactive measures, which were the effects of precaution and policy; and have turned to scorn what ought to have been considered as the great glory of his reign, his unwillingness to involve his subjects in foreign and distant wars. In reality, his love of peace did not proceed from want of military skill, or deficiency of personal courage; as he had distinguished himself both for address and valour in the campaign of 1544, against Francis I., and in the war of Smalkalde. It was derived from a conviction, that Germany and his hereditary countries required repose and tran-

quillity, after a long period of contention and war; and
that the preservation of peace was the only means of sooth-
ing those religious and political animosities which had been
derived from the stupendous revolutions in church and
state. With him, therefore, the desire of aggrandisement
was but a secondary consideration; the maintenance of
peace, which he deemed the greatest blessing he could confer on his people, was the ruling principle of all his actions.
From the adoption of this principle, Germany and the
dominions of the house of Austria, except Hungary, enjoyed under him a series of almost uninterrupted peace;
while the rest of Europe was exposed to all the evils of
civil commotion, religious discord, or foreign war.

No stronger proof of his great and amiable qualities can
be given, than the concurring testimony of the historians
of Germany, Hungary, Bohemia, and Austria, both Catholics and Protestants, who vie in his praises, and in representing him as a model of impartiality, wisdom, and benig-
nity; and it was truly said of him, what can be applied to few
sovereigns, that in no one instance was he impelled, either
by resentment or ambition, to act contrary to the strictest
rules of moderation and justice, or to disturb the public
tranquillity. Germany revived, in his favour, the surname
of Titus, or, the Delight of Mankind; and if ever a christian and philosopher filled the throne, that christian and
philosopher was Maximilian II.*

The wife of Maximilian was Mary, daughter of Charles V.,
who was born in 1528, and married in 1548. She was a
princess of exemplary life, considerable beauty, and personal
accomplishments; but she forms a strong contrast with
her husband, from her ardent and superstitious attachment

---

* Oratio de Maximiliano II. a Johanne Barone de Polheim. This
interesting oration, from which most authors have drawn their accounts of Maximilian, was written by a person resident in the court of
Vienna, and whose father attended Maximilian in Spain. Chrytæi
Saxonia, p. 629. Besides this narrative, for the reign of Maximilian
have been consulted the histories so often quoted: Struvius Heiss,
Schmidt, Heinrich, Puetter, Pfeffinger's Vitriarius, Pinacotheca
Austriaca, Vie de Commendon, Reisser, and Wraxall's Introduction to the History of France, art. House of Austria, which con-
tains a good delineation of the character of Maximilian, vol. i.
p. 370-372.

to the Catholic faith. For this attachment she has been highly praised by the Catholic writers; she received from pope Pius V. the eulogium that she was worthy of a place among those women who were worshipped on earth for their sanctity, and she was justly called, by Gregory XIII., the firm column of the Catholic faith. On the death of Maximilian, she retired into Spain, and with an inveterate bigotry, congenial to the mind of her brother Philip, testified her joy at returning to a country where there was no heretic. She soon afterwards entered into a nunnery of the order of St. Clare, at Villamonte near Madrid, where she terminated her days, in 1603. It is much to be regretted, that the enlightened Maximilian should have principally intrusted the religious education of his children to this bigoted woman, as from the principles infused into their infant minds they imbibed the spirit of intolerance and persecution. Mary was the fruitful mother of sixteen children, of whom three daughters and six sons attained the age of maturity:

1. Anne, the eldest daughter, was born in 1549, and was engaged to Don Carlos, prince of Spain; but, after his imprisonment and death, espoused his father Philip. She died in 1580, and, by bearing male issue to Philip, but off the expected succession of her own family to the Spanish dominions.

2. Elizabeth, born in 1554, espoused, in 1570, Charles IX., king of France. She was a woman of consummate beauty and unsullied purity of morals, which she preserved uncontaminated in a licentious and voluptuous court. Although only twenty at the death of Charles, she rejected the offers of Henry III., Philip of Spain, and of other sovereigns, and faithfully fulfilled a promise which she had made to her dying husband, that she would never again enter into the married state. She terminated her days in 1592, in the monastery of St. Mary de Angelis, at Vienna, which she had built and endowed, with such a reputation for sanctity, that she was supposed to have wrought miracles.

3. Margaret, who was born in 1567, and accompanied her mother into Spain, from motives of religion refused the hand of Philip, and, immuring herself in a convent, died in

1633, with a reputation for sanctity not inferior to that of her sister Elizabeth.

1. Rhodolph, the eldest son of Maximilian, succeeded his father.

2. Ernest, the second son, was born in 1553, and principally educated in Spain with his brother Rhodolph. He inherited the infirm constitution, mild and pacific qualities of his father, and resembled him in his knowledge of languages; but he was cold and reserved, and such a prey to morbid melancholy that he was scarcely ever seen to smile. After being disappointed of the throne of Poland, he was nominated, by his brother Rhodolph, governor of Hungary and regent of Austria. He was intrusted with the government of the Netherlands by Philip, who promised to confer on him the sovereignty of those countries, with his daughter Isabella in marriage. His endeavours to restore peace and tranquillity were exerted too late; for the United Provinces had already declared themselves independent, and formed that union which became the foundation of their republic; and his death prevented the fulfilment of the promises made by Philip. He died in 1595 of a fit of the stone, to which disorder he had been long subject.

3. Matthias, who expelled his brother Rhodolph from the thrones of Hungary and Bohemia, and succeeded him in the empire, will occupy his proper place in the subsequent pages.

4. Maximilian, the fourth son, born in 1558, was, on the 25th of January, 1588, elected, by a strong party, king of Poland, in opposition to another party, who chose Sigismond, son of John, king of Sweden, by the Polish princess Catherine Jaghellon. Both candidates supported their cause by arms, and the contest was dubious until Maximilian was defeated and taken prisoner by the primate of Poland, and purchased his liberty by renouncing his right to the throne. After being guardian to Ferdinand, prince of Styria, during his minority, he was, in 1595, elected grand-master of the Teutonic Order; and, on the death of his uncle Ferdinand, obtained the government of the exterior provinces. He signalised himself against the Turks, and, in conjunction with the other Austrian princes, resigned his right to the succession in favour of his ward.

He died on the 2nd of November, 1619, without issue,
and unmarried.

5. Albert, the youngest son of Maximilian, was destined
for the ecclesiastical profession. Being sent to Spain, he
obtained, with the dignity of cardinal, the archbishopric of
Toledo, the primacy of Spain: he was also appointed
governor of Portugal, and soon afterwards, relinquishing
the ecclesiastical profession, espoused Isabella, daughter of
Philip, and received the Netherlands as an hereditary
sovereignty, in conjunction with his wife; a measure which
was adopted by Philip to conciliate those whom he had
driven into rebellion by his tyranny and intolerance, and
to prevent the total loss of a territory so important to the
crown of Spain.

Since the pacification of Ghent, an essential change had
taken place in the situation of the Netherlands. Don John
of Austria, natural son of Charles V., whom Philip had
appointed governor, had ratified that confederation for the
sole purpose of infringing it; but his perfidious designs
being discovered, the natives disowned his government,
and chose in his place the archduke Matthias, though
without throwing off their allegiance. The war was renewed with advantage by Don John, and, after his death,
by his successor the celebrated Alexander Farnese, duke of
Parma, who detached from the league the southern, or what
were called the Walloon Provinces.* This defection occasioned an attempt to revive the pacification of Ghent, by an
engagement called the Union of Utrecht, comprising those
provinces which afterwards formed the United States, besides Ghent, Bruges, Antwerp, and several considerable
towns of the other provinces.

The successes of the duke of Parma, joined to the incessant disputes between the Catholics and Protestants, and
the repeated defections of many of the towns, convinced
the prince of Orange, and the chiefs of the revolt, that they
could not maintain their liberties without foreign assistance. Disappointed in those hopes of support from the
emperor which had induced them to call in Matthias, they
finally threw off their allegiance to Spain, in July, 1581,
and conferred the sovereignty of their country on Francis,

* Artois, Hainault, and the other southern provinces.

duke of Anjou, on the condition of maintaining their civil
and religious rights, and carrying on the war principally
at the expense of France.   This change was not attended
with the desired effects : although the duke of Anjou had
entered into an alliance with queen Elizabeth, the trifling
support which they received from France and England was
insufficient to enable them to resist the power of Philip,
and baffle the military skill and address of the duke of
Parma.   The new sovereign, at variance with the prince
of Orange, and dissatisfied with the limited authority
allowed him by his subjects, after a perfidious attempt to
seize Antwerp, abandoned a short-lived sovereignty, and in
1584, retired ignominiously into France.   The misfortunes
attending their disunion were aggravated by the assassination of the prince of Orange; and before the close of 1594,
the duke of Parma was enabled to recover all the seventeen provinces, except Holland, Zealand, and Utrecht.

In this situation the states were unable to prevail on
Elizabeth of England, or the king of France, to accept the
sovereignty; but their declining cause found a chief in
Maurice, eldest son of the deceased prince, who inheriting
the splendid qualities of his father, and succeeding to his
influence and power, recovered Guelderland, Groningen,
Overyssel, and Friesland, and, uniting them with the three
other states, established the republic of the Seven United
Provinces.

Such was the situation of the Netherlands when Albert,
with his wife Isabella, succeeded to the sovereignty, which
had been conferred on him by Philip II., and was confirmed
by his successor Philip III.   The seventeen provinces,
under the name of an independent sovereignty, were
granted to them and to their heirs, but, in failure of their
issue, were to revert to Spain.   They were to take an oath
of fidelity to the crown of Spain, to agree not to permit the
exercise of any other religion except the Catholic, to prevent their subjects from trading to the Indies, to receive
Spanish garrisons in the principal towns, and, finally, none
of their descendants were to marry without the approbation of the Spanish court.   On the breach of any of these
conditions, the grant was declared null, and the territories
were to revert to their original sovereign.   Such a grant,

which was evidently intended only to cheat the revolted
provinces into submission, was attended with a contrary
effect, and they exerted themselves against Albert with the
same spirit as against the preceding governors. Albert,
however, omitted no effort to secure and enlarge his sovereignty ; he carried on the war with a skill and enterprise
little to be expected from his former profession and habits
of life, gained Calais, Ostend, and several of the towns,
which still adhered to the seven united provinces, and
completed the reduction of the country, afterwards called
the Spanish or Austrian Netherlands. But, not being sufficiently supported by the court of Madrid, which found
full employment in its other vast projects and ambitious
views, he was unable to make any effectual impression on
the consolidated body of the new republic; he therefore
discontinued a fruitless contest, and, with the permission
of Spain, concluded, in 1609, a truce for twelve years, in
which he virtually acknowledged the independence of the
United Provinces. He afterwards interfered in the contests
for the succession of Juliers, in favour of the count Palatine of Neuburgh, and exerted himself in support of the
Catholic interest in Germany.

He lived long enough to see the renewal of the war with
the United Provinces, and died in 1621, at the time when he
was endeavouring to overcome the obstinacy of the Spanish
court, and to procure the continuation of the truce. As
he left no issue, the sovereignty of the Netherlands fell to
his wife ; and, on her death, reverted to Spain.

CHAP. XL. — RHODOLPH II. — 1576–1603.

ON the death of Maximilian, Rhodolph succeeded of course
to the empire, Bohemia, and Hungary, in consequence of
his prior coronation ; and, for the first time since the
transfer of Austria to the reigning family, he, as eldest
son, obtained the sole possession of that archduchy ; while
his numerous brothers, instead of a joint share in the
government, were provided with annual pensions. Whe-

ther this change, which virtually established the right of primogeniture, was arranged during the reign of Maximilian, or settled by a family compact, is uncertain; but it was of the greatest advantage to this illustrious family, the aggrandisement of which preceding dismemberments had contributed to retard.

Rhodolph, at his accession, was in the twenty-fifth year of his age; he was, like his father, naturally mild and pacific, possessed a quick apprehension and extensive capacity, evinced talents for business, and was no less distinguished for sobriety and decorum of deportment than for literary acquirements. He ascended the throne at a time when religious animosity had begun to subside, and when tranquillity was restored throughout Germany and his hereditary dominions. The prudent conduct of his father had removed or lessened the principal obstacles which had so greatly embarrassed his immediate predecessors; and it required no arduous exertions of body or mind, no daring enterprise or complicated scheme of policy; but the same mixture of prudence, moderation, and firmness to maintain the tranquillity so happily established.

The early habits of the new emperor and the defects of his education frustrated all the hopes derived from these happy auspices. Brought up till his twelfth year under the care of his bigoted mother, he was deeply imbued with her superstitious sentiments, and that tincture was strengthened instead of being weakened by his removal to the court of Madrid, whither he was sent as presumptive successor to the Spanish monarchy.* His education was there completed under the auspices of Philip by the Jesuits, who possessed the art of fixing an almost indelible impression on youthful minds, and whose mode of education tended rather to fill and occupy, than to expand and exercise the understanding; to render their pupils sedentary and contemplative; and to inure them to the petty arts of intrigue and dissimulation, rather than to fit them for the cares of

---

* Philip II. having for a considerable period only one daughter, purposed to continue his dominions in his family, by marrying her to one of the princes of the German branch. For this reason, Rhodolph and his brother Ernest were educated in Spain till the birth of a son, afterwards Philip III.

government or the duties of active life. Hence, his mother, though distant, possessed the same influence over his mind when arrived at years of discretion as in the pliancy of youth ; and by her means, as well as by the agency of the Jesuits, he was during his whole reign rendered totally subservient to the court of Madrid. Even his learning, which in a person of a different character might have tended to counteract this predominant influence, contributed to rivet the fetters of early habit and education. His love and application to the arts was not such as became an enlightened sovereign, but the passion and mechanical dexterity of a mere artist. He was greatly addicted to alchemy, which of all sciences tends the most, by its golden dreams, to absorb and fascinate the mind ; and still more to judicial astrology, which filling the imagination with vain hopes and groundless fears, renders its professors the prey of uncertainty, gloom, reserve, and suspicion.

Unfortunately for Rhodolph, the conduct of his father had left him scarcely any alternative but open toleration, or at least tacit connivance at the Protestant doctrines. Although Maximilian had publicly forbidden the Protestant worship to the burghers, yet towards the close of his reign he suffered those of Vienna to attend divine service according to the Lutheran ritual, when performed before the nobles and equestrian order in the House of Assembly. He even did not prohibit the private celebration of the reformed worship at the houses of individuals, nor prevent the burghers from repairing to the Protestant churches in the neighbouring villages. The consequence of this toleration and forbearance gave the Protestants the ascendency in the states : they deterred, by contempt and insult, the Catholic prelates, and even many other members of that persuasion, from appearing in the diet ; and filled the committees of revenue, and all the inferior departments of the magistracy and administration with those of their own communion. The professors of the university of Vienna, except those in the class of theology, and the masters of the inferior schools, were of the same persuasion. Stimulated by the near prospect of the errors and corruptions of the church, and animated by that ardour with which the human mind is impelled to embrace and propagate religious truths, their preachers frequently passed the bounds of discretion, by indulging themselves in the most bitter and unqualified invectives against the established church. This evil had arisen to such a height that even the tolerant Maximilian at length found it necessary to interpose his authority; and almost the last act of his life was a sentence of suspension against Opitz, one of the most violent of these preachers, who acted as minister for the body of nobles and knights at Vienna, and whose sermons drew an unusual concourse of people. The death of Maximilian suspending the execution of his sentence, Opitz, with his fervid eloquence, continued to rouse the passions of his numerous auditors, and daily to increase the number of converts.

It is therefore but justice to Rhodolph to observe that had he been more inclined to toleration, he would have found it extremely difficult to restore the equilibrium between the two parties, or to check the progress of religious truth, without the strongest exertions of authority. His attempts to attain this object occasioned all the misfortunes of his reign. He confirmed the toleration granted by his father to the nobles and equestrian order within the bounds of their own dependencies; but, in conformity with the letter of that grant, he forbade the burghers of his own towns from assisting at or professing the Protestant worship, and at Vienna he compelled the nobles and knights of that persuasion to perform divine service in an apartment which was too small to admit any other audience except their own body. At the same time he deprived Opitz and two of his most ardent coadjutors of their offices, and commanded that no other priest should be appointed without his approbation.

The states considered these restrictions as the commencement of a system of persecution; after consulting their own preachers and foreign universities, they refused to carry the order into execution, asserting that "they were bound to obey God rather than man." This act of disobedience, which was not justified by prudence or by the existing laws, furnished the emperor with a pretext for measures calculated to suppress the Protestant and restore the Catholic worship. He banished the deposed preachers from his territories, forbade the appointment of others in their places, and abolished the exercise of the Protestant worship in the royal towns, and even in Vienna itself.

He next adopted a regular and systematic plan to restore the preponderance of the Catholic religion. He encouraged the Catholic prelates and other members of the states to resume their places in the diet, exhorted them to act with concert and unanimity, and again filled the vacant committees and subordinate offices of justice and revenue with Catholics. He forbade any cure or benefice to be conferred on any person who was not devoted to the church, or academical degree or professorship to be granted to any member of the university who did not sign the formulary of the Catholic faith. He subjected the schools to new regulations, and published new catechisms for popular use; he permitted no town to appoint a clerk or secretary without the approbation of the sovereign; admitted no person to the rights of burghership who had not undergone a religious examination, and taken an oath of submission to the Catholic priesthood. Finally, he shut up many churches in the neighbourhood of Vienna which were appropriated to the Protestant worship, because they were frequented by the burghers. By these means the preponderance of the Catholic worship was in a few years restored; and he cannot be accused of any glaring breach of the religious peace or the established regulations, although he may be condemned on the score of policy and toleration, in thus shocking the feelings and wounding the consciences of so great a majority of his subjects.

The Protestants were too well aware of his real principles, and his subordination to the intolerant court of Spain, to be deluded by the caution with which these restrictions were imposed; and they were justly apprehensive lest these reforms should prove only the prelude to the abolition of all religious immunities. From these causes, aggravated at the same time by civil grievances, a revolt broke out in 1595 among the peasants, attended with all those excesses which usually accompany popular commotions. It was scarcely suppressed, before a more dangerous rebellion took place in Austria above the Ems, which was directed and organised by the states themselves. The consequences of this ineffectual resistance. however, only served to strengthen the power of the sovereign, and to furnish him with a pretext for overturning the whole system of the Protestant worship in every part of his dominions.

Although in the present enlightened age, when the principles of toleration are understood and duly appreciated, and speculative points of doctrine reduced to their intrinsic value, we may condemn the impolicy of the emperor in alienating so large a portion of his subjects, and leaving them no alternative, except sinning against their consciences or open resistance ; yet the Protestants of the age had little right to censure his conduct, as they acted with the same spirit of persecution in their own dominions, not only against the Catholics, but even against those who equally differed from the church of Rome. The schism, which, in a very early period of the Reformation, had occasioned such a spirit of disunion in the Protestant body, now became an open breach, and divided them into distinct sects or parties.

We have already observed, that Frederic III., elector Palatine, had by force introduced Calvinism into his dominions, and had given publicity and consistence to his doctrines by the catechism of Heidelberg. His eldest son Louis, however, who succeeded him in the electorate, was as much attached to the Lutheran principles ; and under the sanction of the peace of religion, which empowered every sovereign to introduce his own tenets into his territories, he proceeded to extirpate the Calvinistic doctrines, by banishing the Calvinist teachers, and restoring the Lutheran worship as ordained by the confession of Augsburgh. Louis dying in 1583, leaving his son, Frederic IV., under age, his brother John Casimir, who assumed the administration during the minority, in his turn drove out the Lutherans, and again reinstated the followers of Calvin.

Unfortunately the palatinate was not the only theatre of religious persecution among the Protestants. During the reign of Christian I., the son and successor of Augustus, elector of Saxony, the doctrines of Calvin found many adherents even in Saxony, the seat of Lutheran orthodoxy, and many powerful partisans in the court and family of the elector, among whom the chancellor Krell was the most zea-

lous and persevering.   By his influence, joined with that of
the higher orders of the clergy, many changes were made in
the Lutheran worship, which gradually approached the
simple ritual of Calvin, the priests who opposed these innovations were persecuted and driven from the country,
and even the book of concord was abandoned as a religious
test.   The death of the elector, who, if he did not support,
connived at these alterations, occasioned their suspension.
His relative, Frederic William, duke of Saxe Weimar, who
became guardian to his son, not only restored the Lutheran
worship, but persecuted all who adhered to the recent
changes, and introduced a new religious test, which all
who held civil or ecclesiastical offices were compelled to
sign under pain of banishment.   The partisans of Calvinism
were arrested; Krell, who was the most considerable and
most active, was brought to a public trial, and after a confinement of nine years, expiated his religious offences on
the scaffold, on the 9th of October, 1601.

Hitherto, notwithstanding all diversity of doctrine, and
the persecution of the Lutherans, the princes of the reformed religion had, without distinction, sheltered themselves under the confession of Augsburgh ; but the progress of Calvinism, and its intolerant spirit at length
induced the Lutherans to form a barrier of separation, and
to exclude the Calvinists from the peace of religion ; and,
by this measure, they were themselves led to the same acts
of persecution, which they condemned in others.   Under
the auspices of Augustus, elector of Saxony, and Ulric,
duke of Wirtemberg, both strenuous partisans of the doctrine of Luther, a symbolical formulary, or creed, called
the Book of Concord *, had been drawn up by the Saxon
divines, containing an explanation of the principal points
of controversy, deduced from the confession and apology
of Augsburgh, the peace of Smalkalde, and the two catechisms of Luther.   It was published at Torgau, on the
25th of June, 1580†, under the signature of the three

* Concordienbuck.   It might more properly be called the book of
discord.

† This particular day was chosen by the elector of Saxony, because
it was the anniversary of the day the original confession of Augsburgh
was presented to Charles V. by the diet.

secular electors, Augustus of Saxony, John George of Brandenburgh, and Louis, elector Palatine, twenty-two princes, the same number of counts, and thirty-five imperial towns. It was introduced into all the dominions of the Lutheran princes; and all priests and schoolmasters were ordered to give their public assent to its doctrines, under the pain of instant deprivation.

John Casimir, count Palatine of Lautern, who afterwards became administrator of the palatinate during the minority of his nephew, endeavoured to prevent or retard the publication of this creed. His instances were ineffectually seconded by William, landgrave of Hesse Cassel, and even by the ambassador of Elizabeth, queen of England; and the consequence was, a schism of the two parties, to the inconceivable detriment of the whole Protestant body. For had the two sects formed a system of doctrine on the points in which they both agreed, in opposition to the church of Rome, instead of one derived from those abstruse doctrines on which they differed, we can scarcely doubt that their party must have become predominant, when we consider their physical strength and local situation, and their numerous partisans in every part of Catholic Germany, particularly in the dominions of the house of Austria. But by this impolitic separation, and the consequent dissensions, the equipoise which subsisted between the ecclesiastical and secular electors was destroyed; and the event proved the truth of the prediction made by cardinal Commendon at the first rise of the schism, that the spirit of party and theological hatred, if let loose among the Protestants, would of itself deliver the church of Rome from the danger of that total apostacy with which she was threatened in Germany.

The Jesuits, the great advisers and directors of Rhodolph, took advantage of these dissensions, and with consummate ingenuity, turned the arguments adduced, and the precedents established by the Protestants against themselves. They urged that the religious peace, which originally was only temporary and without legal permanency, was now abrogated; for it was not applicable to the Calvinists, because the Lutherans themselves had disclaimed them as brethren; nor to the Lutherans, because, by adopting a

new creed they no longer adhered to the Confession of
Augsburgh, which was the basis of the religious peace.
With the same address they brought forward the mutual
persecutions of the Protestants, as an argument that Catholic sovereigns had as much right to deprive their Protestant subjects of religious toleration, as the Protestant
princes had assumed by forcibly establishing, in their respective dominions, their own peculiar tenets. But they
directed their principal attention to the support of the
ecclesiastical reservation, as the great barrier of the Catholic church in Germany.

In conformity with their suggestions, the Catholic body
adopted a systematic plan for the gradual extirpation of
the Protestant tenets, which they carried into execution
under the popular name of a reform. The grand principle
of this system was, to force the Protestants to insurrection,
by executing strictly the letter of the peace of religion,
and other compacts between the Catholics and Protestants,
by interpreting in their own favour every stipulation which
was left doubtful, and by revoking every tacit concession,
which had been yielded from fear rather than from conviction ; and thus to make every new restriction appear
not an act of persecution, but a just chastisement of disobedience and insurrection. As a part of this plan, it was
their purpose to lessen the authority of the imperial chamber, by discontinuing the annual visitation, and gradually
to transfer religious causes before the Aulic council, which
was composed of Catholic members, and solely under the
control of the emperor. This project was carried into
execution with uniform consistency and perseverance by
the ministers who directed the counsels of the emperor,
and was supported by all the weight of the Spanish court
under Philip III., who was enabled to detach for its execution a part of the great military force which he maintained
in the Netherlands.

Numerous pretexts were soon found to carry this plan
into execution. Aix-la-Chapelle, at the conclusion of the
peace of religion, was considered as a Catholic city, but
contained a number of Protestant emigrants from the Low
Countries, who daily increasing during the persecutions of
Philip, at length required from the diet of Augsburgh, in

1559, the free exercise of their worship. This demand was refused, but the numbers, wealth, and influence of the Protestants continuing to augment, they succeeded in procuring admission into the magistracy, and renewed their petitions for freedom of conscience. Not deterred by the rejection of their demand, they assumed a right which they could not legally obtain, and in 1580 publicly established their form of worship, notwithstanding the remonstrances of the duke of Juliers, the protector of the town. The emperor being appealed to by the Catholic magistrates, deputed commissaries to take cognisance of the dispute and suppress all innovations; yet, notwithstanding their orders, the Protestants who were grown too powerful to be controlled, raised two of their body to the office of burgomasters. In consequence of this contumacy, the imperial commissaries required, in the name of the emperor, the dismission of the burgomasters, and the keys of the town; and this rigorous proceeding occasioned an insurrection among the Protestant populace.

This was the point to which the Catholics desired to bring the dispute. The emperor reiterated his former mandate, and the town, continuing disobedient, was blockaded by the duke of Juliers and the bishop of Liege, the two imperial commissaries, assisted by a corps of Spanish troops, notwithstanding the instances of the electors of Saxony and Brandenburgh, to whom the Protestants applied. The blockade, however, being raised by the spirit of the inhabitants, the dispute continued in suspense until the progress of events presented a more favourable opportunity for enforcing the ban of the empire.

The execution of the ecclesiastical reservation was another cause of incessant disputes between the two sects, and furnished the Catholics with endless pretexts for harassing and weakening their antagonists. The Protestants had gradually secularised or appropriated several prelacies, some before and some since the religious peace. These instances could not, however, be considered as formal infringements of the ecclesiastical reservation, even had that article been acknowledged by both parties; for the prelates had not themselves quitted their religion, but the whole or the majority of the respective chapters becoming

Protestants, had filled the vacancies with chiefs of their
own persuasion, and some of these elections had taken
place with the connivance, if not the approbation of the
emperor.

The Catholics had, though reluctantly, submitted to
these innovations ; but a change which occurred in 1577,
relative to the electorate of Cologne, was precisely a case
on which the disputes of the two parties had originally
occasioned the insertion of the ecclesiastical reservation in
the peace of religion. Gerard, count of Truchses, had
been chosen elector of Cologne, in opposition to a prince of
Saxe Lawenburgh, on the marriage and consequent resignation of Salentine, count of Isenburgh. Being enamoured
of Agnes, countess of Mansfield, and canoness of Girn-
sheim, a lady of exquisite beauty and accomplishments, he
abjured the Catholic religion, and espoused his mistress ;
but he did not follow the example of his predecessor, in
resigning his electorate, and announced his resolution in a
public declaration, in which he observed, " Since God has
delivered me from the darkness of popery, and endued me
with the pure knowledge of his Holy Word, I am determined not to resign the electorate, as has been maliciously
reported, but to retain it during my life ; confirming at the
same time the chapter in all its privileges, and particularly
its right of election on my death, or voluntary resignation."
He hoped to derive support from the Protestant body, who
had never acknowledged the validity of the ecclesiastical
reservation ; and he expected assistance from Elizabeth of
England, and Henry IV. of France, and still more from
his own subjects, the majority of whom were Protestants.

The Catholic part of the chapter, headed by his former
rival, the prince of Saxe Lawenburgh, opposing his designs, were seconded by the magistrates of Cologne. An
appeal was made to the emperor and to Rome, and the
pope issued a sentence of excommunication and deposition
against the elector, which was confirmed by the emperor.
A civil war ensued, in which Gerard maintained the
advantage, till the chapter raised a powerful rival, by
electing Ernest, brother of William, duke of Bavaria,
who was supported by the pope and the emperor, and still

more assisted by the forces of his brother, and by an army of veterans detached from the Low Countries.

In this extremity, Gerard was urged to resign the contested dignity, and offered an annual pension as a reward for his compliance ; but he imprudently rejected this offer, from the expectation of being assisted by the Protestants, who had made him promises of immediate and effectual support. As he had unfortunately embraced the tenets of Calvin instead of those of Luther, the only German prince from whom he derived assistance was John Casimir, brother of the elector Palatine, a zealous Calvinist. The Lutheran princes suffered their religious prejudices to outweigh their political interests; and the secular electors contented themselves with a bare remonstrance against permitting the pope to deprive a prince of the empire of his dignity.

Henry IV. of France, who had not yet embraced the Catholic religion, saw the advantages to be derived from this opportunity of securing a Protestant majority in the Electoral College, and of lowering the interest of the house of Austria in the empire, by raising an emperor of that persuasion to the throne : he therefore despatched his chancellor Segur to unite the Protestants in behalf of the deposed elector. He urged that as the two sects differed only on the single point of the Lord's Supper, it would be easy to form an union of the two churches, by means of a general synod ; but their answer proves how little he appreciated their prejudices, and how little they were swayed by enlarged notions either of religious or political interest. They replied, that the difference of sentiment was far from consisting in the single point of the Lord's Supper; "the partisans of Calvin," they urged, "have accumulated such numberless errors in regard to the person of Christ, the communication of his merits, and the dignity of human nature; have given such forced explanations of the Scripture, and adopted so many blasphemies, that the question of the Lord's Supper, far from being the principal, is become the least point of difference. An outward union, merely for worldly purposes, in which each party is suffered to maintain its peculiar tenets, can neither be agreeable to God, nor useful to the church. These considerations induced us to insert into the formulary of concord a condemnation of the Calvinistical errors ; and to declare our public decision, that false principles should not be covered with the semblance of exterior union, and tolerated under pretence of the right of private judgment, but, that all should submit to the word of God, as the only rule to which their faith and instructions should be conformable." They concluded with declaring, that even if Henry himself and the French churches were desirous of an union, they must submit to sign the formulary of concord.

In addition to these motives which influenced the whole Lutheran body, peculiar and personal interests actuated the two branches of the house of Saxony, who disputed the succession of the county of Henneberg ; and, as the affair depended on the decision of the imperial tribunals, they were unwilling to offend the emperor by countenancing a prince whom he opposed. John Casimir, being therefore afraid of drawing on himself the whole force of the Catholic body, of the house of Austria and Spain, seized the pretext of his brother's death, in April, 1584, to withdraw from the contest. The deposed elector, disappointed in all his hopes, and left without assistance, was driven into exile* ; and Ernest, being established in the electorate, abolished the exercise of the Protestant worship, which his rival had tolerated.

The dispute for the electorate of Cologne gave rise to a similar contest at Strasburgh. The three Protestant canons of Cologne being deposed by the pope for their adherence to Gerard, retired to Strasburgh, where they also possessed stalls, and where Protestants were admitted under the guaranty of the peace of religion. But as they were considered as deprived of their benefices by the papal excommunication, the Catholic part of the chapter, who then formed a majority, refused to receive them. The three canons, joined by the count of Mansfield, another

* He first found a temporary asylum at Delft, under Maurice, prince of Orange. Maurice being unable to afford him effectual support, Gerard sent his wife into England, to solicit the assistance of Elizabeth. But the queen, who at first received her with great marks of kindness, becoming jealous of her frequent interviews with the earl of Essex, drove her from England. Her husband retired to Strasburgh, of which chapter he was dean, and died in 1601 without issue.

Protestant, and secretly supported by the magistrates, forced open the magazines of corn and wine*, and seized a sufficient portion for their maintenance. The dispute being referred to the arbitration of the magistrates, who decided in favour of the Protestants, the Catholic party on their side took possession of the money, plate, and archives, retired to Saverne, the residence of the bishop, and under his protection formed a separate chapter; while the Protestant canons took up their abode in the canonical houses, and appropriated the rents in the town, and all other revenues which they could obtain.

Rhodolph sent commissioners to deprive the Protestants of the houses and revenues which they had appropriated; but they refused to obey his injunction, and the magistrates to enforce it, because the affair had not been submitted to the cognisance of a competent tribunal. In this situation affairs remained until the death of the bishop, in April, 1592. On that event, Rhodolph proposed to put the bishopric in sequestration, under the care of his uncle, Ferdinand of Tyrol and Alsace; but the Protestant canons, whose number had been increased so as to form a majority, assembling in the chapter house, the usual place of election, chose John George, margrave of Brandenburgh, son of Frederic, administrator of Magdeburgh, hoping by this nomination to secure the support of his powerful house. At the same time the Catholics at Saverne elected Charles, cardinal archbishop of Mentz, son of Charles, duke of Loraine. The margrave of Brandenburgh immediately levied troops, and, being countenanced by the magistrates, took possession of Kochenberg and Dichstein, two strong fortresses in the vicinity, and prepared to conquer the other territories of the see; on the other hand, the cardinal of Loraine supported his election with an armed force, and occupied Saverne and the neighbouring districts. Hostilities ensued, and the domains of the see became the theatre of a civil war, in which neither party gained the ascendency; and as the cardinal was supported by his father and

* As the chapters in general received the produce of their lands and tithes in kind, large stores of corn and wine were accumulated in the magazines, part of which was appropriated for their maintenance, and the remainder sold.

the Catholics, and the margrave by some of the Protestant princes, as well as by Zurich and Bern, which were in alliance with Strasburgh, the war seemed likely to spread into Germany. All the attempts of the emperor to terminate the dispute in his individual capacity, were frustrated by the Protestants ; till at length, in 1593, he prevailed on both parties to lay down their arms, and refer the cause to the arbitration of three German princes of each religion. This mediation, however, produced no effect, as neither party would relinquish their supposed right of choosing a bishop ; and, after an interval of eleven years, the dispute was terminated in 1604 by the mediation of the duke of Wirtemberg. The margrave of Brandenburgh resigned his dignity, and in return was to receive from the duke 16,000 florins, with an annual pension of 10,000, for the discharge of which the rich baillage of Oberkirchen, belonging to the see, was to be sequestered in the hands of the duke. At the same time a truce of fifteen years was arranged between the hostile canons, by which both Protestants and Catholics were to retain all they then possessed; and the cardinal of Loraine was soon afterwards duly installed. Thus for the time, though the dispute could not be considered as terminated, the balance was at least turned in favour of the Catholics.*

The unfortunate schism which subsisted in the Protestant body, paralysed all their efforts. In the midst of all these encroachments of the Catholics, instead of the promptitude and decision with which their predecessors had frustrated the views of Charles, scarcely the consideration even of personal safety was sufficient to awaken them from their indifference. A few, indeed, less influenced by religious prejudices, were alarmed by the constant interference of the Spanish troops, and the views which the imperial court evinced by its continued innovations. Among these, the most considerable was Frederic IV., elector Palatine ; but, as he professed the Calvinistic doctrines, he was unable to overcome the jealousy of the Lutheran chiefs, many of whom continued aloof, particularly the electoral courts of

---

* The truce was afterwards renewed for seven years, and the contest finally determined in favour of the Catholics, by the imperial rescript of Ferdinand II.

Brandenburgh and Saxony, and even Philip Louis, count Palatine, head of the collateral branch of Neuburgh.

Notwithstanding this want of concord, the elector Palatine, on the 16th January, 1594, united several of the minor princes* and states, and even Frederic, duke of Wirtemberg, in a confederacy, at Heilbrun, to withhold the succours which the emperor demanded against the Turks, until their grievances were redressed. A list of those grievances, presented at the diet of Ratisbon, will show that their alarms were not without foundation. They enumerated the repeated attempts of the pope and his nuncios to extend their ecclesiastical jurisdiction, which was limited by the peace of religion ; they remonstrated against the exclusion of Protestant prelates from the diet, the diminution of the Protestant members in the imperial chamber, and the intermission of the annual visitation. They likewise complained that the emperor arrogated an unconstitutional share in the decision of affairs, first, by employing imperial commissaries, and afterwards by referring the contested points to the Aulic council, whose proceedings were full of partiality and injustice. Finally, they inveighed against the efforts made by the pope and the Catholics to calumniate and represent the confession of Augsburgh as a proscribed religion. They concluded with some objections which were without foundation, if not frivolous, particularly to the article of the peace of religion, which prohibited the introduction of the Protestant poctrine into places where it was not professed at that period, and even the attempts of the emperor to introduce the Gregorian calendar.†

* John, count Palatine of Deux-Ponts, Ernest Frederic of Baden Durlach, George Frederic of Brandenburgh Anspach, and Joachim Ernest, son of the elector of Brandenburgh, and administrator of Magdeburgh, and the duke of Wirtemberg.

† The calendar, known by the name of the Gregorian, from pope Gregory XII., by whose order it was framed, rectified the Julian calendar, and introduced the new style, by striking off ten days, which the current year had then advanced before the real time. This reformation of the calendar, however correct and necessary, was adopted only by the Catholic princes and states ; but opposed by all the Protestants, because it originated from the pope. They continued to adhere to the ancient mode of computation, and they added, in the

As they could not induce the Lutheran chiefs to unite in the common cause, their efforts were of no avail; for great succours were granted to the emperor against the Turks, without any promise of redress. The united princes were not, however, discouraged, although deserted by the duke of Wirtemberg, whom the emperor had detached, by changing the tenure of his dominions from a mediate to an immediate fief, and, soon after the diet of Ratisbon, their number was increased by the junction of the duke of Brunswick, the landgrave of Hesse, the prince of Anhalt, and John, count of Nassau. Encouraged by these accessions, they not only continued to withhold their contributions, but even entered into a confederacy at Frankfort, on the 12th of December, 1598, which bears all the characteristics of a defensive if not offensive alliance, and by which they agreed to unite in resisting the aggressions of the pope, in maintaining their civil and religious rights, and in continuing to withhold their contributions till their grievances were redressed. Other circumstances contributed to strengthen their party, of which the most essential was the death of John George, elector of Brandenburgh, and the accession of his son, John Frederic, to their confederacy. They continued, in various meetings and negotiations, to increase their numbers, and give consistency and strength to their union; and the activity and perseverance of their chief, being seconded by the support of Henry IV., they formed, on the 12th of February, 1603, the celebrated offensive and defensive alliance of Heidelberg. Of this alliance the principal articles were a reciprocal engagement to unite in defence of their civil and religious liberties; to resist the unjust jurisdiction of the Aulic council, and the

celebrated list of grievances presented at the diet of Ratisbon, the complaint, that the pope and his nuncios, aided by the Jesuits, presumed to change the order of times and years.

It is easy to imagine the confusion which must have arisen from the use of the two calendars in an empire like Germany, where the diets and other national assemblies are held on stated days, and where one part of the people celebrated Easter, Whitsuntide, Christmas, and the commencement of the new year, ten days before the other; this confusion afforded fresh matter for complaints and disputes between the sovereigns and their subjects, and involved the states of the empire in continual disturbances.

resumption of the secularised property of the church.
The respective contingents in men and money were specified ; and deputies from the different princes were to form
a general council at Heidelberg for the conduct of their
affairs.   They demanded succours from the king of France
and from the United Provinces ; and they entered into a
correspondence with the disaffected subjects in the Austrian
dominions.   Still, however, the duke of Wirtemberg, the
electoral count of Saxony, and the count palatine of Neu-
burg, kept aloof, more from apprehensions of disobliging
the emperor, and from jealousy of a Calvinistic director,
than from sentiments of religion and equity ; nor could all
the efforts of Henry IV. overcome the repugnance, even of
those who had joined the union, to take decisive measures.

CHAP. XLI. — 1576–1609.

THE imperial court, less deterred by these threatening
appearances and the interference of France, than encouraged by the indecision of the united Protestants, and
stimulated by the incessant representations of Spain, not
only suppressed the Protestant worship in Austria, but
even attempted to annihilate the religious immunities so
long enjoyed by the natives of Hungary and Bohemia, and
pursued their designs against the Protestants in the empire
with a rashness bordering on infatuation.

In Bohemia, the administration of Rhodolph had commenced and for some time continued in peace; he conciliated his subjects, who, since the death of Louis, had not
been often gratified with the presence of their sovereigns,
by making Prague his principal residence, and from them
he obtained large and repeated contributions against the
Turks.   But the same impolitic intolerance which he had
hitherto adopted in Germany and Austria soon subverted
the happiness of his government in Bohemia.   Having
abolished the Protestant worship in Austria, the next object
of Rhodolph was to destroy that general liberty of con-

science in Bohemia which had been granted by his father, and to restore the purity of the Catholic religion. As he declined confirming the edicts of Maximilian, the compacts which only tolerated the Catholics and Calixtins continued in force; and he accordingly forbade all meetings of the Lutherans and Calvinists, declared them incapable of holding official employments, abolished the schools which had been founded for the instruction of their youth, and shut up the Protestant churches, or provided them with Catholic ministers. His next purpose was, to restrict the liberty granted to the Calixtins in such a manner as to prevent the Protestants from sheltering themselves under the appellation of Calixtins, and even to bring the Calixtins themselves back to the primitive doctrines of the church. In obedience to his orders or in conformity with his views, the archbishop of Prague held, in 1605, a synod of his clergy, in which all the decrees of the council of Trent were ordered to be received, and such severe restrictions were established, that, to use the expressions of the Bohemian historian, " the way to the Catholic church, instead of being opened, was shut up to the Protestants, and even the Calixtins themselves were driven from the pale of the church to the Lutheran profession, notwithstanding all the proscriptions with which it was loaded." These innovations spread mutual hatred and jealousy among all ranks and orders, and were attended with the same discontents against the sovereign as those regulations which had already produced such troubles in Austria and Hungary.

While Austria, Hungary, and Bohemia, were thus driven almost to insurrection, the same system was pursued among the Protestants in the empire, where the imperial court no longer deigned to colour its intolerant purposes with the semblance of law and justice, or to hold them forth as the merited chastisement of disobedience. The ban of the empire, which for five years had been suspended over Aix-la-Chapelle, was executed with the most rigorous and unrelenting severity. The electors of Treves and Cologne, the duke of Juliers, and the bishop of Liege, to whom the execution of the act was intrusted, made themselves masters of the town, expelled the Protestants from the magistracy, drove the two burgomasters into exile, by the imposition of exorbitant fines, and finally abolished the exercise of the Protestant religion.

Another dispute was evidently provoked by the Catholics, for the purpose of depriving Donawerth of its civil and religious liberties. Donawerth, situated in the Bavarian dominions, and formerly belonging to the Bavarian house, was at the peace of religion a Protestant and imperial city, and consequently entitled to the protection of that peace. A few of the inhabitants were Catholics, and the only Catholic religious establishment was a Benedictine abbey within the walls, wholly subordinate to the jurisdiction of the town. The friars enjoyed the undisturbed exercise of their religion, but were not allowed to make public processions, with the forms and ceremonies of their church, in the streets. After various attempts of the diocesan, the bishop of Wurtzburgh, to remove this restriction, the convent submitted for almost half a century, until the known views of the imperial court and the plans of the Jesuits encouraged the abbot to extort that permission by force which he could not obtain by persuasion.

Having succeeded in making some trifling encroachments on the established usage, the abbot, on the 16th of May, 1605, sent out a procession with torches, colours, and all the other pageants of the Catholic worship ; but it was stopped in the streets by order of the magistrates, the colours sent back to the convent, and the remainder suffered to proceed. This act was laid before the Aulic council, as a breach of the peace, by the bishop of Wurtzburgh, who in October obtained a citation requiring from the magistrates a justification of their conduct. The abbot received this citation, and kept it secret for several months, till an opportunity offered for reducing the magistrates to the alternative of disobeying the order or submitting quietly to the infringement of their jurisdiction ; and it was not delivered till the 28th of February, 1606, two hours before the commencement of a funeral procession. The magistrates remonstrated, and being unable to prevail on the abbot, suffered the ceremony to proceed without molestation, but soon afterwards sent a reply to the citation of the Aulic council, proving the incontestable right of their jurisdiction over the convent. While this affair was pending, the abbot prepared to repeat his former experiment at the ensuing festival of St. Mark. The magistrates finding all their remonstrances ineffectual, endeavoured to prevent a breach of the peace by enjoining the people to abstain from tumult or outrage, and to enforce the necessity of obedience, published the citation of the Aulic council. The procession passed without hindrance through the town ; but, on its return, was assailed by the populace, who demolished the pageants, and drove the friars and their attendants through the mud and mire back to their convent. This popular. commotion being represented by the bishop before the Aulic council in the most exaggerated colours, produced, on the 3rd of September, a new citation and a new reply from the magistrates, and a commission of inquiry, which was granted to Maximilian, duke of Bavaria. The Bavarian deputies arrived at Donawerth, April 23rd, 1607, two days preceding the anniversary of St. Mark, when the contest was renewed by the preparations of the abbot to repeat the procession, and they presented a letter from the emperor to the magistrates, announcing the purport of their commission, which was to prevent the Catholics from being insulted and disturbed in the exercise of their worship. This concurrence of circumstances, joined to the tenor of the letter, contributed still more to exasperate the populace. Notwithstanding all the attempts of the magistrates, they assembled tumultuously in the market-place, venting their fury in invectives against the emperor, the Aulic council, and the duke of Bavaria ; and the deputies, after prevailing on the abbot to relinquish the procession, hastened to quit the town, where they did not consider themselves in safety. The magistrates took instant measures to suppress the tumult, arrested two of the ringleaders, and sent a justification of their conduct, with expressions of regret, to the emperor and the duke of Bavaria. But notwithstanding this submission, and even the testimony of the Bavarian deputies, the imperial court was not inclined to relinquish so fair a pretext for the fulfilment of its plans. On the 3rd of August, 1607, the ban of the empire was issued against Donawerth, and the execution intrusted to the Duke of Bavaria, who was eager to recover possession of a place which had belonged to his family.

Having disdainfully rejected repeated proposals of accommodation, he sent an army against the town, and the magistrates, unsupported and unable to resist, surrendered on the condition of retaining their freedom of worship, and the maintenance of their civil rights. But under the frivolous pretence that the burghers had delayed fulfilling the conditions, the Bavarian troops took possession of the town in the name of their sovereign, abolished the Protestant religion, and delivered the churches to the Catholics. Thus, from an imperial and Protestant city, Donawerth was reduced to a Catholic and provincial town.*

The Protestants were naturally roused by these illegal proceedings of the Aulic council, in issuing, of its own authority, the ban against an imperial city and state of the empire. Their resentment was still further provoked by the violation of an established rule, in not committing the execution of the decree to the duke of Wirtemberg, as director of the circle of Suabia, but to the duke of Bavaria, a Catholic prince, and suffering him to appropriate the town. Nor was the conduct of Rhodolph on this occasion calculated to diminish their dissatisfaction; for, in reply to the remonstrances of the duke of Wirtemberg, he disdainfully warned him not to presume to protect a town under the ban, lest he should himself incur a similar fate.

The Protestants were at length convinced that their own disunion and indecision only exposed them to the aggressions of the imaerial court and the Catholics; and they saw that the critical moment was arrived when they must either resist by open force, or tamely suffer themselves to be stripped of the civil and religious immunities for which their ancestors had bled. They derived fresh courage and strength from the death of the duke of Wirtemberg, and

* The account of this transaction, however inconsiderable in itself, has been thus minutely given, as well from the importance of its consequences as because it has been garbled and misrepresented by the Catholics. Struvius, p. 1183. ; Barre, tom. ix. p. 360. ; Schmidt, b. iii. ch. 15.; and particularly Heinrich, vol. vi. p. 163-171., who has given a minute, perspicuous, and interesting account, principally drawn from the reports of the process.

the hearty attachment of his son John Frederic, and no less from the junction of the count Palatine of Neuburgh, who saw his claims on the succession of Juliers and Berg endangered by the entrance of Spanish troops into the country, and the disposition evinced by the imperial court to appropriate so important a territory.

In this situation of affairs, the diet being opened at Ratisbon, on the 12th of January, 1608, the discussions of a public assembly were not calculated to allay the resentment which the injuries and aggressions of the imperial court had awakened in the breasts of the Protestants. The appointment of Ferdinand, the bigoted duke of Styria, at the recommendation of the court of Spain, to preside, was considered as an additional insult.

The essential proposition of the emperor was the usual demand of succours against the Turks, to which were added, for the sake of form, four projects, for the reformation of justice, the public coinage, and the matricula, and an invitation to consider on the means of terminating the religious disputes. With a view to secure the desired succours, it was proposed to treat them according to the order in which they stood, and this plan was warmly supported by the imperial party; but the Protestants were too much inflamed and too powerful to be baffled or amused by this petty artifice. "Fifty years' experience," they exclaimed, "has taught us, that the imperial court always presses the decision of matters interesting to itself, and, having obtained its purpose, no longer cares for the redress of grievances." They therefore declared, that they would take no share in the deliberations of the diet, until the illegal jurisdiction of the Aulic council was abolished, Protestant assessors admitted into that tribunal, Donawerth re-established in its civil and religious rights, and all processes between the Catholic clergy and the Protestants annulled. Finally, they required, as an indispensable condition, that the plurality of suffrages should no longer be admitted in affairs of religion or the grant of subsidies. These pretensions gave rise to vehement discussions, till at length this diet, which was the most turbulent and stormy since the accession of Rhodolph, separated without deliberating on the affairs proposed for its consideration.

The diet was scarcely closed, when the chiefs of the Protestant confederacy assembled at Aschhausen, in Franconia ; they there established their confederacy for the term of ten years, arranged their specific contingents, re-appointed the elector Palatine their chief, and constituted as their generals prince Christian of Anhalt and the margrave of Baden Durlach. In 1609, the confederacy was augmented by the admission of Strasburgh, Nuremberg, Ulm, and other imperial towns ; and the united Protestants sent the prince of Anhalt, at the head of an embassy, to present a list of their demands to the emperor.

CHAP. XLII. — 1576–1606.

HUNGARY and Transylvania now claim our attention as the theatre of those events which led to a more important revolution than any before recorded in the Austrian annals.

The first object of Rhodolph had been to secure his dominions in Hungary against the Turks. In order to diminish the enormous expense of defending the distant fortresses on the side of Croatia, he transferred that country, as a fief of the empire, to his uncle Charles, duke of Styria, who, from the contiguity of his dominions, was better able to provide for its security. Charles accordingly constructed the fortress of Carlstadt, on the Kulpa, which afterwards became the capital of Croatia, and a military station of the highest importance. He also divided the ceded territory into numerous tenures, which he conferred on freebooters and adventurers of every nation, and thus formed a singular species of military colony. This feudal establishment gradually extended along the frontiers of Sclavonia and Croatia, and not only contributed, at the time, to check the incursions of the Turks, but afterwards supplied that lawless and irregular, though formidable military force, inured to and delighting in desultory warfare, who under the names of Croats, Pandours, and other barbarous appellations, spread such terror among the enemies of Austria on the side of Europe.

Another military community, which formed a part of
the same system, is no less remarkable for its daring enterprises and singular constitution than for being the cause of
a long and bloody war between the house of Austria and
the Turks, and the germ of those troubles which disturbed
the whole reign and ended in the deposition of Rhodolph.

During the reign of Ferdinand, several bodies of Christians, quitting the provinces which had been recently conquered by the Turks, obtained from the Austrian sovereigns a refuge at Clissa, in Dalmatia, under the condition
of forming themselves into a frontier militia continually in
arms against the infidels, and from their emigration, received the name of Uscocks, which, in the language of the
country, signifies wanderers. They fulfilled the purpose
of their establishment; and, being at length expelled by
the Turks, received a new asylum at Senga, a ruined
fortress in Croatia, on the coast of the Adriatic gulph.
Here their numbers increasing, by the accession of Italian
banditti and other marauders, they were rendered more
formidable than before; for they no longer confined their
predatory incursions to the land, but became pirates by
sea, and pushed their enterprises with that daring valour,
which, like the deeds of the American buccaneers, almost
surpasses belief. Their audacity increasing with success
and plunder, they pillaged, without distinction, the vessels
of all the nations who traded in the Adriatic. The Venetians, having in vain made repeated complaints to the
Austrian princes, took measures to expel this nest of
pirates, and their endeavours produced a short though
fruitless war with the Styrian line, which was terminated
by the interference of Philip II. But the most powerful
and important attack against this settlement was made by
the Turks, who suffered still more than the Venetians from
their aggressions.*

* As the fate of the Uscocks is lost in the more important transactions of the Austrian annals, we deem it necessary to gratify the curiosity of the reader, by observing, that their depredations, and the
protection afforded them by Ferdinand, duke of Styria, afterwards
emperor, involved him in a war with the Venetians, in which his ill
success compelled him to purchase peace, by sacrificing this predatory
horde. Segna was demolished, and the Uscocks being transplanted to
Carlstadt, soon lost their name and distinction.

Notwithstanding the armistice concluded with the sultan by Maximilian, and its renewal by Rhodolph in 1584 and 1591, a predatory warfare had never ceased along the frontiers. These contests were, however, not likely to produce an open rupture; for they were regarded, both by the Austrian and Turkish courts, not as a breach of the peace, but as excesses which could not be restrained, or as affording an exercise for personal bravery, and an employment for their turbulent subjects. At length, the constant aggression and the daring bravery of the Uscocks, could no longer be endured with the same indifference.

Amurath, having terminated his wars with Persia, took this opportunity to break the truce, which in 1591 he had concluded with Rhodolph, under the pretext of extirpating this band of robbers. With the connivance, if not the orders of the sultan, the bashaw of Bosnia made an irruption into Croatia, captured the fortresses of Wihitz and Petrina, and, in the following year, resuming his operations with a more considerable force, laid siege to Siseck, situated at the confluence of the Kulpa and the Save, with a view to open a route along the course of the Kulpa. The Austrians did not tamely submit to this invasion of their territories, but, assembling their forces at Carlstadt, attacked the Turks before Siseck, and totally defeated them with the loss of 12,000 men, among whom were the bashaw himself and a nephew of the sultan. Irritated by this defeat, and affected by the loss of his nephew, Amurath published a formal declaration of war, and poured his numerous hordes into Hungary and Croatia. The two following years were passed in various sieges and engagements, attended with alternate success and defeat; but the advantage ultimately rested on the side of the Turks, by the capture of Siseck and Raab.

In 1595, a more favourable though temporary turn was given to the Austrian affairs, by the defection of the prince of Transylvania from the Turks. On the elevation of Stephen Bathori to the throne of Poland, his brother Christopher succeeded him as waivode of Transylvania, and dying in 1582, left an infant son, Sigismond, under the protection of the Porte. Sigismond, who possessed the high spirit and talents of his family, had scarcely as-

sumed the reins of government, before he liberated himself from the galling yoke of the Turks, and in 1595 concluded an offensive alliance with the house of Austria, on
conditions highly honourable to both parties. He was to
retain Transylvania as an independent principality, the
part of Hungary which he still held, and Moldavia and
Wallachia, of which the waivodes had submitted to his
authority, and to receive the order of the golden fleece,
with the rank of a German prince. The conquests of both
parties were to be equally divided; Sigismond, if driven from
Transylvania by the Turks, was to receive a compensation
from Rhodolph ; and his territories were to revert to the
house of Austria, in failure of heirs male. The alliance,
after being confirmed by the states of Hungary and Transylvania, was cemented by the marriage of Sigismond with
Christina, daughter of Charles, duke of Styria.

By this important alliance the house of Austria was delivered from an enemy who had always divided its efforts,
and made a powerful diversion in favour of the Turks.
Sigismond signalised himself by his heroic courage and
military skill; uniting with the waivodes of Moldavia and
Wallachia, he defeated the grand vizir, Sinan, took Turgo-
vitch by storm, and drove the Turks back in disgrace towards Constantinople. Assisted by this diversion, the
Austrians in Hungary were likewise successful, and not
only checked the progress of the Turks, but distinguished
their arms by the recovery of Gran and Vissegrad.

This turn of success roused the sultan Mahomet, the son
and successor of Amurath, who inherited the warlike and
ferocious character of his ancestors. To restore the lustre
of his arms, he put himself, in 1596, at the head of his
forces, led them into Hungary, took Erlau, and defeating
the Austrians under the archduke Maximilian, the lateness
of the season alone prevented him from carrying his arms
into Austria and Upper Hungary, which were exposed by
the loss of Raab and Erlau. As Mahomet could not a
second time tear himself from the seraglio, the war was
carried on without vigour, and the season passed rather in
truces than in action. But this year, though little distinguished by military events, was memorable for the cession
of Transylvania to Rhodolph, by the brave yet fickle Si-

gismond, in exchange for the lordships of Ratibor and Oppelen in Silesia, with an annual pension. The emperor was acknowledged by the states, and the archduke Maximilian was appointed governor; but while he was about to take possession of his charge, he was anticipated by Sigismond, who under the influence of the same caprice which had induced him to abdicate, escaped from the languor of a private life, and easily regained his abandoned territory. Being soon disgusted with so troublesome a government, which he was unable to retain without becoming dependent on the Turks or the emperor, he again resigned in 1599 his dignity to his uncle, Andrew, cardinal bishop of Wermia, and retired into Poland, where he resided with his brother-in-law, the great chancellor Zamoiski. But the new prince did not long enjoy his precarious sovereignty; Michael, waivode of Wallachia, who, on the first abdication of Sigismond, had returned to his alliance with the sultan, was once more gained by the imperial court, and, after defeating the Turks, united his forces with the Austrians to expel Andrew from Transylvania. Andrew being defeated, and killed in his flight, Michael endeavoured to appropriate Transylvania; and a contest ensued between him and the imperial general Basta, in which he was worsted. Sigismond took advantage of these dissensions, again emerged from his retreat, and appearing in Transylvania, was joyfully received and acknowledged by his subjects, by whom, notwithstanding all his caprice, he was still beloved. Michael, however, reuniting with Basta against a prince whose presence was equally fatal to the pretensions of both, Sigismond was defeated with the loss of 10,000 men. To prevent a new contest for the sovereignty, the imperial general procured the assassination of his dangerous coadjutor; and on the 1st of March, 1602, Sigismond, again resigning his dignity, retired to Lobcovitz, in Bohemia, with an annual pension, under the protection of the emperor.* On this event Basta took possession of the country without opposition, received the allegiance of the natives, and, in the name of the emperor, confirmed, as before, all their civil and religious privileges.

* Sigismond continued in this retreat, and closed his turbulent life in tranquillity, in 1613. — Isthuanfius, lib. 22, 23.

His cruel and despotic administration driving the natives to despair, they found a chief in Moses Tzekeli, who, with other magnates, after ineffectually opposing the establishment of the Austrian government, had sought a refuge among the Turks. Tzekeli, at the head of his fellow exiles, assisted by bodies of Turks and Tartars, entered the country, was joined by numerous adherents, and, having obtained possession of the capital and the adjacent fortresses, was elected and inaugurated prince of Transylvania. His reign, however, was scarcely more permanent than that of his predecessor; for, before he could expel the Germans, he was, in 1603, defeated by the new waivode of Wallachia, and killed in the confusion of the battle. In consequence of this disaster, his followers dispersed, and Basta again recovered possession of the principality.

During these revolutions in Transylvania, Hungary had been the scene of incessant warfare between the Austrians and the Turks, which exhausted both parties with little advantage to either. The attention of Mahomet was too much occupied by frequent rebellions in his Asiatic dominions, and by mutinies of the turbulent janissaries, to carry on the war with effect; while, on the other side, the great obstacle to the progress of the imperial arms was, the want of money, which rendered it necessary to disband the troops at the close of every campaign. Hence the imperial generals had annually a new army to form; the troops were each season to be again inured to the Turkish tactics, and to the climate and diet of Hungary; and thus were lost the winter and commencement of spring, which, in the marshy soil of that country, were the most proper seasons for action.

Rhodolph had long lost the confidence of his Hungarian subjects. He never, like the former sovereigns, assisted at the diets, nor paid any attention to the interior and exterior concerns of the country; he neglected to fill the great civil and ecclesiastical offices, or conferred them on foreigners, and suffered the important charge of Palatine to remain vacant. He treated the complaints and remonstrances of his subjects with contempt and indifference; and the German troops being free from control, filled the country with devastation and pillage. While, however, he abandoned the civil and military affairs to chance, or to the will of his officers, he laboured to fetter his subjects with religious restrictions, and the most intolerant edicts were issued against the Protestants, in various parts of the kingdom.

Cassau, the seat of the government in Upper Hungary, which was remarkable for the number and prosperity of the Protestant inhabitants, was in a peculiar degree exposed to these persecutions. Twenty villages, belonging to the town, were occupied for the maintenance of the military; the governor Belgioso, not only prohibited the exercise of the Protestant worship, under pain of death, but, adding insult to cruelty, paraded the city with executioners in his train, and devoted to public punishment those who presumed to murmur against these violations of their rights.

Even in matters which did not relate to religion, the conduct of Rhodolph was equally impolitic. He suffered his rapacious generals to irritate the magnates, on whose good-will the peace and safety of the country more depended than on the strength of his army. Various estates, appropriated by the nobles during the troubles, were reclaimed by the fiscal of the crown; count Illeshasy, a Protestant, the most distinguished of these magnates in authority and influence, whose great civil and military services deserved a better reward, was deprived of two lordships, and, when he presumed to complain, was accused of high treason and driven into exile.

The disaffected increasing in numbers, soon found a leader in Stephen Botskai, the principal magnate of Upper Hungary, uncle of Sigismond Bathori, a noble of distinguished eloquence, enterprising spirit, and military skill. When he repaired to Prague, to represent the deplorable situation of his country, he was never admitted into the presence of the sovereign, and scarcely even of the ministers; and, while he was passing hours in the antechamber, was exposed to all the insults of the court minions. Such contemptuous treatment naturally irritated a man of high rank and independent spirit; but his resentment was still further inflamed, when, on his return, he found his estates plundered and devastated by order of the governor. Private

insults and injuries, thus added to public grievances, drove
him into rebellion; he appealed to his countrymen by a
spirited manifesto, in which he called upon them to extort
by force of arms that redress which was refused to their
remonstrances and complaints.

The people exulting in the prospect of speedy deliverance, flocked in crowds to his standard; he was joined by
numbers of heyducs, or foot soldiers, who deserted from
the imperial service, and soon found himself at the head of
a body of troops sufficient to lay under contribution the
estates of the Austrian partisans. On the first intelligence
of this revolt, Belgioso collected the troops scattered
in the vicinity of Cassau, and marched against him to
suppress the rising rebellion ; but the heyducs in his army
joining their brethren, the Germans were defeated with
great slaughter, and the capture of two generals. Encouraged by this success, the inhabitants of Cassau expelled the Austrian troops, and surrendered the town to
Botskai. This loss drew general Basta from Transylvania,
who, uniting with Belgioso, laid siege to Cassau, but the
want of provisions, and the approach of Botskai, compelled
him to retire, while the insurgents rapidly increased in
numbers, and made themselves masters of several fortresses
in the vicinity.

The discontents in Transylvania, arising from the same
causes as the rebellion in Hungary, greatly contributed to
the success of Botskai. After the death of Tzekeli, the
government of Basta becoming still more cruel and intolerant than before, the country was at once a prey to all
the terrors of despotism, and all the horrors of famine and
disease. All traces of human industry were swept away
from its once fertile plains and fruitful hills; towns and
villages offered nothing but the spectacle of ruin and desolation; corn was bought at the price of gold; horses, and
even domestic animals, were used as food; and, at length,
the people were driven to the tombs to seek a wretched
sustenance from the putrid bodies of their fellow creatures.
The most dreadful disorders were produced by these execrable aliments, and pestilence swept away many of those
who had escaped from famine and from the sword.

From these accumulated calamities the natives of Transylvania sought a deliverance, by applying to Botskai, who had been joined by the remnant of the Transylvanian exiles under Bethlehem Gabor. Botskai was not tardy in obeying their summons. Being in 1604 assisted by a Turkish army, which the new sultan, Achmet, despatched into Transylvania, he soon expelled the Austrians, and was formally inaugurated sovereign. Returning into Hungary in the ensuing year, he was received with regal honours by the Turkish army in the plain of Rakoz. Achmet sent him a club, a sabre, and a standard, and the grand vizir himself placed on his head a diadem which had been worn by the despots of Servia, and proclaimed him king of Hungary and prince of Transylvania. But Botskai was too disinterested or too prudent to accept the regal dignity, which he could not claim without the free choice of the nobles, or maintain without being dependent on the Turks; he therefore declared that he only accepted these honours as proofs of the sultan's friendship, and as the means of recovering the liberties and rights of his aggrieved countrymen. He acted, however, with the same vigour and activity as if he had a crown to acquire; before the close of the campaign he conquered all Upper Hungary, almost to the walls of Presburgh; at the same time the Turks reduced Gran, Vissegrad, and Novigrad; while his partisans threatened the frontiers of Austria and Styria, and made an irruption almost to Brunn, in Moravia.

Such was the deplorable state of affairs in a kingdom for which the Austrian princes had maintained nearly eighty years of continual contests, and drained the blood and treasures of their subjects. Almost all Hungary, with Transylvania, which had submitted to the sovereignty of Rhodolph, was possessed either by Botskai or the Turks; and, in another campaign, the house of Austria would not only have been deprived of the small remnant of its Hungarian possessions, but have seen the enemy in the very heart of its hereditary dominions. Nor was the state of those dominions such as afforded the slightest hope of resisting for a moment these accumulated dangers. Bohemia and Austria, with their dependencies, were exhausted and dispirited by a long succession of bloody contests; the people groaning under a despotic and intolerant government, and indignant at the violation of their civil and religious rights, were ready to hail the approach of Botskai, from whom, as a Protestant prince, they expected their deliverance. The empire likewise, which, in former and even recent periods, had poured forth men and treasures against the enemy of Christendom, was again divided by religious feuds, derived from the impolicy and intolerance of Rhodolph ; the Protestants, whom he had offended in the same manner as he had alienated his own subjects, not only withheld the contributions voted by the diet, but were now forming those combinations against their chief, which renewed the civil wars of Germany. The only ally on whom he was reduced to depend was the Spanish court ; but, in return for their assistance, he was compelled to become the dishonoured instrument of their policy, and, under their impulse, to adopt measures which aggravated his distress, and increased his unpopularity.

The astonishing apathy displayed by Rhodolph, in the midst of calamities and disorders sufficient to have roused the most stoical indifference, was derived from a change which had been gradually wrought in his character, manners, and temper. Unfortunately his love of science had induced him to patronise the celebrated Tycho Brahe, whose acquirements and character were exactly conformable to his own, and who dishonoured his great talents and real science by a superstitious attachment to the reveries of judicial astrology and alchemy. By his prognostications, Rhodolph was persuaded that his life would be endangered by one of his own blood. This prediction increased the natural distrust of his temper, and contributed to alienate him still more from his brothers and family. In order not to increase the number of his fancied enemies, he evaded the numerous matches which were proposed to him from all quarters ; notwithstanding all the instances of his mother, he declined the hand of Isabella, princess and apparent heiress of Spain, and endeavoured to prevent his brothers from marrying. This fear sunk so deeply into his mind, that he never made his appearance in public, nor attended the worship of the church ; he even caused covered galleries to be built, with oblique windows, that he might pass from his apartments to his stables and gardens, without being exposed to the danger of assassination. While his dominions were ravaged by the Turks, or desolated by civil war, while enemy on enemy was rising against him, he secluded himself in his palace at Prague, absorbed in gloom and suspicion, or haunted by all the apprehensions which prey on weak, indolent, and superstitious minds. He sought a refuge from his terrors in his favourite studies and occupations ; he spent his whole time among his astrologers, chemists, painters, turners, engravers, and mechanics, or in his botanical gardens, galleries of antiquities and natural history ; at his easel, or in his laboratories and observatory. He became hypochondriac and impatient, irritable almost to frenzy ; refused to admit foreign ambassadors ; drove even his confidential ministers from his presence ; and strangers, who were induced to visit the emperor of Germany, could not otherwise gratify their curiosity than by introducing themselves into his stables in the disguise of grooms. He resigned himself to the sway of low-born mistresses, whom he was continually changing ; and, abandoning the reins of government to his ministers and generals, relieved them from all fear of revision or control, by refusing to receive the remonstrances and complaints of his subjects.

CHAP. XLIII.— 1606–1609.

THE incapacity of Rhodolph, and the troubles which had resulted from his neglect of affairs, alienated his whole family, and induced Matthias, his brother and presumptive heir, to rescue his illustrious house from impending destruction, by wresting the reins of government from so feeble and inefficient a hand.

Matthias, the third son of Maximilian, was born in 1557, and, under the celebrated Busbequius, received an education far different from that which his brother owed to the Jesuits. He imbibed a considerable degree of learning and a general knowledge of the arts and sciences ; but his predominant passion was for the art of war and military exercises, in which he excelled : from the instructions of his enlightened preceptor, who had passed many years at the court of the sultan, he acquired an intimate acquaintance with the manners, customs, and tactics of the Turks, acquisitions which were of the greatest advantage to him when intrusted with the command of the imperial troops in Hungary.

His active, restless, and ambitious character was so incompatible with the cautious and suspicious temper of his brother Rhodolph, that they lived in perpetual bickerings. At length Matthias, whose mind panted for employment, entered into a secret connection with the contending chiefs of the Netherlands, and, contrary to the will of his brother, as well as the interests of Philip II., accepted the government of the insurgent provinces. He secretly quitted Vienna, in 1577, and, unexpectedly appearing at Antwerp, was installed as governor-general, and the prince of Orange appointed his lieutenant. But his authority was of short duration ; for the chiefs of the respective factions only wished to rule under his name ; for the States, who had called him to the government with the hope of obtaining foreign assistance, were disappointed when they perceived that he was not supported by his brother, or by the empire, and conferred the sovereignty on Francis, duke of Anjou, brother to the king of France. In 1580, Matthias resigned his difficult sovereignty with good humour, and received the public thanks of the States. Being left destitute of support, and unable to return home, or repair to Spain, he applied for the bishopric of Liege, through the interest of the prince of Orange ; but was thwarted by the interposition of the Spanish and imperial courts, and obtained with difficulty the grant of a pension from the States, which was ill paid and soon withdrawn. At length, by the mediation of his mother, he received permission to return into Austria, in 1581, yet he was not admitted into the presence of the emperor, and was compelled to take up his abode at Lintz, where he lived for some time in a state of humiliation, neglect, and penury. This abject state deeply affecting his sanguine and ardent mind, he offered to resign all pretensions to the Austrian succession, for the petty lordship of Steyer, as an independent establishment. On the death of Stephen Bathori, he presented himself, in 1587, as a candidate for the throne of Poland, but met with no encouragement, because the emperor gave his whole support to his younger brother Maximilian.

At length the embarrassments of Rhodolph compelling him to have recourse to the services of his humiliated brother, Matthias was appointed governor of Austria. He was, in 1593, intrusted with the command of the army in Hungary, where he signalised himself, on different occasions, against the Turks.

In 1595 he became, by the death of his brother Ernest, the presumptive heir to Rhodolph, and from that period seems to have held offices of high trust and command. But the suspicion which Rhodolph had conceived from his former conduct, and the jealousy arising from their discordant characters, was never obliterated; while the disgust which Matthias, on his part, fostered against his weak and imprudent brother, was aggravated by the refusal of Rhodolph to give him a proper establishment, and permit him to marry. He bore, however, these mortifications with more policy or patience than seemed consistent with his ardent temper, and, as administrator of Austria and governor of Hungary, performed essential services. At the same time he was silently preparing to avail himself of that crisis which he foresaw must soon arrive, from the impolicy and weakness of Rhodolph; he was careful not to create alarm or provoke opposition by a premature disclosure of his plans, till circumstances imperiously called for his presence. He laboured to conciliate his brothers and relatives, and to obtain the confidence of the Catholics; he also acquired the good-will of the Protestants, both in the empire and the Austrian territories, by affecting the candour and toleration of his father; and even when he had reduced the rebellious peasants of Austria by arms, he retained a claim on their gratitude, by softening the rigour of the conditions which Rhodolph had imposed.

He thus increased in popularity and influence, in proportion as Rhodolph sunk into contempt and ridicule; and when total ruin seemed to impend over the house of Austria, he was pointed out, by the hopes and wishes of all, as the only prince who could avert the impending calamities. At the commencement of the disastrous year of 1606, he held a meeting with his brother Maximilian, and his cousins Ferdinand and Maximilian Ernest, two princes of the Styrian line, and on the 25th of April, 1606, concluded with them a secret compact, by which, in consequence of the incapacity of Rhodolph, they declared him the head of their house, promised their counsel and assistance, and engaged to support his interests at the next election of a king of the Romans. This compact was soon afterwards confirmed by the archduke Albert, sovereign of the Low Countries.*

Matthias, though thus far successful in the most difficult part of his plan, could not avail himself of the compact until he was secure on the side of Hungary. He gained Illeshinsky, the prime minister of Botskai, by the offer of the dignity of palatine; and by his intervention, proposed to his master the most liberal terms, from a consciousness that Botskai was labouring under a mortal disorder. As the favourable tenor of these conditions, and the situation of both parties, did not admit of contention or delay, a peace was concluded at Vienna, on the 23rd of July. Botskai was to retain Transylvania, with the whole district of Hungary beyond the Teiss, the fortresses of Tokay and Zatmar, and the two provinces of Bereg and Ugotz, as an hereditary sovereignty, to revert, on his death without heirs, to the house of Austria. Matthias, in the name of the emperor, not only granted general toleration to the Protestants, whether Lutherans or Calvinists, but declared them eligible to all offices and dignities. The office of palatine was to be again restored, and all charges to be conferred only on natives. Finally both parties agreed to unite against the Turks, should they refuse to accede to honourable terms of peace.

Assisted by the intervention of Botskai, Matthias afterwards completed the pacification of Hungary, by concluding a truce with the sultan for twenty years, on the condition that both parties should retain possession of the territories which they then held. This truce did honour

---

* See this curious document in Goldastus, Appendix, p. 223.

to the spirit and vigour of Matthias, as it was the first instance in which the sultan had condescended to treat the emperor on terms of equality, or to address him by his acknowledged title. He was, however, to receive 200,000 dollars as a voluntary gift, which was not to be again repeated; and thus ceased the dishonourable tribute, which the two preceding princes of the house of Austria had paid to the enemy of Christendom.

Although Rhodolph had entrusted Matthias with full powers, and although the pacification of Vienna was necessary as well as advantageous, he expressed himself highly dissatisfied with its tenor, withheld his ratification, and even summoned a diet of the empire to demand succours for the prosecution of the war. This refusal was, however, of the utmost disadvantage to his interests; for Botskai dying soon after the conclusion of the peace, the people of Transylvania refused to return under the Austrian yoke, and chose Sigismond Ragotski, who was supported by the Turks; while a disaffected party in Hungary, attempting to prevent the incorporation of the ceded districts, furnished Matthias with a pretext for raising considerable levies of troops. Rhodolph was doubtless induced to adopt this measure from a discovery of the secret compact, and a suspicion of the purposes of Matthias, which could not long be concealed from so distrustful a sovereign. The king of Spain had never forgiven the conduct of Matthias in the Netherlands, and had watched, with a jealous eye, his connections with the Protestants; he therefore seized this opportunity to exert his influence over the timid mind of the emperor; and, by instigating him to bring forward his cousin Ferdinand, of the Styrian line, as his successor, obtained the co-operation of Maximilian and Albert. As the first step for the execution of this plan, Rhodolph appointed, on the 12th of January, 1608, Ferdinand his commissary to preside at the diet of Ratisbon, and endeavoured to excite the states of the empire against Matthias, by a rescript which contained a bitter condemnation of his conduct. He recapitulated all his acts of disobedience, from his imprudent enterprise in the Netherlands, to the conclusion of the peace; he not only stigmatised his real faults and ambitious purposes, but even inveighed against him for persecuting the Protestants, charged him with fomenting rebellion, and attributed to him all the disasters which were derived from the dilatory conduct of the war, and his own refusal to ratify the peace. He expatiated on his presumption, in concluding a dishonourable peace with the Turks ; on his traitorous correspondence in the empire; accused him of endeavouring to prevent the grant of the necessary succours against the common enemy of Christendom, and concluded this philippic with calling on the electors, as the pillars and supporters of the empire, to prevent the diminution of the imperial authority. At the same time he arrested an agent who had been sent by Matthias to the Protestant princes with a copy of the family compact; and, by this discovery, furnished a pretext for Ferdinand, and the other archdukes, to publish a formal renunciation of their agreement, and a protestation against the designs of Matthias.

Matthias had now no other alternative but to yield to his offended brother, or to carry his purposes into execution by open force. He proceeded, however, with the same adroit and measured policy which he had hitherto pursued, and gave to his disobedience the appearance of zeal for the fulfilment of public engagements, concluded under the authority of the emperor, and of a just resentment for unmerited injuries. In February, 1608, he assembled a diet of the Hungarian states at Presburgh, to which deputies from those of Austria were invited; and conciliated the whole body of Protestants by promising to those of Hungary a confirmation of their religious rights, and by granting various civil privileges, which were equally advantageous to both Catholics and Protestants. He therefore easily obtained from the diet a ratification of the peace of Vienna, and induced the states to conclude a confederacy with the deputies of Austria, by which they agreed to resist all who should contravene the execution of the peace, and bound themselves to consider as their enemies all who should injure or attack any member of the league. He then repaired to Vienna, obtained the consent of the Austrian states to the confederacy of Presburgh, and even drew from them a grant of subsidies for the pay of troops, which he was levying to quell the discontents

in Hungary. With his usual good fortune he even succeeded in this object: he renewed the truce with the
bashaw of Buda; by his connections with the Protestant
chiefs, he not only pacified the discontented nobles in Hungary, who were on the point of placing a rival on the
throne, but gained even from them a considerable accession of strength; and left the Transylvanians to exhaust
themselves by their mutual contentions. He thus freed
himself from enemies who would have embarrassed all his
operations if they had not frustrated his enterprise, and
was enabled to direct his whole attention to the execution
of a design which he had matured with such address and
perseverance. Having next gained the Moravians, by
means of the Protestant nobles, who were dissatisfied with
the emperor, the states of the province, in an assembly at
Ewanczitz, acceded to the confederacy of Presburgh. He
thus obtained a virtual if not a formal declaration of war
against his brother; and at the same time collected troops
from all quarters to prosecute his advantages, and avail
himself of the confederacy.

The impending danger did not for some time rouse Rhodolph from his apathy, and he neglected the wise remonstrances of his experienced generals to levy troops, and
crush the rebellion in its infancy. At length he made
tardy preparations for resistance, by drawing troops into
Moravia, and appealing to the states of the empire; but
this measure contributed to ruin his declining cause; for
his levies, though too feeble to render effectual assistance,
aggravated by their licentiousness the discontents in Moravia, and increased the party of his rival. As a last
effort, Rhodolph endeavoured to deprive Matthias of the
pretext, under which he cloked his designs, by sending to
him the cardinal bishop of Olmutz, with a promise to
ratify the peace of Vienna, provided he would dissolve the
confederacy of Presburgh, and follow the example of the
other archdukes in renouncing the family compact. He
offered pardon for all past offences, and promised to hold a
meeting within six months, to enter into a negotiation with
his brother and the states of his different dominions.

But the plans of Matthias being now matured, he did
not suffer himself to be amused with vague proposals. He

replied, that far from wishing to disturb, his intention was to restore the peace of the house of Austria and Christendom ; that his brother, if desirous, might ratify the treaty of Vienna, at a place where he purposed to assemble the principal members of the Austrian states, and where all things might be arranged which related to the safety or grandeur of the family. After appointing Znaim, in Moravia, for the rendezvous of his troops, he left Vienna at the head of 10,000 men ; and, before he quitted Austria, issued an appeal for the purpose of justifying his conduct, and conciliating the Bohemian states. " I could not," he said, " see with indifference the ruin of my illustrious house. To obviate the troubles derived from the delay in ratifying the peace of Vienna, I formed an union at Presburgh between the states of Hungary and Austria, to which the accession of Bohemia and its dependencies is required ; and as the Moravians have already joined the confederacy, I trust that the states of the kingdom, with its other dependencies, will assemble at Czaslau, where I shall appear on the 4th of May, to concert measures for completing this necessary arrangement."

Continuing his march, he found the states of Moravia assembled at Znaim, and was received with general acclamations. He halted a few days to complete the junction of his forces, and when his army amounted to 25,000 men, he passed the frontiers of Bohemia. In his route he was met by two ambassadors from the electors of Saxony and Brandenburgh, who endeavoured to suspend his progress, by declaring that their sovereigns would assist the emperor with their whole force, and by a deputation from the Bohemian states, demanding an explicit declaration of his purposes. But these threats and entreaties had no effect on a prince of so decisive and enterprising a temper, who was sensible that the success of his design solely depended on vigour and celerity ; he briefly replied, that he would arrange the business, and declare his intentions at Czaslau.

Reaching Czaslau on the 10th of May, and finding none of the Bohemian states assembled, he repeated his former summons ; he was instantly obeyed by those whose lands were exposed to his arms, and by those whom his presence encouraged to declare their attachment to his cause. Here he no longer concealed his purposes ; but to those few who appeared announced his resolution to demand the government of Hungary, Austria, and Bohemia, and security for his undisturbed succession after the death of his brother. Without wasting his time in unnecessary delays or useless discussions, he rapidly continued his march towards Prague.

Rhodolph was awakened from his dream of indolence by the first reply of Matthias. The approach of danger increased his alarm ; and when his brother entered Bohemia, he summoned a meeting of the states at Prague. The whole kingdom was instantly in motion ; for all the members of the states, except count Thurn, and a few discontented Protestants, obeyed the summons. Rhodolph, who had so long secluded himself within the precincts of his palace, was induced to open the assembly in person, and the curiosity of the populace, who doubted the existence of their sovereign, could not be gratified till the covered galleries which formed the principal communications of his palace were demolished, that he might be exposed to public view in his passage. This meeting, consisting of so many different sects, surrounded by dangers and alarms, was a scene of altercation and violence. The Protestants, who formed the majority, took this opportunity to extort from the necessities of Rhodolph those civil and religious indulgencies which they could not otherwise obtain. They demanded a general toleration, which had been granted by Maximilian, but not confirmed by Rhodolph, with the abolition of the compacts, except the article relative to the communion under two kinds, and the permission to build churches, and to have their own burial grounds. They required the exclusion of foreigners from civil and ecclesiastical offices, that priests should not be allowed to interfere in political affairs, and that the Jesuits should not purchase lands without the approbation of the three estates. These and other articles were subscribed by two hundred lords and three hundred knights, and by all the deputies of the towns, except those of Pilsen, Budweis, and Kathen. A nobleman, who ventured to express his disapprobation, was threatened to be hurled from the window ; and the subscribers bound themselves to punish severely those who should oppose the confirmation of their demands, and to embrace the party of Matthias, should the emperor refuse his ratification.

In the midst of these transactions, ambassadors arrived from the camp of Matthias; they declared, that his reason for entering Bohemia with an armed force was to compel the weak and indolent emperor to cede to him the crown of Bohemia, and retire into the Tyrol ; and promised, in his name, to confirm all the privileges of the nation. Emboldened by this offer, the members of the states flocked to the palace, tumultuously requiring to be admitted into the presence of their sovereign. When Rhodolph appeared, count Schlick, the head of the Protestant party, delivered to him the articles before detailed, and requested him, in the name of the states, to confirm them. Rhodolph replied, that he must take some time to consult with his ministers, before he could give an answer to such important points ; but they pressed their demand with such vehemence, that the emperor with alarm and amazement exclaimed, " What must I do ? " They replied, that he must quickly declare whether he would or would not consent to their request; and Rhodolph, whose situation did not admit of delay, confirmed most of the articles, but contrived to refer those relating to religion to the ensuing diet.

The deputies and the populace were thus satisfied, and troops, flocking from all quarters to Prague, in a few days formed an army of 36,000 men. The natives, exasperated against the Austrians and Hungarians for the depredations which they had committed in their passage, called upon the emperor to expel Matthias from the country ; but the archdukes Ferdinand and Maximilian, the papal nuncio, and the German princes, recommended an accommodation. Rhodolph, whose spirit sunk under his calamities, consented ; and his ambassadors met those of Matthias at Dubertz, between Prague and his camp. As the deputies of Matthias claimed the confirmation of his succession to the crown of Bohemia, and even insisted that the administration should be immediately vested in him, the conference was broken off, and Matthias advanced still nearer to Prague. On his approach, the inhabitants took up arms, and occupied the Ziskaberg, while the rest of the troops were posted on the surrounding eminences. Skirmishes ensued between the irregulars on both sides; but, as the two armies were on the point of engaging, overtures were again made, and accepted by Rhodolph. The same ambassadors met at Lieben, and, after a negotiation of four days, finally agreed that Rhodolph should cede to Matthias Hungary, Austria, and Moravia, deliver up to him the Hungarian crown and regalia, and confirm the pacification of Vienna; that the states, at the request of the emperor, should declare Matthias his successor to the crown of Bohemia, should he die without issue male, under the condition of ratifying their rights and privileges; and that Matthias should assume the title of appointed king of Bohemia. At the conclusion of this agreement, the crown and sceptre of Hungary being surrendered by order of Rhodolph, Matthias, with great pomp, received them at the head of his army. He soon afterwards quitted Bohemia, and made his triumphant entry into Vienna.

Matthias found it a much easier task to wrest a sovereignty from his indolent and distrustful brother than to satisfy the claims of those whom he had incited by promises and encouragements to revolt. His embarrassments commenced with the first measures of his government. He assembled, on the 12th of July, 1608, the states of Austria to receive their allegiance; but the Protestants, who formed the majority, refused to comply, till he had reestablished the toleration which had been abolished by Rhodolph, and restored many of the civil privileges, of which they had been deprived. The Protestants of the district above the Ems, instead of waiting for his answer, re-established their worship in Lintz, Steyer, and Gemunden; and the lord of Inzendorf, a town near the capital, opened his church to the burghers. Matthias was greatly perplexed by this conduct; for he was not influenced by the liberal principles of his father, nor even inclined to fulfil the promises which he had lavished to purchase the assistance of the Protestants. He therefore arrested the lord of Inzendorf, and commanded his church to be closed; he required from the states a simple homage, unaccompanied by any capitulation; and he endeavoured to justify himself by the quibbling assertion, that as the cession of

Rhodolph had conferred on him an hereditary title, he was
no more obliged to enter into a capitulation than Rhodolph
himself. He attempted to pacify them by a vague and
general promise, that he would confirm all their privileges;
but, at the same time, expressed his resolution to extort
their homage by force.

The Protestants had too recently seen the example of
successful rebellion in Matthias himself, to be alarmed at
his threats, or satisfied with his cajolery. They therefore
retired from Vienna to Horn, and sent a message to the
Catholics, warning them not to yield a separate homage;
they, at the same time, ordered a levy of every fifth man,
occupied and provisioned several of the neighbouring fortresses, claimed the assistance of the Hungarians and Moravians, in virtue of the confederacy of Presburgh, and
leagued with the united Protestants of the empire.

Such being the serious aspect of affairs in Austria,
Matthias hastened to Presburgh with a view to detach the
Hungarians, and prevent the confederacy of Presburgh
from proving as fatal to himself as it had been to his
brother. He made a triumphant entry into the capital,
and carried back the sacred crown and regalia, of which
the kingdom had been deprived seventy years, with a
pomp and splendour, which were calculated to dazzle the
imaginations and flatter the prejudices of his subjects.
But the states were not to be captivated with pageants;
sensible of the value of their support, they determined not
to grant it, except on the confirmation of those privileges,
which he had promised when governor; and they digested
their claims into a regular capitulation which they presented to him for his acceptance. It contained a full toleration for the Lutherans and the Calvinists, and confirmed
their eligibility to all offices of the state. All posts of
trust or honour were to be immediately taken from foreigners, and, in future, conferred on none but natives.
The crown of St. Stephen, and the regalia, were to be
deposited at Presburgh, and guarded by laics; a palatine
was to be immediately chosen from four candidates equally
taken by the king from Catholics and Protestants. The
king was to reside in Hungary, but, if absent, on important
occasions, the government was to be vested in the palatine

and council of regency, chosen jointly by his majesty and the states. In addition to these stipulations, the Jesuits were not to be admitted into the kingdom, and the authority of ecclesiastics was to be lessened. The foreign troops were to evacuate the country, on the conclusion of a peace with the Turks; no German garrisons were to be admitted into the Hungarian fortresses, except Raab and Commora, and even in those places the commander was to be a native Hungarian; finally, war was not to be declared without the consent of the states.

Conditions so hostile to the regal prerogative were far from being grateful to Matthias; but his newly acquired dignities depended on his decision. His Austrian subjects were in open revolt, the Moravians were inclined to join them, and the least hesitation would have added the Hungarians to his enemies. Rhodolph was secretly tampering with his former subjects, and was ready to recover their allegiance, by the restoration of privileges which he had before abolished; above all, Matthias had reason to dread the returning partiality, which, after the first impulse of rebellion, subjects naturally feel for a deposed sovereign. He was therefore reduced to the necessity of signing these conditions, however galling to his feelings or derogatory to his dignity, and to carry them into immediate execution. Though reluctant, he removed the Germans from those posts which were the reward of their faithful services to his family, to confer them on natives, whose fidelity was doubtful; Illeshasy was elected palatine, and was the first Protestant ever raised to that important office. These and the other conditions being scrupulously fulfilled, Matthias was unanimously elected, and on the 19th of November, inaugurated in the usual forms.

This compliance produced the desired effect. The states of Hungary, having secured their own privileges, were unwilling to irritate Matthias, by supporting the interests of others; they, therefore, returned a repulsive answer to the Austrian deputies, exhorting them to make peace with their sovereign, and declaring, that their union was not merely confined to the Protestants, but extended equally to the Catholics.

Having thus arranged this delicate transaction, Matthias

returned to Vienna with the resolution of quelling the Protestant revolt. Instigated by the papal legate, by his cousin Leopold, bishop of Passau, and above all, by his favourite and confidential adviser, Melchior Klesel, bishop of Vienna, and encouraged by the loyalty of the Catholics, who armed in support of his cause, he denounced immediate vengeance against all the Protestants if they persisted in their rebellion. But though he had evaded one difficulty, by conciliating the Hungarians, he had not relieved himself from all. The Moravians, who had been equally applied to by the Austrian malecontents, proffered their mediation, and evinced a resolution to support their Protestant brethren; and he had reason to apprehend that the German Protestants would interfere in the dispute. He therefore prudently accepted the mediation of the Moravian states, and, after some conferences, agreed, on the 19th of March, 1609, to the celebrated capitulation, which restored to the Austrian Protestants all the religious privileges and immunities which they had enjoyed under Maximilian. This accommodation was followed by the general homage of all the Austrian states.

CHAP. XLIV. — 1609–1612.

HAVING thus relieved himself from these embarrassments, Matthias returned into Hungary to keep his turbulent subjects in awe, and was making preparations for the recovery of Transylvania, when the conduct of his brother again recalled him into Bohemia.

The privileges which the Protestants of Austria, Hungary, and Moravia had obtained from Matthias, excited the hopes of their brethren in Bohemia, who aspired to recover all the religious immunities which had been granted by Maximilian and abolished by Rhodolph. Confiding in their numbers, encouraged by the degraded situation of Rhodolph, and secretly abetted by Matthias, they resolved to extort, by force of arms, what they could not obtain by petitions and remonstrances.

When the troops of Matthias had evacuated Bohemia, Rhodolph, in compliance with his promise, summoned a diet to take into consideration the affairs of the kingdom. The Protestants refused to enter upon the discussion of civil affairs, until the freedom of religious worship was unequivocally granted; but the emperor, who had not learnt prudence even from adversity, replied, that he would not contravene the ancient laws, which tolerated only the Catholics and Calixtins; and declared that the religious freedom, granted by Maximilian, was no longer in force. He failed in dividing by this subterfuge the real Calixtins from the Protestants; for the former, foreseeing that their privileges would expire with the exclusion of the other sects, wisely declared themselves in union with the Protestants; but Rhodolph, encouraged by the Catholics, and impelled by the baleful influence of the Jesuits, persisted in rejecting their demands.

After much altercation and clamour, the diet was dissolved without coming to any conclusion. Before the separation, however, the Protestants, who formed the majority, indicated the meeting of a new diet, on the 4th of May, in the council house of the new town of Prague, and sent deputies to Matthias and the Protestant princes of Germany, imploring their mediation and support. They assembled at the appointed time and place, notwithstanding the prohibition of their sovereign, conducted the proceedings in the usual forms, by requiring the attendance of the great officers of state, and prepared to reiterate their demands of religious toleration, if not to extort the acquiescence of Rhodolph by force.

An alarm being either accidentally or purposely spread, that troops were advancing to disperse them, the whole party was instantly in motion : and, in less than half an hour, a body of 1200 horse, composed of the deputies and their retainers, and 10,000 of the populace were in arms. This incident convincing the emperor of the popularity of their cause, and the strength of their party, he endeavoured to pacify them by vague and contradictory promises. His offers inflamed instead of allaying the ferment; the Protestants proceeded to organise a system which might enable them to extort the fulfilment of their demands, and which they termed

" a plan for the defence of their king and country, and the preservation of their civil and religious rights." They decreed the levy of an army, of which they nominated Henry, count of Thurn, and two other nobles, their generals, and appointed thirty directors or deputies, representing the three estates, to act as a permanent council. Finally, they strengthened their cause, by concluding a confederacy with the deputies who had been sent by the states of Silesia to Prague, to obtain freedom of worship.

The effects of this confederacy were instantaneous; the decree was scarcely issued before the generals levied a force of 3000 foot and 2000 horse, and this number was rapidly increasing. The emperor, who had drawn the storm on his head without the means of resistance, still persevered in his infatuation, and was with difficulty induced to yield to the remonstrances of his Catholic counsellors, and even of the Spanish ambassador. At last the apprehension of a new appeal to his brother, extorted from him what neither justice nor policy could before induce him to grant; he signified his unqualified assent to all the demands of his subjects, by the publication of a royal letter, or edict, bearing date July 5. 1609. To all members of the states, who received the communion under two kinds, (under which general expression all Protestants were included,) he granted a full toleration of religious worship, to the same extent as it had been conferred by Maximilian. They were to enjoy the power of building churches and founding schools; to have their own ecclesiastical consistory; and, as a security for their religious privileges, were to choose certain chiefs, under the title of defenders of their faith, who were to be confirmed by the sovereign, and whose office was to watch over the affairs of religion and prevent any infringement of this edict. Finally, to preclude all possibility of change or abrogation, a clause was annexed, declaring null all future ordinances contrary to this act, issued either by the sovereign or his successors.*

The Protestants, however gratified by these concessions, did not lay down their arms until they had obtained similar conditions for their fellow confederates, the Silesians.

* Pelzel, p. 653. ; Goldastus has preserved this curious document, vol. ii. append. p. 368.

They then endeavoured to restore tranquillity, by concluding an agreement with the Catholics for a general amnesty,
and entering into engagements for the preservation of
peace, which were signed by the king, and all the members of the states, except two Catholic nobles, William of
Slavata, and Yaroslaf of Martinetz. In consequence of
this accommodation, the churches where the Protestant
worship had been performed were again opened, and even
in the same villages, instead of mutual jealousy and persecution, the different sects again offered up their respective
devotions in mutual cordiality and forbearance.

Humbled and dishonoured in his own dominions, Rhodolph could not turn his eyes to Germany without behold-
ing new dangers and new humiliations, derived from the
same negligence and the same perverse system of policy
which had given rise to his recent disgraces. In the midst
of his contest with the Bohemians, the embassy from the
united Protestants reached Prague on the 20th of May,
1609. The prince of Anhalt laid before him the list of their
grievances, launched out into the bitterest expressions against
his indolence and the corruption and incapacity of his ministers, and stigmatised, with the most mortifying severity,
his refusal to ratify the peace with the Turks. After a
long and laboured invective, he required him to restore
Donawerth to all its civil and religious rights ; to rescind
the iniquitous processes of the Aulic council ; to reform
that tribunal, and the council of regency, by removing the
corrupt and inefficient members, and admitting in their
stead others chosen equally from the Protestants and Catholics, who should be recommended by the electors as more
experienced in the affairs of the empire, and more inclined
to pacific measures. He concluded with a threat, that, if
these requests were not granted, the evangelical states
would, under the protection of God, take upon themselves
the redress of their grievances.

An equivocal and frivolous answer being returned to
these urgent demands, the prince obtained a second audience. Rhodolph, contrary to his custom, opened the conference by observing, " that he had ordered an answer to
be expedited, which he trusted would be satisfactory, as he

was greatly embarrassed with other affairs ; at the same
time he expressed the hope, that his prince would use his
endeavours to pacify his co-estates, and prevent a repeti-
tion of similar remonstrances." The prince replied in a
language which seldom meets the ear of a sovereign, and
which must have been peculiarly galling to Rhodolph, who
in his seclusion was surrounded only by low-born favourites, or obsequious ministers : " As I fear," he said, " that
this answer will rather tend to prolong the dispute than to
tranquillise the united princes, I am bound in duty to represent to your imperial majesty the dangerous flame which
I now see bursting forth in Germany, and of which the
affair of Donawerth, and the contested succession of Juliers
and Cleves, are the principal causes ; while the Bohemian
commotions are far from being appeased, and a new storm
is gathering in Austria. Your counsellors are ill adapted
to extinguish this rising flame ; those counsellors who have
brought you into such imminent danger, and who have
nearly destroyed public confidence, credit, and prosperity,
throughout your dominions. I must likewise exhort your
imperial majesty to take all important affairs into consideration yourself, entreating you to recollect the example of
Julius Cæsar, who, had he not neglected to read the note
presented to him as he was going to the capitol, would not
have received the twenty wounds which caused his death."
The last remark was a thunder-stroke to the terrified imagination of Rhodolph, who was continually disturbed by
astrological predictions ; nor was he tranquillised until he
had extorted from the prince repeated assurances, that the
allusion to Julius Cæsar was not intended as a threat of
assassination, and that he was unacquainted with any plots
in Bohemia and Austria not already known to the public.
After many representations and remonstrances, the emperor at length delivered a more specific answer ; he promised to expedite the proceedings of the Aulic council, in
such a manner that the princes should have no just cause
of complaint, to ameliorate his administration, and to restore Donawerth to its former condition within four
months, or as soon as the 300,000 florins, demanded by
the duke of Bavaria for the reimbursement of his expenses.

should be repaid.* The fulfilment of these promises, if it was ever intended, was prevented by the civil troubles which soon afterwards arose in the empire, and continued during the remainder of Rhodolph's reign. The principal cause of these troubles was the contest for the succession of Cleves and Juliers, alluded to by the prince of Anhalt.

John William, duke of Cleves, Juliers, and Berg, count of La Marc and Ravensberg, and lord of Ravenstein, dying March 25. 1609, without issue, his succession was contested by various claimants. The first was Joachim Frederic, elector of Brandenburgh, in right of his deceased wife, Anne, for his eldest son, Ernest. She was daughter of Maria Leonora, the eldest sister of the late duke, who espoused Albert, duke of Prussia, and in whose contract of marriage it was stipulated that, in failure of heirs male, the whole succession should revert to her and her heirs. The second was Philip Louis, count palatine of Neuburgh, in right of his wife Anne, second sister of the deceased duke, by whom he had a son, Wolfgang Louis. The third and fourth were, John, duke of Deux Ponts, and Charles of Austria, margrave of Burgau, who had married Magdalen and Isabella, the two other sisters; but they soon ceased to prosecute their claims.

The princes of the house of Saxony at the same time claimed this succession on two grounds: first, in virtue of a grant of reversion, or eventual succession to Juliers and Berg, given in 1483, by Frederic III., to Albert, head of the Albertine line, and by other grants of Maximilian I., which extended the same right to the Ernestine line. On the first grant Christian, elector of Saxony, founded his pretensions, as lineal descendant from Albert; and, on the other, the princes of the Ernestine line, who strengthened their pretensions by adducing their descent from Sibilla, eldest daughter of John III., duke of Cleves, wife of John Frederic, elector of Saxony, by whose marriage contract the succession was to devolve on her heirs, in failure of issue to her family.

These complicated pretensions were rendered still more perplexed by two declarations of the emperor, Charles V.;

* The account of this singular interview is circumstantially given by Schmidt, from the documents of the times, vol. viii. p. 271-278.

the first giving the whole succession to the princes of the
house of Saxony, who were descended from Sibilla ; the
second rendering it a female fief, revertible to daughters,
and to their male heirs, if they were not living when the
succession became open ; the intricacy was increased by
another declaration of Ferdinand, which made the whole
inheritance indivisible, and established the succession according to the right of primogeniture.   If these territories
were to be considered a female fief, which seems to be incontestable, they ought to have been divided between the
four sisters, or their descendants ; but as this was a cause
which was to be decided by force rather than by right, the
claims of the two younger sisters were lost in those of the
two elder, who had married into more powerful families,
and the house of Saxony was enabled to render valid the
pretensions derived from the grants of the emperors.

   The elector of Brandenburgh, and the prince palatine
of Neuburgh, at the same time took possession of the inheritance, and mutually contested their pretensions with a
warmth which threatened immediate hostilities ; while the
elector of Saxony appealed to the emperor, and received
from him assurances that he would favour his claims, if
not a promise that he would grant the eventual investiture.
At the same time Rhodolph issued an edict, declaring that
the territories ought to be put in sequestration till the disputes should be terminated ; he ordered the two princes to
evacuate the places which they had occupied, and cited
them, with the other claimants, to appear before his tribunal within four months, and allege their respective
pretensions.

   The two princes, alarmed at the very mention of a sequestration, and suspecting that the emperor either designed
to appropriate these fiefs himself, or to confer part of them
on the elector of Saxony, hastily terminated their dispute,
by the mediation of the landgrave of Hesse ; and, at Dortmund, on the 10th of June, 1609, entered into a treaty to
share the administration jointly, and to unite their forces
against all who should attempt to appropriate the succession.   In consequence of this agreement, the prince Palatine, and Ernest, prince of Brandenburgh, repaired to
Dusseldorf, obtained from the states of the country a con-

firmation of the treaty of Dortmund, and received the homage of the natives, as possessors of the territory, "without prejudice to the rights of the other claimants."

While they secured Cleves, Wesel, Duisburgh, and other places of importance, the emperor annulled the treaty of Dortmund, and published a mandate, commanding the states and people not to acknowledge any of the claimants before he had given his award, under pain of the imperial ban; he followed this declaration, by despatching the archduke Leopold, bishop of Passau and Strasburgh, to assume the administration. Leopold being admitted into Juliers, by a party hostile to the claimants, issued a writ, declaring the territory under sequestration, obtained some of the neighbouring towns and districts, raised troops, and made preparations for defence.

The conduct of Rhodolph, in placing the sequestrated territories in the hands of one of his own family, joined to the known views of the Spanish court to exclude the Protestants from a district so contiguous to the Low Countries, if not to annex it to the dominions of the house of Austria, changed the dispute, from an abstract question of right, into a political and religious contest; from an opposition of the successful claimants against the head of the empire, to a general league of the Protestant body against the house of Austria and the Catholics.

The cause of the Protestants was soon supported by foreign powers, but none interfered with more promptitude and effect than Henry IV. Besides political interests, which urged him to humble the house of Austria, he had long entertained a personal antipathy against the Spanish branch, whose interference in the affairs of France prolonged the troubles of the league, and nearly prevented his accession to the throne. This antipathy likewise extended to the German branch, as well from the connection of interests with those of the Spanish court, as from frequent attempts to suppress the Protestant cause, which he still favoured, though to pacify his country he had been induced to profess the Catholic faith. The weakness of Rhodolph, the divisions in his family, his unpopularity no less in Germany than among his own subjects, presented the most favourable opportunity for the humiliation of the

German branch; and the dispute relative to Juliers fur-
nished Henry with a pretext to form an alliance with the
Protestant states, and to pour his troops into the empire.
While he was thus preparing his first attack against the
German branch, he was no less watchful to complete the
execution of his great plan, by dismembering the Spanish
dominions; he gained Paul V. by the offer of Naples,
and the duke of Savoy by that of Milan; he secured the
Venetians, who were engaged in constant disputes with the
Styrian line, relative to the demarcation of the frontiers
and the depredations of the Uscocks, by the tender of
Sicily; and he is said to have lured the Swiss with the
hopes of acquiring Alsace, Franche Comté, and the Tyrol.
At the same time he strengthened his cause by negotiations
with England and the principal Protestant states of Europe,
who were alarmed by the exorbitant power and domineering principles of Spain, and dreaded the danger which
might arise from the probable union of the whole house of
Austria. He had been long collecting funds sufficient for
supporting several campaigns, and at this juncture, had
assembled a considerable force on his frontiers, which at
the first signal was ready to burst into Germany.*

Henry had already formed connections with the princes
who composed the Protestant confederacy, and used all his
endeavours to excite them against the house of Austria.
But their well-founded jealousies presented an insuperable
obstacle to his design; for, though willing to raise the
Protestant on the ruins of the Catholic interest, and to
reduce the imperial authority and prerogatives, they were
yet averse to engage in measures which might render them
and the German empire dependent on France, and place
over them a chief who, from his power and abilities, was
far more dangerous than Rhodolph. They therefore re-

---

* The plan of Henry IV. to reduce the house of Austria, and the
secrecy in which his designs were enveloped, have occasioned a variety
of conjectures relative to his ultimate object. Among others, it has
been asserted, that he had projected the formation of Europe into a
christian republic, consisting of five hereditary kingdoms, France,
Spain, Great Britain, Sweden, and Lombardy, and other smaller
states. But the romantic extravagance of this plan carries with it its
own refutation.

fused to contract any general engagement, and would only agree to an alliance, of which the sole object was, to arrange the succession of Juliers.

Meanwhile the encroachments made by the emperor increased, and the contest for the succession of Juliers furnished new causes of alarm to the united Protestants. They accordingly again assembled at Hall, on the 27th of January, 1610, and arranged their celebrated union. In addition to their former resolutions for procuring the redress of grievances, and for maintaining their civil and religious rights, they entered into specific engagements relative to the succession of Juliers, by agreeing to maintain the treaty of Dortmund, expel the imperial administrator, terminate the sequestration, and finally, to effect such an arrangement as should not be disadvantageous to the Protestant interest. They received also an ambassador from the king of France, with whom they concluded an alliance, by which they were to be supported by a succour of 10,000 men, for the arrangement of the disputed succession. They at the same time deputed ambassadors to secure the co-operation of England, Denmark, Venice, and Switzerland ; they succeeded in gaining the concurrence of the United Provinces, who were irritated against Rhodolph for his repeated attempts to embroil them with the empire, and bring them again under the hated yoke of Spain ; and they opened a correspondence with the disaffected Austrians, Bohemians, Moravians, and Silesians. Lastly, as they were desirous to unite the whole Protestant body in a common cause, they endeavoured to gain the elector of Saxony, by promising that the decision of the disputed succession should not be disadvantageous to the interests of his house ; but this lure was of no avail, for Christian, and his adherents in the empire, sent dehortatory letters to several of the imperial cities to dissuade them from joining in the alliance. For this refusal he was rewarded by Rhodolph, with the investiture for himself and the whole house of Saxony, on the 7th of July, 1710.

During these transactions a petty war had continued in the territories of Juliers, and Leopold was reduced to the possession of the capital and the fort of Bredenburgh. His attempts to collect troops in Alsace and his diocese of

Strasburgh occasioned the diffusion of the war into that part of Germany, and induced the neighbouring princes of the Protestant union to expel his troops, and occupy Alsace with the territory of Strasburgh. The war seemed likely to spread on every side, and the dominions of the Catholic states which lay in the march of the Protestant levies, or were exposed to their incursions, became the theatre of the usual devastations which accompany religious contests.

The Catholics had not, however, seen the gradual increase of the Protestant union with indifference, for, as early as the middle of 1609, a league had been formed between Maximilian*, duke of Bavaria, and the bishops of Wurtzburgh, Passau, Constance, Augsburgh, Ratisbon, and other prelates, and soon afterwards joined by the three ecclesiastical electors. It was digested into a general offensive and defensive alliance, in support of the Catholic cause ; the respective contingents were specified, and the duke of Bavaria declared the head ; but from the weak and inefficient character of Rhodolph, he was neither consulted on the stipulations, nor, as emperor, permitted to nominate the chief.

These hostile appearances threatened a speedy rupture. The Catholics were arming ; the Protestants had already commenced aggressions ; the United Provinces were preparing to come forward ; the march of the French troops, who were ready to move at a moment's warning, would have been the signal for a general war, which would have desolated Germany from one extremity to the other, and perhaps ruined the house of Austria, and with it the Catholic cause. Rhodolph, pusillanimous, secluded in his palace, the prey of vain imaginations and hypochondriac melancholy, was a burden to his party, disregarded in the empire, and despised even by his own adherents. Matthias was still at variance with his brother, and only anxious to grasp the remnant of his dominions ; the other members of the family, neither from talents nor situation, were capable of stemming the torrent ; and the Spanish court

---

* William, duke of Bavaria, the most bigoted prince of his age, resigned, in 1596, the government of his territories, from principles of superstitious devotion, and retired to the life of a hermit. He was succeeded by his son Maximilian, who afterwards distinguished himself as the champion of the Catholic cause. — Falkenstein, p. 579.

maintained the most inexplicable apathy and indifference, in the midst of the dangers with which it was threatened from every quarter.

This impending destruction over the house of Austria and the Catholic cause was diverted by one of those incidents which baffle all human foresight, and frustrate in an instant the deepest designs of war or policy. On the 11th of May, 1610, Henry IV. fell by the stroke of an obscure assassin, at the very moment when he was preparing to head his army; and with him fell the stupendous plan, which had been matured by the labour of years, and which could only be carried into execution by a prince of his spirit, talents, and power. The Protestants were astounded by the news of this fatal catastrophe : though they were assisted by the Dutch and French, and did not shrink from the contest, their efforts were confined to the occupation of Alsace, the capture of Juliers, and the expulsion of Leopold. The Catholics, as much encouraged as the Protestants were disheartened, by the death of Henry, assembled their forces with redoubled zeal ; and Rhodolph having, by the intervention of Leopold, collected troops in the diocese of Passau, ordered the duke of Bavaria to expel the Protestants from Alsace, and replace the contested territories under the sequestration. But past calamities had reduced both parties to prudence and moderation; the Protestants were satisfied with having gained their principal object, and the Catholics were careful not to renew the horrors of civil war, for the sake of gratifying the resentment or promoting the interests of Rhodolph. The duke of Bavaria, therefore, neglected his mandate, and concluded, on the 24th of October, a treaty of peace and neutrality with the Protestants, by which they were to evacuate Alsace, and repair the damages occasioned by their troops ; both parties agreed to maintain no more forces than were necessary for their safety, and the principal object in dispute was left in suspense by the declaration, that both might take such a share in the arrangement of the succession of Juliers as should appear most advantageous.

When we consider the weak and degraded situation and the timid character of Rhodolph, we can scarcely suppress our surprise that he did not bury himself in his native obscurity, instead of suffering an impotent resentment to hurry him into a new danger greater than that from which he had escaped.

The injuries and humiliations which he had experienced from Matthias were too flagrant to be forgotten, even by the most placid and forgiving temper ; but they sunk deep into the mind of Rhodolph, distrustful, gloomy, and suspicious, and brooding over his misfortunes in the solitude of his palace. Frequent contentions and disputes aggravated the misunderstanding, and all the efforts of his family could scarcely effect an apparent and temporary accommodation, by which Matthias agreed to humble himself before his brother, to honour him as the head of his house, and to receive the territories which he had wrested from him as marks of favour, and as fiefs. In return, the emperor engaged to consider him as a brother and a friend, and to disband the troops which had been collected in the bishopric of Passau, which he still kept on foot, notwithstanding the termination of the war for the succession of Juliers.

Rhodolph had concluded this agreement only to blind the vigilance of his brother, and now hoped to gratify his resentment, which had increased in proportion as he had been compelled to smother his feelings. As his cousin Ferdinand had formerly offended him by signing the family compact, and recently by his attachment to the duke of Bavaria, who had disobeyed his orders, he now employed Leopold as the instrument of his vengeance, and perhaps intended to secure for him the succession to the crowns of Bohemia and of the empire. With this view he had kept on foot the troops raised in the diocese of Passau, who, with those drawn by Leopold from Alsace, amounted to 16,000 men. He affected, indeed, to fulfil the recent agreement, by commanding them to disband ; but in order to afford them a pretext for invading Bohemia, he withheld their pay. The troops, accordingly, under the command of their leader Ramée, burst into Upper Austria, spreading themselves over the country beyond the Danube, and, after committing every species of devastation, passed into Bohemia, in December, 1610 ; they then directed their march along the Moldau towards Prague, making themselves masters of Kronau, Piseck, Tabor, and Beraun, where they were joined by Leopold.

This inroad spread consternation throughout Bohemia, and a general suspicion prevailed that Rhodolph had called in these lawless troops to force Leopold on the nation, and to annul the religious privileges which he had so reluctantly granted. The states assembled at Prague, and the emperor, whose plans were not sufficiently matured, or who wanted courage to avow his intentions, called God to witness that the irruption was made without his knowledge or consent, recommended the adoption of vigorous measures, and sent a herald, commanding Leopold to retire. The herald met the invaders within a day's march of the capital; but, as Leopold did not yet choose to excite suspicion, by appearing as the principal, he was referred to Ramée, who declared, that he came as a friend, not as an enemy to the emperor, and would arrange an accommodation with the people of the capital. Continuing his march, he encamped on the ensuing morning, on the White Mountain, and issued a manifesto, declaring that he came to defend the emperor and the states from violence.

The states of Bohemia had not suffered this army to approach their capital without making preparations for resistance: before the arrival of Ramée, troops began to flock in from all quarters, while the burghers of Prague flew to arms. The states demanded an explanation of the manifesto, and were promised a satisfactory answer by Leopold, who had paid a visit to the emperor. He repaired to the camp, as if to require instructions, and returning to the city, proposed that the troops should retire and evacuate the towns which they had occupied, on receiving a written security from the states, that they should not be attacked during their march. The states accepted this proposal, apparent cordiality was restored, and the camp was abundantly supplied with provisions from the town. But while suspicion was thus lulled, and while the burghers, relying on the security of this engagement, were indulging themselves in the jollity of a festival, the troops, at the following dawn, seized one of the gates, massacred the guard, killed all whom they met, and made themselves masters of the little town, notwithstanding the opposition of the burghers, and of count Thurn, who opposed them with a body of horse. Flushed with this petty success, they endeavoured to occupy that part of the capital which is situated beyond the Moldau, but were repulsed with great loss.

The emperor, who had hitherto continued inactive, now ventured to disclose his purposes. The invading troops having sworn fidelity to him as their sovereign, he pressed the states to unite their forces with those of the archduke, to yield the town beyond the Moldau, and demolish the intrenchments which they had constructed. Unable to obtain their acquiescence in this singular proposal, he furnished Leopold with five pieces of heavy artillery, which were instantly planted on an eminence commanding the old town.

The success of the invaders, and the conduct of Rhodolph, induced the states to have recourse to Matthias, and to require assistance from the Moravians; they also commanded a levy of troops in all the circles of Bohemia, who flocked to the scene of action, bearing on their standards the inscription "Against Ramée." By the orders of Matthias, 8000 Hungarians instantly advanced by rapid marches to Prague, and were joined in their progress or on their arrival by the levies which were pouring in from all quarters. The troops of Passau were struck with a panic, and, after extorting 300,000 florins from the emperor, retired from Prague in the night ; they were attacked in their retreat, defeated with the loss of 2000 men, and compelled to take refuge in Budweiss ; while Leopold, disheartened by the result of his ill-fated expedition, hastened to hide his chagrin and disappointment at Passau.

So dangerous an experiment was not to be tried with impunity, particularly by a sovereign so weak, despised, and pusillanimous. On the first turn of affairs he condescended to make proposals of accommodation ; but his overtures were disdainfully rejected ; the invaders had scarcely retired, before the troops under count Thurn burst into the little town, and, surrounding every avenue of his palace, rendered Rhodolph a state prisoner. On the 20th of March, Matthias arrived, and was received by the master of the horse, who, at the head of a numerous concourse of nobles, congratulated him in the name of the sovereign, and the three estates. After making a splendid entry into the town, Matthias arranged with the leaders of his party a plan to wrest from his brother the crown of Bohemia. A petition was accordingly presented by the states, in which they requested Rhodolph to call a diet, threatening, in case of his refusal, to convene it by their own authority. The humiliated emperor penetrated the meaning of this demand ; but helpless, degraded, despised, deserted by all, he did not attempt to retard the evil hour, and preferred a voluntary resignation of the crown to a compulsory abdication. He therefore summoned the diet, and sent a message, that, since on account of his advanced age he was no longer capable of supporting the weight of government, he entreated them to crown his brother without delay, and by fixing an early day for the coronation, to prevent those troubles which might arise from a disputed succession.

The princes of Germany, who were attached to Rhodolph, did not see with indifference the deposition of a sovereign, however weak and imprudent ; the electors of Saxony and Mentz sent their ambassadors to threaten the states with the vengeance of the empire, and to declare that the diet would not admit the usurper of his crown on the electoral bench. Although this application was received with scorn and indignation by the states, yet the interference of these two powerful princes was sufficient to raise the hopes of Rhodolph, who in his desperate condition grasped the slightest support ; and his hopes were strengthened by the disputes which arose between Matthias and the states, relative to the articles of the intended capitulation.

The transfer of a crown is usually detrimental to the prerogatives of the sovereign. The states of Bohemia did not omit so favourable an opportunity as the usurpation of Matthias, to attempt the recovery of all their rights, however obsolete ; but, above all, the privilege of election, which they had so recently lost. Matthias, having no other title to the crown, consented to the restoration of the elective privilege, and other rights of scarcely less importance ; but he soon found that these were only the prelude to further demands, and that he must purchase a crown to which he had so long aspired, on conditions which reduced him to a mere cypher. They demanded the right of assembling when and where they chose; required the sole management of military and financial affairs ; the power of removing the great officers of state ; of making foreign alliances, even of entering into a confederacy with the Hungarians and Austrians for the defence of their respective immunities; and, lastly, of being empowered to form an armed force by their own authority.

Matthias, eager as he was to obtain the crown, could not submit to these articles. He did not, however, venture to give a positive refusal ; for Rhodolph, by means of private agents, was tampering with the principal members of the states, and endeavouring to lure them with professions of his willingness to confirm their privileges in their full latitude. Matthias therefore temporised, evaded a positive promise, by agreeing to grant a general confirmation of all their rights, and postponed his decision on the specific articles until he had an opportunity of more mature deliberation, and of consulting a future diet. He had the satisfaction to find that this conduct was not displeasing to the nation at large, and to perceive that well-wishers to the country were not wanting, who dreaded the renewal of former troubles, and were as unwilling to see an exorbitant power lodged in the hands of the states, as in those of the king. These promises were, therefore, sufficient to satisfy the states, who, though they relied little on the sincerity of Rhodolph, might perhaps have availed themselves of his offers to extort the consent of Matthias to their demands.

The hopes of Rhodolph were thus annihilated, and the short remnant of his life was nothing but a series of mortifications and disgraces. On the return of his agents from their unsuccessful mission to the Bohemian states, he started from his seat, threw up the window of his apartment, and exclaimed, in an agony of despair, "Prague, unthankful Prague, who hast been so highly elevated by me; now thou spurnest at thy benefactor. May the curse and vengeance of God fall on thee and on all Bohemia ! " He had, however, a still more severe mortification to endure, before he was delivered from the burden of degraded royalty. The diet having appointed

the 23rd of May for the coronation of Matthias, required
Rhodolph to absolve his subjects from their oath of allegiance. But Rhodolph, who had still fondly hoped by this
engagement to maintain a tie on the inclinations of his
subjects, and clung with singular pertinacity to this remnant
of kingly authority, received the humiliating demand with a
natural but fruitless indignation. He refused for a considerable time to subscribe the instrument, and on being
compelled to affix his signature, in a transport of despair
blotted the writing, and, tearing the pen in pieces, trampled it under his feet.

On the day appointed for the coronation, the city was
filled with troops, and the gates shut and guarded, to prevent the adherents of Rhodolph from making a last attempt
in his favour. The three estates being assembled in the
hall of the palace, the chancellor read to them the following act of abdication which had been extorted from Rhodolph : — " In conformity with the humble request of the
states of our kingdom, we graciously declare the three
estates, as well as all the inhabitants of all ranks and conditions, free from all subjection, duty, and obligation ; and
we release them from their oath of allegiance, which they
have taken to us as their king, with a view to prevent all
future dissensions and confusion. We do this for the
greater security and advantage of the whole kingdom of
Bohemia, over which we have ruled six and thirty years,
where we have almost always resided, and which, during
our administration, has been maintained in peace, and increased in riches and splendour. We, accordingly, in virtue
of this present voluntary resignation, and after due reflection, do, from this day, release our subjects from all duty
and obligation."

This important instrument being read, Matthias was
chosen king, with all the forms of an elective monarchy, on
the 23rd of May, 1611, and after confirming the rights
and privileges of the nation, civil and religious, was
crowned with a splendour and magnificence which were
calculated to captivate the attention and dazzle the minds
of his new subjects.

During this solemnity, Rhodolph had retired to a favourite villa, to avoid hearing the joyful acclamations of the

populace at the coronation of his successor. On the following day he had the mortification to receive a message from Matthias, thanking him for his brotherly abdication of the crown; and, in reply, expressed his hope of fraternal and amicable treatment. He was allowed more favourable conditions than are usually given to deposed monarchs; and had a mind so studious and retired as his been less tormented with a love of rule, he might have enjoyed more happiness in his favourite occupations than when he held a sceptre which he was unable to wield, and filled a throne which he degraded. He was permitted to continue his residence in the palace of Prague, and besides an annual pension of 400,000 florins, was allowed to retain the four lordships of Brandeiss, Lessa, Pardewitz, and Petzarau. He was compelled to publish the imperial ban against the troops of Passau, by whose assistance he had expected to recover his pristine authority; these troops being disbanded, Ramée, the unfortunate instrument of his impotent resentment, became a sacrifice to the weakness of his employer, and was beheaded by the order of Leopold, whose ambitious views he had endeavoured to promote.

Matthias having completed the necessary arrangements for the government of the country during his absence, spared his humiliated brother the pain of a visit, and repaired to Silesia and Lusatia to receive the homage of the natives, whom, like the Bohemians, Rhodolph had released from their oath of allegiance. He then proceeded to Vienna, and espoused Anne, daughter of his deceased uncle, Ferdinand, of the line of Tyrol. *

These important events excited a deep interest in the empire. They were hailed with peculiar joy by the Protestants, who saw the triumph of their cause in the deposition of their great persecutor Rhodolph, in the humiliation of Leopold, a Catholic and a prelate, and in the elevation of Matthias, with whom they had maintained a secret and intimate connection. During the progress of the revolution in Bohemia, they had held several meetings; but none was

* The account of this revolution has been amply supplied by Pelzel, p. 654-678. ; Schmidt, Contin. b. iii. ch. 25, 26. ; Heinrich, vol. vi. p. 256-268, who has principally drawn his account from Kevenhuller's Authentic Annals of Ferdinand II.

more memorable than the congress at Rothenburg, which displayed all the power and splendour of their union, and was attended by the contracting princes in person, by commissaries from the emperor, and ambassadors from Matthias. In this meeting, they formed regulations for the maintenance of their confederacy, which, though ostensibly temporary, were calculated to secure its strength and permanence. They digested articles for the levy of troops and the imposition of contributions, for the formation of arsenals and magazines, and the establishment of a place of arms, which was to contain a regular disposable force.

Rhodolph was reduced to the humiliating necessity of endeavouring to conciliate these princes whom he had so long and so repeatedly offended. But all his promises of redress for their grievances, and all his offers of friendship, were received with contempt and derision. They answered, that they had been too long duped by vague and hollow promises, too long the puppets of perfidious and ambitious ministers, and now expected actions, not words : Donawerth, they said, was not restored ; the iniquitous processes of the Aulic council still subsisted ; the emperor had not changed his weak and wicked administration, and had neglected to fulfil his repeated promises. They closed their invective, by expatiating on his persecution of the Protestants, his enrolment of troops in Alsace and Passau, and his illegal sequestration of the territories of Juliers. The ambassadors of Matthias experienced a far different reception, when they announced the recent events in Bohemia, and solicited assistance if needful. The princes expressed the warmest satisfaction, promised their support, and requested, for the prevention of troubles in the empire, that Rhodolph might be treated with brotherly kindness, and a watchful eye kept over his foreign counsellors.

Rhodolph did not experience a more favourable reception even from the electors, the majority of whom he considered as his friends. Having summoned, on the 14th of December, 1711, an electoral meeting at Nuremburgh, he laid before them a pathetic account of the humiliations which he had experienced from his brother, and drew a melancholy picture of the miseries which attend fallen grandeur. He enumerated his privations and distresses, described his revenues not only as too scanty to maintain his dignity, but even to discharge his debts and furnish necessary comforts; he finally besought them to grant him an establishment proportionate to his station, and not to leave the chief of the empire in his old age a prey to want and dishonour.

The hearts of all seem to have been steeled against the distresses of Rhodolph in proportion as he needed compassion. They refused their assent to his proposal, on the ground that it was an affair which concerned the empire, not the electoral college; and after recapitulating the principal complaints which had been made by the Protestant union, declared the necessity of electing a king of the Romans. A deputation, sent to Prague with this unwelcome message, accompanied the delivery of their commission with a new philippic, which might have been better spared to a sovereign already sunk almost below compassion. The electors did not hesitate to disapprove the conduct of Matthias; but declared, " that the emperor was himself the principal author of his own distresses and misfortunes; the contempt into which he had fallen, and which from him reflected on the empire, was derived," they said, " from his own indolence, and his obstinacy in following perverse counsels. He would have escaped all his calamities, if, instead of resigning himself to corrupt and interested ministers, he had followed the salutary counsels of the electors." They concluded with pressing him to assemble a diet for the redress of grievances, and for the election of a king of the Romans; professing that it was not their intention to remove the imperial crown from the Austrian family, and offering to approve whomsoever of the archdukes he should appoint.

This message was considered by the emperor as a warning to abdicate the imperial throne, and as a prelude to the same scene which had passed in Bohemia. He was not, however, yet sufficiently weaned from grandeur, to yield the last remnant of his frail authority without regret; he was unwilling to nominate Matthias, and afraid to recommend another. He therefore acknowledged the necessity of choosing a successor, and affected to acquiesce in the wishes of the electors; but he continued to evade the fulfilment of his promise by delay. This useless subterfuge was of no avail; for the electors, penetrating his purpose, summoned, by their own authority, the dreaded assembly on the 31st of May.

This was the last mortification which Rhodolph was destined to endure. A constitution, enfeebled by constant seclusion and melancholy, was shaken by his recent distresses, and the chagrin derived from this last warning of the electors brought on a deep dejection, which sunk him into the grave in the sixtieth year of his age, and the thirty-seventh of his reign. He welcomed approaching death with firmness, and even with joy. To the bystanders, he described the exquisite pleasure which he had experienced in his youth, in returning from Spain to his native country; and exclaimed, "How much more joyful ought I to be, when I am about to be delivered from the calamities of human nature, and transferred to a heavenly country, where there is no change of time, and where no sorrow can enter."

The preceding narrative sufficiently exhibits the weakness and incapacity of Rhodolph as a sovereign, and his inability to rule either in peace or war; yet it would be injustice to withhold from the view of the reader those qualities and acquirements * which give a slight relief to the darker shades of his character.

He was of the middling stature, pleasing countenance, and his eyes sparkled with remarkable vivacity. Till the unfortunate dejection of mind which clouded all his faculties, he was elegant in his deportment, affable and unassuming in his conversation. He was wholly devoid of that pride which is often inseparable from exalted dignity, and when reproached by one of his brothers for his excessive condescension and familiarity, he replied, "though elevated

---

* We do not deem it necessary to enumerate among his acquirements his deep knowledge of the occult arts and sciences. Like Roger Bacon, Faust, and other learned men in times of ignorance, he had the reputation of a conjuror, and was said to converse with spirits. Even Kevenhuller, the historian of Ferdinand, partakes of the foolish credulity of his contemporaries, and asserts that, by means of a magnet and magic speculum, he could discover what happened at a distance. Kevenhuller, quoted in Gebhaerdi, vol. ii. p. 463.

above others by our dignity and birth, we ought not to forget that we are allied to the rest of mankind by our weaknesses and defects."

He possessed an extensive knowledge of languages, both ancient and modern ; and his attainments in painting, in the mechanical arts, and in botany, zoology, and chemistry, were far from being inconsiderable. To that attachment to the arts and sciences, which occasioned his failings as a sovereign, his own age and country, and even science itself, are indebted for considerable advantages. His court was filled with artists and men eminent in every branch of learning, and the very name of Kepler, whom he employed in conjunction with Tycho Brahe, to construct the Rudolphine tables, is an honour to his patronage. In a country where the arts were little known and less cultivated, he formed collections which vied with those of more favoured climes, and many of his gems, antiques, and pictures are now distinguished ornaments in the splendid cabinet of Vienna. He assisted the study of natural history by his extensive collections of rare and foreign animals, and promoted the infant science of botany by forming gardens of curious and valuable plants, and by patronising the publication of works on that subject. He cultivated chemistry and mineralogy with considerable effect, and introduced great improvements into the arts of mining and smelting.

Under his reign education was greatly ameliorated in Bohemia, by the endowment of numerous schools ; and the native historian boasts that it was not unusual to find the burghers conversant in Virgil and Horace, and even in Homer and Anacreon. He exultingly adds, the reign of Rhodolph II. was a golden era for Prague ; it was the classical age of his native language, and rivalled that of their favourite sovereign Charles IV.

Chap. XLV.—MATTHIAS.—1612–1618.

THE interregnum in the empire which succeeded the death of Rhodolph commenced with the most alarming appearances of trouble and dissension, and threatened to be longer and more stormy than any in recent periods. Besides the dispute still pending between the Catholics and Protestants, and the unfinished contest for the succession of Juliers, other causes intervened, which were likely to disturb the public peace.

The death of Frederic IV., elector palatine, had occasioned a contest for the guardianship of his son Frederic V., during his minority, between Philip Louis, count palatine of Neuburgh, and John, duke of Deux Ponts, which was aggravated by religious antipathy, the first being a Lutheran, and the latter a Calvinist. The dispute had been suspended by the sentence of the emperor and the electoral college, who awarded the regency and guardianship to the duke of Deux Ponts, in conformity with the testament of the deceased elector ; but the count Palatine refusing to submit to this decision, the quarrel was revived with new acrimony on the death of the emperor, in consequence of the competition for the electoral vote, and the vicariate. At the same time the imperial chamber attempted to introduce an illegal extension of its jurisdiction, by refusing to acknowledge the supreme authority of the imperial vicars, or to pronounce its sentences in their name, under the pretext that there was no precedent for acknowledging Protestant vicars, because there had been no vicariate since the peace of religion.

Notwithstanding these struggles, and the general ferment which pervaded Germany, the interregnum fortunately passed without the slightest commotion. This calm was in a great degree owing to the candour and moderation of the Catholics, who set the example in condemning the illegal pretensions of the imperial chamber, and in acknowledging the supreme authority of the vicars, although Protestants. The contestation between the count Palatine and the duke of Deux Ponts was likewise terminated by the electoral college, which confirmed the award it had before given in favour of the duke of Deux Ponts, by vesting in him the electoral vote and the administration of the vicariate.

Matthias, already king of Hungary and Bohemia, and archduke of Austria, offered himself as a candidate for the imperial dignity; but, from a concurrence of unexpected circumstances, he experienced difficulties which he did not foresee. The Catholic electors, who were alienated by his intrigues with the Protestants, offered the imperial crown to the archduke Albert, sovereign of the Netherlands, and were joined by John George, who had recently succeeded his brother Christian in the electorate of Saxony, and who seems to have been disgusted by the conduct of Matthias towards his deceased brother. Even the electors Palatine and Brandenburgh, notwithstanding their recent connections with Matthias, did not support his nomination; but either from a dread of his power, or from a desire to weaken the head of the house of Austria, offered their suffrages to his brother Maximilian. In this instance, however, both the archdukes acted with equal prudence and policy, and, refusing the proffered dignity, joined their interest in favour of Matthias. Accordingly, Matthias was unanimously elected, after an interregnum of six months, and signed a capitulation, which differed considerably from those of his predecessors. Among the principal articles, one restrained the emperor from employing the grants of the diet for any other purpose except their original destination; another related to the amelioration of the Aulic council and the imperial chamber, and the revival of the visitation. But the most important was a stipulation, intended to prevent the imperial crown from being rendered hereditary in the Austrian family, by empowering the electors to proceed by their own authority, to choose a king of the Romans, if the emperor, after being duly requested, should refuse to consent to an election, or should not give valid reasons for his refusal.*

The spirit, talents, and exploits of Matthias filled Europe with general expectations, that a strong and active government would succeed the weak and indolent adminis-

* Pfeffel, p. 273.

tration of Rhodolph II. But his conduct proved how much easier it is to excite than to appease revolts; to effect a great revolution, or to acquire a crown, than to re-establish institutions which have been overthrown, or to exert usurped power with vigour and discretion.

The civil and religious troubles had been revived in all their fury by the administration of Rhodolph; the empire was divided into three parties of Catholics, Lutherans, and Calvinists, mutually animated with religious hatred, and ready to take arms against each other on the most trifling pretext. In Austria and Bohemia the very foundations of government had been shaken by the recent revolutions; the people, encouraged by the turbulent example of Matthias himself, and rather tempted than gratified by the concessions which had been the rewards of their rebellion, were wholly bent on extending their political and religious immunities. In this situation, had Matthias with his talents possessed the tolerant spirit of his father, he would have found numerous difficulties to encounter; we cease to wonder, therefore, that he was still less capable of overcoming the embarrassments with which he was surrounded when we consider that he inherited no particle of a conciliating spirit, and that the toleration of which he had given proofs was the mere result of interest and policy.

Confiding in the unanimity with which he had been chosen, and in his connections with the Protestants, he flattered himself that he should be able to manage the diet and his own states with the same facility and success as his father; but the very first act of his reign proved the frail foundation on which he rested his hopes.

Although the reversion of Transylvania after the death of Botskai had been secured to the house of Austria by the pacification of Vienna, yet the Turks had prevented the fulfilment of that stipulation, first by supporting Gabriel Bathori*, and, when he threw himself under the protection of Matthias, by extending their assistance to his rival, Bethlehem Gabor†, who, on the 27th of October,

---

* Gabriel Bathori, becoming unpopular by his excesses, was driven from Transylvania, and assassinated by two injured husbands, whose wives he had violated. — Benko, p. 263.

† He is generally known under this appellation, as it is the custom

1613, was chosen by the states of Transylvania. Matthias was naturally desirous to recover so important a territory, and had now a favourable opportunity, as the Turks were involved in intestine commotions and employed in external wars on the side of Poland and in Asia. He therefore summoned a diet of the empire to obtain succours for the purpose of fulfilling the treaty of Vienna, and driving the Turks from Moldavia and Wallachia, where they had recently established their dependent chiefs; he endeavoured to conciliate the Protestants by promising in the letters of convocation to reform the Aulic council and imperial chamber and re-establish the visitation, to restore the privileges of Donawerth, and to redress many grievances of which they complained. But the Protestants were too intimately acquainted with his character to rely on his promises, and were displeased with his revival of the unpopular decree against Aix-la-Chapelle. They, therefore, showed as little confidence in him as they had shown in Rhodolph: they even presented the list of their grievances, with claims of additional privileges, and refused to take part in any discussion before those grievances were redressed. The emperor, unlike his father, who had laboured to prevent all party disputes, imprudently suffered the Catholics to answer this memorial, and to present a counter-list of complaints against the Protestants: by these means the discussions of the diet were diverted from the point in question, and degenerated into reciprocal complaints and mutual recriminations. At length, the Catholics, joined by the elector of Saxony and his Lutheran adherents, voted a succour of thirty Roman months; yet, notwithstanding all representations, and a declaration inserted in the recess, the other Protestants persisted in refusing their concurrence, and the diet broke up in confusion.

Disappointed in his hopes of obtaining succours from the German diet, Matthias applied to the states of all the countries under his domination, and summoned a general assembly at Lintz. The temper of his subjects and the

in Hungary to place the christian after the family name: but his real name was Gabriel Bethlehem.

situation of his affairs rendered this step a measure of the most alarming nature. The Austrians were far from being grateful for the privileges granted as the price of their assistance against his brother, and suspected that he only waited a favourable opportunity for resuming what he had conceded with such reluctance. The Protestants of Bohemia were discontented with some recent restrictions on their worship, which, if not infringements of their rights, were at least a rigorous and impolitic execution of the law ; they clamoured loudly for the presence of their sovereign and the convocation of a diet, in which they hoped to obtain a confirmation, or perhaps an extension, of their privileges. The Hungarians, who had so long groaned under the miseries of war, deprecated the renewal of hostilities, and were little inclined to assist in the recovery of Transylvania, or to risk the tranquillity which they now enjoyed, particularly as the Turks were disposed to peace, and the prince of Transylvania courted with extreme assiduity the friendship of the emperor. It might naturally be expected that all these discontents would be inflamed by the discussions of a public assembly, and that the meeting would afford an opportunity to renew that general confederacy which had already been fatal to Rhodolph.

The eagerness of Matthias, however, inducing him to overlook these dangers, he laid his demands before the assembly. He endeavoured to give weight to his proposals by displaying the ill consequences of suffering Transylvania, with the adjacent provinces, to remain under the influence or in the possession of the Turks ; and argued that while the Ottoman empire was engaged in foreign and domestic contests, a favourable opportunity presented itself to recover possession of those countries, and to secure the Austrian territories from future invasion. To these proposals he received an answer which might have been foreseen from the temper of the assembly. The Hungarians urged the necessity of maintaining peace ; the Bohemians cloaked their refusal under the pretence that they could not decide on so important a point as a Turkish war, without more enlarged instructions from their constituents ; and the Austrians represented that hostilities could not be too anxiously avoided, and even advised their sovereign to commence an immediate negotiation for an accommodation with Bethlehem Gabor.

Thus baffled in all his expectations, Matthias was compelled to relinquish his designs; and a Turkish embassy, which now for the first time arrived at Vienna, afforded an honourable pretext for entering into negotiation. He, therefore, renewed the truce with the sultan Achmet for twenty years, with additional explanatory articles ; to save his honour no mention was made of Transylvania, and thus the right of Bethlehem Gabor was tacitly acknowledged.

While Matthias was engaged in securing a temporary tranquillity in his own dominions, the unceasing enmity of the Catholics and Protestants produced new disturbances in Germany. The first dispute was derived from the revival of the ban against Aix-la-Chapelle, and the establishment of Mulheim, a Protestant town in the duchy of Berg, and in the vicinity of Cologne.

Notwithstanding the exclusion of the Protestants from the magistracy of Aix-la-Chapelle and the banishment of their chiefs, their party was far from being reduced ; for in the midst of the troubles which agitated the latter part of the reign of Rhodolph, they revived the contests with the Catholics, took up arms, expelled the Jesuits, and again established their own magistracy. During the interregnum a temporary accommodation was effected by the award of the duke of Deux Ponts, as administrator of the vicariate ; but both parties appealing to the new emperor, he annulled on the 20th of February, 1614, the award, revived the ban against the Protestants, and intrusted its execution to the archduke Albert and the elector of Cologne.

The dispute relative to Mulheim was another consequence of religious animosity. This town was a Protestant settlement, formed under the auspices of the princes possessors of the succession of Juliers, on the right bank of the Rhine, opposite Cologne, as an asylum for the refugees from all quarters. It was strongly fortified, endowed with extensive privileges, and, what peculiarly served in these times of trouble to attract inhabitants, enjoyed freedom of religious worship. The establishment of this fortress giving the Protestants a military post of great importance, and enabling them to interrupt and appropriate the commerce of the Rhine, produced an appeal from the inhabitants of Cologne, who complained of this settlement as an infringement of their compacts with the ancient dukes of Cleves and Juliers. In consequence of this appeal, the emperor issued an imperial mandate, requiring the princes possessors to demolish the fortifications, and the Protestants to suspend their buildings : this act was to be carried into complete execution within thirty days.

But neither of these acts would have been carried into execution had not the Protestant union been divided and weakened by the disputes which at this time arose between the two princes possessors. The treaty of Dortmund being merely a temporary expedient to exclude the other claimants, gave rise to new contests as soon as the contracting parties were relieved from the fear of external aggression ; as each endeavoured to enlarge his acquisitions, and to grasp at a greater share in the administration. Several attempts to effect an accommodation were made by the Protestants, and as the means of uniting their interests, a marriage was arranged between the prince Palatine and the daughter of the elector of Brandenburgh ; but these expedients were frustrated by new altercations, and at length the quarrel was rendered personal by a blow which the prince received from the elector while in a state of intoxication. This insult was too dishonourable to admit of reconciliation : the prince embraced the Catholic religion and espoused the daughter of the duke of Bavaria, in order to secure the support of the Catholics and the court of Spain ; the elector likewise sacrificed his religion to political interests, and turned Calvinist, with a view to obtain assistance from the prince of Orange and the United States. Both parties, with that spirit of intolerance which now actuated all religious sects, endeavoured to introduce their new tenets, not only in the contested territories, but in their hereditary dominions ; and the prince Palatine, in particular, revoked the privileges with which Mulheim had been endowed, and began to demolish the fortifications, notwithstanding the interposition of the elector of Brandenburgh.

This unfortunate division again rendered the dispute for the succession a religious quarrel ; and, as both princes

held joint possession, the contest ripened into immediate
hostilities. The Dutch troops under the prince of Orange,
advancing to support the elector, gained possession of
Juliers, Emerich, Rees, Goch, and Calcar. On the other
hand, the prince Palatine surprised Dusseldorf, while
Spinola advancing with 30,000 Spanish troops from the
Netherlands, executed the imperial ban and edict against
Aix-la-Chapelle and Mulheim, and, descending the Rhine,
captured Duisburgh, Orsoy, and Wesel, with other fortresses of less importance.

The Spaniards and Dutch mutually avoiding any engagement which might tend to disturb their neutrality,
appeared as if by tacit connivance to divide the territories
which they were called in to protect. The princes possessors, therefore, became jealous of their new allies, and at
length by the mediation of France, England, and the
German states, effected, on the 12th of November, 1614,
an accommodation at Santen, by which the foreign troops
were to quit the country, and the contested territories were
to be divided into two equal parts and assigned by lot,
although the administration was to continue in their joint
names.*   But their new allies refusing to yield the places
which they occupied, both parties appealed to the emperor;
the Catholics against the aggressions of the Dutch, and
the Protestants against the Spaniards. This appeal produced no effect; for Matthias, apprehensive of a civil war
in Germany, while his own dominions were in a state of
ferment, prudently refused to support either party; and
the contested territories remained in the possession of the
foreign troops during the remainder of his reign.

Although Matthias has been censured for this apparent
apathy, so different from his former activity and vigilance,
it is easy to find a justification of his conduct, in his own

---

* The division in the first instance was, on one side, the duchy of
Cleves, the counties of La Mark and Ravensberg, and the lordship of
Ravenstein, with some other lands and fiefs situated in Brabant and
Flanders; and, on the other, the duchies of Juliers and Berg. By a
subsequent division in 1630, Cleves, La Mark, and Ravensberg fell to
Brandenburgh, and Juliers, Berg, and Ravenstein to the house
of Neuburgh. — History of the Succession of Juliers and Berg,
pp. 77, 78.

personal situation and the rising discontents in his territories. Advancing in years, and burdened with increasing
infirmities, he was without the prospect of issue. His next
brother and presumptive heir, Maximilian, was unmarried,
and in his fifty-ninth year; his third brother, Albert, was
fifty-eight, and, though married, was without children.
The whole hope of preserving the German branch rested
on Ferdinand, head of the Styrian line, the only prince
who had issue male, and who was likely to continue the
succession, as his brothers were all ecclesiastics. It became
therefore, a matter not only of policy, but even of necessity, to entail the hereditary countries on this prince, and
to procure for him the reversion of the imperial crown;
because the succession was likely to be contested by
Philip III., king of Spain, as descended from Anne,
daughter of Maximilian, and his contrary claims could not
fail to produce the most fatal dissensions between the two
branches, and threatened the ruin of the Austrian family.

Maximilian was the first who came forward to obviate
these dangers. He offered to resign his own claims to
Ferdinand, procured the resignation of his brother Albert,
and in a memorial presented to Matthias on the 19th of
February, 1616, traced the requisite steps for the accomplishment of this desirable purpose. " The succession," he
observed, " is two-fold; the first in the throne of the empire, the second in those of Hungary and Bohemia. In
regard to the first, it would not be difficult to secure, if
not all, at least a majority of the electors. The ecclesiastical electors are already inclined to forward the recommendation of the emperor; and the elector of Saxony is
much influenced by the elector of Mentz; it would, however, be proper for the emperor himself to make to him a
personal application, not only to secure his concurrence,
but to prevail on him to use his interest with his co-
electors, that the nomination of a king of the Romans
should be committed to the emperor, reserving the right of
election. The emperor must next endeavour to gain the
two remaining secular electors, and though he may not
succeed, still he will have a majority on his side, and the
title of the new king of the Romans will be equally as
valid as the appointment of Ferdinand I., notwithstanding

the protest of the elector of Saxony. But, above all, it is absolutely necessary, for the attainment of this object, that the emperor should arm, as I have before advised, on the occasion of the contest for the succession of Juliers.

"In regard to the succession of the hereditary countries, no time should be lost. All attempts should be made, first, to gain the chiefs of the Catholics, and afterwards those of the Protestants; for this point of the succession being settled, the reversion of the imperial dignity may next be attempted with effect." He concluded by strongly recommending secrecy and silence, as the only means of preventing a disappointment.

Notwithstanding the necessity of the case, Maximilian experienced the greatest obstacles from the disinclination of Matthias, who, besides fostering a personal dislike of Ferdinand, had been too conversant in plots and revolutions not to dread the fate of Rhodolph; and his repugnance was increased by bishop Klesel, his confidential minister, who urged him not to give himself a master. He could not reject the memorial, but submitted it to the consideration of a committee, composed of Klesel, two of his own ministers, and two counsellors of Ferdinand and Maximilian. Although this committee approved the plan, and recommended its adoption, Matthias still found a pretext for delay, by requiring a previous and formal renunciation from Albert, and the approbation of the court of Spain; and while he evinced no apparent dissent from the opinion of the committee, he took no step to carry their advice into execution.

Maximilian, penetrating the views of his brother, vented his indignation against Klesel, to whom he attributed the delay. He was not, however, deterred by these obstacles, but exerted himself with new vigour to procure the fulfilment of his design, and obtained the formal resignation of his brother Albert. He next applied to the Spanish court, from whom he experienced considerable difficulty; for although Philip was desirous to prevent dissensions between the two branches of his house, and was favourably disposed towards Ferdinand, who had given such notorious proofs of zeal for the Catholic faith, yet he was too interested a prince to follow even his own inclinations, without the prospect of advantage. Philip, therefore, de-murred, until he had obtained from all the princes of the German branch a public declaration, that, in failure of male issue, the females of the Spanish should be preferred to those of the German branch, and from Ferdinand a secret engagement for the eventual cession of the Tyrol, and the exterior provinces of Austria.

All the objections of Matthias were thus removed; but, during these negotiations, the design was disclosed by the publication of the memorial, which was probably done with the connivance of Matthias, or at least of his minister, and nearly defeated the designs of Maximilian to the imperial crown. A general alarm was excited among the Protes-tants. Frederic, elector Palatine, who had recently attained his majority, and was desirous of distinguishing himself as the head of the anti-Austrian party, endeavoured to ani-mate his co-estates, by representing it as a breach of the golden bull, an infringement of the constitution, and as a plan to deprive the electoral college of their right of elec-tion, and enable the emperor to force upon them a prince of the most despotic and intolerant spirit. These repre-sentations produced a considerable sensation in the empire, and even influenced the elector of Saxony, the creature of the house of Austria; and the Protestant party evinced a design of choosing their future chief from another family.

The intrigues of the elector Palatine occasioned a revo-lution in the mind of Matthias, which all the representa-tions of Maximilian could not effect. He saw the pretexts which he had alleged for the purpose of delay at length removed; and he began to apprehend that any new demur on his part would occasion the loss of the imperial crown, if not those of Hungary and Bohemia, to his family. He, therefore, prosecuted the plan of Maximilian with his cha-racteristic ardour. He first turned his attention to his own dominions, and proposed Ferdinand to the states of Bohemia, in a manner which left the right of election, or hereditary succession, equally undecided. Repairing to Prague, accompanied by Maximilian and Ferdinand, he addressed the diet in a speech, in which he observed, " As I and my brothers are without children, I deem it neces-sary, for the advantage of Bohemia, and to prevent future

contests, that my cousin Ferdinand should be proclaimed
and crowned king; I therefore request you to fix a day
for the confirmation of this appointment." This proposition was opposed by count Thurn, and a few chiefs of the
Protestant party, who endeavoured to excite the alarm of
the Protestants, by expatiating on the intolerance of Ferdinand; but their representations, though true, produced
little effect.   The states, from a dread of civil troubles, or
from deference to Matthias, readily accepted Ferdinand,
with all his defects; and, on the 10th of June, 1616, he
was duly crowned by the metropolitan archbishop of
Prague, after confirming the privileges of the kingdom in
the usual forms, and promising not to interfere in the government during the life of Matthias.

When we consider the known character and conduct of
Ferdinand, we are unable to account for the little opposition which he experienced from the Protestants.   He was
son of the archduke Charles, by Maria, a princess of Bavaria, and was born in 1578, at Gratz, the capital of Styria.
On the death of his father, he was brought up under the
guardianship of his two cousins, the archdukes Ernest and
Maximilian, who were both zealous for the Catholic faith,
and he completed his education at the university of Ingolc
stadt, under the care of the Jesuits, and of his uncle William,
the fifth duke of Bavaria, a prince who was imbued with
all the fanaticism of his family, and who equalled the most
devout hermit in acts of mortification and self-abasement.
Ferdinand possessed eminent talents, and a quick comprehension; but these talents were perverted by his monastic
education, and it was only owing to native energy that he
did not degenerate into another Rhodolph.   From these
circumstances his mind received an early and irremediable
bias; he displayed an unremitting partiality to his teachers,
passed whole days in their society, and was often heard to
declare that, had he been as free as his brothers, he would
have entered into the order of Jesuits.   From their instructions he derived that inflexible bigotry and intolerance, and that hostility to the Protestants, which, at this
period, formed the great characteristics of their order.   He
frequently expressed a resolution to live with his family in
banishment, to beg his bread from door to door, to submit

to every insult and calamity, to lose even his life, rather than suffer the true church to be injured. When he assumed the reins of government, he proved that these declarations were not the effusions of idle enthusiasm. He refused to confirm the privileges which his father Charles had granted to his Protestant subjects, and sent his commissaries to eject their preachers from the archducal domains; these commissaries being expelled, he collected troops to enforce the execution of his orders. In the interim he made a pilgrimage to Loretto, and bound himself by the most solemn vows, before the miraculous image, not to rest till he had extirpated all heresy in his dominions; at Rome he was consecrated by the hands of Clement VIII. and his resolutions were strengthened by the exhortations of the pontiff.

Animated with a new spirit of intolerance, he returned in 1598 to his dominions. The first act of his government was a new order for the banishment of all the Protestant preachers and schoolmasters, and, in opposition to the remonstrances of the states, he carried this rigorous measure into execution by force. He supplied the place of the Protestant seminaries, by founding two convents of Capuchins at Gratz and Bruck, and colleges of Jesuits at Gratz, Laybach, and Clagenfurth. Although two thirds of his subjects were Protestants, he ordered all who would not embrace the Catholic faith, to quit his dominions; and supplied the places of those who preferred banishment to the desertion of their faith, by introducing numbers of Catholics from Wallachia and the neighbouring provinces. To complete the expulsion of heresy, his commissaries, accompanied by an escort, passed from town to town, and from village to village, restoring the ancient temples to the Catholics, and demolishing the new churches and schoolhouses, which had been erected by the Protestants. Notwithstanding the severity of these measures, he met with little opposition; and he experienced no obstacle to his designs, except a slight and ineffectual remonstrance of the states, and a trifling insurrection of the peasants in Carinthia and the miners of Carniola.

Trifling, however, as was the opposition made against Ferdinand by the Protestants of Bohemia, he experienced still less in Hungary, being chosen successor to Matthias, and solemnly crowned at Presburgh. His interests seemed scarce likely to meet more obstacles even in the empire; for, after his coronation in Bohemia, in 1618, Matthias, repairing to Dresden, gained the elector of Saxony, and thus secured the majority of the electoral suffrages, and nothing was wanting to complete his elevation but the assembling an electoral diet.

CHAP. XLVI. — 1619.

THE auspicious appearances which had favoured the elevation of Ferdinand were soon changed, and the first symptoms of those troubles, which commenced in the Austrian territories and afterwards overspread all Europe, appeared in Bohemia. Ferdinand had not long received the crown before the Protestants perceived that the alarms derived from his principles and former conduct were not without foundation; for, from that moment, a new spirit seemed to animate the counsels of the sovereign, and various acts of hostility to their doctrines, evinced his baneful influence. Slavata and Martinetz, the two nobles who had proved their zeal for the Catholic faith by refusing to sign the peace of religion, were introduced into the council of regency, honoured with an unusual degree of confidence, and displayed their attachment to their future sovereign by persecuting their Protestant vassals. The zealous Catholics followed the example, and exulted in the prospect of a change of government which was likely to restore their ascendency; the Jesuits presumptuously proclaimed the new influence and favour which they had attained; and one of the confidential ministers of Ferdinand himself did not scruple to point out the future objects of their vengeance, and to declare, that the restoration of tranquillity could only be effected by executions and confiscations, and by the revocation of the royal edict which had been extorted by force. These threats and rumours were aggravated by fear and religious antipathy; and the Protestants looked forward to the commencement of the new reign as an era no less pregnant with horrors than the abominable massacre of St. Bartholomew. In the midst of this ferment the disclosure of the treaty with Spain contributed to add civil to religious grievances; the illegal engagement for the eventual transfer of the crown to the Spanish branch, without even the knowledge of the states, alarmed a great part of the Catholics, who were no less tenacious of their elective rights than the Protestants of their religious privileges. In this situation it was impossible to restrain so turbulent a people as the Bohemians, animated with all the fury of political and religious animosity, and in count Thurn appeared another Ziska, who was capable of rousing, directing, and organising an insurrection.

Matthew Henry, count of Thurn, a native of Goritz, was descended from an illustrious family. He embraced at an early period the Lutheran doctrines, and on the death of his father transferred his residence to Bohemia, where he inherited considerable estates. He acquired great reputation by his military services against the Turks, gained the affections of his adopted countrymen by zeal for their civil and religious liberties, and to the distinguished part which he acted during the reign of Rhodolph was attributed the publication of the royal edict. Such services could not fail to endear him still more to the Protestants, and such extensive influence to render him respectable to the crown; his importance to both was evinced by his appointment to the custody of the regalia, as burgrave of Carlstein, and his nomination to the charge of the chief defender of religion, allowed by the royal edict. Affable, liberal, eloquent and popular, he was calculated to become the leader of a party. He possessed an enthusiastic warmth of temper, which gave to all his speeches and actions the appearance of undissembled truth and unaffected sincerity, and he united to these specious and dangerous qualities distinguished military talents, a daring spirit of enterprise, a deep acquaintance with the human heart, and energy and skill to impel or govern its movements. Brought up in the midst of civil and religious feuds, he was inured to the arts of intrigue, and delighted in troubles and commotions, which afforded full exercise to his restless spirit, and full scope to his eminent abilities. Such a man was destined to become the scourge or the glory of his age, the ruin or the safeguard of his country.

The character, talents, and influence of Thurn rendered him highly inimical to Ferdinand, while the active part which he had taken in opposing his election added personal antipathy to the dislike naturally arising from discordant characters and principles. These causes occasioned his abrupt dismission from the burgraviate of Carlstein, which impelled him into inveterate hostility against the court, while it increased his influence among the people, who regarded him as a martyr to their cause. He secretly and silently prepared the means of gratifying at once his vengeance and ambition, and securing the liberties and religion of his adopted country from the dangers with which they were threatened. He laboured with success in increasing his Bohemian adherents, and strengthened his cause by forming connections with the discontented Protestants of Austria and Hungary, and with the members of the Protestant union in the empire.

The impolicy and intolerance of the court soon furnished him with an opportunity to inflame a trivial discussion into open hostilities. It is a misfortune attending religious disputes in a peculiar degree, in which all parties act and reason on such discordant principles, that no public instrument can be worded in terms sufficiently clear and explicit to prevent all occasions of cavil. This was the case of the royal edict, which seems by the spirit to grant liberty of worship with the privilege of constructing churches and schools only to the Calixtine or Protestant members of the states, whether nobles, knights, or towns. But an explanatory clause in general terms, instead of rendering the meaning more specific, only made it more doubtful *, and furnished the towns and vassals of eccle-

---

* This clause is as follows : " If any of the united states of the kingdom, who take the communion under both kinds, should want to erect more churches, places of worship, or schools, whether in towns, villages, or elsewhere, this may be done, without let or hindrance by the nobles and knights, as also by the inhabitants of Prague and

siastics and lay Catholics with a pretext for claiming the same privilege. In consequence of this interpretation, the Protestant inhabitants of the town of Brunau and of Clostergraben, a village in the vicinity of Prague, began to erect churches, and to perform divine service according to the Protestant ritual. The archbishop of Prague and the abbot of Brunau, to whom the respective places belonged, considering these acts as an infringement of their feudal rights, obtained a prohibition from the government. The Protestants, however, instead of obeying the order, were encouraged by the defenders of their religion to persevere; and these and other prohibitions of the sovereign induced the Protestant states of Bohemia and its dependencies to enter into a formal confederacy for the security and defence of their rights and privileges. They followed this engagement by a petition for redress in the affair of Brunau and Clostergraben; and at the same time renewed their compacts and treaties with some of the Protestant princes of Germany.

Encouraged by this confederacy, the Protestants proceeded with new vigour, and the churches were completed, notwithstanding Matthias himself expressed his disapprobation to count Thurn, and declared their conduct an infraction of the royal edict. But though he was disposed to connive at this disobedience, Ferdinand was not inclined to the same acquiescence, and soon after his coronation, an order, obtained by his influence, was issued by the court, commanding the surrender or demolition of the newly constructed churches. The archbishop instantly executed the order at Clostergraben; but at Brunau the people opposed their abbot, and sent deputies to Matthias, requesting the revocation of his mandate. Instead, however, of obtaining redress, their deputies were arrested, and an imperial commission despatched to shut up the church, and suppress the Protestant worship in Brunau.

These acts, of which numerous precedents had been

Kuttenburgh, *and all other towns.*" From the context it is evident that this permission was confined to the Calixtine, or rather Protestant members of the states, and therefore the general phrase, " *all other towns,*" ought to be referred only to those towns which were members of the states, instead of the towns in general.

given in Germany and in the Austrian territories, might at any other time have produced a trifling dispute, which would have soon sunk into oblivion ; but amidst the general ferment, and in the powerful hands of count Thurn, they became the instrument which excited an insurrection, and occasioned the Thirty Years' War. As one of the defenders of religion, he persuaded his colleagues that this prohibition was a breach of the royal edict ; and prevailed on them to summon at Prague a meeting of six delegates from each circle, to take the affair into consideration. The assembly met on the 6th of March, 1618, and was attended by a numerous concourse of people, who were attracted by curiosity or impelled by the spirit of party. The delegates, roused by the eloquence of count Thurn, were easily induced to declare the suspension of the Protestant worship and the demolition of the church a breach of the royal edict ; and to draw up a petition to the emperor, demanding redress, and requiring the liberation of the imprisoned deputies from Brunau. The assembly separated, after fixing a day for a new meeting, to receive the answer of the emperor ; and the delegates who had been wrought upon by Thurn, in returning to their respective circles, contributed to inflame the public mind, by spreading reports among their countrymen, that the court, in imitation of Rhodolph, had adopted a systematic plan for the extermination of the Protestant worship, and were prepared to call in foreign troops for its execution.

These alarms were in a great degree corroborated by the manner and terms in which the answer was conveyed ; for the court, if it had not then formed a regular plan of hostility against the Protestants, certainly evinced a resolution to continue and extend its restrictions. The emperor affected to consider the affair in dispute as a mere pretext for an invasion of his authority. He acknowledged that the churches had been shut up and the refractory deputies imprisoned by his order, and that the Protestant delegates had exceeded the privileges granted by the royal edict, in protecting vassals of other lords, contrary to his express commands. He charged the delegates also with disobedience and revolt, and with spreading injurious reports that he was about to call in foreign troops for the invasion of Bohemia. He observed, that he did not expect such proceedings from those who had abused his lenity, under the sanction of the royal edict, and as it became him as sovereign to extinguish the sparks before they burst forth into flame, he declared that he would act towards the disobedient according to their demerits. He concluded, with forbidding all further assemblies, all interference with the vassals of Brunau, or those of any other lord, and all such attempts to excite commotions till he himself should repair to Bohemia, or give his final decision. This answer, if its tone and spirit had been calculated to satisfy the Protestants, could not fail to irritate them still more by the manner in which it was delivered; for it was not addressed to the delegates, who had presented the petition, and were again assembled, but to the council of regency, of which two members were Slavata and Martinetz*, the nobles so peculiarly unpopular among the Protestants.

This impolitic step did not escape the penetration of count Thurn, and furnished him with another opportunity of exerting his consummate skill in exciting popular indignation. Before the answer was communicated he had already wrought upon the feelings of the delegates; but, after their attendance in the council chamber, whither they had repaired to receive the communication, he again addressed them, roused their anger almost to fury against the obnoxious nobles, whose persecutions he depicted in the most glowing colours, and concluded with representing them as the authors of the insulting answer which they had drawn up themselves, and sent to Vienna for the formal signature of the emperor. Moved by this powerful appeal to their passions, the delegates with their retainers assembled in arms on the following morning, for the purpose of making a reply to the answer of the court. Thurn did not suffer the enthusiasm which he had inspired to subside; taking the chiefs of the delegation apart, he repeated his former accusations, represented that Bohemia could enjoy no free-

* The council of regency consisted of ten members, seven Catholics and three Protestants; but, either by accident or design, six of the number were absent at their country seats, among whom were the three Protestants.

dom of worship while Slavata and Martinetz continued in power ; and urged, that now was the time to deliver themselves from two such deadly enemies to their religion and liberties. The voices of a few who ventured to remonstrate, being drowned in clamour, they burst into the council chamber, where the four regents, the burgrave of Prague, Diepold of Lobcowitz, grand prior of St. Mary's, and the two obnoxious nobles were sitting.

One of the delegates advancing assailed the whole council with the most bitter reproaches ; but he was interrupted by another, Kolon of Feltz, who exclaimed, " We have no complaint against the burgrave and the lord of Lobcowitz ; our business is with Slavata and Martinetz, the persecutors of the Protestants." He then addressed the obnoxious nobles, and demanded, whether they knew who had drawn up the answer, or whether they were themselves its authors. The burgrave interposed, urging, that the affair was improper for disclosure, as a secret of state, and endeavoured to soothe them by persuasion and exhortation. His attempts, however, were fruitless; another delegate exclaimed, " Let us follow the ancient custom of Bohemia, and hurl them from the window ! " The impulse was instantly given ; the burgrave and the grand prior were led out of the room, and Martinetz instantly precipitated into the ditch of the castle. The delegates who had been driven to the brink of rebellion, without adverting to the consequences of their conduct, recoiled with horror, and turned round to each other with looks of confusion and dismay. Their chief alone preserved his resolution and presence of mind ; his penetrating eye saw their emotion, and he recalled their scattered spirits, by exclaiming, " Noble lords, another object waits your vengeance ! " In an instant their passions were again roused ; this appeal inspired the conspirators with all their former resolution, and they completed their atrocious act, by throwing from the window Slavata, and Fabricius the secretary, who was no less unpopular. Thus terminated this singular event, which is rendered still more extraordinary by the wonderful escape of the intended victims. Though precipitated from a height of eighty feet, and fired at from the windows, their fall was broken by the water or mud of the moat, and they made their escape almost unhurt, one by crossing the Moldau, the others by obtaining refuge in a neighbouring dwelling.

Thurn having thus led his associates into the commission of an outrage which precluded all hope of accommodation, now laboured to convince his whole party that the vengeance of the emperor would make no distinction of persons, and that their only safety consisted in unanimous and open resistance. He rode through the streets, accompanied by his colleagues, haranguing the crowd of all ranks and conditions, who had flocked from all quarters, on this memorable occasion. "I do not," he exclaimed, "propose myself as your chief, but as your companion, in that peril which will lead us to happy freedom or glorious death. The die is thrown, it is too late to recall what is past; your safety depends alone on unanimity and courage, and if you hesitate to burst asunder your chains, you have no alternative but to perish by the hands of the executioner." His address raised a thunder of applause, and was attended with an instantaneous effect; those Protestants who disapproved the outrage, considering themselves as involved in the common danger, united in the rebellion for common safety, and even many of the Catholics, detesting the arbitrary principles of Ferdinand, joined with the adherents of count Thurn, as the only means of preserving their civil rights.

Their measures were not, as generally happens in popular commotions, tardy and fluctuating; but vigorous, prompt, and decisive. Two days being spent in arranging their plans, the whole body met on the third, and, with all the forms of the diet, revived the confederacy which had enabled them to give law to Rhodolph. They elected thirty directors, chosen equally from the three estates, for the administration of affairs, issued orders for the levy of troops, and appointed count Thurn their commander. They expelled the archbishop of Prague and the abbot of Brunau, drove out the Jesuits, and appealed to their co-estates of Moravia, Silesia, and Lusatia, as well as to the Hungarians, and to the Protestants of the empire. They concluded with drawing up a public apology for their conduct, and sent it with a respectful letter to the emperor.

That part which relates to their outrage against the council of regency, deserves to be recited as an instance of the customs of Bohemia, and as a proof of the art with which they attempted to colour their designs. " They had thrown from the window," they said, " the two ministers who had been the enemies of the state, together with their creature and flatterer Fabricius, in conformity with an ancient custom prevalent throughout all Bohemia, as well as in the capital. This custom," they argued, " was justified by the example of Jezebel in Holy Writ, who was thrown from a window for persecuting the people of God ; and was common among the Romans, and all other nations of antiquity, who hurled the disturbers of the public peace from rocks and precipices."

Matthias, who had reluctantly sent the fatal answer which had been the pretext of the mischief, was thunderstruck with the intelligence of this revolt. He was well acquainted with the temper of his subjects, with the ascendency of the Protestants in every part of his dominions, and the general dislike against Ferdinand, which prevailed as well in Germany as in the Austrian territories ; he also recollected with terror the ferocious resistance of the Bohemians, in defence of their religion, during the Hussite wars. He was therefore justly apprehensive of aggravating the mischief by severity ; and as his subjects had not yet thrown off their allegiance, he hoped by lenity to bring them back to a sense of their duty. In these sentiments he was encouraged by the advice of cardinal Klesel, who, though a zealous Catholic, was yet a prudent minister, and saw no less than his master the danger of recurring to force. But these benevolent sentiments were far from finding a place in the bosom of Ferdinand ; the Jesuits had instilled into his mind the maxim, that Protestantism and rebellion were inseparably united ; that claims of religious freedom were only pretexts for seizing civil rights, and usurping civil authority ; and the enthusiastic fervour with which he had devoted himself to the cause of the church made him rather court than shun dangers in asserting its honour and authority. He delivered on this occasion a memorial, of which we give the substance, as a singular proof of his character, and as displaying the principles on which he now and afterwards acted.

After observing that all attempts would be fruitless to

bring back to reason a people whom God had struck with judicial blindness, he continued, " Since the introduction of heresy into Bohemia, we see nothing but tumults, disobedience, and rebellion. While the Catholics and the sovereign have displayed only lenity and moderation, these sects have become stronger, more violent, and more insolent; having gained all their objects in religious affairs, they turn their arms against the civil government, and attack the supreme authority itself, under the pretence of conscience. Not content with confederating themselves against their sovereign, they have usurped the power of taxation, and have made alliances with foreign states, particularly with the Protestant princes of Germany, in order to deprive him of the very means of reducing them to obedience. They have left nothing to the sovereign but his palaces and the convents; and, after their recent outrages against his ministers, and the usurpation of the regal revenues, no object remains for their vengeance and rapacity but the persons of the sovereign and his successor, and the whole house of Austria.

" If sovereign power emanates from God, these atrocious deeds must proceed from the devil, and therefore must draw down divine punishment. Neither can God be pleased with the conduct of the sovereign in conniving at or acquiescing in all the demands of the disobedient. Nothing now remains for him but to submit to be lorded by his subjects, or to free himself from this disgraceful slavery before his territories are formed into a republic. The rebels have at length deprived themselves of the only plausible argument, which their preachers have incessantly thundered from the pulpit, that they were contending for religious freedom ; and the emperor and the house of Austria have now the fairest opportunity to convince the world, that their sole object is only to deliver themselves from slavery, and restore their legal authority. They are secure of divine support; every sovereign, both ecclesiastic and secular, who is desirous to maintain his own dignity, must favour their cause; and they have only the alternative of a war, by which they may regain their power, or a peace, which is far more dishonourable and dangerous than war. If successful, the forfeited property of the rebels will defray the expense of their armaments ; and if the event of hostilities be unfortunate, they can only lose, with honour and with arms in their hands, the rights and prerogatives, which are and will be wrested from them with shame and dishonour. It is better not to reign than to be the slave of subjects ; it is far more desirable and glorious to shed our blood at the foot of the throne, than to be driven from it like criminals and malefactors."

Ferdinand was supported in his opinion by the archduke Maximilian, and no less by the Spanish court, with whom he had recently entered into a family compact, of which the object was to afford mutual assistance in furthering the aggrandisement of the Austrian family, and the maintenance of the Catholic religion. Matthias, however, was not hurried away by the ardour of Ferdinand, nor induced to abandon his pacific designs, though with a view to give weight to his proposals, he made levies in his hereditary countries, and obtained a considerable subsidy and troops from Spain. By these means he soon assembled a corps of 10,000 men, of which he intrusted the command to general Dampierre, who had already distinguished himself in the war against the Venetians ; and 8000 Spanish troops were advancing from the Netherlands, under the command of the count de Bucquoy, a pupil of Spinola. At the same time Matthias endeavoured to prevent the German princes from assisting the Bohemians, by prohibiting all levies of troops for their support in the empire. With this force he hoped to awe his subjects, while he proffered them the most favourable terms. He declared that he never intended to infringe the royal edict ; that he was only induced to arm because they had armed ; that, if they would abandon their hostile preparations, he would likewise disband his forces, confirm the royal edict, and give full security for the maintenance of their civil and religious privileges. Having followed these proposals with others still more pacific, he sent two of his ministers to Prague, with a view to conciliate the insurgent chiefs, and displayed the utmost earnestness to effect an accommodation.

The known character and principles of Ferdinand prevented the Protestants from accepting these conditions, and his conduct proved their apprehensions to be not unfounded. Enraged at being disappointed of his expected vengeance against the Protestants, he turned his whole resentment against Klesel, to whose advice and influence he attributed the lenity of the emperor. By the assistance of Maximilian, whom Klesel had equally offended, he, on the 20th of July, 1618, caused him to be arrested in the midst of the court, stripped of his cardinal's robes, and conveyed in a covered carriage, under an escort, to a castle in the Tyrol. When the outrage was committed, he repaired with Maximilian to the royal apartment, to communicate the intelligence to Matthias, who was confined with the gout, and endeavoured to justify the deed by representing the cardinal as a weak and wicked minister, whose views were to divide and ruin the house of Austria. The emperor at first received the account with emotions too powerful for utterance ; but, oppressed with age and infirmity, he felt that he had given himself a master, and, from a dread of being driven from the throne, no less than from a sense of his incapacity, he submitted with sullen indignation to the insult.*

Having thus removed the only minister who was willing or able to oppose his views, Ferdinand pursued his designs without control. He led himself 5000 men to awe the Moravians, while Dampierre was ordered with his army to invade Bohemia ; and nothing was heard in the court, or among his adherents, but boasts and exultations, that the rebellious peasants would soon be overpowered by the disciplined troops of Spain, and the injuries and dishonour of the church avenged ; but he soon experienced the difficulty of subjugating a warlike people, directed by able chiefs and animated by a zeal for religion and liberty.

The directors had not beheld the preparations of the court with indifference, and did not suffer their adversaries to obtain a footing in the country before they commenced hostilities. Almost every town in the kingdom joining in the insurrection, as early as July, count Thurn found him-

---

* Kevenhuller informs us, that his emotion at first choked his utterance ; but, on recovering from the first impulse, he thrust the bed clothes into his mouth, and nearly suffocated himself, to avoid speaking.—Schmidt, vol. ix. p. 79.

self at the head of 10,000 men. His first object was, to
secure Budweis, Pilsen, and Krummau, the only towns
which continued faithful to the emperor; he took Krummau by assault, but was foiled at Budweis by the desperate resistance of the inhabitants and imperial garrison.
Called from the siege by the invasion of Dampierre, who
advanced towards the capital, he defeated the imperial
troops, first at Czaslau, and afterwards at Lomnitz. Bucquoy, who approached on the side of Neuhaus to join
Dampierre, was not more successful than his colleague;
he found obstacles in every pass, and every defile; and the
excesses of his troops increased the number of his enemies,
even among those who had hitherto preserved their
loyalty.

The courage of the Bohemians was raised by the junction of the Silesians and Lusatians, and still more by a
timely succour from the Protestant league of Germany,
which they considered as the harbinger of future support;
for that antipathy to Ferdinand which had driven the
Bohemians into rebellion, had at the same time rapidly extended its influence among the Protestants of the empire.
As the means of preventing a civil war, Matthias endeavoured to obtain the dissolution both of the Protestant
union and the Catholic league, which he foresaw would
only divide Germany into two parties, whose hostility
would endanger the imperial authority. He obtained the
assent of the Catholics, on the 14th of May, 1618; but his
efforts only induced the Protestants to renew their union
for three years. Their chief, the elector Palatine, whose
youthful ambition was inflamed by his recent marriage
with Elizabeth, daughter of James, king of England, took
advantage of the unpopularity of Ferdinand, and of the
troubles arising in every part of the Austrian dominions.
The insurrection of Bohemia presented to him a favourable
opportunity of at once aggrandising himself and humbling
a prince against whom he fostered a deep-rooted antipathy.
He entered into a secret league with the elector of Brandenburgh, of which the object was, to secure for himself
the throne of Bohemia; he hoped to obtain the connivance
or acquiescence of the Catholics, by placing a Catholic
prince on the imperial throne; and he flattered himself

with the support of the future emperor, who might owe so high a dignity to his influence and exertions.

Maximilian, duke of Bavaria, a prince no less distinguished for civil and military talents than zeal for the Catholic faith, was the sovereign whom he fixed upon for the destined dignity, and he hoped to secure his nomination without difficulty, as, besides the influence of Maximilian among the Catholics, the vote of his brother, the elector of Treves, in addition to those of Bohemia, Palatine, and Brandenburgh, would form a majority in the electoral college. Frederic himself repaired to Munich, and used every argument to obtain his concurrence ; but he failed of success, as the duke foresaw that such a project would draw on him the resentment of the house of Austria, to which he was allied by blood and friendship, and would exalt the Protestant interest in the empire to the detriment of his own party.

Though thus unexpectedly disappointed, the elector Palatine, instead of relinquishing his project, made a similar proposal to Charles Emanuel, duke of Savoy, whose ambitious spirit and dislike of the Spanish court afforded him a better prospect of success. The wily duke was well aware of the danger attending such an elevation, but foreseeing in this plan an opportunity of drawing the attention of Spain to Germany, he encouraged his ardour by an affected acquiescence in his views. In consequence of this connection, the elector Palatine, and with him the Protestant union, found more ready means than their own resources afforded for interfering in the affairs of Bohemia. By the subsidies of Savoy a corps of 4000 troops was levied in the empire, under the name of the union, of which the disposition was intrusted to the elector Palatine. This corps was raised and commanded by count Mansfeld*, who had served with distinction in the wars of the house of Austria, but, either from disappointment or from attachment to the reformed religion, had entered into the service of the union, led a detachment to the assistance of the duke of Savoy in his Italian wars, and, at the conclusion of the peace, obtained a commission, which was likely

* Natural son of Ernest, count Mansfeld, who had commanded the Spanish army in the Netherlands.

to favour the Protestant cause, and gratify his own resentment.

The members of the union had watched with jealous
attention the conduct of the imperial court toward the
Bohemians, whose cause they considered as their own.
While they were offering their mediation, and exhorting
the emperor to pacify the rising troubles, the elector Palatine issued his orders, and Mansfeld burst into Bohemia.
Being joined by numbers of the natives, he laid siege to
Pilsen, next to Prague, the most important fortress of the
kingdom, and remarkable for the warlike spirit of the inhabitants, and their attachment to their sovereign. After an
obstinate resistance, the fortress surrendered, and Mansfeld
thus obtained a place of arms, where he could wait for
reinforcements, or from whence he could push forwards to
join count Thurn. This success checked the operations of
the imperialists : Dampierre was compelled to retreat into
Austria, and Bucquoy was driven back to Budweis, where
he intrenched himself, in order to preserve so important a
post, the last remnant of the Austrian possessions in
Bohemia.

During these operations Matthias had endeavoured to
obtain effectual succours from the Austrians and the Catholics of the empire. He convoked the states at Vienna ;
but, in reply to all his proposals, he received only demands
for a redress of grievances, and was reproached for under-
taking a war against the Bohemians without their consent.
He met with no better success even from the Catholics of
the empire. They dreaded a contest with the Protestants,
and deprecated the renewal of the civil war in Germany ;
and therefore the duke of Bavaria and the elector of
Mentz joined with the Protestants in recommending an
accommodation. Matthias, had he not been inclined, had
no other choice but to accede to this proposal, and accepted
the arbitration of the electors of Mentz, Bavaria, Saxony,
and Palatine. The repugnance of Ferdinand was overruled, and even the chiefs of the insurgents were awed by
a strong party in the country, who were already wearied
by the calamities of war, and dreaded the uncertain event
of a contest. Pilsen was first proposed for the intended
congress ; but, after much difficulty and many delays, Egra

was fixed upon for the meeting, which was to be opened on the 14th of April, 1619.

At the moment when all parties had been induced or compelled to enter into a negotiation, the death of Matthias frustrated all these well-meant efforts for the restoration of peace. His health had been long declining, but the recent outrage committed on his confidential minister, and the overbearing conduct of Ferdinand, joined to the disturbances in Bohemia, deeply affected his mind, and reduced him to a state of despondency. He brooded over his degraded situation, and was frequently heard to exclaim, that the conduct of his brother and cousin had inflicted on him greater injuries than all the misfortunes of his reign. He received, also, an irrecoverable shock from the death of his wife, whom he tenderly loved, and whose dissolution was hastened by grief for his humiliations and sufferings. This severe loss overcame a mind already drooping under disease, disappointment, and affliction, and soon exhausted the feeble remains of life. He died on the 20th of March, 1619, deeply regretting his own treatment of his brother Rhodolph, lamenting the ingratitude of Ferdinand, and presaging the calamities in which his bigotry and despotism were likely to involve his own territories and the empire.*

Chap. XLVII.—FERDINAND II.—1619.

On the death of Matthias, Ferdinand had attained his 41st year. He became legitimate sovereign of Hungary and Bohemia in consequence of his prior coronation, and archduke of Austria, by the decease of Maximilian, and the renunciation of Albert; he was, in his own right, duke of Styria, Carinthia, and Carniola, and, in conjunction with his two brothers, Leopold and Charles, he inherited the joint possession, but in reality the paramount authority, in

* For the affairs of Bohemia have been principally consulted Pelzel, the native historian; and, for the other parts of the reign of Matthias, Struvius, Heiss, Schmidt, and Heinrich.

the Tyrol and exterior provinces. He was likewise a
candidate for the imperial throne; and the powerful support of Spain, joined with the interest of his family, seemed
likely to crown his claims with undisputed success.

Had he succeeded to an uncontested possession of all
these territories and dignities, he would have almost rivalled
the power of Charles V., the greatest sovereign of his
house. But of all these possessions and honours he seemed
at the moment of his accession scarcely capable of retaining the most inconsiderable; for in every part of his extensive dominions his authority was either secretly undermined or openly annihilated; wherever he turned his eyes
he saw nothing but the flames of rebellion, or the sparks
glowing beneath the embers, and ready to burst into conflagration.

The prospects of Ferdinand were scarcely more encouraging in the empire. He was opposed by the great body
of the Protestant union, who had supported his rebellious
subjects, and who seized so favourable an opportunity as
that which now presented itself to establish the preponderance of their party. They had two votes in the
electoral college: they were not without hopes of detaching the elector of Saxony by the common interests of religion, and were preparing to place a Protestant prince on the
Bohemian throne, and thus to obtain an additional suffrage.
They were countenanced by the united provinces, and by
the Protestant powers of the north; they relied on the
interest which France was likely to feel for the depression
of the house of Austria, to secure her assistance, and they
expected that James I. would support his son-in-law, the
elector Palatine.

All Bohemia, except Budweis, was in the power of the
insurgents; the Silesians and Lusatians had joined the
insurrection, and the Moravians only waited an opportunity to unite in the same cause. Hungary was agitated
by discontents, which all the efforts of the Palatine could
scarcely repress; and the disaffected eagerly looked forward to the support of Bethlehem Gabor, who was in confederacy with the Bohemians, and preparing to invade the
country. In the Styrian territories the Protestants, who
had been reduced to silence by the dread of banishment

and proscription, were eager to disavow their forced conversion, and to follow the successful example of the Bohemians. The natives of Upper Austria had entered into the confederacy, and, by possessing themselves of the passes, at once cut off the communication of Ferdinand with Bohemia, and afforded the insurgents an advantage to invade the last remnant of his possessions. The Protestants of the lower district were animated by a similar spirit; they refused to swear allegiance, and were only prevented from breaking out into open rebellion by the strength of the Catholics, the presence of the sovereign, and a dread of the force under Dampierre.

Duly appreciating the deplorable situation of his affairs, Ferdinand endeavoured to pacify or divide the insurgents by offers of accommodation. On the very day succeeding the emperor's death, he despatched one of his ministers to Prague, with a letter announcing his accession, and a promise to fulfil all the engagements which he had made at his coronation; at the same time he gave orders to Bucquoy to abstain from hostilities and propose a truce. But in this important and critical step he consulted his own feelings and pride rather than his interests; by the same letter he re-established the obnoxious council of regency; and, instead of addressing his proposals to the directorial government, he sent them through the medium of that council which had already become so unpopular, and had furnished the pretext for the insurrection.

The insurgents considered this conduct as a proof of his inveterate hostility, and as an evidence that he was determined to erase with the sword what necessity compelled him to sign with the pen; and, aware that the proposed truce would give him time to assemble his forces, received his proposals with silent contempt. He made subsequent advances in more conciliating terms, but with no better success, for the insurgents were determined to admit no conciliation which was extorted by necessity, but to exclude from the throne a sovereign whom the absolution of the pope would deliver from the most solemn engagements, and from whose inveterate bigotry their civil and religious privileges would be exposed to continual infringements.

They fulfilled their design with the same vigour and

celerity which they had hitherto displayed. While Mansfeld remained in the neighbourhood of Budweis to watch the motions of Bucquoy, Thurn, with 16,000 men, marched into Moravia. His arrival was the signal of revolt; on the 6th of June, the natives rose, the capital opened its gates, the Austrian government was abolished, the Protestant worship established, and the country placed under an administration similar to that of Bohemia. With his forces greatly augmented by this revolution, Thurn burst into Upper Austria, where he experienced a similar reception, and pushed his march to the gates of Vienna. As he was unprovided with heavy artillery, he did not attempt to commence a siege; but, occupying the suburbs, he blockaded the town, and hoped by the aid of the malecontents within, to obtain without bloodshed possession of the capital and the person of the sovereign. So certain did he seem of success, and so confident that the rigours of a blockade would hasten the crisis in his favour, that he even digested a plan for the government of the country.

Ferdinand had seen this storm approach without the faintest prospect of shelter or assistance. All his offers to conciliate the natives of Upper Austria were received with the same contempt as those which he had tendered to the Bohemians. Although the states of the lower district were at this time assembled at Vienna, the Catholics were unable to carry any resolution in his favour, and the Protestants evinced their determination to join the insurgents. The rapid and unexpected irruption of Thurn had precluded all hopes of relief from those troops which were still in arms under Bucquoy and Dampierre in Austria and Bohemia; the garrison was weak, and discontented for want of pay and provisions; while a numerous party within the walls held a correspondence with the enemy, and only waited the signal for insurrection. At the same time he was destitute of all expectations of external assistance: the sovereigns of Spain and Poland, with whom he was connected by blood and interest, were too distant to afford him relief; and even the frail dependence which he might have placed on the Catholics of Germany was frustrated by their mutual jealousies and divisions.

Ferdinand was sensible that the surrender of Vienna

would occasion the loss of Austria, and with it the loss of the imperial crown. He therefore sent his family into the Tyrol, and prepared to maintain his capital, and meet his impending fate with a firmness from which we cannot withhold our admiration. The Jesuits had implanted their maxims in the heart of a hero; and he found a support in that religious fervour with which he was animated. He threw himself at the foot of the crucifix, poured forth his petitions to the Saviour of all, and rose with the full conviction of divine assistance.* Notwithstanding all the remonstrances of his ministers, all the terrors of his situation; notwithstanding the total failure of his hopes from human relief, and all the entreaties of the ministers of that religion to which he was devoted, he persisted in his resolution of encountering the vengeance of an enraged multitude, and burying himself under the ruins of the palace, which had been the seat of his ancestors.

He found full employment for all his resolution; his dangers increased from day to day, from hour to hour; the walls of his palace were battered by the Bohemian cannon; he heard on every side the cries of vengeance, and exclamations; "Let us shut him up in a convent, bring up his children in the Protestant religion, and put his evil counsellors to the sword!" At length the crisis of his fate arrived: sixteen Protestant members of the states burst into his apartment, and with threats and reproaches, clamorously demanded his permission to join the insur-

---

* We have seldom an opportunity of discovering the secret thoughts of sovereigns on great and trying occasions, we therefore gratify the reader with an account given by Ferdinand himself to his confessor, Bartholomew Valerius, who entered his private cabinet at the moment when he had concluded his devotions. " I have reflected," he said, "on the dangers which threaten me and my family, both at home and abroad. With an enemy in the suburbs, sensible that the Protestants are plotting my ruin, I implored that help from God which I cannot expect from man. I had recourse to my Saviour, and said, Lord Jesus Christ, thou Redeemer of mankind, thou to whom all hearts are opened, knowest that I seek thy honour, not my own. If it be thy will that in this extremity I should be overcome by my enemies, and be made the sport and contempt of the world, I will drink of the bitter cup. Thy will be done! I had scarcely spoken these words, before I was inspired with new hope, and felt a full conviction that God would frustrate the designs of my enemies."—De Luca, p. 335.

M 2

gents.   But at this awful moment a sudden sound of
trumpets announced the arrival of succours.   The deputies,
thunder-struck with the alarm, hastened from the palace,
and with the chiefs of their party sought safety in con-
cealment, or took refuge in the camp of the besiegers.

This succour, which had so unexpectedly saved their
sovereign, was a corps of only 500 horse, which had been
detached from Krems by Dampierre, and secretly descending the Danube, had entered the only gate which was not
guarded by the vigilance of the enemy.   Their appearance
operated like magic ; their numbers were exaggerated by
fear or exultation ; and rumours were instantly spread that
further reinforcements were approaching.   The malecontents shrunk away in silence or fled from the city ; and
those whom fear had hitherto deterred hastened to display
their loyalty.   Six hundred students flew to arms ; the
example was followed by fifteen hundred burghers, additional succours arrived, and, in a few hours, all appearance
of danger and discontent had subsided.   Nor did the good
fortune of Ferdinand end with his deliverance : for in the
midst of his exultation, news arrived that Bucquoy had
defeated and dissipated the army of Mansfeld ; and on the
22nd of June, Thurn was suddenly recalled by the deputies from the blockade of Vienna, to secure the capital
of Bohemia.

Relieved from immediate danger, Ferdinand left the
government of his dominions to his brother, the archduke
Leopold, and hastened into Germany to secure the crown
of the empire, on the acquisition of which the recovery of
his own territories principally depended ; because, without
that dignity, he could not expect assistance from the Catholics in the empire, or maintain that influence in foreign
courts, which was necessary for the suppression of the
rebellion in his own territories.

Fortunately the refusal of the duke of Bavaria to receive
the imperial crown, left the Catholics no other alternative
than to accept Ferdinand ; and while their views were
fixed on him, the Protestant party was weakened and
divided.   The elector of Saxony, from motives of interest, strengthened by political jealousy and religious antipathy, maintained his wonted adherence to the house of

Austria, and rejected all the solicitations of the elector
Palatine, and the instances of the Protestant body. The
elector Palatine himself was unable to infuse unanimity
into the Protestant union; and could not bring forward
any candidate whose influence or power might render him
a dangerous competitor. He had proffered the imperial
crown to the dukes of Bavaria and Savoy, but from both
had only received a positive or evasive refusal.

Besides the trifling assistance which he could expect
from the Protestants of the empire, he had less reason to
rely even on those who were most interested to promote
his aggrandisement. James I. was unwilling to offend the
court of Spain, who lured him with the prospect of a
match between the infanta and his son Charles; Denmark
and Sweden were too jealous of each other to act in concert,
and too much employed in their own contests to engage
in foreign wars; the united provinces, agitated by intestine commotions and religious factions, found sufficient employment in guarding and consolidating their newly-
acquired independence. Above all, the situation of France
annihilated all hopes of efficient assistance in humbling
the house of Austria. With Henry IV., that kingdom
had lost its weight in the balance of Europe; a stormy
minority had annihilated all the benefits derived from
his vigorous and economical administration; Mary de'
Medici, the queen-mother, to whom the regency was
intrusted, was governed by Eleonora Galigai, a mean
Italian, and her husband Concini, who was raised to the
title of Marechal d'Ancre. These obscure foreigners, opposed by the great nobles of the kingdom, and embarrassed
by the insurrections of the Huguenots, purchased the
support of Spain by concluding in 1612 a double marriage,
between the young king and the infanta Anne, the prince
of Asturias and the princess Elizabeth. Louis XIII., on
attaining his majority, was anxious to free himself from the
control of his mother and her upstart favourites. He at
length found a deliverer in de Luines, one of the pages of
his court, who procured the assassination of d'Ancre, and
the execution of his wife; and for that service was rewarded with a dukedom, and the supreme direction of
affairs. The young favourite, however, was too weak to

suppress the contending factions, or curb the powerful nobles; he therefore followed the example of his predecessor, submitted himself to the guidance of the king of Spain, and in compliance with his views, promoted the interest of Ferdinand in the empire.

In consequence of these untoward circumstances, Frederic endeavoured to delay the election, hoping that the formal exclusion of Ferdinand from the throne of Bohemia would prove fatal to his cause. But his attempts were overruled by the rest of the electoral college: the day of election was fixed, and Ferdinand invited to assist as legitimate king of Bohemia, notwithstanding all the remonstrances of the insurgent states. He was accordingly unanimously chosen and crowned emperor, on the 9th of September; the elector of Brandenburgh not venturing to irritate him by a fruitless opposition, and even the elector Palatine himself avoiding the publication of his own defeat, by not making a useless protest.

The capitulation signed by Ferdinand was only distinguished by two additional articles of little importance; the first relating to the exercise of the vicarial authority, the other to the constitution of the Aulic council.

The exclusion of the Bohemian ambassadors, and the certainty that Ferdinand would be raised to the imperial dignity, only induced the insurgents to hasten the execution of their plan for ejecting him from the throne. A general diet of the states of Bohemia, Moravia, Silesia, and Lusatia assembled at Prague, soon after the departure of Ferdinand from Vienna. Having formed a confederacy for the maintenance of their civil and religious privileges, they were joined by the Protestants of Upper and Lower Austria, as well as by many of the discontented magnates of Hungary, and were encouraged by assurances of immediate support from Bethlehem Gabor. They then proceeded to draw up a list of their grievances, in which they urged that the election of Ferdinand had been informal, that he had broken his coronation oath, by interfering in the government during the life of Matthias, had commenced the war by his own authority, and sent foreign troops to devastate their country; finally, that he had infringed their right of election, by entering into engagements, without the consent of the states, to transfer the eventual succession of the crown to the Spanish princes, and thus to reduce them under a foreign, hateful, and despotic yoke. On these grounds they declared that Ferdinand had forfeited his dignity, and, in virtue of their supposed right of election, proceeded to nominate a new sovereign.

On this important article, they were, however, less unanimous than on the point of exclusion. The Catholics being too weak and inconsiderable to take any essential share in the election, the remainder of the states were divided between the choice of a Lutheran or Calvinist sovereign. The Lutherans were the most numerous, the Calvinists the most active and artful, and supported by the Picards, or Bohemian brethren, a remnant of the ancient Hussites. The Calvinists suffered the Lutherans to offer the crown to the elector of Saxony, who, they were aware, would refuse the proffered dignity ; and he had no sooner declined it than they turned the choice of the states in favour of the elector Palatine, who was nominated with only six dissenting voices, two days before Ferdinand was raised to the imperial throne. To give an appearance of greater weight to the new election, the states of Moravia, Silesia, and Lusatia were allowed to participate in the choice, a right before often claimed, but never admitted.

Although Frederic had anxiously laboured to secure this dignity, and had previously resolved to accept it, yet he had no sooner gained his object, than he hesitated to encounter the dangers with which the crown was surrounded. He sought advice and encouragement from those with whom he was connected by blood or interest. He was earnestly dissuaded by his mother, by the electors of Saxony and Brandenburgh, by the duke of Bavaria, and, above all, by his father-in-law, the king of England, who declared, that he would not patronise revolted subjects against their lawful sovereign, and would neither acknowledge his title nor afford him support. On the other hand, the wavering resolutions of Frederic were strengthened by his uncles, Maurice, prince of Orange, and the duke of Bouillon, by his favourite counsellor, Christian of Anhalt, by the majority of the Protestant league, and by Bethelem Gabor,

with whom he had entered into the closest connections.
He was urged at the same time by the instances of the
Calvinistic clergy, who represented the proffered crown as
the gift of Providence, and as a pledge of Divine support ;
and he was assailed by all the arts and persuasion of a wife
whom he adored, and who, feeling the pride of royal blood,
was indignant at being the consort of a simple elector. Influenced by these motives, Frederic accepted the fatal gift,
and as he signed the act of election with a trembling hand,
he bedewed it with his tears ; affording at once a proof of
his weakness, and an omen of the miseries which he was
about to draw on himself, on his family, and on Europe.

He left the government of his electorate to the duke of
Deux Ponts, tore himself from the embraces of his mother,
and accompanied by his consort and family, commenced
his journey to his new kingdom. He was met by the Bohemian deputies at Egre, where he confirmed all the privileges which had been granted by former sovereigns. He
then proceeded to the capital, and, as the archbishop of
Prague refused to assist at the coronation, he was crowned
with a pomp and magnificence surpassing all former examples, by the Calixtine administrator, who had been purposely appointed vicar of the archiepiscopal see.

His reign opened under the brightest auspices. The
Protestants exulted in the happy prospect of living under
a sovereign of their own communion ; the people of every
denomination and every sect were enraptured at their
deliverance from the odious yoke of Ferdinand, and the
restoration of all their valued privileges. Their love rose
almost to admiration, when they regarded a monarch to
whom they owed these benefits, endeared to them by their
own voluntary election, and whose popular manners, and
affable demeanour, formed a striking contrast to the preceding sovereigns of the house of Austria, none of whom, except the reserved and gloomy Rhodolph, had deigned to
reside at Prague. Sweden, Denmark, Holland, Venice,
and many of the German princes, acknowledged his title,
and the cause of his rival seemed hastening to its decline.

During the absence of Ferdinand in Germany, the Protestants of Hungary had thrown off their allegiance, and
called in the assistance of Bethlehem Gabor. The Tran-

sylvanian prince, bursting into Hungary, had captured
Cassau, Tiernau, Nietra, Neuhasel, and other fortresses,
dispersed the imperial forces under Homonai, and after
despatching 18,000 men to reinforce count Thurn in Moravia, had advanced with rapid marches towards Presburgh.
The danger of this invasion compelled the archduke Leopold to recall Bucquoy, who, after defeating Mansfeld, had
captured Piseck, and pushed as far as Tabor ; and Thurn,
who was thus delivered from his apprehensions for Bohemia, again bursting into Austria, advanced towards the
capital.   During these events Gabor obtained possession of
Presburgh by treachery, secured the sacred crown, and
called an assembly of the states, who, under his auspices,
united in the grand confederacy against Ferdinand.   Secure of Presburgh, and a considerable part of the kingdom,
he continued his march into Austria, and joining count
Thurn, their united forces amounted to 60,000 men. They
instantly attacked Bucquoy, who, with 18,000 men, had
maintained the head of the bridge over the Danube against
Thurn, drove him from the entrenchments, and would have
forced their way into the capital, had not the imperial
general broken down the bridge in his retreat.

CHAP. XLVIII. — 1619, 1620.

IN this anxious moment Ferdinand returned from Germany, to behold his capital again exposed to all the dangers
of a siege, and to encounter difficulties as great as those
from which he had recently escaped.   He was, however,
again delivered by a new instance of good fortune, scarcely
less extraordinary than the former. The town already suffered greatly from want of provisions ; but this difficulty
was felt in a still higher degree by the besieging army, and
their distresses were aggravated by the extreme severity of
the season.   In this situation, Bucquoy and Dampierre, by
a bold and successful enterprise, descended on the lower
bank of the Danube, and defeated a Hungarian corps at
Haimburgh ; while Homonai, returning from Poland at the

head of a hasty levy of Cossacs, dispersed a body which had been left at Cassau, under Ragotsky, to cover Upper Hungary. Bethlehem Gabor, who thus saw his communication with Hungary and Transylvania in danger of being cut off, and whose troops were exhausted by the severities of the season, and with the want of provisions, was compelled to relinquish the final object of his expedition. In his return, however, he added Oldemburgh to the places which already acknowledged his authority, was proclaimed king of Hungary by the majority of his party, and the adherents of Ferdinand were proscribed and banished. Thurn at the same time retired into Bohemia, to distribute his troops into quarters; and the operations of this campaign, which had been so fertile in great and unexpected events, were closed by the recapture of Piseck, by Mansfeld. Thus the emperor, notwithstanding the opportune deliverance of his capital, again saw himself excluded from every town of Bohemia, except Budweis, and the greater part of Hungary in the possession of his enemies.

While the allies or adherents of Frederic had thus dismembered the states of the emperor, the members of the Protestant union assembled at Nuremberg, and were joined by deputies from many of the imperial towns, and even from the states of the two Austrias. The meeting of so numerous a party, whose decision might fix the balance, occupied the attention of the contending sovereigns. Frederic had no sooner received the crown than he repaired to Nuremberg, to secure the support of that union, of which he was the head; and the emperor himself sent an agent, hoping, by promising a redress of grievances, to prevent them from joining his enemies. But the influence of Frederic, as head of the union, joined with the common interest of religion, outweighed these offers; a disdainful answer was returned to his proposal, in which, after recapitulating the frequent breaches of his promises, they required him, as a proof of his sincerity, to command the Catholic league to disarm, and offered on their side to follow the example. They also urged him to give peace to Bohemia; and concluded with the declaration, that they would not suffer the new king to be molested in his hereditary territories.

Although Frederic had thus defeated the attempt of the emperor, he was yet anxious to draw the union into a more hearty support of his cause, and to entangle their affairs with those of Bohemia. But he at first found a considerable obstacle to his views. Though the princes were desirous to support him, the deputies of the towns were not guided by a policy sufficiently enlarged to appreciate the advantage of seating a Protestant on the throne of Bohemia, and they were, as on former occasions, dissatisfied with the burdens of frequent contributions for the support of the union. At length the military preparations of the Catholic league convinced them that they were threatened with a common danger. They therefore joined with the princes to demand from Maximilian, duke of Bavaria, as head of the Catholic league, the present redress of all their grievances, with security for the future, and the discontinuance of all military preparations, and required a prompt and unequivocal answer. The suspicions which gave rise to this demand, were justified by the conduct of the Catholics, who, instead of replying, accelerated their preparations, and convened a meeting of their party at Wurtzburgh. The Protestants, therefore, on their side, were not less active; they exerted themselves to cut off the passage of those troops who were marching from the Netherlands and Alsace to the assistance of Ferdinand; and an army under the margrave of Anspach, general of the union, advanced to Ulm to watch the motions of the duke of Bavaria. Frederic deeming himself thus secure of immediate support from his party, returned to Bohemia with the full assurance, that the next campaign would crush the hopes and baffle the efforts of his rival.

But the firm temper and active policy of Ferdinand raised him above the difficulties by which he seemed to be overwhelmed. Soon after his coronation at Frankfort, he obtained a promise of assistance from the three ecclesiastical electors, who could not withhold their support from a prince whom they had raised to the throne, and who was the champion of their religion. He gained a still more important acquisition, by securing the alliance of the duke of Bavaria, the only prince of the Catholic party, who from his military skill and political experience, was capable of taking the lead in the present situation of affairs. He repaired in person to Munich, and availed himself of the intimacy derived from their common education, the ties of blood, the authority of his abdicated father-in-law *, and the jealousy which had long subsisted between the Bavarian and Palatine branches; he overcame the scruples which Maximilian advanced, apparently with a view to enhance the price of his services, and purchased his assistance by the most liberal concessions. He yielded to him the full and absolute direction of all military and political operations, agreed to indemnify him for the expenses of the war, for which he pledged a part of his dominions, and promised an equivalent from his own territories, for all the losses which Maximilian might incur in his cause. He also lured the duke with the promise of sharing the spoils of the Palatine, and the prospect of the electoral dignity, which the line of Bavaria was once supposed to have possessed, and still claimed. In virtue of this agreement, Maximilian was to assist him with his own force, and his influence procured the hearty co-operation of the Catholic league. Ferdinand also obtained from the pope a grant of the tenths of all ecclesiastical property in Spain, Italy, and the Netherlands, and a monthly subsidy of 20,000 zecchines.

While Ferdinand was thus employed in uniting his own party, he laboured to weaken and divide the Protestants. To the elector of Saxony he represented the contest as a civil not a religious affair, and he corroborated this assertion by solemn declarations from the Catholic electors and the duke of Bavaria, who, in the name of their whole body, protested that their views were not hostile to the Protestant religion, or directed to procure the restoration of the confiscated property of the church. He held up also the former bait of the succession of Juliers, and lured him with other temptations. His representations found a ready ear from a prince who was weak enough to be displeased with a loss of a crown which he had not courage to accept, and who fostered against the elector Palatine an hereditary jealousy for his superior influence among the Protestants, and an incurable animosity arising from their

* Ferdinand espoused the daughter of his uncle William, the abdicated duke of Bavaria.

discordant sentiments in religion. The defection of the elector was of the greatest advantage to the cause of Ferdinand; for he drew after him the landgrave of Hesse, with other Lutheran princes and states, and his example contributed to discourage and embarrass the remainder.

Ferdinand applied also with equal success to the court of France; he there described his contest with the elector Palatine, not as a political affair, but as a dispute which involved the honour and interest of the church; and he did not fail to avert to the power and restless spirit of the Huguenots, and to expatiate on the assistance which they had constantly derived from the Palatine family. All these arguments were backed by the court of Spain, who swayed the duc de Luines, the all-powerful minister of Louis XIII., and by his means the young king was induced to abandon that system of political enmity which his predecessors had adopted against the house of Austria. By the same predominant influence of Spain, he fixed the king of England in his pacific resolutions, and notwithstanding all the clamours of the nation, and the remonstrances of the parliament, prevented him from taking any other part than sending 4000 troops into Holland, that the same number might be spared by the states for the defence of the Palatinate.

Notwithstanding the advantages which he derived from the interposition of Spain, Ferdinand yet found great difficulty in persuading the court of Madrid to adopt such vigorous measures as were suited to the extremity of his situation. Though they readily furnished a subsidy of 1,000,000 florins in addition to 8000 auxiliaries, the duke of Uzeda, who governed the Spanish counsels, refused to take a part which might render his sovereign a principal in the war; because the truce concluded with the united provinces being nearly expired, Spain might be compelled to renew it on disadvantageous terms, or be at once involved in hostilities with the German princes and the new republic. His opinion was supported by the confessor, who possessed an uncontrolled influence over the weak and bigoted mind of Philip III. For a long time all the arguments and remonstrances of Ferdinand failed of success, till at length his ambassador, Kevenhuller, demanded an audience of the king, and declared that his master, if not assisted by Spain, would abandon Bohemia to the Palatine, Hungary to Bethlehem Gabor, the Friuli to the Venetians, and would himself unite with the Protestants to obtain a compensation by the conquest of the Spanish dominions in Italy and the Netherlands. These threats, however romantic, produced the desired effect; Philip, by almost the only act of authority which he ventured to exercise during his reign, in opposition to his ministers, ordered Spinola to march from the Netherlands with 24,000 men against the Palatinate.

At the same time Ferdinand opened a negotiation with Bethlehem Gabor, concluded with him a truce till the ensuing autumn, and secured himself for a time from an active enemy, whose attacks might have endangered the remnant of his dominions, and diverted his arms from Bohemia.

The good effects of this well-combined system of policy were soon visible. In the spring, the Protestant union and Catholic league respectively assembled their forces; the Protestants at Ulm, under the margrave of Anspach, the Catholics under the duke of Bavaria in the neighbourhood of Guntzburgh. While the vicinity of these powerful armies held Europe in suspense, and while all were expecting an engagement which was to become the prelude to a civil war in Germany, the French court, in compliance with their promises to Ferdinand, despatched the duc d'Angoulême as their ambassador, to mediate an accommodation. The Protestants, disappointed of the expected assistance from France, dreading the strength of their opponents, alarmed by the approach of Spinola, and divided among themselves, agreed to terms of peace, which were highly advantageous to the emperor, on the 3rd of July, 1620. Both parties promised mutually to abstain from hostilities; the union engaged not to support Frederic as king of Bohemia, the league not to attack the Palatinate. The Catholics were thus enabled to assist the arms of Ferdinand in Bohemia ; and the Palatinate was left open to the invasion of the Spaniards or the emperor, or to any of his allies, except the Catholic league.

This treaty produced an immediate effect in Lower Austria. The majority of the Protestant states, deprived of all hope of assistance from their brethren in the empire, and awed by a corps of Polish Cossacs, were reduced to submission. They united with the Catholics to do homage to the emperor, on receiving the confirmation of the religious privileges, granted to them by Matthias ; and the refractory members were proscribed and treated as guilty of high treason.

Ferdinand now concentrated his attacks against the elector Palatine ; and, after exhorting him to abandon his usurped title, gave orders to the duke of Bavaria to expel him from Bohemia. Dampierre, with a body of troops, was detached to the frontiers of Hungary to observe Bethlehem Gabor ; another corps was drawn from Poland to awe the Silesians, while the elector of Saxony reduced Lusatia, and cut off the resources which Frederic might have drawn from that province as well as from the German empire. While these troops were devastating the dependent provinces, the grand attack was led by the duke of Bavaria, assisted by the counsels of John Tzerclas, afterwards count of Tilly, who had greatly distinguished himself in the wars of Hungary. Delivered from all apprehensions of the Protestant union by the truce of Ulm, he led 25,000 men into Upper Austria, and taking the insurgents unprepared, reduced them to unconditional submission. He pursued his success with equal celerity ; uniting near Weidhofen with Bucquoy, he found himself at the head of 50,000 men. He divided these troops into two bodies ; with the Germans he entered Bohemia on the side of Budweis, while Bucquoy, with the Spanish and Italian veterans, reduced Kummau, Budweis, and Prakatitz, and their forces joined under the walls of Piseck. Without a moment's delay they summoned this important fortress to surrender ; and while the governor was deliberating on the terms of capitulation, the Walloons and Cossacs scaled the ramparts, put the garrison to the sword, plundered and burnt the town, and gratified their thirst of blood by massacring the defenceless inhabitants. Their fury spared neither sex nor age, nor was awed by the sacred asylum of the altar ; the carnage was only arrested by the personal interference of the duke of Bavaria, and

Bucquoy. This dreadful example struck terror into the neighbouring towns, Strakonitz, Winterburgh, Schutten-hofen, Klattau, and other places, hastened to avert a similar fate, by submitting to the imperial arms.

The situation of Frederic was now most alarming. He was deserted by the Protestant union, hemmed in on every side by the imperial troops, or the allies of the emperor; and his Palatinate was overrun by Spinola at the head of 20,000 Spaniards, even in the sight of that army, and that union, on which he had relied for its defence. Within his newly-acquired kingdom, his only foreign force consisted of 8000 Hungarian horse, a small corps of Germans under Hohenlohe, and the army of Mansfeld, which, receiving no pay either from the duke of Savoy or the union, was reduced to subsist on plunder. His chief hopes, therefore, rested on his new subjects ; but their enthusiasm and loyalty had also subsided. They soon perceived that his popular and affable manners were supported by no firmness or energy of mind ; and the magnates, who had revelled in imagination in the enjoyment of Austrian governments and English treasures, were discouraged by the failure of all their expectations. He had alienated the affections of his Lutheran and Catholic subjects, by removing the altars, images, bells, and ornaments of the churches, and by endeavouring to reduce their divine service to the naked simplicity of the Calvinistic worship. He had offended Thurn and Mansfeld, the two great champions of his cause, by giving the chief command to the prince of Anhalt and Hohenlohe, and by placing his confidence on his own adherents. The excesses and devastations of his troops, as well as those of Mansfeld, had provoked the peasants, who rose to defend their possessions, and were scarcely persuaded to disperse by promises of indemnification. During this invasion, however, Frederic seemed to be absorbed in the rejoicings attending his elevation ; infatuated by his first success, he neglected the necessary cares for the preservation of his crown, to figure in balls and pageants, the celebration of public ceremonies, and other useless efforts for the acquisition of popularity.

After an ineffectual attempt to rouse the burghers of

Prague, and obtain a supply of money, the increasing danger induced Frederic to repair to the main army, which, under the prince of Anhalt, had remained at Pritznitz, with the hope of animating his troops and fixing the indecision of his generals by his presence.   Here, however, he experienced new mortifications ; the army, which did not exceed 22,000 men, without supplies of clothing or pay, was discontented and discouraged, and the generals and officers differed in opinion ; some, among whom was the intrepid count Thurn, were anxious to risk a battle ; others, yielding to the sentiments of their commander-in-chief, were desirous to protract the campaign till the approach of winter by defensive operations.   These difficulties and the arguments of the prince of Anhalt induced Frederic to make proposals for arranging an accommodation.   But the duke of Bavaria was too sensible of his own advantages and the necessity of crushing a distressed enemy by vigour and decision, to waste the important moment.   He refused to enter into a negotiation except the elector would previously relinquish his crown, and exerting all his efforts to force the prince of Anhalt to an engagement, successively forced him back to Rokytzan, Rakonitz, and Aunhost, and finally drove him under the walls of Prague. His celerity and decision increased the divisions and distress of the Bohemian chiefs, while the troops in their disorderly retreat, gave way to every species of licentiousness, and clamoured against the foreign generals, whom they accused of betraying them.   They took post on the White Mountain, as the last resource for the defence of the capital, and behind its ravines and declivities began to construct intrenchments, in order to defy the assaults of the enemy. The duke of Bavaria, however, did not allow them time to prepare for defence ; he resolved to drive them from their last refuge before they had recovered from the confusion of a retreat, and while his own troops were warm in the pursuit.   He reached the vicinity of Prague on the morning of the 8th of November, 1620, and ere noon had reconnoitred their position and commenced his attack. His troops overcame all obstacles ; the Hungarian cavalry was instantly defeated and dispersed : and although the

Moravians, under the prince of Anhalt and the young count Thurn, balanced the fortune of the day by their heroic resistance, the victory was decided in favour of the imperialists within the short space of an hour. With the loss of only three hundred men, they took all the artillery, a hundred standards, left 4000 of the enemy dead on the field, and drove 1000 into the Moldau ; and thus, at one blow, dissipated the short-lived hopes of Frederic, and decided the fate of Bohemia.

Before this battle the unfortunate prince had returned to Prague for the purpose of rousing the burghers and collecting reinforcements ; but at the important moment on which his destiny was suspended, instead of rushing into the foremost ranks, and animating his troops by sharing their dangers, he indulged his characteristic love of show and conviviality, and was sitting at table with his whole court, at an entertainment which he gave to the English ambassador. Before the engagement the prince of Anhalt requested him to send all the troops within the city, and represented to him the necessity of encouraging his army by his presence ; but Frederic, with an inconceivable infatuation, declined quitting his company before the close of the entertainment. In the beginning of the combat another messenger was despatched on the same errand, and with the same success ; it was not till repeated couriers announced the misfortune of the day, that the thoughtless or pusillanimous prince could be prevailed on to quit the table. Having at length mounted his horse, he rode to the gate leading to the White Mountain ; but, finding it shut, he climbed the rampart, and saw with his own eyes the defeat of the army on which he had placed his hopes of success, and the terrible carnage of those who bled in his defence. After ordering the gate to be opened to admit the fugitives, he immediately returned to the palace, and was overtaken in his way by the prince of Anhalt and the count of Hohenlohe, who had withdrawn from a hopeless contest. By their advice a messenger was despatched to the duke of Bavaria, requesting a truce for twenty-four hours ; but Maximilian granted only eight, under the condition that Frederic should immediately, by a letter, renounce his pretensions to the crown of Bohemia ; and the desponding prince made no difficulty in acceding to this demand, as he had resolved to depart from Prague.

Although the officers were too much astounded amidst the confusion and dismay of the route to make preparations for defending the city, the burghers, deriving courage from despair, repaired in a body to Frederic, and endeavoured to infuse that spirit into their sovereign which they felt themselves, by offering to defend the ramparts to the last extremity. He thanked them for this proof of their affection, but advised them to make the best capitulation in their power, and announced his resolution to quit Prague before break of day. The citizens conjured him to stay; they exclaimed that they had still strength sufficient to withstand a siege, and offered to maintain as large a body of troops as could be collected within the walls. The young counts Thurn and Schlemmendorf represented to him that seventeen battalions were still entire : " the soldiers," they said, " who have escaped from the engagement only wait the beat of the drum to return to their standards; above eight thousand Hungarians are lying at Brandeiss, the gallant Mansfeld is in the rear of the enemy, and still possesses the strong fortresses of Tabor and Pilsen. The courage of the Bohemians is not yet exhausted ; the recollection of the heroic acts of their ancestors in the Hussite wars will rouse them to similar deeds of glory." But these resources, which, in the hands of his firm and able rival would have become insuperable obstacles to the progress of an enemy, were lost on the weak and pusillanimous Frederic, who was overwhelmed by the tide of misfortune. His timid imagination was terrified by the confusion of the defeat ; and the desponding prince pictured to himself the Bohemians as ready to deliver him to their incensed sovereign as a sacrifice to secure their own safety. In the first impulse of alarm, he prepared to carry away the crown and regalia; but his terrors increasing every moment, he left them in the market-place, and consulted only his personal safety by quitting the town during the night. Accompanied by his wife and children, his generals Anhalt and Hohenlohe, and count Thurn, with some of his principal adherents, he hastened from the scene of danger to Breslau, and from thence took refuge at Berlin.

Chap. XLIX. — 1621–1623.

The victory of the White Mountain was followed by a rapid series of the most fortunate events. The citizens of Prague, deserted by their elected sovereign, had no other alternative than to submit themselves to the mercy of the emperor, and on the following day opened their gates to the conqueror. All the indulgence they could obtain was an exemption from plunder ; the states who were immediately convened, took an unconditional oath of allegiance, dissolved their confederacy, and surrendered their arms. These arrangements being completed, the duke of Bavaria delivered the reins of government to prince Charles of Lichtenstein, in obedience to the appointment of the emperor ; and after leaving a garrison in the town under the command of Tilly, returned triumphantly to Munich, laden with the spoils of the unfortunate kingdom.

Three months elapsed without the slightest act of severity against the insurgents of Bohemia. Many lulled into security by this doubtful calm, emerged from their hiding places, and the greater part remained quiet at Prague, though secretly warned of their danger even by Tilly himself, who was no pattern of lenity or forbearance. But in an evil hour all the fury of the tempest burst upon their heads. Forty of the principal insurgents were arrested in the night of the 21st of January, 1621, and after being imprisoned four months, and tried before an imperial committee of inquiry, twenty-three were publicly executed, their property confiscated, and the remainder either banished or condemned to perpetual imprisonment. A sentence of proscription and confiscation of goods was published against count Thurn, and twenty-seven of the other chiefs, who had fled from the country. Nor were these examples confined only to those who had been openly concerned in the rebellion ; for a mandate of more than inquisitorial severity was issued, commanding all landholders who had participated in the insurrection to confess their delinquencies, and threatening the severest vengeance if they were afterwards convicted. This dreadful order spread general consternation : not only those who had shared in the insurrection acknowledged their guilt, but even the innocent were driven by terror to self-accusation ;

and above seven hundred nobles and knights, almost the whole body of landholders, placed their names on this list of proscription. By a mockery of the very name of mercy, the emperor granted to these unfortunate victims their lives and honours, which they were declared to have forfeited by their own confession ; but gratified his vengeance and rapacity by confiscating the whole or part of their property, and thus reduced many of the most loyal and ancient families to ruin, or drove them to seek a refuge from their misfortunes in exile or death.*

Had justice and moderation guided the sentiments of Ferdinand, the war might now have been terminated with honour and safety. He might have gratified his allies, and reimbursed his expenses with the confiscated property of the rebels, and might have converted the elector Palatine from an enemy into a friend and dependent, by restoring him to the quiet possession of his hereditary territories. The fate of Germany and the tranquillity of Europe depended on his nod, and never did a more important decision rest on the will of a single individual ; never did the blindness and intolerance of a single man produce such an extent of mischief and calamity.

Ferdinand, though firm, patient, and resigned in adversity, was stern, vengeful, and overbearing in prosperity. He was urged by many motives of resentment, policy, and zeal to complete the ruin of the elector Palatine, and he did not possess sufficient magnanimity to resist the temptation.   Having squandered away the confiscated property among his Jesuits and favourites, he had still many allies and adherents whose fidelity he was desirous to reward ; he was anxious to recover Upper Austria, which he had mortgaged to the duke of Bavaria, as a pledge for the

* Pelzel, p. 731–742. Several native and Catholic writers endeavour to extenuate the cruelty of Ferdinand, by declaring that he was with difficulty induced to make these dreadful examples ; and was overborne by the representations of his ministers and the Jesuits. Admitting this fact, it is no exculpation of his conduct to assert that he acted unjustly by the advice of his ministers.   But the preceding and subsequent transactions, as well as the general character, the relentless disposition, and the deep-rooted prejudices of Ferdinand, furnish ample evidence that he wanted no external impulse to commit acts of persecution and cruelty against the Protestants.

expenses of the war; he wished to regain possession of Lusatia, and he was bound in honour to satisfy the elector of Saxony for his opportune assistance. The spoils of the unfortunate elector were sufficient to fulfil all these objects; but he was influenced by another motive, which, to such a furious zealot, was irresistible. The principle which he had imbibed from the Jesuits, that Protestantism and rebellion were inseparable, was more deeply than ever imprinted on his mind; he considered his recent and wonderful escape as a proof of divine interposition, and he burned for an opportunity of evincing his gratitude, by fulfilling the vow which he had made to the Virgin at Loretto, and since repeatedly renewed.

By dividing the territories of the elector Palatine among his Catholic allies, he extended the profession of his faith; by transferring the electorate to the duke of Bavaria, he obtained an additional Catholic suffrage in the electoral college, and reduced the Protestants to only two votes; he thus at once gratified his vengeance and his interest, and fulfilled what he deemed the most sacred and indispensable of all duties.

These motives overbearing all considerations of justice and prudence, Ferdinand published the ban of the empire, of his own authority, against the elector Palatine and his adherents the prince of Anhalt, the count of Hohenlohe, and the duke of Jaegendorf. The execution of this informal sentence he intrusted to the archduke Albert, as possessor of the circle of Burgundy, and to the duke of Bavaria, commanding the former to occupy the Lower, and the latter the Upper Palatinate. This vigorous act was instantly followed by the most decisive effects; for the Protestants were terrified by the prospect of sharing the fate of the unfortunate elector. The members of the union now felt the fatal consequences of their own indecision and want of foresight; they had suffered their chief to be driven from a throne which might have served as an insuperable barrier against the Catholic body and the house of Austria; their army had tamely looked on, while Spinola was subjugating the Palatinate; they had no other alternative than to submit to the will of that chief whom they had braved and insulted, and were compelled to purchase an uncertain and temporary safety by the dereliction of those objects which during twelve years they had laboured to attain. Threatened at once by Spinola and the duke of Bavaria, and confounded by the growing power of the emperor, they vied in abandoning a confederacy which exposed them to his vengeance. On the 12th of April, 1621, they concluded at Mentz a treaty of neutrality, by which they promised not to interfere in the affairs of the Palatinate, agreed to disband their troops within a month, and to enter into no new confederacy to the disadvantage of the emperor. This dishonourable treaty was followed by the dissolution of the union, which, on its expiration, was not renewed.

During these events, Spinola, having completed the reduction of the Lower Palatinate, was occupied in the siege of Frankendahl, which was on the point of surrendering, and its capture must have been followed by the submission of Heidelberg and Manheim. The duke of Bavaria had been still more successful in the Upper Palatinate, and had rapidly subjugated the whole province, together with the district of Cham.

The elector Palatine, deserted by the Protestant union, and almost abandoned by his relatives the kings of England and Denmark, owed the first revival of his hopes of restoration to Mansfeld, an illegitimate adventurer, with no other resources than plunder and devastation. Christian of Brunswick, administrator of Halberstadt, distinguished indeed by illustrious birth, but equally an adventurer, and equally destitute of territory or resources, espoused his cause, as well from ties of affinity* as from a chivalrous attachment to his beautiful consort ; and George Frederic, margrave of Baden, even abdicated his dignity to devote himself to his support.

Mansfeld had continued to maintain possession of Pilsen and Tabor ; and, by the march of Bucquoy against Bethlehem Gabor, and the diminution of the forces under Tilly for the conquest of the Upper Palatinate, had been enabled, with only 8000 men, to resist all the efforts of the impe-

---

* Elizabeth, the mother of Christian, was daughter of Christian II. of Denmark, and sister of Anne, the wife of James I., mother of the electress Palatine. Christian is said to have worn a scarf, or favour, with the motto, " *For God and for her.*"

rialists, to capture several fortresses, and spread alarm to the gates of Prague. But destitute of resources, with no other authority than the respect inspired by his superior talents, proscribed by the emperor, a price fixed on his head, and every avenue apparently closed by the enemy, he could not long maintain his position against the skill of Tilly and the strength of a powerful monarchy. Tilly being reinforced with 5000 men, the elector of Saxony advancing to Egra, and his followers yielding Pilsen by treachery, Mansfeld abandoned the posts which he had so bravely maintained, and suddenly passing into the Upper Palatinate, entrenched himself at Roszkopf, a strong post on the Prignitz, in the vicinity of Nuremberg. He was closely followed and surrounded by the army of Tilly, and seemed on the point of being overpowered by superior forces. But his firm spirit was not subdued, nor his fertile genius exhausted. He lulled his vigilant antagonist by feigned proposals for surrender, and, on the 4th of October, 1621, while the terms were adjusting, suddenly breaking from his confined situation in the night, pushed, by forced marches, into the Lower Palatinate. Here he found a more favourable field of action ; for Spinola being recalled with the greater part of the Spanish forces, had left the remainder to Gonzales de Cordova, who, after reducing several minor fortresses, was pressing the siege of Frankendahl. The name of the brave adventurer drew to his standard multitudes of the troops, who had been disbanded by the Protestant union, and he was joined by a party of English, who had been sent for the defence of the Palatinate. Finding himself at the head of 20,000 men, he cleared the country in his passage, relieved Frankendahl, and provided for the safety of Heidelberg and Manheim. Unable, however, to subsist, in a district so recently the seat of war, he turned into Alsace, where he increased his forces ; from thence he invaded the neighbouring bishoprics of Spire and Strasburgh, levying heavy contributions, and giving up the rich domains of those sees to the devastations of his troops.

Encouraged by this gleam of hope, the elector Palatine quitted his asylum in Holland, passed in disguise through Loraine and Alsace, joined Mansfeld, and gave his name and countenance to this predatory army. Animated by his presence, Mansfeld crossed the Rhine at Germesheim, effected a junction with the margrave of Baden Durlach, and captured Sinzheim, Eppingen, and Ladenburgh. On the other hand, Christian of Brunswick levied a predatory army, after the example of Mansfeld, pillaged the rich sees of Lower Saxony, and returning from his incursion enriched with plunder, and strengthened by an accession of force, took the route through the Upper Palatinate to unite with Mansfeld. At the same time the duke of Wirtemberg, the landgrave of Hesse, and other Protestant princes, began to arm, and hopes were even entertained of the revival of the Protestant union.

Tilly, who had followed Mansfeld from Bohemia, had in vain endeavoured to prevent his junction with the margrave of Baden. Defeated at Mingelsheim by Mansfeld, on the 29th of April, 1622, he had been reduced to the defensive, and in this situation saw a powerful combination rising on every side against the house of Austria. He waited therefore for an opportunity of attacking those enemies singly, whom he could not resist when united, and that opportunity was presented by the separation of the margrave of Baden from Mansfeld, and his attempt to penetrate into Bavaria. Tilly suddenly drew together the Spanish troops, and with this accession of force, defeated, on the 6th of May, the margrave at Wimpfen, with the loss of half his army, and took his whole train of artillery and military chest. Leaving Mansfeld employed in the siege of Ladenburgh, he next directed his attention to Christian of Brunswick, routed him on the 20th of June, at Hoechst, as he was crossing the Main, pursued him till his junction with Mansfeld, and drove their united forces beyond the Rhine, again to seek a refuge and subsistence in Alsace.

These successes revived the cause of Ferdinand; the margrave of Baden retired from the contest; the duke of Wirtemberg and the other Protestant princes suspended their armaments; and although Mansfeld and Christian of Brunswick laid siege to Saverne, and evinced a resolution to maintain the contest to the last extremity, yet the elector Palatine again gave way to that weakness which had already lost him a crown. The king of England, who had been lured with the hope of procuring the restitution of the Palatinate, through the mediation of Spain, had opened a negotiation with the emperor, in conjunction with the king of Denmark. This overture presented to Ferdinand a favourable opportunity of consummating his vengeance, and of procuring, without risk, the unconditional submission of the elector Palatine. He therefore affected to listen to the instances of Spain, while he amused the king of England with equivocal promises and vague offers of reconciliation ; at the same time he refused to debase his dignity as sovereign, by treating with a prince who was yet in arms, and who countenanced adventurers proscribed by the ban of the empire. These lures were irresistible to a prince like James, so tenacious of the honour of sovereigns, so averse to war, and so vain of his talents as a negotiator. By his exhortations Frederic was easily prevailed upon to disavow his intrepid defenders, to dismiss them from his service, to retire again into Holland, and wait the mercy of the emperor. By this disavowal, Mansfeld and Christian were left without a name to countenance their operations ; and after various negotiations, feigned or real, for entering into the service of the emperor, Spain, and France, they accepted the overtures of the prince of Orange, and forced their way through the Spanish army which attempted to oppose their passage, to join at Breda the troops of the United Provinces.

The places in Alsace and the bishopric of Spire, which had been occupied by the enemy, were recovered by the archduke Leopold ; and Tilly, having completed the conquest of the Palatinate by the capture of Heidelberg and Manheim, directed his attacks against the forces which Mansfeld and Christian of Brunswick had again assembled.

After a short continuance in Holland, Mansfeld, in November, had led his predatory army into the rich province of East Friesland, conquered the principal fortresses, and extorted enormous contributions from the duke, who was in alliance with Spain. On the other hand, Christian passing into Lower Saxony, persuaded the states of the circle to collect an army of observation amounting to 12,000 men, and intrust him with the command ; and he soon increased this army to almost double that number, by the usual incitements of pillage and plunder. These levies attracting the attention of the emperor, his threats, together with the advance of Tilly, compelled the Saxon states to dismiss Christian and his army. Thus left a second time without authority, he pushed towards Westphalia, with the hope of joining Mansfeld, and renewing hostilities in the Palatinate ; his design was however anticipated by Tilly, who overtook him at Loen, in the district of Munster, and defeated him with the loss of 6000 killed, and 4000 prisoners, in August, 1623. The victorious general then turned towards East Friesland, but Mansfeld, who had hitherto maintained himself in that country, avoided an unequal contest, by disbanding his troops, and withdrawing into Holland, in January, 1624.

During the war in Bohemia, Bethlehem Gabor had been encouraged by the promises of the Turks, by the instances of count Thurn and the duke of Jaegendorf, and by the support of a party among the Hungarian nobles, to assume the title of king, and break the truce which he had recently concluded with Ferdinand. In October, 1619, he sent a reinforcement of horse into Bohemia, and prepared to invade the hereditary countries. Dampierre, who was left to observe his motions, was killed in an attempt to surprise Presburgh, and his troops dispersed on the loss of their general. The defeat at Prague, and still more the pusillanimous flight of the elector, enabled Ferdinand to detach a part of his forces to resist the aggressions of the Transylvanian prince ; and Bucquoy, after reducing Moravia, compelled him to retreat to Cassau. Presburgh, Moder, Rosendorf, Tirnau, Altenburgh, with the isle of Schut, were either taken by force or surrendered to the imperial arms ; while a detachment sent into Lower Hungary reduced Guntz and Oedemburgh, with other places of less importance. Bucquoy pursuing his success, laid siege to Neuhasel ; but in his career of victory was killed in a sally, on the 10th of July, 1621, and his troops, discouraged by the loss of their able commander, retreating towards Commora, were soon reduced by sickness and desertion to 8000 men.

In consequence of this retreat, Bethlehem Gabor resuming offensive operations, recovered Tirnau, and laid siege to Presburgh ; and he was here joined by the young count

Thurn, and by the duke of Jaegendorf, who had made themselves masters of the towns of Glatz and Troppau, in Silesia. His detachments burst into Upper Hungary and Moravia, where they levied contributions and devastated the country, and his partisans spreading themselves on both sides of the Danube, made incursions even to the walls of Vienna. Encouraged by this success, he purposed to carry his arms into Bohemia, where he hoped to rouse the adherents of Frederic, and he flattered himself with the co-operation of the German princes. But his plans were frustrated by the bravery and perseverance of the governor of Presburgh, by the failure of the promised succours from the Turks and the German princes, and still more by his disputes with the duke of Jaegendorf, and the defection of the Hungarian magnates. He accordingly made overtures of accommodation, which were readily accepted by the emperor, who was anxious to turn his forces against the adherents of the elector Palatine in Germany. Both parties being equally desirous of a respite, a treaty was concluded without delay, at Niclasburgh in Moravia, on the 26th of January, 1622. Bethlehem renounced his pretensions to Hungary, and restored the sacred crown, with all his conquests; and Ferdinand purchased these cessions by yielding to him, for life, seven provinces of Upper Hungary, contiguous to Transylvania, with the town of Cassau, and the principalities of Ratibor and Oppelen in Silesia, and by conferring on him the rank of a prince of the German empire. In consequence of this peace, Ferdinand soon afterwards held a diet at Presburgh, where he restored the sacred regalia with the utmost pomp and solemnity; and had the satisfaction to see the crown of Hungary placed on the head of his empress Eleonora, daughter of Vincento I., duke of Mantua, whom he had recently espoused. Sensible of the great advantages resulting from the pacification of Hungary, he even departed from his usual principles, and not only conciliated his subjects by granting them a general amnesty, with the confirmation of their civil and religious rights, but even by approving the choice of a Protestant Palatine. The immediate effects of this pacification were the recovery of Glatz and Troppau.

Fortunately for Ferdinand, this peace, by delivering him

from a dangerous enemy in the heart of his own territories, enabled him to combat the new and alarming confederacy which was forming against him, in consequence of his illegal conduct towards the Protestants, and the elector Palatine in particular.

Having despoiled the elector Palatine of all his dominions, and delivered himself from his enemies in Germany, Ferdinand had proceeded to carry his plans into execution, by transferring the electoral dignity to the duke of Bavaria, and dividing the conquered territories among his adherents. In the fulfilment of this project, however, he had reason to expect the greatest difficulties, from the opposition of the whole Protestant body, from the collateral branches of the Palatine house, from his adherent the elector of Saxony, the kings of Denmark and England, and even from the king of Spain, who was unwilling to offend the English court, with whom he was then negotiating a marriage between the infanta and the prince of Wales. But Ferdinand was not daunted by these obstacles; he gained the elector of Saxony, by promising him the revenues, and perhaps the cession of Lusatia; and the landgrave of Hesse Darmstadt, by offering to favour his pretensions to the succession of Marburgh, which he was contesting with the landgrave of Hesse Cassel; he also persuaded the court of Spain to acquiesce in a transfer which was calculated to strengthen the Catholic cause, and benefit the house of Austria. Having thus gained those whose opposition was most likely to frustrate his design, he paid little regard to the feeble threats of James, and to the remonstrances of the king of Denmark, who was sufficiently employed in his contests with Sweden; he despised the efforts of the Protestant body, when not supported by the elector of Saxony, and he endeavoured to quiet the clamours of the Palatine house, by promising them a portion of the spoils.

His measures being thus prepared, he summoned, on the 25th of February, 1623, a meeting of the electors and princes who were most devoted to his cause at Ratisbon, and, in concurrence with the majority of this irregular assembly, transferred the Palatine electorate, with all its honours, privileges, and offices to Maximilian, duke of Bavaria. To keep up, however, the hopes of the elector

Palatine and his adherents, and not to drive his family and connections to desperation, the whole extent of the plan was not developed : the partition of his territories was deferred, the transfer of the electorate was made only for the life of Maximilian, and the rights of the sons and collateral heirs of the unfortunate elector were expressly reserved. Against this transfer, Wolfgang William, duke of Neuburgh, as head of the collateral line of the Palatine house, made the warmest remonstrances, and he was seconded by the elector of Brandenburgh. The elector of Saxony also, in order to avoid the appearance of deserting the cause of his religion, presented a protest, but previously apprised the emperor that his opposition was merely for the sake of form. With the same insincerity the Spanish ambassador quitted the assembly, that his presence might not be considered as an approbation of the transfer. In the ensuing year another electoral assembly was held at Nuremberg, in which Maximilian was formerly installed on the electoral bench ; the elector of Saxony, having been gratified with the mortgage of Lusatia as a compensation for his expenses, seized this opportunity to revoke his feigned protest, and the single dissenting voice of the elector of Brandenburgh was disregarded.

The Protestants who had seen the ruin of the elector Palatine with the most cruel indifference, were thunderstruck with the transfer of his electorate to a Catholic, and the purposed division of his territories. Their alarms were increased by the dreadful persecution of the Protestants which now commenced in the Austrian territories, and the forcible introduction of the Catholic religion into the Palatinate ; they were convinced that the emperor had formed a systematic design for the depression of their party, by the resolution which he did not conceal, to recover the sees and ecclesiastical property appropriated since the peace of religion, and their fears led them justly to apprehend that his designs would not terminate with this resumption. They could not behold with indifference the close connection between the German and Spanish branches of the house of Austria ; they were alarmed by the vast and ambitious projects of Olivarez, the all-powerful minister of Philip IV. ; and they considered the recent occupation of the small but important district of the Valteline, by their joint forces, as a step towards opening a direct communication between the Austrian territories and the Spanish dominions in Italy, and preparing for the subjugation of Germany and of Europe. Their own union was dissipated; while the emperor and the Catholic league continued in arms; and the troops of Tilly, which, instead of being disbanded, were suffered to spread over the country as far as the Weser, convinced them that more dangerous projects were yet in agitation.

Chap. L.—1624–1629.

The first combination derived from this alarm arose in Lower Saxony, of which the princes and states possessed the principal portion of the ecclesiastical property, and were therefore most exposed to the aggressions of the emperor. Their great object was, to procure foreign support, and they found several of the European powers no less eager than themselves to oppose the aggrandisement of the house of Austria.

An essential change had taken place in the counsels of England. The intended marriage between the prince of Wales and the Spanish infanta having been broken off by the influence of Buckingham, that haughty minister had exerted all his influence over the mind of his timid master, to impel him to vigorous measures for effecting the restoration of his son-in law, instead of trusting to delusive negotiations. An alliance was formed with France, and a treaty of marriage concluded between the prince of Wales and the princess Henrietta; Mansfeld was employed and despatched with an army of 14,000 men, for the re-conquest of the Palatinate, and, although this expedition was frustrated by the refusal of France, and the repugnance of the united states to allow the troops a passage through their territories, the British cabinet stimulated Sweden and Denmark to support the states of Lower Saxony, and offered to assist with subsidies and troops.

The court of France, which under Richelieu had revived the political system of Henry IV., was no less inclined to oppose the views of the house of Austria from policy than England from resentment. Richelieu had already prevented the partition of the Genoese territories between Spain and the duke of Savoy; and, by an armed mediation, obtained the evacuation of the Valteline. Anxious, however, to restore the royal authority, by suppressing the powerful party of the Huguenots, he did not venture to engage in a foreign war, while a domestic enemy remained unsubdued; but he omitted neither lures nor intrigues, and spared neither promises nor money, to inflame the spirit which he saw rising in Germany.

Above all, the two northern sovereigns were most capable from their situation, and most interested by religion and policy, to oppose the extension of the imperial authority in the north of Germany. Both were also stimulated by personal antipathy against Ferdinand. Gustavus Adolphus was offended by the assistance which he had afforded to his rival, Sigismond, king of Poland, who had been driven from the throne of Sweden by his father, and had since incessantly disturbed his government by private cabals or open attacks. Christian IV. was influenced by various motives equally urgent; by his relationship * to the elector Palatine, by his apprehensions that Ferdinand would resume the sees of Bremen and Verden, which he designed for the younger branches of his own family, and by the permission of the imperial court to the counts of Schaumburgh to assume the title and arms of the duchy of Sleswick, which their ancestors had possessed, and which was still contested with the house of Oldenburgh.† Although their mutual

* Elizabeth, the mother of the elector, was daughter of Anne, sister of Christian.

† The counties of Holstein and Sleswick had been held by the counts of Schaumburgh, as fiefs of the crown of Denmark. On the extinction of the direct male line, by the death of Adolphus in 1459, Christian I., king of Denmark, had claimed these territories as reverted to his crown; but as several of the collateral branches yet existed, he endeavoured to render his claims valid, by submitting himself to the choice of the states. Being accordingly chosen count of Holstein and Sleswick, he either forced or persuaded the collateral branches of the house of Schaumburgh to be satisfied with a sum of money. Holstein was

jealousies prevented them from uniting in the same cause, yet they both aspired to head the proposed confederacy, and held forth every encouragement to rouse the Protestant states of the empire.

The whole of the year 1624 was spent in negotiations and contests between the rival sovereigns for the direction of the league. The king of Denmark was supported by all the credit of his brother-in-law, the king of England ; he derived great advantage from his own connection with the circle of Lower Saxony, as count of Oldenburgh and duke of Holstein ; and his continental territories formed a support for his intended operations ; he was besides of mature age, distinguished for prudence and policy, and had acquired considerable fame by his military exploits. On the other hand, Gustavus Adolphus, notwithstanding his great civil and military talents, could not rival the superior reputation and influence of his competitor, and as he possessed no territories in Germany, he required, as the condition of his assistance, the previous cession of some important fortresses on the Baltic, a demand which naturally excited the umbrage of the German states. These considerations giving the preponderance to Christian IV., Gustavus Adolphus withdrew from the contest.

The result of this intricate negotiation was soon afterwards displayed by a meeting of the states of Lower Saxony, at Segeburgh, on the 25th of March, 1625. They entered into a confederacy, in the usual terms, for the preservation of their religion and liberties, and settled the specific contingents and contributions for the intended armaments. Finally, they chose Christian, king of Denmark, as head of their league, in the place of the duke of Brunswick, who adhered to the emperor. Although Tilly remonstrated against this confederacy, as a breach of the Germanic constitution, his interference stimulated instead of abating their ardour ; for within two months they held

erected into a duchy in his favour, by the emperor Frederic III., and these territories had since continued in the possession of the royal line of Denmark. The representatives of the family of Schaumburgh took this opportunity to revive their claims, and being Catholics, obtained the support of the emperor.—Suhm's Geschichte Daennemarks, p. 111-117. ; Hansen's Sleswic, passim.

a new meeting at Brunswick, in which they greatly augmented their former contingents.

Christian, having assembled his own forces and those of the confederacy, published a declaration, that his sole purpose was to secure the peace and liberties of the circle of Lower Saxony. In consequence of subsidiary treaties, or private engagements, he expected considerable succours in men and money from England and the United Provinces; he hoped also to be joined by Mansfeld and Christian of Brunswick, who, with their usual success and celerity, were collecting a new predatory army on the side of France and the Low Countries. The banks of the Weser instantly became the theatre of war; and after a campaign which was principally confined to posts, the advantage remained on the side of Tilly, who made himself master of Hameln and Minden, besides other towns of less consequence, crossed the Weser, and pushed his troops into the principality of Calemberg, and the territories of Hildesheim and Brunswick.

The emperor, who had kept a watchful eye on the progress of this new confederacy, was now in a delicate situation. He had hitherto carried on the war in the empire principally with the Bavarian forces and those of the league; Tilly, the instrument of all the recent victories, commanded in the name of the duke of Bavaria, as charged with the execution of the sentence against the elector Palatine: all military orders emanated from the court of Munich; and the whole conduct of affairs was rendered subservient to the advantage and purposes of the league, not to the views and aggrandisement of the house of Austria. Ferdinand was anxious to emancipate himself from this dependence; but as he had no other army to resist the rising combination, except that of the league, he was sensible that the least ill success, or the defection of the Catholics, would raise a new host of enemies, and reduce him to still greater difficulties than those which he had before experienced. When he considered the exhausted state of his treasury, and the disturbed situation of his hereditary countries, the difficulty of assembling and maintaining an efficient army appeared insurmountable. But Mansfeld had set the example, in raising and supporting a military force without revenues, without territory, and without authority; and, fortunately for Ferdinand, an individual now came forward with talents equal to Mansfeld, and capable of copying and extending his plan. This individual was the celebrated Wallenstein.

Albert Wenceslaus Eusebius Waldstein, commonly called Wallenstein, descended from an illustrious family of Bohemia, and son of William, lord of Waldstein and Hermenetz, was born at Prague, in 1583. He was designed for a learned education, but his turbulent and refractory spirit, repelling all the shackles of school discipline, obliged his father to place him as a page in the family of Charles, margrave of Burgau, who held his petty court at Inspruck.* In early youth he displayed that self-confidence and ardour of imagination, which are often an earnest, and no less often the cause of future greatness. He had been educated by his parents in the Protestant religion, but in consequence of a providential escape in falling from a window, he was induced to embrace the Catholic faith. He afterwards travelled through Holland, England, France, Spain, and Italy, and made a considerable stay at Padua, where he first displayed an inclination for science. He there diligently applied himself to the study of history and the mathematics, and particularly devoted himself to judicial astrology, which is so captivating to an ardent mind, and which inflamed his romantic imagination with predictions of future greatness.

On his return to Bohemia, he was inclined to embrace the military profession; but his straitened circumstances and want of connections prevented the accomplishment of his wishes. Having, however, improved his fortune by espousing a rich and aged Moravian widow, he was enabled to attract attention, and to give full scope to his military genius. During the war of the Friuli, between Ferdinand, when archduke of Styria, and the Venetians, he levied a small corps of horse at his own expense, and with the rank of colonel led them to the siege of Gradiska, where he acquired by his liberality the love of his soldiers, and by his activity the notice of Ferdinand. At the conclusion of the war he repaired to Vienna, and being a

* Charles was son of the archduke Ferdinand of Tyrol, by Philippa Welseren.

widower, increased his influence at the court by espousing the daughter of Charles, count of Harrach, one of the imperial ministers. Adhering to the royal cause in the troubles of Bohemia, he was banished and deprived of his estates by the predominant party. After having endeavoured to suppress the rising rebellion in Moravia, he raised at his own expense a regiment of 1000 cuirassiers, with the rank of major-general, took an active share in the subsequent war, and signalised himself in particular in the defeat of Mansfeld, and at the battle of Prague. On the triumph of Ferdinand he was rewarded for his eminent services, and, besides recovering his estates, received a considerable gratification from the confiscated property of the insurgents.*

Such were the character and actions of this extraordinary man, when the circumstances and situation of his sovereign enabled him to act a part which has not been surpassed by any subject in ancient or modern times. Ambitious of distinction, full of confidence in his happy destiny, relying on the fertility of his resources, and master of a plan which he had duly weighed and meditated, he offered the emperor to levy, equip, pay, and maintain an army of 50,000 men, provided he was intrusted with the absolute command, and permitted to appoint his officers.

Such a plan, proposed by a single individual, who, though possessed of great talents, was known to be a man of fervid imagination, was treated by the imperial ministers as the wandering of a heated brain. But the emperor had himself experienced too many extraordinary events, to consider a project as impracticable because it was vast and difficult; he no doubt augured favourably of the result, from the example and success of Mansfeld, and from the fertile genius and activity of Wallenstein. He therefore readily accepted the proposal, appointed particular districts in Bohemia for the commencement of the levies ; and, to give greater authority to his new general, honoured him with the dignity of duke of Friedland. The success fully answered his most sanguine hopes. Wallenstein soon collected 22,000 men in the appointed districts, and, in his

* Pelzel, passim; Heinrich, vol. vi. p. 458. ; Schmidt, vol. ix. p. 273. ; Schiller's Thirty Years' War.

march to the frontiers of Lower Saxony, augmented their number to 30,000. The hope of advancement, and a thirst for pillage, attracted adventurers from all quarters ; even sovereign princes offered to levy troops for the service of the house of Austria ; and in a short time this army was augmented to an amount far beyond the stipulated number.

Being ordered to join Tilly in Lower Saxony, Wallenstein advanced by rapid marches to Gottingen, as if to effect the intended junction; but, suddenly turning towards the Elbe, he secured a passage at Dessau, and flushed his troops with the plunder of the rich districts of Grubenhagen, Halberstadt, and Magdeburgh. The states of Lower Saxony, thus hemmed in by the imperialists and the army of the league, seeing their territories exposed to the incursions of the enemy, made overtures for peace; and a congress was opened at Brunswick, in November, 1625, under the mediation of the electors of Saxony and Brandenburgh. They were, however, persuaded to try again the event of war, by the king of Denmark, who, besides his subsidiary treaties with England and Holland, had now concluded an offensive league with Bethlehem Gabor, and formed connections with the malecontents in the Austrian states. On the rupture of the congress the campaign opened. The king, joined by Mansfeld and Christian of Brunswick, found himself at the head of 60,000 men, and hastened to commence offensive operations. He detached Mansfeld to keep Wallenstein in check, drew Tilly from the Weser, by sending a corps into the territories of Osnabruck, and endeavoured to push forward a considerable force through Brunswick, in order to occupy Hesse and the Palatinate, and separate the armies of Tilly and Wallenstein. But his design, however well laid, was frustrated by the vigilance and activity of his antagonist. Though embarrassed by the excursion into Osnabruck, Tilly soon discovered the real point of attack, hastened to the confluence of the Weser and the Fulda, took Minden and Gottingen, and thus covered Hesse and the Palatinate. Baffled in his attempt to capture Nordheim, by the approach of the king, he fell back to Gottingen ; but being reinforced with 10,000 men from the army of Wallenstein, he prevented the attempt of the Danish monarch to pene-

trate through Thuringia, by Duderstadt, and driving him
from post to post, totally defeated him at Lutter, near
Wolfenbuttel, on the 27th of August, 1626. The king
having 5000 of his men killed, 2000 made prisoners, having
lost half his officers, and the whole of his artillery and
baggage, effected a difficult and arduous retreat through
Wolfenbuttel to Holstein. Tilly followed his victory by
inundating the territories of Lunenburgh with his troops;
while the king, though joined by a reinforcement of 8000
English and Dutch, was reduced to the defensive, and
scarcely able to maintain himself on his own frontiers.

On the other side the fortune of Ferdinand equally prevailed. Mansfeld confiding too much on his own intrepidity
and success, had imprudently attacked the intrenchments
of Wallenstein, at the bridge of Dessau. Though repulsed
with great loss, he rose with new vigour from his defeat. He fell back into the Mark of Brandenburgh, where
he raised fresh levies, and collected the remnant of his
forces. Being strengthened by 5000 Danes under the
duke of Saxe Weimar, he made a sudden push into Silesia,
defeated the imperialists at Oppeln, in June, and forced a
passage into Moravia, by capturing Ratibor, Jaegendorf, and
Troppau. He left the duke of Weimar with 5000 men to secure those important posts, and descending along the Wag,
routed another imperial corps in the vicinity of Presburgh.
In September he was joined by Bethlehem Gabor, whom
his approach encouraged to recommence hostilities; at the
same time the bashaw of Buda made an irruption with
30,000 men into Lower Hungary, captured various fortresses in the district of Gran, and laid siege to Novigrad,
while the malecontents in Upper Austria flew to arms.

Meanwhile, Wallenstein, unable to prevent or retard the
march of Mansfeld, followed him with 30,000 men, and
appeared in Hungary soon after his junction with Bethlehem Gabor. The two armies remained some time on the
defensive; but disease and the effects of the climate made
greater ravages among them than the sword. At length
Bethlehem Gabor, discouraged by the defeat of the king
of Denmark, and apprehensive of drawing on himself the
whole force of the emperor, concluded a new truce, and
the bashaw of Buda seemed inclined to follow his example.

The insurgents of Austria, who by foreign assistance might have become dangerous, were soon suppressed by count Pappenheim.* Mansfeld, thus abandoned to his fate, and seeing his troops daily diminishing by the effects of disease, disbanded his army, sold his artillery and military stores to the bashaw of Buda, and with only twelve officers, passed through Bosnia, with a view to reach the territories of Venice, and again return to the scene of action. But in his route, a fever, derived from the effects of the climate, and aggravated by chagrin, terminated his extraordinary career at Zara. Thus was Ferdinand delivered from an irreconcilable enemy, who without subjects or revenues, had found inexhaustible resources in his own genius; who, though often defeated, was never dismayed nor discouraged; who had risen with new vigour from every depression, and for seven years had always baffled the designs, and even endangered the safety of the house of Austria.†

This campaign proved no less fatal to his friend and companion in arms, Christian of Brunswick, who died in his 29th year at Wolfenbuttel, not in the field where he had so often courted danger, but a victim to a slow and painful disease, which, without diminishing his spirit or activity, gradually sunk him into the grave.‡

* Godfrey Henry, count of Pappenheim, was son of Weiten of Pappenheim, vice-marshal and count of the Germanic empire. He was born in 1594, received a learned education, and was distinguished for his progress in letters, and, like Wallenstein, travelled through different countries of Europe. The military ardour of the times, however, seized the young student, and his first essay in arms was as a captain of cavalry in the regiment raised by the count of Herberstorff, who had espoused his mother. He joined the Bavarian army at Lintz, and was soon raised to the rank of lieutenant-colonel. He distinguished himself at the battle of Prague, where he received twenty wounds, and was left for dead on the field; after an almost miraculous escape, he recovered from his wounds, and as his exploits had conciliated the favour of his superiors, was raised to more important commands. He is said to have been born with the mark of two swords in saltire (the arms of the vice-marshal of the empire) in his forehead.—Histoire de Gustave Adolphe, tom. ii. p. 82.

† Struvius, p. 1251. note 72. ; Schmidt, vol. ix. p. 283.

‡ His death was attributed to poison; but, on opening his body, the cause of his disease was discovered to be a tape-worm, several ells in length.—Struvius, p. 1251. note 68.

Wallenstein having delivered Hungary, turned against the corps left by Mansfeld on the frontiers of Silesia, of which the command, by the death of the duke of Weimar, had devolved on the younger count. Thurn recovered the fortresses which they had garrisoned, and following them into the Mark of Brandenburgh, compelled the elector to revoke his protest against the transfer of the palatine electorate.

The hereditary countries of the house of Austria being thus delivered from external invasion, and the internal commotions suppressed, Ferdinand had no obstacle to prevent him from dissolving the confederacy, which had a second time endangered his safety. The king of Denmark, unable to cope with Tilly alone, was still less capable of resisting the united attacks of Tilly and Wallenstein. By their concerted and well-directed efforts, all Lower Saxony was overrun, and every member of the circle either exposed to proscription or reduced to submission. The territories of the king of Denmark then became the theatre of war; he was driven from place to place, and from post to post, the troops which he ventured to bring into the field were scattered in all directions, and, before the close of 1628, Gluckstadt was the only fortress which remained in his possession, of the whole country stretching from the Elbe to the extremity of Jutland.

During this series of misfortunes, the king had been induced to make proposals of peace, and the elector Palatine offers of submission; even the Catholic body, who had hitherto so constantly supported the emperor, began to be jealous of his power and success, and evinced a resolution to procure the restoration of peace, and to free themselves from the burden of supporting the imperial army. But Ferdinand was too much flushed with success to listen to the dictates of prudence and justice; he therefore received the proposals of the king of Denmark and the deposed elector with contempt, and required from them concessions too exorbitant to be complied with by any sovereign, however humiliated. He found means also, not only to quiet the clamours of the Catholic body, but even to render their interference subservient to his purposes. A meeting of the Catholic states took place at Wurtzburgh, to deliberate on the means of restoring peace to Germany, and putting a stop to the devastations of both armies; but the emperor availing himself of the jealousy of some, the timidity of others, and the animosity of all against the Protestants, rendered their deliberations fruitless, and their attempts ended in a deputation, entreating him to set bounds to the oppressions of Wallenstein's army. The electors likewise, who assembled at Mulhausen in September, 1627, for the attainment of these objects, far from effecting their purpose, were by the same means rendered totally subservient to the wishes of Ferdinand, and all their resolutions produced only general representations against the licentious conduct of the imperial forces, and a request that he would raise no more levies, but on the first opportunity disband all useless troops. They faintly indeed recommended the conclusion of peace with Denmark; but with respect to the elector Palatine, they declared that, as author of the troubles, he should renounce the crown of Bohemia and the electoral dignity, and that the emperor should indemnify himself for the expenses of the war by the confiscation of the whole or a part of the palatine dominions. Should the elector refuse to submit to these conditions, they announced their resolution to unite with the emperor against him and all his adherents. Finally, at the instigation of Ferdinand, the Catholics reclaimed the restitution of all ecclesiastical benefices which had been appropriated by the Protestants since the treaty of Passau in opposition to the ecclesiastical reservation.

Ferdinand being now too powerful to apprehend any opposition from the adherents of the elector Palatine, rendered the transfer of his electorate permanent, by entailing it on all the princes of the Bavarian house. At the same time he conferred on the elector of Bavaria, as an imperial fief, the Upper Palatinate, with that part of the Lower Palatinate which lay on the right bank of the Rhine, and thus recovered Upper Austria, which had been retained till this time by the new elector; but he was obliged to accompany the grant with the promise of an indemnification, should the house of Bavaria be despoiled of this acquisition at a future peace.

While his troops kept the circle of Lower Saxony in awe,

Ferdinand availed himself of so favourable an opportunity
to diminish the Protestant interest, and procure for his
family the rich benefices which had been wrested from the
church since the peace of Passau. The see of Halberstadt becoming vacant by the death of Christian of Brunswick, he compelled the chapter to choose his son Leopold
William, who had been recently elevated to the sees of
Strasburgh and Passau, on the resignation of his brother
Leopold. The archbishopric of Magdeburgh being also
considered as vacant by the proscription of the administrator Christian William of Brandenburgh, the terror of
Wallenstein's arms induced the canons to declare the see
escheated to Augustus, son of the elector of Saxony, who
had before been chosen coadjutor or successor. But this
choice being contrary to the views of the emperor, he persuaded the pope to annul the nomination, and appoint
Leopold William archbishop. He endeavoured to secure
the transfer, by forbidding the elector of Saxony to accept
the appointment of his son, although after some contestation he gratified him, by allowing the prince a temporary
possession of the see and revenues in the name and under
the authority of the archduke. He also procured for Leopold William the papal nomination to the rich abbey of
Hirtzcheld, which he wrested from the landgrave of Hesse,
and to the archbishopric of Bremen.

The victories which had hitherto crowned the arms of
Ferdinand were, however, far from either gratifying or
bounding his ambition. Indignant at being checked in his
progress by the Baltic, he resolved to occupy its shores,
and acquire a naval force, as well to prevent the northern
powers from opening a new way into Germany, as to pursue the king of Denmark into his isles. He was also
eager to dethrone Gustavus Adolphus, and to restore the
crown of Sweden to Sigismond, king of Poland, his brother-
in-law and ally, who was connected with him by the double
interest of blood and religion. For this purpose he had
endeavoured to obtain the assistance of the fleet belonging
to the Hanseatic towns, and, with the concurrence of Spain,
offered to Lubec the monopoly of the Spanish trade, and
great commercial privileges in Germany. Baffled in this
attempt by the refusal of Lubec, which was too wise to

contribute to its own ruin by concurring in the ruin of others, the next view of the emperor was, to form a naval force of his own, and appropriate all the ports from Kiel to Colberg. For this purpose, as well as for rewarding past services, he put, on the 21st of April, 1628, the two dukes of Mecklenburgh under the ban of the empire, transferred their territories to Wallenstein, and appointed him his generalissimo by land, and admiral of the Baltic Sea.

Wallenstein, whose romantic imagination was never startled by the grandeur or difficulty of a project, exerted himself with his characteristic ardour to fulfil the views of his master. He made Wismar, the principal port of his new territory, his great maritime station, and, by borrowing or hiring ships from every quarter, soon assembled a force of fifteen sail. He then invaded the duchy of Pomerania, although the duke had given no plea for hostility, under the pretext of securing the reversion of that duchy to the empire, of which it was a fief. He took the isle of Usedom, made himself master of the different ports on that part of the Baltic, and suddenly laid siege to Stralsund, a Hanseatic town, remarkable for the capacity and excellence of its harbour, and the extent of its commerce, and which, from its situation and navy, would greatly facilitate his meditated attacks against Denmark and Sweden. Finally he occupied the isle of Rugen, with a view to hasten its reduction, and exclude foreign succours.

The views which the emperor had displayed for establishing himself on the shores of the Baltic, allayed the long-pending jealousies between Sweden and Denmark, and induced the two sovereigns to form a temporary union against the common danger. As early as 1626 they concluded a treaty for the protection of Stralsund, and a Danish garrison was admitted into the place. This garrison, assisted by the inhabitants, by repeated succours from the other Hanseatic towns, and by the fleets of Denmark and Sweden, baffled all the attacks of Wallenstein, although he made assault after assault, and used the most extraordinary exertions to realise his proud and impious threat, that " he would reduce Stralsund, even if bound to heaven with chains of adamant ! " His perseverance would have finally succeeded ; the garrison, worn out by these

continued attacks, must have surrendered had not the inhabitants thrown themselves under the protection of Gustavus Adolphus, who replaced the Danes with Swedish
troops. In consequence of this reinforcement, at the time
when the imperialists were exhausted by fatigue and
thinned by the sword, Wallenstein indignantly relinquished
his enterprise; but endeavoured to save his honour, and
secure some compensation for his failure, by the capture of
Rostock.

Meanwhile the king of Denmark, reduced to the last
extremity, exerted himself with all the vigour of despair.
He was too weak to recover his losses by land; but he
fully availed himself of his superiority by sea, annihilated
the newly-created imperial navy, and by bold and sudden
descents on the shores of the Baltic, greatly harassed
Wallenstein, and contributed to prolong the siege of Stralsund. These gleams of success were, however, merely
temporary. Christian, deserted or feebly supported by his
allies, at length yielded to the clamours of his subjects, and
renewed his overtures for peace. He found a more ready
acquiescence than before from Ferdinand, whose lofty
views were somewhat changed with the situation of his
affairs. The emperor now discovered the vanity of his
attempts to form a navy, and contest the mastery of the sea
with a maritime nation. Notwithstanding the succours
which he had furnished to the king of Poland against Gustavus Adolphus, he saw his ally reduced to the necessity of
concluding a humiliating peace; and he was apprehensive
lest Sweden should unite with Denmark for their common
defence. Embarrassed likewise in a war for the succession
of Mantua, he was sensible that it would require his whole
power and attention to reduce the Protestant body and free
himself from the trammels of the Catholic league, which
began to display symptoms of jealousy and disaffection.
Above all, Wallenstein, his all-powerful general, who dictated no less to his sovereign than to Germany, was anxious
to secure the possession of his new dominions, by persuading the king of Denmark to sacrifice the dukes of Mechlen-
burgh. A congress was accordingly opened at Lubec, in
May, 1629, under the mediation of the elector of Brandenburgh. Notwithstanding some difficulties derived from

the lofty pretensions of the emperor, the influence of Wallenstein procured though not more honourable at least more favourable terms than had at first been offered to the king of Denmark. He was to receive all his conquered dominions ; to agree not to interfere in the affairs of the empire, except when his interests as duke of Holstein were concerned ; to renounce all his pretensions to the archbishoprics and bishoprics which he designed to secure for his family ; and his unfortunate allies, the dukes of Mecklenburgh and the elector Palatine, were tacitly abandoned to their fate, by being passed over without any mention in the treaty.

It is likewise a remarkable circumstance attending this negotiation, that the ambassadors of Sweden, who had repaired to the congress, were refused admission by the imperial general, and even the title of king withheld from their sovereign ; an insult which it was scarcely prudent to offer in the midst of unbounded success, and which Ferdinand had afterwards ample reason to repent.

Chap. LI. — 1628–1630.

On the conclusion of the treaty of Lubec, Ferdinand had a second time an opportunity of restoring tranquillity to Germany. Not a single enemy remained in arms ; the Protestants were awed into submission ; he might have quieted the alarms of the Catholics, by showing that his object was not rule and dominion, but the restoration of the Catholic church and the vindication of his own authority : and he might have satisfied the friends of the elector Palatine, by restoring to him a portion of his dominions. But the unbounded success of his arms, the implicit obedience which followed his decrees, the instigations of the Spanish court, filled him with presumption, and induced him to form the wildest plans of conquest and dominion. It is impossible to produce specific documents of all his designs ; yet, to judge from the declamations of the Jesuits, the discorses of Wallenstein, the observations of the Spanish ambassadors, and the general tenor of his own conduct, his intentions were evidently directed to extirpate the Protestant doctrines by the assistance of the Catholics, and then to reduce the Catholics themselves to dependence. He was likewise anxious to aid the Spaniards in recovering the United Provinces, and he hoped, by opening a communication through the Valteline with their dominions in Lombardy, to give law to Europe by the weight of their united forces.

He imagined that no power was capable of making any effectual opposition to his designs. Charles I., king of England, was embarrassed by the fatal disputes with his parliament, and involved at once in hostilities with France and Spain. The court of France, besides the contest with England, and disputes with Spain relative to the succession of Mantua, was still involved in a civil war with the Huguenots. The Dutch were awed without by the united forces of Austria and Spain, and divided within by civil and religious commotions. The Turks, hitherto the constant and formidable enemy of the house of Austria, were agitated by intestine troubles, and, far from being able to counteract the projects of Ferdinand, deemed themselves fortunate in escaping an attack. Bethlehem Gabor, who had so frequently carried terror to the walls of Vienna, sinking under a fatal disorder, and satisfied with securing the dominions which he had acquired in a more active season of life, concluded, in 1628, a peace, on terms which seemed to ensure its duration. In the north, Ferdinand had reduced the king of Denmark to submission; he had found a faithful ally in Sigismond, king of Poland; and, in the career of victory, he cannot perhaps be accused of overweening confidence, in despising the efforts of Gustavus Adolphus, whose exploits, however remarkable, had been confined to a narrow and distant theatre, and whose troops and revenue, in regard to number or amount, could scarcely deserve a comparison with the vast resources and numerous armies of the head of the house of Austria, and the chief of the empire.

Such being the condition of the European powers, and such the situation and views of Ferdinand, he scarcely waited for the conclusion of peace with Denmark before he hastened the execution of his extensive designs. The object which he had most at heart, from interested as well as religious motives, was the extirpation of the Protestant doctrines.   In all his territories except Hungary, where he was restrained by the vicinity of Bethlehem Gabor and by the fear of Turkish interference, he proceeded without compunction, not only to the revocation of the privileges granted by his predecessors to the Protestants, which he had not confirmed, but even of those which had received his own unqualified approbation.

In Austria he abolished by force the Protestant worship in the district above the Ems, where he was not bound by formal engagements; even in the lower district, where he had solemnly ratified the religious rights granted by Matthias, he acted with the same rigorous severity, imposed successive restrictions on the Protestants, and finally completed their proscription by a general mandate, dated April 10th, 1628, prohibiting all Lutheran books; annulling all baptisms, marriages, and other religious acts performed by Protestant preachers; expelling all Protestants from civil offices; and obliging all persons, of every rank and condition, to receive instruction only from Catholic priests, and attend the Catholic worship.

But it was in Bohemia, so long exposed to his antipathy as the seat of religious liberty, and where three fourths of the natives were Protestants, that he acted with a rigour and cruelty which surpassed all the horrors of the inquisition itself.   He commenced his persecutions by ejecting the preachers, schoolmasters, and professors, and delivering the churches to monks, whom he collected indiscriminately from all quarters of Europe.   He then prohibited all persons who were not Catholics from exercising any trade or handicraft, laid the severest fines on those who preserved even in secret the slightest remnant of their former worship, declared Protestant marriages and baptisms null, wills made by Protestants invalid, and even drove the poor, the sick, and the distressed from the almshouses and hospitals. Then began a series of persecutions, from the recollection of which the mind recoils with horror.   In the capital the Protestant burghers were expelled with their wives and children, and the poorer orders compelled to become Catholics.   The other towns, and even the remotest villages,

were visited by missionary deputations of Jesuits and
Capuchin friars, accompanied by a military force, and were
abandoned to every species of monkish barbarity and military licentiousness.   Those who were enabled to seek a
refuge in exile were comparatively fortunate. The slightest
degree of persecution inflicted on those who remained was,
to imprison the men, give up their houses to pillage, and
expose their wives and children to all the outrages of the
soldiery.   Some were massacred without mercy ; some
hunted and driven like wild beasts to the woods and
mountains, some dragged to processions and masses with
every species of insult and cruelty, and those who ventured
to oppose these enormities were racked and mutilated, or
put to death with tortures too shocking for humanity to
describe.

In the midst of these horrors Ferdinand himself repaired
to Prague to nominate and crown his son as his successor.
After affecting to display his clemency, by confirming to
the states their power of taxation and other civil privileges,
he abolished their right to elect a king, forbade the use of
the Bohemian tongue in all public transactions, and set the
seal to all the enormities which had been perpetrated under
his authority, by abrogating the royal edict of toleration.
He formally restored the order of the clergy to their rank
in the states, from which they had been expelled during
the Hussite wars ; finally, he consummated his vengeance
against the Protestants, by declaring that he would tolerate
no religion except the Catholic ; and he banished all those
who within a specified time refused to return to the bosom
of the church.   By this act of persecution he drove 30,000
families, with all their servants and retainers, from the
kingdom, including the most learned, the richest, and most
industrious portion of the community, and thus inflicted on
Bohemia a wound from which it has never recovered.

It is a tribute of justice to sound policy, as well as to
humanity, to finish this picture by introducing the reflections of the native historian, who, being a Catholic and a
subject of the house of Austria, cannot be suspected of
exaggeration or partiality. " The records of history scarcely
furnish a similar example of such a change as Bohemia
underwent during the reign of Ferdinand II.   In 1620, the

monks, and a few of the nobility only excepted, the whole country was entirely Protestant; at the death of Ferdinand it was, in appearance at least, Catholic. Till the battle of the White Mountain the states enjoyed more exclusive privileges than the parliament of England; they enacted laws, imposed taxes, contracted alliances, declared war and peace, and chose or confirmed their kings; but all these they now lost. Previous to that period the Bohemians were considered as a warlike nation, and had often won military fame; the annals of history recorded, 'The Bohemians took the field; the Bohemians stormed the fortifications; the Bohemians gained the victory;' but they are now blended with other people, they are no longer distinguished as a nation in the field of battle, and no historian has consigned their posterity to glory. Till this fatal period the Bohemians were daring, undaunted, enterprising, emulous of fame; now they have lost all their courage, their national pride, their enterprising spirit. They fled before the Swedes like sheep, or suffered themselves to be trampled under foot. Their courage lay buried on the White Mountain. Individuals still possessed personal valour, military ardour, and a thirst of glory, but, blended with other nations, they resembled the waters of the Moldau which join those of the Elbe. These united streams bear ships, overflow lands, and overturn rocks; yet the Elbe only is mentioned, and the Moldau forgotten. The Bohemian language, which was used in all the courts of justice, and was in high estimation among the nobles, fell into contempt; the German was introduced, became the general language among the nobles and citizens, and was used by the monks in their sermons; the inhabitants of the towns began to be ashamed of their native tongue, which was confined to the villages, and called the language of peasants. The arts and sciences, so highly cultivated and esteemed under Rhodolph, sunk beyond recovery. During the period which immediately followed the banishment of the Protestants, Bohemia scarcely produced one man who became eminent in any branch of learning. The Caroline university was under the direction of the Jesuits, or suppressed; by order of the pope all promotions were stopped, and no academical honours conferred. A few patriots, both among the clergy and laity, murmured openly, though ineffectually ; others sighed in secret over the downfall of literature. The greater part of the schools were conducted by Jesuits, and other monkish orders, and nothing taught therein but bad Latin. It cannot be denied, that several of the Jesuits were men of great learning and science ; but their system was, to keep the people in ignorance ; agreeably to this principle, they gave their scholars only the rind, and kept to themselves the pulp of literature. With this view they travelled from town to town as missionaries, and went from house to house, examining all books, which the landlord was compelled, under pain of eternal damnation, to produce. The greater part they confiscated and burnt, so that a Bohemian and a rare book are synonymous terms. They thus endeavoured to extinguish the ancient literature of the country, laboured to persuade the students that, before the introduction of their order into Bohemia, nothing but ignorance prevailed, and carefully concealed the learned labours, and even the names of our ancestors. Such was their despotism, that the collections and writings of the patriotic Balbinus, on the literature of the ancient Bohemians, could not be published till after the extinction of their order. In a word, from this period the history of Bohemia ceases, and the history of every nation in Bohemia begins."

A sovereign, who could thus act in his own dominions, did not want inclination to pursue the same measures in Germany. He could not, however, venture to drive the Protestants to desperation, by overturning at once the whole fabric of their system, or to alienate both Catholics and Protestants, by any glaring act of authority ; but he imitated the insidious policy which had been traced by the Jesuits, and adopted by Rhodolph, with equal art and address, and with more vigour and perseverance. Like Rhodolph, he availed himself of the terms in which several articles of the peace of religion had been framed ; assuming as a judge and supreme arbitrator the right of interpreting its meaning, and deciding contested points, he declared the Ecclesiastical Reservation valid, and the annexed declaration of Ferdinand I. null. On these principles he published his celebrated Edict of Restitution, dated the 6th of March,

1629, in which he enjoined the restoration of all ecclesiastical property secularised since the peace of Passau, and ordered the Protestants to relinquish to the Catholics all benefices which they had appropriated contrary to the peace of Passau and the Ecclesiastical Reservation. He also authorised Catholic prelates to use every means for the extirpation of the Protestant doctrines in their territories, and confined the benefits of the religious peace only to the Catholics and the members of the Confession of Augsburgh, excluding all other sects, particularly the Calvinists, by name. He concluded with denouncing the ban of the empire against all opposers of this ordinance, and commanding the states without distinction to assist in its execution.

No Protestant prince could venture to resist the execution of a decree supported by the powerful army of Wallenstein. Although the elector of Saxony and others presumed to make remonstrances, their remonstrances were treated with neglect, and the elector alone was suffered to retain the benefices appropriated by his family. In Lower Saxony the dukes of Brunswick were stripped of all the property which they had obtained from the see of Hildesheim; at Halberstadt and Magdeburgh the Protestant canons were ejected; the archbishopric of Bremen was annexed, by the nomination of the pope, to the vast possessions of the church already heaped on the son of Ferdinand. The same innovations were introduced into Suabia, Franconia, and Westphalia. All the convents and ecclesiastical property without distinction were restored to the Catholics, and the Protestant religion excluded from Augsburgh, Ulm, Ratisbon, and the other imperial towns of those circles. Many of the Catholic prelates also, hastening to avail themselves of the authority conferred on them by the emperor, used every exertion to exterminate the Protestant religion in their territories.

The resumption of this vast property, which, besides convents and other inferior benefices, consisted of two archbishoprics and twelve bishoprics *, was adopted as a

---

* Magdeburgh and Bremen; the bishoprics of Minden, Halberstadt, Verden, Lubec, Ratzeburgh, Meissen, Merseburgh, Naumburgh, Brandenburgh, Havelbergh, Lebus, and Camin.

prelude to the total extermination of the Protestants. Their ruin was however suspended, and the projects of the emperor checked by the Catholics themselves, at whose instigation the edict had been issued. They began now to be alarmed at the enormous power which they had contributed to raise ; they were offended by seeing the convents conferred on the Jesuits instead of being restored to the original possessors ; and they were at length convinced that all the spoils of the Protestants would be monopolised by the emperor for his family and dependents, and afford the means of reducing them in their turn to submission. Above all they were indignant at the licentiousness and depredations of the imperial army, which was augmented instead of being diminished on the conclusion of the peace, and was scattered over the empire, levying enormous contributions, and preying alike on friends and foes. The feelings of the high-born princes were wounded by the pride of its upstart commander, who assumed the authority and surpassed the state of a sovereign ; and who unequivocally developed his own designs, and the views of his master, by repeated declarations, that the electors must be reduced to the condition of Spanish grandees, and the bishops to the rank of chaplains to the emperor. Their alarms at this critical juncture were increased by an attempt of the emperor to procure the dismission of their troops who were stationed in Franconia and Suabia, a measure which they with reason considered as the first step to the dissolution of their league.

These sentiments, though common to all, made the deepest impression on the duke of Bavaria, the rival of Wallenstein in fame, talents, and influence. He was disgusted with his rapid rise and superior ascendency ; his jealousy was roused by the formation of an independent army, which far overbalanced the forces of the league, and by the attempts of the emperor to reduce that league, from which he derived his authority. He considered the transfer of the electorate, and the territorial gifts which he had received, as a compensation not more than adequate to his great services and expenses ; and, like Maurice of Saxony, he was alienated by the evident intention of the emperor to reduce the value of that dignity to which he had been raised. These considerations absorbed all sentiments of gratitude, friendship, and affinity ; and even overbore his zeal for the Catholic faith. He therefore caballed with cardinal Richelieu, and the other enemies of the house of Austria, and consolidated the first opposition which humbled the domineering spirit and checked the designs of Ferdinand. At his instigation, the members of the league assembled at Heidelberg, in March, 1629, and requested the emperor to convoke a diet for the restoration of peace, and for remedying the evils occasioned by his army. In reply to his demand, requiring the dismission of their troops, in the circles of Franconia and Suabia, they expatiated on the great services which they had rendered to the house of Austria ; and concluded with the spirited declaration, " Till we have received an indemnification, or a pledge for the payment of our expenses, we will neither disband a single soldier, *nor relinquish a foot of territory,* ecclesiastical or secular, DEMAND IT WHO WILL!" *

It is a singular proof of the presumption and infatuation which accompanied the despotism of the emperor, that at the very moment when he was preparing to crush the Protestants, and when symptoms of discontent had appeared among the Catholics, he should have sent the flower of his troops on foreign expeditions. Besides a considerable force which he despatched to the assistance of Sigismond, king of Poland, and another corps against the united provinces, he interfered in the war which had taken place in Italy for the succession of Mantua.

On the death of Vincent II., duke of Mantua, in 1627, without issue, the succession to the duchy devolved on Charles, duke of Nevers, descended from a collateral branch of the family of Gonzaga, who had been acknowledged by the deceased duke as his heir, and had taken undisputed possession of the territories. But the succession was claimed by Ferdinand, duke of Guastalla, a representative of a more distant collateral branch, and the Montferrat by Emanuel, duke of Savoy, in consequence of his descent from a princess of Montferrat. As the king of Spain was unwilling to see a territory contiguous to Milan possessed by a vassal and dependent of France, he supported the duke of Gua-

* Heinrich, vol. vi. p. 500. ; Falkenstein, vol. ii. p. 648.

stalla, and at the same time concluded a treaty with the duke of Savoy for the purpose of dividing the Montferrat. Accordingly the Spanish troops laid siege to Casale ; while those of Savoy overran the remainder of the duchy. At the same time the emperor ordered the Mantuan territories to be put under sequestration, and published the ban of the empire against the duke of Nevers, for refusing to deliver the duchy to the imperial commissaries.

The duke of Mantua, who was feebly supported by Venice, would have been unable to make effectual resistance, had he not found a powerful protector in the king of France. Louis himself crossed the Alps with an army of 25,000 men, raised the siege of Casale, compelled the duke of Savoy to enter into an accommodation, to cede his pretensions for the district of Trino, and to give temporary possession of Suza and St. François to the French.

Such was the situation of affairs when Ferdinand interfered in the contest. In the spring of 1629, he sent an army of 30,000 men, who forced their way through the country of the Grisons and the Valteline, and spread general alarm throughout Italy ; and in July the following year, took Mantua by storm, and expelled the duke from his territories.

Towards the close of this transaction, the emperor complied with the request of the Catholic league, by assembling an electoral diet at Ratisbon, at which he presided in person. From this diet he hoped to draw succours against the adherents of the elector Palatine, for the prosecution of the Mantuan war, and for opposing Gustavus Adolphus, who was now preparing to carry his arms into Germany ; but his great and principal object was, to obtain the election of his son as king of the Romans. He therefore accompanied these demands with a conciliating offer to provide means for remedying the disorders arising from the licentiousness of his troops, and for the restoration of internal peace. But his hopes were disappointed. The disposition of the German princes, and the meeting of this diet, presented a favourable opportunity for his enemies to interfere with effect. Nor was this opportunity lost on cardinal Richelieu, who having firmly established his power, and restored the vigour of the royal authority by the subjugation of the Huguenots, turned his whole attention to fulfil the grand plan of Henry IV. for humbling the house of Austria. He accordingly sent Leon Brulart as ambassador to the diet, for the ostensible object of accommodating the dispute relative to Mantua, but for the real purpose of carrying on his intrigues with the German princes, and influencing the emperor; he joined in the embassy the celebrated Capuchin friar, father Joseph, the confidant of his secrets, the soul of his plans ; who, under the cowl of a monk, and the exterior of sanctity, concealed the most consummate address, and spirit of intrigue not inferior to his own. The object of this agent was to obtain the reduction of the imperial army, and the dismission of Wallenstein, and frustrate the design of Ferdinand to procure the election of his son ; for the fulfilment of these purposes he was empowered to make any promise or concession, however extravagant. He intrigued with both Catholics and Protestants, and had little difficulty in influencing princes who were already alienated from their chief; but he found the most active and most devoted coadjutor in the duke of Bavaria, who employed all his influence among the Catholics, and by whose intervention the whole conduct of the diet was directed.

Ferdinand had flattered himself with such a ready and unequivocal submission on the part of the diet, and deemed himself so secure of his son's election, that the imperial laureat was suffered to print a congratulatory ode. He was therefore surprised and confounded, when, instead of a complete acquiescence, the diet replied to his demands by expatiating on the dreadful excesses of his troops, and by requiring a prompt remedy to so insufferable a grievance, as a preliminary to the discussion of any business. The duke of Bavaria even declared, that their deliberations could not be free while the emperor maintained an army of 150,000 men ; and these remonstrances were followed by positive and unequivocal demands for the reduction of his troops, and the dismission of Wallenstein. This opposition on the part of the Catholics revived the spirit of the Protestants ; the whole body, particularly the elector of Saxony, made the strongest remonstrances against the edict of restitution, and their instances were supported by the duke of Bavaria and the majority of the Catholics. The duke proposed a suspension of the edict for forty years; some of the Catholics even required its abrogation; others urged the necessity of granting indulgence to the Protestants, to prevent them from uniting with the king of Sweden, or assisting the enemies of the empire.

These instances for the suspension or abrogation of an edict which Ferdinand had not deigned to mention to the diet, for the reduction of an army to which he owed his independence, and for the dismission of a general whom he himself had raised, and whose talents and influence were now more than ever necessary, inflicted a deep wound on his proud and inflexible spirit. He was inclined himself, and he was instigated by Wallenstein, to resist such imperious demands, to pour his forces into Bavaria, and after punishing the refractory chief of the Catholics, to extort the obedience of the rest. But the absence of his best troops in Italy rendered this a dangerous if not impracticable attempt, and reduced him in a great degree to his former dependence on the Catholics. He was besides, in consequence of his other disappointments, more anxious than ever to secure the election of his son. Of this anxiety the duke of Bavaria and the agents of France adroitly availed themselves. On one side the duke assailed him with representations that he could only obtain the suffrages of the electors by acquiescing in the just demands of the Catholics, and granting indulgences to the Protestants. On the other, father Joseph insidiously represented that Wallenstein, though dismissed, might soon be restored to the command, and the deficiency of the troops supplied by fresh levies; he likewise employed all those blandishments, exerted all that subtlety for which he was remarkable, and omitted neither promises nor cajolery to calm the fears and blind the suspicions of the emperor. His arts, covered with the most exemplary severity of manners, and the outward appearance of sanctity, overcame the repugnance of a prince whose only vulnerable side was religion, and who respected even the habit of a monk.

Ferdinand, who hoped at a more favourable opportunity to resume his ascendency, and despised the power of the king of Sweden, yielded to these insidious counsels. He instantly dismissed 18,000 of his best cavalry, and agreed to suspend the edict against the Protestants till the ensuing February, when a meeting was to be held at Frankfort for effecting a compromise. These concessions were matters of little difficulty; but it was a far more delicate and dangerous task to obtain the resignation of a proud and imperious general, at the head of a numerous army, independent of control, and flushed with success, adored by troops who looked up to him alone for their pay and subsistence, and revered by his officers, whose hopes and fortunes depended on his nod. Even Ferdinand trembled at the fatal consequences which might attend the refusal of Wallenstein; he employed two of his most intimate friends to execute the unwelcome commission, and accompanied the request with every proof and every expression of regret, respect, and gratitude.

His apprehensions were fortunately without foundation; for this great and singular man disappointed alike the fears of his friends and the hopes of his enemies. He was persuaded by a favourite astrologer, who could alone bend his intractable mind, that the stars prognosticated future grandeur, that his present disgrace would be only temporary. This augury produced its full effect on the romantic temper of Wallenstein; he received the imperial messengers with mildness and composure; he laid before them an astrological calculation, and observed, "By these signs I knew your message; the ascendant of the duke of Bavaria is superior to that of the emperor; I therefore cannot attach any blame to his conduct, though I regret that he should have so easily sacrificed me. I will obey." He dismissed the envoys with presents, wrote a submissive letter, supplicating the future favour and countenance of his sovereign, and retired with dignity to a private station.

Besides these sacrifices the agents of France, by the intervention of the electors, extorted from the emperor his consent to an accommodation of the affair of Mantua. Ferdinand agreed to grant the investiture of Mantua and Montferrat to the duke of Nevers; a trifling compensation was to be made to the dukes of Savoy and Guastalla for their claims; and in return the ambassadors of France entered into the most solemn engagements not to afford either counsel or assistance to the enemies of the emperor and empire.

After having completed these sacrifices, Ferdinand was still more disappointed than before by the failure of his efforts to procure the election of his son. The electors having gained their objects, not only postponed the intended nomination, but evinced a design to choose the elector of Bavaria. Ferdinand, thus duped and deceived in every instance, abruptly terminated the diet, as well to hide his own disappointment as to put a stop to the intrigues of his enemies. He had soon, however, the additional mortification to see the ambassadors of France disavowed, to witness the public breach of those engagements on which he had placed his principal reliance; and he had even reason to suspect that the same hand which had signed the treaty with him, had at the same moment signed a convention with Gustavus Adolphus. He equally felt for the deception, and for the manner in which it was effected, under the guise of religious faith and private friendship; and was frequently heard to exclaim, "A Capuchin friar has disarmed me with his rosary, and covered six electoral caps with his cowl."

CHAP. LII. — 1630, 1631.

THE resentment which Ferdinand felt for his recent disappointment would probably have urged him to gratify his vengeance against the elector of Bavaria and the Catholics, had not a new enemy called forth all his attention. This enemy was Gustavus Adolphus.

Since the time of Gustavus Vasa, Sweden had been agitated by intestine commotions, and its foreign wars confined to the neighbouring powers of the north. Eric, the eldest son of Gustavus, was dethroned by his brother John, who having espoused Catherine Jaghellon, a princess of Poland, in compliance with her instances endeavoured to restore the Catholic religion. This attempt exciting general discontent, the Protestants found a protector in Charles, the youngest brother ; a civil war was prevented only by the interposition of the senate, and John, in his turn, was compelled to yield to Charles the principal share in the administration of affairs. Such was the situation of the country when John died, leaving two sons, Sigismond, who had been chosen king of Poland during the lifetime of his father, and John, who was brought up a Protestant, and had resided in Sweden. Charles was therefore enabled to retain and increase his influence during the long and frequent absences of his nephew, till the bigoted attempts of Sigismond to change the religion of the country at length roused the whole nation, and occasioned his exclusion from the throne. He was formally deposed by the diet, the crown conferred on Charles, and the duchy of Ostrogothia given to John, who resigned his pretensions.

This revolution occasioned a war between the nephew and uncle; and Charles during his whole reign found constant employment in defending on one side his crown against Sigismond, and on the other in resisting the attacks of Russia and Denmark. On his death in 1611, his son Gustavus Adolphus ascended the throne, in the midst of a war with the three powers. Although only eighteen, he had evinced such great civil and military talents, joined with a prudence above his years, that the states abrogated the law which declared the king a minor till his twenty-fourth year, and liberated him from the tutelage of his mother and the other guardians appointed by the will of his father. The prudence and vigour of the young monarch soon justified this extraordinary confidence. He directed his first attention to the Danes, who had obtained possession of Calmar and Elfsborg, and even threatened Stockholm itself; he baffled all their attempts to penetrate into the heart of Sweden, recovered some of the fortresses which they had captured, and finally purchased peace by the payment of a sum of money, and the cession of his obsolete pretensions to the sterile district of Lapland.

Thus relieved from his most dangerous enemy, he next attacked the Russians, and procured, in 1617, from Michael

Feodorovitch an honourable peace for forty years, and an ample compensation for his sacrifices to Denmark, by the acquisition of Finland, Carelia, and Ingria, which, in addition to Esthonia, conquered by his father, excluded the Russians from the shores of the Baltic. These successes enabled him to concentrate his whole force for the prosecution of the war against his cousin Sigismond, king of Poland, who rejected with disdain all his proposals of peace, and spared neither private intrigues nor open force to recover possession of the throne from which he had been expelled. In this war, the youthful hero gave full scope to those great and splendid talents which had dawned during his contests with Denmark and Russia, and found an ample theatre for the perfection of his military skill, for inuring his troops to that strict and ready obedience to discipline, and that patient endurance of hardships, and inspiring them with that irresistible intrepidity, which ought to be the characteristics of a soldier. By a series of successful enterprises, he overran the greater part of Livonia and Prussian Poland ; and reduced Sigismond to the necessity of concluding a truce for six years, during which he was to retain all his conquests.

As a zealous Protestant, Gustavus considered it a sacred duty to prevent the depression of his religion ; as a sovereign he was interested to check the overgrown power of the house of Austria. These motives were strengthened by the personal resentment which he felt for the support afforded by Ferdinand to the king of Poland, for his refusal to grant him the title of king, and his contemptuous exclusion of the Swedish ambassadors from the congress of Lubec. To these motives of religion and interest, were added an ardent thirst for glory, and a desire to raise his country to that rank and influence among the powers of Europe from which it had been long excluded by its remoteness, internal dissensions, and incessant wars with the neighbouring states.

Soon after the commencement of his reign he endeavoured to form a connection with the Protestant powers of Germany ; and offered his assistance both during the troubles relative to the succession of Berg and Juliers, which had revived under the reign of Matthias, and at the com-

mencement of the contest in Bohemia. Although his overtures were declined, he never lost sight of this great object,
and became a candidate with the king of Denmark for
heading the confederacy of the Protestants in Lower
Saxony. Disgusted with the preference given to his competitor, he took no part in the subsequent contest, till
Christian was driven from his continental territories in
Germany, and the emperor manifested a design of becoming master of the Baltic. He then forgot his former disappointment, entered into an alliance with Denmark, and
sent succours to the relief of Stralsund, when besieged by
Wallenstein.

His character, designs, resources, and military talents,
had not escaped the vigilant eye of Richelieu; and that
great minister selected him as the only agent capable of
fulfilling his plan for humbling the house of Austria. By
the powerful mediation of France, the conclusion of the
truce with Poland was accelerated, and Gustavus was encouraged by promises of support, to become the champion
of the Protestant cause. These offers were too agreeable
to the views of Gustavus to be neglected; but he declined
making any engagement which was likely to shackle his
independent spirit, or compromise his honour. His resolution was strengthened by the conduct of the French
court, who refused to treat with him on terms of equality;
he therefore contented himself with general promises and
professions, waiting till success had given him a claim to
the co-operation, not to the protection of France.

He applied to the Protestant states of Germany, but his
overtures were received only by a few of the minor princes;
while the elector* of Saxony, and even his brother-in-law,
the elector of Brandenburgh, suffered their jealousy of his
talents and ascendency, and their dread of the authority
and power of the emperor, to outweigh their interests. He
was not, however, discouraged by these unpromising appearances; for he was aware that success would gain adherents, and he relied on the advantages which he could

* John George I. was elector of Saxony, and George William
elector of Brandenburgh, who is chiefly known in history as the father
of Frederic William, the great elector. Gustavus had espoused his
sister, Mary Eleonora.

derive from the dissensions between the emperor and the
Catholic league. From these motives he accelerated his
preparations, made levies in every quarter of Europe, and
took into his service the officers and soldiers whom the
emperor had been compelled to disband. He also obtained
promises of support from England, the United Provinces,
and the Hanseatic league; he held an interview with the
king of Denmark, in order to terminate their personal
rivalry, and secure his neutrality; and he omitted no precaution to ensure the safety of his dominions, by stationing
a force sufficient to protect the frontiers from the aggressions
of the neighbouring powers. Finally he assembled the
states of Sweden, to obtain their consent and support, and
to entail the succession on his only child Christiana.

In a speech with which he opened the meeting, he detailed the motives of his enterprise, and proved that he
was not about to engage in a war of conquest or ambition,
but to vindicate his own honour as well as that of the nation, and to protect his religion. After hinting at the
dangers he expected to encounter, and presaging that he
should meet his fate in the field of battle, he added, " If
it be the will of heaven that I should fall in the defence of
liberty, my country, and mankind, I pay the tribute with
thankful acquiescence. It is my duty as a sovereign to
obey the King of kings without murmuring, and cheerfully
to resign the authority delegated to me for his all-wise
purposes. I shall yield up my last breath with a firm persuasion, that Providence will support my subjects, because
they are faithful and virtuous; and that my ministers, generals, and senators, will punctually discharge their duty to
my child, because they love justice, respect me, and feel for
their country!" The sentiments and spirit of this speech
drew tears from all who were present: the assembly, impelled by the enthusiasm which it inspired, instantly announced the warmest approbation of his proposals, voted
the desired succours in men and money, and declared their
resolution to sacrifice their fortunes and lives in support of
their beloved monarch.

The fleet destined for this memorable expedition was
assembled at Elfsnaben. A force of 15,000 men was collected, and, after being detained a short time by contrary

winds, Gustavus took his departure amidst the tears and acclamations of a vast multitude, who were drawn together by a spectacle so extraordinary and so flattering to a warlike nation. He landed on the 24th of June, 1630, on Ruden, an islet in the mouth of the bay, formed between the isles of Usedom and Rugen ; and, first setting his foot on the German soil, prostrated himself in the presence of his army, to return thanks to Heaven for the safety of his voyage. He instantly made himself master of the isles of Rugen, Usedom, and Wollin, to secure his communication with Sweden ; and on the 20th of July advanced without delay to occupy Stettin, the capital of Pomerania, which commanded the course of the Oder, and, if possessed by the imperialists, would have arrested his further progress. He overcame the feigned or real hesitation of the aged duke, and obtained not only his consent to receive a Swedish garrison, but his accession to an offensive and defensive treaty, by which he was to conclude no alliance without the approbation of the king of Sweden, and the forces of Pomerania were to unite with the Swedes. And as the duke was without issue, the treaty was worded in such a manner as to secure the possession of the duchy to the Swedes, at least until the close of the war, although the elector of Brandenburgh was the presumptive heir. As the duke dreaded the vengeance of the emperor, the king allowed him to introduce a clause into the treaty, stating that this engagement was solely to protect his territories from the devastations of the imperial troops, who, after pillaging and wasting his duchy, had left him defenceless, and not to separate the bonds which connected him with the emperor and empire.

Fortunately for Gustavus his promptitude was crowned with success ; for only two days after he obtained possession of Stettin, Conti, the imperial commander in Pomerania, advanced with a force of 17,000 men ; but, finding himself anticipated by the Swedes, threw garrisons into Gart and Grieffenhagen, and, intrenching himself under the walls of Gartz, became master of the upper course of the Oder. After an ineffectual attempt to draw him from his post, Gustavus did not venture a battle till he had secured his rear. Being reinforced by troops from Sweden

and by English auxiliaries, he left a corps for the defence
of Stettin, and expelled the imperialists from the principal
posts of Pomerania, except Demin, Griefswald, and Colberg, which he closely blockaded. He even affected to
make an irruption into Mecklenburgh, pushed on to Stralsund, captured Damgard and Ribnitz, the keys of the
duchy, and defeated an imperial corps near Demin. All
these enterprises did not induce the imperial general to
abandon his important position; he sent, however, various
detachments to embarrass the operations of the Swedes,
continued to succour Colberg, and availed himself of the
king's absence to make an attempt on Stettin, which only
failed from the wonderful promptitude and intrepidity of
the Swedish troops. Had he been properly supported, he
would have greatly embarrassed the operations of the king,
if he had not frustrated his enterprise at its commencement; but left to combat alone with such an antagonist as
Gustavus, seeing his troops gradually diminish from sickness and desertion, and in the midst of a country drained
by their devastations; while the Swedish army was continually increasing, and supplied with every necessary from
the ports of the Baltic, he resigned in disgust, and was replaced by count Schaumburgh.

The new general having sent a part of his forces into
winter quarters, Gustavus, whose troops were hardened by
a northern sky, and defied the severities of a German winter, resumed his design of expelling the imperialists from
the post which they had so long maintained. Sending a
flotilla up the Oder, to cut off the communication between
Gartz and Grieffenhagen, he attacked Grieffenhagen, and
compelled the garrison to retire in the night. Master of
this important post, he pushed across the river against
Gartz, but found it deserted by the imperialists, who, after
setting fire to the place, retired towards Frankfort and
Landsberg. He followed them with his characteristic celerity, harassed them in their retreat into the Mark of
Brandenburgh; he would probably have gained Frankfort, and from thence pushed his successes at once into the
heart of Germany, had he been joined as he expected by
the elector of Brandenburgh; but that prince, from the motives already mentioned, from resentment for the occupa-

tion of Pomerania, and from the influence of his ministers, who were bribed by the emperor, after allowing a passage to the imperial troops, refused him entrance into Custrin. Gustavus, irritated by this conduct, occupied the town of New Brandenburgh, levied heavy contributions, and suffered his troops to overspread the country, and imitate the devastations of the imperialists.

The successes of Gustavus, and the favourable aspect of his affairs, now enabled him to negotiate with France on terms of equality, and soon led to the conclusion of a treaty, which was signed in his camp at Barwalde, on the 13th of January, 1631.

The intent of this treaty was declared to be for the defence of the common friends of the two monarchs; for establishing the security of the ocean and the Baltic, and the liberty of commerce; for protecting the injured states of the empire; and for procuring the demolition of the forts erected on the shores of both seas, and in the country of the Grisons. To fulfil these purposes, the king of Sweden was to receive an annual subsidy of 1,200,000 livres* from France, in return for which he was to maintain at his own expense, and under his own direction, an army of 30,000 infantry and 6000 horse. At once to save the honour of France and conciliate the Catholics, it was further stipulated that Gustavus should grant a neutrality to the duke of Bavaria, and the other members of the league who did not unite with the emperor, and, if successful, he was to make no change in the state of religion. The duration of the treaty was for six years; and, as a compensation for past expenses, the king was to receive, exclusive of the annual subsidy, an immediate advance of 300,000 livres.

Gustavus had accompanied his invasion by publishing a manifesto, recapitulating his personal grievances against the emperor, and appealing to the Protestant body to support a cause in which they were equally interested. Such however was the dread inspired by the power of Ferdinand, and such the jealousy entertained by their two chiefs, the electors of Saxony and Brandenburgh, against Gustavus, that the only Protestant princes who declared in his favour

* Equal to 50,000l. sterling.

were one of the dukes of Saxe Lauenburgh, and the deposed administrator of Magdeburgh.

A meeting of the Protestant states was however held at Leipzic, which, notwithstanding all the prohibitions and remonstrances of the emperor, continued its sittings from the commencement of February to the month of April. The elector of Saxony, under whose auspices the meeting assembled, took this opportunity to resume the predominance of his house in the Protestant body, and persuaded his co-estates not to become subservient to either of the contending parties, but to adopt a line of conduct which would enable them to dictate to both.   At his proposal they required from the emperor the immediate abolition of the edict of restitution, and announced their resolution to employ force, if necessary, in preventing the passage and quartering of troops, levying men and contributions, and the devastations, excesses, and plunder committed contrary to the capitulation and the laws of the empire.   To fulfil this declaration they entered into a resolution to raise a force of 40,000 men, and to form a permanent council for the direction of their affairs.   In order not to appear as the aggressors, or give jealousy to the Catholics, they accompanied the publication of these resolutions with a letter addressed both to the emperor and the Catholic league, declaring that their levy was not intended for hostile purposes, but to preserve the peace, laws, and constitution of the empire.   Although they declined all the overtures of Gustavus, and did not even mention his invasion, their conduct was of the highest disadvantage to the cause of the emperor; for they cut off the resources which had hitherto enabled him to maintain his army ; and they were about to raise a considerable army which contributed to embarrass and suspend his movements, and was ready to declare against him on the first favourable opportunity.

It is a matter of astonishment that the imperial forces who first checked the efforts of Gustavus, should not have been supported; and that with so small an army he should have been suffered gradually to establish himself in Pomerania, particularly when we consider the character of Ferdinand, who was not of a temper to abandon his advantages without a contest, or suffer his troops to continue inactive.

But our astonishment must subside, when we reflect on the proceedings and temper of the diet of Ratisbon. At the very moment when the king of Sweden was expelling the imperialists from Pomerania, Wallenstein was absent at Ratisbon, endeavouring to awe his enemies by his presence, and to suspend his fall; and his officers, left without control, acted without order or concert. The emperor, occupied in baffling the intrigues of the Catholics, or in eluding their demands, was duped by the insidious promises of the French agents, and the counsels of the duke of Bavaria. His deception was increased by the contemptuous idea he was taught to entertain of the king of Sweden, whom Wallenstein boasted that he would whip back with rods to his country, like a truant school-boy, and whom the courtiers call a king of snow, who would melt as he advanced towards a southern climate. At the very time likewise when Ferdinand had most occasion for an increase of troops, and the services of a skilful commander, his inconsiderate eagerness to obtain the election of his son, the promises of France, and the clamours both of Catholics and Protestants, induced him to reduce his forces, and dismiss the only general who possessed skill and resources equal to the exigency. In consequence of this imprudent acquiescence, the troops whom he disbanded enlisted under Gustavus, and the best officers entered into foreign service, or withdrew from Wallenstein into retirement. France broke her promised neutrality to support Gustavus, and the Catholics viewed with indifference, if they did not exult in the distress of the emperor. To add to these difficulties a contest ensued for the vacant command, which was claimed by the duke of Bavaria, while the emperor wished to confer it on his son Ferdinand; and after a delay, which at this important juncture suspended the military operations, a compromise was effected, by which it was conferred on the Bavarian general Tilly, whose active services and military skill qualified him for so arduous a post. The embarrassments of the emperor were augmented by the rising spirit among the Protestants, who, recovering from their dread of that power which had driven them to the brink of ruin, renewed their meetings, and clamoured for the revocation of the edict of restitution.

The diet, indeed, issued a declaration of war against
Gustavus, but made no adequate preparations for the prosecution of hostilities; and the emperor, instead of opposing him with an efficient army, sent a letter, threatening
to attack him with his whole force, if he did not instantly
retire from Germany. Such a mission appeared ridiculous
to the Swedish hero; and he evinced the contempt in
which he held his antagonist, by a derisory and allegorical
reply, " That he would despatch an answer as soon as he
had recovered from a wound given him by an eagle."*

While the king of Sweden had succeeded in expelling
the imperialists from the greater part of Pomerania, some
of the lesser German princes had ventured to take arms,
and avenge the injuries which they had suffered from the
tyrannical conduct of the emperor. Francis Charles, of the
house of Saxe Lauenburgh, assembled a corps of troops in
the neighbourhood of Hamburgh, captured a few posts on
the Elbe, and threw himself into Ratzeburgh, the residence
of his brother, from whence he hoped to make irruptions,
if not to establish himself in Mecklenburgh. But his
enterprise was soon crushed; for the imperial general
Pappenheim followed him at the head of 6000 men,
blockaded Ratzeburgh, and took him prisoner in his attempt
to escape.

A similar enterprise deprived the emperor of the important post of Magdeburgh, which had preserved its attachment to its former administrator, and had resisted the
attempts even of Wallenstein to introduce an imperial garrison. Before the Swedish invasion, Christian William, the
ex-administrator, had repaired to Sweden, and obtained
from Gustavus Adolphus a sum of money, and promises of
support. He returned in disguise to Magdeburgh, and
found little difficulty in rousing the people, and inducing
the magistrates to enter into a formal treaty with Gustavus,
soon after his landing in Pomerania. He obtained the
command of a force raised by the magistrates, and drove
the imperialists from various posts in the neighbourhood of
the town. His troops increasing by new levies, and being
assisted by the skill of the Swedish general Falkenberg,
who had been sent by Gustavus, he prosecuted his advan-

* Alluding to the imperial eagles.

tages, and for several months maintained with success a petty warfare against the imperialists.

Ferdinand at length perceiving that he had been duped by France, and that Gustavus was not so contemptible an adversary as he had been taught to imagine, omitted no effort to resume the advantages which he had lost. He secured himself on the side of Hungary, recovered the ceded provinces, and baffled the intrigues of Gustavus by acknowledging George Ragotski, who had been chosen prince of Transylvania on the death of Bethlehem Gabor. He repressed his indignation at the conduct of the duke of Bavaria and the Catholic league; persuaded them to reject the neutrality offered by Gustavus, and to consider his cause as their own. He at the same time prepared to draw his veteran troops from Italy; and, notwithstanding the remonstrances of Spain, entered into negotiations for terminating the dispute relative to the succession of Mantua.

While these events were passing, Tilly had commenced the campaign by assembling the forces of the league to the amount of 20,000 men, and in February hastened to unite them with the remnant of the imperialists, who under Schaumburgh occupied the Mark of Brandenburgh. But he found the imperial army reduced to 8000 men, without clothes, pay, provisions, or ammunition, unable to draw resources from a country which they had rendered a desert by their excesses, and desponding from their recent defeats. Advancing to Frankfort he received the intelligence that Gustavus, after leaving a corps of observation on the frontiers of Brandenburgh, had returned, as if with an intention to penetrate into the duchy of Mecklenburgh, and laid siege to Demin. He therefore left a garrison of 8000 men in Frankfort, took New Brandenburgh by storm, put the Swedish garrison to the sword, and hastened to cover Mecklenburgh. But on his route he received the mortifying intelligence that Demin had surrendered from the pusillanimity of the governor, after a siege of only three days, and that Colberg had likewise submitted to the Swedish arms. He had the additional mortification to discover that the threatened attack of Mecklenburgh had been only a feint, and that Gustavus, after drawing him from the Oder, had returned towards Brandenburgh, left a corps to cover his march in the strong intrenched post of Schwedt, and directed his attack against Frankfort. Tilly hastened to save a place which was the key of Brandenburgh, and protected the hereditary countries. But although he pushed forward with his usual celerity, he was again anticipated by the superior promptitude of the Swedish monarch, before he could arrive near the scene of action. Frankfort was carried by assault, and the greater part of the unfortunate garrison suffered the fate of the Swedes at New Brandenburgh. The loss of Frankfort was instantly followed by the surrender of Landsberg; the remnant of the imperialists was driven in disorder into Silesia, and the posts on the frontiers were occupied by the Swedes. In consequence of these sinister events, Tilly, unable to maintain himself in the vicinity of the Oder, fell back toward Magdeburgh, to restore the lustre of his arms by the acquisition of so important a post, to draw the Swedes from the Austrian territories, and to wreak his vengeance on the inhabitants, who had been the first in Germany to declare against the emperor.

Pappenheim, after his successful enterprise against the duke of Saxe Lauenburgh, had driven the forces of the administrator from the posts which they wrested from the imperialists, and gradually confined them to the walls and fortifications of Magdeburgh. In this situation Tilly arrived with the main army; and the garrison, exhausted and reduced by the preceding attacks, were still less able to resist this augmentation of force. They abandoned the suburbs to the imperialists, broke down the bridge over the Elbe, and armed the burghers. Their situation became hourly more deplorable; the people were divided by intestine feuds; the lower orders clamoured against the exemption of the higher from military duties; the garrison was continually diminished by hardships and the sword; yet the burghers were urged to reject the repeated overtures of Tilly, and to tempt their impending fate, by the exhortations of their administrator, the sermons of their preachers, and the prospect of immediate assistance from the king of Sweden and the Protestant league.

Gustavus had not seen with indifference the distresses and danger of the only state of Germany which had voluntarily espoused his cause, and a town which he was bound by every motive of religion and policy to save from the hands of the enemy. After the capture of Landsberg, he wrote to the inhabitants, exhorting them to hold out, and promised them speedy support. He hastened to fulfil his promise; yet, too prudent to advance against Tilly without a chain of posts to secure his rear, and to which he could retreat in order to avoid a battle, he applied to the elector of Brandenburgh for the temporary cession of Custrin and Spandau. But notwithstanding the danger of a place so important as Magdeburgh to the Protestant cause, the jealousy and repugnance of the elector were only overcome by the dread of an immediate attack, and the advance of the Swedish army towards Berlin. After some delay Spandau was yielded on the 4th of May, until the siege of Magdeburgh was raised, and the return of the king secured; and Gustavus exulted in the prospect of carrying relief to those who had already suffered so much in his cause. At this critical juncture, when the delay of a single day was fatal, he experienced a new check from the refractory spirit of the elector of Saxony, whom no arguments, no motives of religion or policy, could induce to grant him possession of Dessau, and a passage through his territories, or even to afford the smallest supply. Gustavus was unable to repress his indignation at this impolitic or pusillanimous obstinacy; and exclaimed, "If these people will perish, let them perish! I will retreat into Pomerania, and there wait till these half-witted politicians are driven to the very brink of the precipice, and compelled to implore my assistance. Is it possible they can calmly see their neighbour's house in flames, without assisting to extinguish the conflagration! This unfortunate city must then perish, and with it perhaps the last remnant of German liberty!"

This presage was but too fully verified. During these tedious negotiations Tilly had pressed the siege; and, taking advantage of a moment of repose and security, carried the town by assault on the 10th of May. All the horrors ever exercised against a captured place were repeated and almost surpassed on this dreadful event, which, notwithstanding all the subsequent disorders, and the lapse of time, is still fresh in the recollection of its inhabitants and of Germany. Neither age, beauty, nor innocence, neither infancy nor decrepitude, found refuge or compassion from the fury of the licentious soldiery; no retreat was sufficiently obscure to escape their rapacity and vengeance; no sanctuary sufficiently sacred to repress their lust and cruelty. Infants were murdered before the eyes of their parents, daughters and wives violated in the arms of their fathers and husbands. Some officers of the league, recoiling from this terrible scene, flew to Tilly, and supplicated him to put a stop to the carnage; but the barbarian replied, "Stay yet an hour, let the soldier have some compensation for his dangers and fatigues." The troops left to themselves, after sating their passions, and almost exhausting their cruelty, in three hours of pillage and massacre, set fire to the town, and the flames were in an instant spread by the wind to every quarter of the place. Then opened a scene which surpassed all the former horrors; those who had hitherto escaped, or were forced by the flames from their hiding places, experienced a more dreadful fate; numbers were driven into the Elbe, others massacred with every species of savage barbarity; the wombs of pregnant women ripped up, and infants thrown into the fire, or impaled on pikes and suspended over the flames. History has no terms, poetry no language, painting no colours, to depict all the horrors of the scene. In less than ten hours the most rich, most flourishing, and most populous town of Germany was reduced to ashes; the cathedral, a single convent, and a few miserable huts, were all that were left of its numerous buildings; and scarcely more than a thousand souls, all that remained of thirty thousand inhabitants. The Swedish general Falkenberg was killed at the first entrance of the enemy; the administrator wounded and taken prisoner; and the few soldiers who escaped from the carnage were compelled to enter into the imperial service.*

After an interval of two days, when the soldiers were fatigued, if not sated with devastation and slaughter, and when the flames had begun to subside, Tilly entered the

* Accounts of the wonderful escape of two individuals, a priest and a fisherman, are given in the Histoire de Gustave Adolphe, tom. iii., p. 157-174.

town in triumph. To make room for his passage, the streets were cleared, and six thousand carcasses thrown into the Elbe. He ordered the pillage to cease, pardoned the scanty remnant of the inhabitants who had taken refuge in the cathedral, and surrounded by flames and carnage, had remained three days without food or refreshment under all the terrors of impending fate. After hearing a Te Deum in the midst of military pomp, he paraded the streets; and though even his unfeeling heart seemed touched with the horrors of the scene, he could not refrain from the savage exultation of boasting to the emperor, and comparing the assault of Magdeburgh to the sack of Troy and Jerusalem.

This dreadful example diffused as much exultation among the Catholics as terror and dismay among the Protestants; the league, in a general assembly at Dinkespuhl, announced the most hostile disposition against the Protestants, and declared their resolution to support the chief of the empire. Ferdinand, exulting in this favourable aspect of his affairs, hastened to take advantage of the sensation produced by the capture of Magdeburgh. He had already commanded the confederates of Leipzic to dissolve their union, he now determined to enforce the execution of that mandate which they had hitherto contemned, and announced his resolution to prosecute his designs against the Protestants, by summoning a diet of deputation at Frankfort, in the ensuing August, for fulfilling the edict of restitution. The peace of Chierasco, which he had recently concluded, and by which he restored the duchy of Mantua to its sovereign, and relinquished the Valteline, gave him an opportunity of adding his veteran forces, amounting to 24,000 men, to that army which under Tilly had spread terror throughout Germany. Their march was instantly commenced under the command of the prince of Furstemberg; they passed the Alps, and in their route through Suabia and Franconia forced the duke of Wirtemberg, with the other members of the confederacy, to renounce their alliance, to obey the edict of restitution, to pay heavy contributions, to give up the levies which they had recently made for their own defence, and to assist in the prosecution of the war against Gustavus Adolphus.

On the other hand, Tilly having extorted a similar submission from the archbishop of Bremen, had left Pappenheim with a corps of observation at Magdeburgh, and
directed his attack against 'the landgrave of Hesse, one of
the most zealous partisans of the Protestant cause. He
pushed his march through Thuringia, marking his footsteps with his usual devastation and pillage, occupied Erfurth, and from Mulhausen sent an insulting message to
the landgrave, commanding him to receive imperial garrisons in two of his principal fortresses, to supply the
imperial army with pay, ammunition, and provisions, and
to disband or give up the levies which he had assembled
in consequence of the confederacy of Leipzic. A positive and contemptuous refusal from the landgrave galled
his haughty and presumptuous mind ; he declared his resolution to inflict on every town of the landgraviate a more
dreadful vengeance than he had inflicted on Magdeburgh,
and to render the country more solitary and waste than a
desert. He followed these menaces by inundating the surrounding district with his troops ; but was prevented from
fulfilling his threats by the progress of Gustavus.*

CHAP. LIII. — 1631, 1632.

THE Swedish monarch felt the most poignant sorrow at
the capture of Magdeburgh, and published a narrative for
the justification of his conduct in the eyes of Europe. At
the very moment when the loss of that important fortress
enabled the imperialists to carry the war into Mecklenburgh, and when the fate of that unfortunate city spread
terror throughout Germany, he was still further embarrassed by the conduct of the elector of Brandenburgh, who
clamoured for the restitution of Spandau, in conformity
with the recent agreement. In this critical dilemma,
threatened by equal danger, whether he advanced or re-
ceded, Gustavus acted with his characteristic vigour and

* Schiller's Thirty Years' War — Puffendorf — Struvius — Barre —
Schmidt — Harte's Life of Gustavus — Vie de Gustave Adolphe.

integrity; he replied that he would fulfil his engagement by delivering up the fortress, but from that moment would treat the elector as his enemy. On the very day therefore in which he yielded Spandau, he appeared at the head of his army before Berlin, and after a short parley, on the 11th of June, 1631, extorted from the elector the surrender of Spandau, Brandenburgh, and Ratenou, a free passage through Custrin, and a monthly contribution of 30,000 crowns.

Thus relieved from his difficulties on the side of Brandenburgh, he hastened back to Stettin to attack Griefswald, the only post in Pomerania which was now held by the imperialists; and he had the satisfaction to hear in his journey that the place had already surrendered. After leaving a sufficient number of troops to protect the frontiers of Pomerania, he assembled the principal part of his army in the neighbourhood, pushed towards the Elbe, captured Tangermund, and threatened Magdeburgh. Being checked by the approach of Tilly, he reduced Havelberg, and fell back to Werben, at the confluence of the Elbe and the Havel, a post which from its strength enabled him to defy all the efforts of the imperialists, and from its position to cover Mecklenburgh, to secure his communications with the Baltic, and deprive his antagonist of all the advantages derived from the possession of Magdeburgh and the command of the Elbe. While he remained in this situation, his queen landed at Wolgast with a reinforcement of 8000 Swedes; and the marquis of Hamilton with 6000 English volunteers in the isle of Usedom. The English were sent to make a diversion on the side of Silesia; while the Swedes, joined by a corps under the dukes of Mecklenburgh, recovered the whole of that duchy, except Wismar and Rostock; and the king himself had the satisfaction of formally reinstating the dukes in their lawful possessions. Soon afterwards he concluded an offensive and defensive alliance with the landgrave of Hesse, which was the model of all his subsequent engagements with the princes of the empire. On one side, he promised to defend the landgrave against all his enemies, and to procure the restitution of those fiefs which had been confiscated during the Bohemian troubles. On the other, the landgrave agreed to contract no alliance without the consent of Gustavus, to consign to him the supreme command of the Hessian troops, or in his absence to share the command with a Swedish general ; to admit Swedish garrisons into his principal towns, till the conclusion of peace, and to supply the army with provisions.

The advance of Gustavus on the side of Magdeburgh convinced Tilly of his imprudence in turning his arms against the Protestants, instead of carrying the war into Mecklenburgh. Leaving therefore a corps in Hesse, under Fugger, he hastened to cover Magdeburgh, and dislodge the king. A successful attack made by Gustavus on his vanguard, in the neighbourhood of Wolmerstadt, rousing him almost to fury, he made repeated assaults on the Swedish camp with his usual impetuosity, but was as often repulsed, from the strength of the post, the intrepidity of the Swedes, and the skill and promptitude of their monarch. Such a failure in the midst of success could not fail to irritate the presumptuous mind of Tilly, who had been hitherto considered as unrivalled in the art of war, and who constantly boasted that he had gained seven pitched battles, without experiencing a single check. His concern was heightened by the effect which it produced among his troops, who, disheartened by the failure of a chief hitherto considered as invincible, deserted in crowds to secure their booty in retreat, or to join the standard of Gustavus.

To revive the spirits of his soldiers by new plunder, as well as to restore the lustre of his arms by the subjugation of a less powerful enemy, Tilly turned against the elector of Saxony, whose equivocal and wavering inclinations prevented him from joining either the king of Sweden or the emperor. After a haughty summons, commanding him to renounce the confederacy of Leipzic, and unite his troops with those of the emperor, Tilly fell back to Eisleben, united with the corps which had been led from Italy by Furstemberg, and at the head of 40,000 men advanced to Halle, from whence he sent a hostile reply to a respectful refusal of the elector, which he concluded with this declaration, " By your disobedience you have frustrated the good effects of your boasted services to the emperor and the Germanic body, and must be answerable for all the evils which may fall on Saxony or elsewhere. Your formal refusal has left me no other alternative than to compel you to pay that obedience which you owe to the emperor and empire. Reflect on it; grant my army a passage; furnish me with provisions and necessaries; join your own troops with mine, and be assured that the king of Sweden will soon be driven away. Send back my herald instantly with your answer ; time presses; my troops are impatient, and no delay can be granted." He did not even wait for the answer to this threatening message ; but, devastating the surrounding country, advanced towards Leipzic, and within three days compelled it to surrender.

The approach of danger awakening the elector from his dreams of independence, he assembled his forces at Torgau, sent Arnheim*, his favourite general and confidential counsellor, with full powers to the Swedish camp, and after an affected demur on the side of Gustavus, concluded, on the 1st of September, 1631, an offensive and defensive alliance on terms similar to those of the league recently concluded with the landgrave of Hesse. The danger being too imminent to admit of delay, the king passed the Elbe at Wittenberg, and within four days after the conclusion of the treaty, the two armies, uniting at Duben on the Moldau, advanced towards Leipzic to give battle to the imperialists, the very day on which the town had surrendered.

Tilly flattered himself that he should be able to overwhelm the Saxons before the elector had vanquished his repugnance to the king of Sweden ; he was therefore equally surprised and confounded with the sudden junction and rapid advance of the combined forces. After fluctuating for some time between the resolution of giving battle or waiting for a reinforcement of 10,000 men, which he expected from Silesia, he advanced, agitated with doubts and presages to Breitenfield, determined to receive the enemy, who on the following morning, September 7th, appeared defiling by the village of Podelwitz.

This was the first time in which the two armies were opposed to each other in the field, and as they were nearly

* Arnheim had served with great applause under Wallenstein, whose favour he had obtained ; but, on the dismission of his chief, and part of the army, had entered into the service of the elector of Saxony, whose confidence he soon acquired in an eminent degree.

equal in numbers, and commanded by chiefs who had equal pretensions to military fame, the contest was no less to prove the tactics and skill of the respective generals and the bravery of their troops than to decide the fate of Germany and of Christendom. The army of Tilly was formed in a single line, without any body of reserve; the infantry in the centre, and the cavalry on the wings, at the foot of the range of eminences which skirt the plain to the north of Leipzic, between Breitenfeld and Podelwitz. The infantry and cavalry were ranged in large masses of great depth, the artillery placed on the eminences behind, from whence it commanded the plain. The allies formed before the village of Podelwitz; the Saxons occupied an eminence on the left beyond the road leading to Podelwitz, the infantry in the centre, and the cavalry on the wings, and were headed by Arnheim, under the nominal command of the elector. With a considerable interval the Swedes were posted on the right in two lines, each with its reserve, and the artillery distributed along the front of each. Unlike the cumbrous masses of the imperialists, the infantry, who occupied the centre, was formed in small battalions, six deep; and the cavalry on the wings in squadrons intermixed with platoons of infantry. This expedient was adopted by the king to render his small horses capable of resisting the shock of the strong and ponderous cavalry of the imperialists; and for that purpose the musqueteers were ordered to withhold their fire till the enemy had advanced within pistol shot, that they might check them at the moment of the charge.

The event of this battle and the greatness of the stake called forth all the skill and resources of the two commanders, neither of whom had before witnessed a defeat, and the conduct of the two chiefs seemed to presage the fate of the day. Gustavus, though elate and confident, evinced by his dispositions and behaviour the utmost coolness and self-command; Tilly, on the contrary, though equally intrepid and more experienced, seemed bereft of his usual decision and presence of mind. The carnage and horrors which accompanied the sack of Magdeburgh forced themselves on his recollection, and he shuddered with terror, when he observed on the outward walls of the house in which he signed the capitulation of Leipzic, the painted figures of bones and skulls.* Such an impression at such a moment sunk deep in an ardent and superstitious mind; and Tilly, after hesitating whether he should give battle or remain on the defensive, commenced his march full of perturbation, presages, and dismay. From this cause rather than from presumption he took little precaution to harass the march, or prevent the formation of the allies; and when he saw them advance in consummate order and regularity, he seemed struck with astonishment; he leant his head on his hands, and for a considerable time remained absorbed in thought.

His native intrepidity, however, vanquished this depression of spirits, he gave the signal for battle by the discharge of three pieces of cannon, and the thunder of the artillery instantly resounded from wing to wing. After a furious cannonade of two hours the imperialists advanced to the charge, and their right soon broke and dispersed the greater part of the Saxon troops. This successful onset was considered as the omen of victory, and couriers were despatched with the joyful intelligence to Munich and Vienna. At this moment, however, the battle had commenced on the other wing. Pappenheim, with the cavalry, charged the right of the Swedes; but his troops, mowed down by the destructive fire of the musqueteers, after repeated shocks gave way, and abandoned the field in confusion. During these movements the king sent a prompt reinforcement to assist the remnant of the Saxon troops, who still maintained their ground, and, by gradually advancing, gained the flank of the imperialists. On the repulse of Pappenheim, with that intuitive sagacity which seizes the critical moment of action, he pushed forward, mounted the heights on which the imperial artillery was posted, turned it against their own army, and attacked their infantry in flank and rear, while it was warmly engaged in front. The consequence of this charge was the instant and inevitable defeat of the imperialists, who fled

* This house belonged to a grave-digger, and as it was the only habitation in the suburbs not destroyed, it was appropriated for the headquarters of the general. Mr. Harte observes, that he saw these paintings.

in every direction. Four regiments alone, the veteran bands of Tilly, who had been always accustomed to victory, disdained to stain their honour by flight ; they closed their ranks, cut their way through the victorious army, gained the wood of Linchel, and, obstinately refusing quarter, maintained their ground till they were reduced to six hundred, who retreated under cover of the night. The brave and skilful Pappenheim was seven times wounded, stripped and left for dead on the field, and owed his life to the care of a peasant, who conveyed him the following morning to Fulda. Tilly himself was exposed to the most imminent danger. After displaying distinguished proofs of heroism, he headed the remnant of his veterans, who were making their retreat. Surrounded by the enemy, he was attacked by a Swedish officer, who, from his extraordinary stature was called Frederic the Long ; and although he had received three balls, besides several other wounds, he nobly refused to surrender. At the moment when he was sinking under the blows of so powerful an adversary, he was rescued by Maximilian of Saxe Lauenburgh, who shot his antagonist, and conveyed the imperial general, overwhelmed with pain and chagrin, to Halle.* When a little recovered he continued his retreat to Halberstadt, and even at that distance from the scene of his misfortune could scarcely collect 2000 men to his standard. Thus terminated this memorable battle ; 7000 Austrians were left on the field, 5000 taken prisoners, and all the baggage and artillery lost ; on the side of the Swedes only 700 were killed, and 2000 of the Saxons.

The loss of this battle has been attributed to the unskilful conduct of Tilly, who drew up his troops in unwieldy masses, without a reserve, and placed his artillery in a situation which rendered it equally useless whether his troops advanced or retreated. But it was still more owing to the new tactics of the king, whose troops were formed and armed for vigorous, rapid, and decisive movements, and who possessed a considerable advantage over the imperialists by the use of a new species of field artillery, which, being formed with boiled leather, was more light

* Struvius, p. 1274.

and manageable than metal, and less liable to heat in continued firings.

Gustavus had now the choice of two systems of operation; one of directing the war against the hereditary countries of the emperor, the other of penetrating into the heart of Germany, reviving the Protestant confederacy, and crushing the Catholic league. Though victorious, his situation was extremely critical, as on his decision depended not only the prosecution of his designs, but even his own security. He had penetrated into the heart of an empire, which, however disturbed by intestine commotions, had never seen beyond its frontiers the footsteps of a foreign enemy, which had hitherto been preserved from external attacks by the vigilance and union of its princes, the natural strength of the country, the martial spirit of the people, and the number of its fortresses. His progress had been promoted as much by civil and religious troubles as by his own skill and energy; and it was no less necessary to keep open the communication with his dominions on the banks of the Maine, the Rhine, and the Danube, than on those of the Elbe and the Oder. The number of garrisons requisite to maintain this necessary communication could not, however, be supplied from his own troops, without diminishing his army, and exposing himself to the danger of losing, in the prosecution of his success, all that he had gained by his victories. He was likewise advanced to such a distance from his own territories, that it was necessary to render the war the support of itself, and to draw the resources for the maintenance of an army continually increasing, from the contributions of his allies, or the territories of the enemy which had hitherto escaped devastation. He was sensible that his astonishing success had confounded his allies as well as his enemies; he knew that France would be as anxious to check his progress as to humiliate the house of Austria, and if he looked to the greater German princes, he saw them no less jealous of his ascendancy than of the overgrown power of the emperor, particularly the elector of Saxony, whose weak, suspicious, and fluctuating character was likely at every moment to deceive his expectations. He could therefore only depend for support on the smaller princes and states, who did not envy his ascendancy, and looked up to him for protection and reward; and these, from their situation, could only assist him against the Catholic league. Thus, by means of the Germans, he was enabled to conquer Germany : these minor states protected his rear, maintained his communications, opened to him their fortresses, supplied his army with provisions, and lavished their blood in his cause. For these reasons he sent the elector of Saxony to achieve the conquest of Bohemia; while he himself revived and reunited the scattered parts of the Protestant confederacy, and led his victorious troops against the Catholic league, to cut off the resources of the house of Austria in the empire.

His march rather resembled the tranquil progress of a sovereign receiving the homage of his subjects than that of a general through a hostile country. At Erfurth he formed an alliance with the dukes of Saxe Weimar, the most powerful princes of Thuringia, and left to them, and to the landgrave of Hesse, the conduct of the war in that part of Germany. He then directed his course towards the Maine, received the voluntary submission of Schweinfurth, took Wurtzburgh by storm, drove the bishop into exile, and laid his see under contribution. From thence entering the electorate of Mentz, he continued his course down the Maine, captured Aschaffenburgh and Hanau, with the fortresses on both sides of the river; and, after expelling the diet of deputation, which had been assembled at Frankfort for the purpose of enforcing the edict of restitution, was received in that centre of imperial authority with all the honours of a sovereign, and all the gratitude due to a deliverer. In this course he dispersed without a blow the forces of the duke of Loraine*, who, in order to liberate himself from his dependence on France, had

---

* The duchy of Loraine, which formerly was a part of the kingdom of Loraine, had been a constant source of contests between the kings of France and Germany, until it was acknowledged as a dependence on Germany. It continued to be connected with the empire until the male line became extinct in Charles III. (1431), when his eldest daughter and heiress Isabella conveyed it to René, duke of Anjou, titular king of Naples, and duke of Bar, who thus united the duchies of Loraine and Bar. From this transfer of the duchy to a prince of the blood royal of France, the connection of Loraine with the empire was

espoused the cause of the emperor, and advanced with 12,000 men to join Tilly; while the Spaniards, alarmed by his progress, retired from the palatinate, leaving garrisons in Heidelberg, Frankendahl, and Oppenheim.

gradually dissolved, and its sovereigns became wholly dependent on the crown of France.

Charles III., or, as he is generally called, IV., duke of Loraine, the prince mentioned in the text, was son of Francis, count of Vaudemont, brother of Henry, duke of Loraine. He was born in 1604, and educated at Paris. He was brought up to the church, and received two abbies, and other ecclesiastical preferment; but his volatile character and martial propensities soon induced him to abandon the ecclesiastical profession for that of arms. As early as his sixteenth year, he entered into the Bavarian service, and was present at the battle of Prague. As his uncle Henry, the last duke, was without issue male, he espoused his daughter Nicola, to secure the inheritance; and on the death of Henry, in 1624, took joint possession in his own name and that of his wife. But desirous to obtain those territories in his own right, his father claimed and took possession of them as the next male heir, and then resigned them to him; he accordingly excluded his wife from the joint regency, and received in his own name the homage of the states. The position of Loraine rendering its possession of great advantage to France in an attack against the Spanish Netherlands, or the empire, cardinal Richelieu endeavoured to secure so important a territory, either by reducing him to the state of a vassal, or expelling him as an enemy, and he found endless pretexts to colour his designs from the independent, capricious, and enterprising character of the duke. He first secured an entrance into Loraine, by building a citadel at Verdun, and soon afterwards deprived him of the duchy of Bar, because he had not received the investiture as a fief of France, and had excluded his wife from the joint regency.

These designs of the French court, naturally irritating a prince of such an ambitious and enterprising spirit, he entered into alliances with Charles I. of England and the duke of Savoy. He gave protection to Gaston, duke of Orleans, when expelled by the all-powerful minister, promoted a match between him and his sister Margaret, formed secret connections with the emperor, received an imperial garrison in Moyenvic, and began to assemble an army. These preparations and connections giving still further pretexts for aggression, afforded the king of France an opportunity to lead an army to the frontiers of Loraine, and to obtain possession of Marsal, Moyenvic, Stenai, Clermont, and Jametz. These humiliations irritating the duke still more, he took advantage of the civil troubles in France to endeavour to liberate himself from his dependence; he declared openly in favour of the emperor, took possession of the towns in Alsace which had received French garrisons, and led, as mentioned in the text, a considerable force to join Tilly against Gustavus Adolphus.

Continuing his march, Gustavus crossed the Rhine near Oppenheim, at the head of a small corps, in the very face of the Spanish troops, and on the opposite bank erected a column, as a memorial of his first passage. His conquests along the Rhine were scarcely less rapid than those along the Maine; he took Oppenheim, Mentz, Worms, Spire, and all the principal fortresses in the vicinity of the river, from Bacharac to Strasburgh, opened a passage into Alsace, by the capture of Weissemburgh and Landau, and into the Palatinate, by making himself master of Manheim and Wimpfen, two important posts on the Neckar and the Rhine. He expelled the elector of Mentz from his territories, forced the elector of Treves to recede from his alliance with the emperor, and prepared to carry his arms into the electorate of Cologne. Not only the princes and states in his passage sought his friendship, but even those who were more distant. On one side he formed an alliance with the city of Strasburgh; on the other with Bremen, Lubeck, Lunenburgh, and Brunswick; Nuremberg and Ulm claimed his protection. He entered into similar connections with the counts of Nassau Solms, and the other feudal lords of Wetteravia, with the dukes of Brunswick * and the archbishop of Bremen.

While Gustavus thus made himself master of the countries watered by the Maine and the Rhine, his generals and allies were equally successful. The dukes of Mecklenburgh, assisted by the Swedish troops, recovered possession of Wismar, Rostock, and Domitz, and expelled the imperialists from their duchy. Charles, duke of Saxe Lauenburgh, who had purchased his liberty by changing his religion, and by promising not to bear arms against the emperor, forgot at once his conversion and his promise, raised troops in the name of Gustavus, strengthened the army of the Swedish general Todt, and enabled him to secure Stade, the key of the Elbe. Horn occupied the bishopric of Bamberg; Banner drove the imperialists from the ruins of Magdeburgh, and, joined by 10,000 men, whom

---

* The house of Brunswick was at this period divided into two branches, Brunswick Wolfenbuttel, of which Frederic Ulric was the head, and Brunswick Lunenburgh, of which William, duke of Zell and Hanover, possessed the principal territories.

Bernard*, duke of Saxe Weimar, levied in Thuringia, captured Nordheim, Gottingen, Goslar, and Duderstadt; while the landgrave of Hesse laid the bishoprics of Fulda and Paderborn under contribution, and spread terror into Westphalia. By these conquests and alliances Gustavus became master of the courses of the Elbe, the Weser, the Maine, and the Upper Rhine, commanded a vast tract of country, and occupied a continued chain of fortresses, stretching through the heart of Germany, from the Baltic to the frontiers of Switzerland.

While Gustavus and his allies were thus rapidly extending their arms through the heart of Germany, the elector of Saxony achieved the conquest of Bohemia. Before the battle of Leipzic, Goertz and Teuffenbach led the remnant of the imperialists from Frankfort into Silesia, collected the troops scattered on all sides, and, at the head of 10,000 men, overran the greater part of Lusatia. They even sent their partisans as far as Dresden, placed garrisons in the principal towns, and would have maintained themselves against the Saxon army, had not Ferdinand commanded them to retire into Silesia, from the hope of again detaching the elector. This retreat being however considered by the elector as a proof of weakness or fear, he declined all the pressing overtures of the imperial court. The Saxon army, under the command of Arnheim, penetrated into Bohemia, took without opposition Aussig, Leutmeritz, Schlan, Melnick, and Teschen, where the imperialists had formed considerable magazines, and occupied the whole district contiguous to Lusatia and Saxony, with inconsiderable loss.

The natives making no opposition to a Protestant prince in behalf of their intolerant despot, the Saxon troops advanced to Prague; the governor and the principal nobles retired in haste, and the capital capitulated through the mediation of count Thurn, who accompanied the Saxon army on the sole condition that the citizens should be secured from pillage and the quartering of the troops, and that no

* Bernard, afterwards so much celebrated as generalissimo of the Swedish forces, was seventh and youngest son of John, duke of Saxe Weimar, and third in the line of descent from the elector John Frederic I., deposed by Charles V.

injury should be done to the Catholics. Thurn had the satisfaction of returning in triumph over the bridge which he
had before traversed as a fugitive, and where the heads of
twelve of his companions announced to him the fate from
which he had escaped. By his direction they were taken
down, wrapped in a covering of black satin, and interred
with all the honours which could be paid to martyrs for
their religion and country. The presence of the Saxon
army revived the dormant spirit of the Protestants ; the
Lutheran preachers were reinstated, the principal churches,
schools, and universities restored, the Jesuits banished, and
the Protestants again gratified with all their former privileges. Many even returned from exile to recover their
confiscated property, and those who had been driven by
persecution into the pale of the Catholic church joyfully
renounced their restrained conversion, and publicly professed the religion which they had been compelled to abjure. An irruption of the imperial troops on the side of
Nymberg was repulsed by Arnheim ; and before the close
of the year the whole country fell under the power of the
Saxons.

The elector did not attempt to prosecute his success by
carrying his arms into Austria, but considering his possession of Bohemia as only temporary, retaliated on the partisans of Ferdinand the excesses of the imperial troops in
Germany. He not only appropriated the artillery and im-
plements of war, but sent to Dresden fifty waggons laden
with the choicest specimens of those collections which it
had been the great business of Rhodolph to form. His
soldiers followed his example ; the houses of the rich Catholic burghers were plundered, and themselves driven into
exile ; the same excesses extended throughout the country,
and if we may credit the Bohemian historian, scarcely a
nail or a fragment of the cumbrous metals escaped their
rapacity.

During these events Gustavus gave a short repose to his
troops. At Mentz he received ambassadors from the kings
of France and England ; he was also visited by the elector
Palatine, to whom the success of the Swedes had given a
gleam of hope, and whom he received with regal honours.

The fatal defeat of Leipzic, and the rapid series of

disasters by which it was followed, did not shake the firmness of Ferdinand; he used his utmost exertions, both by representations with his allies and levies in his own countries, to strengthen the discomfited army, which, under Tilly, was driven to a distant part of the empire. Ever watchful to improve the least favourable circumstance, he likewise availed himself of the jealousy which the progress of the Swedes had excited in France, to weaken a connection which had been of such essential service to Gustavus. He found an active agent for his purpose in the bishop of Wurtzburgh, who, after his expulsion from his diocese, had repaired to Paris. This artful prelate laboured to identify the Catholic cause with that of the house of Austria, and represented the views of Gustavus not as directed against the emperor alone, but to render his own religion predominant on the ruins of the ancient worship. Assisted by the other agents and partisans of Ferdinand, he endeavoured to justify these assertions by attributing to Gustavus the wildest plans of conquest and dominion. Besides incorporating Poland and Hungary with Sweden, and aspiring to the throne of Germany, he represented his approach to the Rhine as the prelude to an irruption into France to revive the Huguenot cause. He urged also that it ill became a king, who prided himself on the title of Most Christian, and gloried in his attachment to the Catholic faith, to unite in alliance with a heretic, who had already expelled so many prelates from their sees, and who, like another Alaric, at the head of his Goths and Vandals, intended to pass the Alps, and dethrone the head of Christendom. At the same time the duke of Bavaria represented the danger to which he was himself exposed, as head of the league, and claimed by every consideration of honour and religion that support to which he was entitled by positive engagements with France, should his dominions or electoral dignity be endangered.

These representations made a deep impression on the timid and superstitious mind of Louis XIII., and would have greatly embarrassed a minister less determined than Richelieu. He, however, imposed silence on the clamorous bishop, overcame the scruples of his master, and declared that the alliance with the elector of Bavaria was to guarantee him against the house of Austria, not to furnish him with succours against the king of Sweden, with whom France had formed a more ancient and specific connection. To avoid the appearance of oppressing the Catholic religion, and to save the honour of France, he proposed to mediate a treaty of neutrality between Gustavus and the Catholics, by which the expelled bishops were to be restored to their sees ; but the other conditions were calculated to separate the Catholics from the emperor, and reduce their forces to such a degree as to deprive them of the means of affording him assistance.

This neutrality, with the concurrence of Gustavus, was offered to the Catholics. But the elector of Bavaria and the other members of the league, were now convinced that their own safety depended on that of the emperor; and that, by suffering the house of Austria to be depressed, they were concurring to render themselves dependent on France and Sweden. They were therefore not inclined to accept a neutrality on the proffered conditions; and, even during the negotiation, the elector of Bavaria despatched considerable sums of money to Pappenheim, the imperial general in Lower Saxony, and ordered Tilly to attack the posts on the Maine. These circumstances being known to Gustavus, by means of intercepted letters, afforded him and the court of France a pretext for invading the territories of the house of Austria through those of the Catholic league. He prepared to expel the Spanish garrisons from the fortresses on the Rhine and in the Lower Palatinate, as a prelude to his design of penetrating into Bavaria, and from thence pushing his arms into the Austrian territories.

While he was executing this plan, his attention was called to another quarter by the movements of Tilly. After the battle of Leipzic, Tilly had fallen back towards the Weser, united with the corps under Aldringer and Fugger, and drawn reinforcements from the garrisons in Lower Saxony. He intended to make an effort for the relief of Wurtzburgh ; but while he marched to Aschaffenburgh, to effect a junction with the duke of Loraine, and secure provisions and magazines, the town fell into the hands of the king of Sweden. He was soon afterwards abandoned by the duke of Loraine, whom the approach of the Swedes, and an invasion by France had compelled to retire to his own country, and the imperial army was so much weakened by fatigues, by the inclemency of the season, and by diseases derived from unwholesome provisions, that after remaining an idle spectator of the conquests of Gustavus, he distributed the remnant of his dispirited troops into winter quarters, in the vicinity of Nordlingen and the country bordering on the Danube.*

His army being refreshed by a short repose, reinforced with recruits, and supplied with clothing, provisions, and ammunition, in March, 1632, he resumed his former activity, invaded the bishopric of Bamberg with 20,000 men, took the capital, drove Horn, the Swedish general, from the country, and directed his march towards Schweinfurth, to secure that important post on the Maine. The rapid advance of Gustavus, who, after leaving his troops on the Rhine, under Oxenstiern, to make head against the Spaniards, had concentrated the forces under Horn, Banner, and the duke of Saxe Weimar, at Aschaffenburgh, compelled Tilly to retire : he fell back into the neighbourhood of Erlang, ravaging the country, and threatening Nuremberg with the same fate as Magdeburgh. The advance of the king, however, saved the city ; for the imperial general, continuing his retreat, crossed the Danube into Bavaria, and took post behind the Leck, where he was joined by the elector.

As an imperial army was at this time assembling in Bohemia, Gustavus was anxious to engage the Bavarians before the two bodies could effect a junction. He therefore continued his march, took Donawerth by storm, and invested Ingolstadt. Foiled, however, by the resistance of the garrison, he returned to Donawerth, crossed the Danube, and prepared to attack the Bavarians, in opposition to the advice of his most skilful generals, and not-

* The conduct of Tilly has been attributed by some authors to his own discouragement, in consequence of his recent defeat, and by others to the secret orders of the elector of Bavaria not to risk an engagement ; but if we may give credit to his letters, which were published by the elector, in vindication of his conduct, the inactivity of Tilly was derived only from the causes mentioned in the text. Schmidt, vol. x. p. 76.

withstanding the strength of their position, which was equally defended by nature and art. A bend of the Leck near Rain, enabled him to avail himself of his well organised artillery ; and, after a desperate conflict, he, on the 5th of April, succeeded in constructing a bridge and forcing a passage. Tilly, at the head of his veterans, exerted every effort to prevent the passage, but received a mortal wound by the shot of a falconet. Aldringer, the second in command, was soon afterwards desperately wounded ; and the elector, deprived of both his generals, retreated under the walls of Ingolstadt. Here Tilly died, at the age of seventy-three ; a general successful in all his undertakings till the fatal battle of Leipzic, and confessedly the first soldier of his age, till his fame was eclipsed by the skill and prowess of Gustavus. His enemies cannot withhold from him the praise of heroic intrepidity, sobriety, and continence unusual in his profession, and such an uncommon degree of disinterestedness, that he died poor, notwithstanding all his opportunities of acquiring riches ; but his warmest admirers cannot conceal his unrelenting spirit ; and the excesses committed under his auspices, or by his orders, have rendered his very name proverbial for barbarity and devastation.

On the retreat of the Bavarian army, Augsburgh fell into the hands of the Swedes, the Protestant religion was re-established, the Catholic magistrates expelled, and the city took an oath of allegiance to Gustavus and to the crown of Sweden. Having secured this post, the king proceeded to invest Ingolstadt, and opened a correspondence with the inhabitants of Ratisbon, to secure possession of two places which would have rendered him master of the Danube, and enabled him to carry his attacks into Austria ; but the elector of Bavaria anticipated his designs, by throwing a garrison into Ratisbon ; and it was the honour of Ingolstadt to give the first proof that the arms of Gustavus were not invincible. Foiled in his attempts on Ingolstadt, Gustavus reduced the whole country between the Inn and the Leck, and entered Munich in triumph, accompanied by the elector Palatine, who thus enjoyed a momentary exultation in visiting the abandoned capital of his bitterest enemy.

Chap. LIV.—1632.

From the fatal battle of Leipzic a rapid series of disasters had disclosed the weakness of the Austrian empire, the ascendancy of which had been as much owing to the disunion of its antagonists as to its own intrinsic force and resources. The presence of a chief, who, like Gustavus, united in himself all the qualifications of the statesman and the soldier, who gave strength and consistency to his plans, and infused vigour and unanimity into the heterogeneous body of the Protestants, occasioned a change no less astonishing than decisive. The numerous forces who had given law to the empire and to Italy had disappeared, or were reduced to a weak and discouraged remnant, which owed its existence to the other occupations of the enemy. The princes of the Protestant body who had been humbled at the feet of Ferdinand, and despoiled without mercy of their dignities and possessions, had risen with new power, while the Catholics were either wavering or become the prey of the conqueror. The elector of Treves was compelled to throw himself under the protection of France; the bishops of Wurtzburgh and Bamberg, and the elector of Mentz, were driven from their territories, and the elector of Cologne threatened with a similar fate. Loraine, by the forced or voluntary retreat of the sovereign *, had been appropriated by

* Charles returning unsuccessful from his enterprise against Gustavus, with the scanty remnant of his forces, was again exposed to all the vengeance of the French court, which in the interval had suppressed the civil troubles, and again invaded Loraine. He was enticed into the French camp, rendered almost a prisoner, and reduced to the necessity of surrendering Nancy, his capital, and disavowing the marriage of his sister, though he was suffered to retain his revenues. The duchy of Bar was at the same time declared re-united to the crown of France.

After effecting his escape, and resigning his territories to his brother Nicholas Francis, cardinal bishop of Toul, Charles assembled thirteen companies of cavalry, and repaired to join the imperial army in Alsace. His brother, to secure his title to Loraine, espoused his cousin Claude, the sister of the duchess Nicola ; but being arrested by the French court, under the pretence that their marriage was contracted without its consent, they made their escape, leaving their territories in the possession of France, and took refuge at Vienna. The duchess Nicola

France ; the Spaniards retained only three fortresses of all their acquisitions in the Palatinate, and were almost excluded from the banks of the Rhine; and the elector of Bavaria seemed to have no other alternative than to desert Ferdinand, or share the ruin of that house and that cause which he had so well defended. A victorious monarch was in the heart of Germany, at the head of an army, if not more numerous, at least braver and better disciplined than any in Europe, master of the whole country from the Baltic to the frontiers of France, and in the pride of conquest preparing to carry his arms into the heart of the Austrian dominions. Bohemia was occupied by the elector of Saxony, nothing was likely to oppose his advance to Vienna ; throughout the territories, which yet owned the

was conveyed to Paris, and though her husband had divorced her, and even espoused another wife, she nobly refused to sanction any measure in opposition to his interests and those of his brother.

Charles passed the remainder of his life sometimes as a fugitive, sometimes in prison, sometimes as an ephemeral sovereign, continually making and breaking alliances, maintaining a predatory army, which he occasionally sold to all, though he principally exerted his military talents in the service of the house of Austria. The same versatility distinguished his private as his public life. After divorcing his wife, and espousing the widow of the prince of Cantecroix, of whom he formerly had been enamoured, he recalled his first duchess, and then again dismissed her to renew his connection with the princess. He endeavoured, likewise, to obtain a divorce from his second wife, and afterwards entered into various contracts of marriage with different mistresses. He contracted himself with Isabella, countess of Ludre, a canoness of Poussai, and soon afterwards abandoned her for a banker's daughter of Nancy, called La Croisette. He again espoused, for the sake of form, the princess of Cantecroix, on her death-bed, and concluded his numerous connections by marrying in his sixty-first year, a short time before his death (which happened in 1675), Maria Louisa, countess of Aspremont, who was only thirteen. His capricious and volatile conduct was well characterised in an epigrammatic epitaph : —

> " Ci-git un pauvre duc sans terre,
> Qui fut, jusqu'à ses derniers jours,
> Peu fidèle dans ses amours,
> Et moins fidèle dans ses guerres.
> Il donna librement sa foi,
> Tour à tour à chaque couronne
> Et se fit une etroite loi
> De ne la garder à personne."

authority of Ferdinand, the concealed Protestants only waited the approach of a foreign force to throw off the restraints under which they groaned, and a dangerous revolt took place among the peasants of the district above the Ems. The ascendency of the Swedes had cut off all hopes of maintaining, as before, the war at the expense either of allies or enemies, and his own territories being exhausted by so ruinous a contest, he saw himself again driven to the brink of a precipice more dangerous than that from which he had been rescued at the commencement of his reign.

Under the first impulse of desperation, Ferdinand announced a resolution to take the field himself; but he was easily dissuaded by his ministers from adopting an expedient, which would have been rendered fruitless by his own want of military experience. The next alternative was to confer the command on his son, the archduke Ferdinand, who had been recently crowned king of Hungary, and had evinced a spirit and talents above his years. But besides the danger of opposing a general of the age of twenty-three to the matured experience of Gustavus, it required little reflection to discover, that without an army and without the means of inspiring an army with confidence, it was of little use to nominate a commander. In this extremity Ferdinand saw no other resource than applying to Wallenstein, whom he had dismissed with such reluctance, whose genius, skill, and services, his recent reverses had taught him to appreciate; and the haughty emperor did not hesitate to abase himself before his still more haughty subject.

Wallenstein, though deeply affected by his dismission, had retired from his command with the full confidence that his ruling star had not yet attained its zenith, and his fertile genius had devised the means to render his restoration to power almost inevitable. He was followed into his retreat by the principal officers of his army, whom his immense riches enabled him to attach to his person, and who looked up to him for present support, as well as future advancement. He took up his principal residence at Prague, where he built a magnificent palace, and lived in a style of splendour more resembling a king in his glory than a subject in disgrace. The six gates of this magnificent habitation were

guarded by sentinels ; fifty halberdiers clothed in sump-
tuous uniforms waited in his ante-chamber ; a patrol of
twelve watchmen perambulated the apartments and the environs, to prevent the slightest noise or disturbance; and
sometimes even the neighbouring streets were barricaded
to exclude the tumult of carriages, or the concourse of foot
passengers. Six barons, and as many knights attended
his person ; four gentlemen ushers presented those who
were admitted to the honour of an audience ; sixty pages,
belonging to the most illustrious families, were entertained
at his expense, and instructed by the ablest masters in the
whole circle of the arts and sciences. His steward of the
household was a baron of the highest rank, and even the
chamberlain of the emperor quitted the court to exercise
that office in his establishment. His table was served
with more than regal pomp and delicacy, and daily attended by a hundred guests ; his gardens were equal to
the splendour of his palace, and his stables were furnished
with marble mangers, each of which was supplied with the
living stream, by means of artificial fountains. When he
travelled, his numerous suites were conveyed in twelve
coaches of state, and fifty carriages, as many waggons bore
his plate and equipage, and the cavalcade was accompanied
by fifty grooms on horseback, with fifty led horses richly
caparisoned.*

His recent disgrace and increasing anxiety to recover his
former authority, had totally changed the disposition of his
mind, and robbed him of that freedom, openness, and affability which distinguished his early career. In the midst
of splendour and magnificence Wallenstein lived in a state
of gloom, solitude, and impenetrable taciturnity, absorbed
in dreams of past grandeur, or projects of future ambition
and vengeance, maintaining with his own hand an extensive
and regular correspondence with every part of Europe,
and with all the great actors on the scene of affairs. To
complete the portrait of so singular a character, in person

* These accounts of his regal magnificence would appear incredible,
were they not authenticated by contemporary authors, particularly by
Dr. Carve, who was chaplain to colonel Devereux, one of his favourites, and afterwards his assassin, in his itinerary, which was published
in Latin at Mentz. See Schiller, who in his Thirty Years' War has
drawn an animated description of the retirement of Wallenstein.

he was tall and thin, his complexion sallow, his hair red and short, his eyes small and sparkling, his gait and manner indicative of sullenness and distrust, and the few words which broke his habitual silence were uttered in a harsh and disagreeable tone of voice. He was sudden, fierce, and ungovernable in his anger, implacable in his resentment, capricious and fanciful in his commands, extravagant equally in rewards and punishments. He was an enemy to flattery, and insensible to temptation; quick in discovering merit, and ready to reward it. In his dependants he encouraged a spirit of rashness and enterprise; he termed high and magnificent resolutions the effects of a well-qualified soul; a prompt action, a new thought, an unusual audacity, were the surest ways to secure his favour. He was grand and lofty in his ideas, impassioned for glory, and disdained dissimulation, or any vice which evinced baseness and timidity of character. Despising riches, except as the agent of his greatness, he was unbounded in his liberalities, and was accustomed to say, that no gold was equal to the weight of a valiant soldier, that great hopes followed great rewards, and the greatest recompences produced both the best troops and most skilful officers.

On the advance of the Saxons to Prague, Wallenstein refused to take any share in opposing the enemy, and, by his advice and conduct, hastened the surrender of the city. Under the guise of indifference, he exerted all his activity to turn the misfortunes of his sovereign to his own advantage; he maintained a mysterious correspondence with his former dependant Arnheim, and even with Gustavus; and he watched, with peculiar assiduity and attention, all the movements of the court of Vienna, where, besides several of the ministers who were his creatures or partisans, his liberality had gained almost every agent in every sphere, who was capable of furnishing intelligence, or promoting his views.

While the remembrance of his former services was yet fresh in the public recollection, while his liberality and magnificence were the theme of general applause, his numerous partisans beset the emperor, and pointed him out as the only man who was capable of saving the house of Austria.

Ferdinand, who since the death of Tilly, had no commander able to cope with Gustavus, was easily induced to employ a general who had rendered him such essential services, and to whose dismission he had consented with unfeigned regret.

Wallenstein had learnt by experience the difficulty of maintaining such an elevation as that to which he was about to be raised, and adopted every expedient to prevent a second dismission. Amidst all his eagerness for command he affected an indifference and reluctance, which enabled him to enhance his terms, and impose more effectual shackles on his sovereign. Notwithstanding the invitation of the emperor, he refused to repair to court, but advanced to Znaim in Moravia, with a view to facilitate his arrangements. He indignantly rejected the proposal to command under the archduke Ferdinand, with the impious declaration, that he would not serve under God himself; and after a long negotiation, which was conducted by the intervention of his friend the prince of Eggenberg, he affected to yield to threats and entreaties, and offered to raise troops in the same manner as on the former occasion; but he refused to take the command for a longer period than three months, which he deemed a sufficient time to form and discipline an army.

This promise was soon fulfilled; the greater part of the officers had followed him in his retreat, or were dependent on his bounty, and the very magic of his name brought together thousands of veterans, who had either served under his standards, or were anxious to share his glory and his munificence. He hastened his levies by granting rank to the rich who exerted their influence in raising troops, and for the same purpose advanced money to the poorer officers, with whose courage and talents he was acquainted. He even conferred commissions equally on persons of all persuasions, and tranquillised the consciences of the Protestants, by representing the war against Gustavus as a civil not a religious contest. For the formation and maintenance of this force the pope and the court of Spain supplied considerable subsidies. Wallenstein lavished his own private fortune; persons of all conditions and ranks were induced to furnish liberal contributions, and every effort was made, as well in Italy as in the Austrian territories, to replace the arms and accoutrements lost in the recent battle. By these means he assembled an army with a rapidity which astonished even those who had witnessed his former exertions, and before the close of three months was at the head of 40,000 men, well disciplined and better appointed than the troops which had been dispersed at the fatal defeat of Leipzic.

Having now fulfilled his promise, he announced his intention of resigning the command, and affected an eagerness to return to his dignified retreat, far from the dangers of war and the jealousies of a court. But the singular good fortune which had attended his early career did not fail him in this instance. Either by accident or design, he fulfilled his engagement at the very moment which was best calculated to complete all his views ; for, as Gustavus was advancing on the wings of conquest, from the banks of the Rhine to those of the Danube, the last hope of the house of Austria and the Catholic cause seemed to rest on his exertions. His proposals were therefore equivalent to commands; and we scarcely wonder that Ferdinand should purchase the services of his general, on conditions which reduced him to a greater dependence than ever sovereign had before been reduced. Notwithstanding the remonstrances of the elector of Bavaria and the Spanish court, Wallenstein was to be declared generalissimo of the imperial and Spanish forces in the empire, with unbounded authority; the emperor and his son Ferdinand engaged never to enter his camp ; he was to be intrusted with the nomination of all officers, and the distribution of rewards and punishments; and no pardon or safe conduct was to be valid, even though signed by the emperor, without his confirmation. He was to be free from all restriction in levying contributions; to dispose of the confiscated property of the enemy, without being subjected to the control of the imperial chamber or any other tribunal; no peace or truce was to be valid without his privity, if not his consent; and his demands for money and provisions were to be promptly complied with. Finally, he was to receive a remuneration for his expenses, either from the spoils of the enemy or the hereditary countries of the emperor, to be guarantied in the possession of Mecklenburgh, by a specific article in the imperial capitulation ; he was to be allowed a place of retreat in the hereditary countries if pressed by the enemy ; and, on the re-conquest of Bohemia, the emperor promised to reside at Prague.

These conditions being accepted, Wallenstein assumed the command, and prepared to commence his operations. Sensible that the Protestants began to be jealous of Gustavus, he opened a negotiation, by the connivance of Ferdinand, with the elector of Saxony, and made the most liberal concessions to a prince, whose defection would draw after him the majority of his party. These overtures being frustrated by the jealousy and apprehension which the character of Ferdinand naturally inspired, no less than by the exhortations of Gustavus, Wallenstein led his army to Prague, procured its speedy surrender, by allowing the Saxon garrison to retire with their plunder, though without the honours of war ; and a second attempt to negotiate being equally fruitless, he dislodged the Saxons from all their posts in Bohemia. He remained inactive at Leutmeritz, notwithstanding all the exhortations and commands of the emperor, under the pretence of covering and securing Bohemia, but in reality with a secret satisfaction, witnessing the devastations committed in the territories of that rival, the elector of Bavaria, who had procured his first disgrace, and opposed his recent appointment. At length, when the progress of Gustavus endangered Austria itself, he left 8000 men as a corps of observation at Leutmeritz, and advanced to effect a junction with the elector of Bavaria at Egra, a post from whence he awed Saxony, and menaced Nuremberg, which formed a place of arms for the Swedish attack on Bavaria. This skilful movement instantly reduced the king to the defensive, and compelled him to combat for his security, not as he had hitherto done, for conquest and glory. The feigned movements of Wallenstein, on various quarters, kept Gustavus in continual alarm, obliged him to distribute his forces for the defence of the Maine, and the posts in Suabia ; and finally to abandon his designs on Bavaria and Austria, and with an army, scarcely amounting to 12,000 men, to hasten to the defence of Nuremberg.

Wallenstein held an interview with the elector of Bavaria at Lutitz, a town in the vicinity of Egra, on the confines of the Upper Palatinate, where, under the guise of affected condescension, he exulted in his superiority over his humiliated rival. Their united forces were put in motion ; and Wallenstein, finding himself at the head of a spirited and well-appointed army of 60,000 men, could not refrain from giving a public testimony of his joy, at the advantage which he had already gained over the Swedish hero. In the pride of his heart he boasted, that a few days would decide whether Wallenstein or Gustavus was to command the world. To fulfil this boast he advanced towards Nuremberg, with the hope of crushing the inferior forces of Gustavus ; but finding him strongly intrenched, and the numerous inhabitants in arms ready to defend their city, he dreaded the courage, skill, and tactics of the king, when driven to desperation, and took post at the village of Zirndorf, on the Preignitz, with the resolution to reduce him to risk a battle, or abandon his post. Awed by the presence of his illustrious antagonist, he lowered that presumptive tone which had been derived from his former success ; justifying his conduct by the remark, " That the imperial generals had too often staked the fortune of their master on the uncertain fate of battles, and that he was now determined to wage war on different principles." Influenced by these motives, Wallenstein, with a force more than triple in number, remained eight weeks within sight of the Swedish camp, without risking any enterprise beyond the feints and assaults of irregular warfare. In this situation he continued, notwithstanding all the importunities of the duke of Bavaria, and the clamours of the soldiers ; and thus allowed Gustavus to draw his scattered corps from Bavaria, Suabia, Franconia, and Lower Saxony, and to collect reinforcements from his allies. These troops, under the standards of the duke of Saxe Weimar, Banner, and the landgrave of Hesse, gradually united, and were led to the Swedish camp by the chancellor Oxenstiern, who equally served his sovereign in policy and in arms. Although Gustavus braved the imperialists by repeated offers of battle, yet Wallenstein was neither provoked by insults nor encouraged by the advance of reinforcements, to risk an engagement. He strengthened his post with intrenchments, till it resembled a fortress rather than a camp ; and in this situation calmly bore all the extremities derived from want of provisions and supplies, and saw his troops moulder away from confinement and hardships, hoping that the superior distress of the king would compel him first to decamp, and leave Nuremberg to its fate.

But Gustavus bore these difficulties with no less firmness, and even endeavoured to dislodge his antagonist from that position which he could neither provoke nor allure him to abandon. Intrusting the defence of his own camp to the citizens of Nuremberg, he, on the 24th of August, led his army against the enemy. The irresistible impulse of his troops burst through intrenchments which nature and art seemed to have equally contributed to render impregnable. Regiment after regiment was led on to the attack ; nor did the king order a retreat till 3000 of his best troops had fallen, and every part of his army had shared in the danger and the loss of a conflict, which Wallenstein represented in his account to the emperor as the most desperate he had ever witnessed. After this engagement both armies remained watching each other for a fortnight, and Wallenstein had the sterile honour, if it might be so termed, of seeing the king first abandon his position. But the prize for which he had borne these difficulties eluded his grasp, for Nuremberg was secured by a Swedish garrison, and he too much dreaded the tactics of the king to molest his retreat. Thus terminated a struggle, in which the two armies, for seventy-two days, vied in supporting all the miseries of famine, hardship, and sickness, and which was far more fatal to both than the most bloody engagement known in modern warfare. Nuremberg lost 10,000 of its inhabitants ; the king scarcely fewer than 20,000 of his troops ; and Wallenstein led back his army, which at first amounted to 60,000 men, reduced to half its number.

Though this part of the campaign was distinguished by no brilliant action or important acquisition, Wallenstein cannot be robbed of the honour of having first set bounds to the progress of Gustavus, of having saved Bavaria, recovered Bohemia, and secured Austria.

On quitting Nuremberg, the Swedish monarch detached a part of his forces under the duke of Saxe Weimar to cover Franconia and his posts on the Main, which were now peculiarly exposed to the attacks of the imperialists, while with the remainder he returned towards the Danube, to pursue his designs against Bavaria and Austria. But Wallenstein, instead of following him into Bavaria, which would have drawn the war into the hereditary states, pursued the judicious plan by which he had already gained such advantages without risk, and directed his attacks against the elector of Saxony, either to detach or overcome an ally so necessary to the king of Sweden. He suffered the elector of Bavaria to hasten to the defence of his own territories, and occupy the attention of Gustavus, and strengthened his diminished army by reinforcements from the neighbouring garrisons. He then detached Gallas and Holk, with 10,000 men, through the Voigtland, towards the Elbe, to open and secure his communications with Bohemia, and advanced himself into Franconia, either to attack the Swedish posts, or to prevent the duke of Saxe Weimar from anticipating his designs, by joining the elector of Saxony and the duke of Brunswick, who were posted at Torgau and Wittemberg.

After overrunning the territories of Culmbach and Bamberg, he suddenly directed his course through the Voigtland to Weida, sent Gallas with a part of his detachment into Bohemia, to assist in making head against Arnheim; and, recalling Holk with the remainder, marched to Leipzic, which he took after a siege of only three days. Having made himself master of Weissenfels, Merseburgh, Naumburgh, and the neighbouring places on the Saal, he continued to advance against the elector. He had already reached Eilenburgh, midway to Torgau, when he was acquainted with the approach of Pappenheim, who, during the recent events, had gained considerable advantages in Lower Saxony, by a rapid and well-conducted march had eluded the duke of Saxe Weimar, and effected a passage through Hesse. Their two armies, uniting at Merseburgh, amounted to above 40,000 men; with this force Wallenstein hoped to maintain himself on the Saal and the Elster, to capture Erfurth and Weimar, with the other places commanding the passes of Thuringia, and prevent a junction between the Swedes and Saxons till he had overwhelmed the latter by the superiority of his force.

To prevent the ruin or defection of his ally, Gustavus suspended his conquests in Bavaria. Leaving a corps to oppose the elector, he effected a junction with the duke of Saxe Weimar at Arnstad, directed his rapid march through the forest of Thuringia, and, ascending the course of the Saal, advanced at the head of 20,000 men to Naumburgh, to form a junction with the Saxon army, or at least with that of the duke of Brunswick. On his sudden approach, Wallenstein sent courier after courier to recall Gallas, fell back from Weissenfels, detached Pappenheim to reduce Mauriceburgh, the citadel of Hall, which was defended by a corps of Swedish veterans, and prepared to retire behind the Elster, in order to maintain the position between Leipzic and Hall, where he hoped still to prevent the junction of the Swedes and the allies. But in this intention he was baffled by the promptitude of the king, who hastening to attack him in his retreat, and while weakened by the departure of the corps under Pappenheim, came in sight of the imperialists at Lutzen, a town on the high road, midway between Leipzic and Weissenfels. The evening being far advanced, the Swedes fatigued by a long march in miry ground, and impeded by a morass, which was only passable over by a single bridge, the king deferred his attack, and permitted his troops to repose till the morning, although the night was spent in skirmishes between the irregulars of both armies.

Wallenstein passed this awful interval with the same anxiety as he had before felt in the presence of his great antagonist. Aware that a retreat in the night, before so skilful and vigilant an adversary, would be attended with the utmost danger, if not the ruin of his army, that his name would be irretrievably disgraced by giving way before a far inferior force[*], he condescended to call a council of war, and applied to his favourite astrologer, the confidant of all his secrets, and the director of his plans. His

---

[*] Many authors have supposed after the authority of Kevenhuller, that the forces of Wallenstein did not exceed 12,000 men. Such a supposition is disproved by the accounts of other contemporary writers, and by the amount of his forces before his retreat from Weissenfels. From a comparison of various authorities, we may justly estimate his force at 30,000 men, exclusive of the corps under Pappenheim.

officers unanimously advised him to accept the combat, should the Swedes venture to attack a force superior in strength and position ; but his resolution was more decidedly fixed by the opinion of his astrologer, who declared that during the month of November the stars were unpropitious to Gustavus.　In conformity with this advice, Wallenstein determined to maintain his position, made the concerted signals for the recall of Pappenheim, and employed the remainder of the night in widening the trenches * on both sides of the high road in front of his army, throwing up redoubts, and taking measures to strengthen his position.　On the ensuing dawn he drew up his army, and ordered mass to be celebrated throughout his whole camp ; after encouraging his soldiers, by suggesting every motive of hope, honour, and greatness, he quitted his coach, mounted a bay genet, and prepared to receive the attack, which was every moment expected to commence.

Fortunately for Wallenstein the morning of this important day, the 6th of November, was lowering and overcast, and an impenetrable fog suspended the movements of both parties till an hour before mid-day.　When the gloom dispersed, the two armies were discovered in order of battle on each side of the high road which skirts the extensive plain of Lutzen.　The king adopting the same order as at the battle of Leipzic, drew up his troops in two lines, intermixing platoons of musketeers with his cavalry.　On the other side, Wallenstein appears to have formed his in one line, according to the prevailing tactics of the times, the cavalry on the wings, and four ponderous squares of infantry in the centre ; the trenches in his front were lined with musketeers, and flanked with cannon, and the rest of his artillery was distributed principally along his centre and on his right flank, to bear obliquely on the centre and left of the enemy.　The wings of both armies were supported on one side on the Flussgraben, and on the other stretched to Lutzen, which was occupied by the imperialists.　The cannonade and skirmishing commenced with the dawn, but from the darkness of the fog it was eleven before the king could put his

---

* As the country was open, these trenches were dug as fences for the corn fields.

army in motion. After a public prayer, he gave out the fortieth psalm, " God is our refuge and strength," which was sung by the whole army, accompanied by all the military music, and then led forward his troops. The Swedish infantry first advanced against the imperial musketeers, posted along the trenches, but were received with such a galling fire that they gave way. In this extremity the king himself leaped from his horse, flew to their head, and seizing a pike, encouraged them by his voice and gestures to renew the combat; at the same time Wallenstein advanced to animate his men, fresh reinforcements crowded to the point of attack, and the two parties, encouraged by their respective chiefs, fought with unparalleled desperation. The Swedes, though frequently repulsed, as frequently returned to the assault; and at length the imperial infantry were driven from the trench back on their own cavalry. The king seized the moment of this confusion to lead on the cavalry of his right, crossed the ditch, and charged the imperialists. But while the battle was thus in suspense on the right, he was informed that his left had given way before the fire of the imperial army, and was threatened by the approach of Pappenheim, whom the delay occasioned by the fog had allowed time to advance. He instantly galloped to that wing to restore the combat, but in hurrying before his troops to examine the situation of the enemy, accompanied by the duke of Saxe Lauenburgh and by three attendants, he fell in with a party of imperial horse. At this moment his arm was shattered by a ball, and he soon afterwards received a mortal wound in the breast. He instantly fell from the saddle, exclaiming, " My God! my God!"* and his horse, galloping along the

* The accounts of the king's death are so confused and contradictory, that we have not descended to particulars. The few circumstances mentioned in the text are principally drawn from the contemporary Gualdo, because he received his account from the only one of the king's pages who was present with him, and escaped with life. We must not, however, withhold the remark, that his death, like that of his descendant Charles XII., was attributed to treachery, and that the duke of Saxe Lauenburgh, who was with him at the moment he fell, was accused of the crime. But we can scarcely doubt that he received his death from a hostile hand, when we consider how lavishly he exposed his person, that, contrary to the custom of the times, he was without a cuirass,

front of the lines, conveyed the intelligence of his loss to his troops.

The duke of Saxe Weimar, who succeeded to the command, spread a report that the king was not killed, but taken prisoner; and the hope of rescuing their beloved leader roused the soldiers to deeds of almost supernatural heroism. The right wing broke and dispersed the left of the imperialists; the left was equally irresistible; the infantry bore down the imperial infantry by the force and unity of the charge, and the confusion and loss were heightened by the explosion of some powder-waggons. At this moment, when victory had declared for the Swedes, Pappenheim reached the field, and burst on their exhausted ranks with eight fresh regiments of cavalry. The shock was no less desperate than the preceding conflict, until the intrepid Pappenheim received a mortal wound, and was carried off the field. His troops, discouraged by this event, gave a sudden cry, "Pappenheim is killed, and the battle lost!" and, notwithstanding all the exertions of Wallenstein and his officers, the confusion became irreparable. The return of the fog, and the approach of evening, having suspended the combat, Wallenstein retired during the night, leaving the field to the enemy, with all his artillery. The number of killed was nearly equal on both sides; and the Swedes were not apprised of the extent of their advantages, but were deliberating on a retreat, when the ensuing morning saw them masters of the field. Their victory was dearly purchased by the loss of their beloved monarch. His

that at the moment of his fall he was surrounded by the enemy, and that two of his pages shared his fate. Besides the only foundation for the charge against the duke of Saxe Lauenburgh rests on his returning safe from the battle, on his having recently quitted the imperial for the Swedish service, and having, soon after this event, returned to the imperialists, which was a circumstance far from uncommon at that time. As an additional proof, it has been also asserted, that the fatal wound was given to the king in the back; but this is not the fact; for the buff waistcoat which the king wore in the engagement, and which is still preserved in the arsenal at Vienna (where I examined it myself), is only perforated in the front. For a further account of the king's death, the reader is referred to Gualdo's Wars, b. iv.; Harte's Life of Gustavus Adolphus; Struvius, p. 1281, 1282., who has collected from different authors various passages relating to the death of the king; and particularly to the Histoire de Gustave Adolphe.

body, which was discovered stripped, mangled, and covered with gore, under a heap of slain, was conveyed to Naumburgh, and afterwards to Wolgast, from whence it was transported to Stockholm.

Thus fell Gustavus Adolphus, in the thirty-eighth year of his age, one of the greatest monarchs who ever adorned a throne. As an individual, he was religious without bigotry or affectation, temperate, and a pattern of conjugal fidelity and domestic affection. Though unable to conquer at all times a constitutional warmth of temper *, he possessed all the social virtues, and the conciliation of courtesy in so high a degree, that no individual was ever admitted to his converse without being charmed, or left his presence dissatisfied. To all these amiable qualities he united the learning of a scholar, and the accomplishments of a gentleman. As a statesman, he was firm, sagacious, and provident, embracing equally the grand features and minute details of the most extensive plans. As a general, he surpassed his contemporaries in his knowledge of all the branches of the military art, in a bold, inventive, and fertile genius. His intuitive sagacity, undisturbed presence of mind, and extensive foresight, were warmed and animated by an intrepidity more than heroic. No commander was ever more ready to expose his person to dangers, or more willing to share the fatigues and hardships of his troops; he was accustomed to say, " Cities are not taken by keeping in tents; as scholars, in the absence of the master, shut their books, so my troops, without my presence, would slacken their blows." Like many other great men, he was a predestinarian, from a pious submission to the inevitable decrees of an all-wise Providence : to those

---

* The chancellor Oxenstiern, who knew his master well, said of him to Whitelocke, " If any fault might be imputed to that king, it was that sometimes he would be very choleric. It was his temper. He was wont to say to me, ' You are too phlegmatic; and if somewhat of my heat was not mingled with your phlegm, my affairs would not succeed so well as they do.' To whom, with his leave, I would answer ; ' Sir, if my phlegmatic temper did not mingle some coolness with your heat, your affairs would not be so prosperous as they are.' At which answer the king would laugh heartily, and give me my freedom of speaking fully to him." Whitelocke's Journal, vol. i. p. 347.

who urged him to spare his person, he replied, " My hour is written in heaven, and cannot be reversed on earth."*

Gustavus created a new system of tactics, and formed an army which was without a parallel for its excellent discipline and for its singular vigour, precision, and unity in action. He conquered, not by dint of numbers, or the impulse of a fortunate rashness, but by the wisdom, and profoundness of his combinations, by his irresistible yet bridled spirit of enterprise, by that confidence and heroism which he infused into his troops. Since the days of Alexander, the progress of no conqueror had been equally rapid; since the time of Cæsar, no individual had united, in so consummate a degree, all the qualities of the gentleman, the statesman, and the soldier.

The death of Gustavus was soon followed by that of the elector Palatine, who was considered as the original cause of the war. After suffering every extremity of disgrace and poverty which could befal an exiled prince, after wandering from country to country, and seeking in vain an asylum from court to court, his last hopes of restoration had centered in Gustavus. On the victory of Leipzic, he had shared the triumphs of the Swedish hero, and had once more enjoyed the flattering though empty honours of a sovereign. But from some cause, which we have not been able to ascertain, his restoration had been hitherto delayed, although the greater part of his territory was gradually conquered by the Swedes. He was waiting at Mentz, in the hourly expectation that the first decisive success of his protector would be the prelude to his complete restoration; he saw this darling hope frustrated by the fatal event of the battle of Lutzen, and the shock of this melancholy intelligence was too powerful for a frame worn out by chagrin and anxiety, and at this moment labouring under a fever, derived from the mingled emotions of hope and fear. He died in the thirty-ninth year of his age, the victim of imprudent ambition. Happy for himself, his family, and for Europe, had he not mingled in the storm which he was unable to direct, or involved himself in dangers which he wanted firmness and constancy to bear; but had confined

* Gualdo, p. 73.

himself to his proper sphere, the calm enjoyment of domestic life, and the tranquil rule of a small but hereditary sovereignty.

CHAP. LV.—1632–1634.

THE death of Gustavus was received with the highest exultation by the Catholics, and considered as a singular mark of God's immediate interposition. The court of Spain in particular testified the most extravagant joy ; the rejoicings at Madrid were continued twelve days, and so many bonfires were made, that the police interposed to check the excessive consumption of fuel * ; at Vienna also Te Deum was sung for what was termed a victory. Amidst the general joy, Ferdinand received the intelligence of this event with moderation and magnanimity. Far from giving way to exultation, he expressed concern at the death of so great a man, and wished that he had rather returned in peace to his own country. When the buff waistcoat, which the king had worn in the battle, and which was perforated by the fatal ball, was presented to him, he turned with great emotion from the melancholy trophy, and expressed the strongest compassion and regret. This concern may be perhaps compared to the tears of Cæsar over the head of Pompey ; but, whether feigned or real, it proves that Ferdinand possessed the generosity to acknowledge the talents and admire the virtues of his great antagonist.

Whatever were the private sentiments of Ferdinand, the death of Gustavus seemed likely to produce the most favourable change in his affairs as well as in the situation of Germany. The Protestant princes, by their union alone, had been enabled to resist his power ; and their weight and influence had been less derived from the strength of Sweden, than from the talents of Gustavus. The bond of

---

* For an anecdote of the extreme scarcity of fuel at Madrid, see Cumberland's interesting memoirs, p. 382. ; where he mentions, that he burnt, in the only fire-place in his house, carved and gilt remnants of old carriages, which he purchased from a coach-maker.

that union was now broken ; the spirit which had animated their confederacy was fled. It was probable that the discordant mass, when left without a head, would be dissolved by its own weakness ; that the German princes who had reluctantly submitted even to the ascendancy of Gustavus, would burst the bonds which had hitherto kept them united ; and that the different generals, many of whom were Germans, would not willingly obey the orders of a foreign senate or plenipotentiary. Sweden itself was in a situation apparently too weak and precarious to continue the direction of the Protestant league. Christina, the daughter and heiress of Gustavus, was in her seventh year ; the crown was claimed by Ladislaus, who had recently succeeded his father Sigismond in the throne of Poland ; the country was burthened with taxes for the maintenance of the war, and the people, no longer dazzled by the fame of Gustavus, clamoured for the restoration of peace. Such being the state of the discordant parts, which had hitherto composed this formidable league, Ferdinand cannot be deemed too sanguine if he indulged a hope of recovering his former power, more especially as Denmark might again contest the superiority of the north, and Ladislaus, who was of a warlike and ambitious temper, was eager to invade Sweden, in order to recover the crown of his ancestors.

The senate of Sweden, however, acted on this occasion with a firmness and policy unusual in a deliberative body. Convinced that under such an apparent depression they could not obtain either a safe or honourable peace, they formed the resolution to continue the war ; they proclaimed the young queen, and interdicted all allusion to the claims of Ladislaus, under the penalty of high treason ; they appointed a council of regency, voted ample succours in men and money, and consigned the sole conduct of the war, with the superintendence of German affairs, to the chancellor Oxenstiern, who by his great civil and military talents was capable of supplying, if any individual could supply, the place of Gustavus.

Christian of Denmark was lured with the hope of uniting the three northern crowns, by the marriage of his son with the young queen, and instead of attacking Sweden, courted the continuance of her friendship ; while Ladislaus, in the midst of his preparations for war, was reduced to the necessity of defending his own dominions against an irruption of the Russians. A change equally favourable to Sweden took place in the sentiments of the court of France, which had beheld with a jealous eye the progress of Gustavus, and had seen with dissatisfaction his plan of parcelling out the dominions of the Catholic princes, and acquiring territories in Germany. Delivered from an ally, who, instead of being the agent of his views, was become a curb on his designs, Richelieu now saw that no private individual to whom the conduct of affairs might be intrusted could maintain himself without the support of France ; he was sensible that by continuing to assist the Swedish and Protestant party in the empire, he should employ the arms and reduce the ascendancy of the house of Austria, and prevent the interference of the emperor and Spain in those civil troubles which still agitated his own country.

These favourable circumstances did not escape so able a politician as Oxenstiern ; he availed himself of the extensive knowledge which he had acquired of the German nation, and the characters and interests of its princes, to unite, by the dread of common danger, those whom success would have speedily divided. He convinced them, that however powerful when in union, they must, if single, submit to the law of that chief whom they had braved and humiliated, and he did not fail to dwell on the intolerant principles of Ferdinand, and his antipathy to the Protestant doctrines. By these motives, he restrained their impatience to free themselves from foreign dependence ; and of all the princes and states who had been connected with Gustavus, the elector of Saxony, and Frederic Ulric, duke of Brunswick, were alone induced, by a desire of superiority, or jealousy of Sweden, to show even the appearance of dissatisfaction.

The first object of Oxenstiern was to renew the alliances with the German princes, and instead of partial treaties, to fulfil a plan, sketched by the deceased monarch, for uniting them in one general engagement. In April, 1633, he summoned at Heilbron a meeting of the states composing the four circles of Suabia, Franconia, the Upper and Lower Rhine, where he appeared with a pomp and dignity becoming the crown which he represented, and the high charge which he had assumed. The occupation of the principal places in those circles by the Swedish troops, the influence of France, England, and Holland, the presents and promises which Oxenstiern lavished among the German princes, enabled him to counteract the public exhortations and private intrigues of the elector of Saxony ; he obtained the assent of the assembly to a league, in which they agreed to unite with Sweden in carrying on the war, until the liberties and religion of Germany were secured, the deposed princes re-established, and a compensation made to Sweden for her expenses. He likewise succeeded in gaining the most difficult, though most essential point, that he, as plenipotentiary of Sweden, should be entrusted with the direction of the war and all affairs relating to the common cause ; though his authority was shackled by the institution of a council chosen by the states of the league, with which he was to deliberate, and by various regulations which were secretly suggested by the French ambassador.

To strengthen his cause, and still further to conciliate England and Holland, as well as the German princes, the first act of Oxenstiern's administration was the restitution of Charles Louis, son of the unfortunate Frederic, both in the electorate and in that part of his paternal dominions which had been recovered by the Swedes ; the Palatine ambassadors were accordingly admitted into the assembly of Heilbron, and in a subsequent meeting at Frankfort, convened for the purpose of confirming these regulations. He at the same time renewed the alliance with France and obtained the accession of the elector of Brandenburgh, with many members of the circles of Lower Saxony and Westphalia, to the league of Heilbron. But all his endeavours to conquer the jealousy of the elector of Saxony were fruitless ; for that prince, still more disgusted with his popularity and influence than with the ascendancy of Gustavus, secretly thwarted all the views of the Swedish plenipotentiary, and began to enter into private negotiations for renewing his connections with the imperial court.

On the side of the Swedes, the death of the sovereign, and on that of the imperialists, the humiliation of a defeat, occasioned a temporary suspension of hostilities. To avoid

an attack from the fresh troops, under the elector of Saxony
and the duke of Brunswick, Wallenstein had abandoned
Saxony, and fallen back into Bohemia ; and he advised the
emperor to conciliate the Protestant princes, by publishing
a general amnesty, and proposing favourable terms of accommodation. But this wise counsel, which would have
produced an essential effect in the present views of the
Protestant princes, and the situation of the emperor's affairs, was lost on Ferdinand, who considered the death
of Gustavus as more advantageous than a victory, and was
resolved to prosecute hostilities with fresh vigour, for the
fulfilment of all the designs for which he had commmenced
and carried on the war. His infatuation was encouraged
by the exhortations of the Jesuits, and by the influence of
the king of Spain, from whom he received considerable
subsidies, with the promise of additional succours.

The consequence of this decision was the renewal of
hostilities ; but the event did not answer the expectations
which Ferdinand had conceived from the situation of
Sweden. The spirit of the departed hero still seemed to
direct his generals, and animate his soldiers ; the Swedes,
masters of the most important military posts, and most fertile territories in Germany, gained advantages which supported the fame they had acquired under the guidance of
Gustavus. Before the close of the year following his death,
they occupied the whole Lower Palatinate, reduced almost
all Alsace *, except Brisach, drove the imperialists from
the circles of Westphalia and Lower Saxony, and conquered
the greater part of Silesia. The gallant Bernard of Saxe
Weimar, who was entrusted with the principal command,
resumed the plan of his great master for carrying the war
into the hereditary countries ; assisted by the troops which
had conquered Alsace, he captured, Neuburgh Ingolstadt,
Ratisbon, Straubingen, and Cham, and once more threatened Bohemia and Austria with invasion.

Wallenstein has been accused by superficial observers for
not striking a decisive blow when the career of glory was
opened to him by the death of his great antagonist. But

* Many of the towns of Alsace, which had received French garrisons, had been occupied by the duke of Loraine, on his junction with
the imperialists.

his army was considerably exhausted by the efforts of the preceding campaign ; he had lost his bravest troops, with all his artillery in the recent battle, and the rest of his forces were dispirited by their defeat. On the contrary, the Swedes were indeed deprived of their chief, but they had still generals who had been bred in his school, had imbibed his principles, who had been the instruments and companions of his victories, and were capable of extending and completing his plans. That disciplined army, which had humbled the house of Austria, still existed, and occupied the chief posts and communications of Germany ; and that part of it which had given the recent blow to the imperial cause, though diminished, was yet inspired by the confidence of victory, eager to avenge its loss, and might be joined by the fresh troops of Saxony and Brunswick, who had not shared in the engagement.

On returning into Bohemia, Wallenstein endeavoured to diminish the impression made by the defeat of Lutzen ; he executed seventeen officers for cowardice, and defamed fifty others by attaching their names to the gallows. He gave a still greater effect to this instance of severity, by rewarding the bravery or skill of those who had distinguished themselves with his accustomed munificence. He bestowed on Octavius Piccolomini, who had signalised himself in the engagement, 10,000 dollars, presented several of the generals with his medal set with diamonds, and recompensed general Holk, whose estates had been confiscated by his sovereign the king of Denmark, for entering into the imperial service, with the choice of four estates in Bohemia, each of which contained from sixteen to eighteen villages.

He passed the winter in giving repose to his troops, collecting magazines, procuring artillery, and filling with new levies the vacancies which the fatigues and losses of the last campaign had occasioned in his regiments. In May he took the field, and assembled his army between Pilsen and Egra ; but still finding his forces unable to cope with the enemy, he amused the Saxons and Swedes with feigned negotiations for peace, and induced them to suspend their operations by successive armistices. Having increased his army, he detached general Holk, on the side of Egra, with

7000 men to watch the movements of the duke of Weimar, and directed his march towards Konigsgratz, on the frontiers of Silesia.

After new and ineffectual attempts to detach the elector of Saxony, he suddenly passed into Silesia, and would have captured Schweidnitz, had it not been promptly succoured by the allies. He then made a feint as if to enter Saxony, directed his march towards Leutmeritz, and sent Gallas, with 10,000 men, to threaten Dresden ; having thus drawn Arnheim from Silesia, he suddenly returned in October, 1633, surprised a corps of 5000 Swedes under counts Thurn and Duval at Steinau, on the banks of the Oder, and reduced them to purchase their safety by the cession of all the places which they held in Silesia. He fulfilled this agreement, set count Thurn at liberty, and suffered Duval to escape. The consequence of these skilful movements was the capture of Great Glogau Lignitz and Wohlau in Silesia, Frankfort and Landzberg in the Mark of Brandenburgh, and Gorlitz and Bautzen in Lusatia. He now revived his favourite plan, to attack the very root of the Swedish power, by carrying his arms into Mecklenburgh and Pomerania, and once more occupying the shores of the Baltic. To secure his rear and facilitate his communications with the Austrian territories, he likewise resumed his design of either detaching the electors of Saxony and Brandenburgh, or conquering their dominions, hoping that, while awed by the vicinity of his army, they would more readily agree to conditions of peace.

But while he was pursuing this safe and prudent system, his conduct afforded his enemies, at the imperial court, an opportunity of forming an intrigue which terminated in his ruin.

It was natural that Ferdinand should be anxious to relieve himself from the shackles in which he was bound by Wallenstein, as soon as he had secured those advantages which he had so dearly purchased. Hence he lent a more ready ear to the representations of his enemies, and consented to various expedients which gradually tended to reduce the overgrown power of his haughty subject. With this view he approved the levy of a Spanish force in the Milanese, and brought it into Germany, first under the command of the cardinal infant, and afterwards under that of the duke of Feria; he justified the formation of a separate corps, independent of Wallenstein, by urging that his authority, as generalissimo in Germany, did not extend to troops raised in another country; and he likewise endeavoured to weaken his forces, by requiring him to send a detachment to co-operate with this Spanish army.

The conduct of Wallenstein gave effect to the intrigues of his enemies; for, instead of submitting to these encroachments, he arrogantly remonstrated against such flagrant breaches of the agreement which had been the price of his services. His apparent inactivity, his frequent negotiations with the Saxons, and even with the Swedes, were represented by his enemies as a traitorous correspondence; and his liberation of count Thurn, in opposition to the instances of the court, could not fail of being galling to a sovereign, who, like Ferdinand, was so little inclined to show mercy to a Protestant and a rebel. These impressions, strengthened by the monks and Jesuits, whom Wallenstein had offended by sarcasms on their indolence, bigotry, and rapacity, were still further increased by the elector of Bavaria, between whom and Wallenstein existed every motive of personal and political enmity, and by the court of Spain, which had seen with such indignation his restoration to authority.

The progress of the enemy on the side of the Danube contributed to accelerate a crisis which, from the disposition of the court and the general, could not be far distant. At the instances of the duke of Bavaria, the emperor commanded Wallenstein to hasten to the relief of Ratisbon, when besieged by the duke of Weimar. Though indignant at commands which were a breach of his engagement, though unwilling to relinquish his darling project of conquering the north of Germany, especially for the sake of succouring a rival against whom he suffered his personal antipathy to influence his military operations, he did not venture to resist, but he attempted to elude the repeated orders of his sovereign. Though he detached general Gallas with 10,000 men, he strictly enjoined him to maintain himself on the defensive. When new and reiterated commands at length induced him to commence his march, his movements were so tardy that Ratisbon, Straubingen, and Cham were taken by the duke of Weimar before he approached the scene of action. Even these losses did not overcome his repugnance to succour Bavaria; for, after a weak attempt to recover Cham, he hastily measured back his march to Pilsen, on receiving intelligence that the Saxons had besieged Frankfort, and again threatened to penetrate into Silesia; and he soon afterwards closed the campaign, by distributing his troops into winter quarters in Bohemia and Moravia. This contemptuous obstinacy promoted the views of his enemies. The duke of Bavaria and the court of Spain redoubled their instances to procure his downfall: the duke threatened to make a separate peace, and the Spaniards to withdraw their subsidies; while the Jesuits exerted their characteristic ingenuity to bring forward every fretful expression, every mark of disobedience, every negotiation with the enemy, as proofs of a systematic design to usurp the crown of Bohemia, formed from the very moment of his first dismission.

These repeated imputations, rendered plausible by the pride and obstinacy of Wallenstein, could not fail to make a deep impression; and if Ferdinand was before inclined to lessen the overgrown authority of his general, he was now determined to deliver himself from so dangerous a subject. As an abrupt dismission was too critical an experiment to be tried on a general at the head of an army which he had himself created, and which was entirely at his devotion, Ferdinand endeavoured to disarm his power, by weakening and dividing his forces. He ordered him to send part of his troops to Passau, to despatch 6000 horse into the Low Countries, to march with the remainder to the siege of Ratisbon, and after the recovery of that fortress, to take up his winter quarters in the territories of the enemy.

These intrigues had not escaped the vigilance of Wallenstein; but, with his usual presumption, he despised the efforts of his enemies, till these last orders convinced him that they began to take effect. The most natural expedient to be adopted in this situation was, to alarm the emperor with the apprehension that the army would disband, and the officers follow him into his retreat, in the same

manner as on the former occasion; and to this expedient
Wallenstein had recourse. He instantly repaired to Pilsen,
and summoned the colonels of his army. He represented
to them that his enemies at court had persuaded the emperor to remove him from his command, after he had
served the house of Austria thirty years with such fidelity
and success, after he had gained so many advantages, and
delivered the emperor from such imminent danger: "For
my part," he added, "I am determined to resign my command before I am dismissed, and only feel for the fate of
my brave and worthy soldiers, the companions of my victories, and the sharers of my dangers, who are going to be
separated from each other, and ordered to march, in the
midst of a severe winter, from those comfortable quarters
which I had provided for them. I regret still more that I
cannot confer upon them the rewards of their valour,
which they so eminently deserve, and I promised to bestow,
promises which I hoped to fulfil in the next campaign."

After this artful address he retired. His brother-in-law
Tersky, with three of his confidential officers, then easily
prevailed upon the others to intercede with him not to
resign his command, and drew from them a promise to support him at the risk of their lives and fortunes, by sub-
scribing the following memorial.

"We the underwritten generals and colonels, having
been informed that his highness Albert duke of Mecklenburgh, Friedland, Sagan, and Great Glogau, has resolved
to resign his command of generalissimo, on account of the
calumnious imputations against him at the court of Vienna,
and because the emperor refuses to supply the army with
subsistence; we, taking into mature consideration the detriment which will accrue from his resignation, not only to
his imperial majesty, but also to the general welfare of the
state, as well as to the imperial army, which will be utterly
ruined; and since we are convinced that our sole expectations depend on our commander-in-chief, to whom we
have hitherto been true and obedient in all dangers, and
who from his kind affection to us is alone both able and
willing to reward our faithful services; we therefore cannot
but apprehend and testify our concern, lest his resignation
should be followed by the immediate ruin of the army.

For the purpose of preventing this misfortune, we have
unanimously deputed field-marshal Illo, and the four brave
generals, Morvald, Predau, Losy, and Hinnersam, to his
highness the duke of Friedland, to entreat him not to
resign his command, and assure him that we will bind ourselves, our fortunes, and lives, and all the troops under our
command. This true and sincere love towards our dear
father finally prevailed upon him to accede to our request,
and to promise not to abandon the army without our
knowledge and consent. In gratitude for this favour, we
on our parts do freely bind ourselves by oath to remain
true and faithful to him, and shed the last drop of our
blood in his service. We also most solemnly swear that
we will, at the risk of our lives, punish all those who attempt to swerve from this promise, or break this oath ; and
we therefore subscribe our names to this writing, without
reservation or deceit. Given at Pilsen, Feb. 12. 1634." *

This paper was signed by fifty of the principal officers ;
but, as his impending disgrace was now known to the
chiefs of the army, he was deserted by Gallas, the second in
command, as well as by Aldringer, and other officers of
high rank, who declined appearing at Pilsen.

Octavius Piccolomini, who, according to some historians,
was present, and signed the paper, but, according to others,
had likewise, under various pretences, declined appearing
at Pilsen, was the person who gave the first notice of these
proceedings to the emperor. He arrived at Vienna in the
middle of the night, awakened Ferdinand, informed him
of what had recently passed, and exaggerated the account
by adding, that the whole army had risen in rebellion, that
the troops quartered in the environs of Vienna were preparing to attack the city ; that many conspirators were
collected within the walls, ready at a moment's warning to
pillage the town, and massacre the whole imperial family.
Ferdinand, alarmed at the intelligence, ordered the arrest

---

* This document, which has been strangely garbled, mangled and
misrepresented, is given from Pelzel, as the authority, which seems to
be most authentic, without being partial to Wallenstein. Pelzel, p. 777.
The substance, as given by Gualdo, tallies in general with the declaration in the text, though it is more favourable to Wallenstein, p. 222.

of Wallenstein, deprived him of the command, conferred it on Gallas, and intrusted to Piccolomini the arduous task of seizing his person, either dead or alive. Piccolomini instantly returned into Bohemia, while Gallas assembled the greater part of the troops, represented to them the proscription of Wallenstein, and without the smallest difficulty took possession of Prague, Budweiss, Leutmeritz, and Tabor.

During this interval, Wallenstein waited the effect of the declaration signed by his officers, and sent his cousin to Vienna to justify his conduct. He was soon, however, apprised of the fatal change which had taken place; and, though at first not acquainted with the tenor of the orders issued against him, he found that his representations were without effect, and that he had every thing to apprehend from the vengeance of his enemies, and the displeasure of his sovereign. Pride, disappointed ambition, and a natural anxiety for his own safety, drove him into that rebellion of which he had before been only accused. After extorting new promises of attachment from his officers, and publishing a declaration that he had never entertained the slightest thought injurious to his sovereign and the Catholic religion, he despatched a force under Tersky to seize Prague, and sent couriers to the duke of Saxe Weimar, at Cham, offering to surrender Pilsen and Egra, and join the Swedes and Saxons with the best part of his army. But such were the subterfuges which he had before employed to deceive his antagonists, that at the very moment when his defection would have been of the utmost importance, he was not believed.* The duke, surprised at this unexpected proposal, considered it as a new artifice, and instead of accepting the offer, sent back the messenger with plausible excuses.

Wallenstein, thus disappointed on one side by the suspicions which his former duplicity had inspired, was soon

---

* This reluctance of the Swedish generals to accept the first offers of Wallenstein, joined to the extreme caution which they evinced to the very last moment, have sadly puzzled those who criminate the whole conduct of Wallenstein; and no wonder; for they are the most irrefragable proofs that he had entered into no previous conspiracy, and that his treason was only the effect of his danger and resentment at the moment of his proscription.

confounded with the intelligence on the other, that he had
been anticipated in his design to seize Prague, and was
deserted by his officers and a part of his army, that he and
his adherents were declared traitors, and the command
transferred to Gallas. Baffled, abandoned, proscribed, he
was driven to desperation; he sent Francis Albert of
Saxe Lauenburgh with new and pressing instances to the
duke of Weimar, despatched a courier to Oxenstiern at
Frankfort, and another to the Saxon general Arnheim, and
removed 40,000 ducats to Pirna, as a place of safety. He
quitted Pilsen, accompanied by colonel Butler, to whom he
had given a regiment of dragoons, and in whom he placed
implicit confidence, and, escorted by the regiment of Tersky, hastened to Egra. Here he hoped to maintain himself
till he had concluded his arrangements with the Saxons
and Swedes, as the place was strongly fortified, and the
governor, Gordon, a native of Scotland, was a man whose
gratitude he imagined he had secured by raising him from
the rank of a common soldier. Seldom, however, a disgraced favourite experiences a faithful attachment; and it
was the fate of Wallenstein to be betrayed by those whom
he had most served, and in whom he most implicitly
trusted. To Gordon, Butler, and Leslie, another officer
on whom he had likewise conferred his bounties, he expatiated on his injuries with all the bitterness of disappointment, developed his plans of vengeance, and urged them to
espouse his cause. They affected compliance, but one or
all had been gained by the imperial court; and as an attempt to seize his person was equally impracticable and
dangerous, surrounded as he was by his friends and adherents, in the midst of troops devoted to his cause, they
resolved to assassinate him and his immediate partisans, as
the only means to prevent his escape, or disconcert his
projects.

Having strengthened their party by gaining three cap-
tains, Devereux, Burke, and Geraldine, Gordon, on the
25th of February, invited to an entertainment in the castle,
generals Tersky, Illo, and Kinsky, with Nieman, the secretary of Wallenstein. At the close of the evening, Geraldine and Devereux, with fourteen determined men, were
posted in two adjoining apartments, and Burke, with a party

of an hundred, paraded the streets to prevent any sudden tumult. Towards the close of the repast, when the guests were heated with wine, a dispute was purposely commenced by the conspirators, and the noise which it occasioned was the signal for the execution of their design. Two doors being opened on each side of the room, Burke and Devereux entered at the head of their respective parties, crying, "Long live Ferdinand the Second!" The table was overturned in an instant; Gordon and his associates seized the candles, and held them aloft. Illo darted to his sword, but received a halbert through his neck as he was attempting to draw it; Kinsky was slain after a short but manly resistance; Tersky, who had time to seize his sword, killed three of his assailants before he fell; and Nieman was massacred as he descended the stairs.

The enterprise was now begun; but the assassination of the chief, the most difficult and dangerous part, yet remained to be executed. Devereux, seizing a halbert, exclaimed, "I will have the honour of putting Wallenstein to death;" and leading thirty fresh soldiers, hurried with Gordon to his apartments. The sentinels, who knew Gordon, suffered them to pass; but, as they entered the porch, a musket belonging to one of the party was discharged by accident. The dread of discovery gave wings to their impatience: they hurried up stairs, killed a chamberlain, who, awakened by the report of the musket, opposed their passage, and burst open the door of the chamber. They found Wallenstein, roused by the tumult, standing in his shirt at the window, which he had already forced open, and calling for assistance. As he advanced towards them, Devereux demanded, "Are you the traitor who is going to deliver the imperial troops to the enemy, and tear the crown from the head of the emperor?" Receiving no answer, he exclaimed, "You must die!" and offered a few moments for prayer. Disdaining likewise to reply, Wallenstein stretched out his arms, and without uttering a single word, received the halbert in his body.

This deed was scarcely perpetrated before the alarm was spread through the town; the soldiers seized their arms, and flocked in troops to defend the life or avenge the death of their general. Fortunately the effects of this sudden

impulse were prevented by the promptitude and coolness of
Gordon. He addressed them with firmness and moderation, expatiated on the supposed treasons of Wallenstein,
and read the directions of the emperor for securing his
person either alive or dead. The effect of this address
was instantaneous: the troops, perceiving on one hand
their hopes annihilated by the death of their chief, and on
the other dreading the vengeance of their sovereign, were
alarmed at their dangerous situation; and a faint though
unanimous cry of "Long live the emperor!" proclaimed
their return to obedience. The duke of Saxe Lauenburgh,
on returning from his mission, was made prisoner; and the
duke of Weimar, who at length had advanced towards
Egra, only escaped the same fate by his own caution, and
the strength of his escort.

Butler and Devereux instantly repaired to Vienna, and
imparted the welcome intelligence to the emperor. The
assassination of this formidable chief became the signal
for the punishment of his adherents. Several were taken
up at Prague, and privately put to death; others were publicly executed; and at Pilsen seven colonels, and seventeen
persons of inferior condition, were beheaded. Thus, while
his partisans were terrified by the severity of these punishments, the number of executions contributed to spread a
more general belief of the danger and extent of his treasons.
On the other hand, those who had betrayed him, or contributed to his fall, were amply rewarded. Gordon received
the confiscated estates of Tersky; and the princely possessions of Wallenstein were divided among Piccolomini,
Gallas, Aldringer, and Leslie.

To justify the assassination of a general who had twice
delivered the house of Austria from destruction, the court
of Vienna published an apology for its conduct, in a writing
which was called "A circumstantial and authentic narrative of the treacherous conspiracy of Wallenstein and his
adherents." In this paper, which was drawn up with
jesuitical ingenuity, it was not deemed a sufficient justification to deduce his treachery from the moment when his
treason really began, but from the very period of his first
dismission. He was charged with plots which carry their
own refutation in their very extravagance. He was ac-

cused of having formed a systematic plan to annihilate both branches of the house of Austria; and after satisfying himself with the kingdom of Bohemia, he was said to have adopted the system attributed to Henry IV. for the division and dismemberment of the hereditary and Spanish territories. In proof of these accusations, every overture to the enemy, and every subterfuge which he had employed to dupe and divide his antagonists, was made a part of his treasonable correspondence; every violent expression, and doubtless more than one broke from him in the transports of resentment, was registered; and these proofs were attempted to be corroborated by the testimony of those who were his avowed and bitter enemies; who were richly rewarded for becoming his accusers; who had taken part in his assassination, or profited by his fall.

In justice to this arrogant, ambitious, eccentric, and implacable, but great and injured man, we have deemed it our duty to strip his cause of its false colouring and specious exaggerations, and to describe his conduct as it appeared on a candid and unimpassioned review. Though at last driven into treason by pride, indignation, ill-requited service, and self-defence, it was, during the greater part of his splendid career, his honour and his boast to raise the authority and glory of Austria, and to become the sole instrument and supporter of her power. He was far superior to his sovereign in true policy, in liberality of sentiment, in religious toleration; and these qualities (the want of which occasioned all the misfortunes of Ferdinand) became the theme of accusation in a bigoted and tyrannical court. His crime was that of being too powerful, of contemning the prejudices and passions of those on whom he was dependent, and of an overweening confidence in his own good fortune and superior abilities. These were his failings as a courtier; as a general he deserves a high rank in a martial age, and a period of great men. He does not, like his royal antagonist, astonish us by daring efforts, and splendid enterprises; but, though he did not want fire when necessary, his distinguishing characteristics were extreme vigilance and presence of mind, profound judgment and unshaken perseverance; and it is the greatest eulogium we can pay to his character and talents as a soldier to add, that he was the only general who checked the progress or defeated the designs of Gustavus Adolphus.*

Chap. LVI.—1634–1637.

The vigilance of the court, the activity of Gallas, and above all the popularity of the young king of Hungary, who succeeded to the command, prevented the ill effects which were apprehended from the assassination of Wallenstein; for a mutiny of the troops in Silesia, and an insur-

* Numerous publications have been written on the supposed conspiracy of Wallenstein; and the circumstance which has most contributed to keep alive the accusation against him is the romantic nature of his history, which has given such scope to fancy and conjecture. The most singular of these works is the " Conjuration de Wallenstein," by Sarazin, a Frenchman, who resided in Germany at the time, which has become highly popular, from the point and brilliancy of the style. It has contributed to throw an air of romance over his hero, and like the singular work of his countryman, the Abbé St. Real, on the supposed conspiracy of the marquis de Bedmar against Venice, has given to a shadow all the substance of reality.

Some curious accounts of Wallenstein's adventures and death are given in the itinerary of Carve, chaplain to Devereux, who was present at Egra at the time of his assassination. This work, which is extremely scarce, has furnished Harte with the principal materials for his account of Wallenstein, vol. ii. p. 35–57. But as the former work is too fanciful to be considered as history, the accounts of Carve are to be received with caution, as they must have been derived from Devereux, and the other principal actors in this scene, who were interested to justify the assassination of their chief. The most sober, candid, and rational account of Wallenstein, is to be found in Gualdo, particularly in b. 8. Pelzel has also given an impartial narrative, principally derived from the archives of Prague, p. 772. Schiller, in his History of the Thirty Years War, has drawn an animated picture of this singular man, which if it does not carry conviction from its truth, must please by its force and eloquence. The most remarkable is the narrative alluded to in the text, which was published by the court, under the title of " Ausfuerlicher und gruendlicher Bericht der Friedlaendischen und seiner Adherenten Prodition, und was es damit fur eine Bischaffenheit gehabt, &c. in offenen druck gegeben aus sonderbare der Roem. Kais. Majest. Befehl." This document has been followed by most historians, even while they affected to doubt its authenticity; and those who have been most inclined to do justice to Wallenstein have suffered their judgment to be biassed by this artful narrative.

rection among the peasants, the only consequences of this dangerous expedient, were soon suppressed.

Still, however, the affairs of the emperor wore an unfavourable aspect. The states of Lower Saxony had joined the confederation formed by the four circles of the Rhine; Westphalia was on the point of acceding, and in March, 1634, Oxenstiern held a meeting of the Protestants at Frankfort, with a design to allay all jealousies, and unite the whole body against the house of Austria. The duke of Weimar, at the head of 10,000 men, posted at Ratisbon, kept the Bavarians in check; the French possessed Loraine, the Swedes the greater part of Alsace, and the rhingrave Otho, after defeating the imperialists at Warweil, had taken Philipsburgh, Neuburgh, and Friburgh in the Brisgau, and straitened Rheinfelden. In Suabia, Horn moving from Ravensburg, his winter quarters, captured Biberach, Kempten, and Memmingen, and, after routing a corps of Bavarians at Wangen, advanced to the vicinity of Augsburgh. From this situation of the armies, General Banner and the Saxons might have renewed the invasion of Bohemia, while Weimar, Horn, and the rhingrave, uniting in the heart of Bavaria, attacked the most vulnerable part of the hereditary countries, with a force far superior to any which the Austrians could oppose.

Notwithstanding these inauspicious appearances, Ferdinand was induced by various motives to turn the principal effort of the war on the side of Bavaria, which Wallenstein, no less from prudence than caprice, had always avoided. By the recent acquisition of Cham and Straubingen, the Bavarians had opened a passage over the Danube; the cardinal infant of Spain had collected a considerable force in the Milanese for the defence of the Low Countries, and in his passage was empowered to make a diversion, or co-operate with the imperial army. Ferdinand relied also on the secret influence which he had acquired in the venal court of Saxony by means of Wallenstein's intrigues, and on the disgust of the elector of Brandenburgh, who was disappointed in his expectation of obtaining the young queen Christina in marriage for his son, and irritated by his exclusion from Pomerania. He was still more encouraged by the divisions which subsisted between the

Germans, the Swedes, and the French, the growing antipathy of the two great ministers, Oxenstiern and Richelieu,
and the rivalry and altercation which pervaded the combined armies.

By vigour and decision the emperor hastened the dissolution of a confederacy, which in all its parts exhibited
such symptoms of weakness and decay; and it seemed as if
that regularity of design, and promptitude of action, which
had given such astonishing success to the Swedes, was
suddenly transferred to the imperialists. The new generalissimo took the field early in the spring, assisted by the
counsels of Gallas and Piccolomini. He assembled his
army at Prague, and leaving 10,000 men under Colloredo,
to observe the motions of the enemy in Lusatia and Silesia,
advanced rapidly by Egra towards the Danube, joined the
Bavarians and the forces of the Catholic league under the
duke of Loraine, passed the river at Straubingen with
30,000 men, and invested Ratisbon. While the Swedish and
German generals were wasting the time in contentions for
the supreme command, or discussing plans of operation, he
vigorously pressed the siege, and reduced the place to surrender on the 26th of July, 1631, at the moment when
they suspended their rivalry and moved to its relief.*

An irruption of the Swedes and Saxons into Bohemia
gave only a momentary check to his career, while it increased the infatuation of the enemy. Secure that their
divisions would not allow them to act in concert, and relying on the secret jealousies of the Saxon court, the imperial
commander detached only 10,000 men to protect Bohemia,
and pursued his plan of driving the enemy from the Danube.
By a rapid march he anticipated the movements of his anta-

* Count Thurn, the origin of the insurrection in Bohemia, and
the bitterest enemy of Ferdinand, bore a principal share in the defence
of Ratisbon, and by some is said to have been the commandant. But
as he had fallen into disgrace with Oxenstiern since his defeat at
Steinau, he was so sunk from the height of reputation, which he had
attained as a popular leader, and the chief of an insurrection, that he
was suffered even by the imperialists to escape with the rest of the
garrison. From this period his name seldom occurs in history, and all
my efforts have not been sufficient to trace the subsequent events of
his life, or the time of his death. Schmidt, vol. x. p. 185. ; Pelzel,
p. 786. ; Falkenstein, p. 678.

gonists, took Donawerth by storm, and invested Nordlingen, the great support of their hostile operations in Suabia and Franconia. The same divisions among the enemy still favouring his operations, the junction of the Spaniards augmented his army to 40,000 men, and he made a vigorous but fruitless assault to carry the town by storm, before his antagonists recovered from their infatuation.

At length when the apprehension of common danger, and the sense of disgrace, had again allayed the feuds of Weimar and Horn, their tardiness, disputes, and indecision allowed the youthful hero to add another laurel to his military crown. On their advance he recalled his detachments, drew his artillery from the trenches, formed his troops, and occupied the posts commanding his position. By these precautions, by the advantages of ground, the superiority of numbers, the skill of his officers, and the bravery of his soldiers, he on the 6th of September, repulsed the desperate attacks of the enemy. When exhausted by the combat they began to retreat, he pressed on their rear, broke their diminished ranks, and, after a conflict of eight hours, gained a complete victory, with the loss of only 2000 men. Eight thousand Swedes were killed on the field; more were slain in the flight, 4000 were made prisoners; the whole baggage, with eighty pieces of artillery, fell into the hands of the imperialists, besides numerous standards and other trophies. Horn, after courting death in every shape, and receiving several wounds, was captured, with three other generals, and the duke of Weimar himself narrowly escaped a similar fate.

In a conflict where all contended for the palm of glory, the most distinguished were John de Wert, and the duke of Loraine, who with his own hand took the standard of Weimar. The king of Hungary and the cardinal infant exposed themselves to danger with all the ardour of youthful heroism, and vied in displaying the characteristic bravery of the Austrian family. To use the simple expression of a contemporary warrior, "they won immortal glory in this battle; to the wonder of all men were always amidst the musket shot void of fear, nor could they be drawn from thence by any representation, but replied, let such princes as are afraid keep themselves within their royal palaces, and not come to an army." Nor did they less distinguish themselves by moderation and humanity after the victory, than by gallantry in the hour of danger; they received the captives with the utmost respect and compassion; endeavoured, by their conduct to Horn, to alleviate the sense of his misfortune; and the cardinal infant repairing to a petty hovel, relinquished his own quarters to accommodate the Swedish commander.

The victory of Nordlingen produced scarcely less rapid and important advantages to the house of Austria, than the victory of Leipizc had given to the Swedes; by the total rout of the confederates, the destruction of their infantry, and the capture of so many generals, the Swedes lost the reputation of their arms; while the conquerors succeeded to the fame and fortune from which they had fallen, and in their turn became the objects of admiration and terror.

On the surrender of Nordlingen, which yielded the following day, the cardinal infant took the route of Aschaffenburgh and Cologne, to defend the Netherlands against France. Part of the Bavarians were left to clear the banks of the Danube, the Leck, and the Iller; the duke of Loraine directed his march through the Brisgau, with a view to recover his duchy; the troops of the Catholic league, under de Wert, burst into the Upper Palatinate, and a part of the imperialists, under Piccolomini, swept the banks of the Main. The king of Hungary, after driving the forces of the rhingrave, with the remnant of the discomfited army, across the Rhine, took Heilbron, the focus of the confederacy, and established his winter quarters in Wirtemberg, as well to awe the states in the neighbouring circles, as to prepare for the recovery of Alsace and Loraine in the ensuing campaign.

On the rapid advance of the victorious army, the confederates assembled at Frankfort were overwhelmed with consternation. They accused the Swedes as the authors of all the misfortunes which they either felt or dreaded; and the union displayed the same symptoms of dissolution as that of Smalkalde after the defeat of Muhlberg. The contentions among the officers were likewise increased by their ill success, and the remnant of the army which had escaped from Nordlingen, with the troops of the rhingrave, and those drawn in haste from Alsace to the vicinity of Frankfort, were driven to mutiny by the cabals of their chiefs, and the want of pay and provisions. In the midst of this general dismay, Oxenstiern alone stood firm ; but all his efforts could not allay those discords which had been the cause of the recent misfortune. The confederates, who were most exposed to danger, conducted their deliberations with all the tardiness of fear and indecision ; the others pursuing their own particular views, held an insidious neutrality, or entered into negotiations for peace. Holland and England were too distant or too lukewarm to afford him support, and Austria disdainfully rejected all overtures of accommodation. In this desperate emergency, he adopted the only but mortifying alternative now remaining, of allowing France to obtain the direction of the war, and a share in the spoils. As he had already withdrawn the garrisons from the towns on the Rhine and in Alsace, he made a merit of necessity, and offered to cede Philipsburgh with that part of Alsace which was held by the Swedes, except Benfeld*, provided France would augment her subsidy, and act as a principal in the war against the house of Austria.

This was the opportunity which had been long expected by Richelieu. After employing his power and great talents in subduing his own enemies and restoring the tranquillity of the country, in humbling the branches of the royal family, and fixing his authority in the timid mind of the king, he laboured with the same spirit and perseverance to complete his system of external policy, and establish the future prosperity and splendour of that people, whose rights he had violated, and whom he ruled with a rod of iron. He therefore listened to the proposals of Oxenstiern ; but profited by the distress of the Swedes, to render their assistance subservient to his grand principle of operation, which was, to direct his chief efforts against the Spanish territories, with the view of gaining a footing in Italy, appropriating Franche Comté, and extending the French

---

* Benfeld was a small, but important town, affording an entrance into Alsace, from its position on the Ill, which runs through the centre of that country, dividing it in its whole length.

frontier on the side of the Netherlands. He proposed engagements to Oxenstiern, which were calculated to relieve
the Swedes from impending ruin, without affording them
the means of recovering their former ascendency. He sent
an immediate largess to pacify the mutinous soldiers, and
permitted 6000 French troops to join the remnant of the
army under Weimar ; but he firmly refused to engage in the
war as a principal against the emperor. After long discussions, he concluded with the Swedish chancellor a treaty
of offensive and defensive alliance. Besides a continuation
of the former subsidy, France granted 500,000 livres, to
enable the Swedes again to put their army in motion ;
agreed to declare war against Spain ; to furnish a corps of
12,000 men, which was to be placed under the control of
the German directory; and to supply additional forces,
who were to act on the Rhine, as occasion might require.
In return, France, under the terms of protection and deposit, was to retain possession of all Alsace, except Benfeld, with the towns of Philipsburgh and Spire, till the
conclusion of a peace, reserving the rights of the inhabitants and the authority of the empire. The confederates
were to grant a neutrality to any Catholic prince of Germany who should claim the protection of France ; they
were also to assist in the conquest of Brisac, and the fortresses on the Upper Rhine as far as Constance, and in the
recovery of Philipsburgh, which, during the negotiation,
had been surprised by the imperialists.

This agreement, at first privately arranged between the
French and Swedish ministers, was submitted, in March,
1636, to the confederates of Heilbron, and it required all
the influence of Oxenstiern and all the interest of France
to obtain their acquiescence in so dishonourable a treaty,
which delivered the keys of Germany into the hands of a
foreign power so ambitious and enterprising as France, and
enabled her to dictate to that empire which had once given
law to Europe.

The difficulties and delays occasioned by these negotiations suspending the military operations of the confederacy,
the emperor pursued the advantages which he had derived
from the decisive victory of Nordlingen. While the king
of Hungary remained at Heilbron, treating with the

princes and states, who were willing to submit, Bavaria was delivered from the enemy; Ulm, Augsburgh, and Memmingen surrendered; and John de Wert, after reducing the whole Palatinate, except Heidelberg, and taking Spire, joined the duke of Loraine in an attempt to recover his dominions, where his partisans, from their numerous castles and small posts, incessantly harassed the French army under La Force.

Another fruit of this important victory was the reconciliation with Saxony. The elector, who had long waited for a favourable opportunity to desert his allies, had been deterred from accepting reiterated offers of peace, by the superiority of the Swedish arms in his vicinity, or had demurred from a desire to obtain more advantageous terms. The battle of Nordlingen having removed his apprehensions, as well as lessened his hope of dictating his own conditions, he listened to the proposals of Ferdinand, who on his part relinquished some of his prejudices and interests, and tacitly abandoned the edict of restitution in favour of the Lutherans, to detach a prince, the bond of the Protestant union.

Preliminaries were signed soon after the battle of Nordlingen, and on the 30th of May, 1635, formed into a definitive peace, which was concluded at Prague. The members of the Confession of Augsburgh were allowed to possess in perpetuity all the mediate ecclesiastical property secularised since the pacification of Passau, and to retain all the immediate* property seized since the 11th of November, 1627, or for ever, unless a new and amicable arrangement should take place within ten years. The worship of the Confession of Augsburgh was to be tolerated only among the free nobility, or in those imperial cities which were not bound by a previous arrangement with the emperor, and likewise among the natives of Silesia; but from this toleration were formally excluded Bohemia and the other possessions of the house of Austria in the empire. A general amnesty was granted to all who acceded to this treaty, with the restitution of all conquests made since the

---

* Mediate property meant that which was subject to any sovereign or state, and included in their territories. Immediate property depended solely on the emperor and empire.

landing of Gustavus Adolphus. From this clause were, however, excepted the dukes of Wirtemberg, the prince of Baden and the landgrave of Hesse, as well as the subjects of the house of Austria, who had taken up arms against their sovereign. Finally, the two contracting parties, with all who should accede to the treaty, were to unite their arms in expelling foreigners from the empire. The elector of Saxony was to retain Lusatia as a fief relevant from the crown of Bohemia, and the archbishopric of Magdeburgh was assigned to his second son, with the exception of four bailiwicks, which were ceded to the elector himself. The bishopric of Halberstadt was to remain in the possession of the archduke Leopold. The proscription against the elector Palatine continued in force ; but his widow was to receive her jointure from the elector of Bavaria, and his sons a princely establishment, whenever they should return to their duty. With the hope of regaining the elector of Brandenburgh, a clause was introduced, securing to him the eventual succession of Pomerania.

This treaty bears evident marks of that bigotry and political jealousy, which actuated both the contracting parties ; for Ferdinand was unwilling to make any concession which was not extorted by necessity, and he unfortunately found in the elector the same antipathy against the Calvinists, and the same aversion to the Palatine family, with which he himself was animated. Hence both parties concurred in excluding the Calvinists from the peace, and the Palatine family, with their adherents from the amnesty ; and by a subterfuge, which equally accorded with the principles of both, avoided the very mention of the general term Protestants in the treaty.*

The Lutheran princes and states rejected the proffered conditions with indignation ; but their repugnance was speedily overcome by the terror of the imperial arms, the influence and example of the elector, and above all by

---

* Nothing, perhaps, proves more the inaccuracy with which history is generally written, than the account given of this celebrated treaty ; for even the best informed authors have described the toleration established by it, as applying to the whole Protestant body. On the contrary, this treaty, like the peace of Passau, was confined to the members of the Confession of Augsburgh, or Lutherans.

their desire to relieve themselves from a ruinous contest. Frankfort, the seat of imperial power, and the first city of the empire, set the example on the 14th of July, 1635; before the close of September, the confederacy of Heilbron was dissolved, and all the members successively acceded, except those who were formally or tacitly excluded. By this fortunate accommodation Ferdinand gained such a preponderance, that the Swedes would have been speedily crushed, and his authority fully re-established, had not France taken a new and active part in the war.

Richelieu had been long preparing to turn the principal strength of France against Spain. He formed a league with the dukes of Savoy and Parma, for the attack of the Milanese, and entered into an alliance with the United Provinces, for the conquest and partition of the Netherlands. The occupation of Treves, in February, 1635, and the seizure of the elector * by the Spanish forces, gave him a plausible pretext for a declaration of war. Two fleets were immediately equipped, and four armies put in motion. The first, of 26,000 men, was to act in the Netherlands, with the prince of Orange; the second, of 14,000, in Italy; the third, of 4000, under the celebrated duke of Rohan, was sent from Alsace to secure the Valteline, and cut off the communication between the Spanish and Austrian territories, and another under La Force was ready to act on the side of the Rhine.

Yet notwithstanding these vast preparations, the struggles of the Swedes to keep alive the war in Germany, and the intrigues of Richelieu to turn the Dutch and the powers of Italy against Spain, the exertions of the house of Austria for a time triumphed over all his efforts.

In Italy the Spaniards easily resisted an army, whose operations were impeded by misintelligence between the duke of Savoy, and Crequi, the French commander; and not only baffled all attempts to penetrate into the Milanese, but even carried the war into the territories of the duke of Parma, compelled him to quit the alliance of France,

* In consequence of the treaty with the United Provinces, and the occupation of Treves by a French garrison, a detachment of Spanish troops from Luxemburgh surprised that city, and transported the elector to Brussels, from whence he was sent a prisoner to Vienna.

and to give up the fortress of Sabionetta. On this side, therefore, the only advantage gained by the enemy, was the occupation of the Valteline by Rohan, who, with the assistance of the Grisons, maintained possession of this important pass against the Spaniards and Austrians.

In the Netherlands the victory of Avein gained in May, 1635, enabled the French to effect a junction with the Dutch troops under the prince of Orange, to capture Tirlemont and Diest, and spread terror as far as Brussels. But here, as in Italy, their plans were disconcerted by national jealousy, or the effects of personal pique between Richelieu and the prince of Orange. Their progress was impeded by the obstinate resistance of Louvain, and the judicious measures of the cardinal infant, till a succour of 10,000 men detached from the imperial army, under Piccolomini, turned the scale. The united forces were compelled to raise the siege; the Spaniards recalled the prince of Orange to cover Holland, by surprising the fort of Skenk; the French commanders led back the remnant of their army, reduced to half its number, between the Rhine and the Waal; and Richelieu had the mortification to see a predatory corps ravaging Picardy with fire and sword, and preparations made for the invasion of France.

On the Rhine the emperor and his allies secured a passage by the surprise of Philipsburgh and Worms; the duke of Loraine, assisted by the forces of the Catholic league, roused the spirit of his partisans, and regaining a footing in his territories; while Gallas took Gustavusburgh, blockaded Mentz, drove back Weimar with a French army under the cardinal de la Valette, and united with the duke to expel the French from Loraine. Louis himself was necessitated to head his troops, and exact the services of his feudal dependants; and he secured the fidelity of Weimar, who was negotiating with the emperor, by the enormous subsidy of 4,000,000 livres, and the cession of Alsace, as an hereditary sovereignty. Yet with all these exertions and sacrifices, the French with difficulty retained their footing in Loraine, and could not prevent the imperialists from establishing themselves on the frontiers of Franche Comté and Upper Alsace.

The splendid success of the imperial arms seemed to

augur that France would be visited with the same evils which she had inflicted on Spain and Germany, and that the war would be closed with the humiliation of that power by whose intrigues it had been fomented and continued. In the ensuing year, three attacks were at once made on the French territories ; the two principal on the side of Alsace and Picardy, the third against Guienne, where the inhabitants were in a state of ferment and disaffection. The Spaniards, enabled by the inactivity of the Dutch, to pour their principal forces into Picardy, took la Capelle, Roie, and le Catelet, surprised Corbie, and pushed a predatory corps almost to the gates of Paris. John de Wert, the active general of the Catholic league, compelled the burghers of Liege to enter into an accommodation with the emperor, reduced Coblentz, and invested Ehrenbreitstein, which surrendered after an obstinate blockade. Gallas having taken Mentz, crossed the Rhine at Brisac, joined the duke of Loraine, succoured Dole in Franche Comté, which was besieged by a body of troops under the prince of Condé, and bursting into Burgundy, laid siege to St. Jean de Losne, at the confluence of the Euse and the Saone.

These alarming irruptions spread such consternation in Paris, that many of the inhabitants sought safety in flight ; the royal family were about to retire to Orleans ; even the firmness of Richelieu was overcome, and he is said to have meditated his resignation. But he rose from this temporary despondency, displayed all the energy of his genius, and collected with incredible rapidity an army of 50,000 men. With this force the king himself advanced against the Spaniards, drove them beyond the Somme, and recovered Corbie ; at the same time succours were thrown into St. Jean de Losne, which had made a desperate resistance, and the imperialists, exhausted by a tedious siege and the inclemency of the season, withdrew their shattered forces from the frontier of France. On the side of Guienne the campaign began at too late a period to be attended with any essential effect ; the Spaniards who had crossed the Pyrenees, were awed by the presence of the duc d'Epernon, and reduced to retreat after capturing the petty fortress of St. Jean de Leus, with other posts of less importance.

While the emperor turned his principal efforts against

France, the Swedes rose from their depression, and again contested the ascendency in the north of Germany. Though the senate of Sweden were disheartened by the desertion of the German princes, though even Oxenstiern himself meditated the evacuation of Germany, Banner, the pupil and emulator of Gustavus, at the head of only 12,000 men, discontented and mutinous, maintained a defensive war against all the forces of Saxony, seconded by a considerable corps of imperialists. He retarded, though he could not prevent the reduction of Magdeburgh, Werben, and Stargard, and, without risking an engagement, retreated skilfully and gradually, disputing every foot of ground till he reached Pomerania. But the power which still kept up the war in the west of Germany found means to revive the conflagration in the north. After many delays and disputes arising from the opposition of Oxenstiern and the Swedish senate to the encroaching and interested conduct of Richelieu, the dread of common danger produced a temporary union. By the influence of France, assisted by the mediation of England and Holland, the truce with Poland was prolonged for twenty years, for which Sweden restored her conquests in Russia; and soon afterwards the French court renewed the former subsidiary alliance for three years. Assisted by the reinforcements drawn from Prussia in consequence of this truce, Banner resumed offensive operations. He totally defeated the Saxons and imperialists at Witstoch, cleared Pomerania and Brandenburgh, drove the imperialists back into Franconia, took Erfurth and Naumburgh, penetrated into the heart of Misnia, defeated the Saxons in various encounters, reduced Torgau, besieged Leipzic, and before the close of the year, prepared to make Saxony the support of his attack against the hereditary countries.

During this interval the French court again roused the landgrave of Hesse Cassel, enabled him by a new subsidiary treaty to oppose the forces of the emperor, and by his assistance prevented the subjugation of Westphalia till the efforts of Banner restored the preponderance of Sweden.

In the midst of these military operations, all things proclaimed the returning ascendency of Ferdinand in Germany, and proved the advantages which he had derived from his reconciliation with the two chief Protestant princes, the electors of Saxony and Brandenburgh. An electoral diet was assembled at Ratisbon, by the emperor in person, on the 15th of September, 1636, for the ostensible purpose of restoring peace, for which some vague negotiations had been opened under the mediation of the pope and the king of Denmark, and congresses appointed at Hamburgh and Cologne; but with the real view of procuring the election of his son Ferdinand as king of the Romans. Some attempts were made by the Protestants to hasten the negotiations, by requiring that Ferdinand, though elected, should not be crowned till after the termination of hostilities; and by the English ambassador in favour of the unfortunate princes of the Palatine house. But the superior influence of the emperor overruled all opposition; the benefits of the armistice were offered only to the duke of Wirtemberg, on the most rigorous terms, and the instances for the restoration of the prince Palatine evaded by requiring impracticable conditions. The alarms of the diet were excited by an artful rumour that the king of France fostered designs on the imperial crown, in case of an interregnum, which from the declining health of the emperor, was soon likely to happen, and Ferdinand was elected with only the fruitless protest of the Palatine family, and the dissenting voice of the elector of Treves, who was still in custody at Vienna. His capitulation contained no stipulation of importance, except a few temporary regulations occasioned by the war, with the declaration, that the exclusion of the elector of Treves should not operate on any future occasion. He was accordingly acknowledged by all the powers of Europe, except France and Sweden.

The emperor did not long survive this happy event. He died on the 15th of February, 1637, soon after his return to Vienna, in the fifty-ninth year of his age, of a decline, derived from incessant anxiety and continual fatigues of body and mind.

When we review the awful period of his reign, pregnant with such extraordinary events and stupendous revolutions, we cannot but admire, in Ferdinand II., the great qualities which have distinguished the greatest men of

every age and nation ; penetration and sagacity, unbroken
perseverance, irresistible energy of character, resignation
and fortitude in adversity, and a mind never enervated by
success. But these great qualities were sullied and disgraced by the most puerile superstition, inveterate bigotry,
and unbounded ambition. In many features of his public
character, Ferdinand resembled his relative Philip II. ; in
his talents for the cabinet no less than in his incapacity for
the field ; in elevation of mind as well as in bigotry, persecution and cruelty ; in fortitude in adverse, and arrogance in prosperous circumstances. But it is a satisfaction
to record, that in his private character he differed essentially from the gloomy tyrant of Spain. He was a good
and affectionate father, a faithful and tender husband, an
affable and indulgent master ; he was easy of access to the
meanest of his subjects ; compassionate and forgiving,
where his religious prejudices were not concerned. From a
principle of superstitious humility, he admitted into his
presence the poor of all descriptions ; and even beggars,
who were suspected of being infected with the plague,
were not repulsed. He purchased the liberty of many
Christian slaves from their Asiatic or African masters,
gave public entertainments to the needy, at which he assisted in person, and appointed advocates, at his own expense, to plead the cause of the indigent and the helpless
in the courts of justice.

As the virtues of his amiable predecessor and uncle,
Maximilian II., were principally derived from early habits
and education ; so the failings of Ferdinand may be attributed to the early impressions which he received from
his mother, and his uncle William of Bavaria, and to
the prejudices instilled into him by the Jesuits, which
strengthened with his years, and grew up with his growth.
Had he not been influenced by the narrow and jaun-
diced views of superstition and bigotry, he might have
maintained the peace and happiness of his hereditary dominions ; might have ruled the empire not as the head of a
sect or the chief of a party, but as the sovereign and friend
of all ; and might have saved Germany and Europe from
thirty years of anarchy, persecution, and terror, devastation
and carnage. In fine, the defects of education, and erroneous

principles, rendered him the misfortune of his family, the enemy of his country, and the scourge of his age.*

A prince of so superstitious a character as Ferdinand was not likely to be sparing in his benefactions to the clergy. He endowed many religious establishments, and enriched others : for the Jesuits he founded sixteen colleges, and convents for the Barnabites, Capuchins, Camaladunes, Paulines, barefooted Carmelites, reformed Augustins, Benedictines of Montferrat, Servites, and Irish Franciscans. He settled an annual pension of 24,000 florins on the archbishopric of Prague ; the twenty-eighth part of the produce of the gold and silver mines in Hungary on the archbishopric of Gran, and 40,000 florins annually on the Austrian prelates. He founded also four bishoprics in Bohemia, many schools for the education of the clergy, numerous hospitals and almshouses, and gave great presents to the secular clergy of the hereditary countries.

When we consider that his ordinary revenue did not exceed 5,400,000 florins †, and reflect on the enormous expenses of his wars, and the charges of his splendid establishment, it is scarcely necessary to observe that notwithstanding the sums he drew from the confiscated property of his adversaries and rebel subjects, these benefactions contributed to exhaust his resources, to load him with pecuniary embarrassments, and often to retard or prevent the success of his military operations.

Ferdinand was twice married, first to Maria Anne, daughter of William, duke of Bavaria ; and, secondly, to Eleonora, daughter of Vincent, duke of Mantua. He had no children by his second wife, and his surviving issue by his first were : —

1. Ferdinand Ernest, who succeeded him.

2. Leopold William, born in 1604, and devoted to the

---

* Besides occasional references to other works, we have consulted for the narrative of his reign, the English translation of Gualdo, Historia delle Guerre di Ferdinando II., 1647 ; Kevenhuller, Annales Ferdinandi II. ; Struvius ; Heiss ; Schmidt ; Heinrich ; Gebhaerdi ; de Luca ; Puetter ; Schiller's History of the Thirty Years' War ; Pfeffel ; Pelzel and Windisch ; Daniel, Histoire de France ; le Vassor, Histoire de Louis XIII. ; Mémoires de Montglat ; Puffendorf ; Complete History of Europe.

† Nearly 540,000l. sterling. De Luca, vol. ii. p. 332.

ecclesiastical profession.   He was educated by the Jesuits, and, like his father, imbibed from them a singular degree of superstition and bigotry.   He acquired a taste for the arts and botany, and made collections of paintings, curiosities, and rare plants; but from a principle of mortification he denied himself the indulgence of smelling to his flowers, and from rigid notions of continence, shunned even his own sisters.   From this turn of mind he obtained from his father the surname of the Angel; and the courtiers at Vienna believed, or affected to believe, that his prayers contained a peculiar sanctity.   The son of an emperor was not likely to want preferment, and accordingly ecclesiastical benefices were heaped upon him at an early age.   Before he had attained his eleventh year he was nominated bishop of Strasburgh and Passau, and abbot of the rich foundations of Maurbach and Neiders.   About his sixteenth year he received from the pope an appointment to the sees of Bremen Halberstadt and Magdeburgh, of which he was deprived by the Swedish invasion, and renounced all, except Halberstadt, in the peace with the elector of Saxony. He was appointed bishop of Olmutz, grand master of the Teutonic order, and finally nominated successor to the see of Breslau.

Neither his sanctity, nor the disorders of a weak frame prevented him from occasionally exchanging the crosier for the sword; for he appears with distinction among the great military characters in the reign of his brother.   On the death of Ferdinand III., the crown of the empire was offered to him by the electors, who opposed his nephew Leopold; but he refused it from attachment to the interests of his house, and became a guardian to the children of his deceased brother.   He at length relinquished the career of politics and arms, which he had reluctantly entered, and hastened to that retirement which had been the object of his early and constant wishes.   He died in 1662.

The two daughters of Ferdinand were: 1. Mary Anne. She was first betrothed to Gabriel Bethlehem, prince of Transylvania; but refusing to espouse him because he would not embrace the Catholic faith, she married, in 1635, Maximilian, elector of Bavaria.   2. Cecilia Renata, was wife of Ladislaus, king of Poland, and died at Vilna, a widow, in 1644.

We have before observed that, on the death of Maximilian II., the archduchy of Austria was assigned solely to the emperor Rhodolph, the right of primogeniture virtually, if not formally introduced, and the younger children provided with pensions or estates, instead of obtaining a share in the administration. Ferdinand, however, seems to have been the first who formally established the right of primogeniture in all his hereditary territories. By his testament, dated May 10th, 1621, he ordered that all his Austrian dominions should devolve on his eldest male descendant, and fixed the majority at eighteen years. The younger brothers were to receive each an annual salary of 45,000 florins, with a lordship as a place of residence in one of the hereditary countries; and to each of the daughters he assigned a portion of 75,000 florins.

But these regulations could only affect the archduchy of Austria and the Styrian dominions, which Ferdinand inherited from his father Charles; as the Tyrol, and the exterior provinces in Alsace and Brisgau, were the joint property of him and his two brothers, Charles and Leopold. This divided inheritance occasioned disputes, not only between the brothers, but likewise gave rise to claims from the Spanish branch, till after much difficulty the king of Spain was induced to relinquish his pretensions, and primogeniture was likewise established in the succession of these territories. Ferdinand, in 1624, consigned to his only surviving brother Leopold, the possession of the Tyrol, with the exterior provinces, to revert, in failure of issue male, to the elder branch.

CHAP. LVII. — FERDINAND III. — 1637–1641.

As the faintest gleam of light, to those who have been long surrounded with storms and hurricanes, seems to presage a returning calm, so the death of a bigoted emperor, and the accession of a tolerant prince, gave hopes that peace would be speedily restored to Germany. But after so long and dreadful a contest it was no easy task to re-establish tranquillity; for the ravages of the war had impressed the deepest antipathy on the minds of the contending parties, and the varied and contradictory connections of eighteen years, had left an endless variety of jarring interests to accommodate and disentangle. The new monarch, unable to obtain any terms of peace, but such as would have dishonoured the memory of his father, injured the interests of his house, and endangered the Catholic cause, was compelled to continue a contest entailed on him with his inheritance, and of which he had seen and deplored the fatal effects.

The death of Bogeslaus, the aged duke of Pomerania, in March, 1637, enabled the new emperor to prosecute the war in the north with increased advantages. As the Swedes, in virtue of the compulsory treaty concluded by the deceased duke with Gustavus Adolphus, refused to surrender Pomerania, the elector of Brandenburgh made a common cause with Austria, for the recovery of a territory to which he was entitled to succeed, united his forces with the imperialists, and increased their means of attack against the Swedes, by yielding his principal fortresses, or commanding his garrisons to swear allegiance to the emperor. Accordingly Gallas advancing from Wirtemberg, united with Hasfeldt and Goertz, who had been assisted by the troops of Westphalia and Luneburgh, and forced Banner to retire into Pomerania; while a corps of Saxons and imperialists cleared Lusatia and the march of Brandenburgh, drove the troops of Wrangel beyond the Wartha, and retook Landsberg. Banner, endeavouring to divert the war into the hereditary countries, by bursting through the Mark into Silesia, Gallas suddenly penetrated into Pomerania, near Tribsees, surprised the troops of Wrangel, who were left for the defence of the duchy, and reduced all the places west of the Oder, except Anclam, Stettin, and Stralsund. The return of Banner alone saved Lower Pomerania; and the imperial general, after leaving garrisons in the conquered places, as well as in the isles of Usedom and Wollin, cantoned his troops in Saxony.

The preponderance of Austria in the south of Germany was at the same time increased by the decease of William, landgrave of Hesse, who died in September, 1637, at the very moment when he had arranged a league between France, Sweden, and the United Provinces, for the restoration of the Palatine family. Leaving an only son, William, in the eighth year of his age, he committed the regency to his wife Elizabeth ; but this disposition was opposed by his relative George, of the collateral branch of Hesse Darmstadt, who was a zealous partisan of the house of Austria. This event, and the contest which ensued for the administration, not only frustrated the league, which had been the result of the landgrave's negotiations, but diminished the number of Ferdinand's opponents, and deprived the enemy of an active adherent, who, from the local position of his territories, had essentially contributed to their ascendency on the side of the Rhine.

The deaths of the dukes of Savoy and Mantua, together with the contests for the government of their dominions, during the minority of their successors, who were both infants, occasioned a similar change in the affairs of Italy, and suspended the alliance which had been the great support of France in the war beyond the Alps. Mary, the regent duchess of Mantua, abandoned the French, and exerted her influence in favour of the Spaniards. The emperor annulled the will of the duke of Savoy, which consigned the regency to his duchess Christina, and supported the claims of cardinal Maurice, and prince Thomas of Carignan, brothers of the deceased prince, one in the service, and the other an adherent of Spain. These princes, assisted by the Spanish army from the Milanese, and favoured by the people, conquered the principal part of Piemont, surprised Turin, and laid siege to the citadel.

The Grisons also, apprehensive of drawing the war into their territories, and irritated by the interference of the French in their civil and religious affairs, forced the duke of Rohan to quit the Valteline, and renewed the treaty with the two branches of the house of Austria, which again opened a free passage for their troops between Germany and Italy.

During these events a feeble attempt was made by Charles Louis and Rupert, sons of the unfortunate elector Palatine, to recover their lost honours and inheritance.

Having obtained a scanty supply of money from the king of England, they collected 4000 men, penetrated in May, 1638, into Westphalia, where they were joined by a corps of Swedish cavalry, and being supplied with artillery from Minden, laid siege to Lemgau, the capital of the county of La Lippe. But this enterprise was crushed in its infancy by the imperial general Hasfeldt, who, advancing against them with a superior force, overtook them in their retreat to Minden on the 7th of October, and defeated them after an obstinate engagement of two days. Their little army was dispersed, their whole artillery taken, the prince Palatine escaped with difficulty, and prince Rupert, with many of the officers, were made prisoners.*

The success of the imperial arms in the north of Germany, and of the Spaniards in Italy, was however balanced by still greater losses in other quarters. While the prince of Orange in the Netherlands reduced Breda, a French army, penetrating into Hainault, took Landrecies, Maubeuge, Damvilliers, Ivoy, with various smaller posts, and recovered La Chapelle, the last remnant of the Spanish conquests in Picardy. In the neighbourhood of the Upper Rhine, the duke of Weimar again emerged from his temporary eclipse, threw off his dependence on Sweden, treated with France on terms of equality, and laid the foundation of an hereditary sovereignty. Assisted by the subsidies and succours of France, he continued to extend his conquests over the remaining part of Alsace, defeated John de Wert, and drove the imperialists from the greater part of their posts. With the co-operation of the duke of Longueville, he routed the duke of Loraine on the frontiers of his own duchy, dispersed the troops of Franche Comté, and reduced the greater part of the country.

Like Mansfeld, increasing his army with mercenary levies of Germans and Swiss, he affected to distribute his troops into quarters, in the bishopric of Basle; but in the heart of winter he suddenly appeared on the Rhine, surprised Lamfenburgh, Waldshut, and Seckingen, and laid siege to Rheinfelden. Defeated†, with great slaughter by the im-

* This prince was afterwards well known in English history, for his exertions during the civil wars.

† In this defeat, the duke of Rohan, who, after his expulsion from

perial general Savelli, he again attacked the victorious troops, when reposing in the confidence of success, and gained a complete victory, with the capture of the two generals Savelli and John de Wert.   The surrender of Rheinfelden and Rottelen was the fruit of this victory; his force increased with his good fortune, and he laid siege to Brisac, the key of Alsace and the Brisgau.   The imperial generals obeyed the orders of their sovereign, by exerting every effort to save so important a fortress; the whole summer was spent in the most bloody combats; but nothing could resist the skill and impetuosity of the Saxon hero, and the place surrendered on the 7th of December, after suffering such extremities of famine and distress, that guards were set over the burial places to prevent the inhabitants from devouring the putrid carcasses of the dead. Favoured by the possession of Brisac, the duke distributed his troops into quarters beyond the Rhine, and prepared for the execution of more important enterprises on the return of spring.

At the same time Banner had recovered Pomerania, and drove the imperialists beyond the Elbe.   Strengthened by the arrival of 14,000 men from Sweden, he concerted with Weimar a plan for carrying the war again into the Austrian territories by a joint attack, one on the side of Bohemia, the other on that of Bavaria.   He passed the Elbe at Lawenburgh, took his course through the territories of Magdeburgh and Halberstadt, crossed the Saal at Hall, made himself master of Kemnitz and Marienburgh, and besieged Freyberg.   After twice defeating the Saxons, who advanced to its relief, he abandoned an enterprise which would have occupied his forces at a time when celerity and decision were necessary, reduced Pirna, and penetrated into Bohemia, along the northern bank of the Elbe, at the head of 40,000 men.   He published a proclamation calling on the Protestants to unite against their enemies the Catholics, and after routing, on the 20th of May, 1639, a corps of imperialists at Brandeiss, and making their generals Montecuculi and Hoffkirch prisoners, advanced to the walls

the Valteline had joined his friend, the duke of Weimar, to escape the persecutions of Richelieu, was mortally wounded in leading a wing of the army.

of Prague; but, not being joined by the Protestants, and unprovided with battering artillery, he again fell back behind the Elbe, dispersed his detachments over the country to the north of that river, and like another Tilly, spread devastation from the frontiers of Saxony to the borders of Moravia.

He chose this position to wait till the duke of Weimar could co-operate on the side of Bavaria; but his designs were frustrated by one of those events which baffle all human combinations. The duke drew his troops from their quarters early in the year, and laid siege to Thann, almost the only place remaining unconquered in Alsace. The resistance of the inhabitants protracted the siege till late in the spring, and at the moment when he was preparing to co-operate with the Swedes, a fever, derived from excessive fatigue, terminated his brilliant career at Neuburgh, in the 35th year of his age, and thus delivered the house of Austria from the most dangerous of its enemies, and deprived the Swedes of their most active and skilful supporter.*

The duke having bequeathed his army, with Alsace and his other conquests, to his brothers, his bequest was opposed by various competitors: the emperor, the Swedes, the young prince Palatine, and France, contested the acquisition of a well appointed army, and the possession of Alsace. At length the superior address, vigour, and good fortune of Richelieu, prevailed over the other competitors: the brothers of the deceased hero were bribed to relinquish their claims; the young Palatine, who was hastening through France in disguise, was put under a temporary arrest; the army was persuaded to enter into French pay, under the command of Longueville; the generals induced to receive French garrisons in their respective fortresses; and Alsace, of which a part only had been reluctantly ceded by Richelieu, fell entire under the dominion of France.

While these intrigues kept the enemy inactive on the Rhine, Ferdinand amused Banner with feigned negotia-

* History of Ernest the Pious, and Bernard the great duke of Saxe Weimar. It is a sufficient eulogium of the military talents of Bernard, that Turenne acknowledged him as one of his masters in the art of war.

tions, till he had drawn together a considerable force from Westphalia, the Rhine, and from Hungary.   He then threw off the mask, and in February, 1640, the archduke Leopold, to whom the command was intrusted, attacking the quarters of the Swedes, expelled them from Bohemia and Silesia.

On the departure of the Austrians towards Bohemia, the French recovered the ascendency.   The duke of Longueville, descending the Rhine, captured Alzey, Oppenheim, Bingen, and Creutznach, drove the Bavarians into Wirtemberg, crossed at Bacharach, and renewed the war in the circle of Westphalia.   The regent of Hesse, who amused the court of Vienna with illusory negotiations till she had established her government, was encouraged to declare openly against the house of Austria, and to conclude a treaty, by which she agreed to furnish 5000 men to the allies.   Her example was followed by the dukes of Brunswick, who were alienated by the demands of the imperial court for the restoration of their conquests in the see of Hildesheim, and, who, entering into the confederacy against the emperor, supplied 4000 auxiliaries.   These forces and those of France, joining with Banner at Erfurth, saved the Swedish army, which had been driven back into Thuringia, by the united troops of Austria and Bavaria, and advanced against the archduke Leopold, who was posted at Saalfeld. But, after fruitless endeavours to bring the imperialists to an engagement, they were, in December, 1641, reduced, by the judicious dispositions of the archduke, to fall back behind the Weser, and the imperialists approached the Rhine. The Bavarians took quarters in Suabia, the Austrians in Wirtemberg, Franconia, and the Upper Palatinate, while Banner retired into Brunswick, and Guebriant, who had succeeded to the command of the Weimarian troops on the death of Longueville, drew back towards the French frontier.

The joy of the emperor at this success, was, however, considerably diminished by the unfortunate situation of Spain.   Her fleets had been repeatedly defeated by the Dutch and French; in the Netherlands she had lost the important town of Arras, the key of Artois, and in Piemont, deserted by the princes of Savoy, who threw them-

selves under the protection of France, her troops had been
expelled from all their conquests. The natives of Portugal, also irritated by repeated oppressions, threw off, in
1640, the detested yoke of Spain. A plot, arranged and
matured in silence, astounded the court of Madrid, by
its sudden explosion, and in an instant placed John duke
of Braganza on the throne. At the same time the Catalans
were driven to revolt by the violation of their privileges
and the licentiousness of the soldiery quartered on their
frontier, and the spirit of disaffection began to spread into
the contiguous provinces.

During these events the states and princes of Germany,
whose dominions had been so long visited by the dreadful
scourge of war, clamoured for the cessation of hostilities,
and at length extorted from the emperor the convocation
of a general diet, to deliberate on the means of restoring
peace, a measure which had been adopted since the accession of Ferdinand II. The diet assembled at Ratisbon,
and Ferdinand presided in person; but instead of giving
way to the clamour for peace, which would only encourage
the enemy, and lead to the imposition of more onerous
terms, he endeavoured to unite the whole Germanic body
in a declaration of war against France and Sweden, and
to obtain a considerable augmentation of the ordinary
contingents. He indeed succeeded in persuading the diet
to make the peace of Prague the basis of the future accommodation, and to continue the exclusion of the Palatine
family from the amnesty; but he was unable to unite the
whole empire in hostilities, or to obtain the proposed
augmentation of the supplies; for the circles of Austria
and Bavaria alone furnished the stipulated demand of a
hundred and twenty Roman months, while all the other
circles contributed only sixty. All his influence likewise
could not prevent the transfer of the congress from Cologne and Hamburgh to Munster and Osnaburgh, which
were more under the influence of France and the Protestants, nor the mortifying concession that all the states of
the empire should send deputies to that assembly.

The opposition which occasioned these disappointments
was principally derived from the defection of the dukes of
Brunswick, and the influence of Frederic William the new

elector of Brandenburgh, who emancipated himself from the dependence in which his father had been held by the court of Vienna, and, at the early age of eighteen, displayed that consummate policy, independent spirit, and vigour of character, which established the grandeur of his house. The weight of the emperor was also diminished by the introduction of a maxim, now become universally prevalent among the German jurists, that the elective head of Germany was not to be considered as succeeding to the powers and rights of Constantine or Justinian; but that the empire was an aristocratic body, the splendour and authority of which resided in the states, and not solely in the chief. This principle was first exhibited in a systematic form by Chemnitz, chancellor of Stettin, in a work* published at the instigation of the Swedish government; and it was too flattering to the Germanic states, not to obtain a favourable reception. It marks an era in the German law, which distinguished the great decline of the imperial authority, the consequent diminution of the splendour and weight of the empire, and the increasing influence of foreign powers over its component states.

Chap. LVIII.—1640–1648.

In the midst of Ferdinand's endeavours to unite the states of Germany against the French and Swedes, and his preparations to carry hostilities beyond the Rhine, Banner nearly succeeded in dispersing the diet, and diverted the torrent of war into the hereditary countries. He quitted his quarters in the depth of winter, at the head of 15,000 men, and after uniting at Erfurth with 6000 French under Guebriant, he rapidly directed his march by Hof, Amerback, and Schwendorf, cutting off the imperial troops scattered in his route, and reached the neighbourhood of Ratisbon in the middle of January, 1641.

This sudden irruption exposed the emperor and the diet

* De Ratione Status in Imperio nostro Romano Germanico. For an account of this work, see Puetter's Development, b. vi. ch. 7.

to the most imminent danger. Ferdinand narrowly escaped being taken in his way to the chace, by a detachment which passed the Danube on the ice, while a corps advancing to the very walls of Ratisbon, insulted the empire and its chief by a distant cannonade. The firmness of the emperor alone prevented the dissolution of the diet; he declared his resolution to defend the city to the last extremity, and by his presence and exertions restrained the deputies and ambassadors, who were preparing to take their departure. The advance of reinforcements, and a sudden thaw, relieved him from his perilous situation; and the confederate generals, unable to agree in their plans of operation, separated their armies, Banner carrying the war into Bohemia, and Guebriant returning towards the Rhine.

These delays gave time to the imperialists to collect their forces, and avenge the insult offered to the emperor and the diet. Piccolomini, to whom the command was intrusted, harassed the Swedes in their march through the mountainous passes which skirt the frontier of Bohemia, followed them into Saxony, and though they were rejoined at Zwicka by the French, drove them back to Halberstadt, where Banner fell a sacrifice* to his own intemperance, and the fatigues of this arduous expedition. During the contests which ensued for his army, the imperial general pursued his advantages; he cleared Lusatia and Silesia, pressed the retreat of the confederates into the duchy of

---

* This distinguished commander died in his forty-first year. His death, like that of the duke of Weimar, was attributed to poison; but was the consequence of chagrin, and the incessant fatigues of the campaign, as well as intemperance, and indulgence in pleasure, to which he had at all times addicted himself, particularly since his marriage with a beautiful princess of Baden, whom he had recently espoused in a kind of amorous frenzy. The victories of Banner were attested by six hundred standards which decorate the arsenal of Stockholm.

Torstenson, who succeeded him in the command, was also the pupil of Gustavus, and equally emulated the exploits of his great master. He is a singular instance of the power of a vigorous mind over bodily infirmity. Though crippled by the gout, and reduced to the necessity of being always conveyed in a litter, he was the most active and enterprising of the Swedish generals; and it was truly said of him, that while his body was confined to earth, his mind was free as air, and his enterprises had wings.

Luneburgh, and closed his brilliant campaign, by fixing his winter quarters in Luneburgh and Hesse.

Torstenson, the new Swedish commander, with a reinforcement of 8000 men, joined the confederate troops in the duchy of Luneburgh, and by his presence prevented the desertion or dispersion of the army. While Guebriant crossed the Rhine at Wesel, defeated a corps of imperialists under Lamboy at Kempen, on the 7th of January, 1642, and overran the electorate of Cologne, the Swedes again directed their attack against the hereditary countries. Torstenson traversed the territories of Brandenburgh, burst into Silesia, took Great Glogau by storm, and defeated a corps of imperialists under Albert of Saxe Lauemburgh. He followed this success by capturing Schweidnitz, pushed into Moravia, reduced Neustadt, Littau, and Olmutz, laid siege to Brieg, and even spread terror to the gates of Vienna.

Fortunately, the resistance of Brieg enabled the imperialists again to repel the invasion. The archduke Leopold and Piccolomini assembled their forces, and drew them into the hereditary countries; they drove Torstenson through Moravia and Silesia into Saxony, and on the 2nd of November, 1642, the two armies encountered in the plain of Breitenfeld, on the very spot where Gustavus had gained the memorable victory of Leipzic, which opened to him the centre of Germany. The place and the occasion, with all its concomitant circumstances, called forth the emulation and bravery of the contending hosts. The imperialists were flushed with hope derived from recent success, and panted to vindicate their fame on the very ground which had witnessed their former disgrace; the Swedes, driven to desperation, were stimulated by every consideration of safety and honour, to emulate the heroic deeds of those over whose graves they were contending. The battle was fought with all the fury inspired by these motives; and after a long and bloody conflict, the imperialists were totally routed, with the loss of 10,000 killed and prisoners. Leipzic immediately surrendered, and Torstenson, after sending a detachment under Koningsmark to clear Franconia, resumed his design of invading the Austrian territories. On the 28th of December, he laid siege to Freyberg, to open a way into Bohemia, and summoned the French army under Guebriant to concur in the enterprise.

At this period disasters as alarming as those which hung over the emperor, hastened the decline of the Spanish monarchy, and contributed to diminish the weight of the house of Austria.

Olivarez, the enterprising and all-powerful minister of Philip IV., had formed the design of recovering Portugal in the same manner as it was lost, by a secret conspiracy, of which the bishop of Braga, and some Portuguese magnates were the agents, and of reviving the civil troubles in France, by supporting the discontented nobles against Richelieu. But this plan failed of success. The conspiracy in Portugal was discovered and defeated ; the new monarch, John IV., was confirmed by the cortes of the realm, and acknowledged by all the powers of Europe, except the emperor and the pope. In France, the duke of Orleans supported by the discontented nobles, and Cinq Mars, the favourite of the king, entered into a secret treaty with Spain, with the concurrence of the queen, and obtained the acquiescence of Louis himself in the dismission of the minister. But the very means which where employed to further this design, prevented its success. The inroad of the Spanish troops from the Netherlands alarmed the king; the conspirators, jealous of each other and of Spain, did not act with concert and decision ; the minister recovered that ascendency which he derived from his superior talents in times of danger, and obliged the reluctant monarch to abandon the conspirators to his vengeance. The duke of Orleans was disgraced, Cinq Mars brought to the scaffold, and the duke of Bouillon purchased his life by yielding Sedan, the focus of the conspiracy. In Spain, the Catalans acknowledged the sovereignty of France; the veteran troops refused to execute the orders of the minister, and Philip himself, who repaired to Saragossa to encourage the army by his presence, witnessed from the windows of his palace the devastation of Arragon. The capture of Callioure and Perpignan, in September, 1642, completed the reduction of Roussillon, and opened a direct communication between the revolted province and France. In the midst of these reverses the Spanish government suffered a fatal loss by the premature death of the cardinal infant, whose skill and valour had balanced all the efforts of the French during two arduous campaigns, and whose eulogium was proclaimed by the exultation of the enemy, and the regret of his countrymen.

During these events, Richelieu, who had triumphed on the verge of the grave, closed, on the 4th of December, 1642, his splendid administration, and his death was followed by that of Louis XIII., on the 14th of May, 1643. The helm of government was left in the hands of cardinal Mazarin, an Italian priest, and the regency vested in the queen mother, Anne of Austria.

Under the regency of a Spanish princess, and the administration of a foreigner, whose power was not established by time or talents, the house of Austria naturally expected to regain its wonted ascendency; but this gleam of hope seemed only to mock its transient expectations. The spirit of Richelieu still impelled the machine, which his genius had set in motion; Mazarin extorted from the queen the sacrifice of her personal and national feelings to the interest of that country over which she was called to rule, and the Spanish power in the Netherlands received, on the 12th of May, 1643, an irretrievable blow in the memorable defeat at Rocroi, the first fruits of the skill and courage of the duke of Enghein, who afterwards so highly illustrated the name of Condé. At the moment also, when France was bereft of the directing genius of Richelieu, Spain was deprived of Olivarez. The unfortunate issue of all his schemes, the discontent occasioned by the burdens of a long war, the loss of Portugal, the dismemberment of Roussillon, and the rebellion of Catalonia, raised against the great but unfortunate minister a host of foes. The queen, the grandees, the council of state, united in requesting his dismission; the timid and reluctant king was assailed by all, who, from habit or situation, retained an influence over his mind; the discontented were joined even by the family and friends of the minister, whom he had alienated by adopting an illegitimate son; the emperor himself had the weakness to expostulate with Philip, and insist on his disgrace. The credit of Olivarez sunk under these repeated attacks, and Philip unwillingly dismissed the only minister in whom he placed implicit confidence, or who could govern his wavering and voluptuous mind, at a juncture when his genius and talents might have restored the declining fortunes of Spain.

The emperor was equally prevented from availing himself of the changes in France by the deplorable state of his own affairs. After the fatal battle of Breitenfeld, the archduke collected the scattered remnant of the forces in Bohemia, and endeavoured to remove the sense of their disgrace, by inflicting a severe and exemplary punishment on those to whom he attributed the defeat. He disarmed the regiment of Madelon, tore their standards, decimated the soldiers, and ordered the commander to be decapitated. His presence being necessary in the Netherlands, to supply the place of the cardinal infant, the chief command was given to Gallas; but this appointment occasioned great discontent among the officers and troops, and induced those active and experienced generals, Piccolomini and Hasfeldt, to enter into the service of Spain and Bavaria. While the imperialists were reduced to inactivity by these dissensions, and by their endeavours to recruit and discipline the army, the Swedes pursued their operations with their accustomed vigour and decision. Torstenson continued the siege of Freyberg, notwithstanding the inclemencies of the season; but when the imperialists threw succours into the place, he again abandoned an enterprise which could only produce unnecessary delay, drew reinforcements from Lower Saxony and Pomerania, and after insulting Prague and the imperial army, took the route of Chrudim and Leutomischl to Moravia, where his troops still maintained a footing. Having relieved Olmutz, which was besieged by the imperialists, he reduced Cremsier, took post at Dobitschau, and laid the whole country under contribution as far as the Danube.

Thus was the emperor involved in the utmost distress, at the very moment which seemed to afford him the most favourable prospect of changing the fortune of the war. But he met the storm with an undaunted countenance, and called forth the scanty resources which were now left, to increase his adherents in Germany, and turn the tide of hostilities into the territories of the enemy. He effected a reconciliation with the dukes of Brunswick, by restoring Wolfembuttel, and the other fortresses in their territories occupied by his troops. He opened also a negotiation with Christian IV., king of Denmark, and found little difficulty in gaining a prince ardent for military glory, and interested to diminish the power of the Swedes. A secret treaty seems to have been arranged, and while the emperor was recruiting his forces, and recovering his own dominions, the king of Denmark was to make a diversion by invading Sweden.

These designs, however, did not escape the vigilance of the Swedish government. The senate resolved to anticipate the intended attack, by commencing hostilities; and this resolution was taken so secretly that it was not suspected till the moment of execution. On the receipt of a private order, Torstenson abruptly quitted Moravia, in September, 1643, traversed Silesia, crossed the Elbe at Torgau, and threatened the Upper Palatinate. After keeping all parties in suspense, he suddenly directed his march to Havelberg, burst into Holstein with the impetuosity of a torrent, and finding the country unprepared for resistance, in less than six weeks made himself master of the whole peninsula except Gluckstadt and Krempe. While one Swedish army thus subjugated the Cimbric Chersonesus, another under Horn * invaded Skone, Bleckingen, and Halland; and a fleet was prepared to wrest from the Danes their naval superiority in the Baltic. To rescue the king of Denmark from impending ruin, the emperor, whose territories were relieved from the presence of the enemy, collected all his forces in Bohemia, and in the depth of winter despatched the flower of his army towards Holstein under Gallas, enjoining him to imitate the rapid movements of the Swedes, notwithstanding the inclemency of the season, and the length of the march.

Suspending our account of these operations in the furthest extremity of Germany, we turn our attention to France, where the administration of Mazarin had begun to attain strength and consistency. With a less lofty and commanding genius, though with more patience and plia-

* This general had been recently exchanged for John de Wert, who was taken in the battle of Rheinfelden.

bility of temper, the new minister pursued the general plan
of his predecessor ; but from principle as well as necessity,
he made greater exertions on the side of Germany, as the
Bavarians and the troops of Loraine at this time threatened to carry the war into France.

After the defeat of Lamboy, Guebriant hastened into
Saxony to support the Swedes. On the victory of Brietenfeld, he declined concurring in the attack on the Austrian
territories, from the principle now adopted by the French
court, of confining their efforts to maintain the advantages on the side of the Rhine. He turned accordingly
towards the Maine, captured Lohr and Aschaffenburgh ;
but was attacked in his progress by the Bavarians, assisted
by the duke of Loraine *, and driven into the Brisgau.
Here he remained during the winter, struggling with
famine and every species of distress, and afterwards retired
into Alsace to refresh and recruit his troops. Being reinforced by a part of that army which had gained the victory of Rocroy, he re-crossed the Rhine, and pushed
towards Rothweil, to secure the magazines of the enemy,
and force his way into Bavaria. Though he was killed
during the siege, the place was soon reduced to surrender,
and Rantzau, who succeeded him in the command, led the
army towards the Danube. Here, however, their progress
was checked; the Bavarian general Mercy suddenly collecting his forces, surprised the French, who were scattered in quarters in the neighbourhood of Duttlingen, and
obtained a victory which almost annihilated their army.
Rantzau with most of his officers were captured, 6000
men made prisoners, and all the baggage and artillery fell
into the hands of the conquerors.

Although the danger which threatened Bavaria and
Austria was arrested by this signal victory, yet the intrigues
of France excited a new enemy on the side of Hungary,
by gaining Ragotsky †, prince of Transylvania, and obtain-

---

* This extraordinary man, to recover possession of his dominions
had duped even the jealousy of Richelieu, by a feigned treaty ; and
after passing the winter at the French court, had equally surprised his
friends and enemies, by joining the Spaniards in the Low Countries.
After assisting in the operations of one campaign in that country, he
again made Germany the scene of his exploits.

† On the death of Bethlehem Gabor, Ferdinand II. attempting to

ing a promise of support from the Turks. Ragotsky declared against the emperor in the spring of 1644, at the very moment when the French army was expected to appear on the frontier of Austria. He took Cassau, Neusohl, Chemnitz, and other places ; and, with a predatory army, which rapidly increased to 60,000 men, advanced as far as Eperies, where he published an incendiary proclamation exciting the Hungarians against their sovereign. As the flower of the imperial forces were employed in the distant war of Jutland, this sudden irruption threatened the most alarming consequences. But Ferdinand met the danger with equal prudence and firmness. He published a dignified answer to the incendiary proclamation ; drew together 10,000 veteran troops, who checked the numerous but lawless hordes of the enemy; he at the same time renewed the truce with the Turks for twenty years ; and the prince of Transylvania, disappointed of the expected assistance from France and the Porte, fell back towards his own frontiers.

The emperor had scarcely escaped from these dangers before he was threatened with new perils from the attacks of the Swedes. At the commencement of the year, Gallas had rapidly advanced to the assistance of the king of Denmark, left Hatsfeldt * with a strong detachment to join the

re-annex Transylvania to Hungary, in conformity with ancient compacts, the natives opposed this incorporation, and were supported by the Turks. They first assigned the government to Catherine of Brandenburgh, widow of their deceased sovereign, and afterwards to his brother-in-law Stephen Bethlehem ; but as neither possessed sufficient influence to govern so turbulent a people, they elected George Ragotsky, a native noble, cousin of Bethlehem Gabor, and one of the most distinguished generals of Sigismond Ragotsky, who had for a short time (1630) possessed this precarious dignity, before the election of Bethlehem Gabor. Ferdinand opposed the election of Ragotsky, and sent the palatine Esterhasy with a corps of troops to awe the natives; but the new prince being supported by a body of Turks, Ferdinand, who was then embarrassed by the attack of Gustavus Adolphus, withdrew from a fruitless contest, acknowledged Ragotsky as sovereign of Transylvania, and deemed himself fortunate in recovering the seven provinces of Hungary, formerly ceded to Bethlehem Gabor, with most of the fortresses, except Mongatch. — Benko, lib. iv. ch. 4. ; Windisch, p. 408. 414.

* On the disgrace of Gallas, Hatsfeldt and Piccolomini again entered the imperial service.

archbishop of Bremen against a Swedish corps under Koningsmark, united with a Danish force in Holstein, and hoped to shut up the Swedes in the narrow bounds of the Cimbric peninsula. But Torstenson anticipated his design by occupying the pass of Rendsburgh, drove him beyond the frontier of Holstein, where he was abandoned by the Danes, compelled him to fall back to Magdeburgh, and though he was joined by the Saxons, reduced him to the most deplorable distress. Leaving Koningsmark to complete the reduction of these harassed and discouraged troops, who had taken refuge at Yutterbuck, he pushed forward to the defenceless frontier of Bohemia ; and Gallas, reduced to desperation, was totally defeated on the 23rd of November, 1644, in an attempt to cut his way through the enemy.

While this remnant of the imperial army was dissipated at Yutterbuck, Torstenson seized Preisnitz, and advanced into Bohemia. His approach spread universal alarm ; the emperor and the archduke Leopold hastened to Prague, to make preparations for resisting the progress of the invaders ; Gallas was dismissed, the fugitives collected ; a succour of 4000 men obtained from the elector of Bavaria ; different bodies drawn together under Montecuculi, Goertz, and other generals, and the command intrusted to Hatsfeldt, who took post between Budweiss and Tabor. After various feints and marches the two armies came to an engagement at Yankovitz, on the 16th of March, 1645, in which, notwithstanding the utmost efforts of valour and skill, the imperialists were again defeated with the loss of 8000 men, their commander captured, and many of their principal officers killed or made prisoners. The hereditary countries were laid open to the conqueror ; Leipnitz, Pilgram, Iglau, were reduced ; Moravia submitted, the Swedes secured the command of the Danube by the capture of Crems, Stein, Thiernstein, and Korn Neuberg, and even obtained possession of the works which covered the head of the bridge at Vienna. The emperor, who had hastened from Prague to defend his capital, retired to Ratisbon ; the empress, with the principal nobles, took refuge at Gratz, and preparations were made at Vienna for withstanding a siege, and defending the last bulwark of the Austrian empire, in the safety of which, as at the accession of Ferdinand II., the very existence of the family was involved. To add to the distresses, Ragotsky again burst into the northern part of Hungary at the head of 25,000 men, sent his son with 8000 to Brunn, which Torstenson was besieging ; and detached 6000 to join a corps under the Swedish general Douglas, which spread such an alarm to Presburgh, that the sacred crown and regalia were removed.

While the emperor was thus pressed by an enemy in sight of his capital, his allies were reduced to desert his unfortunate cause. Koningsmark, after dispersing the army under Gallas, captured Bremen and Verden, Leipsic, Torgau, and Meissen; forced the elector of Saxony to consent to a suspension of arms, which finally terminated in a peace; and hastened to rejoin Torstenson in the heart of Moravia. The defection of Saxony was accompanied by that of the Danes, who had shared the misfortunes of the preceding campaign. In addition to repeated defeats by land, their navy had been routed in an action between the isles of Aland and Femeren, and Christian, on the 13th of August, 1645, was reduced to sign a peace dictated by Sweden under the mediation of France. In return for the restoration of his dominions, he abandoned the alliance with Austria, left Bremen and Verden in the possession of the Swedes, ceded to them the isles of Oesel and Gothland, and pledged the province of East Gothland for thirty years. The emperor found also a new enemy in the elector of Treves. Liberated for the purpose of attending the congresses opened at Osnaburgh and Munster, he had no sooner recovered his freedom than he renounced a treaty which he had signed from compulsion, was restored by the French army to his see and dominions; and thus the power and influence of France were extended along the banks of the Rhine, from the Alps almost to the frontier of the United Provinces.

The elector of Bavaria, the brother and most powerful ally of the emperor, was doomed to share his misfortunes. After the defeat of Duttlingen, the French army had in vain risked an engagement for the recovery of Friburgh, which was captured by Mercy, and had suffered a considerable check at Mariendahl the ensuing spring. But the

activity of the French court soon retrieved this disgrace.
Turenne being joined at Spire by the duke of Enghien
with 6000 men, their united troops advanced towards
Feuchtwang, where Mercy was posted. The movements
of the French generals brought on another battle in the
vicinity of Nordlingen, on the 3rd of August, 1648; both
parties suffered nearly equal loss; but the fortune of the
day was turned against the Bavarians by the death of
Mercy, who was killed by a musket shot. John de Wert,
on whom the command devolved, retreated beyond the
Danube; Nordlingen, with the neighbouring places, surrendered, and the Bavarian frontier was laid open to the
victorious enemy.

Ferdinand met his accumulated calamities with a magnanimity equal to his father. On the fatal battle of Yankovitz, the archduke Leopold and Gallas, the recollection
of whose misfortunes was lost in those of his successors,
collected the scattered remnant of the army, raised new
levies, and assembled a sufficient force to restrain the incursions of the Swedes to the northern bank of the Danube.
Ferdinand also lessened the number of his enemies by
taking advantage of the bickerings between Ragotsky and
the Swedish commander, and, after a short negotiation,
purchased an accommodation with Ragotsky, by yielding to
him the temporary possession of the provinces which Bethlehem Gabor had held in Hungary, and the fortresses of
Tokay and Regetz.*

This peace produced an instant change in the desperate
fortune of the emperor. He drew a part of his forces from
Hungary, and repaid the service rendered by the elector of
Bavaria, after the battle of Yutterbuck. The archduke
Leopold and Gallas led a strong corps of cavalry into Bavaria, joined de Wert, drove the French under the cannon
of Philipsburgh, and assisted in recovering the places captured after the action at Nordlingen. The Bavarians were
quartered in Suabia to cover their own country; and the
archduke returned into Bohemia to resume his operations
against the Swedes, who during these events had been

* These provinces were Zatmar, Zabatsch, Ugots, Bereg, Zemplin,
Bervel, and Abaiwar; Benko, vol. i. p. 276.; Windisch, p. 413.;
Novotny, p. 209.; Palma Notitia Rerum Hungar. v. iii. p. 174.

wasting their principal efforts against Brunn, but had extended their ravages over the whole country beyond the Danube. The troops drawn from Hungary, the new levies, and the assistance of the Bavarians, enabled the archduke to resume offensive operations with superior force. He drove Torstenson back into Bohemia, where the Swedish general quitted the service, and was succeeded by Wrangel, who had likewise been bred in the school of Gustavus.

The new commander, unable to maintain himself against the increasing force and energy of his antagonist, retreated in the commencement of 1646, from Bohemia through Misnia and Thuringia, towards Hesse, to save his harassed army by a junction with the French. Turenne was to have crossed the Rhine to his support at Baccharac; but some delays intervening, the Austrians, who closely followed the Swedes, united with the Bavarians, placed themselves between the two armies, and hoped to overwhelm them separately. Wrangel, however, disconcerted their design by occupying the strong post at Ameniburgh, where he resisted all their attacks, till the resources and promptitude of Turenne again diverted the war from the frontier of France. He deceived the imperialists, by directing his course towards the United Provinces, crossed the Rhine at Wesel on bridges prepared by the prince of Orange, and then turning towards the Maine, effected a junction with the Swedes at Giessen. Thier united forces reached the Maine by a masterly march, before the imperialists were prepared to obstruct their passage; captured Aschaffenburgh; crossed the Neckar in sight of the archduke; took Schorndorf, Dunkesbuhl, and Nordlingen; traversed the Danube and the Leck, reduced Rain, laid siege to Augsburgh, and forced the elector of Bavaria himself to take refuge at Branau.

Though astounded by the wonderful boldness and rapidity of this expedition, the archduke displayed skill and resources which proved him worthy of his great antagonists. He advanced by Wurtsburgh and Bamberg, through the Upper Palatinate, towards Ratisbon, drew reinforcements from Austria and Bohemia, crossed the Danube at Straubingen, and approached the Leck. He speedily raised the siege of Augsburgh, kept the enemy in check till the close of the campaign, and forced them to take up winter quarters in the vicinity of the lake of Constance.

Although the archduke had delivered the Bavarian territories, the elector, wearied with the continuance of hostilities, and afflicted with the devastation of his country, prevailed on the emperor to open negotiations, at least for the conclusion of a temporary armistice. A congress was accordingly formed at Ulm, by the Imperial, Swedish, and Bavarian plenipotentiaries. As the unexpected conclusion of a peace between Spain and the United Provinces, on the 19th of March, 1647, rendered it necessary for France to turn a greater part of her force to the side of the Netherlands, she omitted no lure to conciliate the elector, and at length obtained his signature to a separate armistice. He yielded to the Swedes, Memmingen and Uberlingen; to the French, Heilbron, Lawingen, Gundelfingen, and Hochstedt, and in return received Donawerth, Rain, and the other places which had been occupied by the enemy. This accommodation was followed by the separation of the confederates. A few days after the signature, the French under Turenne took the route towards the Low Countries, and in their way reducing the landgrave of Hesse Darmstadt, detached the only remaining ally of the emperor. At the same time the Swedes, disappointed in their hopes of making Bavaria again the scene of war and plunder, turned, in July, 1647, towards the Maine, took Schweinfurth, and, directing their march to Bohemia, reduced Egra.

The emperor, so unexpectedly abandoned by his allies, called forth all his resources. He himself superintended the new levies, and as many of his best generals were either captured or had fallen in the contest, and others were employed in distant quarters, he intrusted the command to Melander, a Calvinist, who from disgust had quitted the service of Hesse. The new general hastened to relieve Egra; but arrived only to witness its capture. To appease the discontents in the army which arose from the religion of the general, the emperor himself assumed the command, and took post near the Swedes. The vicinity of the two armies produced continual skirmishes, and Ferdinand himself was in the utmost danger of being surprised by a detachment, which penetrating by night into his camp, killed the sentinels at the door of his tent. He succeeded, however, in keeping the enemy in check till the return of Bavaria to his alliance afforded him the means of resuming offensive operations.

On the defection of the elector, Ferdinand attempted to seduce his army from their allegiance; he claimed their services as troops of the empire, and gained John de Wert, with the principal generals, who were dissatisfied with the conclusion of the armistice. The elector discovered the plot, and forced de Wert to take refuge under the Austrian protection. But he had little reason to congratulate himself on his neutrality; for instead of accelerating, it retarded a peace, by inducing the French to rise in their demands, and encouraging the Swedes to insist on the entire restitution of the palatine dominions, as well as the electorate. He therefore overlooked the affront which had been offered to him by the emperor, and broke the armistice with the same precipitation as he had concluded it. In September, he published a manifesto against the Swedes, renewed his connection with the emperor by the treaty of Passau, sent a part of his troops to assist the imperialists, and despatched the remainder to recover the fortresses which had been yielded to the Swedes. The consequences of this change were as important as instantaneous. Wrangel, in danger of being overwhelmed by superior numbers, retreated with precipitation from Bohemia to effect a junction with Koningsmark, the French, and Hessians. He was followed by Melander, who, after harassing his retreat as far as Weimar, was induced to ravage Hesse, either from personal revenge, or at the instigation of the elector of Bavaria, and thus gave him an opportunity to save his army, and take quarters in Brunswick and Luneburgh.

During these events the emperor had availed himself of the temporary expulsion of the Swedes from Bohemia, to declare his son Ferdinand successor to the crown, and readily obtained the confirmation of the states. In 1647, he made a similar application to the diet of Hungary; conciliated the Protestants by removing the restrictions laid on their worship, restoring ninety of their churches, and restraining, by the strictest penalties, the insults or persecutions of the zealous Catholics. By these prudent concessions he secured the elevation of the young prince, who was crowned on the 16th of July, at Presburgh, in opposition to all the intrigues of Ragotsky, and even while a foreign army was hovering on the frontiers.

On the return of spring, Wrangel and Turenne rejoined and directed their march towards the Danube, behind which the imperialists under Melander were posted. In May, 1647, they passed at Lawenburgh, pursued Melander, who retired towards the Leck, and attacked him in his march near Sustmarshausen. The imperialists were defeated, Melander himself was killed, and the total ruin of the army was only prevented by the skill of Montecuculi, and the courage of Ulric duke of Wirtemberg, who with a part of the cavalry covered the retreat. The victors gained the passage of the Leck, drove the imperialists successively beyond the Iser and the Inn, spread themselves over the whole country, levying contributions on every side, and would have carried the war into Bohemia, had they not been checked by an inundation of the Inn. The delay occasioned by this accident enabled Piccolomini, who was called to the command, to draw reinforcements from Austria and Bohemia, to enter Bavaria with an army of 22,000 men, and again to drive the confederates beyond the Danube. On the close of the season, Turenne took up quarters on the Neckar and the Maine, and the Swedes in the neighbouring parts of Franconia.

Though this success diverted the imminent danger which threatened Bavaria and Austria, the cause of the emperor was far from being prosperous in other quarters. The imperial general Lamboy, who headed the troops in the electorate of Cologne, was defeated by the Hessians and Swedes under Koningsmark, with the loss of 5000 men; at the same time Wirtemberg, who commanded another Swedish corps, levied heavy contributions in Silesia, and not only maintained himself against all the efforts of Montecuculi, but repeatedly reinforced the garrison of Olmutz, and even pushed his parties as far as the frontier of Austria.

But an enterprise, equally brilliant and decisive, was the surprise of Prague by Koningsmark, who in the preceding campaigns had given various proofs of his talents for desultory warfare. During the campaign in Bavaria, he was detached by Wrangel to make a diversion in Bohemia, which, by the march of reinforcements to Piccolomini, was left almost defenceless. From the information of an officer, named Ottoalsky, who had recently quitted the imperial service, he formed the design of surprising the Bohemian capital. Having industriously spread reports of his intention to attack Pilsen, he pushed forwards a corps of 1200 cavalry, accompanied by Ottoalsky, which took possession of Rakonitz, and blocked up all the avenues to Prague. Koningsmark following with the remainder of his forces, left his artillery and baggage at Rakonitz, mounted his infantry on horses which he collected in the vicinity, and reached the neighbourhood of Prague in the evening of July 26. 1648. Concealing his troops in a wood till the advance of night, he approached the walls unobserved, near the gate of Strohof : his dispositions were already made for the attack ; an hundred musketeers followed by thirty pioneers, formed the vanguard ; these were supported by two hundred select troops, and the march was closed by the rest of the infantry and the cavalry. As he drew near the wall, he heard the cries of the patrol, and the bells of a neighbouring convent. Struck with these signals of apparent alarm, he suspected that his design was discovered, and was on the point of ordering a retreat ; but was prevented by the declaration of Ottoalsky, that the sounding of the bells was only the usual call to matins. He suffered the patrol to finish its round, and then gave the signal for the attack. The troops led by Ottoalsky mounted the wall, killed the sentinel, rushed to the neighbouring gate, put the guard to the sword, lowered the drawbridge to admit the cavalry, and the Little Town was in the possession of the Swedes before the citizens suspected the approach of an enemy. Koningsmark instantly occupied the bridge which connects the Little with the Old Town, and seized a tower at its further extremity ; but as the alarm was already given, and as the garrison of the Old Town consisted of 800 men, with 10,000 armed burghers, he did not venture to risk the loss of the advantage he had already gained, but made himself master of the citadel and arsenal, which were both in the Little Town.

Fortunately the active and intrepid count Colloredo, commandant of Prague, made his escape during the tumult of the assault, and crossed the Moldau to the Old Town. He disciplined the burghers, who assembled on the first alarm, secured the principal avenues, and recalled 2000 men who had recently marched to Glatz. Though provided with only two small pieces of artillery, and reduced to strip an armourer's shop to arm the burghers and students, he resisted all the attacks of the Swedes. The danger was increased by the arrival of Wirtemberg, the Swedish general from Silesia, with a considerable force and artillery, who taking post on the Ziskaberg, on the 4th of August, opened five batteries, mounted with forty pieces of cannon, against the New Town. The two pieces of the garrison were soon silenced; but the great superiority of the enemy served only to stimulate the burghers to new exertions; they maintained their posts, though armed only with muskets, spits, and flails, and successfully repulsed repeated assaults of the besiegers.

As the cavalry suffered for want of forage, a single regiment was left in the town, and Buckheim led the remainder towards Budweiss, to form a junction with a corps of troops collected under general Goltsch, to introduce reinforcements and supplies. Wirtemberg, following the imperialists, defeated them near the castle of Hlubocka; and, after wasting the circles of Bechin and Prachin, returned to resume the operations of the siege. Fortunately in this interval, Conti, an experienced engineer, had repaired to the place, and under his skilful direction a new wall, with additional bastions, was raised on the side of the New Town, and the deficiency of artillery supplied by the construction of mines. At the same time provisions and forage were procured by the activity of Goltsch, and the town was placed in a far better state of defence than at the commencement of the siege.

This change induced Wirtemberg to suspend his attacks until the arrival of Charles Gustavus*, prince palatine of Deux Ponts, who had been appointed generalissimo of the

---

* Son of John, duke of Deux Ponts, by Catherine, sister of Gustavus Adolphus, and afterwards, on the abdication of Christina, king of Sweden.

Swedish army, and brought a reinforcement of 10,000 men. The siege was renewed, and the attacks were pressed on both sides of the city with redoubled vigour; batteries were opened on every point which commanded the place ; in a few days numerous breaches were made sufficiently large to admit a waggon, and the artillery was advanced within pistol shot of the walls. The resources of Conti appeared to augment with the danger, and he brought into activity the means which he had before devised for opposing the attacks of the enemy ; they were entangled with harrows and crows' feet in the ditches ; wherever they advanced, the intrenchments seemed to multiply behind the breaches, and they had no sooner effected a lodgment than it was blown up with mines. The inhabitants, under the guidance of their skilful chief, emulated the deeds of their ancestors, and compensated for their rebellion, at the commencement of the war, by their bravery and loyalty at its close. Amidst the general display of personal valour, the students distinguished themselves by acts of heroism ; and even the very monks, forming themselves into companies, exchanged the cross for the sword. Repeated summons being rejected, the Swedes concentrated their whole force, and made a desperate effort to carry the place by storm. Their mines having cleared the breaches, 4000 men steadily advanced to the assault, but had no sooner gained the wall, and were pressing forwards, than a mine was sprung, which swallowed up 500 ; they were attacked in the midst of their confusion and dismay, and, after a contest of five hours, the remnant were with difficulty disengaged by a body of reserve. Such was the dread inspired by the desperate valour of the besieged, that the assailants made only another feeble effort, and, on the approach of succours under Goltsch, raised the siege ; the prince Palatine and Wirtemberg took the route of Brandeiss, and Koningsmark was left with his troops and artillery to maintain possession of the Little Town.

This was the last event of this memorable, long, and bloody war, for, on the following day, October 25th, the inhabitants of Prague received the joyful intelligence of the signature of the armistice, which soon after gave peace to Germany.

The emperor rewarded the bravery and loyalty of the burghers, by raising many of those who had distinguished themselves to the rank of knighthood, by conferring numerous privileges on the town, and by commanding, under severe penalties, that all memory of their former disobedience should be buried in oblivion.

Chap. LIX.—1637–1648.

For the sake of maintaining a due connection, we have hitherto carried on the account of the military operations in a continued narrative; we now trace the progress of the negotiations.

Sensible that the separation of France from Sweden was the only means of procuring more advantageous terms of peace, the emperor and Spain exerted all their address to divide the two allies; and for that purpose proposed separate congresses, of which the proceedings were to be entirely distinct; and appointed, as the places of meeting, Cologne and Hamburgh, which, from their distance, rendered a reciprocal communication slow and difficult. This artifice was too palpable to escape the penetration of the French and Swedish ministry; and as the means of maintaining their union, and securing the advantages for which they had prosecuted the war, France, in 1638, sent ambassadors to Hamburgh, where the Swedish and imperial plenipotentiaries were assembled. The two powers renewed their alliance, and entered into an engagement not to conclude a separate accommodation. But as it was necessary that two places should be appointed for the negotiation, as well to save the honour of the pope, who was one of the mediators, as to prevent disputes between the Catholics and Protestants, the diet of Ratisbon, at the instigation of France, selected Munster and Osnaburgh, which, from their position and contiguity, were not liable to the same objection as Cologne and Hamburgh.

Ferdinand having reluctantly consented to this arrangement, his ambassador at Hamburgh concluded with the French and Swedish plenipotentiaries, under the name of preliminaries, a convention for settling the ceremonial and proceedings of the congresses. Munster was to be the place of negotiation for the empire, Spain, France, and the Catholics, under the mediation of the pope; Osnaburgh, for the empire, Sweden, and the Protestants, under the mediation of the king of Denmark ; and all the princes of Germany, as allies of France and Sweden, were to be admitted. The two congresses were considered as one, and a free communication was to be maintained between the two towns, which were left under the guard of their own magistrates and burghers, and freed from their allegiance to the emperor and empire. Finally, the congresses were to be opened on the 26th of March, 1642.

These conditions, though concluded by the imperial ambassador, and sanctioned by a recess of the diet, were far from being agreeable to Ferdinand. He saw his design of separating France and Sweden by a feigned negotiation disappointed, and he deeply felt the mortification of being reduced to admit the refractory princes to the congress, and a share in the peace. He therefore disavowed his ambassador, and rejected the convention as equally dishonourable to himself and to the empire. A new ambassador sent to Hamburgh to obtain a modification of these conditions, was not received by the two powers; and the emperor temporised till the unfortunate battle of Brietenfeld reduced him to accept the terms which he had before rejected, and to consent that the 11th of June, 1643, should be fixed for the opening of the congress. Still, however, his hopes of more favourable events, the aversion of Spain to enter into negotiation, and above all the deaths of Richelieu and Louis XIII., delayed the intended meeting till September ; and the French ministers did not make their appearance till the following spring.

Never did Europe witness such an era in politics as this celebrated congress, whether we consider the constellation of diplomatic talents which shone on this occasion, the importance of the different interests, and the parties concerned, which, except England, comprised all the great, and almost all the minor powers of Europe. In this assembly were represented the emperor and empire, separately and collectively; Spain, France, and Sweden; the new king of Portugal, and the new republic of the United Provinces; Savoy, Tuscany, Loraine, Mantua, and the Swiss Cantons, besides the pope, the king of Denmark, and Venice, as mediators.

Excessive demands on one side, and on the other the disinclination of Spain to peace, and the hopes of the emperor, that by the prosecution of hostilities he should obtain more favourable terms, retarded, or reduced the proceedings of the congress to mere disputes on forms and etiquette. At length the series of disasters, which commenced with the unfortunate battle of Jankovitz, induced him to negotiate with earnestness and sincerity. In June, 1645, the ministers at length commenced their operations by delivering specific propositions. But the demands of France, Sweden, and their allies, were so exorbitant, and the pretensions of the Catholics and Protestants so contradictory, that, during the two following years, the negotiation varied with the fluctuations of the war.

While the congress was employed in these discussions, Spain was visited with new disasters. The duke of Modena withdrew from her alliance, and two revolutions in Naples, the first under the fisherman Massaniello, the second under the romantic duke of Guise, threatened the loss of her power in Italy. Deeming it therefore impossible to maintain the contest at once against all his enemies, Philip opened a separate negotiation with the United Provinces, alarmed them with a proposal of ceding the Netherlands to France, lured them with commercial privileges, and gained the prince of Orange with the offer of territorial acquisition. A peace was accordingly concluded, on the 30th of June, 1648, by which Spain acknowledged the independence of the new republic, permitted the states to retain their conquests in the Netherlands, with their colonial acquisitions, acquiesced in shutting up the navigation of the Scheld, and conceded several commercial privileges in the trade of the East and West Indies.*

* Among the commercial stipulations of this treaty was the following clause : — " The Spaniards shall keep the navigation to the East Indies in the same manner as they hold it at present, without being

This treaty would have probably encouraged the emperor to prolong hostilities, with the hopes of being assisted by the forces of Spain, had not the events of the ensuing year effected a change in the sentiments of all parties. The firmness of Ferdinand was shaken by the incursions of the Swedes into the hereditary countries, the devastations of Turenne and Wrangel, and the spirit of revolt which again made its appearance in Austria. The Catholic states of Germany were exhausted of men and money, and anxious to deliver their territories from the exactions of the imperial troops their protectors, as well as of their enemies the Swedes. An unfortunate campaign exposed them to ruin; if the emperor's arms should again prove successful, they dreaded lest the destruction of the Protestant liberties should be followed by the extinction of their own; and therefore were anxious for the termination of so long and ruinous a war. Nor were the Swedes less desirous to procure a peace: their finances were exhausted, and their armies dwindled to a few native regiments; while the far greater part of their forces under their standards were Germans, connected by no ties but those of discipline, and ready to desert on the smallest reverse. Even France herself was interested to hasten the conclusion of hostilities. The evils of a minority began to

---

at liberty to extend it further; as also, the inhabitants of these Low Countries shall abstain from frequenting the places which the Castilians possess in the East Indies." This clause afterwards gave birth to incessant disputes between Charles VI., as sovereign of the Netherlands, and the maritime powers. Charles having, in 1722, erected a company at Ostend, for the purpose of carrying on a direct trade to the East Indies, this establishment was opposed by the United Provinces, as trenching on the articles of this treaty, and by both the maritime powers, as an infringement of the barrier treaty, which confirmed that of Munster. The Dutch contending, according to the spirit of the treaty, that the stipulation, relative to the East Indies, interdicted all commerce from the Low Countries with that quarter of the world; the court of Vienna, according to the letter, urging that this stipulation regarded only the Spaniards. It must be confessed that the former interpretation is the most reasonable and just; because throughout the king of Spain is engaged as sovereign of the Netherlands; and because, at the conclusion of this treaty, it was impossible to provide for a case which could not be foreseen, the separation of the Netherlands from the crown of Spain.

be felt ; the flame of civil discord had already burst forth ; the war with Spain still continued, and the peace which the court of Madrid had just concluded with the United Provinces, rendered an accession of force indispensably necessary to maintain the advantages already gained on the side of the Low Countries.

All parties being influenced by these motives, the emperor resisted the solicitations of Spain to continue the war ; France and Sweden relaxed in their demands ; and the terms of peace were finally signed at Osnaburgh, on the 6th of August, 1648, and at Munster on the 8th of September.

The emperor and empire renounced all claims to the bishoprics of Metz, Toul, and Verdun, which France had appropriated in 1552, reserving the metropolitan rights of the elector of Treves ; and also to the city of Pignerol, which the duke of Savoy had yielded in 1632 by the treaty of St. Germain. The emperor, in his own name, and in behalf of his family and the empire, ceded the full sovereignty of Upper and Lower Alsace, with the prefecture of Haguenau, or the ten towns*, and their dependencies. But by one of those contradictions, which are common in treaties, when both parties wish to preserve their respective claims, another article was introduced, binding the king of France to leave the ecclesiastics and immediate nobility of those provinces, in the immediacy which they had hitherto possessed with regard to the Roman empire, and not to pretend to *any sovereignty* over them, but to remain content with such rights as belonged to the house of Austria. Yet this was again contradicted by a declaration, that this exception should not derogate from the supreme sovereignty before yielded to the king of France. As the means of securing the advantages derived from these acquisitions, France obtained the introduction of a clause, that no fort should be raised on the German banks of the Rhine, from Basle to Philipsburgh.

In return for this cession in Alsace, which belonged to

* Haguenau, Schelestadt, Weissemburgh, Colmar, Landau, Oberenheim, Rosheim, Munster in the Val de St. Gregoire, Kaiserberg, and Turingheim.

the archduke Ferdinand, France promised him a compensation of 3,000,000 livres.

Sweden acquired Upper Pomerania, and the isle of Rugen with Stettin, Gartz, Damme, Golnau, the isle of Wollin, Peine, Schweine, and Divenau, in Lower Pomerania; Wismar in the duchy of Mecklenburgh; the archbishopric of Bremen secularised and converted into a duchy; the bishopric of Verden converted into a principality; the whole to be held as a fief of the empire, with three deliberative voices in the diet. In failure of issue male to the house of Brandenburgh, all Pomerania was to devolve on the crown of Sweden. As an indemnification for the expense of maintaining an army till the articles of the peace were carried into execution, 5,000,000 crowns were to be levied on the circles of the empire, Austria, Bavaria, and Burgundy excepted.

The elector of Brandenburgh was indemnified for the part of Pomerania ceded to the Swedes, with the archbishopric of Magdeburgh secularised under the title of a duchy, and the bishoprics of Halberstadt, Minden, and Camin as secular principalities, with four voices in the diet.

The house of Brunswick Luneburgh was gratified for the loss of the archbishoprics of Magdeburgh and Bremen, and the bishopric of Halberstadt and Ratzeburgh, to which some of that family had been appointed coadjutors or successors, with the convents of Walkenried and Groningen, and by vesting the succession to the bishopric of Osnaburgh alternately in a Catholic bishop and a younger prince of the house of Hanover.

The dukes of Mecklenburgh received, in return for Wismar, the bishoprics of Schwerin and Ratzeburgh, converted into secular principalities, and two commanderies of the order of St. John, with two voices in the diet.

The Lower Palatinate was restored to Charles Louis, son of the unfortunate elector Palatine, with all his paternal possessions, except the Upper Palatinate, and the county of Cham, which were confirmed to the elector of Bavaria; and an eighth electorate, with the office of great treasurer, was established in his favour. If the Bavarian line became extinct, this new electorate was to be suppressed, and the palatine family restored to the electorate which had been granted to the house of Bavaria, and the possession of the Upper Palatinate and county of Cham.

William, landgrave of Hesse Cassel, obtained the princely abbey of Hirschfeld as a secular domain.*

The other princes and states of the empire, who had been proscribed or troubled in their lawful rights, were restored to all the possessions, rights, and prerogatives which they had enjoyed before the troubles of Bohemia in 1619.

The Helvetic confederacy was exempted from the jurisdiction of the empire.

The affairs of the empire may be subdivided into the two heads of religious and civil regulations.

The religious affairs, which had been the principal cause of the war, were the primary objects of the negotiation, and comprised in the treaty of Osnaburgh alone ; the civil regulations were arranged jointly with France and Sweden, and inserted in both treaties.

In regard to religion, the treaty of Passau, and the religious peace of 1555, were confirmed. The spiritual authority of the pope and the Catholic prelates over the Protestants was suspended till a final accommodation of all disputes should take place, or in other words be abolished. The Calvinists were included in the religious peace under the denomination of " Reformed," which they had assumed, and admitted to the same privileges as the Lutherans. A general equality was to be maintained among the princes and states of the empire, whether Catholics, Lutherans, or Calvinists. The dispute concerning the ecclesiastical reservation was finally settled by the declaration, that all ecclesiastical benefices, mediate or immediate, should remain in or be restored to the same state as on the first of January, 1624, which was termed " the definitive year." But in regard to the dominions of the elector Palatine, the margrave of Baden, and the duke of Wirtemberg,

---

* He was the only prince who acquired any accession of territory, without a particular claim for satisfaction or indemnity. He owed this entirely to the gratitude and support of the Swedes, his father, William V., being the first among the German princes who joined Gustavus Adolphus, and on his death in 1637, his mother continued firm to that alliance during his minority.

1618 was fixed as the definitive year, on account of the changes in civil and ecclesiastical affairs, introduced by the imperialists and Spaniards during their invasion of the palatinate. The article of the ecclesiastical reservation was recapitulated almost in the same words as in the peace of religion, but, instead of being confined to the Catholics, was extended to the members of the Confession of Augsburg ; by the stipulation that, if an incumbent of an ecclesiastical office, whether Catholic or Protestant, should change his religion, he should be considered as having vacated his office, and another person of the same religion be appointed in his place.

All other princes and states, immediate members of the empire, and possessing sovereign power, were allowed to change their religion, or reform the public worship of their dominions, in all cases not limited by the treaty, or by compacts with their subjects. Unfortunately, however, the disputes subsisting among the Protestants occasioned the introduction of a clause to explain this right of reformation, by which a Lutheran or Calvinist prince, possessor of territorial sovereignty, or patron of any church, who should change his religion, or acquire a territory of which the subjects enjoyed the public exercise of a different religion, was allowed to retain preachers for his own residence and court, and permit his subjects to embrace the same persuasion, but was not to make any innovation in the established worship. Although no similar regulation was mentioned, or even necessary in regard to the Catholics, and although this clause is specifically described as a convention between the two Protestant sects, yet the Catholics afterwards availed themselves of this article to arrogate the same privileges as the Lutherans and Calvinists conceded to each other.

The subjects of either church, differing from their lord or sovereign, possessed in the definitive year of ecclesiastical property, or enjoying the free exercise of their religion, were still to retain that property, and enjoy that toleration in perpetuity, or till a final arrangement of religious disputes. Even Catholic subjects of a state which adhered to the confession of Augsburg, or members of the confession of Augsburg, subjects of Catholic states, who did not enjoy the public or private exercise of their worship, in the definitive years, or who, after the peace, should embrace a different religion from their territorial lord, were to be tolerated, and not prevented from performing their devotions in their own houses, or even assisting at the public exercise of their worship, in places where it was tolerated in the vicinity. They were also permitted to provide for the education of their children, either by sending them to foreign schools of their own persuasion, or by entertaining preceptors in their houses; and they were to enjoy the same rights and privileges, personal, civil, and commercial, as their fellow-subjects. But this toleration was in a great degree rendered dependent on the will of the sovereign, by the addition, that all subjects, who in the definitive year did not possess the free exercise of their worship, and should be inclined to change their place of residence, or should be dismissed from their sovereign on the same account, should, in the first case, be allowed five, and in the last three years, to dispose of, or carry away their goods and property.

The point for which the Protestants had long laboured was also terminated in their favour. No decree of the diet was to pass by a majority of suffrages, but by amicable accommodation; first, in all causes of religion, secondly, in all other affairs where the states could not be considered as a single body, and, thirdly, in all cases in which the Catholics and Protestants should divide into two parties. In regard to the mode of voting public impositions, the question was referred to the ensuing diet. Diets of deputation likewise were to be composed of equal numbers of the two religions; and, in extraordinary commissions, the officers or commissaries were to be all Protestants, if the affair concerned the Protestants; all Catholics, if the Catholics; and an equal number of each, if it concerned both religions. Finally, the dignity of the Protestant body was secured by guarantying to their beneficiaries, who were entitled to seats in the diet, or in the college of princes, a peculiar bench between the Catholic ecclesiastics and the secular members, with the distinction of "Postulated" annexed to their respective dignities.

With respect to the Aulic Council and Imperial Chamber, the amendment of the abuses which had been the early and constant theme of complaint among the Protestants, was referred to the ensuing diet; but, in the present instance, a few general regulations were established, tending to secure to the Protestants the impartial administration of justice, and an equal share in those tribunals.

The rights of the pope, in regard to Catholic sees and benefices, were guaranteed; and the privileges of presentation, which belonged to the emperor, were confirmed, both with regard to Catholic and Protestant benefices, with the sole restriction that he was to replace Catholic with Catholic, and Protestant with Protestant ecclesiastics. Finally, all dubious expressions were to be interpreted and decided by a full diet, or settled by amicable accommodation between the states of both persuasions.

As insuperable difficulties occurred, relative to the restoration of Donawerth to its liberties and privileges, the consideration of an affair which so warmly interested both parties was referred to the ensuing diet.*

The civil regulations established and limited the prerogatives of the emperor, as elective head of Germany, and defined the Germanic body as a grand union, combining for common good, and bound by those principles and regulations which constitute the public law of the empire. The electors, princes, and states, were confirmed in all their prerogatives and privileges, particularly the right of suffrage in all deliberations on the affairs of the empire, in framing or interpreting laws, making war or peace, and concluding alliances. In all other respects, each sovereign and state was at liberty to conclude alliances with foreign powers, or perform every act of sovereignty, not contrary to the public law and the interests of the general association. The imperial towns also were to possess the same deliberative voice in the diets of the empire, as in the particular diets of the circles.

Other regulations were proposed, tending to circumscribe the prerogatives of the emperor, and diminish the influence of the house of Austria. These were, to establish regular sessions of the diets; to prevent the election of a king of

* To prevent any further reference on this subject, we shall only observe that Donawerth was never reinstated in its former privileges and liberties, but has continued subject to the house of Bavaria.

the Romans during the life of the emperor, or at least to exclude the family of the reigning sovereign ; to introduce a perpetual capitulation, and to prevent the proscription of any prince or state without the consent of the diet.   But, by the influence of Ferdinand, the decision of these points was referred to future consideration.

Other stipulations, merely temporary, were admitted to hasten the conclusion of hostilities, or promote the execution of the treaties.   The emperor and the empire agreed to grant no succours to Spain in defence of the circle of Burgundy, though its connection with the empire was still to be maintained after the peace.   A similar stipulation was introduced in regard to the duke of Loraine, and it was agreed that the discussion relative to the state of his territories should be referred to arbitrators, or settled in the treaty between France and Spain.   On the same principle, the dukes of Savoy and Modena, and the other allies of France, were not to be exposed to any detriment on the part of the emperor, for the war which they carried on against Spain in Italy.

As the protests of the pope and the king of Spain were foreseen, a particular clause, expressed in the strongest and most precise terms, established these treaties as a perpetual law and pragmatic sanction, and declared null and ineffectual all opposition made by any ecclesiastic or secular prince, either within or without the empire.   Temporary regulations were likewise introduced for securing and accelerating the execution of the treaties, such as making the stipulated restitutions and satisfactions, disbanding the troops, and restoring the captured fortresses ; but of these we spare the reader a minute detail, after the extended account we have given of the essential and permanent articles.

The peace was concluded under the guaranty of all the contracting parties, and by the sole mediation of the republic of Venice ; for that of Denmark had been terminated by the war with Sweden, and the pope, after taking a share in an early stage of the negotiation, had withdrawn his interference, from unwillingness to acquiesce in the secularisation of the ecclesiastical property, and the concessions granted to the Protestants.   The principal contracting parties were allowed to include their allies, if nominated within a certain period, and received by common consent ; and the different powers, specified under the sanction of this article, comprised all the European states, except the pope and the Turkish sultan.

Although compelled to desert Spain by imperious necessity, and to agree to conditions which militated against his rights as emperor, no less than against the interests of his family, Ferdinand displayed the spirit of a sovereign in all cases which regarded his own religious principles, or the government of his hereditary states.   Notwithstanding all the instances of the Swedes, and the solicitations of the Protestant body, he refused to include his rebellious subjects in an unlimited amnesty ; and would not relinquish a tittle of that right which was confirmed to the other princes, of re-establishing his own religion in his own territories, except the concessions which had been already made in the peace of Prague.   He allowed the dukes and princes of Silesia, with the town of Breslau, the same exercise of their religion which they had enjoyed before the war ; and permitted the construction of three Protestant churches, without the towns of Schweidnitz, Jauer, and Glogau.   As to the other Protestant nobles of Silesia and Austria above the Ems, he only agreed not to force them to emigrate, or prevent them from assisting at the exercise of their worship in places beyond the bounds of the Austrian territories.   Those who had emigrated from his dominions, particularly from Bohemia, during the war, were allowed to return, on the condition of submitting to the laws, and conforming to the established rules relative to religion ; and those only were restored to their confiscated property, who had taken up arms since 1630, and were considered and termed, not disobedient subjects, but adherents of France and Sweden.   He also maintained the honour and rights of his family by refusing to admit the ministers of Portugal into the congress, as well as by protesting against the nomination of John king of Portugal in the treaty, and he renewed his declaration, frequently made in the course of the negotiation, that he acknowledged no other king of Portugal than Philip of Spain.

We close our account of the negotiation with a few remarks on this celebrated treaty, which forms an era in the political state of Europe.

The Catholics undoubtedly derived advantages from the restoration of that ecclesiastical property which had been confiscated before 1624, and from the uncontroverted establishment of the ecclesfastical reservation. Their pride was also gratified by the preference given to the Catholic as the dominant religion; by the reference continually made to some future re-union of the church; and by the terms in which the concessions were granted to the Protestants, not as matters of justice and right, but of toleration and favour. Yet, although none lost any portion of their hereditary possessions, the weight of their body, and the power of the church, which formed the bond of their union, were greatly diminished by the extensive secularisation of the ecclesiastical property, most of which was transferred to Protestants.

On the contrary, the Protestants lost little advantage by the arrangement relative to the ecclesiastical reservation, which they had never had power or unanimity to set aside, and which had involved them in continual disputes with the Catholics. They saw their own religion secured from the consequences of apostacy by an insuperable barrier, themselves admitted to an equal share of influence in the tribunals of justice and the diet, and, by uniting in a body, they possessed a legal expedient to deprive their antagonists of the advantage derived from superior numbers. The inclusion of the Calvinists in the peace diminished that fatal jealousy which had so long reigned between the two sects, and, by their consequent union into a compact body, removed that weakness and discordance which had often exposed them to the aggressions of the Catholics. From this time the Protestants, though differing in religious principles, were, as a political body actuated by the same views and guided by the same interests; and the heads of the electoral house of Saxony unanimously chosen their chiefs, instead of fomenting their disputes, were the champions of their cause and the supporters of their interests, though they afterwards became members of the Catholic body.*

* Augustus, elector of Saxony, renounced the Protestant and embraced the Catholic religion, on his elevation to the throne of Poland, in 1697.

By this treaty the king of France was enabled to secure passages into Germany and Italy ; to avail himself of those regulations which rendered the empire an aristocracy, by detaching the minor states from their chief ; and to form, on every occasion, a powerful party against the emperor or the house of Austria. Under the pretext of the joint guaranty, to which he was entitled by this treaty, he found a never-failing excuse for interfering in the affairs of the empire ; he assumed the protection of the weaker states, by affecting to support their liberties ; and seized continual opportunities of increasing that influence, which was already too predominant, and afterwards became fatal to Germany.

The advantages acquired by the Swedes were scarcely less important than those of the French. Though by local position apparently excluded from any share of influence among the civilised states of Europe, they rose to a height of fame far beyond their physical strength or extent of territory, obtained a footing in Germany, which gave them the command of two of its principal rivers, the Elbe and the Oder, and acquired a degree of influence which enabled them frequently to turn the scale in favour either of France or Austria.

As emperor, Ferdinand saw himself stripped of a great part of that authority which he derived from prerogative or prescription, reduced to admit to a share of sovereign power and dignity the states whom preceding emperors had treated as vassals ; and, as head of the house of Austria, he lost, with the important territory of Alsace, his footing beyond the Rhine. By these restrictions and dismemberments he was deprived of that preponderance in Europe which his family, by its own weight, had hitherto maintained over France.

To the empire, as a great political body, this peace can scarcely be considered in any other light than as a fatal blow to its strength and influence. The different states were indeed gratified with an appearance of independence, but purchased this shadow of sovereignty by foregoing the advantages derived from concord and union. The right which they acquired of concluding alliances with other states often rendered them the mere instruments of intrigue in the hands of foreign powers ; and the king of France in particular, by the assistance of the Germans themselves, exerted and extended the ascendency which he had gained by breaking down the barriers of the empire. To a few of the greater states, the peace of Westphalia became the foundation of independence ; but to the smaller it was the ultimate cause of weakness and degradation, and led to the subjugation of most of the imperial towns, once the chief seats of German wealth, prosperity, and commerce.

Chap. LX. — 1648–1657

As the early part of Ferdinand's reign had been devoted to war, the remainder was employed in carrying the peace into execution, and healing the wounds of a long and destructive conflict.

A treaty, comprising such concessions, embracing such great and contradictory interests, trenching on so many deep-rooted prejudices and established regulations, met with almost innumerable obstacles in the execution. Pope Innocent X. annulled it by a formal bull : the king of Spain also protested against the article which bound the empire not to assist the circle of Burgundy, as well as against the cession of Alsace, and the evacuation of the Lower Palatinate, of which he claimed a part, and refused to restore the fortress of Frankendahl. But this opposition produced little effect ; the protest of the pope was invalidated by the stipulation which had been inserted in the treaty by way of precaution, and that of Spain only induced France to suspend the payment of the 3,000,000 livres intended as an equivalent for the cessions in Alsace. The emperor yielded Heilbron as a temporary compensation to the elector Palatine, and afterwards purchased the restoration of Frankendahl by the surrender of Besançon to Spain.

After the exchange of the ratifications, a congress, assembled at Nuremberg, employed two years in settling the mode of making the restitutions, granting compensations, and disbanding the troops; and it was not till the close of 1651, that these tedious arrangements were completed, and the empire relieved from the presence of a foreign army.

This business being terminated, the emperor, in conformity with the stipulations of the treaty, summoned, in 1652, a general diet at Ratisbon, for the purpose of confirming the peace, and deliberating on the propositions left undecided. But the object which he had most at heart, was to obtain the crown of the empire for his son Ferdinand, at a time when intestine troubles prevented France from exerting her usual interference. By the intervention of the Spanish ambassador he wrought on the romantic temper of Christina, queen of Sweden, who, being eager to exchange the cares of royalty for philosophic retirement, and purposing to abjure the Protestant religion, was desirous to conciliate the pope, and acquire the favour of the Catholic princes. Thus relieved from opposition on the part of France, and secure of support from Sweden, he procured a meeting of the electors* at Prague, under the pretence of renewing the union of 1521, and obtained, by lures and promises, their tacit or formal engagement to appoint his son. He prevented the interference of the princes and states, who were eager to share in the election and the arrangement of a permanent capitulation, by alarming the electors for their privileges, and prevailed on them to hold in the following year a separate and private meeting at Augsburg, where, to the astonishment of all, Ferdinand was unanimously chosen king of the Romans. Still, however, anxious not to offend the other members of the diet, he persuaded the electors to request their advice on the subject of the capitulation, and induced them to insert in the preamble the unusual declaration that it was drawn up with the concurrence of the princes and states. All parties being conciliated, the new king of the Romans was, on the 18th of June, 1653, crowned at Ratisbon by the elector of Mentz.

Besides the attainment of this important object, the

---

* As Maximilian, elector of Bavaria, died in 1651, leaving Ferdinand Maria his successor, at the age of sixteen, his representative at this meeting was his mother, Mary Anne, sister of the emperor.

same fortunate concurrence of circumstances favoured the attempts of the emperor to procure the ratification of the peace of Westphalia, without the discussion of the principal points left undecided; and during his whole reign he evaded the establishment of the proposed restrictions on his prerogative, by obtaining the reference of those points to the consideration of subsequent diets. He had also the satisfaction to gain an additional weight in the college of princes, by the admission of eight new members, whom he and his father had created, and who were principally subjects of Austria. He even promulgated, of his own authority, statutes or instructions for the proceedings of the Aulic council and Imperial chamber; and succeeded in enforcing them, notwithstanding the remonstrances of the diet, and the provisions of the peace of Westphalia.

The joy of Ferdinand at securing the reversion of the imperial crown for his son, was of short duration, for, on the 9th of July, 1654, the young prince fell a victim to the small-pox. Nothing now remained for the disconsolate father but to confer the same honours and dignities on his second son Leopold. He accordingly procured the homage of the Austrian states, and the crowns of Hungary and Bohemia, but he failed in his attempts to gain the German electors, because the restoration of internal peace enabled the French court again to interfere with effect in the affairs of the empire.

Ferdinand acquired the confidence of Germany by his firm and moderate conduct, and frustrated all attempts to renew hostilities, which were excited by the discontent and ambition of the powerful princes, or by the mutual jealousy and hatred of the Catholics and Protestants.

The affair of Juliers and Berg, which had been neglected amidst the more weighty concerns of the thirty years' war, had continued in the same state of suspense as during the reign of Matthias. The peace of Westphalia, instead of deciding this difficult point, referred it to a subsequent and particular accommodation; and the business seems to have been tacitly arranged in 1650, when the foreign troops evacuated the fortresses, and the claimants entered quietly into possession of their respective portions. The prince of Neuburgh occupied Juliers, Berg, and Ravenstein; the

elector of Brandenburgh, Cleves, La Mark, and Ravensburgh. Such a divided possession, however, between two
princes, who equally grasped at the whole, could not long
be maintained in tranquillity ; and disputes soon arose
which threatened the peace of the empire. Although it
was a part of the private agreements between the princes
in possession that the affairs of religion should remain in
the same state as in 1612, or before the troubles ; and
although such agreements were ratified by the peace of
Westphalia, the prince of Neuburgh, under the sanction
of that article, which in general fixed 1624 as the definitive
year, endeavoured to restore the Catholic worship in every
place where it had been then exercised. The elector of
Brandenburgh, eagerly seizing a pretext for dispute, stood
forth as the champion of the persecuted Protestants, and
claimed the execution of the private agreements. In June,
1651, he made an irruption into the territory of Berg, and
hoped to be assisted by the United Provinces, France,
Sweden, and the Protestants of the empire, who were interested to maintain the peace of Westphalia. The prince of
Neuburgh, on his part, prepared for resistance, and was assisted by the duke of Loraine, who, expelled from his own
territories, and at the head of a mercenary army, interfered
in every adventure which was likely to produce either
employ or emolument.

A dispute, at so critical a period, called forth the earliest attention of the emperor. Anxious to terminate the
contest before foreign powers could interfere, he sent his
monitory to the elector of Brandenburgh, commanding him
to desist from his aggressions, and refer the cause to the
proper tribunals of the empire. At the same time he
claimed the assistance of the other electors, and found a
ready acquiescence from those of Cologne and Bavaria,
who were swayed by the interests of their religion, and
even from the elector of Saxony, who joined in discoun-
tenancing the conduct of the elector of Brandenburgh.
Fortunately the foreign powers were neither able nor inclined to interfere ; France, embarrassed with civil troubles, was not in a situation to revive a foreign contest ;
Sweden was alienated from the elector of Brandenburgh by
disputes for the possession of Lower Pomerania ; and the

governing party in Holland withheld their assistance. Frederic William, thus deprived of any countenance in the empire, and hopeless of succour from abroad, reluctantly abandoned his hasty enterprise. On the 11th of October, 1651, an accommodation was concluded through the mediatioh of Holland and Cologne, by which former treaties of partition were confirmed, and the Protestants allowed to retain that liberty of conscience which had been secured to them by the private compacts between 1612 and 1647.

Ferdinand had scarcely enjoyed the satisfaction of terminating this contest, before Germany was threatened with new troubles by the attempts of the Swedes to subjugate the imperial city of Bremen. Although the emperor, by a particular decree, confirmed the privileges and independence of Bremen, the Swedes, as possessors of the archbishopric, claimed the sovereignty, and general Koningsmark even obtained possession of the citadel. Ferdinand opposed this violation of the rights belonging to a state of the empire, and the firmness which he displayed finally induced the Swedish government to agree to an accommodation, concluded by the mediation of Holland, on the 4th of December, 1654. The dispute was to continue in suspense till settled by treaty; in the mean time the city was to enjoy its rights, to be protected by Sweden in its commerce and manufactures, but was to do homage to the crown of Sweden in the same manner as to the last archbishop, and the citadel was to remain in possession of the Swedish troops.

By these timely interventions Germany enjoyed a peace of almost seven years, and began to recover from the devastations of the war. But the animosity inspired by the preceding contest did not readily subside, and like a half-extinguished conflagration was no sooner smothered in one place than it burst forth in another.

Christina, the eccentric daughter of Gustavus Adolphus, had scarcely arranged the complicated business of the peace of Westphalia, before she executed her romantic project of abdicating the crown, and was succeeded by her cousin, Charles Gustavus, prince palatine of Deux Ponts. The new sovereign, brought up in arms, inspired by the heroic deeds of his uncle, and impelled by youthful ardour, attacked John Casimir, king of Poland, under pretence of the ancient dispute for the family succession. He found little resistance from the Poles, who were divided by party feuds, and enfeebled by inroads of the Muscovites, and insurrections of the Ukraine Cossacks. Before the close of the year he drove John Casimir into Silesia, received the submission of the principal towns, and of the waivodes or governors of provinces, with the allegiance of the militia, and induced the Lithuanians to accept his protection. He next attacked the elector of Brandenburgh, who, during his invasion, had occupied Royal Prussia, with a view to make a diversion in favour of Poland, routed his troops, and forced him to acknowledge Ducal Prussia as a fief of Sweden, and enter into the war against the Poles. Their armies, however, had scarcely united, before they were called into action by the Polish monarch, who in the interval had recovered possession of Warsaw, by the assistance of the Turkish hordes, and drawn to his standard a considerable number of his volatile subjects. After different combats, which were attended with varied success, the contending parties concentrated their principal force in the vicinity of Warsaw; and a dreadful conflict, which lasted three days, ended in the total rout of the Polish troops.

Ferdinand, however anxious to preserve peace, could not behold with indifference, the alarming progress of the Swedes, which threatened to destroy the balance of power in the north. He demanded succours from the diet of deputation assembled at Frankfort; and, when disappointed in this application, attempted to unite those princes and states who were equally interested to oppose the progress of the Swedes. He stimulated the commercial jealousy of the Dutch, and induced the czar of Muscovy to make an irruption into Ingria and Carelia; he formed an alliance with the Poles, and promised to support them with an army, on condition that they should choose one of his sons on the next vacancy of the throne; he entered into a negotiation with the king of Denmark and the elector of Brandenburgh, and had even arranged an offensive and defensive alliance. But this was the last act of his reign;

for he died on the 3rd of March, 1657, at the very moment when his army was preparing to march, only three days after the signature of the treaty with Poland.

Without those energies of mind, without those splendid talents or striking defects which marked the character of his father, Ferdinand III. was mild, prudent, attentive to the affairs of state, and skilful in conducting them ; and so great a lover of justice, that his own declaration may be with truth applied to him, "During his whole reign no one could reproach him with a single act which he knew to be unjust." He was conversant in various languages, and a lover and patron of the arts and sciences. He was not deficient in military skill, and, from his conduct in the battle of Nordlingen, and his campaign in Bohemia, we may conclude that he would have distinguished himself as a warrior, had he not been kept from the field by the weakness of his constitution, which, at an early period, suffered from the effects of the gout. Though educated by Jesuits, and brought up under the auspices of his bigoted father, he rose superior to that intolerant spirit which gave rise to all the miseries of Germany, and even liberated himself from the trammels which his preceptors usually fixed on the minds of their pupils ; for he took from their society the direction of the Caroline university, and confined them to deliver lectures on philosophy and theology.

Ferdinand III. was thrice married.

His first wife, Marianne, daughter of Philip III., king of Spain, was the princess who makes so conspicuous a figure in English history, as the object of the romantic expedition of Charles I., when prince of Wales, to Madrid. She was equally remarkable for beauty of person and purity of morals, and with less flattery than the compliment is usually applied, is said to have resembled the angelic nature, both in body and mind. She was born in 1606, and died in childbed, in 1646.

2. His second wife, Maria Leopoldina, was still more nearly related to him, being a daughter of his uncle Leopold, of the line of Tyrol. She was married to Ferdinand in 1648, and died likewise in childbed the ensuing year.

3. Maria Eleonora Gonzaga, daughter of Charles of

Nevers, duke of Mantua and Montferrat. She was a princess of great talents and acute understanding ; and, after the death of her husband, possessed considerable influence in the administration of her son-in-law Leopold. She was born in 1630, married in 1651, and died in 1686.

By his first wife Ferdinand had two sons.

1. Ferdinand, who was born in 1633, chosen king of Hungary and Bohemia, and elected king of the Romans, but died in 1654, before his father.

2. Leopold, who succeeded.

By his first wife, Ferdinand had also a daughter, named Maria Josepha, who was born in 1635, and died in 1696. She was first affianced to Balthazar Charles, prince of Spain ; but, on his premature death, espoused his father Philip IV., and brought into the world Charles II., the last sovereign of the Austrian race who filled the Spanish throne, and whose will occasioned the contest for the succession.

By his second wife, Ferdinand had a son, Charles Joseph, who was a prodigy of quick comprehension and acute understanding. He inherited a weak constitution, which he seems to have undermined by intense application, and died at the early age of fifteen. He was bishop of Passau, and grand master of the Teutonic order.

The third wife bore Ferdinand a son, Ferdinand Joseph, and two daughters.

The son was the innocent cause of accelerating his father's death. A fire breaking out in the apartment of the young prince, one of the guards seized the cradle and, in conveying it into the chamber of the emperor, who was then sick, struck it with such violence against the wall, that it was broken in pieces, and the child thrown to the ground. The danger to which the infant was exposed, produced such an effect on the debilitated sovereign, that he died within an hour after the accident. The child escaped unhurt, but expired the following year.

The two daughters were : 1. Eleonora Josepha, who espoused Michael Viesnovitsky, king of Poland ; and, after his death, Charles, duke of Loraine. She died in 1697, and her grandson Francis again united the houses of Loraine and Austria, by his marriage with Maria Theresa.

2. Maria Anna Josepha, who married William Joseph, elector Palatine, of the house of Neuburgh, and died in 1689.

Chap. LXI. — LEOPOLD I.—1657–1660.

Leopold had not attained his eighteenth year when the death of his father called him to the succession of Hungary and Bohemia, and to all the Austrian dominions, except the exterior provinces, and the possessions in Alsace, which had been ceded to France. He was placed under the guardianship of his uncle Leopold; and the first object of the Austrian cabinet was to compose the dissensions of Germany, and secure for their young sovereign the imperial crown, which had been so long worn by his family, that it was considered almost as a prescriptive right.

The attainment of this object was, however, no easy task. France having acquired a predominant influence in Germany by her recent victories, and as guarantee of the peace of Westphalia, Mazarin, the all-powerful minister, exerted all his intrigues to wrest the crown of the empire from the house of Austria, and was joined by Charles Gustavus, who was influenced by personal motives of resentment against Leopold, for taking part in the war of Poland.

Mazarin first attempted to procure for his youthful and ambitious sovereign, Louis XIV., that crown which Francis I. had in vain contested with Charles V., and to revive the empire of Charlemagne in the person of his descendant. He gained the electors of Cologne, Mentz, and Palatine; but he was foiled, no less by the unwillingness of the others to choose a foreign and powerful prince as their chief, than by the secret opposition of the king of Sweden, who, while he openly affected to concur in the views of France, secretly thwarted a design, which was still more fatal to his interests than the elevation of an Austrian prince.

The French minister, unable to realise his own splendid project, next offered the crown to Ferdinand Maria, the young elector of Bavaria, with an annual subsidy of

3,000,000 livres, to support the dignity of his court, and secured the influence of his wife Maria, a princess of Savoy. He found, however, a new obstacle in the refusal of the elector Palatine to vote for a rival, whose father had humbled his family and dismembered its territories, and with whom he was now contesting the vicariate of Germany. Mazarin was still more effectually foiled by the mother of the elector, an Austrian princess, and the Bavarian minister, count Curtz, who prevailed on the young prince himself to reject a temporary and uncertain dignity, and spurn the offer of a pension, which would render him a dependent on France.

After an ineffectual attempt by the king of Sweden to recommend the prince Palatine of Neuburgh, who was rejected for his insignificance, the last resource of the French minister was, to divide the house of Austria, by proffering the crown to the archduke Leopold ; and he obtained from some of the electors a more ready concurrence than he had experienced in his former proposals. But the archduke himself imitated the example of his patriot ancestors, by warmly recommending his nephew to the choice of the electors.

The electoral diet, which was opened in August, 1657, five months after the death of Ferdinand, was attended by the electors of Mentz, Treves, Cologne, Palatine, and Saxony, in person, by deputies from the others, and by ambassadors from France and Sweden. But, as Leopold had not completed his eighteenth year*, the Austrian ministers amused the diet by promoting frivolous discussions, or by caballing with the electors, till he had attained the age which obviated all objections derived from his minority, and permitted him to exercise the vote of Bohemia. During this interval they also strained every nerve to conciliate the majority of the electors. Fortunately their views were promoted by the concurrence of Frederic William, elector of Brandenburgh. That enlightened prince foresaw the ambitious designs of Louis XIV.; he perceived

---

* Though there was no regulation in regard to the age of an emperor, yet eighteen being the period fixed by the Golden Bull for the majority of an elector, objections were made against the election of an emperor under that age.

that the peace of Westphalia had changed the psoition of affairs, and that the house of Austria was no longer the scourge, but the supporter of German independence. Though offended by the refusal of the Austrian court to restore the duchy of Jaegendorf, which Ferdinand II. had wrested from a collateral branch of his family, he sacrificed his private disgust and personal feelings to the permanent interest of the Germanic body. He represented, with manly eloquence, the danger of raising the head of the house of Bourbon, or a petty prince dependent on France, to the vacant throne; and strenuously enforced the necessity of electing a sovereign, whose hereditary dominions would afford the means of maintaining his dignity and resisting the aggressions of France. His opinion weighed with that part of the electoral body which had been lukewarm in the cause of Austria, and the three electors who adhered to France, perceiving all opposition ineffectual, concurred with the majority. Accordingly Leopold was unanimously chosen, and crowned at Frankfort, by the elector of Cologne, on the 31st of July, 1657.

Many difficulties occurred, and much time was employed before the capitulation was arranged. Although it was the longest since that of Charles V., and was swelled to no less than forty-five articles; yet in the grand and principal points relating to the empire, it differed little from those of his predecessors, except in confirming the internal regulations settled by the peace of Westphalia, and in comprising a solemn engagement to preserve the liberties of the ten towns in Alsace, with the prefectural jurisdiction. To all these Leopold submitted without much reluctance; and even consented to a clause which restrained him from assisting Spain in the wars of Italy. But though attempts were made to extend the same restriction to the war of the North, he had influence sufficient to obtain the rejection, and spurned, with becoming dignity, a proposition that, on the breach of this or any of the articles, the emperor should be considered as dethroned. His spirited opposition being seconded by the patriotic members of the empire, who were indignant at this attempt to secure a pretext for reviving the civil troubles of Germany, it was disdainfully rejected.

Though Leopold obtained this triumph over the French and Swedish party, yet all his influence could not prevent the conclusion of a formidable alliance, which greatly weakened his authority in the empire. The three ecclesiastical electors, the bishop of Munster, the count Palatine of Neuburgh, the landgrave of Hesse, and the king of Sweden, as lord of Bremen Verden and Wismar, on the 14th of August, 1658, entered into an alliance, which, from the situation of the contracting parties, was called the league of the Rhine. This league was an offensive and defensive engagement for three years, by which the different powers agreed to maintain a standing army of 10,000 men for mutual protection, if attacked in contravention of the peace of Westphalia, and to prevent the passage of troops through their territories, or the exaction of levies and contributions. The accession of France, which was deferred a single day for the sake of form, extended these stipulations to the circle of Burgundy. Leopold indeed soon found means, by the intervention of the pope, to detach the elector of Treves and the bishop of Munster; but this league prevented him from carrying the war into all the German territories of Sweden, and precluded him, as well as the Catholic states of the empire, from furnishing succours to Spain in the Netherlands. It besides formed the foundation of a systematic combination, which was frequently renewed, and by means of which France extended her influence over all the western states of Germany.

Leopold being precluded from interfering in the war between France and Spain, turned his whole attention to prosecute the contest against Sweden. Soon after his succession he renewed the alliance which his father had concluded with Poland, induced the king of Denmark to declare war against Sweden, and the Dutch to join in the confederacy, and obtained a secret promise from the elector of Brandenburgh to desert his alliance with Charles Gustavus. He sent a corps of 16,000 men, under Hatsfeldt and Montecuculi, from Silesia into Poland, who joining with the Polish forces, took Cracow and Posen, and drove Ragotsky, the ally of Sweden, back into Transylvania. At the same time the king of Denmark occupied Bremen and Verden, and an united English and Dutch squadron blockaded Dantzic, to intercept the only communication which Charles Gustavus maintained with his own dominions.

With their superior forces the emperor and his allies hoped to crush the Swedish monarch before he could escape from Poland ; but their hopes were frustrated by his surprising skill and celerity. Leaving garrisons in the most important posts, he reached the Oder before the elector of Brandenburgh was apprised of his march, passed rapidly through the circle of Lower Saxony, and drove the Danes from Bremen and Verden. Assisted by the city of Hamburgh, and secure of support from his brother-in-law, Frederic duke of Holstein Gottorp*, with whom he had formed a secret alliance, he burst into Holstein, and penetrated without opposition into Jutland. Leaving Wrangel to besiege Fredericsodde†, a strong fortress on the narrow part of the Little Belt, he returned to Pomerania, to su-

* From the mischievous custom of dividing territorial possessions among different branches of the same family, the throne of Denmark had been weakened by the establishment of different collateral lines, which formed as many subordinate sovereignties, dismembered from the duchies of Sleswic and Holstein. The line of Holstein was divided into two branches, royal and ducal. The royal branch was formed by John, second son of Christian III., and his descendants were divided into the lines of Sonderborg, Augustusborg, Beck, Weissenborg, Norborg, Luxborg, and Ploen. The ducal line was formed by Adolphus son of Frederic, the first duke of Holstein and Sleswic, who became king of Denmark on the deposition of his nephew, Christian II. This line possessed several important posts which commanded the eastern part of the duchy of Holstein, namely Kiel, Altenberg, and Cismar on the Baltic, with the isle of Femeren, Neuminster on the Stoer, Bortisholm on the Eyder, Tremsbuttel near the sources of the Trave, and Rembeck near Altona on the Elbe. In the duchy of Sleswic they possessed Sleswic, with the palace of Gottorp, from which they derived their title of Holstein Gottorp, and Tonningen at the mouth of the Eyder. By the position of these places, they maintained a communication both with the German ocean and the Baltic, and separated the Danish dominions in Sleswic and Holstein. Many of their domains were so blended with those of Denmark as to form a mixed jurisdiction. Hitherto the dukes had intermarried with the royal family of Denmark, and preserved their fidelity to that crown, till Charles XI., king of Sweden, in 1654, espoused Eleonora, daughter of the reigning duke Frederic. From this alliance they may be considered as having broken off their natural connection with the crown of Denmark. — Hansen's Schleswic, passim.

† Now called Fredericia.

perintend, as from a central point, his extensive system of operation, and to hasten the equipment of a fleet for conveying his troops across the straits which separate Jutland from the Danish isles. Fredericsodde being soon taken by storm, Czarnesky, who was hastening to Jutland with a corps of 10,000 auxiliary Poles, abandoned his design, and the king of Denmark was exposed alone to all the forces of an active, ambitious, and inveterate enemy.

To preserve their ally, Leopold, with the other members of the confederacy, made astonishing exertions. The states general hastened their succours; the elector of Brandenburgh joined all his forces with those of the confederacy *; the Swedish fleet was shattered, if not defeated, in an engagement with that of the Danes; the czar of Muscovy burst into Livonia, and the garrisons in Poland were successively reduced by the imperial and Polish troops. By another desperate enterprise, however, Charles Gustavus again surmounted the dangers with which he was threatened, and turned the war into the heart of Denmark. He hastened to Jutland, on the 9th of February, 1658, availed himself of a severe frost to transport his army over the Little Belt, between Arroe and Fredericsodde, to the isle of Funen, and defeated a corps of Danes posted to oppose his descent. Having made himself master of the whole island, he drew his troops to the eastern shore in the vicinity of Nyborg. Encouraged by his former success, he effected the still more perilous passage of the Great Belt, by taking a circuitous route over the icy sea, by the isles of Langeland and Falster, and on the 21st of February, reached Wordenborgh in Zealand without opposition.

This astonishing enterprise, which scarcely has a parallel in the annals of history, or even the tales of romance, spread instant terror through the court and kingdom. The hero who had surpassed the barriers of nature, found no obstacle to arrest his progress, and advanced to the very gates of Copenhagen, while a Swedish army invaded the continental province of Scone, Bleckingen, and

---

* The price of his important accession was the independence of Ducal Prussia, which was a fief of Poland, and which he obtained from John Casimir, through the mediation of the Austrian court.

A A 2

Halland. The king of Denmark was reduced to the most deplorable state; without hope of assistance from his allies; shut up in his capital ill-provided for defence; surrounded by treacherous counsellors, and a factious nobility; in the midst of a people agitated with endless feuds, and struck with terror and despondency. Thus circumstanced, he submitted to the terms dictated by the conqueror, under the mediation of France and England, and by a treaty, concluded on the 26th of February, at Roskild, ceded Halland, Scone, and Bleckingen, the isle of Bornholm, the district of Bohus, and the province of Drontheim in Norway. In return for some acquisitions too inconsiderable to deserve mention, he relieved the duke of Holstein Gottorp from his dependence on the crown of Denmark; exempted the Swedish vessels from search, and from the tolls of the Sound and Belt; agreed to shut the Sound against hostile fleets, and to abandon his alliances with the enemies of Sweden. Soon after the signature of this treaty, the Swedes evacuated Falster and Zealand; but retained possession of the other islands, under pretence of securing its fulfilment.

The ministers of Vienna, had deeply felt for the humiliation of a faithful ally, whom they had themselves plunged into such fatal disasters. But doubtful of the empire, and unwilling to irritate the Germanic body by attacking the territories of Sweden, at a time when the elevation of their young sovereign was opposed by such powerful enemies they could only venture to continue the war in Poland as simple auxiliaries of the Poles. They had no sooner secured the imperial crown, than they endeavoured to prevail on Frederic to risk a new war; and they made the most active preparations to assist him by a direct attack, in conjunction with the elector of Brandenburgh, on those German territories of Sweden which were not protected by the Rhenish alliance. The elector, at the head of 7000 of his own troops, 10,000 Austrians, and 6000 Polish cavalry, marched towards Holstein, in September, 1658. After reducing the duke of Holstein, who had joined Sweden in the war, to surrender Gothorp, and withdraw all his troops to Tonningen, he pushed in winter into Jutland, and drove the Swedes into Fredericsodde. Assisted by a Danish squadron, he obtained possession of the isle of Alsen, and would have passed over to Funen or Zealand, had not the advance of the season compelled the Danish admiral to return to Copenhagen ; and the same cause preventing the siege of so strong a fortress as Fredericsodde, he distributed his troops into quarters.

Notwithstanding this prompt and powerful diversion, the king of Denmark was still exposed to dangers, and surrounded by difficulties scarcely inferior to those from which he had recently escaped. Charles Gustavus regained possession of Zealand, captured Kronborgh, and besieged the capital ; while his fleet stationed at the entrance of the Sound, shut up the sea, and blockaded that of the Danes. Frederic defended his capital with a spirit worthy of his exalted station ; and at the moment when he was reduced to the last extremity, a Dutch squadron under admiral Wassenaer, forcing the passage of the Sound, worsted the Swedes, and brought a reinforcement of men, with a supply of provisions. The return of spring would have enabled him to recover possession of his territories, by the assistance of his allies, and preparations were made for transporting the troops from Holstein, when the appearance of an English squadron, sent by Richard Cromwell to the assistance of the Swedes, or rather to dictate peace to both parties, awed the Dutch, and frustrated the intended expedition.

Notwithstanding this unexpected obstacle, the allies, in May, 1659, retook Fredericsodde by storm, and having collected a flotilla of boats and transports, endeavoured to cross the straits which separate Funen from the continent. Failing in this attempt from the spirited resistance of the Swedes, and the loss of their flotilla, which was destroyed by an English squadron, they made a powerful diversion in Pomerania. On one side general Souche, at the head of 10,000 men drawn from Poland, forced the lines of Greiffenhagen, took Damme and Camin, occupied the isle of Wollin, and reduced the whole country east of the Oder. At the same time the imperial general Montecuculi, with a considerable part of the allied forces from Holstein, captured Tribsees Demin and Griefswald, and united with the troops of Souche to besiege Stettin.

Meanwhile the affairs of Denmark assumed a no less favourable aspect. De Ruyter, arriving with a new squadron, and a reinforcement of 4000 troops, effected a junction with Wassenaer. The two powerful fleets of England and Holland, awing the Baltic, affected to act in concert to support the mediation of their respective courts for the conclusion of a peace. France likewise took part in the negotiation, and two conventions were concluded by the mediating powers, conjointly or separately, for maintaining the equilibrium of the North, and accelerating the termination of hostilities. This interference equally displeased the two rival monarchs : Charles Gustavus indignantly repelled their attempts to set bounds to his conquest ; and Frederic was no less averse to accept the dishonourable treaty of Roskild, as the basis of the peace. In this suspense, the English fleet being recalled in consequence of the revolution in England, which restored the long parliament, the Dutch squadron remained master of the Baltic ; and the combined powers were enabled to act directly against the king of Sweden, who had recovered Laland and Falster, and again obtained a footing in the isle of Alsen. Ruyter sailed to Kiel with the 4000 men whom he had brought from Holland, and transported them, with an equal number of the allied and Danish forces, to Funen. They defeated the Swedes posted in the vicinity of Nyborg with great slaughter, and forced the remnant which had retired into Nyborg to surrender at discretion.

Charles Gustavus himself saw, from the top of a tower at Corsoer, in Zealand, this fatal defeat, which in a moment annihilated all his high-flown hopes, and threatened to involve him in a danger greater than any to which he had exposed his antagonist. But the Dutch admiral, true to the policy of his government, which was unwilling to retard the conclusion of peace by giving the preponderance to Denmark, refused to transport the victorious troops to Zealand ; and a part being sent to secure Funen, the rest were re-conveyed to Holstein. In this situation of affairs, Charles Gustavus condescended to accept the mediation of the states general which he had before rejected ; but with a secret resolution to continue the war. He secured the posts which he still held in the Danish isles, and repaired

to Gottenborg, where he assembled the states, and prepared, by an expedition into Norway, to compensate for the
failure of his enterprise against the capital of Denmark ; but
he was hurried to the grave in the midst of his preparations
by a fever, derived from fatigue and chagrin, the result of
his failure, leaving an infant successor, an exhausted kingdom, and a host of enemies.

Encouraged by this event, Frederic made active preparations to prosecute the war with redoubled vigour.   But
the emperor, eager to take advantage of the revolutions in
Transylvania*, was unwilling to continue the contest, and
the other allies were influenced by his example.   The mediating powers, therefore, found no difficulty in effecting a
separate peace between Sweden and Poland, which was
concluded in May, 1660, at Oliva, a convent in the vicinity
of Dantzic.   The allies of Denmark being thus detached,
and their conquests restored, Frederic had no other resource
than to accept the terms dictated by the mediating powers,
and to accede to a treaty, which within the space of a
month was signed at Copenhagen.

By the treaty of Oliva, peace was established between
Denmark and Poland, including the emperor and the
elector of Brandenburgh.   The king of Poland renounced
all right to the crown of Sweden, engaging not to use the
title and arms in his intercourse with the court of Stockholm.   The king and republic of Poland ceded to Sweden
that part of Livonia which is situated on both sides of the
Duna, and which they possessed in 1635, with the isle of
Runen, and the rights of Poland on Esthonia and Oesel.

The emperor and the elector of Brandenburgh gave up
to Sweden all their conquests in Pomerania, Mecklenburgh,
Holstein and Sleswic, and restored the possessions of the
duke of Holstein Gottorp.†   All parties joined in mutual

---

* See chapter lxii.

† Frederic had died at Tonningen in 1659, and was succeeded by
his son Christian Albert.   By the liberation of Sleswic from its feudal
dependence on Denmark, the dukes were still more closely united with
Sweden, by whose assistance they could alone maintain that independence which they had acquired by her support.   Hence they were
always exposed to an attack in case of a war between Denmark and
Sweden, because they either opened their territories to Sweden, or
were invaded by Denmark, to anticipate their enmity.   Hence, like-

securities for the fulfilment of these conditions, and France in particular charged herself with this guaranty, in favour of the kings of Sweden and Poland, and of the elector of Brandenburgh, at their own desire. By a separate article the particular treaties between the elector of Brandenburgh and Poland were confirmed, and the independence of Western or Ducal Prussia established.

The treaty of Roskild was made the basis of that of Copenhagen, the only change being the cession of the right which Sweden possessed to the province of Drontheim. By a separate convention, which was not concluded till 1661, the isle of Bornholm was also assigned to Denmark, and the rights and privileges of Swedish subjects secured to the natives of Scone, Halland, and Bleckingen.

The pacification of the North was preceded by an event of far more consequence to the house of Austria, the peace of the Pyrenees. Since the treaty of Westphalia, hostilities between Spain and France had continued with varied success. Notwithstanding the desertion of the German branch, Spain, favoured by that civil war in France which is distinguished by the whimsical appellation of La Fronde, reconquered Catalonia, and recovered Dunkirk, with many of the French conquests in Flanders. The suppression, however, of civil broils, and the re-establishment of Mazarin's authority, restored the ascendency of France; and Spain unequal to resist alone, was borne down by an attack from Cromwell. The united forces of France and England gave a fatal blow to her declining power. In the West Indies she lost Jamaica; in the Netherlands, her army, scarcely recovered from the bloody conflict of Rocroy, was totally routed in the no less fatal battle of the Dunes; Dunkirk was surrendered to England; Dixmude, Gravelines and Ypres to France ; the same misfortunes attended her affairs in Italy ; and in Portugal, defeats heaped on defeats completed the establishment of the rival monarchy.

The haughty spirit of the Spanish monarch bent under these disasters. But his repeated proposals of accommodation were frustrated by the refusal of France to conclude

wise, their interests were warmly espoused in every negotiation by Sweden, and their territories, if conquered, restored by every treaty.

peace, unless the eldest infanta was given in marriage to Louis XIV. As long as Philip was without male issue, he firmly rejected this demand; because with a natural partiality to his own family, he destined his daughter, the apparent heiress of Spain, for his relative Leopold. But increasing difficulties, the birth of a son, and another pregnancy of the queen overcoming his objection, the preliminaries of peace were signed at Paris, on the 7th of November, 1659, and the treaty, with the contract of marriage, concluded in the isle of Pheasants, situated in the river Bidassoa, at the foot of the Pyrenees, by the two prime ministers, cardinal Mazarin and don Louis de Haro.

By this memorable treaty, which laid the foundation of so many future wars, France acquired the whole county of Artois, except St. Omer, and Aire, with the important chain of fortresses stretching almost from the coast of the channel to Luxemburgh. At home, Spain was likewise stripped of Roussillon, and Conflans, with part of the county of Cerdagne, and thus lost her footing beyond the Pyrenees. She also yielded Dunkirk with its dependencies, and Jamaica, to England; confirmed the treaty of Munster, and agreed to restore Juliers, which had been retained since the commencement of the dispute for the succession. In return for all these important concessions, the king of France relinquished his conquests, and engaged to afford no assistance to Portugal. The duke of Loraine was to be re-established in his territories on the condition of dismantling Nancy, and maintaining no army; the dukes of Savoy and Modena were replaced in the same situation as before the war.

This peace was followed by the solemnisation of the marriage between Louis and the infanta, at St. John de Luz, on the 9th of June, 1660, and the ceremony was preceded by a general renunciation made by Louis and his bride to every part of the Spanish succession.

Chap. LXII. — 1660–1664.

Scarcely was tranquillity restored in the South and the North, by the peace of the Pyrenees and Oliva, before a series of revolutions called the attention of Leopold to Transylvania and Hungary, and revived the war with the Turks.

Almost from the beginning of the century, Constantinople had been the scene of incessant commotions ; the turbulent janissaries, like the Pretorian guards of Rome, had alternately raised and deposed their sovereigns, and sultan after sultan had been driven from the throne. At the same time the Turks had waged an unsuccessful war with the Persians and the Poles, and had recently commenced hostilities against the Venetians by the celebrated siege of Candia. These revolutions and contests diverted their force from the Austrian territories, and reduced their efforts to a covert interference in the civil troubles of Hungary and Transylvania, instead of the continual and alarming invasions of preceding times.

In 1648, nine years before the accession of Leopold, Mahomet IV. was raised to the throne in the fifth year of his age. The commencement of his reign was troubled by struggles for power among the women in the harem, which occasioned a civil war between the two great military bodies of janissaries and spahis. After a long and bloody contest, the authority of the sultan was restored by the transcendent talents of the two grand viziers, Mahomet and Achmet Kiupruli, who directed the reins of government. Under their vigorous administration the evils of a minority ceased to be felt ; internal dissensions subsided, the banners of the crescent were unfurled, and the house of Austria was again visited by those dreadful irruptions, which had so often wasted its fairest provinces, and threatened the extinction of its empire.

As soon as they had recovered from the effects of internal troubles, the Turks found a favourable opportunity for interfering in the affairs of Transylvania. George II. had succeeded his father Ragotsky in the principality, with the consent of the states, and the confirmation of the Turks. His administration was splendid and successful both at home and abroad; till excited by a desire to obtain the reversion of the Polish throne, he entered into an alliance with the king of Sweden, and made a predatory irruption into Poland at the head of 25,000 men. On the departure of the king for Holstein, the Transylvanian prince was overwhelmed by the united army of Austrians, Poles, and Tartars, and driven back in disgrace. The Turks, irritated by his irruption into Poland, expelled him as a refractory vassal, and forced the states to elect in his stead two successive princes, Redei and Bartzai, who are only known for their temporary elevation. Ragotsky retiring to his Hungarian territories, collected an army, and after in vain soliciting assistance from Leopold, marched against the Turks. On the 17th of May, 1660, he was killed in a battle near Clausemburgh, in the moment of victory, leaving a widow, and a son, Francis, aged fifteen, who had been appointed his successor, and who was intrusted to the guardianship of John Kemeny, one of his most skilful generals.

By the death of Ragotsky, Bartzai regained possession of his precarious dignity; and the Turks, after placing garrisons in the principal fortresses of Transylvania, laid siege to Great Waradin, and prepared to wrest from the family of Ragotsky those towns in Hungary which they had obtained from the house of Austria. At the request of his partisans, and with the consent of the Hungarian states, Leopold despatched general Souche, with 10,000 men, for the purpose of garrisoning the Hungarian towns, and throwing succours into Great Waradin. By force, or persuasion, the imperial general obtained from the widow possession of Tokay, Zatmar, Erschit, and Onod; but was too late to succour Great Waradin, which in September, 1660, fell into the hands of the Turks.

Meanwhile Transylvania was subjected to new revolutions. Kemeny seduced the army of Bartzai, and extorted his abdication; he gained the adherents of Ragotsky, obtained from the states his own election on the 24th of December, and secured his elevation by the assassination of the abdicated prince. Aware, however, that he could not singly maintain himself against the whole force of the Ottoman empire, he solicited the assistance of Leopold, and was warmly seconded by the Hungarian states, who were alarmed by the capture of Great Waradin, and the progress of the Turks.

Leopold did not neglect so favourable an opportunity of interfering in the affairs of Transylvania. He ordered his generals in Hungary to support Kemeny, and the imperial commandant of Zatmar received from the Transylvanian prince the possession of Zekelheid, Kovar, and Samosvivar. A horde of Turks and Tartars having expelled Kemeny, and appointed in his stead Michael Abaffy, Montecuculi, with 16,000 men, advanced from the isle of Schut; and though his march was delayed by the refractory Hungarians, who refused him quarters and provisions, he joined Kemeny in the county of Zatmar, forced the passes, and drove the Turks from Transylvania. Unable, however, to maintain himself in a country so long the seat of war, and disappointed of the expected succours from the Hungarians, he left 1000 horse with Kemeny, and a garrison in Clausemburgh, and fell back with a reduced and dispirited army towards Cassau. On his retreat, Kemeny was defeated and killed in a skirmish with the Turks, on the 23rd of January, 1662, and Abaffy restored to his nominal sovereignty. In this crisis, a temporary and tacit suspension of arms took place; the Turks not deeming themselves sufficiently prepared to pursue their success, and the emperor with a diminished army, and embarrassed by the opposition of his turbulent subjects, unwilling to draw the enemy into his own dominions.

During this interval, Leopold summoned a diet at Presburgh, for obtaining succours against the Turks, and allaying the discontents in Hungary. These discontents were principally derived from the wretched form of government, which united the evils of an elective monarchy, with those of feudal licentiousness. The king was a mere cypher; unable to make war, conclude peace, levy taxes, or exercise any other act of authority, without the consent of the diet, which was a heterogeneous body composed of the prelates, magnates, and high officers of state, with representatives from the counties, or equestrian order, and royal cities.* The scanty prerogatives of the crown were circumscribed by the office of palatine, who was nominated by the king from four candidates presented by the diet, whose duty was, to secure the laws from infringement, to act as viceroy, to command the army, and to mediate between the sovereign and the subject. By the extent of his privileges, the Palatine was always a powerful, and often a dangerous opponent; and the office was now filled by Wesselini, a zealous Protestant, of an unquiet spirit, and great influence, who was irritated by recent severities against the members of his persuasion. A constant and legal pretext was also afforded for insurrection by the celebrated clause in the coronation oath of Andrew II., in which the king himself acknowledged that the nobles possessed the right of opposing his authority without incurring the guilt of treason, whenever he acted contrary to their privileges. Another restriction, which was equally dangerous to the sovereign and subject, in a country threatened by so powerful and enterprising an enemy as the Turks, was the law which prohibited the introduction of foreign troops without the consent of the states, and compelled the king to rest the defence of the country on an army of insurrection, an heterogeneous and tumultuary force, raised on the principles of the feudal system.

As head of such a government, the sovereign was involved in endless disputes with the states, and harassed with continual opposition to all his designs. Unfortunately these contentions were aggravated by the arbitrary conduct of the court of Vienna, and by recent persecutions of the Protestants. A perpetual jealousy therefore existed between the sovereign and the nobles. The sovereign, de-

---

* In early times, the diets were formed by the whole body of nobles, or proprietors of land in fee, who assembled in person, in the plain of Rakoz near Buda, mostly on horseback, and sometimes to the number of 80,000. But these tumultuary assemblies producing great confusion, the mode of representation by deputies was adopted under Sigismond, in 1411; the higher orders, consisting of the bishops and magnates, only appearing in person, and the rest by deputies. The principal place of meeting was Buda; but after that city was conquered by the Turks, the assemblies were transferred to Presburgh, and occasionally held in other places. The session of the diet was annual, and afterwards triennial, or oftener, according to necessity.

sirous of abridging a liberty, which always degenerated
into licentiousness, was unwilling to authorise the arming of a turbulent nobility, who maintained constant
connections with his enemies ; while the nobles saw with
alarm the introduction of foreign troops, and considered every measure of the court, however indifferent,
or however salutary, as tending to the annihilation of their
darling privileges. In such a temper on both sides, and
with a system of government, which could neither maintain internal tranquillity, nor resist foreign invasion, the
crisis was rapidly approaching which must turn the balance
in favour of the sovereign or the nobles, and deliver over
the country to all the evils of anarchy, and the miseries of a
foreign yoke, or establish the regal power on a permanent
basis.

On the first interference of the Turks in the affairs of
Transylvania, the nation clamoured for assistance ; and
the Palatine promised quarters and subsistence for foreign
troops. Yet the danger had scarcely subsided, before the
jealousy of the nobles revived, and at the commencement
of winter the troops under Souche could only obtain quarters by forcing an entrance into Cassau. Irritated by the
difficulties of finding subsistence, and left to struggle with
the severities of the season, they gave way to every species
of licentiousness, while the inhabitants retaliated by insults
and assassination. The nobles also inveighed against the
emperor for placing garrisons in the towns belonging to
Ragotsky, and clamoured for their own army of insurrection. The expulsion of Kemeny, and the advance of the
Turkish hordes, again suspended the jealousy of the nation;
but Montecuculi had no sooner commenced his march,
than the same contests revived with redoubled acrimony ;
he was unable to obtain quarters or provisions, and reduced to force his way through a country which he had
been called to defend, as if marching through the territories of an enemy. New insults and new outrages awaited
the termination of his expedition : when he quitted Tran
sylvania, his troops, like those of Souche, were refused a
shelter, and after the fatigues of their arduous campaign,
exposed to perish by hardships, disease, and famine, or by
the insidious attacks of the natives. New clamours arose

against the imperial court, and the excesses of the troops; exclamations resounded on all sides, that the emperor intended to extirpate the Protestants of Hungary, as his predecessor had extirpated those of Bohemia, and that his design was rather to subjugate than to defend the country, to reduce the natives rather than to resist the Turks.

All the attempts of Leopold to reconcile the minds of his Hungarian subjects were fruitless. The diet, which was convoked at Presburgh for the purpose of terminating these disputes, assailed him with remonstrances upon remonstrances, and, as the only means of preventing a civil war, or the junction of the malecontents with the Turks, he entered into a compromise with the states. Nine thousand of his troops were to be withdrawn to the frontiers; the remainder to be paid at his expense, and subjected to the laws of Hungary, and the jurisdiction of the Palatine. In regard to quarters, all privileges and exemptions were to be respected, and in case of necessity, the army of insurrection was to be raised, in conformity with the constitution. This compromise, however, did not restore tranquillity, or give unanimity to the diet; for the remonstrances of the Protestants against the recent persecutions giving rise to disputes with the Catholics, they abruptly retired, and the assembly broke up without arranging any plan for executing the agreement with the emperor.

This disappointment induced Leopold to open a negotiation with the Turks; and the terms of peace were speedily arranged in a congress assembled at Temeswar. But, encouraged by the defenceless and distracted state of Hungary to prosecute the war, the grand vizir Achmet Kiupruli had no sooner lulled the imperial court into security, than he burst into Hungary with an army of 100,000 men. Meeting with no opposition from the forces under Montecuculi, who were exhausted by the hardships of the preceding winter, he crossed the Drave at Esseck, and the Danube at Buda; cut off a corps posted at Parkan, captured Neuhasel, Neutra, Novigrad, Leventz, and Freystadt, and detached a predatory corps of Turks and Tartars, who, after threatening Vienna, spread their customary devastations as far as Olmutz. On the other side, the imperial garrisons of Zekelheid and Clausemburgh surrendered to the prince of Transylvania, and Croatia and Styria were only saved from the same inroads by the valour and skill of Nicholas Zrini, ban of Croatia.

In a danger so imminent and unexpected, the embarrassments of the imperial court were increased by the indisposition of Leopold, who was seized with the small-pox, that disorder which had already proved so fatal to his family. By this unfortunate accident the ministers were rendered still more dilatory and indecisive. Montecuculi with difficulty maintained himself in the strong position of the isle of Schut; and a tardy attempt to raise the army of insurrection was unsuccessful in the face of an enemy. The emperor, left without any other resource than an appeal to the powers of Christendom, after a fruitless attempt to obtain succours from the individual princes and states, hastened to the German diet, which was assembled at Ratisbon in December, 1663. The same disputes, however, arose as on former occasions, whether the demand of succours against the Turks should be first taken into deliberation, or be preceded by the decision of the points left for future discussion by the peace of Westphalia. After much altercation, the contest was terminated in favour of the emperor, with the unanimous consent of the electors, and the majority of the princes. A subsidy of fifty Roman months was voted, and the league of the Rhine agreed to maintain a body of 6500 men men for a year, on condition that the diet should not be dissolved till the other articles were settled. Still, however, this succour was opposed by the disaffected party, under pretence that grants of taxation ought to be passed only by common consent; and this opposition suspended the march of the troops and the payment of the contribution till the capture of Neuhasel in February, 1664, awakened the states to a sense of their danger. Succours were at length granted; the former contribution was tripled by unanimous consent; Leopold William, prince of Baden*, was appointed to the command

* Leopold William was brother of Ferdinand Maximilian, the reigning margrave of Baden, and uncle to prince Louis, who distinguished himself in the war of Hungary, and was the colleague of Marlborough in the contest for the Spanish succession.

of the German army; and the prince of Hohenloe, to that of the auxiliaries furnished by the league of the Rhine. The other states of Europe also vied in furnishing assistance against the enemy of Christendom. The pope, besides a subsidy of 700,000 florins, allowed the emperor to tax the ecclesiastical property in the Austrian dominions; the king of Spain, the republics of Venice and Genoa, the dukes of Tuscany and Mantua, supplied money or magazines, and even the king of France despatched 6000 men under the comte de Coligni, and the marquis de la Feuillade. By these contributions and succours, an auxiliary army to the number of 30,000 men was collected, and commenced its march to the scene of action.

At the close of the year, the grand vizier, leaving garrisons in the conquered places, drew his troops into the Turkish territories; and both parties prepared to open the ensuing campaign with redoubled vigour. Souche, at the head of 8000 men, routed the Turks in various encounters, retook Neutra and Leventz, defeated the bashaw of Buda with a body of 25,000 men at Parkan, secured the frontier of Austria north of the Danube, and straitened the Turkish garrison of Neuhasel.

On the other hand, the active count Zrini laid a plan for surprising or reducing the fortress of Canisia on the Drave, which would have covered the frontiers of Styria. But so much important time was wasted in waiting the tardy deliberations of the council of war, and in disputes between Zrini and Montecuculi, that the grand vizier was enabled to assemble his troops, and advance to its relief. On the approach of the Turks, Zrini united with Montecuculi; but all their operations were retarded by the jealousies between the Hungarians and Germans, and the disputes derived from the discordant characters of the two chiefs; Zrini being ardent and active, accustomed to the daring enterprises of desultory warfare; Montecuculi, cautious and deliberative, a strict adherent to the formalities of regular discipline, and exasperated against the Hungarians, for their treatment of his troops during the preceding campaigns. An army so constituted could not act with effect; and, in addition to the failure of the enterprise against Canisia, the commanders had the mortification to witness the reduction of Zrinevar, a fortress built by Zrini himself on the Mura, to restrain the incursions of the Tartars. This ill success, and the constant refusal of Montecuculi to attack the enemy, irritating the haughty mind of the Croatian chief, he quitted the army in disgust, to lay his complaints before the emperor.

The grand vizier, unwilling to waste the campaign in besieging those fortresses which covered Austria on the side of the Danube, directed his march towards the frontiers of Styria, with a view to penetrate through a defenceless country ; and Montecuculi drawing together all the forces, poured in from Germany and France, at the head of 60,000 men, took post behind the Raab, in the strong position of St. Gothard, to arrest his progress. Notwithstanding his presence, a body of janissaries crossed the river on the 1st of August ; but a sudden rain prevented the passage of the whole army. While the hostile troops were preparing for the engagement, a young Turk, mounted on an Arabian courser, and covered with splendid habiliments, darted from the ranks, flourishing his scimitar, and in the spirit of ancient chivalry defied the bravest of the Christians to single combat. He was opposed by the chevalier de Loraine, who in a few minutes extended him lifeless on the earth, and led off his horse in triumph. The event of the combat proved ominous of the fate of the day. The janissaries who had passed the river were attacked early in the morning, and thrown into confusion ; but being supported by a body of spahis, began to cover themselves with intrenchments. The combat was renewed by additional reinforcements, which continually crossed the river ; and the Christian troops were at one time so broken, that some fugitives who fled to Gratz announced the total defeat of their army. But the fortune of the day was restored by the skill and valour of Montecuculi. While he sent his cavalry to keep the spahis in check, he led the flower of his infantry against the janissaries. The spahis were driven back ; the janissaries broken by the steady discipline of the Germans and the heroic intrepidity of the French ; 8000 fell in the conflict, and more were lost in attempting to climb the craggy and abrupt banks of the Raab. Among the slain were the bashaw of Buda and a son of the chan of

Crim Tartary, and the loss of the Turks did not fall on the desultory hordes of irregular troops, but on the disciplined bands of janissaries and spahis, who are called in the emphatic language of the East, the Sword and Shield of the Empire.

The despondency and rout of the enemy, and the enthusiasm of the victors, gave hopes that this success would open the way to the destruction of the infidel power in Hungary. But the heterogeneous mass of the Christian army was neither animated with the same spirit, nor actuated by the same views. The German troops were anxious to retire as soon as their term of service was expired; the French caballed with the discontented natives, and held a secret correspondence with the Turks; the Hungarians renewed their clamours for the dismission of foreigners, and were more solicitous to thwart than to forward the military operations. Leopold himself was desirous to prevent the renewal of the disputes, which in preceding years had occasioned the loss of so many brave troops, for want of quarters and subsistence. He felt the impoverished state of his finances, and his attention was called to the distracted situation of Germany and the increasing influence of France. He was likewise anxious to terminate the Turkish war, lest the death of Philip IV., and the accession of his son, a feeble and unhealthy infant, should encourage Louis XIV. to grasp the Spanish succession, to which, notwithstanding all renunciations, his views were invariably directed.

Influenced by these motives, Leopold accepted the overtures of the grand vizier, and, to the astonishment of Europe, within nine days after the victory, concluded a truce with the Turks for twenty years. Transylvania was confirmed to Abaffi, evacuated by both armies, and declared independent; the fort of Zekelheid was demolished, the Turks retained Great Waradin, Neusohl, and Novigrad; the emperor, the provinces of Zatmar and Zambolicz, with the towns which he had taken from the house of Ragotsky; and, as a security for his Austrian dominions, was allowed to erect fortresses on both sides of the Wag.

The Hungarians were no less offended by the terms of the treaty than irritated by its conclusion, contrary to the

laws of the kingdom, without the knowledge or consent of
the states.   They even arrested the secretary of the imperial resident in the Turkish camp, as he was carrying the
treaty to Vienna, and were with difficulty persuaded to
restore his despatches and papers.   But after much delay,
and repeated instances, the emperor obtained the ratification
of the states, by promising to build the fortresses on the
Wag at his own expense ; to replace the German troops
with Hungarian levies ; and to grant no office of trust or
profit without their consent.   He likewise gratified his
subjects by restoring to Presburgh the crown of St. Stephen, which during the war had been conveyed to Vienna.

CHAP. LXIII.—1664.

As the treaties of Westphalia, Oliva, and the Pyrenees,
together with the truce concluded with the Turks, occasion
a total alteration in the balance of power ; and as subsequent events revived with new fury that jealousy, and
those opposite claims between Austria and France, which
had already deluged Europe with blood ; we pause to
review the situation of the contending parties, and the
relative connections and interests of the other kingdoms
and states.

Under the administration of Richelieu and Mazarin, the
intestine factions of France had been finally crushed, and
the royal authority established ; the finances were ameliorated, the army disciplined, and a succession of generals
formed, who rivalled the military characters of every age
and nation.   Her political importance was augmented by
territorial acquisitions, which opened a passage into Spain,
Italy, Germany, and the Netherlands ; the conquests in
the Netherlands were secured by the purchase of Dunkirk,
Mardyke, and their dependencies, from Charles of England ; and those on the side of Germany consolidated, by
extorting from the duke of Loraine the surrender of his
principal fortresses.   The house of Austria was humbled

in both its branches, and France acquired that paramount influence in Europe which was before possessed by her rival.

Hitherto, from youth, habit, and inexperience, Louis had implicitly submitted himself to the conduct of Mazarin; but on the death of the minister, on the 1st of March, 1661, he assumed the reins of government, and adopted the system of policy which had been planned by Henry IV., and which by the able execution of Richelieu and Mazarin, had so highly exalted the splendour of his crown. Louis, in the twenty-seventh year of his age, was endowed with every quality calculated to flatter the pride or conciliate the affection of a vain, volatile, and high-spirited people. He was distinguished for manly beauty and majestic deportment ; fond of show and magnificence ; and devoted to that specious gallantry which was the characteristic of his nation. Though deficient in knowledge, neither skilful in military affairs, nor remarkable for personal bravery, he was animated by an ardent love of fame, and possessed the talent of inspiring his generals and troops with enthusiasm ; and he showed his discernment in the choice of able ministers, who, under his ostensible superintendence, directed the administration with as much vigour and address as their skilful predecessors.

Spain, once the preponderant monarchy of Europe, was rapidly sinking into a state of weakness and degradation. During the recent war, her formidable infantry, the pride and terror of the world, had been almost annihilated, her navy ruined by the contests with England and Holland, her finances exhausted, her population diminished, and her commerce destroyed. This long and ruinous conflict had given birth to popular commotions and open rebellion. She had seen her colonies captured, her provinces torn from her empire, and Portugal again erected into a rival monarchy. She had purchased a peace with France, by ceding Roussillon, her barrier on the side of the Pyrenees, by diminishing the remnant of her Burgundian inheritance, and by concluding that sinister marriage of the infanta with Louis, which, in spite of engagements and renunciations, threatened ultimately to render her dependent on France.

Although Spain still possessed resources in the native

energy of the people, in the extent of her territory, and in
the inexhaustible mines of the new world, the genius of
the nation was shackled by the indolent and voluptuous
character of Philip IV. and the feeble administration of the
ministers, who ill supplied the talents of Olivarez. Of all
her former grandeur little remained but the recollection ;
the haughtiness of her counsels began to subside ; the
nation which had so long awed and controlled Europe was
foiled by the petty kingdom of Portugal, and reduced to
solicit the assistance of those United Provinces which had
recently thrown off her yoke. Besides the natural connection of Philip and Leopold, as descended from the same
ancestors, they were united by the ties of frequent marriages, and still more by the bonds of political interest,
derived from a common dread of France, whose encroachments had reduced their respective dominions, and whose
systematic enmity and ambitious designs furnished continual causes of alarm.

The revolution of Portugal was less owing to the exertions of the new monarch, who was indolent, indecisive,
and unwarlike, than to the zeal of the nation, and the mas-
culine spirit of his queen, Louisa de Gusman, a daughter of
the duke of Medina Sidonia. John IV. died in 1656, leaving two minor sons, Alphonso and Peter; and this great
woman maintained that crown on the head of her son
which she had secured for her husband, by conciliating the
affections of her subjects, and by obtaining the assistance of
England and France. She was afterwards driven from the
government by Alphonso, whose weakness of intellect rendered him unfit to fill the throne, and who rivalled the
follies and barbarities of Commodus or Caracalla. Fortunately the count of Castel Melhor, prime minister, possessed
her spirit and followed her example ; while the military
operations were directed by the count of Schomberg, who by
the victory of Villa Viciosa in 1665, secured the independence of Portugal. Such was the situation of the kingdom
at the present period; but in 1667, the excesses of Alphonso occasioned his deposition, and the establishment of
his brother Peter on the throne. The new monarch, after
concluding, in 1668, a peace with Holland and Spain,
maintained tranquillity both at home and abroad, and for

a period of thirty years took no share in the contests of Europe.

Italy had lost its weight in the balance of power. The Milanese and Naples were provinces of Spain, and the only states still retaining a portion of their ancient importance, were Venice, the duke of Savoy, and the pope.

Venice was no longer the same republic, which had almost monopolised the commerce of the world, aspired to the dominion of Italy, and excited dread or jealousy among the powers of Europe. Her continental possessions, indeed, remained nearly in the same state as before the league of Cambray ; but her relative importance had been greatly reduced by the increase of the houses of Austria and Bourbon ; while the progress of maritime discovery had annihilated her eastern commerce. Deprived of the great source which had enabled her to employ the best generals, and maintain a formidable army, she confined her warlike exertions to the Turks, by whom her commerce to the Levant was continually threatened, and by whom her maritime possessions were considerably reduced. Thus situated, she endeavoured, by the wisdom of her counsels and the moderation of her conduct, to maintain that consideration which her former wealth and vigour had assigned her among the states of Europe. From her position between the Milanese, and the dominions of Leopold, she was naturally jealous of the house of Austria, although mutual apprehensions of the Turks occasionally produced a temporary union.

Although the popes had increased their dominions by the acquisition of Ancona Urbino Ferrara, and the provinces of Castro and Ronciglione, yet they retained little or no weight among the great monarchies of Europe. Neither their spiritual nor temporal arms were sufficient to protect them from repeated humiliations, and instead of dictating, as in former ages, to emperors and kings, rousing whole nations, vacating or conferring thrones, their principal influence was derived from their flexible, profound, and persevering policy, and from the extensive connections which they maintained by means of the religious orders, interfering in every court, and scattered through every Catholic country of Europe.

The dukes of Savoy had derived their consequence from the interposition of their territories between France and the Milanese, and the command of the principal passes into Italy. But their dominions, as well as the advantages of their local position, were considerably diminished; the Pays de Vaud and the county of Romand had been conquered by the Swiss, and Bresse, Bugey, and Gex ceded to France, with the important fortresses of Pignerol and Coni. Charles Emanuel, the reigning sovereign, had employed the interval since the peace of the Pyrenees, in healing the wounds occasioned by his long and stormy minority; and he bore with impatience the humiliating state in which he was held by France, anxiously watching for an opportunity to rescue himself from a bondage so intolerable to a prince of high spirit and superior talents.

The Helvetic States still preserved the principles of their union in its primitive simplicity. Since the establishment of their independence they invariably maintained peace, because they had little farther advantage to expect, and much to lose from war; but they kept up the military spirit of the people by subsidiary treaties with France, Spain, Venice, Savoy, and Holland, and thus retained on foot a force of 40,000 men, who, in cases of necessity, could be recalled to defend their native soil. From local situation, and the natural strength of their Alps, their concurrence, or even neutrality, was necessary in an Italian war; and, except the Grisons, who were closely connected with the court of Vienna, they preferred the friendship of France, as well from habit and interest, as the national jealousy derived from their ancient dependence on the house of Austria, and the preponderance of Spain in Italy.

Detestation of civil and ecclesiastical tyranny gave birth to the revolution which established the republic of the United Provinces. Their independence being acknowledged by the peace of Westphalia, they turned their attention to the improvement of that commerce which had formed the source of their prosperity, had furnished resources for maintaining an efficient army, and supporting a navy which enabled them to expel the Spanish fleets from the Channel, to dictate in the Baltic, and contest with England the command of the ocean. Excluded by Philip II.

from the port of Lisbon, then the great emporium of the world, they conquered all the Portuguese settlements in the east, except Goa, founded the central establishment of Batavia in the isle of Java, secured the exclusive trade of China and Japan, and settled a colony at the Cape of Good Hope, as a connecting link between their European and eastern possessions. The separation of Portugal from Spain gave them an opportunity to consolidate these acquisitions by a peace, which they concluded with Portugal in 1661.

The weakness of their complicated government, which was a singular mixture of aristocracy and democracy, ancient and modern institutions, was obviated by the predominant influence of the house of Orange, which seems to have been destined by Providence for the maintenance of civil and religious liberty, and furnished a succession of men as great in arms and policy as any recorded in the pages of history. To family connections and extensive possessions the three first princes, William, Maurice, and Henry Frederic*, owed the elective office of stadtholder, or governor of five of the provinces; from their superior talents and eminent services, no less than from the gratitude of their countrymen, they derived a principal share in the direction of affairs, under the titles of captain-general and admiral, or president of the council of state. Such an authority, in such "a many-headed headless government," and among people so jealous of their liberties, excited violent opposition, and gave rise to the formation of a republican party. This faction, with difficulty suppressed even by the superior genius of the three first princes, rose with new vigour during the short administration of William II., and generated a civil contest, which was only terminated by his death. Being succeeded by a posthumous son, William, the republican party, headed by the celebrated brothers de Wit, availed themselves of his long minority, procured a decision that the high offices and dignities, held

---

* William was assassinated in 1584. He was succeeded by his two sons. The first, Maurice, died unmarried in 1625. The second, Henry Frederic, dying in 1647, was followed by his son William II., who signed the treaty of Munster, and was the father of our glorious deliverer, William III.

by the princes of Orange, should remain vacant, and afterwards effected their formal abolition, by the perpetual
edict of 1668.

England had recently been the scene of one of the most
memorable revolutions recorded in history, whether we
consider its effects on the country, or its consequences in
the affairs of Europe. Charles I., gifted with talents superior to the common order, adorned with all the domestic
virtues of an individual, and the graces of a sovereign, had
been led by his own imprudence, and still more by the
difficulties of his situation, and the wiles of the republican
party, into a contest with his parliament and people, which
terminated in his deposition and public execution. But
the nation soon groaned under a burden far more galling
than that for which it had sacrificed its own tranquillity
and the life of its monarch. The republican government,
established on the ruins of the throne, was overturned by
Cromwell, who replaced it with a military despotism, and,
under the title of protector, exercised greater power than
the most arbitrary king of England. He made, however,
some amends for the vices of an usurper, by displaying the
talents of a great statesman. He suppressed the numerous
factions which had hitherto agitated the nation, distributed
justice with an impartial hand, and increased the military
and naval resources of the country. Under his administration England, which, during the reigns of James and
Charles, had been treated with little consideration, if not
contempt, again gave terror to Spain, and awed even
France in the height of her prosperity. To gratify that
national antipathy, which had been fostered against Spain
since the time of Philip II., and to recover that footing
which had been lost on the opposite coast, he united with
France, and was highly instrumental in forcing Spain to
agree to the humiliating peace which she had recently
signed. Jamaica and Dunkirk, with its dependencies, were
the fruits of this contest, and had the protector lived, he
would probably have extended his acquisitions on the
Continent, for he seems to have entered into a plan for the
partition of the Netherlands with France.* He died be-

* As a statesman, Cromwell seems to have been very unjustly
censured for his conduct in this instance. He duly appreciated the

fore the conclusion of the peace; and after the feeble government of his conscientious but timid son, and, a vain attempt of the republicans to regain their ascendency, the voice of the nation, seconded by the agency of general Monk, restored Charles II. to the throne of his ancestors. Charles, on his accession, held in his hands the balance of Europe; but that pre-eminence which the nation had attained under the vigorous rule of Cromwell, was soon lost under his profuse, voluptuous, and dissipated reign; and, by his dishonourable dependence on Louis XIV., he contributed more than any other prince of Europe to the humiliation of Austria and the preponderance of France.

Frederic III., king of Denmark, had compensated for his recent losses by effecting a singular revolution in the form of government. Aided by the clergy and commons of the realm, he overthrew the aristocracy, which had long kept the crown and nation in the most oppressive bondage, and, in place of a feudal elective and limited, established an absolute and hereditary monarchy. The executive authority deriving new vigour from this change, he crushed the factions which had hitherto agitated the kingdom, lessened the public debts, improved the internal polity, ameliorated the army and navy, and placed himself in a situation to command the attachment of his friends, and the respect of his enemies. His recent misfortunes naturally rendered him desirous to maintain peace; but he was sincerely disposed to cultivate the friendship of the house of Austria, as the surest protection and safeguard against the strength which Sweden had acquired from her recent acquisitions, the fruit of her alliance with France.

value of the Netherlands in a military, political, and commercial view, and considered the acquisition of Dunkirk as the first step of a plan to appropriate a considerable part of those countries. Had Charles II. followed and extended this plan, he might have fixed an insuperable barrier to the ambition of France, and placed the balance of power on a more permanent foundation than it has ever been since established. Even at the peace of Utrecht, had England retained a portion of these territories, as a compensation for her expenses, instead of engaging in the impracticable stipulations, and endless discussions of the Barrier treaty, she might have maintained her footing on the Continent, on less onerous terms than the expenses incurred in the subsequent wars, and afforded a more effectual assistance to Austria and to Europe, than by subsidies and auxiliary troops.

The military exploits and successes of the Swedes had
heightened the splendour, and extended the influence of
their country, but at the same time exhausted her physical
strength, and dissipated her revenues. By the possession
of Pomerania, Bremen, and Verden, derived from the
thirty years' war, and of Deux Ponts, the family inheritance of the king, as well as by the authority annexed to
the guaranty of the peace of Westphalia, Sweden attained
considerable influence in the empire, which she had hitherto
preserved by her union with the house of Bourbon. By the
acquisition of Sconen, Haland, and Bleckingen, she not
only gained an important accession of territory, but secured
herself from the invasions of Denmark, her ancient rival,
and she commanded the Gulf of Finland, by appropriating
Livonia and Esthonia. But these very acquisitions exposed
her to the enmity of the neighbouring states, particularly
the house of Austria, Denmark, the elector of Brandenburgh, the Poles, and Russia; and from this cause, joined
to the distractions of a minority, Sweden, which, from the
accession of Gustavus Adolphus, had interfered in all the
wars of Europe, was reduced to a state of comparative
weakness and temporary tranquillity.

Poland, which once gave law to the North, and possessed a greater extent of dominion than any other state in
Europe, had gradually diminished in power, territory, and
influence, since the establishment of that mischievous law,
which prevented the reigning sovereign from procuring
the nomination of his successor, and thus rendered the
monarchy purely elective. From this period it became the
scene of anarchy and confusion; the turbulent nobles seized
that authority which was once possessed by the crown; its
fairest provinces were dismembered; Prussia, formerly a
fief, was declared independent; Livonia and Esthonia were
appropriated by Sweden; and the Poles, weakened by intestine divisions, and exhausted by unsuccessful wars, were
still involved in that contest with Russia which finally
stripped them of the eastern provinces and the Ukraine.

John Casimir was now the reigning sovereign; but, in
1668, he quitted his throne to become the head of an
abbey, for which he was better fitted than to direct and
curb the energies of a military and turbulent people; by

recent treaties he was to have been succeeded by an Austrian prince, but this design having been frustrated, by the death of Charles Joseph, the only brother of Leopold, the nation elected to the vacant dignity Michael Viesnovitsky, a native Pole. Pressed by the Turks on one side and by the Russians on the other, the king and republic placed their principal reliance on the friendship of Austria, and the new sovereign soon after his election cemented their mutual interest by espousing the sister of Leopold, as his predecessor had married the daughter of Ferdinand II.

Russia was governed by Alexey Michaelovitz, the second sovereign of the dynasty of Romanof, under whom the country has risen to so great a height of power and splendour. Though generally known only as the father of Peter the Great, he deserves our attention equally for his beneficial regulations and military exploits. He new-modelled and disciplined the army, and laid the foundation of the Russian navy, by building vessels on the Caspian Sea. Besides continual contests with the Tartars on the south and east, he ventured to cope with the Swedish troops, at that time the terror of Europe. Though often vanquished, he was, like his son, still unsubdued, and secured Marienburgh by a truce, in order to turn his arms against the Poles, from whom he recovered the provinces of Smolensko, Severia, and Tchernichef, which had been wrested from his father, and the sovereignty over the Cossacs of the Ukraine, which was the source of long and bloody wars with the Turks and Poles. This contest between Russia and Poland was peculiarly advantageous to the house of Austria, as it induced them both to court her alliance, and the connection was strengthened by mutual dread of the Turks, which often compelled them to suspend their own disputes, and to join Leopold in resisting the common enemy.

Such were the situation and interests of the European states, when Leopold suspended his wars with the Turks, and was enabled to direct his attention to the empire and to Europe.

His influence and power may be considered under the two-fold light of head of the house of Austria and emperor of Germany. In addition to the dominions which he inherited from his father, Leopold had recently succeeded to

the Tyrol, and all the exterior provinces, which escheated
to him by the death of his cousin Sigismond Francis, on
the 15th of June, 1665, the last representative of the collateral branch, without issue. Although these important
territories could before be scarcely considered as a distinct
sovereignty, because the princes had always been subservient to the head of their house, yet this fortunate re-union,
at the same time that it brought an accession of revenue
and military force, prevented a renewal of those feuds
which had formerly weakened the Austrian family, and
would have revived when the ties of affinity became more
distant and faint.

In Austria and Bohemia, with their respective dependencies, the authority of Leopold was more firmly established
than that of his predecessors. The evils occasioned by the
long and ruinous war of thirty years, had been gradually
remedied by a prudent and economical administration.
That spirit of disobedience, against which his predecessors
had struggled in vain, had been suppressed by the gradual
restoration of the Catholic religion, which took place during the war, and was established by the peace. The people
of Bohemia and Austria, no longer split into different persuasions, and animated against their sovereign by religious
antipathy; no longer the instruments of foreign intrigue or
domestic feuds, became tranquil and loyal, followed his
standards, and granted their subsidies with cheerfulness
and alacrity. Instead of a tumultuary force, the army of
Leopold consisted of veterans inured to dangers, accustomed
to discipline, and commanded by officers who had been
formed in a conflict of thirty years, with the most skilful
generals and bravest troops of the age ; and the same long
and bloody struggle, by diffusing a warlike spirit throughout his dominions, gave birth to that military system which
became permanent during his reign. In Hungary and its
annexed provinces his authority was still circumscribed,
no less by the vicinity of the Turks and the princes of
Transylvania than by the constitutions of the country, and
the opposition of a brave but turbulent nobility. The
scanty remnant of that kingdom, which he had purchased
with the loss of so much blood and treasure, was intrinsi-
cally rather a burden than an advantage, and could only

be maintained against his rebellious subjects and foreign
enemies by exhausting the strength of his other dominions.
By the cession of the Brisgau and the loss of the possessions in Alsace, he was deprived of a territory, which,
though distant and isolated, gave him a footing beyond the
Rhine, formed a barrier against the encroachments of
France, and enabled his predecessors to attach to their
cause the neighbouring princes of Germany and the dukes
of Loraine.

Under Leopold the scanty influence in Germany possessed by former emperors was considerably reduced by the
recent changes, as well in its constitution, as in the situation and interests of the component states.

The diet, from being temporary, and convoked only at
the will of the emperor, was rendered permanent. Leopold
had assembled the German states at Ratisbon, for the purpose of obtaining succours against the Turks, and would,
like his predecessors have dissolved the meeting as soon as
he had attained his object; but this design was prevented
by the princes, who were not inclined to relinquish the
privilege secured to them by the peace of Westphalia, of
sharing in the election of an emperor or king of the Romans,
and assisting in the arrangement of the capitulation. For
this purpose they formed a princely, in imitation of the
electoral, union, and extorted from the emperor, as the
price of their succours, a promise not to dissolve the diet,
till these and the other points left undecided in the peace of
Westphalia were finally settled. Accordingly, after the
grant of succours, the states proceeded to arrange the capitulation; but the electors being unwilling to admit the
claims of the princes, no specific plan could be adjusted,
and the question was perpetually adjourned. In consequence of these and other delays, the diet was unusually
prolonged, and at last virtually rendered permanent by a
decree, authorising the princes and states to levy taxes on
their subjects for defraying the expense of sending lega-
tions or deputies. Hence the diet, instead of an assembly
composed of the emperor, electors, and princes in person,
became a mere convocation of representatives, similar to a
congress of ministers, to which the emperor sent his commissary, the electors and princes their envoys, and the

towns a particular or common agent. Thus the emperor
was unable to prevent disagreeable discussions by dissolution, or the representatives to decide any question, without
previous reference or continual appeals to their principals.
Thus the usual tardiness of their proceedings was aggravated, and the influence of the chief diminished, while
greater opportunities were afforded for the interference of
foreign powers. The right also, granted to the Protestants
by the peace of Westphalia, of voting as a separate body,
and preventing the decision of a majority in all matters
which were considered as affairs of religion, afforded a
constant pretext to embarrass the measures of their chief,
and enabled them even to oppose the levies of troops and
subsidies, by pleading the privilege of religion.

Above all, the imperial prerogatives were circumscribed
by the privilege which each prince and state enjoyed, of
concluding alliances with each other, or with foreign powers,
without reference to the great body of the empire. This
mischievous privilege threatened to reduce Germany to
the same situation as before the suppression of private
warfare ; for the greater princes maintained standing
armies, in order to take advantage of the weakness or embarrassments of their neighbours, or to subjugate the
imperial or independent towns situated within their respective territories. The warlike bishop of Munster, by
uniting with Austria, reduced his capital Munster, which
had long refused to acknowledge his sovereignty. Erfurth,
which had hitherto enjoyed and improved its extensive
trade under the protection of Saxony, was subjugated by
the elector of Mentz, with the assistance of a French
force; Magdeburgh was deprived of its independence by
the house of Brandenburgh ; Brunswick by its dukes ; and
the cities of Bremen and Cologne were only saved from
the attacks of the Swedes and the elector, the first, by
the interference of the emperor, the last by that of the
United Provinces. From this mischievous privilege also
arose the league of the Rhine, which, more than any other
cause, contributed to strengthen the power of France, and
became the foundation of a dangerous schism in the empire, which for a time palsied all the efforts of its chief.

From this review of the principal changes in the Germanic body in general, we proceed to examine the situation and interests of the most remarkable princes and states.

The dominions and resources of the ecclesiastical electors had diminished with the aggrandisement of the neighbouring states; while by the increase of the French territory towards the Rhine, and the occupation of Loraine, they were overawed; and, however attached to Austria, were prevented from uniting with those members of the Germanic body who adhered to the cause of the emperor.

The house of Bavaria was considerably aggrandised no less by the extinction of the collateral lines, the re-union of its territories, and by establishing the right of primogeniture, than by the acquisition of the electoral dignity with the Upper Palatinate and the county of Cham. Still it could scarcely be considered as more than a secondary power among the German states, from the indolent and unambitious character of the reigning sovereign, Ferdinand Maria, who inherited the superstitious zeal, without the great and splendid qualities of his father. Although connected by blood and principle with the emperor, the acquisitions of France on the side of the Rhine rendered him anxious not to offend a monarch by whose attacks his territories were endangered; and his inclination to peace was strengthened by the prospect held out to him by Louis, of a match between his sister and the young dauphin, which afterwards took place.

The Palatine house, which in former periods possessed a predominant influence in the empire, had been gradually weakened by the partition of its territories among the collateral branches; and its humiliation was completed by the disasters of the thirty years' war. Charles Louis, son of the unfortunate Frederic, though invested with the electoral dignity, possessed only half his paternal dominions; while the consequence of his family was diminished by the rise of Bavaria, and by the reviving influence of the elector of Saxony, who again became head of the Protestant body. He was attached to France and to the enemies of Austria, no less from gratitude for their protection, than from enmity to those who had occasioned the depression of his family.

Of the collateral branches of the Palatine house, it will be sufficient to mention the lines of Neuburgh and Deux Ponts. The head of the first was Philip William, who had so long contested the succession of Juliers and Cleves with the house of Brandenburgh, and nearly involved Germany in a religious war. His ardent zeal for the Catholic faith, and his devotion to the court of Vienna, were afterwards rewarded by the marriage of his daughter with the emperor; a connection which gave splendour to his family, by promoting numerous alliances with the great princes of Europe*, and procured him the subsequent investiture of the Palatine electorate on the extinction of the branch of Simmeren. The line of Deux Ponts derived little consideration from its own scanty territories, but was illustrated by the elevation of its head, Charles X., to the throne of Sweden.

The Albertine or electoral branch of Saxony, which had lost its preponderance among the Protestants by the mercenary and equivocal conduct of John George I., recovered its ascendency by the depression of the Palatine family, and the regular formation of the Protestants into a separate body in the diet, of which he again became the chief. He died in 1656, and at his death contributed ·to weaken his family by dismembering his territories, to give separate establishments to his younger sons, who formed the three lines of Weissenfels, Merseburgh, and Zeitz. John George II., the reigning elector, had no other object in view than to preserve his own dominions and Germany in peace; and though from long habit, and the connections of his family, attached to Austria, he was not inclined to take a more active part in a war against France than was required by his duty as a member of the empire.

The Ernestine or elder branch of Saxony, irremediably depressed by the loss of the electorate, and the principal part of its possessions, was reduced to insignificance by the

---

* He was father of thirteen children. His eldest daughter espoused the emperor Leopold; Maria Sophia, Peter, king of Portugal; Marianne, Charles II. of Spain; Dorothea, first, Edward Farnese, duke of Parma; and secondly, Francis, brother of her deceased husband; Hedwige, James the eldest son of John Sobieski.

separation of its scanty dominions into several portions, for the maintenance of eleven separate lines. *

The whole power and influence of the house of Brandenburgh centered in the elector Frederic William, who, from the extent and position of his dominions, and his personal qualities, was the most considerable prince of the empire, and justly surnamed the Great. On the decease of his father George William, in 1640, the greater part of the electorate was occupied by the Swedes; the fortresses of Custrin and Spandau, which domineered the capital, were in the possession of the emperor. This unfortunate tract of country exhibited ruined cities, and depopulated districts, and the wretched people who had escaped from the sword and famine, were alternately exposed to the rapine of the imperialists and Swedes. The duchy of Cleves and counties of La Mark and Ravensburgh were occupied by the Dutch, and the natives exhausted by exorbitant contributions; while Eastern Prussia still groaned under the load of oppressive imposts exacted by the Swedish troops, and being feudatory to Poland, and governed partly by its own states, formed a kind of republic, which took little interest in the misfortunes of its sovereign. Pomerania, which ought to have escheated to the house of Brandenburgh, was appropriated by the Swedes, and the elector possessed only the empty title of duke, with the right of giving, in that capacity, his suffrage at a diet of the empire. The annual revenue paid into the electoral treasury did not exceed £100,000.

In this desperate situation, Frederic William began his reign; to use the words of the royal historian, "a sovereign without states, an elector without power, a successor without inheritance;" himself only in the dawn of manhood, and unacquainted with business. But he had fortunately acquired firmness and self-confidence, on being removed by the jealousy of a corrupt minister, count Schwartzenberg, to a distance from his father's court, had been seasoned by hardships and disappointments, and had learned the military art under his illustrious uncle Frederic Henry, prince of Orange.

* Altenburgh, Weimar, Isenach, Jena, Gotha, Coburgh, Memmingen, Rombild, Eusenburgh, Hilburghausen, Saalfeld.

He had no sooner succeeded to his inheritance, than he developed the talents nurtured in the school of adversity. He regained by force and address the fortresses of Spandau and Custrin, and thus emancipated himself from that dependence on the house of Austria, to which the treachery of count Schwartzenberg had subjected his father. He had no sooner attained this important object, than he negotiated with Ferdinand III., on terms of independence and equality, which the Austrian court did not expect from an elector of Brandenburgh; and when the emperor refused to restore the principality of Jaegerndorf, of which Ferdinand II. had deprived a branch of his family, for supporting the elector Palatine at the commencement of the thirty years' war, he applied to the Swedes, and partly by address, partly by the payment of a large subsidy, prevailed on them to evacuate the Mark of Brandenburgh. In 1647, by an agreement with the house of Palatine Neuburgh, he secured the duchy of Cleves, and the counties of La Mark and Ravensberg. At the congress of Westphalia, he made the most conspicuous figure among all the German princes, assisted the Calvinists, of which church he was a member, in procuring the same rights as the Lutherans, and obtained as an indemnification for that part of Pomerania which was assigned to the Swedes, the bishoprics of Halberstadt, Camin, and Minden, with the reversion of the archbishopric of Magdeburgh. During the wars of the North, he drew advantages from all parties, relieved Prussia from its feudal dependence on Poland, calmed the commotions of the natives who opposed this transfer, and received their homage at Konigsberg.

With dominions scattered from the Vistula to the Rhine, deprived of communication, he was under the necessity of adopting a versatile system of policy, and varying his connections as his dominions or interests were endangered. We have already seen him forming alliances with the Swedes and Poles, in order to preserve or augment his territories on the Vistula, the Oder, and the Elbe; and we shall hereafter find him, from the same motive, alternately courting the friendship of Austria and France, for the recovery or security of his territories on the Weser and the Rhine. Yet with this temporising policy, he never lost sight of the grand principle, to maintain the balance of power in Europe, and the peace of Germany, and for this object he generally sacrificed his partial views, personal feelings, and even his private interests. Although differing from Leopold in religious principles, and conscious that the house of Austria was watchful to prevent his aggrandisement, he did not hesitate to support with his influence the election of Leopold to the imperial throne, in opposition to France and Sweden, and he united with Austria and Sweden to save Holland from the invasion of Louis. At this period he yielded to the difficulties of his situation, and the disposition of Europe, but he saw with anxiety the aggressions of France, and was afterwards among the first of the German princes to unite with the emperor in opposing the aggrandisement of a power whose domineering spirit, and ambitious principles, threatened the tranquillity and independence of Germany. At the head of a well-appointed army of 20,000 men, with an administration which by wisdom and economy compensated for the scantiness of his revenues, he obtained a degree of consideration above his means, and was at once courted, respected, and feared by the greater powers of Europe.

Of the other princes, besides the electoral houses, none were sufficiently prominent, either for influence and character, to demand our notice, except the dukes of Brunswick, and the bishop of Munster.

The powerful house of Brunswick, from ancient lineage and extent of territory, took precedence of all the princes of the empire, except the electors and the archduke of Austria. Notwithstanding its division into several lines, the family maintained a constant and almost uninterrupted union among themselves; and this union joined to the extent of their territories, the amount of their revenue, and the respectability of their military force, as well as their warlike character, had rendered the dukes of Brunswick conspicuous during the thirty years' war, and insured to them the preponderant influence in the circle of Lower Saxony. But from this period they ceased to follow the same uniform system of policy ; the different members of the family embracing at the same time the opposite interests of Austria and France.

The house was divided into the two lines of Wolfembuttel, and Luneburgh or Zell. Augustus, the head of the
former line, to whose exertions and abilities his family
owed much of its preponderance, was now alive; but in the
ensuing year closed his long and splendid administration,
and was succeeded by Rhodolph Augustus, who inherited
his prudence, without his military talents.

George William who had recently succeeded to the
duchy of Zell, and was head of the line of Luneburgh, was
a prince highly distinguished for personal qualities and
military skill, and possessed an active and enterprising
spirit, which led him to take a considerable share in the
affairs of Germany and Europe. No other eulogium of his
merits and character is necessary, than that he was the
friend of William prince of Orange, the depository of his
secrets, and the soul of his counsels. His second brother,
John Frederic, was duke of Hanover, and had embraced
the Catholic religion during his travels in Italy. The
third, Ernest Augustus, now bishop of Osnaburgh, and
afterwards duke of Hanover, became eminent in the annals
of Germany, as the prince in whose favour Leopold created
the ninth electorate, and who by his marriage with Sophia
grand-daughter of James I. secured to his descendants
the succession to the throne of England.

Of these four princes, Rhodolph Augustus and John
Frederic may be considered as attached to France, with
whom they entered into subsidiary treaties; while George
William and Ernest, devoted to the Protestant cause, and
the principles of German independence, were among the
most zealous members of the empire in supporting the
house of Austria.

Matthew von Galen, bishop of Munster, was the only
German prelate who took a considerable share in the subsequent transactions. He was a native of Westphalia; and
his father being proscribed for murder, was placed under
the care of his uncle, who was dean of Munster, and by
whose influence he obtained a canonry in the chapter. He
passed his youth in arms, and till the age of fifty had rendered himself notorious for the irregularity of his conduct;
but on the death of Ferdinand of Bavaria, elector of Cologne and bishop of Munster, he surprised the votes of the

canons in a moment of jollity and intoxication, and the
ensuing morning was elected bishop by the majority of the
chapter. Fitter for the sword than the cross, he employed
his newly acquired power to indulge his lust of dominion,
and thirst for military renown. He collected troops, interfered in all the petty contests of his neighbours, and hired
out his services to the best bidder. He was involved in
incessant contests with the Dutch, the dukes of Brunswick,
and the princes of East Friesland, and he had recently
succeeded in reducing the city of Munster, notwithstanding
all the remonstrances of the German princes, and the succours of the Dutch. At this period he was at the head of
no less than 18,000 men, for whom he was subsidised by
England, and was at once the terror and the scourge of the
neighbouring states.*

The internal resources of the empire were considerably
reduced by the decline of commerce, and the diminution of
the towns, in number, wealth, and consequence. We read
with surprise of the splendour and population which distinguished the German cities at the commencement of the
sixteenth century, when it was a proverb, that the kings of
Scotland would gladly be lodged like the common burghers
of Nuremberg, which contained 52,000 souls; Lubec
armed 5000 shopkeepers and porters to suppress a commotion of the burghers, and when Strasburgh and Aix-la-
Chapelle each mustered 20,000 men capable of bearing
arms. We are no less astonished when we consider the
strength and resources of the Hanseatic League, which extended its ramifications to every country of Europe, concentrated in Germany the trade of the North and the East,
and contested the mastery of the Baltic with the united
fleets of Denmark, Sweden, and Norway. But of all this
splendour and strength little more remained than the recollection. The Hanseatic League, from seventy-two opulent
towns, was reduced to the three cities of Lubec, Hamburgh,
and Bremen, and these were watched and circumscribed by
the jealousy of the neighbouring states. The population
and wealth of the imperial cities had been exhausted by the

* Sir William Temple, from personal knowledge, has drawn, in his
Political Memoirs, an animated portrait of this singular man. Bas-
nage, Hist. de la Hollande, tom. i. p. 495.; Barre, tom. ix. p. 879.

thirty years' war; many never rose from their ashes, others were appropriated by the neighbouring princes ; the whole trading system of Germany was diverted into other channels, by the fall of the Venetian commerce, the establishment of new sources of trade in England, Portugal, and the Netherlands, and the shutting up of the navigation of the Rhine by the Dutch. The decline of these towns was hastened by the establishment of manufactures, under the patronage of the neighbouring sovereigns, nobles, and states, and still more by the increasing weight of perpetual taxes, which augmented with the diminution of their resources. Their depression was a fatal blow to the imperial power ; for from these towns, which found a sure protection under the shelter of the throne, preceding emperors had drawn their most effectual support against the greater princes, and from their resources and population had derived the means of maintaining internal tranquillity, or waging external war.

From this rapid sketch of the state of Germany, we may calculate the trifling assistance which Leopold could draw from so heterogeneous a mass, even when not influenced by any common motive of opposition. Still less, therefore, may the imperial dignity be considered as an essential weight in the scale of Austria, when we recollect, that the majority of the princes and states had not yet shaken off that jealousy and dread which had been inspired by the despotism and intolerance of Charles and Ferdinand II. ; and still regarded France as their great support against the encroachments of their chief. Hence, although the states willingly furnished succours against the Turks, they were not inclined to concur with the emperor in a war against France, and Louis exercised an authority in the empire, which was more implicitly obeyed than that of Leopold himself.

Chap. LXIV.—1664–1679.

We have already observed that Philip IV. destined his eldest daughter for his relative Leopold, from a natural desire of preserving the Spanish monarchy in his own family. When, in compliance with the treaty of the Pyrenees, he reluctantly gave her hand to Louis XIV., he adopted every precaution to obviate the fatal effects of the marriage, and affianced to Leopold his second daughter, who, by the renunciation of the first, was justly considered as his eventual heiress. Before the age of the princess permitted the solemnisation of this marriage Philip died, on the 17th of September, 1665, leaving a daughter by his first wife, Maria Theresa, married to Louis ; by his second, Margaret, who was betrothed to Leopold, and an infant son, Charles, who succeeded to the throne, under the regency of his mother, Ann, a daughter of Ferdinand III.

Under the weak government of a regency, Spain sunk into a most deplorable state. The queen, inordinately fond of power, without the abilities or discretion to use it, was governed by her confessor, father Nitard, a German Jesuit of obscure extraction. This low-born foreigner was elevated to the office of grand inquisitor, and engrossed the administration of affairs. Accustomed only to the petty arts of monkish intrigue, he proved himself unequal to the government of a great monarchy, with exhausted resources, a dispirited army, and still involved in the unsuccessful war for the recovery of Portugal ; and he alienated the Castilian grandees, by assuming the austerity and haughtiness of Ximenes. The general discontent against his feeble administration was fomented by Don John of Austria, natural son of Philip, who had signalised himself both as a statesman and a soldier, who was respected by the nobles, and adored by the people. Being excluded from the government, he exerted his whole influence and power to overthrow a proud and narrow-minded monk, and to attain that share in the administration to which he was entitled by his talents, rank, and services. Such was the state of Spain in September, 1666, when Leopold solemnised his marriage with the infanta Margaret.

Soon after this marriage Louis was encouraged, by the embarrassments of the Spanish government, to grasp a part of the succession, so solemnly renounced, although he had acknowledged the young king as heir of the whole monarchy. Scarcely a year elapsed after the death of Philip, before he claimed a large portion of the Netherlands. He founded his pretensions on what was called the right of devolution, by which the daughter of the first marriage was entitled to succeed in preference to the son of the second; a right which, far from being the law of succession in any country of Europe, was only an uncertain, obscure, and local custom, confined to a few districts in some of the provinces. He justified the breach of the solemn engagements at his marriage, by the quibbling subterfuge, that the infanta, being then a minor, had no power to make a renunciation, and still less to annul the rights of her children.

Louis had been long preparing for this hostile aggression. By employing threats and promises, he gained the neutrality or acquiescence of the German states; he bound Sweden by a subsidiary treaty; he deemed himself secure from any opposition on the part of England, which was engaged in war with Holland, and on the part of Holland, with which he was in alliance. He seems even to have opened some negotiations with the court of Vienna, and acquired considerable influence in the imperial cabinet. Having matured his preparations, he, in May, 1667, poured his troops into the Low Countries, leading himself the principal army of 30,000 men, without publishing a declaration of war; but simply notified his resolution in a letter to the queen regent, declaring his intention to take possession of what had been usurped from his wife, or to secure an equivalent. He added mockery to aggression, by disavowing any design to break the peace. He experienced no resistance in a country unprovided for defence; and in less than three months made himself master of the principal fortresses on the frontier between the Scheldt and the Channel. He increased the embarrassments of the regent, by entering into an offensive alliance with Portugal; and, in the depth of the ensuing winter, added Franche Comté to his conquests.

The court of Spain appealed to the German diet against

the invasion of territories which formed part of the circle of Burgundy; and solicited assistance from Leopold in particular, both as chief of the empire, as a member of the Austrian family, and as the next heir to the succession by right of descent and marriage. But this appeal was not attended with the slightest effect. As Louis had gained the states of the empire, several offered him the possession of their fortresses, others raised troops to prevent any opposition to his designs; and even the elector of Brandenburgh, the most powerful and independent of the German princes, was induced to join the league of the Rhine. Thus thwarted by the empire, and embarrassed by new discontents rising in Hungary, Leopold had no other alternative than to maintain a state of neutrality, and acquiesce in the dismemberment of territories, which he had so powerful an interest to preserve.*

From the apathy of the empire, the acquiescence of Leopold, and the weakness of Spain, Louis would have found no obstruction to the conquest of the whole Netherlands, had not the United Provinces taken the alarm, and had not the spirit of the English nation and parliament forced Charles II. to join in opposing the aggrandisement of France, which endangered the safety of England, and the liberty of Europe. The war, which had divided the two countries, was suddenly terminated by the peace of Breda, in July, 1667, and this peace was followed by the triple alliance between the two maritime powers and Sweden, to whom France had also given umbrage by withholding the stipulated subsidies. The object of this league was, to reduce Louis to enter into an accommodation, on

* Voltaire has assigned as a reason for the conduct of Leopold, that he had concluded a secret treaty with France for the partition of the Netherlands, should Charles die without issue ; and that the original was deposited in the hands of the duke of Florence. This assertion is confirmed even by Torcy ; but the embarrassed situation of Leopold, and the singularly impolitic conduct of the German states, sufficiently accounts for his acquiescence in the incroachments of Louis, without recurring to the improbable supposition that a sovereign of so firm a temper, and so tenacious of his rights as Leopold, would voluntarily relinquish those rights by a treaty ; and the still greater absurdity of imagining, that he should intrust the original of such an engagement to a petty prince of Italy.

the condition either of retaining his conquests in the Netherlands, or of accepting as an equivalent Franche Comté, or the duchy of Luxemburgh, with the Cambresis, Douai, Aire, St. Omer, and Furness.

Louis, apprehensive of being involved in a war with the two maritime powers; aware that a peace, recently concluded with Portugal, would enable Spain to bring forward her whole force; dreading the interference of Leopold, and the defection of his adherents in the empire, accepted, though indignantly, the terms prescribed by the triple alliance. By the mediation of the pope, he, on the 2d of May, 1668, concluded a peace with Spain, at Aix-la-Chapelle, on the condition of restoring Franche Comté, and retaining his conquests in the Netherlands * ; but he had the address or the firmness to evade even the mention of his former renunciation of the Spanish succession, and by thus virtually abrogating the essential stipulations in the peace of the Pyrenees, reserved his pretensions to be again brought forward on the first favourable occasion.

The only object remaining for the three contracting powers was, to remedy the uncertainty of this treaty with Louis, by securing the remainder of the Netherlands, with Franche Comté, to Spain. But more than a year elapsed before this essential object was attained by the treaty of the Hague, on the 9th of May, 1669, between England, Holland, and Sweden. To this treaty Spain afterwards acceded; and bound herself to discharge the arrears of the subsidy due to Sweden. The contracting parties ought to have strengthened this league by the accession of other powers, particularly the emperor; but so discordant were their views, and so greatly was the influence of Louis increased over Charles II., that the British court declined, under various pretences, accepting the accession of Leopold, who had been formally invited to enter into the treaty.

* It is barely sufficient to enumerate these places, and refer to their situation, commanding the three principal rivers of the Low Countries, and a passage into Brabant, to prove the magnitude of their loss to Spain. The places now ceded were Charleroi, Binche, Aeth, Douay, with Fort Scarpe, Lille, Oudenarde, Armentieres, Courtray, Bergue and Furnes, with their dependencies. — Peace of Aix-la-Chapelle.

An alliance, founded on such discordant principles, and forming so feeble a bond of union, could not long subsist, or oppose a permanent barrier to the increasing power of France. Although Louis had obtained a considerable accession of territory in the Netherlands, he was not satisfied with a part, however vuluable, when he aspired to the possession of the whole; and as he was sensible that he could not consummate his schemes of aggrandisement while Holland formed a point of union for the European states, he next directed his attack against a country so interested to oppose his conquests. He gained Charles II., whose ruling principle was the love of pleasure, and whose extravagance reduced him to the humiliating necessity of becoming a pensionary of France; and recovered his influence with the Swedish government, which was dissatisfied with the delays of Spain in discharging the stipulated subsidies. All the German princes, except the elector of Brandenburgh, were again secured by bribes or alliances; by a promise not to attack Germany or the Spanish dominions, he obtained from the states on the Rhine a passage through their territories; and he induced the elector of Cologne and the bishop of Munster to concur in the intended invasion. He contrived to embarrass Leopold, by fomenting the discontents in Hungary, gained some of his ministers, and by representing the intended invasion as directed solely against the Protestant religion, induced him to sign a treaty of neutrality, by which he promised not to oppose the arms of France in any war against England, Sweden, or the United Provinces.

Having thus isolated the Dutch from the other powers of Europe, Louis commenced his operations. He attacked Charles IV., duke of Loraine, who was collecting a subsidiary army for the service of the United Provinces; by the occupation of his duchy, opened a direct communication with the Alsatian territories, and thus delivered himself from an enemy who might have made a dangerous diversion. Notwithstanding the interference of the emperor and empire in behalf of a sovereign under their protection, he retained possession of Loraine; and the tameness with which this aggression was borne, proved the extent of his influence, and the terror inspired by his arms. The

United Provinces were thus deprived of every ally except
Spain, with whom mutual danger had induced them to sign
a defensive alliance, on the 17th of December, 1671.

The storm which had been long gathering at length burst
forth. England and France declared war almost at the
same moment : and, while their fleets united by sea, Louis
commenced his memorable attack by land. He collected
his forces at Charleroy, crossed the Meuse at Viset and
Maestricht, and turned into the electorate of Cologne.
From Bonne, Nuys, and Kayserswerth, where the elector
permitted him to form magazines in the preceding winter,
he descended the Rhine, captured, almost without opposition, all the fortresses belonging to the elector of Brandenburgh in the duchy of Cleves, forced the passage of the
Rhine at Tollhuys, and poured his troops like an inundation over the United Provinces. With astonishing rapidity he made himself master of Grave Doesburgh and
Zutphen on the Yssel; Nimeguen and Bommel on the
Waal; Grave and Crevecoeur, on the Meuse; the fortresses on the Rhine as far as Woerden, and even captured
Naarden within three leagues of Amsterdam. At the same
time the bishop of Munster, assisted by a French corps
under the duke of Luxemburgh, penetrated through Overyssel into the provinces of Groningen and Friesland.

In this extremity the Dutch burst open the dikes to in-
undate the country, separated their army to form a line of
defence between Muiden and Gorcum, and removed their
archives and magazines to Amsterdam. But their situation was most perilous and alarming. Their troops undis-
ciplined, weak, and discouraged, were commanded by officers
without skill; the people enervated by a long peace, and
absorbed in commercial speculations, had lost the spirit
which enabled them to defy the best troops of Europe,
though directed by an Alva, a Farnese, and a Spinola. In
the midst of universal dismay, the country was divided
between the Republican and Orange parties, who were more
anxious to weaken and embarrass each other than to resist
the common enemy. The fleet alone acting with the national spirit, attacked the united squadrons of France and
England at Solebay, and maintained the equality, if not superiority, in a series of engagements. But this advantage,

if it might be called an advantage, was far from being decisive; they might have been annihilated as a nation by
land, while their fleet rode triumphant by sea; and so great
was the general despondency, that many, like the Athenians
of old, even proposed to abandon their native shores, and
remove their empire to the colonies in the East.

The approach of such stupendous danger, the unprovided
state of the garrison towns, the weakness of the army, the suspicion of treachery which naturally arose from a rapid series
of disasters, and the known connections of the two de Wits
with France, excited general indignation. The public misfortunes being attributed to their improvident counsels, they
fell a sacrifice to the fury of the people; the prince of Orange
was intrusted with the supreme command of the army and
navy, and appointed stadtholder of the five provinces which
his ancestors had governed under the same title. Party
animosities subsided, and all, from fear, prudence, or pa-
triotism, suppressed their own grievances to turn their
efforts against the common enemy. Under the guidance of
the young prince, who proved himself worthy of that heroic
family from which he was descended, the army was restored
to discipline, the officers who had betrayed or ill served
their country were dismissed or punished, and the people,
who were recently inclined to receive a foreign yoke, unanimously concurred to defend the last remnant of their
native soil, of which neither the arms of the French, nor
the inundation of waters had yet bereaved them.

But neither this reviving spirit, nor the heroism of the
young prince, would have saved the republic without the
assistance of the emperor and the elector of Brandenburgh.
As early as May, the elector concluded a subsidiary treaty
with the republic for a succour of 20,000 men. The almost
inevitable loss of the Low Countries, should France maintain
possession of Holland, and the occupation of Loraine, at the
same time induced the court of Vienna to break the recent
treaty of neutrality, and unite with the elector in assisting
the Dutch. A league was accordingly concluded in August,
1672, between the emperor, the elector, and the states;
and 16,000 imperialists uniting with the forces of Brandenburgh at Halberstadt, advanced towards the bishopric of
Munster; but being opposed by Turenne, they spent the

whole season in fruitless efforts to pass the Rhine. This inactivity created disgust, jealousies, and mutual recrimination. The elector, shackled in his command by the imperial court, seeing on one side his fortresses on the Rhine in the possession of the French, and alarmed on the other by an invasion of his Westphalian territories, concluded on the 10th of April, 1673, the truce of Vossem, by which he promised to take no part in the war against France, except as a member of the empire.

Yet this diversion, however fruitless in the event, by giving a temporary respite to the United Provinces, enabled them to make the most strenuous exertions both by sea and land. They repulsed the efforts of the French against Amsterdam, and secured the province of Broningen by reducing the fortress of Coevorden ; while the prince of Orange called the attention of the enemy to their own frontiers, by an enterprise, in conjunction with the Spaniards, against Charleroy. The states also redoubled their exertions to augment their navy, and repulsed the projected descent of their united enemies on the coasts of Holland and Zealand.

Meanwhile Leopold supplied the defection of the elector of Brandenburgh by new efforts. After attempting in vain to rouse the empire, he placed garrisons in Coblentz and Ehrenbreitstein, by which he secured a passage over the Rhine, and obtained a post which gave him the command of the Moselle, and the means of invading Loraine. He entered into alliances with Spain, the United Provinces, and with the ejected duke. A combined army of 18,000 men was speedily formed on the side of the Low Countries, while Montecuculi, with 30,000 Imperial troops, drew towards the Maine. The effect of these movements was decisive ; Turenne was driven out of Franconia, whither he had advanced to oppose the imperialists ; Montecuculi passing the Rhine at Coblentz, joined the prince of Orange with the confederates at Andernach, and their united forces took Bonne. The French, apprehensive of losing their communications with their own country, withdrew their garrisons from most of the conquered places, except Grave and Maestricht ; and this sudden reverse was followed by the defection of all their adherents except Sweden. The king of England was again forced by his parliament to make peace with Holland, and the presence of the confederate armies, induced the bishop of Munster to abandon France, and join his co-estates of the empire.

A no less sudden and important change took place in Germany. The aggressions of Louis, the devastations recently committed in the Palatinate by the French troops under Turenne, the occupation of Treves and Loraine, the seizure of the ten imperial towns in Alsace, a long series of arrogant declarations, and unprovoked aggressions, all gave weight to the representations of the emperor, and the whole diet concurred in a declaration of war against France. Besides their ordinary contingents, many of the states entered into separate alliances with the emperor and the United Provinces, particularly the elector of Brandenburgh, the dukes of Brunswick, and the elector Palatine; and the king of Denmark promised a succour of 16,000 men, if the Swedes should declare in favour of France.

Before, however, the allies could assemble their forces, the French conquered Franche Comté, and not only reconciled the Swiss to this aggression, but even prevailed on them to shut the passage from Italy against the Spaniards. During the two succeeding years, the war between France and the emperor was chiefly confined to Alsace and the neighbouring countries on the Rhine, where the caution of Montecuculi, and the enterprising spirit of Turenne, were so nicely balanced that the contest produced no permanent advantage on either side. Soon after the death of Turenne and the retreat of Montecuculi, the war assumed a new aspect. The Swedes, again co-operating in favour of France, drew off the troops of Brandenburgh, Brunswick, and Munster to the north of Germany, and thus enabled the French to regain the ascendency on the Rhine and in the Low Countries. The imperialists under Charles, the new duke of Loraine, who inherited the talents and ruined fortunes of his uncle, recovered Treves, reduced Philipsburgh, and even approached the frontiers of Loraine; but the French compelled a corps which had penetrated into Alsace to capitulate, drove the duke from Mentz, prevented him from crossing the Meuse to join the Dutch, and closed the campaign by the capture of Friburgh. The prince of Orange, assisted by the Spaniards and auxiliary troops of the empire, for some time balanced the forces of the enemy, though defeated at Senef and Montcassel; till the French, favoured by the diversion of the Swedes, concentrated the principal part of their strength in the Netherlands, and not only frustrated the attempt of the allies to penetrate into France, but before the close of 1679, extended their conquests by the capture of the fortresses which formed the great barrier of the Spanish provinces.*

Meanwhile, according to the usual custom of blending negotiations and arms, a congress of ministers from the belligerent powers assembled in March, 1679, at Nimeguen, under the mediation of England. France exerted her usual artifices to divide the allies; but was foiled in all her attempts by the spirited opposition of Leopold and the prince of Orange. The first required the restitution of Loraine and Franche Comté, the re-establishment of the imperial rights over the ten towns in Alsace, and full security on the side of the Rhine against future aggressions; the latter insisted that France should be reduced to her original boundaries before her encroachments on the empire and Spain. They were supported by the king of Denmark, the elector of Brandenburgh, and the princes in the north of Germany, who were not merely desirous to recover their losses, but to retain the conquests which they had now made or expected to make from Sweden.

Foiled in all attempts to weaken the confederacy, Louis redoubled his efforts to gain the Dutch, and succeeded in persuading the governing party in Holland to listen to separate overtures, by luring them with commercial privileges, and the offer of a sufficient barrier in the Netherlands. His intrigues were, however, again baffled by the prince of Orange, who repaired to England, negotiated a marriage with the princess Mary, presumptive heiress of the crown, and by the influence which he acquired in the English ministry and nation, persuaded Charles to send an ambassador to Paris, insisting that Louis should restore all his conquests from the emperor and empire, reinstate the duke of Loraine, give up Maestricht to the Dutch, and

* Bouchain, Valenciennes, Condé, Cambray, Maubeuge, Bavay, Aire, St. Omer, Warwick, Warneton, Poperingen, Bailleul, and Cassel.

cede to Spain, Ath, Charleroy, Binche, St. Guillain, Condé, Valenciennes, Courtray, and Tournay, as a barrier for the Low Countries. Charles even promised to declare war should the French refuse to comply with this demand; entered into a treaty at the Hague with the United Provinces, for enforcing the acceptance of these terms, and obtained, in the commencement of 1678, a supply from his parliament for the maintenance of ninety sail, and an army of 30,000 men.

These warlike appearances encouraged the allies, and active preparations were made for carrying hostilities into France. Leopold exerted himself with unusual vigour to assemble an army, which was to enter Alsace under the command of the duke of Loraine; the states of Lower Saxony were to furnish troops to act on the Moselle; and the prince of Orange was to attack the northern frontier of France, with the Dutch and Spaniards. But while the allied powers were holding councils of war, and discussing plans of operation, the French drew their troops to the frontiers; after threatening the empire on the side of the Upper Rhine, and alarming the whole extent of frontier as far as the Meuse, they suddenly burst into Flanders, and in the course of a few days captured Ghent and Ypres. In the midst of the alarm occasioned by this success, Louis made specific propositions to the congress of Nimeguen on the 15th of April, 1678. He demanded full and entire satisfaction for Sweden, for the duke of Holstein Gottorp, and for the bishop of Strasburgh, whose territories had been occupied by the allies. To the emperor he held forth a vague promise to fulfil the peace of Westphalia, and allowed him to purchase the restoration of Philipsburgh, by the cession of Friburgh as an equivalent. To Spain he offered Limburgh, Ath, Charleroy, Binche, Oudenard, Courtray, Ghent, and St. Guillain, affecting to consider this barrier as sufficient to gratify England and Holland, and in return demanded Franche Comté, with all the towns which he had conquered during the war. To the Dutch he tendered the same commercial advantages as before, with the restitution of the principality of Orange, which he had seized at the commencement of the war. He proposed to reinstate the duke of Loraine, either on the terms stipulated by the peace of the Pyrenees, or of ceding Nancy to France in exchange for Toul, with passages half a league in breadth through his territories to Alsace and Franche Comté ; the provostship of Longwy, which belonged to the duke, was likewise to be exchanged for a provostship in one of the three bishoprics. Louis delivered these terms with the imperious tone of a conqueror, declaring, that his enemies had now the option of peace or war, and that if his proposals were not accepted before the 10th of May, he should deem himself at liberty to make new demands, and produce new restrictions.

Such conditions, dictated in the most haughty language, could not fail to be highly galling to the allies, particularly to Leopold, who was aware that the empire, and his own territories, were exposed to the most imminent peril, by the proposed transfer of Franche Comté to France, by the cession of a free passage through the territories of Loraine, by the loss of his sovereignty over the ten towns of Alsace, and by the establishment of two passages over the Rhine. However desirous of peace, he disdained to accept conditions so degrading and dangerous ; and as he deemed himself secure of support from England, Denmark, Brandenburgh, and the allies of Lower Saxony, he resolved to continue the contest. He endeavoured to rouse the spirit of the Spaniards and the Dutch, and made active preparation to push military operations with vigour and effect.

But Louis had already taken measures to dissolve the union of the allies, by gaining the powers on whom the continuance of the contest principally depended. He palsied the efforts of England, by alternately bribing and threatening the king ; by caballing with the leaders of the popular party ; by inflaming the jealousy of the king against the parliament, and of the parliament against the king ; and succeeded in inducing them, by common consent, to disband that army for which the nation had clamoured *, at the very moment when Charles had recalled the English troops from the service of France, and sent a part of his forces into Flanders. He was still more successful with the Dutch :

* This dishonourable conduct of all parties in England is ably developed by Dalrymple, in his interesting Memoirs of Great Britain and Ireland, ch. ii. and iii. with the two Appendices.

he represented to the popular party the opposition of the prince of Orange as the sole obstacle to peace, excited their jealousy against his connections with England, alarmed them with hints of a projected cession of the Netherlands for Roussillon, and again lured their commercial cupidity. By this series of intrigues and artifices, he induced the Dutch government to sign a temporary armistice, for the purpose of effecting a general peace on the proffered conditions, and promise to abandon the alliance if those terms were rejected. This armistice was afterwards prolonged to the close of the year.

The Dutch being thus detached, he found little difficulty in gaining Spain, exhausted by the contest, and agitated by intestine feuds. Don John had obtained the disgrace of Nitard, the imprisonment of the queen mother, and the banishment of Valenzuela, an intriguing poetaster, who was raised by her influence to the post of prime minister. But though the greatest statesman who had directed the counsels of Spain since Olivarez, he was unable to infuse spirit into the weak mind of the king, or to combat the factions of a turbulent nobility in the midst of an unsuccessful war. Being therefore desirous of peace, no less to recover his exhausted country than to establish his own authority, he accepted without hesitation the offers of France, and soon after the accession of Holland, agreed to the proffered terms.*

The other allies astounded by this defection, vented their reproaches against the Dutch for setting the example in deserting a contest which had been commenced for their safety. The ambassador of Leopold, in particular, observed : " Although some provinces may now reap a temporary advantage, all will eventually be swallowed up by so powerful a neighbour. France proposes conditions of peace, to which neither the emperor nor his allies can consent with honour and safety. As a proof that her design is only to divide and subjugate the allies one after the other, she does not even specify the satisfaction which she requires for Sweden. If there be an absolute necessity for peace, the emperor offers to agree to terms which shall prove his moderation ; but can it be believed without doubting the for-

* Memoirs of the Bourbon Kings of Spain, Introduct. sect. 2

titude, prudence, and justice of the states general, that they
will precipitately desert their faithful confederates, and thus
expose them to the most imminent danger The enemy requires a speedy determination, because he wishes to hurry
us to the brink of the precipice ; yet, for that very reason,
we ought to proceed with caution and deliberation. If the
king of France succeeds in treating separately with Holland,
he will gain her wishes, and there is an end to all hope of
a general peace."

Similar remonstrances were made by the king of Denmark and the elector of Brandenburgh, and still more by the
prince of Orange, who used every representation to combat
the commercial prejudices and petty views of his countrymen. But all these representations were lost on the short-
sighted politicians of Holland, who sacrificed their own
honour and safety for the sake of illusory advantages, and
a temporary respite, by ordering their ambassador to conclude the peace within the space of a month.

On the 22nd of June, 1678, the very day in which it was
to have been signed, an incident happened which revived
the spirit of the allies, and seemed even to rouse the Dutch
themselves from their lethargy. Although no mention of
Sweden had been made in the treaties between France,
Spain, and Holland, Louis refused to surrender Maestricht
and the Spanish towns, before the allies had restored on
their side all the conquests wrested from Sweden. This
unexpected demand prevented the signature, and war
seemed on the point of being renewed. Even the king of
England felt the dishonour of his recent dependence on
France ; again concluded, on the 26th of July, a treaty with
the Dutch, binding himself to declare war against Louis, if
he did not within fourteen days restore the ceded towns;
and earnestly appealed to his parliament for supplies. Unfortunately, he had acted with too much duplicity to obtain
the esteem or confidence of any party. His parliament
considering this effort as a mere pretence to extort money,
or raise a standing army, rejected his demand, and Charles
again fell into his shameful dependence on France. Although he had not the effrontery to recall his declaration,
he endeavoured to obtain from the French king an increase
of his pension, not only by offering to preserve his accus-

tomed neutrality, but even to declare war in favour of Sweden. Louis skilfully cajoled the needy monarch, while his hostility would have been dangerous ; but at the same time disclosed his perfidious conduct to the Dutch. By these manœuvres, he gained the signature of the states to the definitive treaty, on the 10th of August, at the last moment of the very day appointed by Charles for his ultimate determination ; and their example, as before, was, on the 17th of September, followed by Spain.

Even after this formal signature, Leopold and the allies conceived new hopes of renewing the war ; for, on the ensuing morning, the prince of Orange attacked the French forces under marshal Luxemburgh, who, notwithstanding the conclusion of the armistice, had blockaded Mons, and drove him from his position, with the loss of 5000 men. At the same moment the king of England, irritated against Louis for suspending the payment of his pension, for once appeared sincere, ratified the treaty with Holland, hurried the embarkation of his troops for Flanders, used every exertion, and employed every argument to induce the states to continue the war. But the Dutch had been too often deceived by Charles to rely on his sincerity, and Louis having submitted to the insult offered to his arms by the prince of Orange, the ratifications were exchanged without delay. Still, however, the instigations of the emperor, and the prospect of assistance from England, induced the king of Spain to withhold his acquiescence, until the French troops invading the Netherlands, exacted such heavy contributions, and committed such devastations, that he, on the 15th of December, 1678, acceded to the treaty, to relieve his subjects from evils greater than any which they had suffered during the war itself.

The French, secure on the side of the Netherlands, soon recovered the trifling advantages which the imperialists obtained at the commencement of the campaign, and inundated the electorate of Cologne, and the territories of Juliers. The princes who were most exposed to danger hastened to desert the alliance. The elector of Brandenburgh, anxious to retain Pomerania, which he had wholly subjugated, made indeed a chimerical proposal for raising an army of the empire, amounting to 80,000 men, of which he promised to furnish one-fourth ; but Leopold declined trusting to so uncertain a resource, and was too jealous of the elector to continue the war for the sake of his aggrandisement. He therefore entered into a separate negotiation with France, notwithstanding all the reproaches of the elector and his allies, who in their turn inveighed against his desertion as he had inveighed against that of the Dutch and Spaniards. The conclusion of the peace was suspended by his attempts to retain Philipsburgh and Friburgh, to recover the rights of the empire over the fiefs and towns of Alsace, and still more to obtain the complete restoration of the duke of Loraine. But Louis, who could not be induced to yield a tittle of these important points in the midst of a general war, was still less inclined to concede them to the emperor, when deserted by the principal members of the alliance. After long discussions, Leopold submitting to necessity, relinquished his pretensions, abandoned Brandenburgh and Denmark, and, on the 5th of February, 1679, signed the peace with France and Sweden. He retained Philipsburgh in exchange for Friburgh ; left all points in dispute, in regard to himself or the empire, on the same vague footing as they were left by the peace of Westphalia ; and acquiesced in the conditions offered to the duke of Loraine ; but to save his honour, and justify himself to the empire, he published a fruitless protest, reserving his own rights and those of the empire over the fiefs and towns of Alsace. As he had made this peace without the formal concurrence of the Germanic body, he submitted an apology to the diet, and obtained the ratification of all the states, except the elector of Brandenburgh, the king of Denmark as count of Oldenburgh, the dukes of Brunswick, and the bishop of Munster. He, however, soon afterwards procured the acquiescence of the dukes of Brunswick, and the new bishop who succeeded Bernard von Galen in the see of Munster ; and a French army penetrating into Lower Saxony, overcame the repugnance of Brandenburgh. But the elector still displayed so much spirit and policy, that he obtained more advantageous terms than any other member of the alliance, by securing a small district on the left bank of the Oder, half the tolls of Colberg, and receiving from France the payment of

300,000 crowns. The king of Denmark reduced to follow the example, restored the duke of Holstein Gottorp, and renewed the treaties of Westphalia, Roskild, and Copenhagen.

The duke of Loraine was the only sovereign who was not reinstated in his dominions. The high-spirited prince, disdainfully rejected terms which reduced him to total dependence on France, and retiring under the protection of his brother-in-law the emperor, became the great ornament of his court, the prime mover of his counsels, and the director of his military operations.

Chap. LXV. — 1679–1697.

THE peace of Nimeguen could only be considered as a temporary truce ; for, instead of setting bounds to the ambition and encroachments of Louis XIV., the security with which it crowned his aggressions encouraged him to persevere in his projects of aggrandisement.

The purpose now appeared for which he had so artfully introduced the contradictory stipulations into the peace of Westphalia, relative to Alsace, and the three bishoprics, and of which he had refused to admit any explanatory clause. For the peace was scarcely signed, before he commanded the towns and nobles to renounce their connection with the empire ; and established three tribunals, or chambers of re-union, at Brisach for Alsace, Metz for the three bishoprics, and Besançon, for Franche Comté. The object of these tribunals was, to investigate musty records, and worm-eaten manuscripts, to collect traditional information relative to all the obsolete rights which had been enjoyed, or were supposed to have been enjoyed by former sovereigns, in order to appropriate the territories subject to such rights, as fiefs and dependencies. These re-unions did not merely comprehend towns and districts, but extended to whole principalities, duchies, and counties. Such were Deux Ponts, Saarburgh, Weldentz, part of the bishoprics of Strasburgh and Spire, Sponheim, and Montbeillard, with numerous other places, which had long ceased to have any connection with the ceded territories. On the side of the

Netherlands, Louis likewise claimed the county of Chinay, with the town of Alost or Luxemburgh, and several districts between the Sambre and the Meuse belonging to the archbishopric of Liege. The proprietors of all these territories were ordered to do homage to the crown of France, under pain of confiscation.

The small towns and states, who were unable to resist, complied; but the greater carried their complaints before the emperor and empire. The king of Sweden, as possessor of Deux Ponts, the Palatine family as proprietors of Weldentz and Germesheim, and the duke of Wirtemberg as sovereign of Montbeillard, assailed the emperor with clamours for redress, and with reproaches for neglecting the security of their interests in the recent peace. When Leopold made the warmest remonstrances against these usurpations, Louis coldly referred him to the tribunals which he had himself instituted to judge his own cause. But while he amused both the empire and Spain by affecting to enter into negotiations, he continued his encroachments, extorted the county of Chinay from Spain, suddenly invested and reduced Strasburgh, and at the same time took possession of Casale, an imperial fief, which he had obtained by purchase from the duke of Mantua.

Trusting that these aggressions would rouse the spirit of the empire, Leopold prevailed on the diet to place the military system on a more consistent and advantageous footing. As the contingents had hitherto been united according to the rank and order of the states in the matricula, troops had been drawn from one extremity of Germany to join with those of another, from whom they differed in language, manners, and military institutions. This heterogeneous mixture was now avoided by assembling the troops according to vicinity of territory, and apportioning the contingents on the respective circles. By this system arrangements were made in October, 1681, for forming an army of 28,000 infantry, and 12,000 cavalry, which could be raised to 80,000 or 120,000 men, by merely doubling or tripling the contingents. For the regular payment of this force, the particular funds of each state and circle were to be united, and form a common military chest.

At the same time, Leopold encouraged the formation of

defensive leagues or associations, as well among the German states themselves, as with foreign powers. He himself acceded to the association of the four circles of the Rhine, and concluded alliances with the dukes of Brunswick Luneburgh, and Maximilian Emanuel, the new elector of Bavaria. He also gained the king of Sweden, who was alienated from France by the seizure of Deux Ponts, and entered into a defensive league for twenty years with Sweden, Spain, and the United Provinces. He expected to obtain a declaration of war from the empire, and hoped, by means of the prince of Orange, even to draw England into the quarrel. But all these expectations were frustrated by the intrigues and superior influence of France. Louis detached the king of Denmark by a subsidy of 800,000 crowns, and by luring him with the promise of supporting his pretensions to the duchy of Holstein Gottorp, as well as to the towns of Lubec and Hamburgh; and he successfully tampered with the governing party in Holland. He at the same time secured the neutrality of England, by remitting to Charles II. sufficient sums of money to supply his profusion, without being reduced to the necessity of assembling a parliament. In the empire he found a partisan in the elector of Brandenburgh, who equally dissatisfied with Spain for withholding the arrears of his subsidy, and with the emperor for forcing him to accede to the treaty of Nimeguen, and for taking possession of the Silesian duchies *, employed all his efforts to prevent the diet from declaring war against France; and even entered into a treaty with the king of Denmark, and the bishop of Munster, to preserve the neutrality of Germany. Above all, Louis gave sufficient employment to Leopold, by fomenting the rebellion in Hungary, and inciting the Turks to invade the Austrian dominions.

Trusting to the effect of these intrigues and negotiations, he commenced, in 1685, aggressions against Spain by invading the Netherlands, captured Courtray and Dixmude, and after dismantling Treves, made himself master of Luxemburgh. This series of aggressions divided or intimidated

---

* The elector claimed the principalities of Lignitz, Brieg, and Wohlau, in virtue of a compact of inheritance, concluded in 1557. But on the death of the last duke, Leopold took possession of these principalities as fiefs reverting to the crown of Bohemia.

the other European powers; for the unfortunate divisions
in the empire, the impolitic neutrality of England, the
apathy of the Dutch, and above all, the increasing dangers
of Leopold, enabled Louis to consolidate the greater part
of these acquisitions by a truce which was concluded at
Ratisbon, on the 26th of August, 1684, for twenty years,
between France on one side, and Spain and the emperor
on the other. During this period France was to retain
Luxemburgh, Bouvines, Beaumont, and Chinay, with their
dependencies, as well as all the places in the Netherlands
re-united before August 20. 1683. From the empire, Louis
acquired Strasburgh, Kehl, and the places re-united before
August 1. 1681, with the rights of supreme sovereignty in
Alsace, which were not in future to be contested. He
promised in return to confirm the territorial proprietors
who should do homage, or take an oath of allegiance, in all
their rights civil and religious, and agreed in a separate
article, not to disturb the Catholics, Lutherans, or Calvinists,
in the free exercise of their religion, or in the enjoyment of
their ecclesiastical property.

On the conclusion of this truce, the power of France and
the glory of Louis had attained their highest elevation.
Under the celebrated Colbert, the finances had been placed
in excellent order, justice ameliorated, the police improved,
commerce extended, colonies and manufactures established ;
canals and communications were opened, new ports and
arsenals formed or forming at Dunkirk, Toulon, Brest,
Rochfort, and the places on the channel ; a navy of 100
sail, manned by 60,000 sailors, spreading terror through
the Mediterranean, and contesting the mastery of the ocean
with England and Holland. These improvements were
accompanied with the patronage of all the arts which improve or adorn life, and with the protection of letters and
science ; nor was the munificence of the sovereign confined
to his own subjects, but men of genius distinguished in every
branch of knowledge, and in every quarter of Europe,
were taught to look up to the French monarch as their
patron and protector.

Louvois placed at the head of the war department, raised
the military system to the same degree of perfection as
Colbert had raised the civil institutions and naval force

The standing army, commanded by the most skilful generals of the age, was greatly augmented and strictly disciplined; schools were instituted for the education of officers in the higher branches of their art; while the indefatigable perseverance and stern severity of the minister, maintained a wonderful promptitude and order throughout a military establishment the most extensive in Europe. He introduced the plan of subsisting armies by means of magazines, stored the frontier places with every requisite for defence or attack; and whenever the caprice or ambition of Louis induced him to meditate an irruption or siege, however distant or however sudden, the regulations were arranged for assembling the troops, their marches calculated, their quarters fixed, and every necessary provided for the enterprise. The recent acquisitions, as well as the original boundaries of the kingdom, were strengthened with new fortifications, and a double or triple line of fortresses at the same time rendered the frontier impenetrable, and furnished on every point the means of aggression into the neighbouring countries. The perfection to which this branch of the military system was raised, was principally owing to the skill of Vauban, who, though he has less attracted the notice of history than Turenne, Condé, or Luxemburgh, contributed as much, by his talents as an engineer, to the extension and establishment of the French power, as any other man in the age of Louis XIV., so fertile in great men. To him France was indebted for new modes of fortification, and still more for a new species of attack, which, by reducing the duration of sieges almost to the certainty of calculation, introduced an essential change into the art of war, and gave that vast predominance to the arms of Louis, and that celerity to his conquests, which confounded his enemies, and secured him the superiority, till the same inventions were adopted by his adversaries.

Puffed up with uninterrupted success; exulting in the dread or the admiration which he inspired throughout Europe; impelled by inordinate love of glory, Louis disdained the artifice and colouring with which he had hitherto cloaked, and the address and caution with which he had carried on his first aggressions. He threw off the mask, openly trampled on the most solemn engagements and established rights, treated the other states of Europe as a master, a judge, and a conqueror; and insulted his contemporary sovereigns with the arrogance of a feudal lord towards his vassals. He had recently dictated a peace with all the authority of a master ; and while most of the other states disbanded or reduced their forces, he still maintained his army and navy at their full complement, and seemed watching for the moment when he might proceed to new usurpations ; careless of the means, and employing alike the pen and the sword, violence and deceit.

Inflamed by superstitious fervour, Louis aspired no less to shackle the consciences and the persons of his subjects, than to awe the other states of Europe. Hitherto he had sullenly confirmed the toleration granted by Henry IV. to the Huguenots, from respect to the remonstrances of Colbert ; but in 1683, after the death of that great minister, he revoked the edict of Nantz, and followed the revocation with persecutions, which recalled the memory of the barbarities exercised against the Protestants in the early stages of the Reformation. Their ministers were banished, their churches destroyed, liberty of conscience abolished, children torn from their parents to be brought up in the Catholic religion, every species of severity adopted to prevent adult persons from seeking that freedom of worship in another land which was denied in their own, and the plans of Jesuits and monks executed with all the military despotism of the relentless and unfeeling Louvois. The effects of this intolerance were similar to those which followed the fatal persecutions in Bohemia. Notwithstanding all the vigilance of civil and military tyranny, above 500,000 persons found means to emigrate, carrying with them their riches, their industry, their manufactures ; and, what was still more fatal to France, spreading throughout every country of Europe where they found an asylum, that detestation with which they were themselves animated by the cruelties of their persecuting sovereign.

While Louis tyrannised over his subjects at home, and domineered over Europe, he did not intermit his aggressions against the empire. Notwithstanding the recent truce, he continued his system of re-union, by appropriating the possessions of the Teutonic order and of the chapter of

Strasburgh in Alsace, confiscated the territories annexed to the university of Friburgh, and extorted from the elector of Treves an annual tribute, under the name of a due to the duchy of Luxemburgh. He made other encroachments of less importance, though not less galling, in the Brisgau, and, contrary to the fate of treaties, persecuted the Protestant inhabitants of Saarwarden and Saarbruck. He continued to multiply the means of invading the German empire by additional fortifications on the banks and islands of the Rhine, the Moselle, and the Saar, most of which were erected on the territories of the German princes, and at the same time he evinced his hostile designs by maintaining a formidable army on his frontier.

These aggressions, together with his unfeeling and domineering character, gradually alienated many of those princes who had hitherto been warmly attached to his cause. Of all his allies he could only depend on the king of Denmark, who was animated by dislike of Austria and Sweden, and the dukes of Brunswick Wolfembuttel, whom he held by a subsidiary treaty. Even though he shackled James II. of England with the same golden fetters with which he had entangled Charles, he was opposed by the rising spirit of the British nation. The people who had borne with the vices and servility of Charles from a love of his easy character and popular manners, as well as from a dread of returning anarchy or republican despotism, were roused by the designs which James did not affect to conceal against their religion and liberties, participated in the common aversion of Europe against the despotism and persecutions of Louis, and looked up to the prince of Orange for support against the arbitrary schemes of their sovereign and the ambition of his protector.

While most of the European states were awed into submission, or sunk into apathy, Leopold was not insensible of his own humiliations nor of the danger arising from the ascendency of the house of Bourbon; but embarrassed with the wars in Hungary, and curbed by the opposition of the elector of Brandenburgh, and the adherents of France in the empire, he submitted with silent indignation to his wrongs, and watched with sedulous attention for an opportunity to rouse the dormant spirit of Europe. He found an able coadjutor in William, prince of Orange, who, besides the same political grievances, was animated against Louis by motives of religious and personal anti-pathy, and at this time was anxious to employ the arms of France on the Continent, that he might comply with the general voice of England, in overthrowing the civil and religious tyranny of James.

These two princes united to take advantage of the gene-ral antipathy against the common enemy. William, avail-ing himself of the abhorrence excited even among the French party in Holland, by the persecutions of the Hugue-nots, effected a revolution in the sentiments of his country-men, animated them with his own fervour, and with no less effect exerted his personal and political influence over the king of Sweden and the members of the empire. Leo-pold himself, equally active and successful, again drew to his party the elector of Brandenburgh, by sacrificing to him the circle of Schweibus, as a compensation for his claims on the Silesian duchies, and obtained the hearty co-operation of the powerful princes of Brunswick Luneburgh, by luring them with the prospect of the electoral dignity.

Fortunately at this momentous interval a dispute for the succession of the Palatinate afforded the emperor and prince of Orange a pretext for resistance against France, and an object for uniting the empire and their adherents in a general association.

On the death of Charles Louis, elector Palatine, the last male of the house of Simmeren, in April, 1685, the succes-sion was disputed by the lines of Neuburgh and Weldentz, and the allodial property claimed by his sister, Elizabeth Charlotte, who was married to the duke of Orleans, brother of Louis XIV. After a short contest, the suit being de-cided in favour of Philip William, duke of Neuburgh, the brother-in-law of the emperor, he received the investiture of the electorate, and was acknowledged by the diet. But the duchess of Orleans claimed, under the title of allodials, all the moveable property of her deceased brother, even his artillery and ammunition ; and finally extended her pre-tensions, under one title or another, to the greater part of the territories which belonged to the house of Simmeren. Louis, ever eager to pursue his usurpations in the empire, supported these pretensions by threatening to invade the Palatinate.

The emperor and the prince of Orange took advantage of the alarms excited by these designs. By their mediation, alliances were formed between the United Provinces, the elector of Brandenburgh, and the king of Sweden ; and a subsidiary treaty concluded between Leopold and the elector. Finally, Leopold, the king of Sweden, as possessor of Pomerania and Bremen, and the principal members of the empire, united in the celebrated League of Augsburgh, which was concluded June 21. 1686, of which the object was to resist the aggressions of France, under the pretext of maintaining the treaties of Munster and Nimeguen and the truce of Ratisbon. Arrangements were settled for assembling an army of 60,000 men, which was to be intrusted to the command of the elector of Bavaria, the prince of Waldeck, and the margrave of Bareith.

Alarmed at this rising opposition, Louis suspended his intended invasion of the Palatinate. He proposed to convert the truce of Ratisbon into a peace, and permitted the duchess of Orleans to accept the sum of 100,000 livres, in compensation for her claims. But the empire, at the instigation of Leopold, refusing to secure him in his recent encroachments, by rendering the truce of Ratisbon permanent ; this refusal, joined to the hostile aspect of Germany, the successes of Austria against the Turks, and the expedition which the prince of Orange was forming against his father-in-law, induced him again to become the aggressor, in order to dissipate the combination before it had attained consistency. He revived, and even extended, the claims of the duchess of Orleans, and took advantage of a disputed election in the see of Cologne. By supporting William, count of Furstemberg, who was chosen by a part of the chapter, against Joseph Clement, brother of the elector of Bavaria, whose cause was espoused by the pope and the emperor, he obtained possession of Bonn, Kaiserswerth, and the principal places of the electorate, except the capital, which admitted the troops of the empire. He followed this aggression by sending an army of 80,000 men into the Palatinate, under the command of the dauphin, despatched other bodies on the side of Treves and the Low Countries, and before the close of 1687 captured Philipsburgh, conquered the whole Palatinate, reduced Spire, Worms, and many other fortresses on the Rhine, with Treves and Huy in the bishopric of Liege. At the same time he displayed his resentment against the pope, by the sequestration of Avignon. To these irruptions he experienced little opposition. The emperor being eagerly employed in pushing his success against the Turks and the rebels of Hungary, no other proof of hostility was shown than the dismission of the French ambassadors from Vienna and Ratisbon.

Fortunately for the house of Austria, Louis poured his troops into Germany, with a view of effecting a diversion in favour of the Turks, instead of invading Holland; and by this oversight, allowed the prince of Orange time and opportunity to achieve the revolution in England, which ultimately put a period to the continental despotism of France.

The people of England had submitted to the arbitrary measures of James in sullen silence, with the hope that his death would deliver them from his tyranny, and that the constitution would be restored under the reign of his daughter Mary, and the administration of her husband, the prince of Orange. But the birth of a prince of Wales spread general consternation, lest a son, educated by so bigoted and arbitrary a father, or succeeding a minor to the crown under Catholic guardians, should entail popery and absolute power on the nation. On the delivery of the queen, rumours were spread and readily believed, that the child was supposititious; and these rumours, however improbable, found a ready relief both in England and Holland. A general combination was formed to exclude the young prince, and William was invited by the principal nobility, clergy, and gentry, to assist them in the recovery of their constitutional rights.

He accordingly made active preparations, both by land and sea; assembled an army, in 1688, on the side of Germany, as if to concur with the league of Augsburgh; and, when his measures were ripe for execution, drew his forces rapidly to the coast, and embarked them at Helvoetsluys. With a fleet of fifty armed ships, besides numerous transports, and a body of 15,000 men, he landed at Torbay on the 5th of November, 1688, a day already memorable in the annals of England, for the discovery of the popish plot. After a trifling suspense, he was joined by the principal nobles and gentry, received with enthusiasm by the people, and became master of England, without shedding a drop of blood. He connived at the escape of James, summoned a parliament, and, after some difficulties, which arose from the attachment of the nation to the right of hereditary succession, the throne was declared vacant, the crown conferred on William and Mary, and the sole administration vested in the king. Thus terminated a revolution so happy for England and so fortunate for Europe, which every circumstance however discordant, every interest however adverse, almost miraculously combined to promote. James himself, though frequently apprised by Louis of the intentions of his son-in-law, acted with equal presumption and infatuation, taking no measures to discover or defeat the enterprise till the very moment of execution. Louis, though acquainted with the whole progress of the design, instead of attacking Holland, which would have prevented the departure of the prince, pushed his troops into a distant quarter of Germany. So general, indeed, was the detestation fostered against France, that every power concurred in furthering the expulsion of James, as the means of lowering the interest of the common enemy. The heterogeneous mass of the Germanic body joined with the court of Spain to protect the United Provinces during the absence of William, while Leopold, and even the pope, preferring their political interests to their zeal for the Catholic faith, countenanced the expulsion of a Catholic, and the accession of a Protestant prince.

The revolution in England produced a great and instantaneous change in favour of the allies. The empire was encouraged, by the instances of Leopold, to issue a formal declaration of war against France; the allies of Augsburgh assembled their contingents, and early in the spring troops advanced from every quarter towards the Rhine. Alarmed by these preparations, Louis abandoned his design of maintaining himself in Germany, and withdrawing his forces, gave orders to lay waste the Palatinate and the neighbouring provinces, as an additional means to secure his frontier.   These cruel orders were too rigidly obeyed, and a scene of devastation was exhibited to the eyes of mankind, which is scarcely paralleled in the annals of the most barbarous people.   Above forty towns, besides innumerable villages, were given up to the flames; the unfortunate inhabitants, driven into the open fields then covered with snow, were exterminated by famine, by hardships, or the sword; and the most fertile country of Germany was rendered almost a desert.   These horrible devastations committed on a defenceless and unresisting people, roused to detestation that general horror against France which pervaded all Europe; increased and confirmed the influence of Leopold, and encouraged the allies to redouble their efforts for reducing a monarch who had violated the laws of nations, and trampled on the rights of humanity.

Frederic, who, on the 20th of April, 1688, succeeded his father as elector of Brandenburgh, espoused the cause of the house of Austria with the most ardent zeal, and his conduct was emulated by the princes of Brunswick Luneburgh.*   Their troops, assisted by those of the neighbouring states and the Dutch forces, drove the French from a considerable part of the electorate of Cologne, and recovered the territories of Treves.   Another army, composed of Austrians, Saxons, Bavarians, and Hessians, led by the duke of Loraine, traversed the desolated fields of the unfortunate Palatinate, reduced Mentz, and uniting with the forces under the elector of Brandenburgh, by the capture of Bonn, deprived the French of a post which enabled them to endanger the very existence of the United Provinces.

The combined princes, no less active in negotiations than in arms, increased their party, and concentrated their efforts by alliances.   After various leagues and separate combinations, Leopold was enabled to lay the foundation of a grand alliance, which ultimately united all the powers of Europe against France, except Portugal, Russia, and a few of the Italian states.   The commencement of this confederacy, was the league between the emperor and the

* George William duke of Zell, and Ernest Augustus duke of Hanover.   See chapter 64.

states general, concluded at Vienna, on the 12th of May, 1689. It was couched in the usual terms of an offensive alliance; the two parties agreed to exert their whole force by sea and land against the common enemy, till all things were restored to the same footing as was settled by the peace of Westphalia and the Pyrenees, and they engaged to make no truce or peace without mutual consent. They bound themselves also to procure the re-establishment of the duke of Loraine ; by secret articles the emperor or his heirs were to be supported in their right of succeeding to the Spanish monarchy should Charles II. die without issue; and the contracting parties were to further the election of the archduke Joseph as king of the Romans. Finally, the adherents of France were to be treated as enemies ; all the allies of both parties were to be admitted, and they even engaged to maintain a perpetual league against France after the conclusion of peace. On the invitation of the United Provinces, William acceded as king of England ; the king of Spain on that of Leopold, and the example was followed by the empire, the duke of Savoy, and the king of Sweden. The dukes of Luneburgh compelled the house of Wolfembuttel to secede from its connections with France, and the king of Denmark entered into a subsidiary treaty with England, to furnish 8000 men against his former ally. The revolution, by placing England and Holland under the same chief, allayed that commercial and national jealousy which had exhausted their strength in efforts for mutual destruction, and enabled them to employ their vast resources in the cause of public liberty and the house of Austria.

From this period the disposition of Europe presented a new aspect. France, instead of being assisted by a multitude of allies, friends, or adherents, was left singly to combat a host of foes. The same enthusiasm which had thrown the empire under the tutelage of France, turned in favour of the house of Austria ; the German states, who adored Louis as their great supporter against the tyranny of their chief, now considered him as the most dangerous enemy of their liberties, and regarded his power as a destructive torrent against whose ravages they could not oppose too strong a barrier.

The first proof of this surprising change in the empire was the unanimity with which the archduke Joseph was chosen king of the Romans, on the 4th of January, 1690, although he had not yet completed his eleventh year. In an electoral meeting assembled at Augsburgh, Leopold himself even ventured to state the pretensions of his son in a style which savoured of hereditary right. All ideas of a permanent capitulation were abandoned, and not a single article was added to that which had been signed by Leopold, except one temporary regulation arising from the nonage of the young king. A momentary clamour of the princes against the mode of this election, ended in the presentation of a strong, though fruitless protest.

The strict union of the empire, and the formation of a vast combination, seemed likely to overwhelm Louis XIV. But France, by her compact territory, by the strength and valour of her disciplined armies, the order of her military system, the skill of her generals, and above all by the enthusiasm of her people, triumphed by land over all the attacks of this host of foes. In the Low Countries, marshal Luxemburgh defeated, in July, 1690, the prince of Waldeck at the battle of Fleurus; Louis himself took Mons and Namur, in April, 1691; and the allies under the command of William were routed at Steinkirk and Nerwinden, in 1692. On the Rhine, the German allies, who on the death of the duke of Loraine, were commanded by the electors of Saxony and Bavaria, were reduced to inaction, and afterwards had the mortification to see the French renew their devastations in the Palatinate and ruin Heidelberg, which had begun to rise from its ashes.

But these successes were counterbalanced by the failure of the different expeditions fitted out by Louis to reinstate James on the throne of England. With the assistance of France, James recovered possession of all Ireland; but William had no sooner suppressed the internal factions in England, than he poured his forces into the sister island, and by the splendid victory of the Boyne, on the 4th of July, 1690, dissipated at once the hopes and resources of his abdicated father-in-law. James was reduced again to seek a refuge in France, and before the close of the ensuing year, Limerick, the last remnant of his power, submitted to the conqueror. Louis, not discouraged by this failure, made new and greater efforts. His fleet under Tourville having defeated the English and Dutch off Brest, he availed himself of his naval superiority to make an attempt against England itself. Two great armaments were formed at Toulon and Brest; a considerable army was assembled in Normandy, and James himself repaired to the coast to head the expedition. Louis, confident of success, relying on the discontents in England, and on the supposed partiality of the fleet to its former sovereign, did not wait the arrival of the Toulon squadron, but ordered Tourville again to attack the English and Dutch fleets, though they were far superior in number. The consequence of this rash attempt was, the destruction of the Brest squadron off La Hogue, in May, 1692, and the loss of that naval superiority which Louis had acquired with such labour, expense, and perseverance.

Thus secured on his throne, William turned the whole force of England and Holland against France, and arrested her progress in the Low Countries. He recovered Namur in the sight of an army, which vainly endeavoured to regain its honour, or disconcert the designs of the allies, by the capture of Dinant, and the bombardment of Brussels. He increased the lustre of his military reputation, which had shone even in the midst of failures; and Europe saw a French force far more powerful than that which had so rapidly overspread Holland, and twice given law to Spain, reduced almost to the defensive, and its operations confined to marches and countermarches, or bounded by the capture of a few towns from which it drew no essential advantage.

In the midst of these transactions the war had languished on the Rhine. Notwithstanding the zeal of Leopold, and the unanimity of the diet, all the efforts of the Germans terminated in a faint attempt to penetrate into Franche Comté, and a temporary irruption into Alsace. On the other side, the French having exhausted their principal efforts in their navy, and in the Low Countries, Spain, and Italy, their army effected nothing more than inroads into the unfortunate Palatinate, in which the former devastations were repeated.

E E 4

In Italy and Spain the French were completely victorious. Victor Amadeus, duke of Savoy, being subsidised by the Maritime Powers, collected a considerable body of troops, and was strengthened by reinforcements from the Milanese and Germany. Yet though at the head of superior numbers, he was unable to cope with the talents of Catinat; he was routed at Staffarda, and his defeat was followed by the loss of Saluzza and Susa; Savoy was soon afterwards overrun, Nice and Montalbano were taken, and his whole territory to the walls of Turin laid under contribution.

In this situation of affairs, the enthusiasm which had animated the German empire gradually subsided, and at the same time its exertions were enfeebled by religious disputes and civil discords.

Of these the principal was derived from the creation of a ninth electorate in favour of the house of Hanover, and the attempts of Leopold to revive the electoral privileges of Bohemia.

In reward for the services rendered to Austria during the wars with France and Hungary, by George William duke of Zell, and Ernest Augustus duke of Calemberg or Hanover, Leopold proposed to raise a ninth electorate in favour of their house. Having in 1690 gained the electoral college, he profited by his own popularity, and the antipathy which he had excited against France, to carry this design into execution, and concluded, on the 22nd of March, 1692, with the two princes a treaty of hereditary union and defensive alliance at Vienna. He promised to confer on Ernest Augustus, in whose favour George William renounced his pretensions, a ninth electorate, with the office of arch-banneret, and the reversion of the arch-treasurership of the empire on the extinction of the eighth electorate, and engaged to assist in defending their dominions if attacked. In return, the two princes stipulated to maintain, besides their ordinary contingent, a corps of 6000 men in the service of the emperor, as long as the war with France and in Hungary should continue; to pay during the same period a subsidy of 100,000 crowns, to assist with their whole force in raising the archduke Charles to the throne of Spain, should the king die without issue; to contribute a subsidy of 144,000 crowns, or supply 2000 men, should Hungary be invaded by the Turks ; and to use their influence in recovering to the kingdom of Bohemia the exercise of its electoral rights. Ernest Augustus bound himself and his successors for ever to vote in all elections, during the vacancy of the imperial throne, in favour of the eldest member of the house of Austria ; both princes agreed to act in concert with the imperial court in all the general and particular assemblies of the empire, and to confer on the Catholics the free exercise of their religion at Zell and Hanover.

In virtue of this treaty, the emperor proposed the intended creation to the electors assembled in the diet of Ratisbon. But he experienced an opposition which he had little reason to expect ; for even Mentz, Saxony, Brandenburgh, and Bavaria, who had before promised their concurrence, began to waver, and the three others protested against it as an infringement of the Golden Bull, which had fixed the number of electors, and as a measure which would give too great a preponderance to the Protestant interest. Rhodolph Augustus, duke of Brunswick Wolfembuttel, as chief of the elder branch, reprobated the elevation of the younger to a superior dignity ; while the duke of Wirtemberg objected to the post of arch-banneret, as an invasion of his rights as arch-standard-bearer. The formal investiture of the new electorate, before the close of the year, gave new fury to the dispute. Still more irritated by this disregard of their remonstrances, the college of princes presented to the diet a solemn protest against the investiture, and followed this measure by concluding a league, under the name of the Corresponding Princes, against the ninth electorate. The construction of new fortifications at Ratzeburgh furnished a pretext for hostilities between the king of Denmark and the house of Luneburgh, and in the commencement of 1693, the corresponding princes assembled their troops to support their ally. As the affair now bore the most serious aspect, and afforded an opportunity for the interference of France, Leopold prudently waived his designs, and with the concurrence of the new elector, informed the diet, that he would suspend the effect of his investiture till he could obtain the consent of the states. He at the same time negotiated an accommodation with the king of Denmark, and induced the duke of Zell to sacrifice the fortifications of Ratzeburg for the sake of the general tranquillity. These concessions pacified the diet, and prevented the extension of a dispute which might have enabled France to recover her influence in the empire, and given birth to a civil war.

To obviate the objections of the Catholic body against the establishment of a new Protestant electorate, as well as to attain an object much coveted by his predecessors, Leopold proposed to reinstate Bohemia in all the electoral rights, which from various causes had been either lost or suspended, and for this purpose procured for the Bohemian plenipotentiaries a share in arranging the capitulation of his son Joseph. The proposal, however, was violently opposed by the corresponding princes, who were joined by the Protestant body, and the question became identified with the dispute relative to the new electorate. The corresponding princes renewed their league; and these rising troubles contributing to divide and weaken the Germanic body, Leopold could only quiet the ferment by withdrawing his proposal, and deferring his design to a more favourable opportunity.

These concessions, and the conciliating conduct of Leopold, restored the union of the empire. In 1695 he procured the renewal of the grand alliance, and the accession of the bishop of Munster, with several other princes, and afterwards effected a grand association between the five circles of Franconia, Suabia, Westphalia, and the Upper and Lower Rhine; but all these engagements could not overcome the natural tardiness, nor remove the incurable jealousy of the Germanic body, and the whole empire clamoured for peace.

The other members of the Grand Alliance were equally anxious to withdraw from the contest.

England, drained of men and money, had seen her trade interrupted by the enterprises of the French, notwithstanding her superiority by sea, and had been the scene of incessant struggles for the restoration of the abdicated monarch, which had been fomented by the intrigues of France. The sentiments of William himself had undergone a material change. He was alarmed with the renewal of immense preparations for the invasion of England, and with the discovery of a plot to assassinate him; and in this uncertain state he was unwilling to carry on a war merely for the sake of entailing the whole succession of Spain on the house of Austria, when the other objects of the Grand Alliance, which peculiarly regarded England and Holland, were attained. The United Provinces were still more anxious for peace than England; because they had borne a more onerous part in the burdens of the war than the other members of the alliance; and because, in case of a reverse, they were more immediately exposed to danger. Spain had little or no hope of preserving the Netherlands, without the assistance of the allies; a French army in Catalonia threatened to penetrate into the heart of the kingdom ; the people were in a general ferment; the court, distracted by contending parties, the treasures of America expended by anticipation, and the most dishonourable expedients, for raising money, still unequal to furnish means for the continuance of hostilities. The duke of Savoy, disappointed in his expectations, seeing his own territories overrun by the French, recurred to that versatile system of policy which every weaker state is obliged to adopt with its more powerful neighbours, and after the fatal battle of Marsaglia, in October, 1693, tampered with the court of France; though for his own safety, as well as to enhance his terms, he still affected to adhere to the Grand Alliance.

Leopold was in no better situation than the rest of the allies. Compelled to feed the war at the same time on the side of the Rhine, the Netherlands, in Italy, and in Hungary, his forces were inadequate to act with effect in so vast a sphere. Hence he lost the ascendency which he had gained over the Turks at the commencement of the war with France; and nothing but the skill of his generals, the valour of his troops, and the distracted state of the Ottoman empire, enabled him to maintain his footing in Hungary and Transylvania. His finances were exhausted; his people irritated by the imposition of new taxes; and he was constrained to employ the credit or voluntary loans of his loyal subjects. To fill the vacancies in his regiments, he had recourse to the doubtful and dangerous experiment of engaging the magnates to levy troops at their own expense; and he could only raise a weak flotilla on the Danube, by granting to individuals monopolies and privileges highly detrimental to commerce. Yet all these expedients did not meet the exigency of his situation ; his troops were ill paid and ill provided, and seldom able to take the field till the season of action was nearly past. Yet in this embarrassed situation, he was of all the allies the least desirous of peace ; because he trusted that on the death of the king of Spain (which, from his declining health, could not be far distant), the assistance of the grand alliance would enable him to realise his pretensions to the Spanish succession; and he foresaw, in the conclusion of hostilities, the necessary dissolution of that confederacy on which he relied for support.

The king of France no longer maintained his former superiority. In the first campaign, the promptitude, energy, and order of his military system had as usual given to his arms the most decisive advantages. But at length the phlegm of Leopold and the perseverance of William damped his spirit and activity. Although the French generals gained battles and captured places in the Low Countries and Germany, they no longer made the same rapid strides as in preceding wars ; and were completely successful only in Italy, where they were favoured by the lukewarmness or jealousy of the duke of Savoy. The death of Louvois, in 1691, deprived Louis of the only person capable of directing the vast and complicated system which he had himself created, and the armies had since felt the want of his vigilant and superintending genius. France was deprived of her naval superiority, and all her maritime efforts terminated in interrupting the commerce of England and Holland. Her vast armaments by sea, with the maintenance of a force amounting to 450,000 men, exhausted her revenues ; and the country, depopulated by the war, was at the same time afflicted by famine. Besides these motives for terminating the contest, Louis wished for peace, that he might traverse the designs of the emperor on the Spanish succession.

After separate attempts to divide the allies, and some general overtures, he applied, in 1695, with effect to the Victor Amadeus, induced him to intermit hostilities, suffered him by connivance to take Casale, and finally purchased his defection by restoring all conquests with Pignerol dismantled, by arranging a marriage between a princess of Savoy and the duke of Burgundy, and granting him a subsidy of 400,000 livres, to maintain his troops until the conclusion of peace. In consequence of this engagement, the duke, after formally tendering his mediation to the allies, joined his forces with those of France, and extorted their consent to a treaty of neutrality for Italy, on the 7th of October.

In the midst of the general suspicion and distrust occasioned by this defection, Louis proposed to the allies certain preliminaries, which he affected to hold forth as founded on the treaties of Westphalia and Nimeguen. He offered also to restore Strasburgh dismantled, to annul all the re-unions since the treaty of Nimeguen, to give up all the conquests made during the war from the empire and Spain, to re-establish the duke of Loraine on the terms settled by the treaty of Nimeguen; to acknowledge William as king of England, restore the principality of Orange, refer the claims of the other princes to the future treaty, and not to support the pretensions of the duchess of Orleans.

William and the Dutch being satisfied with these conditions, over-ruled the objections of Spain, of the emperor and empire, and, on the 9th of May, 1697, a congress was opened under the mediation of Sweden, at Ryswick, a village near the Hague. Besides the plenipotentiaries of the belligerent powers, for the first time, on a similar occasion, a deputation was admitted on the part of the empire, consisting of four members for the electoral college, twenty-four for the princes, and four for the towns, equally drawn from Catholics and Protestants. But this numerous deputation, though appointed in conformity to the peace of Westphalia, and the capitulation of Leopold, was wisely excluded from the general discussions of the congress, and only allowed to confer with the imperial plenipotentiaries on the affairs of the empire.

At the commencement of the negotiation, new difficulties arose on the part of the emperor and of Spain. Leopold, far from admitting the preliminaries as the basis of the treaty, insisted on the unconditional restoration of Strasburgh with all its dependencies, and the surrender of Brisac; the abrogation of all the re-unions effected by the chambers of Metz, Brisac, and Besançon, and the re-establishment of the duke of Loraine. Above all, he demanded that the contested sovereignty over the ten towns and other

places in Alsace, should be referred to impartial arbitration
and in the interim placed in the same situation as in 1673,
or, in other words, before the sovereignty of France was
established ; he likewise demanded a compensation for the
injuries suffered by the empire since the commencement of
the war. Spain, at his instigation, required the restitution
of all the places and territories of which she had been
deprived since the peace of the Pyrenees.

These terms were undoubtedly consistent with the true
sense of the Grand Alliance, justified by every principle of
sound policy, necessary for effecting a salutary reduction in
the power of France, and lessening her means of aggression
against the house of Austria, the empire, and the Netherlands. Unfortunately, however, jealousy and disunion had
hourly spread further among the allies ; and the discussions
to which this heterogeneous meeting gave birth afforded
the French court an opportunity to employ its usual address.
While the emperor was maintaining his demands with firmness and dignity, France tampered with William, on whom
the prosecution of the war principally depended. By means
of private conferences between the earl of Portland and
Boufflers, general of the French army in the Netherlands,
Louis, besides acknowledging the title of William, agreed
not to assist James either directly or indirectly ; and held
forth his former lures to the Dutch, of restoring their commercial privileges, and permitting them to form a barrier
in the Spanish Netherlands. Having obtained the concurrence of William and the states, he, with their approbation,
presented his ultimatum at the congress, founded on the
basis of the former preliminaries, with the additional option
either of Strasburgh, or Friburgh and Brisac as an equivalent, but still reserving, by vague modifications, the power
of changing the articles of the treaty of Nimeguen, which
he affected to consider as the basis of the peace. He allowed
only six weeks for the acceptance of these conditions.

Though Leopold could scarcely doubt that he should be
deserted by England and Holland, he firmly persisted in
his former demands, and endeavoured to rouse the allies to
a sense of their honour and safety. But in the midst of
these fruitless altercations, France broke the frail bonds
which united the remnant of the confederacy, by a new

attack against Spain. Barcelona was invested by Vendome, a Spanish army which advanced under the viceroy to its relief was defeated, and the place, though defended by 15,000 men, surrendered after an honourable resistance of fifty-three days, on the 27th of August, 1697. The feeble king, whose natural apathy rendered him insensible to distant failures, or whose extreme ignorance exposed him to constant deception, was panic struck with a loss which was too near to be concealed or palliated. The same consternation spreading through the court, over-ruled the influence of the Austrian cabinet, which had hitherto been predominant, and Spain prepared to abandon the contest. During this interval also, the proffered alternative of Strasburgh, or Friburgh, and Brisac, which had been artfully thrown out by France, to divide the emperor and empire, produced its effect. The time allowed for decision was spent in disputes ; Leopold, from self-interest rather than sound policy, preferring Friburgh and Brisac as possessions of his family; the deputies of the empire, Strasburgh, as an imperial city. Their discussions being prolonged till the expiration of the six weeks, the king of France produced new propositions still more unfavourable to the emperor, refusing, in particular to cede Strasburgh, and granted an additional term of twenty days for the acceptance of these conditions.

Leopold, however, still disdained to accept such onerous terms so insultingly proposed, and renewed his endeavours to rouse England and the states. He made every exertion which the exhausted condition of his treasury and his numerous embarrassments would permit, to augment the army on the Rhine, and sent his troops from Italy under prince Eugene, to strengthen the force acting against the Turks. He entered into a new alliance with Peter, czar of Muscovy; by his co-operation he counteracted the designs of France to place the prince of Conti on the throne of Poland, vacant by the death of John Sobieski, and secured the election of his friend and ally, Augustus of Saxony. By this advantage he relieved Hungary from the danger to which it would have been exposed, had the French been able to create a dependent king. But all exhortations and exertions were lost on the members of the grand confederacy. William and the Dutch, having secured their own objects, were unwilling to risk the renewal of the war for the sake of the house of Austria and the empire ; while Spain, unable to defend herself, had no other alternative than to follow their example. Accordingly the English, Dutch, and Spanish plenipotentiaries signed separate treaties on the very day on which the period of acceptance elapsed, allowed two months to the emperor and empire for their accession, and even concluded an armistice in the name of the Germanic body, although the imperial minister refused to witness the signature, and published a formal protest against their proceedings.

Leopold, however averse to this dishonourable treaty, did not venture, by rejecting the armistice, to expose the empire and himself to the whole burden of the war. He recalled the margrave of Baden, who had passed the Rhine, took Eberenberg, and invested the fort of Kirn ; but he still negotiated with a dignity and firmness which deserved better success. Deserted by his allies, and feebly supported by the empire, he could not obtain the restitution of Strasburgh, or Landau and Saar Louis, which he endeavoured to procure as an equivalent, nor could he refuse to acquiesce in the re-establishment of his nephew *, the duke of Loraine, on conditions which rendered him a vassal of France ; but he opposed with resolution and success the new encroachments of Louis, particularly an attempt to sequestrate the territories of Simmeren and Lautern, till the claims of the duchess of Orleans were satisfied. At length the interference of the Dutch brought back Louis to the terms which he had himself originally proposed ; and after a series of complicated negotiations, a treaty between the emperor and France was signed on the 30th of October, 1697, only two days before the expiration of the limited term.

By the peace of Ryswick, Louis acknowledged William as king of England, and solemnly engaged not to assist his enemies, directly or indirectly, or trouble his government ; he promised also to restore the principality of Orange, and repay the arrears of the revenue since its sequestration.

* Leopold, son of Charles IV., and father of Francis, who espoused Maria Theresa.

The treaty with Holland contained little more than the ordinary stipulations for the re-establishment of commerce. By that with Spain, Louis gave back all his conquests, except a few inconsiderable places in the vicinity of Tournay, surrendered Luxemburgh with its duchy, and the county of Chinay, and agreed to relinquish all the re-unions which he had made in Namur, Luxemburgh, Flanders, Brabant, and Hainault, except eighty towns, villages, or hamlets, which were calculated to secure his own frontier fortresses.

In regard to the empire, all places occupied, and all rights assumed by France out of Alsace, were to be restored. Leopold recovered Friburgh and Brisac, with all military works in the Black Forest, and in Brisgau ; the empire preserved Philipsburgh, and obtained Kehl, which had been recently constructed by Vauban himself. By the general outline of the treaty, all the other fortifications erected by France on the right bank, and in the islands of the Rhine, were to be demolished. The fortifications of Mount Royal, and the works at Traerback, with the fort of Kirn and Eberenberg, were to be razed before they were yielded up to their legitimate possessors. In return, the empire ceded Strasburgh in perpetuity to France, and permitted the demolition of the bridges and tête du pont at Philipsburgh. The claims of the duchess of Orleans on the Palatine succession were to be settled by amicable accommodation, and in the interim she was to receive from the elector Palatine an annual payment of 200,000 livres.

The prince of Bavaria was acknowledged elector of Cologne, and the cardinal of Furstemberg reinstated in all his rights as bishop of Strasburgh. The duke of Loraine was re-established in his dominions, and the roads before ceded to France, re-incorporated, on the condition of razing the fortifications of Nancy, ceding Longwy and Saar Louis in perpetuity, and allowing the French troops a free passage through his territories.

The treaty with the duke of Savoy, and another which had been likewise recently signed between France and the elector of Brandenburgh, were confirmed ; and the king of

Sweden, in return for his office as mediator, was to participate in all the advantages of the peace.

These were the general conditions arranged by the common consent of the plenipotentiaries from the emperor, and the deputies of the states. But at the very moment of the intended signature, and at the approach of midnight, the French ambassadors brought forward a new clause in addition to the article for the re-delivery of the French conquests and re-unions, importing that in the restored places the Catholic religion was to continue in the same state as it was then exercised. As the French had introduced the Catholic worship in many parts, where the Protestant doctrines were professed, the clause thus perfidiously intruded excited general alarm among the Protestant deputies, who considered it as an infringement of the religious peace and constitutions of the empire; and the majority, in conjunction with the Swedish plenipotentiary, refused to affix their signatures. But as it was brought forward with the connivance of the emperor and the Catholic body, the French persisted, and even threatened to continue the war against those who should withhold their signature beyond the six weeks allowed for their ratifications. Accordingly the treaty was signed by the imperial plenipotentiaries and Catholic deputies, their example was followed by those of Wirtemberg, Frankfort, and Augsburgh, and of the bench of Wetteravia, from a dread of being exposed to the vengeance of France.

When it was presented to the diet for ratification, the Protestant states renewed the remonstrances made by their deputies at the congress. They appealed to the emperor and empire against such a flagrant breach of the civil and religious regulations of Germany, and claimed support from the Protestant members of the grand alliance. But the emperor and the Catholic states, who considered themselves interested to support the clause, refused to risk the continuance of the war for a matter which they affected to regard as of little importance, while the foreign powers, careless or ignorant* of its consequences, confined them-

* The extreme ignorance of the English plenipotentiaries is evident from a remarkable passage of Burnet: — " The king was troubled at this treacherous motion ; but he saw no inclination in any

selves to remonstrances. The Protestant states, thus abandoned, vainly endeavoured to prevent the encroachments which might follow the introduction of this precedent, by proposing, as a postscript to the ratification, an assurance that the clause should be considered as a subject of dispute merely between the empire and France ; and that the Catholics should not take advantage of a stipulation which the French themselves confined to a few churches. Even this expedient was rejected ; for the emperor, in his own name and in that of the empire, ratified the treaty, without adverting to the claims of the Protestants ; and, after a violent discussion, the dispute was only suspended. This unfortunate contest produced, however, the highest detriment to the emperor and empire in general. It weakened the Germanic body, by furnishing new causes of disunion between the Catholics and Protestants, and alienated from the emperor many of his faithful adherents. The grievance was aggravated by the conduct of the Catholic princes, particularly the electors of Mentz and Palatine, who, instead of adopting the literal and obvious sense of the article, restored the Catholic religion wherever an itinerant preacher had once performed divine service. The number of these places, instead of sixteen or twenty-nine, as originally represented, amounted to no less than one thousand nine hundred and twenty-two, according to the list presented by the French envoy to the diet of Ratisbon.

If we consider the contents of the former treaties, the peace of Ryswick may be deemed comparatively advantageous to the house of Austria and the empire. Leopold recovered possession of Brisac and Friburgh, and Louis was arrested in his career of spoliation, which operated more effectually in time of peace, than his arms in time of war. But though confined to the left bank of the Rhine, he still retained abundant means of aggression, to which, on the principles of the confederacy, nothing but extreme weakness and disunion could have induced the allies to submit.

of the allies to oppose it with the zeal with which it was pressed on the other hand. The importance of the thing, *sixteen* churches being only condemned by it, as the earl of Pembroke told me, was not such as to deserve he should venture a rupture upon it."—Vol. iv. p. 293. 8vo. ed.

Louis acquired undisputed sovereignty in Alsace, which had not been yielded by preceding treaties ; and he secured that country on the side of Germany, by the permanent acquisition of Strasburgh. By the demolition of the fortifications of Nancy, and the cession of Longwy and Saar Louis, with a free passage for his troops, he obtained the means of appropriating Loraine, opening a direct communication with his Alsatian territories, insulating Franche Comté, overrunning the rich countries to the west of the Rhine, and pouring his troops into the heart of Germany. Finally, he indeed gratified the honour of the empire, by demolishing his fortifications on the right bank of the Rhine ; yet we must deem that boundary little more than ideal, when we compare a frontier covered with fortresses, with one left almost to its natural defence ; the promptitude, energy, and order of the military system in France, with the slowness and discordance of that in Germany; the difference between a great nation acting uniformly, vigorously, and systematically, under one absolute head, and a mixed multitude of states, at variance with each other, jealous of their chief, the instruments of foreign intrigues, and without a fixed or certain principle of action. Subsequent events proved the advantages arising from the acquisitions which France was thus permitted to appropriate.

The house of Austria and Europe derived permanent benefit from the expulsion of James, and the establishment of William on the British throne, which deprived France of a friend and ally, and united the vast resources and spirit of the two maritime powers, in raising a formidable barrier against the house of Bourbon. On the side of Italy, the advantage which the duke of Savoy drew from the cession of Pignerol, was rather nominal than real, because that fortress dismantled could no longer prevent the passage of a hostile force. To Spain Louis granted concessions which scarcely could have been expected, even if he had been unsuccessful ; but in reality he made these concessions from views of consummate policy, hoping, by an appearance of generosity, to eradicate from the minds of the natives the antipathy derived from his past aggressions, and thus to prepare the way for acquiring the whole Spanish monarchy.

The question in regard to the Spanish succession, which had formed a secret article of the Grand Alliance, was neither alluded to in the treaty, nor even brought forward in the negotiation. As Leopold was unwilling to relinquish a tittle of his claims ; as the allies were not inclined to prolong the war for the sake of supporting those claims in their full extent, and as Louis was equally resolved not to yield his pretensions, all parties seem by mutual consent to have passed it over in silence, although, from the declining health of Charles, the throne was likely soon to become vacant. By the shameful and impolitic precipitation with which the grand confederacy was thus dissolved, it was evident that Europe was again to become the theatre of a new war, derived from the very evils which that alliance was intended to obviate. But we suspend our account of these transactions, to resume the affairs of Hungary and Transylvania, in which the house of Austria was so deeply interested.

CHAP. LXVI. — 1667–1699.

DURING these transactions with France, Leopold was involved in a war with the Turks and the malecontents in Hungary, and finally compensated for his losses on the side of the Rhine, by driving the infidels beyond the Danube, and re-annexing all Hungary and Transylvania to his dominions.

The conclusion of the truce with the Turks only aggravated the discontents in Hungary. The continuance of the German troops, the erection of Leopoldstadt on the Wag, which, though necessary to secure the Austrian frontier, was considered by the natives rather as a curb on themselves than on the Turks, furnished new subjects of dissatisfaction, and the irruptions of the Ottoman hordes increased the ferment. The magnates collecting their retainers, under pretence of resisting the Turkish aggressions, frequently gratified their party hatred or personal revenge, by attacking each other, and the whole country became a scene of devastation and anarchy.

Mutual jealousies likewise reigned between the sovereign and the nobles : they suspected Leopold of a design to subvert their liberties, and he attributed, to a party of the most violent, a plot to assassinate him. In the midst of these contentions, a secret conspiracy was actually formed by the intrigues of the Palatine Wesselini, under the sanction of that clause in the coronation oath, which authorised the nobles to associate in defence of their privileges. The designs of the conspirators were at first obstructed by disputes for ascendency, as well as by jealousies between the Catholics and Protestants, and afterwards by the death of Wesselini ; but count Peter Zrini*, ban of Croatia, who was disgusted by the refusal of the court to confer on him the government of Carlstadt, revived the confederacy. He secured count Frangipani, a young magnate of great talents, spirit, and influence ; gained Tattenbach, governor of Styria ; Nadasty, president of the high court of justice, and finally attached to his party the young count Ragotsky, by giving him in marriage Helena, his beautiful and accomplished daughter.

The conduct of the imperial court greatly increased the strength of this faction ; for Leopold not only declined assembling a diet, and filling the office of Palatine, but connived at the excesses of his troops, and encouraged the Catholics to persecute the Protestants. Discontents, therefore, spread rapidly through the nation. The chiefs of the confederacy formed connections with Abaffy, prince of Transylvania, by his intervention, secretly appealed to the Porte, and, in 1670, assembled a diet at Cassau, in virtue of that law which allowed the nation to elect a Palatine, if the office remained vacant for three years. This meeting enabling them to consolidate their union, they made arrangements for raising a military force, and thirteen of the counties entered into a formal association. Ragotsky assembled 2000 of his retainers, and was joined by considerable numbers of insurgents ; but was prevented

---

* His brother Nicholas was accidentally killed in hunting the boar ; but, in this ferment of party, his death was attributed to the machinations of the court of Vienna.

from surprising Tokay by the resistance of the garrison, and afterwards from occupying Mongatz, where the treasures of his fathers were kept, by the opposition of his mother, who, more prudent or more timid, turned the artillery of the place against his troops.

Meanwhile Leopold was acquainted with the progress of the conspiracy, by the rebel agents at the Ottoman court, and by a servant of Tattenbach. The extent of the plot, as well as the plans of the conspirators, were also disclosed by the papers of Wesselini, which were found in the fortress of Muran, by the confession of his widow, and by the depositions of a secretary to the rebels. Aware of his danger, Leopold acted with a vigour and promptitude which confounded the insurgents. Troops were detached into Upper Hungary against Ragotsky, and into Croatia and Styria against the other chiefs ; Tattenbach, Zrini, Frangipani, and Nadasti, being secured, either by artifice or force, were conveyed as state prisoners to Vienna and Neustadt; Ragotsky, defeated in various encounters, purchased a pardon through the intervention of his mother, by admitting imperial garrisons into his principal fortresses, and betraying the intrigues of his father-in-law. From his information, and the confessions of the conspirators, Zrini, Nadasti, Frangipani, and Tattenbach were found guilty of rebellion, and publicly executed ; the sons of Zrini were sentenced to perpetual imprisonment, and as the means of rooting out their family influence, the children of the delinquents were compelled to change their names.

The emperor took advantage of this success to change the constitution of Hungary, and render the monarchy hereditary, like that of Bohemia. He published the acts of the process, declared that the whole nation, by participating in the conspiracy, had forfeited its freedom, and summoned a diet at Presburgh. As the majority of the nobles, instead of obeying the summons fled into Transylvania, he issued a proclamation on the 21st of March, in which he declared, " Having, by our victorious arms, suppressed a wicked rebellion, in which the principal ministers of the crown were implicated, and had seduced the other orders, attacked and killed our soldiers, assumed a part of our prerogatives in raising troops, levying contributions, calling assemblies, and seizing our treasures, and even engaged in a conspiracy against our life, which was frustrated by the providence of God : And whereas it is a duty incumbent on us to provide for the safety of the people who are committed to our charge, and to prevent Hungary and Christendom from being again exposed to similar disorders; We, by our absolute authority, have ordered regulations for the quartering of our troops ; and we enjoin all persons to submit, without excuse or delay, to that power which we have received from above, and are determined to maintain by force of arms. We require our subjects to give this proof of submission, lest, contrary to our natural clemency, we should be forced to execute our wrath against those who abuse our indulgence."

In conformity with this declaration, 30,000 additional troops were quartered in Hungary ; and the natives, besides being loaded with unusual taxes, were reduced to pay contributions for the maintenance of that army which awed them into subjection. Having occupied the principal fortresses, banished, ruined, or executed the chiefs, humbled the spirit, and exhausted the resources of the country, the emperor deemed his plans sufficiently matured to make a formal change in the constitution. In another proclamation, issued in 1673, he announced that, for the purpose of remedying abuses, and preventing future rebellions, he had established a new form of government, which was to restore the kingdom to its ancient splendour. He vested the supreme administration of affairs in a council consisting of a president and counsellors, whose number and appointment depended on his will ; and he nominated, as president and governor-general, John Gasper Ampragen, a native indeed of Hungary, but devoted to his service as a prince of the empire, and grand master of the Teutonic Order. His next object was to extirpate the Protestant religion. Under the pretence of being implicated in the rebellion, and inflaming the people with their discourses, the pastors were involved in a general proscription ; courts were instituted for the punishment of heresy ; the Protestants were subjected to vexatious persecutions, and deprived of their churches ; their preachers sent to the galleys*; and the whole country abandoned to all the excesses of military despotism, and the horrors of inquisitorial cruelty.

These accumulated oppressions at length drove this brave though turbulent people to despair; and both Catholics and Protestants repressed their mutual jealousies to unite for common safety. The insurgents, assisted by the prince of Transylvania, supplied with money and provisions by the French, and secretly aided by the neighbouring bashaws, maintained an arduous struggle against the superior discipline and military spirit of the German troops. But, at the moment when they were likely to be overpowered, they found an able chief in Emeric Tekeli, son of Stephen count of Kersmark, a noble implicated in the former conspiracy. Losing at once his father and his property at the early age of sixteen, Tekeli had sought an asylum in Poland, and in vain appealed to the court of Vienna for the restoration of his patrimony. Inheriting against the house of Austria an antipathy as deep-rooted as that of Hannibal against Rome, he repaired to Transylvania, gained the favour of Abaffy, at first served as a volunteer in the army sent to the assistance of the malecontents; and by the powerful influence of his family, joined to his own military talents, gained the command before he had attained his twentieth year. At the head of 20,000 men, who were rapidly joined by new followers, he made, in 1678, frequent irruptions into Hungary, secured the towns and rich mines in the mountains, continued to gain strength amidst alternate successes and defeats, and extending his conquests towards the Danube, even

* Two hundred and fifty of these ministers were sentenced to be either stoned or burnt; but their punishment was commuted for hard labour and imprisonment. Their firmness under sufferings, and their exemplary piety inspiring general compassion, their cruel judges, to remove them from the public eye, sold them at fifty crowns each to serve in the galleys of Naples. They found, however, a deliverer in the celebrated admiral de Ruyter, who after defeating the French squadron, protected the bay of Naples, by whose powerful mediation with the viceroy Los Velos, they were restored to liberty. He took them on board his fleet, and treated them with the greatest compassion and beneficence, an action which honours his name no less than his most splendid exploits.—Sacy, tom. ii. p. 315.

pushed his predatory parties into Moravia, Austria, and Styria.

The emperor, unable to recruit his troops, who were thinned by desertion and the sword, and foiled in repeated attempts to divide or gain the insurgents by partial con- cessions, abandoned his impolitic system, and offered a complete re-establishment of the constitution, with a full restoration of all civil and religious privileges. At the same time he adroitly sowed divisions among the chiefs : he lured Tekeli with the prospect of consenting to his mar- riage with Helena, the beautiful widow of Ragotsky,* and by frequent negotiations rendering him suspected by his colleagues, obtained the acquiescence of the other chiefs. A diet being assembled at Oedenburgh, on the 4th of Feb- ruary, 1681, Leopold abolished the new form of govern- ment, published a general amnesty, confirmed the election of Paul Esterhazy as Palatine, abrogated the illegal im- posts, re-established the frontier militia, granted liberty of conscience to the Protestants, and agreed to restore the confiscated property, with the power of resuming the family names, to the heirs of those nobles who had suffered for the former conspiracy. Besides these concessions, the disputed points relative to the maintenance of foreign troops, and subjecting the nobles to their own tribunals, were to be settled in conformity with his engagements at his coronation, and the other constitutions of the kingdom.

Tekeli suspecting the sincerity of the imperial cabinet or relying on the assistance of the Turks, declined com- plying with the proffered conditions, though he was pre- vailed upon, by the instances of the diet, to prolong the armistice for six months. During this interval, the em- peror despatched an envoy to Constantinople, with a pro- posal for renewing the truce of 1664, which was on the

* Francis Ragotsky dying in 1667, soon after his accommodation with the imperial court, left by his wife Helena, daughter of count Zrini, two sons, of whom the eldest, Francis, afterwards made so con- spicuous a figure in the affairs of Hungary. With a view to obtain possession of the fortress of Mongatz, and the treasures of the family, Tekeli solicited the hand of the widow ; but his suit had been hitherto frustrated by the mother of Ragotsky, who still retained Mongatz, and being a zealous Catholic, opposed the union of her daughter-in- law with a Lutheran.

point of expiring, hoping to deprive Tekeli and his adherents of that assistance which encouraged them to continue the contest. But France having commenced her encroachments by the system of re-union, exerted her powerful influence in the divan, and persuaded the Turks to evade the proposal, by demanding conditions which would have left Leopold scarcely the shadow of authority even in his hereditary dominions. He was required to pay an annual tribute, to demolish the fortifications of Gratz and Leopoldstadt, to yield Neutra, Eschkof, the isle of Schut, and the fortress of Muran to Tekeli, to restore to the malecontents all their property and rights, and to the nation all its ancient privileges.

These conditions were equivalent to a declaration of war. Tekeli, who had temporised till he could obtain external assistance, renewed hostilities on the expiration of the armistice, and being joined by Abaffy with an army of Transylvanians, reduced the imperial troops under Caprara to the defensive, and levied contributions on every side. Soon afterwards he increased his influence and power, by espousing the widow of Ragotsky, who, being freed from constraint by the death of her mother-in-law, conferred on him, with her hand, the treasures and possessions of the family, and the strong post of Mongatz. Encouraged by this accession of strength, he, in 1682, made a triumphal entry into Buda, and was inaugurated prince of Upper Hungary by the bashaw, who, in the oriental manner, gave him the investiture with a sabre, a vest, and a standard. Being joined by numbers of Protestants who were irritated at the attempts of the emperor to elude the fulfilment of his promises in regard to their religion, and assisted also by the bashaws of Buda and Waradin, he captured Zatmar, Cassau, Titul, Eperies, Leventz, and Neutra. At the same time the Turks made the most formidable preparations for the invasion of Hungary; and early in the ensuing year, the grand vizir Cara Mustapha, with an army of 200,000 men, advanced to Essec, where he was joined by Tekeli. The insurgent chief published a manifesto calling on the natives to join his standard, offered the protection of the sultan, with security for their religion, property, and privileges; and declared that no quarter should be given to those who neglected his invitation. This manifesto, and a dread of the Turks, occasioned the surrender of Vesprin and other towns, and the emperor withdrew the rest of his garrisons from the distant parts of Hungary, to save them from being delivered up by the inhabitants, or from falling into the hands of the enemy.

Meanwhile Leopold made preparations to oppose the approaching storm. He obtained a vote of succours from the German diet, entered into private alliances with the electors of Bavaria and Saxony, concluded, on the 31st of March, 1683, a subsidiary treaty with John Sobieski, king of Poland, for 40,000 men, and employed the palatine Esterhazy to levy an army of insurrection. Such however was the apathy of the imperial court, the tardiness of the German succours, and the desertion of the troops, that on the 7th of May, when the emperor reviewed his army in person at Presburgh, scarcely 40,000 men had joined his standard. The duke of Loraine, to whom the command was intrusted, attempted with this inadequate force to open the campaign by the siege of Neuhasel, but was speedily reduced to retreat by the approach of the Turkish army. He threw the principal part of his infantry into Raab and Commora, and retiring with the remainder and his cavalry, wasted the country in his passage till he reached Vienna.

He found the inhabitants in a state of confusion and terror. On the preceding night, the emperor, with his whole court, had departed amidst the clamours of the people; nothing was heard but reproaches against his ministers, and the baneful influence of the Jesuits, and execrations against a sovereign who, after drawing on them the enmity of the Turks, had left them without protection. The city was unprepared for resistance, surrounded with an extensive suburb, the fortifications dilapidated, and the garrison unequal to its defence. On one side, people were hurrying from the country to the capital as to an asylum; on the other, the burghers followed the example of their sovereign, in flying from a place which seemed devoted to destruction. The roads were crowded with fugitives, and covered with carriages laden with valuable effects; the churches and public places filled with the aged and the helpless, imploring Heaven for protection.

The presence of the duke calmed the general apprehension. In conjunction with Rudiger count Staremberg, the intrepid and skilful governor, he placed the city in a posture of defence. The suburb was destroyed, the fortifications hastily repaired, the citizens and students trained to act with the garrison. Having left a reinforcement of 8000 infantry, he fell back with the cavalry beyond the Danube, to harass the movements, and interrupt the communications of the vizir, who appeared before Vienna on the 14th of July, in the space of a few days completed the investment, and commenced his attacks.

During the progress of the siege, the duke of Loraine acted with a degree of skill and promptitude which reflects high honour on his military talents. After employing every effort to interrupt the operations of the vizir, he rapidly marched to Presburgh, defeated Tekeli, who had been detached to secure that important passage over the Danube, and repressed the incursions of the Tartars and malecontents on the side of Moravia. But still the besieged were driven to the last extremities for want of provisions ; thinned by sickness and the sword, they saw the enemy in possession of the principal outworks, and were in hourly expectation of being taken by storm. Every hope of relief seemed extinct, every exertion unavailing. The German succours had not arrived, and the Polish army had scarcely begun to assemble on the frontiers of Silesia. The duke of Loraine sent messenger after messenger to quicken their motions, and the emperor himself, driven to despair, pressed the king of Poland to hasten his march, without waiting for his army. "My troops," he said, "are now assembling ; the bridge over the Danube is already constructed at Tuln, to afford you a passage. Place yourself at their head ; however inferior in number, your name alone, so terrible to the enemy, will ensure a victory!"

These instances prevailed ; Sobieski ordered his army to commence its march, and at the head of 3000 horse, without baggage or incumbrance, traversed Silesia and Moravia with the rapidity of a Tartar horde. On his arrival at Tuln, he found the bridge unfinished, and no troops except the corps under the duke of Loraine. Stung with disappointment, his impatient spirit broke out with the exclamation, "Does the emperor consider me as an adventurer! I quitted my army to command his. It is not for myself but for him I fight." Being however pacified by the duke of Loraine, he awaited the arrival of his own army, which reached the Danube on the 5th of September, and the junction of the German succours was completed on the 7th. Eight thousand men were furnished by Suabia and Franconia, the elector of Saxony led 10,000, and the same number was supplied by Maximilian Maria, the young elector of Bavaria. With an army which thus amounted to above 60,000 men, the two commanders advanced against the Turks; on the night of the 11th, the spirit of the citizens and garrison was revived by the concerted signals; and on the following morning they descried with rapture the Christian standards floating on the Calemberg.

The rapid and unexpected approach of this powerful army confounded the vizir, whose troops were greatly discouraged and reduced by the efforts of the siege. On the memorable 12th of September, at the moment when he had been repulsed in a last and desperate attempt to carry the town by storm, his consternation was increased by the vigorous attack of the Christian army, in which the Polish monarch and the imperial general vied in skill and bravery and their respective troops in coolness and intrepidity. He suddenly drew off his forces in the night, and fled rather than retreated with such precipitation, that his vanguard reached the Raab before the ensuing evening. When the Turks gave way, the Christians burst into their lines, and on the dawn of morning were equally gratified and astonished by the booty which had been abandoned by the enemy. They found a camp stored with all the luxuries of the east, all the tents, baggage, ammunition, and provisions; an hundred and eighty pieces of artillery, the ensigns of the vizir's authority, and even a standard, which was supposed to be the sacred banner of Mahomet. The magnitude of these spoils induced Sobieski, with his characteristic pleasantry, to write to his queen, "The grand vizir has left me his heir, and I inherit millions of ducats. When I return, I shall not be met with the reproach of the Tartar wives, 'You are not a man because you are come back without booty.'"

The king of Poland, to whom the victory was principally attributed, received the warmest and most unfeigned congratulations on the field of battle. On the ensuing morning he entered Vienna, and as he passed through the camp and the ruins of the town, was surrounded by the inhabitants, who hailed him with the titles of Father and Deliverer, struggled to kiss his feet, to touch his garment or his horse, and testified their gratitude by marks of affection which rose almost to adoration. With difficulty he penetrated through a grateful people, to the cathedral, and threw himself on his knees to thank the God of battles for the recent victory. After dining in public, he returned amidst the same concourse to his camp, and with truth exulted in declaring, that this day was the happiest of his life.

The entrance of Leopold, on the 15th of September, was far different from that of the Polish monarch. He keenly felt the humiliations which had accompanied his departure; the clamours and execrations of the populace still resounded in his ears; no honours, no crowds, no acclamations marked his passage; at every step which brought him nearer to his capital, he had the mortification to hear the sound of cannon, which proclaimed the triumph of Sobieski. He shrunk from honours which he knew were undeserved, or which he dreaded to see withheld. With mingled emotions of joy and sorrow, he beheld the works of the besiegers, and the desolation of the city. To return thanks to heaven for his providential deliverance, he repaired to the cathedral, not as a prince in triumph, but on foot, carrying a taper in his hand, and with all the marks of humility. A heart far more phlegmatic than that of Leopold, must have deeply felt the difference between the unbridled effusions of gratitude and joy which had welcomed Sobieski, and the faint, reluctant, studied homage which accompanied his own return. In the anguish of his soul, he vented his indignation against count Sinzendorf, to whose sinister advice he attributed his calamities and unpopularity, and reproached him with such

bitterness, that the unfortunate minister within a few hours
fell a sacrifice to chagrin.

These feelings overcame all sentiments of admiration or
gratitude. Instead of hurrying to the Polish camp to
pour forth his acknowledgments to the conqueror, he
seemed anxious to evade a meeting, and made inquiries
whether an elective monarch had ever been admitted to an
interview with an emperor, and in what manner he should
be received. "With open arms," replied the duke of
Loraine, who was disgusted with his pride and apathy, and
alive only to sensations of reverence for the deliverer of
Vienna; but Leopold wanted liberality of sentiment to
bear an obligation, and settled the formalities of the interview with the punctilious spirit of a herald. The two
monarchs met on horseback, between the Austrian and
Polish armies. The emperor plainly clad and meanly
mounted, stiff and awkward in his address and deportment;
Sobieski, habited as on the day of battle, rode a superb
courser richly caparisoned, and the natural gracefulness of
his mien was dignified by a consciousness of his former
triumphs, and recent victory. On a concerted signal, the
two sovereigns advanced, saluted each other at the same
moment, and embraced. The conversation was short and
formal. Sobieski, frank, cordial, and tremblingly alive to
fame and honour, was disgusted with his punctilious reception; he impatiently listened to faint, embarrassed, and
reluctant expressions of gratitude which Leopold was endeavouring to articulate, and after a second embrace withdrew to his tent, leaving to his chancellor Zaluskı to
accompany the emperor in reviewing those troops who had
defeated the Turks, and saved the house of Austria.

The desire of the Poles to secure their booty, as well as
the dissatisfaction of the German princes at the ungracious
deportment of Leopold, prevented the victorious troops
from completing the destruction of the enemy by an immediate pursuit, and it was not till five days after the
battle, that the army was again put in motion. Being
increased by reinforcements, the victors continued their
progress after the flying enemy, and on the 27th of October, crossed over to the northern bank of the Danube, to
attack a corps of Turks posted at Parkan. Sobieski, yield-

ing to the fire of his temper, and his ambition for glory, pushed on at the head of his cavalry; but though accustomed to desultory warfare, he was enveloped in an ambuscade, and owed his life or safety to the bravery of his guards, and to timely succours from the duke of Loraine. The ardour of the Polish hero being tempered by the phlegm of the German chief, they waited the arrival of the infantry, and on the following day wiped off their temporary disgrace by a complete defeat of the enemy; 7000 men were killed, many threw themselves into the fort of Parkan, and the rest were drowned in attempting to cross the Danube. The allies carried the fort sword in hand, and after driving the terrified remnant of the infidels into the river, invested Gran, and compelled the garrison of 4000 men to yield a place which had remained seventy years in the possession of the infidels. This success was followed by the surrender of the towns which had submitted in the first panic of the invasion, and again hastened to acknowledge their sovereign, while the Turkish army, continuing their flight to Belgrade, abandoned Hungary.

The Christians soon afterwards separating, the greater part of the German auxiliaries returned to their respective countries. The disgust of Sobieski seems to have been increased by the jealousy of the emperor, who was offended at his attempts to mediate a reconciliation with the malecontents, and suspected him of intriguing with Tekeli to obtain the crown of Hungary for his son. He therefore drew his troops into Poland; and declared, that although he would prosecute the war against the Turks, he would not turn his arms against the insurgents.

But the imperial forces still remaining in Hungary were sufficient to pursue their advantages. The offers of the emperor, and the terror of his arms, induced the greater part of the malecontents to implore his clemency, and Tekeli was gradually insulated from those who had formed the great support of his cause. Leopold fomented those jealousies between Tekeli and the Turks which were derived from their ill-success, till the failure of Tekeli in an attempt to relieve Cassau induced the bashaw of Great Waradin to arrest him, and send him in chains to Constantinople. This impolitic act ruined the party of the malecontents; the chief who succeeded to the command joined the imperialists, and the surrender of Cassau again threw the principal part of northern Hungary into the power of the emperor. The release of Tekeli in the ensuing year produced no effect; and from this time the confidence of his adherents in the Turks was irrecoverably lost. New victories followed the imperial arms, under the direction of the duke of Loraine, the margrave of Baden, the duke of Bavaria, and prince Eugene. They captured Neuhasel, Erlau, and Buda, the ancient capital of Hungary, and the seat of the infidel power since the time of John of Zapoli ; and the battle of Mohatz, gained by the duke of Loraine, on the 18th of August, 1687, retrieved the disgrace which the crown of Hungary had suffered on the same ground under the unfortunate Louis. This splendid victory was purchased with the loss of only 600 men, while, by the acknowledgment of the vizir himself, 20,000 Turks were either killed or captured, and the plunder equalled, if it did not exceed, that taken under the walls of Vienna.

In the midst of these successes, Leopold completed his long-meditated design of rendering the crown hereditary. He availed himself of the disaffection still subsisting among those who had submitted to his authority, and either surmised or really discovered a correspondence which the discontented had opened with Tekeli. This conspiracy, the extent, nature, and even existence of which is doubtful, furnished the court with a pretext to break the spirit of the nation by the severest punishments, as a prelude to the abolition of the elective monarchy. For the purpose of examining and punishing the delinquents, a horrible tribunal was instituted at Eperies, headed by Caraffa, a foreign general of a sanguinary disposition, and composed of officers ignorant of the laws, with a few natives attached to the court. Before this tribunal every person distinguished for wealth, popularity or influence, or suspected of disaffection, was arraigned, and parties of horse scouring the country, brought daily new victims, of every age, sex, and condition. In vain the accused persisted in their innocence ; in vain those who had taken up arms appealed to the general amnesty ; a vague charge of having corresponded with Tekeli or his wife, though unsubstantiated by proofs, was sufficient to procure their condemnation, and on the slightest suspicion numbers were sacrificed to party rancour or private vengeance.

To execute the sentences of this horrible tribunal, whose cruelties scarcely find a parallel in the proscriptions of Marius and Sylla, or the massacres of the cold-blooded legal Tiberius, thirty executioners, with their assistants, found constant employment, and a scaffold erected in the midst of the town, as the place of execution, is commemorated in history by the expressive appellation of the Bloody Theatre of Eperies. The accused were thrown into dungeons, and tortured, for the purpose of enforcing confession, or the discovery of their accomplices. If they possessed strength of body and mind sufficient to support their torments, they were subjected to heavy penalties, or to a confiscation of property ; and if the smallest confession escaped in the midst of excruciating agonies, they were consigned to the executioner, in contradiction to the merciful provision of the laws, which required a confirmation of what was uttered on the rack.

The ministers and Jesuits, who, as on the former occasion, had instigated and profited by the persecutions of Leopold, again pressed him to take advantage of his successes, and the terror inspired by these severities, to revoke his concessions, establish an arbitrary government, and abolish the Protestant worship. But Leopold had learnt prudence from past experience, and appreciated the danger of driving a brave people to desperation. He rejected this infamous advice, and satisfied himself with abrogating the right of electing and of resisting the sovereign, two privileges which, without producing a single advantage, had always been injurious to the real happiness and tranquillity of the kingdom, and furnished pretexts for endless insurrections.

He delivered to a deputation of the nobles the sacred diadem, which had been transported to Vienna, and accompanied this favour by convoking a diet at Presburgh, to crown his son Joseph, " as the only means of restoring his ancient kingdom to its pristine splendour and felicity."

Though his arms were all-powerful, he did not attempt to found his pretensions on the odious right of a conqueror. He laid before the diet a declaration, deducing the claims of his house to the hereditary succession, from the ancient compacts between his ancestors and the kings of Hungary, and from the marriage of the princess Anne with Ferdinand I. He accompanied this deduction with an offer to publish a general amnesty, to suppress the tribunal of Eperies, to confirm all the civil and religious privileges of the nation except the obnoxious clause in the coronation oath, and to incorporate with the kingdom all his conquests, present and future.

Notwithstanding the wretched state of Hungary, and the humiliation of every foreign power from whom the natives could expect assistance, they adhered with singular pertinacity to the mischievous though darling privilege of electing their monarch ; they employed every subterfuge, and offered every expedient, to save a right which they considered as the palladium of their liberties. When all the threats, bribes, or concessions of Leopold could not extort their consent to render the succession hereditary in the female line, he prudently yielded to their prejudices. The states agreed to the coronation of Joseph as an hereditary sovereign, and confirmed the succession in the males, both of the German and Spanish branches ; but still reserved to the nation the right of election on the extinction of the male line. The emperor on his part nominated counsellors to examine the grievances of the people, by whose award the criminal tribunal of Eperies was suppressed, and the great and original dispute was terminated by the arrangement that the quartering and pay, both of native and foreign troops, should be settled by Hungarian and German commissaries, and that a chamber of finance, composed of both nations, should be established at Buda.

These arrangements were followed, on the 9th of December, 1687, by the coronation of the new king, who had not yet attained his tenth year, with great pomp and magnificence, and with a minute observance of all the ancient forms and ceremonies.

This advantageous change in the government, by strengthening the power of the sovereign, was the prelude to greater successes. The progress of the imperial arms was promoted by the number of enemies which the court of Vienna succeeded in raising against the Turks. The Venetians, who had joined the alliance between the emperor and Poland, conquered the Morea, with the adjacent parts of Greece, and the coast of Dalmatia. The king of Poland was again induced to resume hostilities, and succoured the house of Austria by a powerful diversion; and even Russia, won by the cession of the sovereignty over the Cossacs, heightened the distresses of the Porte by an invasion of the Crimea. The effects of these diversions, and of the pacification of Hungary, were the total defeat of Tekeli, and repeated discomfitures of the Turks; the subjugation of the whole country as far as the Save, the reduction of Belgrade, Orsova, and Widdin, and even the conquest of Servia and Bosnia. Erlau was recovered, together with the neighbouring districts of Hungary; the strong fortress of Mongatz taken, and the wife of Tekeli, with her two sons by Ragotsky, reduced to throw herself under the protection of the emperor. Michael Abaffy, prince of Transylvania, renounced his connection with the Turks, and received imperial garrisons in his fortresses; even the natives of Wallachia offered their submission, and before the close of the year 1689, Great Waradin and Temeswar were all which remained of the extensive possessions so long occupied by the infidels to the north of the Danube.

By these disasters, the Turkish empire was shaken to its very foundations. The ill success of the first memorable campaign in Hungary, and the failure of the siege of Vienna, occasioned the deposition of the chan of Crim Tartary, the execution of four distinguished bashaws, and even of the grand vizir, Cara Mustapha, nephew of the celebrated Kiuprugli, and son-in-law of the sultan. The defeat of Mohatz led to the resignation of another vizir; and the internal discontents which arose from the subsequent misfortunes added another to the many revolutions at Constantinople. Mahomet IV. was deposed in 1688, and Solyman his brother placed on the throne. The Ottoman pride was humbled by these accumulated calamities, and the new sultan proved the distresses of his situation, by repeated and pressing instances for peace.

Leopold, on his side, elated by success, with no less imprudence than haughtiness, required such exorbitant concessions, as indicated a resolution to drive the Turks from
Europe ; and thus unfortunately afforded the French
monarch an opportunity to revive the drooping spirits of
the Ottoman court, while by an irruption into the empire,
he drew a considerable part of the Austrian forces from
their conquests on the side of Hungary.

The effects of this diversion were soon manifest. As
Leopold could not pursue the war with the same vigour as
before in Hungary, the splendour of the Ottoman arms
was for a time restored by the new grand vizir of the illustrious house of Kiuprugli. He collected a numerous army,
re-established discipline, recaptured Semendria, Widdin,
and Belgrade, and recovered the provinces beyond the
Danube. At the same time Tekeli, with a Turkish force,
burst into Transylvania, which was under the nominal
government of Michael Abaffy, a youth of fourteen. Joined
by tumultuary hordes from the neighbouring provinces,
he declared himself prince by the authority of the Porte,
defeated the united imperialists and Transylvanians, captured general Heusler with other Austrian officers, confined Abaffy almost to the walls of Clagenfurth, and extorted the homage of the states.

A month, however, scarcely elapsed, before the margrave
of Baden, leaving the Danubian provinces to their fate,
forced the passes of Transylvania, surprised and drove
Tekeli into Moldavia, and, with the consent of the states,
reinstated Abaffy   Having intrusted the defence of
Transylvania to general Veterani, and the government to
a provisional regency. he maintained this administration
itself until the conclusion of the war, in opposition
to the combined efforts of the Turks and Tekeli.   Notwithstanding the vast superiority of the enemy, who in the
ensuing year again poured into Hungary, to the number of
100,000 men, the imperialists recovered Sclavonia, and the
margrave of Baden, on the 19th of August, 1691, once
more delivered Hungary by the splendid victory at Sal-
ankamen, where 20,000 Turks were left on the field, and
the vizir himself was among the slain.   The lateness of
the season, joined with the inability of the emperor to

reinforce his army, prevented the margrave from pursuing his advantages. He himself quitted Hungary to succeed the duke of Loraine* in the command of the German army, and the generals La Croix and Caprara employed the three ensuing campaigns in reducing the Five Churches, Great Waradin, and Giula. The two following years, Augustus elector of Saxony, at the head of the imperialists, was opposed to the new sultan Mustapha, who commanded his army in person; and though he had the mortification to witness the defeat of 7000 men under general Veterani, and to suffer considerable loss at the doubtful battle of Olatz, on the 26th of August, 1696, he awed the Turks by his firmness and decision, and the success of the sultan only produced the recapture of Titul and Lippa, Lagos and Caransebes.

The campaign of 1697 bore a far different aspect. As the neutrality of Italy enabled Leopold to draw new forces into Hungary, the most active preparations were made by the Turks, as well as the imperialists, for a vigorous contest. An insurrection excited in Upper Hungary by the adherents of Tekeli, who. took Tokay and Bazar, drew the two armies into the field at an early period. The Turks were again led by their sultan; the imperialists by prince Eugene of Savoy, who was now for the first time placed at the head of an army. The sultan collecting his forces at Belgrade, took Titul by storm, and threatened Peterwaradin; but on the approach of the imperial general, who had sent detachments to reduce the rebels, and strengthened himself with reinforcements from Transylvania, he suddenly crossed the Danube, and ascended the Teiss with the intention of surprising Segedin, and subjugating Upper Hungary or Transylvania. Eugene, however, instantly threw a garrison into Segedin, and followed the movements of the enemy. Learning from his parties that the Turks had abandoned their design on Segedin, and were crossing the Teiss at Zenta over a temporary bridge, he hastened to attack one part of their army while separated from the other. When he had approached within a league of the enemy, a courier arrived from Vienna, with

* Charles IV., duke of Loraine, died in 1690, and was succeeded in his nominal sovereignty by his son Leopold.

peremptory orders from the emperor not to risk an engagement; but such an opportunity was too favourable to be
lost, and the youthful hero ventured to disobey the
mandate of his sovereign. On the 11th of September, his
army advanced in twelve columns, and by four in the
afternoon was formed in sight of the enemy, the left flank
supported on the Teiss, the right stretching into the
country. As the Turkish cavalry had already passed, and
the day was rapidly declining, he did not hesitate to commence the attack, although their bridge was covered by a
triple entrenchment, defended with seventy pieces of
artillery. Having reconnoitred the disposition of the
enemy, he bent his army into the form of a crescent to
embrace the works, strengthened the flanks with bodies of
cavalry and cannon, turned several pieces of artillery
against the bridge, to prevent the Turkish horse from re-
passing to the assistance of the infantry, and attacked the
entrenchments in every quarter at the same moment. The
assault was made with a vigour and promptitude which
surprised even the commander himself; the cavalry accompanied and supported the infantry to the very foot of
the lines, and formed a passage by filling the ditch with
the dead. The enemy, surprised by this sudden and
desperate assault, hastened their defeat by their own terror
and confusion. Numbers rushed tumultuously to gain the
opposite bank, forced their way through a body of cavalry,
which was drawn up to prevent them from deserting their
post, and in a paroxysm of terror and despair, massacred
the vizir with many of the principal officers. In the
midst of this confusion and dismay, the imperialists successively carried the intrenchments. While those who had
first effected an opening cut off the fugitives from their
bridge, the others pressed on them in front, and when they
were driven from their last rampart, a carnage ensued
which baffles description. The soldiers heated by the fury
of the attack, fell on the terrified and defenceles multitude,
and put all to the sword, not sparing even the bashaws,
who supplicated for mercy, and held out rich jewels and
purses of gold for their ransom. Above 10,000 were killed,
numbers were precipitated into the Teiss, and of 30,000
who had not crossed the river, scarcely 1000 escaped alive.

This complete victory, which cost only 500 men, was gained within the short space of two hours; and, to use the emphatic expression of the heroic commander. "The sum seemed to linger on the horizon, to gild with his last rays the victorious standards of Austria."

During the carnage, the sultan was seen on the opposite bank, displaying every gesture of consternation and despair. Flying with the first who fled, he did not rest till he had secured himself within the walls of Temeswar. He placed garrisons in Temeswar and Belgrade, abandoned the open country and the discomfited remnant of his army to the fate of war, and hurried to Constantinople to repress by his presence the commotions which this defeat was likely to excite among his turbulent subjects.

The season being too far advanced for the operations of a siege, Eugene, instead of attacking Temeswar or Belgrade, poured his victorious troops into Bosnia, and reduced the capital Serai. After laying the country under contribution, he drew his forces, laden with booty and honours, into winter-quarters, and returned to Vienna, to receive from a proud and punctilious court a reproof for disobedience, instead of a recompence for victory.

Leopold being delivered from his embarrassments in Germany by the peace of Ryswick, was at liberty to pursue his advantages against the Turks ; but the exhausted state of his treasury, and, above all, the prospect that the Spanish succession would soon become vacant, induced him to terminate the Hungarian war, that he might turn all his attention to Europe. After an inactive campaign, he listened to the overtures of the Turks, and Carlovitz, a small town near Peterwaradin, midway between the two armies, was selected as the place of conference. Plenipotentiaries were assembled on the 14th of November, 1697, from all the powers in alliance against the Porte ; the negotiations were conducted under the mediation of England and Holland ; and in little more than two months, a general accommodation was effected. Russia entered into a truce of two years, by which Peter the Great maintained possession of Asoph. By a peace signed with the Poles and Venetians, the Turks ceded to the first Kaminiec, with the province of Podolia, and the sovereignty over the Cossacs ; to the latter the Morea, with several places in Dalmatia. With Austria, a truce was concluded for twenty-five years. The emperor retained possession of Transylvania, all Hungary north of the Marosch, and west of the Teiss, and all Sclavonia, except a small district between the Save and the Danube, in the neighbourhood of Belgrade. The Turks were permitted to continue the protection which they had granted to Tekeli and his adherents, but were to give no future refuge or assistance to the malecontents; and both parties mutually agreed to punish the rebel subjects who might escape into their respective territories. An article in the peace of Carlovitz secured to the house of Austria the possession of Transylvania, although that principality was still under the nominal sovereignty of Michael Abaffy. But since the exclusion of Tekeli*, Transylvania had been

* From this period, Tekeli passed the remainder of his active and enterprising life in obscurity. As the emperor refused either to restore his confiscated property, or grant him an equivalent, the sultan Mustapha conferred on him Ley or Caransebes, and Widdin, as a feudal sovereignty. Mahomet, the successor of Mustapha, transferred him to Nicodemia, where he for a time gave him a splendid establishment; but he was afterwards neglected by the Turkish government, lodged in one of the vilest streets of Constantinople, among Jews and the meaner sort of Armenians, and receiving only a paltry allowance for himself and his family, was even reduced to carry on the trade of a vintner. It is singular that this extraordinary man, after having roused the Protestants of Hungary in defence of their doctrines, should have embraced the Catholic religion towards the close of his life. He lamented to prince Cantemir the caprice of his fortune, which had urged him to abandon his lawful sovereign, to throw himself under the protection of infidel princes whose inclinations were as wavering and changeful as the crescent in their arms. He fell a sacrifice to chagrin, and dying at Constantinople in 1705, in about his fiftieth year, was buried in the Greek cemetery, the place appropriated for the interment of foreign ambassadors. — Sacy, tom. ii. p. 499. ; History of Europe, 1706, p. 472.

His death was preceded by that of Helena, his once beautiful wife. She deserves to be commemorated for the unshaken firmness with which she bore her own misfortunes and those of her family, and her invariable attachment to her husband in exile and disgrace. After defending the castle of Mongatz with great gallantry, she was overpowered by the forces of the imperialists, and to save her own life, and the property of her family, resigned herself and her children to the protection of the court of Vienna. She herself was thrown into a convent, and her children educated under the auspices of the emperor. She was ex-

really an Austrian province; for the young prince had chiefly resided at Vienna, and soon after the conclusion of the peace, made a formal transfer of his sovereignty to Leopold, which was ratified by the states. In return he received an annual pension, with the dignity of a prince of the empire, and lived and died a subject of the house of Austria.

The peace of Carlovitz forms a memorable era in the history of the house of Austria and of Europe. Leopold secured Hungary and Sclavonia, which for a period of almost two hundred years had been occupied by the Turks, and consolidated his empire by the important acquisition of Transylvania. By these possessions, joined to the change of government, he annihilated one great source of those discontents and factions which had hitherto rendered Hungary little more than a nominal sovereignty. At the same time the sultans lost nearly half their possessions in Europe, and from this diminution of territorial sovereignty the Ottoman power, which once threatened universal subjugation, ceased to be formidable to Christendom.

CHAP. LXVII. — 1697–1700.

WE now reach that important period in the Austrian History in which commenced the contest for the Spanish succession, derived from the ominous marriage of Louis XIV. with the eldest infanta of Spain ; a contest of which Austria and Europe still deplore the fatal effects.

From his infancy Leopold had been flattered in expectation of succeeding to the Spanish throne, and in different periods of his reign had employed various expedients to prevent the alienation of so valuable a domain. Besides the constant renewal of family compacts between the two

changed for general Heuster, and permitted to join her husband, though compelled to abandon her children ; and from that period, she shared the fortunes and vicissitudes of his fate, and died in 1703.—History of Europe for 1703, p. 494.

branches of the house of Austria, for the mutual succession to their respective territories, and frequent intermarriages, Leopold had been originally affianced to the eldest daughter of Philip IV. when presumptive heiress. This hope was frustrated by the birth of a son, and the marriage of the princess to the king of France; but still, with a view to secure the eventual succession, a solemn renunciation was exacted both from Louis and his queen, and Leopold espoused the second infanta, Margaret Theresa. The union producing only a daughter, he endeavoured to prevent the transfer of her rights to another family by inducing her to renounce her claims, on her espousal with Maximilian, elector of Bavaria. He engaged also the members of the Grand Alliance to concur in support of his pretensions; and to remove the apprehension entertained by the European powers, lest the whole dominions of the two Austrian branches should be united under one head, he promised to relinquish his own claims to Charles, his second son by his third wife. But in these expectations he was also disappointed by the birth of an electoral prince of Bavaria; for the allies considering his elevation to the Spanish throne as far less dangerous than that of an archduke, became lukewarm to the interests of Leopold, and from this change of sentiment concluded the peace of Ryswick, without even the mention of the Spanish succession, though it was considered as likely to become the cause of a new war.

Charles II., the last male of the Spanish branch, was weak in body and feeble in mind, a prey to hypochondriac melancholy, and like the phantom kings of the Merovingian race, secluded in his palace, a mere puppet in the hands of those who held the reins of government. His ruling passion was an hereditary antipathy to the house of Bourbon, which was aggravated by the repeated aggressions of his brother-in-law, Louis XIV., as well as inflamed by his mother, an Austrian princess. Though by the instances of Don John he had been induced to espouse a French princess, Maria Louisa, daughter of Philip duke of Orleans, he could not conquer his inveterate antipathy, but with the imbecility of a weak mind, displayed his prejudices in the most trifling occurrences of domestic life, as well as on great occasions.* On the death of Don John, he again resigned himself to the guidance of his mother; and on the decease of his queen without issue he espoused the Palatine princess Marianne, sister to the empress, who was introduced to his bed by Leopold, with the hope of increasing that partiality for the Austrian branch, which he had fostered from his infancy.

The three principal pretenders were, 1. The dauphin of France. 2. Joseph Ferdinand, the electoral prince; and, 3. The emperor Leopold.

The pretensions of the dauphin were deduced fron his mother, Maria Theresa, eldest daughter of Philip IV., and his right would have been undoubted, had not his mother on her marriage formally renounced, for herself and her children, all title to the succession of the Spanish throne; a renunciation confirmed by the will of Philip IV., as well as by the cortes, and ratified in the most solemn manner by Louis himself.

If the dauphin's pretensions were set aside, the electoral prince of Bavaria was the undoubted heir, in right of his mother, whose renunciation was considered invalid, because it had never been approved by the king of Spain or ratified by the cortes.

The emperor Leopold claimed first, as the only remaining descendant of the male line from Philip and Joanna; and secondly, in right of his mother Mary Anne, daughter of Philip III. the legitimate heiress, in virtue of the aforesaid renunciations.

The cause of Leopold, besides, was not only supported by the two queens, but by count Oropesa, prime-minister and president of the council of Castile, by Portocarrero, cardinal archbishop of Toledo, and by almost all the members of the cabinet. Charles himself at first acknowledged the justice of his claims, by acceding to the Grand Alliance,

---

* Madame de Villars says, "le Roy a une haine effroyable contre les François." In the Memoirs of the court of Spain, it is said the queen never demanded her parrots and dogs whenever the king was in her apartment, for he would not suffer those little creatures, because they came from France, and he was out of humour whenever the queen looked at a Frenchman passing through the court of the palace. He was pleased with the duchess of Terranova, who strangled one of her favourite parrots because it could speak nothing but French.

and by a will in favour of the archduke, which he made during a dangerous illness. But the birth of the Bavarian prince produced the same change in the councils of Madrid as among the powers of Europe. Even the queen-mother deemed his rights better founded than those of the archduke, and her opinion was adopted by Oropesa, and a considerable party in the cabinet.

The death of the queen-mother, in 1696, and the retirement of Oropesa, however, allowing the influence of the queen-consort again to operate in favour of the Austrian family, Leopold sent to Madrid, Ferdinand Bonaventura count of Harrach, one of his principal ministers, who had grown grey in diplomatic intrigues, to secure the nomination of the archduke before the close of the war, that he might obtain the guaranty of the Maritime Powers in the ensuing treaty of peace. Harrach found the court divided into two parties: the queen, cardinal Portocarrero, the admiral of Castile, and the majority of the cabinet supported the Austrian candidate; Oropesa, who though in retirement was often consulted by the king, and the marquis of Mancera, were attached to the interests of the Bavarian house; the count of Monterrey, a member of the council of state, was the only considerable person devoted to France. The king himself, if so weak and fluctuating a prince could be considered as having any fixed principle, preserved the impressions which he had received from the queen-mother, in favour of the Bavarian claims. The queen, vain and imperious, without talents for business, was governed by the countess of Berlips, a German lady, who accompanied her into Spain, and by her confessor, father Gabriel Chiusa, a capuchin monk. Her German partialities, and the venality of her favourites, disgusted a people remarkable for the strength of their national prejudices; and at the same time the Austrian party, thus rendered unpopular, was weakened by contests between the cardinal and admiral for pre-eminence, and by the antipathy of the native Spaniards to the German junta.

After considerable delays and innumerable difficulties, Harrach found means to infuse unanimity into so heterogeneous a body; and obtained from the king a promise to nominate the archduke his successor, provided the emperor would send him to Spain with an auxiliary force of 10,000 men. But this opportunity was lost by the indecisive conduct of Leopold, who, from want of troops and money on one hand, and from fear of exposing the person of his darling son on the other, made endless objections. He also at length alienated his partisans by demanding for Charles the government of Milan, which was considered as a proof that his views were rather fixed on dismembering the Spanish monarchy, than securing its indivisibility.

These divisions, demurs, and punctilios having protracted the negotiation till the conclusion of the war, Louis turned his whole attention to secure the succession of Spain. He brought forward no specific claims, for fear of provoking opposition among the powers of Europe, but he kept up his military establishment, increased his army on the Spanish frontier, formed magazines, and filled the neighbouring harbours with ships of war. He at the same time despatched the marquis, afterwards duke of Harcourt, one of his most able negotiators, to Madrid, to counteract the intrigues of Harrach and the Austrian party ; and directed him, if he could not secure the nomination of a French prince, to support the Bavarian claims, or even to procure the elevation of a Spanish grandee, if more agreeable to the nation.

While Harrach, with German stiffness and phlegm, and with all the pride and punctiliousness of the imperial court, expatiated on the justice of the Austrian claims, Harcourt employed the silent influence of bribes, promises, and personal flattery, and was ably seconded by his lady, a woman of the most accomplished and winning manners. His house was open to all ; and his table, at once the scene of elegant conviviality and princely magnificence, attracted even those who were adverse to his cause, and formed a striking contrast with the formal and inhospitable establishment of the imperial ambassador. He likewise conciliated the clergy, who possess such extensive influence in Spain ; he availed himself of the divisions of the Austrian party, and the unpopularity of the German junta; he gained the majority of the cabinet, and found means to secure Portocarrero, who was disgusted with the superior influence of his rival the admiral. He applied with success to the rapacity of the countess of Berlips, roused her resentment against Harrach, who had endeavoured to procure her dismission, as the means of diminishing the odium against her nation; and tampered with the no less powerful confessor, whom he lured with the prospect of a cardinal's hat. By their influence and intervention he opened a communication with the queen herself, inflamed the dislike which she had conceived against Harrach for his harsh remonstrances and incessant importunities, presumed to hold forth the prospect of a marriage with the dauphin after the death of her husband, and succeeded in rendering her lukewarm in her efforts, if he did not wholly datach her from her Austrian connections.

During these intrigues at Madrid, Louis secured the powerful influence of the church, by conciliating Pope Innocent XII., who was irritated against Leopold, for reviving some obsolete pretensions on the Romanfiefs. He fomented also that jealousy between the elector of Bavaria and the emperor, which arose from their contrary claims on the Spanish succession, offered to support his pretensions, and attached to his cause a prince, who held the government of the Netherlands, whose dominions favoured an attack against the Austrian territories, and who gratefully proposed to repay his support, by laying at his disposal any part of the contested succession.

At length the emperor, alarmed at the growing influence of France, and freed from the embarrassments of the war, proposed to accept the offer of the Spanish court, by sending the archduke into Spain with a force of 10,000 men. But this expedient was adopted too late, for the French party in the cabinet was now sufficiently powerful to procure its rejection. Harrach, also, feeling the decline of his influence, obtained his recall from a court where he could expect nothing but disgrace and disappointment, and aggravated the general dislike which was rising against the house of Austria by impolitic reproaches and ill-timed resentment. He was succeeded by his son Louis, who, without his talents or sagacity, inherited his haughty and unconciliating manners, and, by his imprudence, widened that breach which had been effected by the intrigues of Harcourt.

While Louis was employing every art to establish his influence at Madrid, he endeavoured to amuse the other states of Europe, and prevent the renewal of the Grand Alliance. Aware that the Maritime Powers were no less unwilling to see Spain annexed to the possessions of the house of Austria than to those of the house of Bourbon, he secretly applied to William, and proposed an expedient which seemed calculated to prevent either from acquiring a dangerous preponderance. This specious project produced its effect; and after some negotiations an arrangement was concluded on the 11th of October, 1698, which bears the name of the first Partition Treaty, between Louis, William, and the United Provinces. Spain itself, the Netherlands, and the colonial possessions, were assigned to the prince of Bavaria; Milan to the archduke Charles; Naples and the Two Sicilies, with the rest of the Spanish dominions in Italy, and the province of Guipuscoa, to the dauphin. Should the electoral prince die without issue, after his accession to the Spanish throne, his share was to be entailed on his father. The contracting parties agreed to enforce the execution of this treaty, and to maintain the strictest silence to all, except the emperor, to whom it was to be communicated by William, for the purpose of obtaining his assent.

It is difficult to ascertain what were the real motives or hopes of William in consenting to this treaty; whether he suffered his jealousy of the house of Austria to overcome the just apprehensions which he ought to have entertained of Louis, or whether, embarrassed by the factious opposition in parliament and the reduction of his military force, he adopted an expedient which seemed at least likely to prevent the renewal of war. With regard to Louis, the treaty was a mere subterfuge; for with an army of 100,000 men on his frontiers, and with every means to appropriate the Spanish succession, it is not probable that so ambitious a prince should relinquish an object to which all his designs had long tended, to fulfil the stipulations of a compact, which, except the trifling acquisition of territory on the side of Navarre, gave France only a distant and

uncertain possession in Italy. On the contrary, by this
refined stroke of policy he kept the Maritime Powers in
suspense; alarmed the court and people of Spain, and
prepared them to throw themselves under the protection of
France, as the only means of preventing a dismemberment.
In fact, his motives were evident from his conduct; for
while William was vainly endeavouring to obtain the
consent of the emperor, he betrayed the secret of the
intended partition to the court of Madrid, threw the whole
blame on the Maritime Powers, and earnestly exhorted
the Spaniards to maintain the integrity of their monarchy.

The disclosure of the treaty excited the strongest
sensations at Madrid and Vienna. Leopold resented the
attempts of the Maritime Powers to compensate for his
claims by the petty cession of the Milanese, which he considered as a fief of the empire, and was still more indignant
at the exclusion of his family from all hopes of future succession, by entailing the crown on the elector of Bavaria.
The court of Madrid displayed still greater marks of indignation and horror. All parties united in condemning
the arrogance of the partitioning powers, who thus parcelled
out their country; the weak and irritable mind of the king
was roused almost to frenzy, and with a view to prevent
the fulfilment of a treaty no less hostile to his honour than
offensive to his feelings, he resolved to nominate his successor.

Louis was fully prepared for this turn of affairs. Unwilling to provoke opposition, or unite those powers whom
he had recently contrived to divide, he kept his own claims
in silence, and suffered his partisans at Madrid to support,
or at least not to oppose, the pretensions of the Bavarian
house, as the means of excluding the archduke, and de-
stroying that influence which the Austrian party might
derive from the declaration of the king in its favour. His
purposes were forwarded no less by the agency of Portocarrero, and the influence of the pope, than by the re-
establishment of Oropesa in the post of prime-minister.
The queen, who was influenced by the countess of Berlips,
remained neuter; and the adherents of Bavaria, assisted
by the agents of France, persuaded the king to consult the
council of state, the pope, and the most celebrated jurists

in Spain and Italy. The council almost unanimously re-commended the adoption of the Bavarian prince; the same sentiment re-echoed from the professors of Salamanca and the jurists of Italy; and the decision was sealed by the sacred authority of the pope. This unanimity decided the wavering mind of the king. A will was drawn up, signed, and, on the 28th of November, 1698, delivered in the usual forms, before the council of state, appointing the Bavarian prince his successor. The secret was confined to Oropesa, Portocarrero, and the secretary by whom it was drawn; but, the very same evening, the intelligence was imparted to the French ambassador, by means of the cardinal.

Louis received the account with coolness and even com-placency, and made no other opposition than a mild remonstrance against the exclusion of the dauphin. But the effect of this testament was still more striking at Vienna than even the treaty of partition; for Leopold, who had hoped, by rejecting so offensive an engagement, to conciliate the king and nation, and to see his family called to the succession, was equally confounded and pro-voked by this unexpected decision. He loudly remon-strated with the court of Spain ; the empress reproached her sister in the bitterest terms; above all, Harrach irretrievably offended the queen, by the most disrespectful expostulations, and every court of Europe was filled with the complaints of the imperial ministers.

In the midst of this general ferment, the death of the electoral prince, on the 6th of February, 1699, gave new hopes to the emperor. The partiality of the queen for her family revived; her venal and rapacious favourite seems to have again embraced the Austrian interest; Oropesa became as zealous for the Austrian, as he had been for the Bavarian succession, and he was joined by the admiral of Castile. Above all, the court of Vienna relied on the disposition of the king, and trusted that he would not remove the crown from his own family, to confer it on the hereditary and detested rival of his house, who had recently incurred his bitterest resentment, by joining in the treaty to dismember his monarchy.

In proportion, however, to the difficulty of the crisis,

Louis redoubled his activity, and he found a most subtle and indefatigable agent in Portocarrero. By a series of intrigues and artifices, assisted by fortunate accidents, the cardinal procured the removal of the king's confessor, and intimidated the queen; he availed himself of a popular commotion to obtain the dismission of Oropesa and the admiral, replaced them with his own creatures, and appropriated the direction of affairs. His influence being now predominant, the agents of France began to act more openly in favour of the dauphin, circulated papers enforcing his claims, and used every expedient to influence the public mind.

As in the former instance, Louis did not solely trust to his own exertions or the activity of his partisans at Madrid; but again endeavoured to embarrass and deceive the other powers of Europe. While he fomented the troubles of England, and renewed his cabals with the Jacobites, he opened a new negotiation with William, for another treaty of partition. The archduke was to have Spain, the Netherlands, and the colonial possessions, and the dauphin, in addition to the share assigned by the former treaty, the Milanese, or Loraine and Bar, as an equivalent. In the midst of the negotiations for settling the intended partition, the project was again artfully disclosed to the king of Spain. The intelligence produced a still greater sensation than on the former occasion; Charles made the most violent remonstrances at Paris, London, and the Hague, and with England, in particular, his representations occasioned a public breach of the correspondence between the two courts.

The activity of the French agents at Madrid having excited the suspicions of William, he threatened to break off the negotiations. But Louis disavowed the transactions of his ambassador, and solemnly declared that he would abide by the treaty, even should a will be made in favour of his family. These professions weighing with a prince who was swayed by the strictest notions of probity, the treaty was signed and ratified. In addition to the former stipulations, it was declared, that the crown of Spain was not to be united either with that of France or the empire, and therefore should the archduke die without issue, Leopold or his successor was allowed to nominate another

prince of his family on the same terms. Louis likewise
engaged that Spain should never revert to the possessor of
the French crown. Three months were allowed for the
accession of the emperor, and on his refusal, the contracting parties were to nominate another prince to the Spanish
throne; finally, a secret article contained engagements to
prevent by force of arms the passage of the archduke either
into Spain or Italy.

Nothing but the extreme embarrassment of William, the
discontents in England, and the impossibility of raising a
new combination against France, could justify a prince of
his sagacity for concluding a treaty, which left him no
resource, but reliance on the good faith of a monarch who
had long sported with the most solemn engagements. This
treaty, in fact, was a virtual exclusion of an Austrian
prince. It afforded Louis an opportunity to revive the
alarms of the Spaniards against the dreaded dismemberment; it enabled him to increase his army on the frontiers,
under pretence of taking upon himself the whole burden
of its execution ; while by excluding the archduke from
Spain, it prevented the king from securing the fulfilment
of his dispositions by the presence of his intended heir.

On considering the situation of Leopold, our surprise
may perhaps be excited, that he did not embrace an offer
which seemed to afford him the prospect of securing for
his son, Spain, the Indies, and the Netherlands, with the
support of the Maritime Powers, and even the guaranty
of France. He was threatened with the renewal of civil
contests in Germany, as the corresponding princes against
the ninth electorate were assembling troops, and preparing
for hostilities, and were instigated by the promises of
France. The elector of Bavaria, from a dependent, was
become a rival and enemy ; the elector of Saxony found
sufficient employment in securing possession of the throne
of Poland, and the war was now beginning which soon
afterwards involved all the powers of the North and the
contiguous states of Germany. His hereditary countries
were exhausted by a long and ruinous contest, and his
chamber of finance had barely sufficient credit to supply
his household with necessaries. The discontents in Hungary were only suspended, and he had reason to apprehend

lest the Turks, who were still disputing for the arrangement
of the frontiers, should be encouraged, by the prospect of
a new convulsion in Europe, to attempt the recovery of
their territories.

Notwithstanding these embarrassments, Leopold was
swayed by motives of superior strength and interest to
reject the treaty. From the recent defection of the Maritime Powers, he placed little reliance on their support ; he
justly doubted the sincerity of France, and he was unwilling
to relinquish the Milanese, which would give him a footing
beyond the Alps, and afford him the means of increasing
his territories and influence by new acquisitions in Italy.
These motives were strengthened by the apprehension of
alienating the king and Spanish nation, should he give
countenance to a treaty so offensive to their pride and feelings. In this resolution, he was still further strengthened
by the revival of his party at Madrid. The queen, for the
sake of popularity, dismissed her confessor and the countess
of Berlips, and obtained the recall of Harcourt, by betraying to the king his intrigues, and the offer of a future
marriage with the dauphin. A general sentiment also
prevailed throughout Spain, that the only means of securing the indivisibility of the monarchy was to nominate the
archduke, and hasten his arrival. Military preparations
were commenced; the duke of Medina Celi was sent to
Naples to receive imperial troops ; similar orders were despatched to Milan ; and negotiations were opened with the
duke of Mantua, to obtain the admission of a German garrison into his capital. The king even promised to execute
a testament in favour of the archduke, and sent the duke
of Moles, a warm partisan of the house of Austria, to
Vienna to convey the joyful tidings and make the necessary arrangements; while courier after courier was despatched to hasten the departure of Charles with 15,000
men.

A vigorous struggle now ensued between the contending
parties at Madrid. While the stipulations of the secret
article in the last treaty of partition deterred the emperor
from sending the archduke to Spain, or German troops into
Italy, the French agents redoubled their activity and vigilance. Blecourt remained as French envoy to Spain, to

carry on the intrigue ; Harcourt, under the pretence of commanding the army on the frontier, directed the movements of his party, and formed a chain of communication between Paris and Madrid. Portocarrero, and his subordinate agents, roused the national resentment against the Maritime Powers, and increased the general clamour for appointing a successor to the crown. In the different discussions which took place on this subject, they artfully turned the dispute on the claims and power of France. They displayed the danger of civil commotions, represented that internal contests would enable the various pretenders to dismember the succession, and enforced the necessity of appointing an heir, whose right was indubitable, and who was sufficiently powerful to sustain the weight, and preserve the integrity of so vast a monarchy. Providence, they urged, had afforded such an heir in the house of Bourbon, possessing such claims to the succession, and capable, by its arms and situation, of rendering Spain a province of France ; while the emperor was either unable or unwilling to support his pretensions at such a distance from the scene of action, or even to send the archduke to take possession of the inheritance. To obviate, therefore, a danger so imminent, to prevent a partition so dishonourable, to revive the glory, and establish the independence of the nation, they proposed to confer the crown on Philip, the second son of the dauphin ; and to take measures that Spain and France should never be united.

These discussions increased the perplexity of the timid and irresolute monarch. He considered the renunciation of Louis and his queen as valid ; he was unshaken in his attachment to the German branch of his family, and his antipathy to the house of Bourbon ; yet he wavered between the fear of involving his country in foreign and domestic war, and the desire of doing justice to his own blood. To remove, therefore, this reluctance, Portocarrero laid before him the different opinions of the adverse parties, threw him into perplexity, persuaded him as before to consult the most celebrated divines and jurists, and induced him to have again recourse to the pope, as the father of Christendom, whose profession was peace, and whose decision must derive irrefragable strength from the sanctity of his high office.

The opinion of the jurists was accordingly despatched to Rome, accompanied by a letter from the king. "Having no children," he observed, "and being obliged to appoint an heir to the Spanish crown from a foreign family, we find such great obscurity in the law of succession, and in the circumstances of the case, that we are unable to form a settled determination. Strict justice is our aim, and to be able to decide with that justice, we have offered up constant prayers to the Supreme Being. We are anxious to act rightly, and we have recourse to your holiness, as to an infallible guide, entreating you to consult with the cardinals and divines whom you judge to be most able and sincere, and after having attentively examined the testaments of our ancestors, from Ferdinand the Catholic to Philip IV., the decrees of the cortes, the renunciations of the infantas Anne and Maria Theresa, the marriage articles, compacts, and all the acts of the Austrian princes, from Philip the Handsome to the present time, to decide by the rules of right and equity." Charles concluded with declaring that he was not guided either by love or hatred, and only waited the decree of the holy pontiff to regulate his conduct.

Innocent, already prepared for this appeal, affected to refer the case to the cardinals Albani, Spinola, and Spada, who, after an examination of forty days, decided in favour of the dauphin. He therefore artfully replied to the king, in a style calculated to influence a conscientious prince on the verge of the grave. "Being himself," he said, "in a situation similar to that of his Catholic majesty, on the point of appearing at the judgment-seat of Christ, and rendering an account to his sovereign pastor of the flock which had been intrusted to his care, he was bound to give such advice as would not be a reproach to his conscience at the day of judgment. Your majesty," he added, "ought not to put the interests of the house of Austria in competition with those of eternity, and of that dreadful account of your actions which you are soon to give before the great judge of kings, who admits no excuse, and is no respecter of persons. Neither should you be ignorant that the chil-

dren of the dauphin are the rightful heirs of the crown,
and that in opposition to them, neither the archduke, nor
any member of the Austrian family, has the smallest legitimate pretension. In proportion to the importance of the
succession, the more crying will be the injustice of excluding the rightful heirs, and the more will you draw upon
your devoted person the vengeance of heaven. It is therefore your duty to omit no precaution which your wisdom
can suggest, to render justice where justice is due, and to
secure, by every means in your power, the undivided succession of the Spanish monarchy to a son of the dauphin."

Notwithstanding this decision, Charles yet hesitated
between his affection for his own family and his dread of
occasioning the dismemberment of his country, or involving
it in a war with the house of Bourbon. He was pressed on
one side by the queen, his confessor, and the inquisitor
general; on the other he was assailed by the cardinal, and
almost all the members of the council of state; and he
was beset by attendants from whom he heard nothing but
arguments in favour of the Bourbon claims. These disputes were agitated with the utmost virulence and fury,
and not only the antechamber, but even the apartment of
the sick monarch, resounded with indecorous debates. He
alternately waved between the houses of Austria and
Bourbon; at one time encouraging the hopes of the emperor, and at another, doubting whether he should bequeath
the succession to the duke of Anjou, lest the king of France
should prefer to execute the treaty of partition.

Agitated by these doubts and anxieties, his health rapidly
declined; and at the moment when his disorder had reached
a crisis, and when his frame was exhausted by the effects
of disease and the struggles of contending passions, the
cardinal persuaded him to admit some divines of exemplary learning and piety to assist him in his devotions, and
prepare him for the awful moment of dissolution. These
divines opened their office by terrifying the king with the
prospect of immediate death; and in the midst of the
lugubrous ceremonies with which the Roman Catholic
church appals the mind of the dying, impressed on his
morbid imagination the danger to which his soul would be
exposed, if he entailed on his country the miseries of a

disputed succession. They insisted that it was his duty as a true son of the church to conform to the opinion of the pope and of his council, the disinterested advocates of justice, and the interpreters of the national voice. They terrified him with the vengeance of an offended deity, if in the disposal of his crown he suffered himself to be swayed by partial love or hatred. They argued that the Austrians were not the relations, nor the Bourbons the enemies of his soul; and they exhorted him not to listen to the bastard voice of natural affection, which soothes and flatters in life, but is reduced to dust and ashes in the grave.

Weak and exhausted, sinking under anguish and disease, appalled by the terrors of eternal punishment, Charles yielded to these representations. He imparted the substance of his testament to Ubilla, secretary of state, in the presence of Portocarrero, and Arias, president of the council of Castile. A will, instantly drawn up, or already prepared, was presented for his signature, and attested by Ubilla, who was made notary public for that purpose.* On the 2nd of October, it was inclosed in a cover, which was sealed and endorsed by seven witnesses, the cardinals Portocarrero and Borgia, the president of Castile, the dukes of Medina Sidonia, Sessa, and Infantado, and the count of Benevento; and three days after a codicil was annexed, containing further arrangements in regard to the queen and the regency. But to the last moment the king testified his reluctance to disinherit his own family; he endeavoured to reconcile himself to this disposition by the reflection, " God gives kingdoms, because they are his; " and, when he affixed his signature, he burst into tears, exclaiming, " I am already nothing ! "

Within a few days after the signature, his disorder took a more favourable turn. He was no sooner flattered with

---

* It is neither easy nor important to ascertain in whose presence this will was read and signed; but in the codicil, Ubilla, who is called secretary of state, and notary public, is mentioned as a witness. The will was dictated in the presence of Portocarrero and Don Miguel Arias; but probably no one except Ubilla was present when it was executed, to avoid suspicion ; for we are informed by St. Philippe, that Ubilla was constituted notary public, on this occasion, to fulfil the formalities of the Spanish law

the hopes of recovery, than he relapsed into his former inclination for the Austrian family, expressed the strongest resentment against those who had recently deceived his conscience, and sent a courier to the emperor announcing his resolution to appoint the archduke his heir. But he was unable to execute his purpose. The change of health which had revived his spirits was but a transitory gleam ; exhausted nature sunk under accumulated infirmities, and he expired on the morning of the 1st of November, in the fortieth year of his age, and the thirty-sixth of his reign.

On the very day of his decease, the will was read in the presence of the council of state, by order of Portocarrero. In regard to the succession it declared, " It appears from various consultations of the ministers of state and justice, that the reason on which the renunciations of the infantas Anna and Maria Theresa, the queens of France, our aunts, were founded, was the danger of uniting the succession of France and Spain in the same person. That fundamental objection being removed, the right of succession subsists in the nearest relation, conformably to the laws of Spain ; and this relation is the second son of the dauphin of France. For this reason he is declared successor to the Spanish dominions ; and all subjects and vassals, of all our kingdoms and lordships, are required to acknowledge him." Should the duke of Anjou die without issue, or become heir to the French crown, the duke of Berry was to succeed on the same conditions ; and after him or his posterity, the Spanish territories were entailed on the archduke Charles, on the same terms, to prevent the union of the crowns of Spain and the empire ; and finally on the duke of Savoy and his issue. The remainder of the will related to regulations for the appointment and conduct of the regency. The administration of affairs till the arrival of the new king, or till he had attained his majority, if a minor, was committed to the queen, and to a junta of eight ministers, headed by Portocarrero, in whom centered the supreme authority.*

* The council of regency was composed of the queen, Portocarrero, don Manuel de Arias, the duke of Montalto, head of the council of Arragon, the marquis of Villafranca, of the council of Italy, the count of Monterrey, of that of Flanders, the inquisitor general, the count of

The contents of this testament excited the utmost astonishment in the queen and the Austrian party, who had been so confident of success, that Harrach was waiting in the antechamber to receive and impart the earliest intelligence of the archduke's appointment. To this surprise was probably owing the extreme tranquillity with which the change was attended; for the nation submitted in silence, if not with pleasure, to a disposition which removed the fear of a dismemberment. The government was established in conformity with the provisions of the will; the regulations of the deceased monarch were notified by the regents to Louis XIV.; the most earnest representations were made for his acceptance of the testament, and the departure of the new monarch; and formal orders were given to the courier, in case of his refusal, to proceed without delay to Vienna, and tender the succession to the archduke Charles.

Louis, who was previously apprised of the contents of the will, had recourse to the most puerile subterfuges to justify his breach of faith towards the Maritime Powers. Affecting to waver between a resolution of maintaining the treaty of partition and of accepting the will, he submitted the question to different councils of state, and listened with affected gravity and attention to their discussions. He suffered himself also to be assailed with the warmest reproaches from the dauphin, Madame de Maintenon, and the ministers, for neglecting the interests of his family. At length, with prudish reluctance, he seemed to yield to their remonstrances, concluded the farce by presenting the young monarch to his obsequious court, and finally endeavoured to justify himself to Europe, by publishing a manifesto fraught with eloquence, artifice, and sophistry.

Little time intervened between the acceptance of the testament and the departure of Philip. The acknowledgment of his title at Paris was the prelude to his accession in Spain; he was proclaimed on the 24th of November at Madrid, in December was joyfully received by his new subjects, who were won by his personal comeliness and devout deport-

Benevento, as representative of the grandees, and the count of Frigiliano, as counsellor of state. — St. Philippe, tom. i. p. 51. See a copy of the will in Dumont, vol. ii. part 2. p. 485.; Lamberti, v. i. p. 191.

ment, and took quiet possession of the throne. He found the Austrian party suppressed; the queen had been compelled, by an order given under his name, to retire from Madrid, for expressing a doubt concerning the authenticity of the will; the confessor was banished; and the two Austrian partisans, Frigiliano and the inquisitor general, removed by their colleagues in the regency; and Harrach, after making an ineffectual protest, quitted the kingdom. The ministers, eager to display their zeal, submitted the whole administration to Louis, and acted with such servility as to draw from him the remark, that they had made him prime-minister to his grandson. From the unexpected tenor of the will, and still more from the precautions adopted by Louis, the prince of Vaudemont, though promoted to the government of Milan by the influence of the queen and William III., received a Spanish garrison, while the duke of Medina Celi followed his example in Naples, and all the foreign territories acknowledged the new sovereign with the same facility as Spain itself.*

* On a subject so important as the transfer of the Spanish monarchy, various and contradictory accounts have been given. Many of the early authors, both native and foreign, even those who were partisans of France, and attached to the court of Madrid, have asserted that the whole conduct of Louis was a series of mere deception and intrigue, and that his design, from the very commencement of the contest, was to appropriate the succession. Torcy, however, in the strongest terms combats this assertion; declaring that the transfer of the monarchy "was the work of Providence, and conducted without the intrigues of man;" and the declaration of a statesman who possessed the character of integrity, and was himself concerned in the negotiation, has weighed with later authors. We have not however differed from such authority without cogent reasons. Without adverting to the strong counter testimony of other writers, we discover, in an attentive perusal of Torcy's own Memoirs, various proofs that Louis directed the intrigues at Madrid and Rome, that he was acquainted with the appeals of Charles to the pope, and that constant communications took place between Portocarrero and the French ministers at Madrid. This being the case, it is absurd to doubt that Louis was previously ignorant of the movements of his partisans, or that he did not even dictate the conditions of the will. In fact, whoever compares the work of Torcy with other authentic sources, will be convinced that it is an artful narrative, drawn up to colour the perfidy and justify the negotiations of Louis XIV.

On this occasion we quote the various authorities which we have consulted and compared. Memoires de Torcy, tom. i., passim — du

CHAP. LXVIII. — 1702, 1703.

WHILE Philip was thus seated on the Spanish throne, without opposition from his subjects, he was no less quietly acknowledged by all the powers of Europe except the emperor.

The court of Vienna, which had confidently relied on the inclinations of Charles, and the reviving strength of the Austrian party, was confounded by the intelligence of the testament made in favour of a French prince, and the acceptance of it by Louis. A general indignation prevailed among all ranks against France. The popular fury was with difficulty restrained ; the ministers, headed by count Harrach, urged the emperor to the most violent measures ; the king of the Romans, whose ardent temper was ungovernable, could not refrain from invectives and personal insults against the marquis of Villars, the French ambassador. Leopold himself was transported beyond his characteristic caution and phlegm. In the height of resentment he forgot his embarrassments, and, in conformity with his own feelings, the sentiments of his family, and the general wishes of his people, resolved to assert his pretensions by force of arms. He made military preparations, sent commissaries to obtain possession of the Italian territories as imperial fiefs, and despatched envoys to rouse the empire and the other states of Europe.

But his emissaries were refused admittance into the Milanese ; and of those whom he sent to Naples, one, who attempted to inflame the populace, was arrested and decapitated. He was equally foiled in his endeavours to persuade the diet of Ratisbon to attempt the recovery of the Milanese as an imperial fief; and the five circles of

Comte de Harrach ; de St. Simon, liv. 6. ; de St. Philippe, t. i. p. 1-61.; De la Torre Tesse, t. 1. ; Ottieri Historia della Guerra, &c., per la successione alla Monarchia di Spagna ; Desormeaux, Hist. de l'Espagne, tom. v. p. 147-174.; Targe, Histoire de l'Avenement de la Maison de Bourbon au Tròne d'Espagne, lib. i. ch. 1-4. ; Lamberti, tom. i. passim. ; Milbiller's Continuation of Schmidt, b. ix. ch. 19-22 b. x. ch. 1. ; Heinrich, vol. vii. p. 367-422. ; Mably and Koch, Art. de la Succession d'Espagne.

the Rhine even united in an association to prevent the interference of Germany in the war for the Spanish succession.

His appeals to the other powers of Europe were equally fruitless. The northern sovereigns were too deeply engaged in their own contests to interfere in the concerns of the house of Austria; the pope, with the dukes of Savoy and Mantua, were gained by France; and from Venice he obtained only vague and secret promises of neutrality. He experienced a still greater disappointment from the Maritime Powers. In England, the factions in parliament had risen to an alarming height; William, after suffering a personal insult in the dismission of his Dutch guards, had seen his military and naval establishment reduced, had been compelled to dissolve the Whig parliament, and to accept a Tory administration, who joined in the national clamour against foreign entanglements, and in particular reprobated a war for the Spanish succession. The death of the young duke of Gloucester diminished that influence which he derived from the prospect of a Protestant successor; and he was reduced to the necessity of sacrificing his own feelings and delicate sense of honour to conciliate the different parties, for the sake of entailing the British crown on the house of Hanover. He had experienced all the virulence of popular fury for concluding the partition treaties; and was scarcely able to save his late ministers, who were impeached for advising measures considered as hostile to the trade and welfare of England.

The Dutch, exposed to immediate danger from the increase of the French power on the side of the Netherlands, were almost unanimous in their resolution to assist the emperor; and, as early as the commencement of 1701, concluded a subsidiary treaty with the king of Denmark for a succour of 12,000 men, and hired troops from the elector Palatine and other princes of Germany. But Louis disconcerted their designs with his usual address, promptitude, and vigour. By the connivance of the elector of Bavaria, he introduced a military force into the Low Countries, and at the same moment became master of the principal fortresses, and captured 15,000 troops who garrisoned the chief towns on the frontier, in virtue of the arrangement with the king of Spain. This master-stroke of policy instantly changed the conduct of the Dutch, who, to obtain the release of their captive troops, and divert the impending danger, acknowledged Philip as king of Spain. Their example was followed by William, who yielded to their earnest entreaties, and the clamours of his parliament and nation, on the 17th of April, 1701.

Besides these events, a strong combination was formed in favour of the new monarch; and France secured considerable advantages for offensive operations, should the contest terminate in a war, which now seemed inevitable. Victor Amadeus, duke of Savoy, was gained by a marriage between his daughter Maria Theresa and Philip, and by a treaty, which assigned to him the supreme command of a Spanish and French army in Italy, with a monthly subsidy. The duke of Mantua was induced to admit French garrisons into his capital and other fortresses. The elector of Bavaria was secretly bound to support the projects of Louis in the empire; his brother, the elector of Cologne and bishop of Liege, received garrisons in all his fortresses on the Rhine and the Meuse; and the dukes of Brunswick Wolfembuttel and Saxe Gotha, the bishop of Munster, and the landgrave of Hesse, engaged to furnish troops for the service of France; even the king of Portugal, whose political interests and personal sentiments attached him to the house of Austria, was forced to conclude an alliance in support of Philip's pretensions. Louis, as before, endeavoured to employ the emperor by his intrigues at the Porte, and among the malecontents in Hungary; and opened a secret correspondence with the young Rogotsky, whose hereditary antipathy to the house of Austria was heightened by personal resentment.

Notwithstanding the unfavourable situation of Europe, and the formidable posture of France, Leopold was not discouraged. He pressed his military preparations, and assembled a force of 80,000 men, part of which was destined for the protection of the hereditary countries, and the remainder to act on the Rhine, and in Italy, where he purposed to make his principal effort. He relied on the jealousy which the unprincipled ambition of Louis had excited, and he was secretly encouraged by William, who only temporised till he could allay the discontents of his subjects, and re-unite the scattered parts of the Grand Alliance. Leopold checked the rising rebellion in Hungary by arresting Ragotsky, whose designs were discovered by a confidential agent ; and he obtained from the Venetians a promise to supply him with guides and provisions, and connive at the passage of his troops through their territories.

Early in spring, Catinat, one of the most able of the French commanders, led an army through Piedmont, and united with the prince of Vaudemont, who commanded the Spaniards in the Milanese. They threw garrisons into Mantua and Mirandola, concentrated their forces on the right bank of the Adige, the furthest natural line of defence to prevent the entrance of the Germans into Italy, and strongly fortified the ordinary passes leading from the Tyrol on both sides of the Adige. Relying on the strength of their position, and on their own numbers, they tauntingly defied the Germans to pass the rugged mountains which divided the Vicentino from the Trentin, without the wings of birds.

Eugene, the imperial generalissimo, was neither embarrassed by difficulties, nor daunted by dangers. Early in April he assembled at Roveredo, in the bishopric of Trent, a force of 32,000 veterans, habituated to camps, and hardened in the wars of Hungary ; and while he amused the enemy with movements as if he intended to force the passages on the side of the Adige*, he suddenly directed his march over the Alps, which separated the Trentin from the Vicentino. Led by Venetian guides, the cavalry wound its way along the circuitous valley of the Brenta ; the infantry, shod with crampons, and handing their arms to one another, passed the frightful chasms and precipices towards the head of the Astico ; the baggage and artillery were conveyed partly on roads constructed over the rugged mountains with incredible labour, or raised from height to

---

* The only two practicable passages from Roveredo to the Vicentino ran, the first between the Lago di Garda and the Adige, the second on the other side of the river at the foot of the impending mountains, and defended by the celebrated fort of Chiusa, from which the pass derived its name.

height by means of machines. After penetrating through a district hitherto impervious to all but hunters and mountaineers, the whole army united in the plains at the foot of the Alps; and Eugene, leaving a corps of 2,000 men on the frontiers of the Vicentino, suddenly appeared in the vicinity of Verona, before the enemy suspected that he had commenced his march.

Even the matured skill of Catinat was embarrassed by this bold and decisive movement. He made, however, every preparation to defend the Adige, and by the warmest remonstrances, endeavoured to dissuade or terrify the Venetian senate from supplying the imperialists with guides and provisions. He kept a considerable corps on the side of the Lago di Garda, to watch the troops still remaining in the mountains, and prevent the enemy from effecting an opening in his rear into the Brescian; he placed troops in the neighbourhood of Verona and Legnano, and ocupied Carpi and Castagnaro, which command the two principal passages over the Adige, and the only great roads across the marshes of the Val di Verona. But Eugene did not relax in the vigour and decision with which he had commenced the campaign. He still amused the French with various movements along the banks of the Adige and towards the Po, effected a passage near Castel Baldo, occupied the island formed by the canals of Castagnaro and Malopera, and constructed a bridge across the Po at Palantone. By these means he induced Catinat to draw the principal part of his forces to Ostiglia, as a central position, to defend the country either above or below the Po. He kept up the illusion of the enemy by false attacks against the posts along the Adige, and by pushing a corps into the Modenese; while he suddenly crossed the Tartaro at Trecento, with a detachment of 11,000 men, defeated the French corps at Castagnaro, on the 7th of July, reduced Carpi after an obstinate engagement, and would have captured the troops at St. Pietra di Legnano, had not the march of the columns intended to cut off their retreat been delayed by accident.

The French, separated by the loss of these posts, and in danger of being cut off in detail, precipitately retired behind the Mincio, leaving the imperialists masters of the whole

country between that river and the Adige. Nor did the
junction of the duke of Savoy enable them to retard operations so skilfully commenced; for Eugene, having effected
the passage of the Mincio near Peschiera, drove them
behind the Oglio, occupied the fertile territory of the
Brescian, forced an entrance into Chiari, notwithstanding
the opposition of the Venetian governor, and by taking
post under the walls, secured an impregnable camp, and
ready communication with the Tyrol.

Louis, astounded at the retreat of his army, deprived
Catinat of the command, and despatched a reinforcement
of 20,000 men under Villeroy, with orders to risk a battle.
But if Catinat, with all his military talents, had been foiled,
still less was the vain and presumptuous Villeroy able to
withstand the rapid and complicated movements of Eugene.
The new general prepared to restore the honour of the
French arms by a battle, and confiding in superior numbers, boasted that he would drive the German rabble from
Italy. Deceived by the report of spies, that the imperialists were retiring, he crossed the Oglio, and pushed on to
Chiari, hoping to fall in with their rear guard. But his
troops, having to encounter with the whole army, secured
with every advantage of art and nature, were repulsed in
all their attempts to force the imperial intrenchments,
after a battle, as long contested and destructive as any conflict during the whole war in Italy.

The French being too much discouraged by their defeat
to resume their attack, and Eugene too prudent to risk, in
the open field, the advantages which he had obtained by
his position, the two armies remained in sight of each other,
vying which could longest keep the field, till the approach
of winter compelled the French to retire into quarters
behind the Oglio. On their retreat, Eugene reduced the
whole duchy of Mantua, except the capital and Goito,
which he closely blockaded, and soon afterwards extended
his quarters beyond the Po, by occupying Mirandola and
Guastalla.

The glory and advantage which Leopold gained in this
campaign, by singly defeating the united forces of France,
Spain, and Savoy, fixed the smaller states of Italy in his

interest, revived the spirit of the Maritime Powers, and effected a total change in the disposition of Germany.

William gradually quieted the discontents in England, and after a feigned negotiation with Louis, in which both engaged for the sake of colouring a rupture, alarmed the nation with apprehensions of a French invasion, which was to be assisted by an insurrection of the Jacobites. By a firm, dignified, yet temperate policy, he conciliated the house of lords and the people; and, being assisted by the public voice, overruled the opposition in the house of commons. He induced the States, who were endangered by the hostile preparations of France on their frontier, to require from England the succours stipulated by former treaties; he also obtained from parliament a vote for the promised assistance, and an engagement to support him in such measures as should be necessary for the common safety, according to the tenor of the Grand Alliance. He hastened the embarkation of the troops, repaired to Holland, and before the commencement of September, renewed the Grand Alliance between England, the States, and the emperor. The object of this engagement was to secure satisfaction for the claims of the house of Austria on the Spanish succession, to recover the Italian territories, to wrest the Netherlands from France, and to prevent the union of France and Spain in the same family. The Maritime Powers, as a compensation for their exertions, were to retain all their conquests in the two Indies; and the contracting parties mutually agreed to conclude neither truce nor peace till this security and compensation were obtained, and allowed two months for procuring the satisfaction demanded, by amicable negotiation.

Fortunately, the views of William were furthered by the conduct of Louis himself. For James II. dying soon after the signature of the treaty, Louis, on the 16th of September, acknowledged his son king of Great Britain and Ireland, contrary to the stipulations of the peace of Ryswick and was followed by the pope, the king of Spain, and the duke of Savoy. William, returning to England, availed himself of the indignation excited by this premeditated affront among all ranks and parties, and by dissolving the parliament, enabled the Whigs to recover their

ascendency.   An animated and dignified address from the
throne increased the general enthusiasm : the new parliament attainted the pretended prince of Wales, and passed
the celebrated act of abjuration; both houses presented
warm and affectionate addresses, declaring their resolution
to support the king in resenting the insult offered to the
nation.   The lords, in a subsequent address, expatiated on
the danger which threatened Europe from the accession of
the duke of Anjou to the crown of Spain, stigmatising the
French king as a violator of treaties, and declaring, that
" his majesty, his subjects, and allies, could never be secure
till the house of Austria should be restored to its rights,
and the invader of the Spanish monarchy brought to reason."   The commons, though less ardent in their expressions, were not less zealous in their grants.   Without one
dissenting voice, they voted 40,000 sailors, and the same
number of troops, and passed the subsidiary treaties with
Denmark, Brandenburgh, and the other powers of Germany.   All the animosity of contending parties was turned
against the common enemy; and the king saw a gleam of
popularity close the evening of his tempestuous reign.

The death of the illustrious monarch, which happened
on the 8th of March, was received with a momentary
exultation in France and Spain, but was attended with no
material change in the counsels of the Maritime Powers.
Anne, his successor, though attached to the claims of her
family, and timid beyond her sex, fortunately intrusted the
whole administration to Marlborough and Godolphin, one
the greatest general, the other the greatest financier of the
age.   Connected by family interests and political views,
these two great men conducted with equal harmony, prudence, and vigour the affairs of England: they acquired
an influence at home and abroad not inferior to that which
had been exercised by William, maintained compact and
entire all the parts of the Grand Alliance, and communicated a rapid and vigorous motion to the whole machine.
Marlborough, despatched to Holland with the title of
ambassador extraordinary, revived the drooping spirit of
the States, and counteracted the deadly feuds which, in
such a government, followed the death of their beloved
chief, and again led to the abolition of the offices held by

the house of Orange. Connected no less by friendship
than congenial views with pensionary Heinsius, he conciliated while he awed the republican party, and turned
against Louis that faction which had hitherto been his
great support. The States cordially united with England,
and prevented the disunion which arises from a competition for military power, by intrusting to Marlborough, as
generalissimo, the same authority over their forces which
he possessed over those of England.

Meanwhile Leopold had acted with equal vigour and
address. He had acquired a cordial supporter in Frederic
elector of Brandenburgh, by acknowledging him as king of
Prussia : he found steady adherents in the dukes of Brunswick Luneburgh, and he appeased the discontents in
Germany by renewing his former concessions to the corresponding princes against the ninth electorate, and luring
the Protestants with the hope of repealing the obnoxious
clause in the treaty of Ryswick. He gradually led the
majority of the empire into his views. By the apprehension of common danger, he first induced the four circles
of Franconia, Suabia, and the Upper and Lower Rhine,
to unite with that of Austria, and accede to the Grand
Alliance. By means of the dukes of Brunswick and Luneburgh he again forced the houses of Wolfembuttel and
Saxe Gotha to relinquish their connections with France ;
he finally procured from the diet of Ratisbon a declaration
of war against Louis XIV., and the usurper of the Spanish
throne ; and on the 15th of May, 1702, hostilities were
denounced against France at London, the Hague, and
Vienna.

In the midst of these negotiations, the allies opened the
campaign in the Netherlands, Italy, and Germany. In the
Netherlands, the combined army of the Maritime Powers
assembled in the neighbourhood of Nimeguen, and was
opposed by the French under the duke of Burgundy and
marshal Boufflers. They commenced their operations
with the siege of.Kaiserswerth, an important fortress on
the Rhine, which was occupied by a French garrison, and
might have again afforded a place of arms for an attack
against the United Provinces. It was besieged by the
prince of Nassau Saarbruck with a strong detachment,

and, after a defence of six weeks, was reduced in spite of the succours which were poured in from the French army, and all attempts to make a diversion. At the same time a corps, under the celebrated engineer Cohorn, demolished the French lines constructed between the forts of St. Donat and Isabella, and laid the district of Bruges under contribution.

Such was the state of the war when Marlborough assumed the command. The plan of the campaign was to conquer the places on the Meuse, while the imperial army on the Rhine penetrated through the heart of Alsace. Loraine, of which the sovereign was only waiting the approach of the imperialists to declare in their favour, was to be the point of union for the two attacks, and from that centre the allies would have cut off the communications of the enemy between Flanders and the Upper Rhine, while they opened a way into the defenceless provinces of France. Marlborough collected the troops in the vicinity of Nimeguen, recalled those who had been employed in the siege of Kaiserswerth, with the forces of Luneburgh and Hesse, and formed an army of 60,000 men. He crossed the Meuse at Grave, and by continually advancing on the flank of the enemy, forced them to retreat to the frontiers of Brabant, where the duke of Burgundy quitted the army, to avoid the disgrace of witnessing the disasters of the French arms. This retreat enabled Marlborough to invest successively the places on the Meuse. Assisted by the skill of Cohorn, he captured in less than two months, Venloo, Ruremond, Stevensward, and Maseich, and closed the campaign with the reduction of Liege.* While the Maritime Powers were pushing their victorious career on the Meuse, Louis margrave of Baden† assembled the German army on the Rhine to the number of 40,000 men, and having secured the lines on the Lauter, on the 16th of June, invested Landau, where he was joined by the king of the Romans. The presence and exertions of the young prince gave spirit to the troops ; the attacks were pushed

* For a more detailed account of this campaign, see Memoirs of the duke of Marlborough, vol. i. cap. 12.

† The same commander who had so highly distinguished himself in the preceding war, both in Germany and Hungary.

with the utmost vigour ; Catinat, who commanded in Alsace, was repulsed in his attempts to succour the place ; and Melac, the governor, surrendered on the 10th of September.

The two armies were on the point of uniting, and France was threatened with an attack on the most vulnerable part of her territory ; but at this crisis the plan of the campaign was suspended, by the appearance of a new enemy in the heart of Germany. The elector of Bavaria suddenly broke his feigned neutrality, and while he amused count Schlick, who was sent by the imperial court to detach him from France, surprised Ulm, occupied Memmingen with the territory of the Nordgau, and sent his general D'Arco with 10,000 men to open a communication with a French army, which, under the command of Villars, was drawn towards the Rhine, to penetrate through the Black Forest. This danger was, however, diverted by the interference of the Helvetic States, and the skill of the German commander. The corps under D'Arco, stopped near Schaffhausen by a body of Swiss, returned to Bavaria ; and the margrave, by vigilance and firmness, arrested the progress of the French, even after they had passed the Rhine, and worsted him in the engagement of Friedlingen. After various movements, Villars re-crossed the Rhine, took Treves and Traerbach, secured Loraine by the capture of Nancy, and distributed his troops in Alsace, while the imperialists took up their quarters on the Kintzig.

In Italy, Eugene passed the commencement of the year in blockading Mantua, and on the 1st of February, 1702, made a bold but fruitless attempt to surprise Cremona, in which he was repulsed, after capturing the French commander Villeroy. But as the reinforcements which he received from Germany did not exceed 15,000 men, it required all his ability and resources to withstand the vast superiority of force which the French court poured into Italy, commanded by the enterprising Vendome in place of the vain and presumptuous Villeroy, and animated by the presence of Philip himself.

While the prince of Vaudemont, with 20,000 men, on the Fossa Maggiore observed the imperialists, who were still employed in the blockade of Mantua, Vendome and

the young monarch, with 30,000, crossed the Po, to cut off
their communications with the territories of Moneda and
Mirandola ; defeated three regiments of cavalry posted as
a corps of observation at Santa Vittoria, and speedily reduced all the fortresses of the Modenese except Bercello.
To obviate this danger Eugene hastily quitted the blockade of Mantua, crossed the Po on the 15th of August, and
advanced with the hope of surprising the enemy near
Luzara. He, indeed, attacked them unawares ; but was
unable to prevail over superior numbers, directed by a
resolute and active general, and inspired by the presence
of a young monarch. Yet, though foiled in this attempt,
he awed his antagonists by perseverance and firmness, and
maintained himself on the south bank of the Po till the
close of the campaign, though he could not prevent the
reduction of Guastalla, Luzara, and Borgoforto. When
the French separated their troops, Eugene established his
quarters in Mirandola and the Lower Modenese, between
the Sechia and the Po ; and, by the occupation of Ostiglia
secured his communications with the Adige and the Austrian territories.

At sea, the result of the war was no less unfavourable
to the house of Bourbon. The first object of the British
court was to execute a plan formed by the late monarch,
on the information of the admiral of Castile, for a descent
on Spain. An expedition of fifty sail of the line, besides
numerous frigates, fireships, and smaller vessels, was fitted
out by England and Holland, under Sir George Rooke,
with 14,000 troops under the duke of Ormond. They
effected a landing in the neighbourhood of Cadiz ; but the
licentiousness of the troops, the vigilance of the enemy,
and the loyalty of the people, frustrated the enterprise.
They compensated, however, for this failure, by an attack
on the rich fleet from the new world, which had taken
refuge at Vigo, carried the forts, and forced an entrance
into the harbour; twelve ships of war with eleven galleons
were captured, and the whole fleet, with a considerable
part of the treasure, either taken or destroyed.

Chap. LXIX. — 1703, 1704.

In the Netherlands, the campaign of 1703 was not fertile in events. The allied armies were increased by considerable reinforcements, and Marlborough was again intrusted with the command; but the divisions in their councils, the mutual jealousies of the generals, and the feuds in Holland, prevented them from deriving any essential advantage from superior numbers. The result of the campaign was, however, not unfavourable to the allies; for although a corps of Dutch under Opdam received a check at the battle of Echeren, and Marlborough, by the opposition of the Dutch deputies, was compelled to abandon his plan of forcing the lines with which the French had covered the whole frontier of the Netherlands, from Antwerp to the Meuse; yet the capture of Huy and Limburgh secured the electorate of Cologne and the bishopric of Liege, and the surrender of Guelders completed the reduction of Spanish Guelderland.

During these transactions, Germany became the principal theatre of the war. Leopold turned his whole efforts to achieve the conquest of Bavaria, no less to chastise the elector for his defection, than to secure the hereditary countries from invasion. The contingents of Franconia were preparing to assemble under general Stirum near Neumarkt, to act against the Upper Palatinate; while a corps of Austrians and Saxons was collecting under general Schlick, to make an attack on the side of the Inn. At the same time every precaution was taken to secure the Rhine and the avenues of the Black Forest, and the margrave of Baden took up his head quarters at Kehl as a central point, to superintend the operations on either side of the Rhine as soon as the campaign should open. But the orders of Louis were issued to make every effort for a junction with the elector; and as the means of effecting this junction, to capture Kehl. Villars, the French commander, carried this order into execution with equal vigour, promptitude, and ability. Having induced the margrave, by various movements, to separate his troops over the space between the Rhine and the Black Forest, for the purpose of defending the numerous defiles between Brisach and Kehl, he suddenly crossed the Rhine between Hunningen and Brisac, dispersed the troops posted on the Eltz, passed under the cannon of Friburgh in a fog, broke up the quarters of the margrave, which were formed along the Kintzig, and drove him back to Stolhoffen. He made himself master of no less than fifty forts and posts occupied by the imperialists between the Rhine and the mountains, captured the towns which command the entrance of the valley watered by the Kintzig, and obtained abundant supplies of stores and ammunition. Before the Germans had recovered from their confusion, Kehl was invested; the trenches were opened under the direction of Terrade, by whom its construction had been superintended, and the attacks pushed with such rapidity and success that in March the place capitulated, after a siege of only thirteen days. Villars having reduced Kintzingen, secured additional supplies of provisions and ammunition, shut up the valley to the right and left of the Eltz, and after alarming the posts in the vicinity of Friburgh, returned across the Rhine to recruit his exhausted army, and wait till the advance of spring should open the passages of the mountains.

As the intention of the French to penetrate into Bavaria was no longer doubted, the Germans employed the interval, after the retreat of Villars, to strengthen their position. The margrave took post behind the rivulet which falls into the Rhine near Stolhoffen, formed lines and inundations, and obtained reinforcements from Holland. He sent also a considerable force under general Furstemberg, assisted by the militia of Wirtemberg, to occupy the passes of the Black Forest, and multiplied the obstacles in the valley of the Kintzig, the way by which the French were expected to force their passage.

To penetrate through a mountainous and woody district not less than sixty miles in extent, affording no subsistence, traversed by only three practicable roads*, and these narrow

* These roads were, first through the valley of the Kintzig, which was the most practicable of the three; the second skirted the walls of Friburgh, and traversed the valley of St. Pierre; the third branched

and rugged, with an enemy ready to hang on his rear, and
a corps in front occupying the numerous defiles with
fortifications, was an enterprise which called forth all the
resources and activity of Villars. He continued his preparations with unremitting diligence; distributed his
troops at proper distances along the Rhine to assemble on
the first signal; and by the construction of three new
bridges, obtained five passages, at Strasburgh, Altenheim,
Cappel, Neuburgh, and Hunningen. On the advance of
spring the troops destined for the expedition, as well as a
corps under Tallard to cover their march, were put in
motion. While Tallard kept the margrave in check,
Villars crossed the Rhine at Strasburgh, and made a real
or feint attack on the lines at Stolhoffen. He then pushed
forward a strong corps up the valley of the Kintzig, to
prevent the margrave from throwing new obstacles in his
way, and while he waited the arrival of his baggage and
artillery, distributed twelve days' provision among his
troops. His preparations being speedily completed, he
forced the intrenchments which covered the heights, or
were drawn across the valley, carried Haslach and Hornbeck by storm, by his vigorous attacks terrified the
Germans, who were scarcely recovered from their former
panic, and drove them from the passes between Hornbeck
and the summit of the mountains, where, to use his own
expression, "fifty trees would have arrested the progress
of an army, or the removal of a little earth rendered it
impossible to pass except by constructing scaffolds." After
the most arduous exertions, and a march of eleven days,
he reached Villingen, at the point where the mountains
terminate; but the want of provisions not allowing him to
attempt its reduction, though necessary to secure his communication with France, he left it behind, and joined the
elector of Bavaria near Dutlingen on the 12th of May.

During the interval in which the French army was
preparing to advance to his assistance, the elector himself
surprised Neuburgh on the Danube. He likewise diverted

out near Friburgh, and passed the Val d'Enfer, so called from its
ruggedness and horror. These three passages opened almost at the
same point, near the head of the Danube. From thence the principal
road proceeds through the celebrated pass of Stockach into Bavaria.

the danger with which his country was threatened by the
attacks of Schlick and Stirum, the former of whom entered
Bavaria on the side of the Inn, the latter forced the lines
at Dietfurth, captured Neumarkt, and laid siege to Amberg.
Having sent reinforcements to keep Stirum in check, the
elector marched towards the Inn, drew off a part of the
Austrian forces by threatening Passau, and then crossing
the river, defeated the remainder near Scharding, and
made himself master of all the artillery, tents, and baggage. Next directing his attack against Stirum, he raised
the siege of Amberg, defeated the margrave of Anspach,
who had been detached to secure the passes on the Wiltz,
worsted the main body at the village of Einhorf, and after
reducing Ratisbon, returned towards the sources of the
Danube to unite with the French.

Bavaria and the greater part of the Upper Palatinate,
being thus delivered, and the junction of the French and
Bavarians effected, the Austrian territories, which were
totally unprepared for resistance, were laid open to invasion. But in this critical juncture the emperor was
saved by the divisions of his enemies. The proposal of
Villars to march directly to Vienna was overruled by the
elector, and, after great difficulties, it was settled that the
French commander should remain in Bavaria to watch the
motions of the margrave, while the elector penetrated
through the Tyrol, and opened a communication with
Vendome in Italy; their united forces were then to terminate the war by pouring into the heart of Germany or the
Austrian territories. In pursuance of this plan, the
elector, with 15,000 men, took Kuffstein, the key of the
Tyrol, in less than ten days made himself master of Ro-
temberg and Hall, entered Innspruck in triumph, spread
his troops through the surrounding valleys, and rapidly
marched towards the Trentin, to open the intended communication with the Italian army. But fortunately the
peasants of the Tyrol rose in arms ; and being supported
by a corps of regulars and by reinforcements from the
Grisons harassed the march of the elector, and assailed
him in the defiles of the mountains. The burghers of
Innspruck and of the other towns followed the example;
and the elector was reduced to force back his way by

continual combats, owing his personal safety to the bravery of his troops. After losing half his army, and evacuating all his conquests in the Tyrol except Kuffstein, he rejoined Villars to defend in his turn his own country from the danger with which it was now threatened.

During the expedition into the Tyrol, the margrave of Baden hastened from Stolhoffen, united with the troops in the Upper Palatinate, left Stirum with a corps to observe Villars, who was posted between Lawingen and Dillingen, crossed the Danube, and ascending the Iller, occupied Augsburgh at the moment when the French and Bavarians were in full march to secure so important a post. At the same time Stirum descended the Danube, with an intention to cross and place himself between the Gallo-Bavarian army and a corps of 12,000 men left by Villars to maintain the camp at Dillingen. The French and Bavarians were rescued from their critical situation by an accident which delayed the march of Stirum, and still more by the promptitude and skill of Villars. Shut up between the two German armies, he directed his whole force against that of Stirum, which was the weakest, overpowered him by superior numbers, and drove him, with the loss of 6000 men, and great part of his artillery, to take refuge under the walls of Nuremberg. But the indecision of the elector prevented him from completing his success by attacking the margrave. After endless contentions and delays, the Gallo-Bavarians captured Memmingen and Kempten, which opened a communication with France; Villars abruptly quitted the army in disgust; and Marsin, who succeeded in the command, closed the campaign with the recovery of Augsburgh and the reduction of Passau.

After the departure of the margrave of Baden for Bavaria, the duke of Burgundy had assumed the command of the French army on the Rhine, which amounted to 30,000 men. But instead of opening a way into Bavaria, and supporting the operations of Villars and the elector, he invested Brisac, captured the place after a siege of only fourteen days, and hastened to Paris to receive the congratulations of the court. On his departure, Tallard led the army towards the Moselle, invested Landau, defeated on the Spirebach a corps of 10,000 men, which had been detached from the Low Countries for its relief, and after a long and arduous siege did not complete its reduction till the 6th of November, 1703, when the advance of the season precluded all further operations.

In Italy, notwithstanding the loss of Bercello, which surrendered after a blockade of eleven months, Staremberg retarded the operations of Vendome by a spirited defence of Ostiglia, and prevented him from concurring in the attack on the side of Bavaria with that concert and promptitude which was necessary to ensure success. Thus foiled in his attempts to exclude the imperialists from the country north of the Po, Vendome at length led a considerable part of his forces toward the Trentin. He directed his march along the shores of the Lago di Garda, made himself master of the forts commanding the passes on both sides of the lake, and towards the beginning of August appeared before Trent. The place, though garrisoned by 4000 men, being defended only by antique fortifications, could not long have arrested his progress ; but as the insurrection of the Tyrolese compelled the elector to retrace his footsteps, a change of another kind recalled Vendome into Italy.

Victor Amadeus had been long disgusted with his French and Spanish allies. He had already gained the principal object of his alliance with France, the establishment of his two daughters, and was aware that the consolidation of the Bourbon power beyond the Alps would lead to the loss of his own independence. He therefore listened to the overtures of the allies, who offered him a monthly subsidy of 80,000 crowns, the supreme command in Italy, with a reinforcement of 20,000 men ; and in addition to that part of the Montferrat which belonged to the house of Mantua, the cession of Allessandro, Valenxa, Lumellina, and the Val di Sesia. Having accepted these terms, he prepared to seize the favourable opportunity afforded by the absence of Vendome in the Trentin to declare in favour of the emperor.

The French court, which had long watched his intrigues, could only anticipate his design at the moment of execution. Vendome having suddenly returned to his head-quarters at Mantua, on the 29th of September, surrounded the troops of Savoy, arrested the officers, and incorporated the soldiers with those of France. While an army under Tessé advanced on the side of the Savoy, Vendome pushed forward to the frontiers of Piedmont, and a menacing but laconic letter, sent by a trumpet from Louis, required the duke, within twenty-four hours, to renounce his connections with the allies, or to expect the vengeance of an offended sovereign.

The duke was not daunted by these menaces, nor alarmed at the dangers to which he was exposed. On the 25th of October he publicly acceded to the Grand Alliance, arrested all the French within his territories, seized their magazines, armed his people, made every preparation for defence, and called for the assistance of his new allies. The principal places of Piedmont were, however, speedily reduced by Vendome, and all Savoy conquered by Tessé, except the strong fortress of Montmelian. Bnt fortunately the attachment of his subjects and the approach of winter enabled the duke to make head till he could receive assistance from the emperor. On the first advance of the French troops towards Piedmont, a corps of 1700 horse was despatched by Staremberg to his support; but these were intercepted at St. Sebastian, and only a small number reached the place of destination. The failure of this attempt only rendered the imperial general more vigilant in succouring so important an ally. As the enemy were far superior in numbers, and masters of all the communications, he waited till they had separated their army. Having formed secret arrangements for provisions, and relays of carriages, he suddenly broke from his quarters on the Secchia in the depth of winter, took his route along the south of the Po, defeated all the attempts of Vendome to check his progress, joined Victor Amadeus at Canelli, in January, 1704, and inspired him with fresh resolution to maintain the contest.

As the defection of the duke of Savoy saved the hereditary countries and secured the passages of Italy, the emperor obtained equal advantages from the increase of his party in Spain and the accession of the king of Portugal, which placed in his power the means of contesting the possession of the Spanish territories on Spanish ground.

After the first burst of enthusiasm derived from the presence of the young monarch had subsided, Spain was torn by the struggles of contending parties, and agitated by discontents arising from the influence of strangers and the innovations of a foreign government. Louis XIV. in accepting the will of Charles II. was less swayed by the desire of fixing his grandson on a powerful throne, than the hope of exerting the force of Spain for the aggrandisement of France. From motives of prudence he at first avoided every measure which might excite the slightest suspicion of foreign interference, carrying his delicacy even to affectation; but he took care to throw the government into the hands of his creature, Portocarrero. Not content, however, with the implicit obedience derived from the gratitude and deference of his grandson, and the servility of Portocarrero, the object of Louis was to provide against every event which might tend to diminish his influence. Sensible that Philip was incapable of continued application, and averse to business, and that from constitution and principle he was likely to be swayed by his queen, who was a woman of great spirit and talents, it was thought necessary to attach to her person an adherent of France, who, by her means, might govern the king. For this purpose the important post of camerara mayor, or superintendent of the queen's household, which gave constant and intimate access to the presence of the sovereigns, was conferred on the princess of Orsini, a native of France, who was the widow of the duke of Bracciano, a Spanish grandee, and head of the Roman family of Orsini.* This extraordinary woman was calculated by the blandishments of her manners and the brilliancy and intelligence of her conversation, to relieve the tedium of a monotonous court, and conciliate the affections of a young and lively princess, surrounded with the formality of Spanish etiquette. She had acquired at Paris all the polish of French courtesy; by a long residence at Rome, of which she was the principal ornament, she was equally mistress of Italian finesse; and she was intimately acquainted with the language, manners, and customs of Spain. She accompanied the young queen to

* This extraordinary woman was of the illustrious family of Tremouille, and daughter of Louis duke of Noirmoutiers. She was very young when she espoused Adrian prince of Chalais (1659); after his death she married Flavio duke of Bracciano, in 1675; and again became a widow in 1698. She is generally known in the French and foreign and contemporary Memoirs, by the name of the princess des Ursins.—See Memoirs of the Kings of Spain, chap. iv.

Madrid, and by the dismission of her Piedmontese adherents, became her sole companion and confidant. During the absence of Philip in Italy, she increased her ascendency, and governed her young mistress with absolute sway. To strengthen still further the influence of France, the embassy to Spain was conferred on the cardinal d'Etrées, who had recently filled the same office at Rome, and, by his recommendation, had contributed to the rise of the princess Orsini. At the same time the revenues were placed under the superintendence of Orri, another native of France, who had risen from obscurity by his talents for finance.

These three persons monopolised the whole power of government, alienated the grandees who would not submit to their nod ; and even Portocarrero had the mortification to see himself excluded from all influence and authority by the very persons whom he had introduced into the government. The unpopularity of the French was increased by various innovations which militated against the prejudices of the natives. The Castilian pride was mortified by a decree of Philip, which gave to the peers of France the same distinctions at Madrid as the grandees of Spain. The national feelings, wounded by the loss of the Vigo fleet, were still more irritated by the seizure of the treasure saved from the wreck, of which a considerable part was sent to France. The introduction of unusual taxes, innovations in the modes of collection, and numerous abolitions of offices in the civil and military departments, at once alienated a great body of those who were attached to the court, and disgusted a nation so tenacious of ancient customs. The clamour was heightened by the attempts of Louis to appropriate the Netherlands, for which he extorted the consent of Philip, notwithstanding his frequent and solemn declarations that he would not dismember the Spanish monarchy.

In the midst of these discontents the authority of Philip was shaken by the escape of the count of Melhor, admiral of Castile. This grandee, descended from the royal line, connected with the principal houses of Spain, and equally distinguished by his talents and extensive property, was disgusted by the appointment of Portocarrero to the direction of affairs, and the increasing influence of the French. He had long maintained a secret correspondence with the

court of Vienna ; and, after affecting to accept the embassy
to France, made his escape into Portugal with a considerable treasure and a numerous train of adherents, and found
an honourable asylum at Lisbon. Encouraged by the
example of so powerful and popular a noble, people of all
ranks poured into Portugal, carrying with them jewels and
money to a vast amount, and increasing by their emigration the odium against the French government. At the
same time the duke of Moles, Spanish ambassador at the
court of Vienna, joined with the admiral in representing
Spain as an easy conquest, and urging Leopold to secure
possession of a kingdom which had been unjustly arrested
from his family, and of which the natives were eager to
receive an Austrian prince.

Leopold embraced this favourable opportunity, and
found a cordial support from the Maritime Powers. By
their assistance, by offers of territorial acquisition, and by
the exaggerated representations of the admiral of Castile,
he gained Peter, king of Portugal, who had seen with
aversion and alarm the Spanish throne filled by a Bourbon
prince. Peter privately acceded to the Grand Alliance, on
the 16th of May, 1703, agreed to acknowledge Charles, to
give him an entrance into Portugal, and, for the purpose
of assisting in the conquest of Spain, to maintain an army
of 28,000 men. In return for these services he was to receive from the new king of Spain the frontier towns of
Badajoz, Albuquerque, Valencia, and Alcantara, in Estre-
madura, the important posts of Bayonne and Vigo, with
Guardia and Tuy in Gallicia, and a considerable district
in South America, to the north of the Rio de la Plata.
The new king was to espouse his daughter, and the Maritime Powers were to subsidise 13,000 men of the army
which he had agreed to maintain.

Having by this alliance secured the means of attacking
Spain, Leopold and his son Joseph renounced their claims
on the Spanish succession, and Charles was solemnly proclaimed king at Vienna, in September, 1703. Leopold,
however, still hesitated to expose his darling son to the
dangers of such an enterprise, till the near prospect of a
splendid establishment, the representations of the Maritime
Powers, the accession of the king of Portugal, and the
urgent solicitations of his party in Spain, overcame his

paternal apprehensions. The young king, after being formally acknowledged by all the members of the Grand Alliance, passed through Holland to England, embarked on
board a fleet commanded by Sir George Rooke, and landed
at Lisbon, in March, 1704. The recent death of the infanta, whom he was to have espoused, made no change in
the sentiments of the king of Portugal; he was received
with every testimony of respect and affection, and the
court of Lisbon concurred with the allies in active exertions to wrest the Spanish crown from the house of
Bourbon.*

CHAP. LXX. — 1704.

NOTWITHSTANDING the accession of the duke of Savoy and
the king of Portugal to the Grand Alliance, and the progress of the confederates on the side of the Netherlands,
the affairs of Leopold were in an alarming situation. His
forces could scarcely make head against the French in
Italy; Passau, which covered Austria and commanded the
Danube, was in the hands of the enemy; an hostile army
in Bavaria was ready to penetrate into the heart of the
hereditary countries, and co-operate with the malecontents
in Hungary, who had broken out into a new and dangerous rebellion.

The majority of the Hungarian nobles, irritated by the
establishment of an hereditary monarchy, and the rigorous
measures with which it had been preceded and accompanied, waited in sullen silence for an opportunity to throw
off the yoke which their habits, manners, and prejudices
rendered peculiarly irksome. Their discontents, increased
by new persecutions of the Protestants, by forced levies of
men, and by the extortion of illegal contributions, were
continually fomented by the agency of France. Disaffection spread rapidly among a turbulent and high-spirited
people; and at the very moment when the arms of the
emperor were unsuccessful in Germany, and Austria was

* See Memoirs of the Bourbon kings of Spain, anno 1703, 1704;
Memoirs of the Duke of Marlborough.

threatened with invasion by the united forces of France
and Bavaria, the flame, which had been smothered by the
dread of punishment, broke forth with redoubled violence.
The malecontents found a chieftain whose influence commanded a number of adherents, and whose talents were
fitted to excite and direct a rebellion, in Francis Ragotsky.
Left an orphan by the death of his father, he had been separated from his mother on the surrender of Montgatz,
and brought up under the auspices of the court of Vienna.
He was removed to Bohemia during the rebellion of Tekeli,
and placed under the care of the Jesuits, who in vain used
all their influence and persuasions to induce the representative of so powerful and dangerous a family to embrace
the ecclesiastical profession. Having completed his studies,
he was permitted to travel through various parts of Europe,
and after suffering a temporary disgrace on account of his
marriage with Eleonora, princess of Hesse Rheinfeld, returned to Hungary, and fixed his residence in his patri-
monial domains.

An irreconcilable jealousy and irritation naturally subsisted between the court of Vienna and the young magnate. The mind of Ragotsky perpetually brooded over
the faded splendour of his family, and the calamities which
it had suffered from the court of Vienna ; his grandfather
and great uncle decapitated, his cousin condemned to perpetual imprisonment, his father reduced to the state of a
private individual, his father-in-law proscribed, and his
mother driven into exile ; the sceptre of Transylvania
wrested from his grasp, his minutest movements watched
by the court, his pride and interest wounded by the refusal of the emperor to transfer the confiscated property of
his father-in-law, Tekeli, to his second son. These grievances exasperated his sensitive and aspiring mind; and the
angry words which broke forth in the hours of conviviality and confidence were conveyed in aggravated terms to
a suspicious court. On the other hand, the emperor dis-
trusted the descendant of the Transylvanian waivodes,
from habit and principle inimical to his government, whose
spirit and talents contributed to render still more dangerous his family influence over the minds of his countrymen.
He regarded with jealousy and alarm the correspondence
which Ragotsky maintained with his mother, who had

taken refuge at Constantinople, and considered all his actions as proofs of a design to recover the lost honours of his ancestors.

The French court did not omit so favourable an opportunity of working upon the feelings and ambition of Ragotsky. On the prospect of a war for the Spanish succession they opened a secret correspondence with a prince who was so capable of making a powerful diversion, lured him with the prospect of recovering Transylvania, and restoring the splendour of his family; promised large supplies of men and money, and encouraged him with the hope of assistance from the Turks. At an early period Ragotsky seems to have formed designs to excite a commotion in Hungary, which was to be supported by France and the Porte.* But at the moment when he was making the necessary arrangements with Bertzeny and Syrmai, two Hungarian nobles, his plot was discovered by the treachery of Longueval, his confidential agent. Ragotsky and Syrmai were arrested, and Bertzeny fled. Ragotsky was conveyed to Neustadt, and confined in the same apartment from which his maternal grandfather, count Zrini, was led to the scaffold; but during his examination he gained his liberty by bribing the officer to whose care he was intrusted. After a series of hair-breadth escapes and romantic adventures, he joined his friend Bertzeny at Warsaw, lay concealed a year and a half in Poland, and in that interval completed his arrangements with the disaffected nobles of Hungary. At length, when the emperor had drawn the principal part of his troops from Hungary, to defend his hereditary territories against the attack from Bavaria, Ragotsky, in 1703, suddenly descended from the Carpathian mountains into the plain of Mongatz, at the head of a 'predatory and half-armed multitude, published a bitter manifesto, calling on his countrymen to shake off the detested yoke of Austria,

* This conspiracy, like all other plots, was exaggerated by one party, and extenuated by the other. The court of Vienna described it as a regular design to seize or assassinate the emperor and his family ; Ragotsky and his adherents, as an association merely to remedy the grievances of their country. Without entering into the arguments or allegations of either party, there is no doubt, that a design was formed to raise an insurrection.

and pushed into the town with the hope of surprising the castle, which was defended by only 500 men, some of whom were his secret adherents. But this first attempt was premature; for, on the approach of the imperial general Montecuculi with a detachment of cavalry, he was surrounded, and by singular good fortune and presence of mind escaped to the frontier of Poland. Having received fresh supplies of money and officers from France, and being joined by count Bertzeny with two corps of regular cavalry, he again descended into Hungary, and was more successful than on the former occasion. The country being left to the protection of the garrisons, who could not be drawn together in a body, he found no troops to impede his progress. He strengthened his party by the reduction of Kalo and Somlio, and being joined by continual swarms of adherents, gradually increased his army to the number of 20,000 men; he became master of the principal communications, by capturing the smaller forts in the east of Hungary as far as the Teiss, blockaded the imperial garrisons in the greater fortresses, and before the commencement of the ensuing year reduced Zolnoc and Tokay, on the Teiss, with the central fortress of Erlau. While he was thus employed, his adherents were no less successful; the flame of rebellion spread into Transylvania. Count Bertzeny overran the mountainous district of Upper Hungary, took Scepus and Leuitsch, obtained possession of Neusohl, Chemnitz, with the other towns in the neighbourhood of the mines, blockaded Neuhasel, and pushed his predatory corps into Moravia and Austria. Count Caroli, a powerful magnate of Lower Hungary, who was alienated by the neglect of the court, joined the rebels, roused the people of Lower Hungary, occupied the open country below the Danube, and established a communication with Bertzeny. At the same time Simon Forgatz, count of Borsod, a major-general in the imperial service, quitted a cause which he had zealously supported, and drew to his party even the nephews of the palatine Esterhazy.

This rebellion, as general as it was unexpected, caused the utmost consternation at the court of Vienna. General Heuster was despatched with a considerable corps to the south of the Danube, and even the garrison of Passau was drawn out under Schlick to oppose the rebels in the north.

But though these generals dispersed some of the predatory corps which swarmed on every side, they were unable to make any impression on an armed nation, and fell back, the one to Presburgh, and the other to cover Vienna. Negotiations were opened with the rebels, first by Eugene, afterwards through the intervention of the archbishop of Colotza, and finally by the mediation of the Maritime Powers. These repeated offers, however, only encouraged the insurgents to rise in their demands, and they delivered preliminaries, which show the confidence inspired by their success, and the increasing embarrassments of the emperor. They required Leopold to acknowledge Ragotsky as independent prince of Transylvania, to consent to the abolition of the hereditary monarchy, and the revival of the article in the oath of king Andrew, which sanctioned the resistance of the subjects to the regal power; to expel the Jesuits and other members of religious orders, who were considered as dangerous; to remove the foreign officers and foreign garrisons; to appoint Bertzeny palatine, restore the confiscated estates, grant the Protestants the free exercise of their religion, and reinstate them in four hundred churches, of which they had been deprived. These negotiations accordingly produced only temporary suspensions of arms, which enabled the rebels to continue, without interruption, the blockade of the imperial garrisons. They secured passages over the Danube, the March, and the Wag, concerted with the French a joint attack against Vienna, and at the moment when the Gallo-Bavarian army threatened the frontier on the side of the Inn, Caroli, with a considerable body of insurgents, spread such terror to the capital, that the citizens prepared to retire, and the king of the Romans threw up works to defend the suburbs.

In this emergency, Leopold was induced, by the advice of Eugene, to neglect the distant affairs of Italy, concentrate his principal force to drive the enemy from Germany, and prevent their co-operation with the Hungarian malecontents. By the intervention of Marlborough, he obtained the effectual support of Great Britain. But as the whole success of the plan depended on secrecy, and as the same dangers were to be apprehended from the indiscretion of the Dutch, as from the vigilance of the enemy, Marlborough was forced to undertake this momentous enterprise with only the troops in British pay. He purposed to lead the English forces from the Low Countries, prepared to draw 10,000 British auxiliaries who were employed on the Rhine, and relied on his address, and the progress of events, to obtain the co-operation of the Dutch. At once to deceive the enemy, and quiet the alarms which the States might have conceived in consequence of the removal of so considerable a force from their frontier, he made preparations as if he intended to open a campaign on the Moselle, a project which was equally calculated to forward and conceal his real design. But in the midst of these preparations, new dangers gathered round the house of Austria, and hastened the crisis which rendered his assistance necessary. The elector of Bavaria was joined by 15,000 French troops, who had broken through the defiles of the Black Forest, and at the head of 40,000 men, took post behind the rivulet which falls into the Danube, near Ulm, while Tallard, with 45,000, remained on the banks of the Rhine, ready to advance towards the Moselle, to penetrate through Wirtemberg, or to support the invasion on the side of Bavaria. The margrave of Baden, after exerting in vain all his skill and vigilance to secure the passes of the Black Forest, was watching the elector with 25,000 men at Blauberen; and an inconsiderable corps was left rather to observe the movements of Tallard, than to defend the lines of Stolhoffen, or cover Suabia.

Such was the critical situation of affairs when Eugene arrived to command the troops on the Rhine, and Marlborough commenced his memorable expedition. At the beginning of May he assembled the British forces, amounting to 15,000 men, in the vicinity of Maestricht, crossed the Meuse between Venloo and Ruremond, and bending his course towards the Rhine, reached Coblentz on the 25th. The direction of his march, the formation of magazines at Coblentz, joined with the reports which were industriously circulated, alarmed the French court with apprehensions of an attack along the Moselle. Villeroy was detached with troops from the Upper Rhine to secure the frontier of Loraine, and to divert or delay the progress of Marlborough, preparations were made on the side of the Netherlands for the siege of Huy. Of these movements the British commander adroitly availing himself, obtained the consent of the States that the Danish and other auxiliaries in their pay should be detached to his support from the army on the Meuse. From Coblentz he sent his baggage and artillery up the Rhine to Mentz, recommenced his march, himself preceding with the cavalry, while his brother led the infantry, crossed the Main, and directed his course to Ladenburgh, where he passed the Neckar. This progress held all Europe in awful suspense. As his arrival at Coblentz had spread apprehensions of invasion by the Moselle, his advance to Mentz equally threatened Alsace; his subsequent movements afforded no indication of his ultimate design; and the construction of a bridge over the Rhine, by the governor of Philipsburgh, seemed preparatory to the siege of Landau. Villeroy accordingly drew back towards the Upper Rhine, and Tallard re-crossed at Altenheim, with a view to unite, at the first signal, for the protection of Alsace or Loraine.

Having thus induced the French to concentrate their force for the defence of their own frontiers, and reached the point where the object of his march could be no longer concealed, Marlborough ordered the auxiliaries in British pay on the Rhine to move towards the neighbourhood of Ulm, which was fixed as the point of junction, and extorted from the States permission to employ in the empire those auxiliaries which were already on their march from the army on the Meuse. He immediately continued his route, himself as before pushing on with the cavalry, and the infantry following with the artillery and baggage. After again crossing the Neckar at Lauffen, he left his troops to pursue their march, and held an interview at Mondelsheim with Eugene, where these great generals, who now met for the first time, contracted for each other that mutual friendship, cordiality, and confidence, which animate congenial souls, and which contributed to the success of the allied arms. After concerting the plan of the campaign, they were joined at Hippach by the margrave of Baden, who, though distinguished for military talents, was proud and punctilious, and arrogated the supreme command as general of the empire. Marlborough employed all his address, and Eugene all his influence, to soothe his feelings and conciliate his pride, and obtained his acquiescence in their arrangements. The forces under the

margrave were to join with those under Marlborough, in the
vicinity of Ulm, and to avoid the mischiefs of a competition for superiority, they were to command each day alternately.   Eugene, with the troops on the Rhine, amounting
to 23,000 men, was to defend the lines of Stolhoffen, and
observe the motions of Tallard, and the place of the auxiliaries in British pay was to be supplied by 9000 Prussians,
and 3000 imperial horse from the German army.   After
these arrangements, Eugene repaired to the Rhine, the
margrave returned to his camp, and the duke rejoining his
cavalry, continued his march.   He united with the auxiliaries at Lauenstein, with the margrave at Westerstetten,
and was joined by the infantry, artillery, and baggage at
Giengen.   Having thus happily effected the junction of
troops drawn from such distant points, he pushed forwards
at the head of 40,000 men, with a resolution to penetrate
into the heart of Bavaria.

As the elector, to protect his territories, took post in the
intrenched camp at Dillingen, and detached d'Arco with
12,000 men to defend the heights of Schellenberg, which
covered the passage into Bavaria, by Donawerth, Marlborough overruled the captious or timid opposition of the
margrave, passed in front of the electoral army, forced the
lines of Schellenberg after a short but desperate conflict,
and drove the corps of d'Arco across the Danube, with the
loss of 5000 men, and all their baggage and artillery.   Being
reinforced by the Danish horse, who arrived the following
day, he crossed the Danube, advanced up the Leck, compelled the elector to take refuge under the walls of Augsburgh, and secured his communications by the capture of
Neuburgh on the Danube, Rain on the Leck, Aicha and
Friedberg in the vicinity of Augsburgh, and thus cut off
the communication of the elector with the Bavarian territory.   Hoping, in this critical situation, to detach the
elector from France, he opened a negotiation, in conjunction with count Wratislaw, the imperial minister, and
proffered the most favourable terms of peace.   Besides the
restoration of the Palatinate and all other conquests, they
promised, in the name of the emperor, to cede to him the
duchy of Neuburgh ; to confer on him the perpetual government of the Netherlands ; to pay 500,000 crowns for the
redemption of his jewels, which had been pledged in

Holland ; and to subsidise all the troops which he should furnish for the service of the allies. To these terms the elector affected to accede, but only temporised till he could be joined by Tallard, who, at the head of 30,000 men, was advancing from the Rhine, and on the approach of this succour, he threw off the mask. Irritated by this act of duplicity, the confederates gave up his country to military execution, and on the 5th of August, drew back towards the Danube ; Marlborough took post at Rain, to watch the Gallo-Bavarians, and the margrave repaired with 20,000 men to besiege Ingoldstadt, which contained the principal magazines of the enemy, and would have formed a point of support for a new invasion of Bavaria.

The Gallo-Bavarians, in their turn acting on the offensive, crossed the Danube at Dillingen. They hoped either to overpower the inferior force of Eugene, who, with 18,000 men, had followed Tallard from the Rhine, and reached Munster, a small town near the Danube, the same day in which he joined the elector ; or at least they purposed to separate the two armies, and force them to quit Bavaria, by cutting off their communications with the countries from whence they drew their supplies. This design was, however, frustrated by the promptitude and skill of the allied generals. While Eugene maintained his position on the Kessel with his cavalry, and detached his infantry to secure the passage at Schellenberg, Marlborough rapidly pushed his army across the Leck and the Danube, and on the ensuing morning their whole force united at Munster. They hastened towards the strong position of Hochstedt ; but in this they were less fortunate than in their junction, for they found the enemy already occupying the very spot on which they intended to fix their camp.

As they were greatly distressed for forage, and as Villeroy had pushed a considerable corps from the Rhine into Wirtemberg, to intercept their communications, they resolved to risk an engagement before the enemy had secured themselves in their new position. At break of day their armies moved in eight columns, and appeared in sight of the Gallo-Bavarians, who, far from suspecting an attack, were scarcely apprised of their junction. The enemy, however, recalled their foragers, drew in their outposts, and in he utmost haste formed in order of battle. Their situation was admirably calculated for defence, and their arrangements judiciously adapted to the advantages of the ground. Before their front were swamps and marshes formed by the Nebel*, a rivulet which rises in the vicinity of Lutzingen, and falls into the Danube near Blenheim. Their armies were drawn up in two continued lines, though under separate commanders ; the right consisting of the troops led from the Rhine by Tallard ; the left, of the united French and Bavarians, headed by Marsin and the elector. They stretched from the Danube to Lutzingen ; their right flank was covered by Blenheim, and their centre by Oberclaw, both hastily fortified ; their left was supported on Lutzingen, and enveloped by an extensive wood. Of their first line, the infantry was posted to defend or sustain Oberclaw and Blenheim ; the cavalry, drawn up on a gentle ascent behind the two villages, and beyond Oberclaw towards Lutzingen, where the open ground allowed it to act with effect ; their second line was disposed in the usual manner, the infantry in the centre and the cavalry on the wings ; and their whole front was defended with ninety pieces of artillery.

The confederates on reaching the verge of the swamp, drew up in order of battle. On the left Marlborough headed the British troops and auxiliaries, to attack the right and centre of the enemy ; and Eugene on the right led the German force against the electoral troops on the left. The battle began with the attack of the two villages. A part of the British infantry passing the marshes, advanced against Blenheim ; but were repulsed after repeated encounters, attended by a dreadful carnage ; the same ill success attended the attempt against Oberclaw. Foiled in these attacks, the skilful eye of Marlborough discerned fluctuation in the hostile ranks ; and he formed the perilous design of directing his whole force against their centre. He paused, checked the ardour of his troops, masked the villages with a part of his infantry, and prepared to lead his cavalry across the Nebel and adjacent marshes. At this critical moment a cannon ball grazing his horse, threw him to the ground ; the troops trembled for their leader, the fate of Austria hung suspended on the life of the general. But Providence had destined this great man for higher

* This rivulet is sometimes called the Hasel.

fortunes and more splendid successes. He rose unhurt, though covered with mire and dust; he led forward the troops animated with new spirit by his marvellous escape, and the cavalry pushed across the swamps on bridges of fascines and planks, collected in haste, or torn from the neighbouring buildings. The French making no movement to interrupt their passage, either from presumption or inadvertence, Marlborough formed his cavalry in a double line at the foot of the ascent, led them against that of the enemy, and after four charges drove them on their second line. The infantry having now passed to sustain the cavalry, the compact body overbore all the efforts of the enemy, which at every shock became more feeble ; the foot, intermixed with the exhausted squadrons, were cut to pieces, and the centre irrecoverably broken. The remnant of the cavalry which escaped captivity or the sword was driven into the Danube, and Tallard himself, swept away in his vain attempts to rally the fugitives, was made prisoner. Marlborough instantly put a stop to the pursuit, enclosed the infantry in Blenheim, and turned with his victorious troops on the side of Oberclaw to attack the flank of the electoral army. But the defeat of the right had already decided the fortune of the day. Eugene, after numerous difficulties in crossing the marsh, emulated the example of Marlborough, by a spirited attack on that part of the line which was formed between Oberclaw and Lutzingen, while by extending his line round the sources of the rivulet, he endeavoured to turn the flank supported on Lutzingen. Though his efforts were unsuccessful, he was undaunted by repeated repulses, and in the third charge so eagerly exposed his person, that he was with difficulty rescued, at the moment when he was on the point of being cut down by a French or Bavarian dragoon. With all the disadvantages of ground and inferiority of force, he kept the enemy in check, prevented them from sending succours to the army of Tallard, and vigorously pressed on their rear, when the rout of the right decided the contest, and the electoral troops were withdrawn from Oberclaw and Lutzingen. He then co-operated with Marlborough in reducing the forces inclosed in the village of Blenheim. This gallant remnant of an unfortunate army, amounting to 13,000 of the choicest soldiers of France, would have dearly sold their honour and liberty, had they not been bereaved of every resource by the retreat of the elector, and abandoned by many of their officers, who shrunk from a hopeless conflict. Their commander rushed into the Danube, and was drowned ; many of the officers followed his example, and shared his fate; and the troops, after tearing their colours and indignantly burying their arms, were soothed by the exhortations of Marlborough and Eugene, and surrendered prisoners of war.

On the side of the allies, 4000 were killed and 7000 wounded ; the loss of the enemy exceeded 40,000 men, including prisoners and deserters, besides 120 pieces of artillery, 300 colours and standards, and the principal part of the military chest.*

The elector and marsin covered the retreat with the cavalry of their left, passed the morass of Hockstedt, crossed the Danube at Dillingen, and continued their flight with precipitation towards the Rhine. Broken, dispersed, and ruined, the enemy left a free and uninterrupted march for the confederates from the Danube to the Rhine ; and the wretched remains of that army, which had threatened Germany with bondage, and spread terror to the gates of Vienna, was driven back in dismay to the foot of the Vosges. The victors pressed on their retreat, crossed the Rhine at Philipsburgh, entered Alsace, and, before the close of this eventful campaign, the fortresses of Landau, Treves, and Traerback surrendered to their victorious arms. The success of the allies was at the same time followed by the reduction of all Bavaria. Augsburgh and Ulm were the first fruits of their victory ; and the electress, to whom her husband had consigned the administration of affairs, on his retreat from the unfortunate plains of Blenheim, was reduced to accept the terms of accommodation dictated by the conquerors. By a treaty concluded at Munich, she restored Passau and the other places taken from the Austrians, surrendered the fortresses of Bavaria with the artillery and ammunition, disbanded the troops, resigned the revenues, and reserved only the capital dismantled, as a residence for herself and her children.

* It appears that the French and Bavarian force amounted to 56,000, that of the allies to 52,000 men. — Memoirs of the Duke of Marlborough, chap. xxvi.

At the same time the affairs of Hungary assumed a more favourable aspect. Ragotsky had continued his successful career by the capture of Cassau and Eperies; amused the emperor with feigned negotiations while he reduced Neuhasel, and collected an army of 30,000 men to blockade Leopoldstadt, the only fortress remaining to cover the Austrian frontier. But the success at Blenheim enabling the emperor to draw reinforcements into Hungary, Heuster obtained a splendid victory over the insurgents, in which he killed or made prisoners the greater part of their infantry, secured the Austrian frontier, and confined their subsequent operations to the precincts of their own country.*

The splendid victory which opened this career of success warmed even the phlegmatic heart of Leopold; and in his letters to the queen and the States he expressed the strongest sense of his obligations for their assistance. On the general who was the great agent of his preservation he offered to confer the dignity of prince of the empire, and announced the promotion in a letter written with his own hand, with an unusual warmth of gratitude. We preserve this epistle as a monument equally honourable to the feelings of the monarch, the spirit and generosity of our nation, and the merits of our great countryman.

"Most illustrious cousin, and most dear prince,—I do gladly call by these names your dilection†, whom I have freely and of my own accord admitted among the princes of the holy Roman empire, not so much in consideration of your ancient family as on account of your personal merit and great deserts towards my august house and the holy Roman empire. I have been willing that this supreme honour in Germany which I have so deservedly conferred on you, should remain, that it may more and more appear to all the world how much, as I freely own, I and the empire owe to the most serene queen of Great Britain, for sending her powerful assistance as far as Augsburgh and Bavaria under your conduct, when my own affairs and those of the empire were so much shaken and disordered by the perfidious defection of the Bavarian to the French; and also to your dilection, by whom all things have been so

* Windisch, p. 472.
† The title used by the emperor to the princes of the empire.

prudently, so vigorously, and so successfully transacted. For not only fame, but likewise the generals of my forces, the companions and sharers of your labours and victories, attribute the same chiefly to your counsels, and the valour of the English and other troops who fought under your command. These actions are so great, and particularly that of Hockstedt (past ages having never witnessed the like victory over the French), that we may rejoice to see not only the pernicious efforts of the common enemy repulsed, and Europe rescued from its uncertain situation, but we may reasonably hope that the liberty of the Christian world will be rescued from the impending power of France. Being entirely persuaded that your dilection will, without intermission, apply all your care and industry towards that end, there remains nothing for me but to wish you a prosperous success, and to assure you that I shall seize every occasion to give you still greater proofs of my esteem and gratitude." *

Chap. LXXI.—1705.

The general exultation with which the wonderful victory of Blenheim, and the subsequent success was received, evinced the prevalence of that dread which had been inspired by the power of Louis ; and the reports of prodigies proved that it was generally considered as superior to human agency.

Leopold is said to have had a mysterious presentiment of the awful event which decided the fate of the house of Austria. In Italy, the centre of superstition, the figure of an angel in the chapel of Loretto was reported to have moved its wings ; a rich candlestick, the gift of Louis, suspended before the shrine, sunk down, while another, presented by the emperor, rose above its usual place. Even in England, where the public mind is less susceptible of superstitious impressions, reports of similar prodigies gained credit. The clashing of arms, and

* For a more particular account of this transaction, the reader is referred to the Memoirs of the Duke of Marlborough.

shouts of contending hosts were heard in the air ; and an apparition mounted on a white steed, rode through the fens of Lincolnshire, announcing, on the very day of the battle, the triumph of the British army at Blenheim, as the apparition of Castor and Pollux had proclaimed in the forum the victory of Regillus over the Tarquins, which established the liberties of infant Rome.

The nation, mindful of the glories won in the fields of Cressy and Agincourt, hailed so splendid a proof of British valour and skill, and exulted in the prospect of again seeing the star of England predominant over that of France. The factious clamours against Marlborough were hushed ; the Tories were driven from power ; the pacific queen was borne away by the general ardour ; Marlborough and Godolphin were supported with the Whigs, who were animated with fresh spirit ; the new parliament was filled with members of the prevailing sentiment ; and from this period may be dated the commencement of that glorious administration, which carried the power and fame of England to so great a height. In the speech from the throne the queen spoke the sentiments of the nation, when she encouraged the parliament " to continue the war until the monarchy of Spain was restored to the house of Austria, and the faithless king of France reduced." The arrival of Tallard and the captured generals in England revived the memory of those days when a king of France was brought prisoner by a prince of Wales, and the nation gave the most striking proofs of its gratitude to the general who had so ably exerted its force and vindicated its fame. Marlborough received the thanks of parliament ; was rewarded with a perpetual pension, and with the manor of Woodstock, the residence of several sovereigns ; and honoured with the construction of a splendid palace, which still commemorates in its name the victory of Blenheim.

During winter the most active preparations were made, by all the allies, to prosecute their advantages. Leopold obtained large supplies of money and provisions from his hereditary countries, and the Maritime Powers used similar exertions to reinforce their armies. But he lived only to witness the dawn of success : a lingering disorder, which had induced him to consign the administration of government to his son Joseph, on the 5th of May, carried him to the grave in the sixty-fifth year of his age and the forty-sixth of his reign ; the longest in the Austrian annals except that of Frederic III.

Leopold was surnamed the Great, an appellation flattering to his own character or talents, but true if applied to the great events of his reign. He was of a weak and sickly constitution, low in stature, of a saturnine complexion, ordinary in countenance, and distinguished with an unusual portion of the Austrian lip. His gait was stately, slow, and deliberate ; his air pensive, his address awkward, his manner uncouth, his disposition cold and phlegmatic. He was attached to the Spanish dress, customs, and etiquette, and usually appeared in a coat of black cloth, ornamented with a large order of the golden fleece, scarlet stockings, and a Spanish hat, decorated with a scarlet feather. So reserved was his disposition, and so recluse his way of life, that he was scarcely known even in his own court, except by those who constantly attended his person. On this subject, an anecdote is related by a contemporary author. One of his chamberlains, who was not in constant attendance, being suddenly called on some extraordinary occasion, met a little dark ordinary figure in the antechamber, and familiarly inquired Where is the emperor ? A solemn voice replying in hollow accents " It is I," so confounded the astonished chamberlain, that he hastened out of the palace, and never again ventured to return to court.

Leopold possessed all the private and domestic virtues ; he was pure in his morals, faithful to the marriage-bed, a good father and a kind master. Though reserved in public and with strangers, he was open and facetious with those who formed his private society ; and he delighted in the tricks of buffoons and dwarfs, who, according to the custom of the times, formed a part of his establishment.

Being originally educated for the church, the Jesuits his preceptors acquired such an influence over his mind that he professed a resolution to enter into their order, and even passed through the probationary exercises. To them he owed the acquisition of multifarious knowledge, and such an intimate acquaintance with theology, jurisprudence, metaphysics, and the speculative sciences, that he was called the most learned prince of his age. When the death of his brother Ferdinand opened a more flattering prospect, he could not throw off his early habits and principles, but still displayed rather the virtues of the recluse and the acquirements of a professor, than the qualifications of a prince. He was minute in acts of devotion, much addicted to judicial astrology and alchemy, and proud of displaying his knowledge of Latin style. He wrote epigrams, anagrams, inscriptions, and fables ; he possessed great judgment in painting, was distinguished both as a performer and composer of music, and considering the scantiness of his revenues, may be ranked among the most liberal patrons of the arts and sciences. He improved the university at Olmutz, founded two universities at Innspruck and Breslau, patronised several colleges and literary establishments at Vienna, and greatly augmented the imperial library. To his preceptors also, like Ferdinand II., he owed the principal defects of his character, and the great embarrassments of his administration : at their instigation he was induced to persecute the Protestants, and to commit those frequent breaches of faith, which diminished the confidence of his subjects, and tarnished the lustre of his reign.

He was unbounded in his charities to the poor and needy, but this virtue partook of that excessive and affected humility which characterised Ferdinand II. He gave audience to persons of the lowest description, even to beggars, and distributed among them considerable largesses with his own hand. When told that such benefactions, as well as his munificence to the Jesuits and other religious orders, drained his finances, he was accustomed to reply, with an allusion to Louis XIV. that if he lavished the same sums on mistresses and useless luxuries, he should be commended instead of being blamed. For these virtues and charities he was deemed worthy of canonisation by Pope Innocent XI. ; and a Spanish priest at Rome actually dedicated a chapel to his honour.

Notwithstanding, however, his own predilection to the Jesuits, and his attachment to the minute forms of his religion, he gave an unusual proof of liberality for a mind so tenacious of its prejudices. Feeling from experience that his own education was ill suited to the duties of a sovereign, and sensible that the Jesuits sacrificed every consideration for the advancement of their own order, he departed from the custom of his family, and did not intrust to them the education of his children. With the same degree of magnanimity he commanded the governor of the archduke Joseph not to conceal from his pupil the defects of his own administration, but to hold them up as a warning against similar errors.

The despotism and intolerance of Ferdinand II. had rendered him the object of jealousy and terror, and led to those restrictions of the imperial authority which were established under his successor by the peace of Westphalia. All the moderation and prudence of Ferdinand III. could not remove the prejudices derived from his father's arbitrary measures; and the imperial authority would have suffered new diminution, if in such a difficult situation an active and aspiring prince had ascended the throne. Fortunately the phlegmatic character of Leopold was suited to the times. The mild and moderate system introduced by the father was matured by the son; and the most inactive prince who since Frederic III. had held the reins of empire, aided by a concurrence of fortunate events, and assisted by great generals and able ministers, restored the imperial authority, and revived the declining grandeur of the house of Austria.

The reign of Leopold forms a new era in the military and civil institutions of his country. Since the invention of gunpowder the incessant wars in Europe had occasioned progressive changes in the military art. The artillery had been gradually lightened, and received most of the improvements which at present subsist. The same innovations had taken place in the form and use of the musket; the pike had been superseded by fire-arms, and its place supplied by the introduction of the bayonet. The regiments had been lessened and equalised, formed into regular divisions and subdivisions, supplied with additional officers, and the files gradually reduced to three. The armies, instead of small bodies, seldom exceeding 30,000 or 40,000 men, encumbered with little baggage, drawing their provisions from the country which was the theatre of their operations, and accustomed to quarter in towns and villages, now took the field to the number of 100,000, directed their movements by plans previously calculated, encamped with the same regularity as they marched and fought, and in all seasons drew their principal subsistence from magazines. Thus their movements became slow, confined, systematic, and complicated, instead of the bold and rapid inroads and singular surprises so frequent in the thirty years' war, and preceding periods.

These progressive improvements in the art of war induced Leopold, with the advice of Eugene, to meliorate the military system of his own dominions, as he had already done that of Germany. The regiments of infantry, hitherto of unequal force, were all established on the same footing, in number, divisions, and discipline; and similar changes were extended to the hussars and other irregulars. Beneficial regulations were likewise introduced into the internal economy of the army; many grievances with respect to quarters, which bore heavy on the public and on individuals, were removed; and the fortifications of the principal places strengthened and augmented. By these measures Leopold left a permanent force amounting to 74,000 men, consisting of twenty-nine regiments of infantry, eight of cuirassiers, six of dragoons, two of light horse, and three of hussars. *

Leopold also deserves peculiar praise for an unwearied attention to jurisprudence, and beneficial regulations in the civil and criminal courts, in imitation of similar changes to which the progress of knowledge had given birth in other countries. Without descending into a minute detail of a subject so dry and complicated, it will be sufficient to observe, that he laid aside the Caroline code, so severe in its punishments, for a more mild and lenient form. He also forbade the customary appeals to foreign tribunals, introduced the use of the German tongue instead of the Latin, which had hitherto been the language of the courts, formed a digest of the common law of Austria, as a systematic regulation for all judicial proceedings, encouraged the study of the laws, and made various modifications in the subordinate tribunals of his other territories.

* Each regiment of infantry consisted of a company of grenadiers of 100 men ; and twelve others of 150 each, forming three battalions. The horse regiments consisted of ten companies of 100 men each, forming five squadrons.—Le Luca Lesebuch des Oesterreichischen Staaten, v. i. p. 392.

To him also the capital was indebted for a more regular and better police, and the establishment for lighting the streets, the expense of which was defrayed by a tax on foreign wine; a benefit which, though it may seem too inconsiderable for the notice of history, is highly advantageous to domestic intercourse.

Leopold was thrice married.

His first wife, Margaret Theresa, daughter of Philip IV., king of Spain, became, by the renunciation of her elder sister, presumptive heiress of the Spanish dominions. She was of a meek and humble disposition, and chiefly distinguished for attention to her husband, and for skill and industry in working and embroidering coverings of altarpieces, and paraphernalia for the church. She gained the affection of her husband by her domestic virtues and endearing attentions. She had a weak and sickly constitution; and, after bearing four children, died in childbed in 1673.

Maria Antonia, her only surviving daughter, was in her right undoubted heiress of the Spanish dominions, but was compelled by Leopold to renounce her claims on espousing Maximilian Emanuel, elector of Bavaria. She died in 1692, leaving her pretensions to her only son Ferdinand Joseph, who, by the first partition treaty was appointed king of Spain and the Indies, and afterwards nominated, by the will of his uncle Charles, heir of all the Spanish dominions. His death in 1701 happened so opportunely, that both the French and Austrian parties mutually charged each other with recurring to poison, but both without foundation.

Claudia Felicitas, the cousin and second wife of Leopold, was the daughter of Ferdinand Charles, head of the Tyrol line. Her hand was first demanded by James Stuart, pretender to the crown of England; but his suit was rejected in favour of the emperor. The nuptials took place at Innspruck in 1663, and almost the first use which she made of her influence was, to exclude the queen-mother from the share which she had hitherto borne in the government, and to obtain the disgrace of the prime-minister, prince Lobcowitz, who had opposed her marriage, and recommended the princess of Neuburgh. Claudia was a woman of great beauty, discretion, and vivacity, and par-

ticularly attentive to the taste and inclination of her consort. She sung and performed delightfully, and introduced
order and economy into the household. She was so fond
of the chace that her incessant fatigues brought on a decline, which carried her to the grave in 1676.

His third wife, Magdalen Theresa, was daughter of
Philip William, first elector Palatine of the branch of
Neuburgh. She was born in 1655, and brought up, under
the auspices of her zealous father, in the constant practice
of every species of mortification and gloomy superstition.
With such an education the young princess contracted the
austerity of an anchorite. She rejected the harmless plea-
sures of society, panted for religious retirement, and even
exposed herself to the sun and wind, that her complexion
might disgust Leopold, who, after the death of his first wife,
offered her his hand. On the decease of his second wife
her repugnance was overcome by the persuasions of her
family, who represented that Providence had destined her
to fill the first throne of the universe for the advantage of
the Catholic faith. But amidst all the pomp and splendour
of a court, she still preserved the same gloomy notions,
the same disdain for the vanities of the world, the same
inclination for mortifications and self-abasement. She
visited the sick and prisoners, wrought ornaments for the
church and garments for the poor, kept a severe register of
her thoughts and actions, condemned herself to stigmas for
real or imaginary faults : she wore bracelets not as usual
decorated with precious stones, but armed with iron spikes,
which lacerated her flesh, walked barefoot in processions,
and frequent pilgrimages, and inflicted on herself the
severest discipline, till her blood flowed on the ground.
While she prepared with her own hand the most exquisite
delicacies for her husband, she kept frequent and rigid
fasts, and condemned herself to the most ordinary fare.
These austerities, however, she practised in the utmost
secrecy, and several were never known till after her death,
when the instruments of her penance were found in a box
tinged with blood. With a commendable degree of self-
denial, she burnt also, with her own hands, a detailed
history of her life and actions, which had been written by
her confessor, who considered her as a saint.

These religious practices did not divert her from the

duties of the wife and the empress.. She complied in appearance with the taste and inclinations of her husband, frequented the opera with the psalms bound like the books of the performance, and exerted her skill in music for his solace and amusement. Knowing the aversion of Leopold to the French language, she made, for his use, extracts in German from the best French publications on political economy; and, though not anxious to interfere in political affairs, assisted him with her counsels. On the death of her eldest son Joseph, she was intrusted with the regency; and after conducting the reins of state with vigour and prudence, in the short but critical period which elapsed before the arrival of Charles, she resigned her power without regret, to resume her darling course of life. She possessed an active and versatile genius; and, besides her native tongue, was well acquainted with the Latin, French, and Italian languages, and mistress of music both as a performer and composer. She turned the psalms into German verse, and set them to music; and besides numerous versions of devout and edifying works, translated from the French "Pious Reflections for every Day of the Month," which was printed at Cologne.

In the last illness of her husband she was indefatigable in her attendance, scarcely allowing herself rest, or quitting the sick-bed till she was exhausted with fatigue. Except the short interval in which she was intrusted with the reins of government, she renounced all wordly occupations, and resumed that course of austerity and abstraction which had been the delight of her youth. She died in 1720; was buried, at her own desire, without pomp or parade, and her coffin was distinguished with no other inscription than—

"ELEONORE,
"Pauvre Pecheresse,
"Morte le 19 Janvier,
"1720:"

leaving behind her a singular example of a princess, who with talents, qualities, and accomplishments to adorn the highest station, suffered them to be perverted and obscured by superstitious practices and gloomy austerities, both equally contrary to the real spirit and temper of the Christian religion.

Of ten children by Leopold, five survived ; two sons, Joseph and Charles, who succeeded, and three daughters.

Mary Elizabeth, born 1680, compensated for an ordinary person by an excellent understanding, an extensive knowledge in various branches of science and literature, an intimate acquaintance with the Latin, French, and Italian languages, and a proficiency in the lighter accomplishments of her sex. After ruling the exterior provinces, she was appointed governess of the Netherlands, fixed her residence at Brussels, and conducted the helm of state with a prudent and steady hand till her death in 1741.

2. Mary Anne, born in 1683, espoused in 1708 John the sixth king of Portugal, a marriage which cemented the attachment of her husband to the principles of the Grand Alliance. She combated by mildness and discretion his ardent passions, and bore with exemplary patience his licentious amours and numerous infidelities. During the long illness of her husband, who, in the latter part of his life, was afflicted with a paralytic disorder, she obtained the chief share in the administration of affairs, which, in conformity with the principles of her family, she placed in the hands of the clergy ; but she is little remarkable in the History of Portugal, except as the foundress of an edifice for the convent of barefooted Carmelites at Belem, where she was buried in 1654.

3. Of Mary Magdalen, the third daughter, little is known, except that she was born at Vienna in 1689, and died in 1743.

END OF THE SECOND VOLUME.

LONDON :
SPOTTISWOODE and SHAW,
New-street-Square.